Zeb Vance

Zeb Vance

NORTH CAROLINA'S

CIVIL WAR GOVERNOR

AND GILDED AGE

POLITICAL LEADER

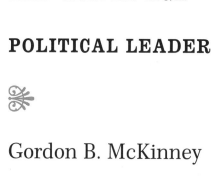

Gordon B. McKinney

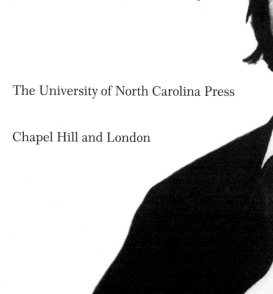

The University of North Carolina Press

Chapel Hill and London

© 2004 The University of North Carolina Press
Set in Ruzicka and Monotype Clarendon
by Tseng Information Systems
Manufactured in the United States of America

Publication of this book was made possible in part by a
generous gift from Ben M. Jones III.

Portions of Chapter 20 were previously published as "Zebulon Vance
and His Reconstruction of the Civil War in North Carolina," *North Carolina
Historical Review* 75 (January 1998): 69-85.

Portions of Chapter 21 were previously published as "Zeb Vance and the
Construction of the Western North Carolina Railroad," *Appalachian Journal* 29,
nos. 1-2 (Fall 2001-Winter 2002): 58-67; © 2002 by *Appalachian Journal* and
Appalachian State University; used with permission.

The paper in this book meets the guidelines for permanence and durability
of the Committee on Production Guidelines for Book Longevity of the Council
on Library Resources.

Library of Congress Cataloging-in-Publication Data
McKinney, Gordon B., 1943-
Zeb Vance: North Carolina's Civil War governor and Gilded Age political leader /
Gordon B. McKinney.
     p. cm.
Includes bibliographical references and index.
ISBN 0-8078-2865-3 (cloth: alk. paper)
1. Vance, Zebulon Baird, 1830-1894. 2. Legislators—United States—Biography.
3. United States. Congress. Senate—Biography. 4. Governors—North
Carolina—Biography. 5. North Carolina—History—Civil War, 1861-1865.
6. North Carolina—Politics and government—1861-1865. 7. North Carolina—
Politics and government—1865-1950. I. Title.
E664.V2M34   2004
975.6'03—dc22
2003027749

08 07 06 05 04   5 4 3 2 1

CONTENTS ✖

ILLUSTRATIONS ✻

PREFACE ❈

When I first started working on Zeb Vance as a research topic, I had an opportunity to share some of my ideas with a group of senior citizens at a meeting in Black Mountain, North Carolina. During the discussion period that followed my presentation, one woman made several very insightful comments. After the end of the formal program, she came forward and introduced herself as Mrs. Glenn Tucker, the wife of the best scholarly biographer of Vance. She shared with me some of the challenges that she and her husband had faced in working on *Zeb Vance: Champion of Personal Freedom*, a work that has stood as the finest study of Vance's life for nearly four decades.[1]

Unfortunately, the challenges that the Tuckers faced forced them to neglect the period after the Civil War. Since the publication of *Zeb Vance*, the amount of scholarship on the Civil War, Reconstruction, and the Gilded Age has expanded enormously. Making use of new analytical approaches and ideas, including gender analysis and modernization theory, scholars have developed much different perceptions of topics such as the role that race played in shaping the United States during the latter part of the nineteenth century. The result is the need for a new biography of Zebulon Vance that places him in the context of historians' rapidly changing perceptions of the American South. Many of the interpretations in this study that differ from those offered by the Tuckers were first presented by other scholars in articles and monographs. I have sought to convey the breadth and depth of this exciting new work as accurately as possible. Where I disagree with some scholars on a point, I have tried to explain why in some detail, using primary sources to support my assertions.

The Tucker biography was not the first scholarly attempt to understand Vance's historical reputation. As early as 1914, J. G. De Roulhac Hamilton discussed important parts of Vance's career in his highly partisan *Reconstruction in North Carolina*. In this detailed account of events between 1861 and 1876, Hamilton wrote approvingly of virtually everything that Vance did during the period, and he used quotations from Vance letters to support his analysis. Unfortunately, Hamilton's determination to attack African Americans and Republicans—especially William Woods Holden—at every point limited the value of his study. In 1925, Frank Owsley took the opposite stand on the value of Vance's contribution during the Civil War.

In his monograph, *State Rights in the Confederacy*, Owsley accused Vance and Georgia governor Joseph E. Brown of undermining the Confederate war effort. Owsley was particularly critical of Vance's unwillingness to share state resources with the Southern government.[2]

The Civil War centennial in the 1960s encouraged many writers and publishers to produce studies of topics that had been neglected for decades. Like many other works from this period, John G. Barrett's *The Civil War in North Carolina*, published in 1963, concentrated on battles and the movements of armies. Barrett's book, however, was the first of these centennial monographs to also examine the contributions that Vance made during the war. The picture of Vance that emerges from his study is one of a skilled administrator who kept North Carolina's troops well supplied.[3]

Starting in the 1970s, however, scholars began to examine Vance's career in a much more detailed manner. The result of their investigations was a considerably more nuanced depiction of his life. For example, William T. Auman challenged the picture of Vance as a champion of constitutional rights. In several studies, Auman argued that Vance sanctioned harsh tactics, including torture, against opponents of the Confederate war effort. Paul D. Escott confirmed Auman's assertions and went on to point out that Vance employed a subtle strategy of alternating leniency and firmness toward peace advocates. Escott also analyzed the controversies between Vance and Jefferson Davis that had prompted Owsley to claim that Vance undercut the Confederacy. Escott recognized that Vance was actually attempting to ensure that North Carolina's fragile Confederate nationalism was nurtured and sustained. Finally, analyzing the opposition to Vance by Republicans in western North Carolina, I demonstrated that Vance's postwar career was as full of controversy and partisan competition as was the case during the war.[4]

In the last thirty years, a great many new studies have been published that provide fuller information about several of the men with whom Vance interacted. Max Williams continued the massive task of publishing the manuscripts of William A. Graham, one of Vance's mentors during the war. In a biography of Henry K. Burgwyn Jr., Archie K. Davis gave a much needed corrective to our understanding of Vance as a soldier. William C. Harris provided a definitive biography of Vance's political nemesis William Woods Holden, and Horace Raper and Thornton Mitchell published the surviving Holden manuscripts through 1868. E. Stanly Godbold and Mattie U. Russell wrote a valuable biography of William Holland Thomas, a persistent Vance opponent in western North Carolina. Jeff Crow composed a sympathetic sketch of Vance's 1876 gubernatorial opponent Thomas Settle Jr. that uncovered some previously unrecognized features of that contest. Finally, Thomas E. Jeffrey produced an outstanding study of Thomas Lanier Clingman, the major roadblock to Vance's political advancement as a young man.[5] All of these works taken together made it obvious that Vance was not a lone actor at any time in his career, and that any Vance biographer needed to be aware of the actions of many other historical figures.

Other scholars sought to place Vance in the context of his native mountain region in western North Carolina. Phillip S. Paludan described Vance's angry attempt to gain a measure of justice for the victims of an atrocity in Madison County. John C. Inscoe provided the first convincing description of the mountain slaveowning class; Vance was a self-conscious member of this group. John and I chronicled Vance's efforts as governor to relieve the suffering of the civilian population in the Appalachian counties. We also related how Vance tried, with far less success, to counter the growing war-weariness in the region. Kenneth W. Noe and Shannon H. Wilson edited a series of essays that explored the impact of the entire war on the mountain South; these essays helped to place Vance's efforts in a broader perspective. Martin Crawford, in his study of Ashe County, allowed scholars to consider the impact of the war on small mountain communities.[6]

Another group of historians evaluated Vance through the lens of their more complex understanding of the Confederate experience. Richard E. Beringer, Herman Hattaway, Archer Jones, and William Still Jr. tried to explain why the Confederacy failed. In the process, they absolved Vance of any blame for the result and cited his imaginative supply policies as an example of his positive contributions. George C. Rable examined the revolt against partisan politics within the Confederacy and cited Vance as the prime example of a successful state leader. Rable's portrait of Vance as a master political craftsman who sought to aid the Confederacy by maintaining a tenuous political truce in North Carolina is especially convincing. My own interpretation of Vance's war governorship closely follows Rable's.[7]

Other scholars investigated the roles played by larger forces in creating the world in which Vance lived. Paul D. Escott drew a very convincing picture of the North Carolina political and economic elite during the last half of the nineteenth century. Escott featured Vance as one of the leaders of this group and showed how the war governor became a major architect of the postwar political system that limited the underclass's access to power. On a broader scale, Laurence Shore described the ideological consistency of Southern capitalists. His study also placed Vance within a much broader perspective than had previous studies. Anne C. Rose made a similar point when she used Vance as an example of elite adjustment to Victorian America. In her insightful study, Rose examined Vance's domestic and public life in relation to the lives of middle-class men and women throughout the nation.[8]

This study is, then, an attempt to evaluate the life of Zebulon Vance within the context of our best understanding of the times in which he lived. They were turbulent times. Debates about slavery, the Civil War, the modernization of Appalachia, Reconstruction, and Gilded Age politics still provoke controversy in and outside of the academic world. Zeb was a public figure for virtually his entire life, and he took very definite stands on the major issues of his time. Most of the time, there was little ambiguity in his statements; it is clear that he said and wrote what he meant. In many cases, his contemporaries disagreed with him and argued back with considerable vigor. Thus, many of the current controversies about Zeb's legacy first arose while he was still alive and capable of replying. Since Zeb had a well-developed historical perspective, he offered rebuttals to many of the arguments that are made about him today. This makes the role of Zeb's biographer a most interesting one, as his perspective must be regularly addressed in the text.

Another important consideration that every biographer must address is the personality and individuality of the subject. In Zeb's case, it is clear that virtually from childhood he was recognized as a unique character. First, he was physically arresting. He was always large; he appears to have been big-boned. He stood an inch below six feet tall and weighed nearly 200 pounds as a young man; as he matured he reached an approximate weight of 230 pounds. Everyone also noticed Zeb's abundant hair. It was dark black and very unruly when he was young, but in his thirties it turned to gray, and it looked increasingly distinguished as he attained middle age. Many observers were struck by Vance's eyes, as well. Apparently they twinkled with goodwill, with a touch of mischievousness always present. Zeb radiated wit and humor. He was a masterful storyteller who was also very adept at the quick quip. All indications are that he never met a stranger, and that he was able to converse on a seemingly equal basis with all classes, sexes, and races. He also struck most of his contemporaries as intellectually acute— if not too deep. As a result of all these pleasing attributes, Zeb was a widely admired public figure.

After considerable study, I have concluded that any understanding of Zebulon Vance must begin and end with the recognition that he was first and foremost a politician. Even in the midst of the Civil War, many of his actions were based on political considerations. Zeb read the public mind very accurately on many occasions and often pursued policies that reflected his understanding of the public's needs. This ability made him an extremely effective governor of North Carolina during the Civil War and led him to champion the small farmers during the Gilded Age. But Zeb never lost sight of his own political needs. He sought election to public office for four decades with an almost frantic energy, and he was very unhappy when he was a private citizen. Other aspects of Zeb's life—especially his family—were important to him, but he neglected them if they came into conflict with his political ambitions.

The compulsion to pursue political power is part of the core of many successful public figures. When it is harnessed to a good cause, and the person is placed in the right place at the right time, astonishing accomplishments can be the result. Unfortunately, this same drive continues to work when the individual is in a position to cause harm. This was true for Zeb. On a number of occasions, he pursued policies or espoused positions that severely damaged the lives of other people. Generally, he did not recognize that what he was doing was undesirable, and he rarely expressed regret about the actions that he had taken.

One of the areas in which Zeb did the most damage was race relations. William Cooper, in his biography of Jefferson Davis, noted that although Davis was a consistent racist, his biography would not take special note of that fact.[9] Cooper's decision was a valid one, because Davis lived most of his life in a society in which race relations were rigidly bound by law and custom. In that sense, Davis had few options, and his opinions were not a matter open to discussion or dispute. Zeb Vance lived in a very different world, however. Throughout his public life, race relations were an important part of the public discourse. Between 1862 and 1894, government policies evolved rapidly, and law and custom were in a state of flux. In the midst of these momentous changes, Zeb refused to modify his positions in any meaningful way. He firmly believed in the mental inferiority of African Americans and never deviated from that belief. As the people of the United States tried to adjust to emancipation and black citizenship, Zeb sought to limit African American access to political power. He used negative stereotypes of African Americans in political campaigns, in congressional speeches, and in his public and private writings. All of this material helped to shape the public dialogue about race relations in North Carolina to the detriment of the new black citizens. Unlike Jefferson Davis, Zeb lived at a time when he had the option to adopt different attitudes and change his public stands. He chose not to do so.

One of the reasons that Zeb's position on any issue was important is that he was one of the great public speakers of his day. At a time when public speaking was both a form of communication and a form of entertainment, Zeb was a master of both elements. He had a commanding voice that could reach large crowds in the days before mechanical amplification. In addition, Zeb was capable of speaking for as long as three hours at a time. Although he often did not prepare formal addresses, his surviving speeches indicate that he followed a rough outline that led to obvious conclusions. He made many of his most telling points through the use of short and humorous stories that listeners recalled long after they forgot the main subject of the speech. Because this talent was relatively rare among speakers of the period, Zeb was justifiably celebrated as an outstanding humorist and public speaker. It is difficult to recapture all of the magic of Zeb's public addresses today, but they are covered in some detail in the text that follows.

Finally, Zeb participated in a highly competitive political system that contained many men who were as ambitious as he was. In order to demonstrate the challenges and constraints that Zeb faced, this study provides a great deal of information about his allies, his opponents, and the political milieu in which they operated. The enduring image of Zeb is that of a massively popular figure who won elections to public office with ease. That was usually not the case. Zeb was challenged by people within his own party as well as those in opposition parties on a consistent basis. On a number of occasions, Zeb was defeated or won very narrow victories. Thus, to properly understand his life, it is essential to understand how the world of politics and politicians operated throughout his lifetime. Politics was the world in which he thrived and prospered, and in it he expressed the essence of his being.

ACKNOWLEDGMENTS ❧

When one works on a project for two decades, it becomes a collective enterprise rather than an individual effort. In 1983, I signed a contract with the North Carolina Division of Archives and History to continue their Zebulon Vance Papers publication project. I hoped to edit the remaining three projected volumes in the series while preparing myself to write a biography of North Carolina's Civil War governor. After many eventful and fruitful detours along the way, I have finally completed the contemplated biography.

The first change in plans was imposed from the outside. Finding it difficult to prepare a volume of the Vance Papers while teaching a full load of classes at Western Carolina University, I applied to a number of funding agencies for sufficient support to allow me to work on the project full time. The National Historical Properties and Records Commission made me a counteroffer: it would give me a one-year grant if I would prepare a microfilm edition of the entire body of Vance Papers. With the support of the people at the Division of Archives and History, I accepted the offer. When I started on the project, I soon realized that I could not do it alone. Fortunately, Richard McMurry, then at North Carolina State University and a former colleague of mine at Valdosta State University, agreed to be coeditor. Richard did an outstanding job, and the work proceeded smoothly. University Publications of America published our guide and thirty-nine reels of microfilm in 1987.

Only the support of many individuals at several institutions allowed the two of us to finish the massive project in a timely manner. Carolyn Wallace of the Southern Historical Collection at the University of North Carolina, Mattie U. Russell at Duke University, and David Olson and Ed Morris at the North Carolina Archives provided us with complete access to the Vance Papers and other assistance as we needed it. My colleagues at Western Carolina University, including Max Williams, Tyler Blethen, Curtis Wood, Theda Perdue, Bill Anderson, and Alice Mathews, supported my efforts and created a stimulating atmosphere in which to work. Archivist George Frizzell and the Hunter Library staff at Western Carolina were also of great assistance and willingly purchased a copy of the microfilm edition to assist me with my later research.

After the publication of the microfilm, I resumed work on the volumes of the letterpress edition. That project ended abruptly in 1989, when I accepted a position in the Research Division of the National Endowment for the Humanities (NEH). Ironically, one of my responsibilities at the NEH was acting as a program officer for several scholarly editions similar to the Vance Papers project. In 1992, I accepted the position of executive director of National History Day at the University of Maryland. In both of these positions, I had interesting colleagues who kept me intellectually stimulated. But the demands of the work at both institutions made further in-depth research difficult.

It was at this point that my good friend and fellow Appalachian historian John C. Inscoe made me a most attractive offer: he proposed that we coauthor a history of the Civil War in western North Carolina. Since I had done virtually all of my previous Vance research on the period through 1865, with an emphasis on western North Carolina, I could immediately start writing on this topic. The subject was clearly important, and my work on the manuscript further acquainted me with the world that produced Zebulon Vance. We were greatly aided in our analysis of the broader developments in the history of western North Carolina by the innovative work on Appalachia during the Civil War by Ralph Mann, Tracy McKenzie, Todd Groce, Martin Crawford, Shannon H. Wilson, and Kenneth W. Noe. As the manuscript neared completion, I accepted a position at Berea College as director of the Appalachian Center and professor of history. My fellow historians at Berea, including David Nelson, Katherine Christiansen, Rob Foster, Al Perkins, and Shannon H. Wilson, created a most hospitable environment for completing the manuscript. Ann Chase and Gerald Roberts at Hutchins Library greatly facilitated my work by acquiring a copy of the Vance Papers on microfilm for the library. David Perry at the University of North Carolina Press gave patient and sustained support as we brought the book to fruition and publication.

Starting in the summer of 2001, I was able to take the first regular sabbatical of my academic career. John Bolin, the dean of Berea College, aided my work by allowing me to take this break one year ahead of schedule. I was financially able to afford to take a full year away from my work at Berea College thanks to a John B. Stephenson Scholarship from the Appalachian College Association (ACA). Alice Brown and J. P. Brantley of the ACA were especially supportive during the 2001–2 academic year. Special thanks are due to Jacqueline Burnside and the Professional Growth Committee at Berea College for financial assistance during the editing process. My colleagues at the Appalachian Center have been exceptionally tolerant of a coworker who seems to spend his time in the nineteenth century; Genevieve Reynolds and Lori Briscoe Pennington have been particularly helpful. Once again, David Perry at the University of North Carolina Press has shown extraordinary patience and editorial expertise in preparing this manuscript for publication. His assistant, Mark Simpson-Vos, also provided me with much timely aid.

My family has had to endure the inconveniences of this drawn-out process the most. Notecards by the thousands invaded many rooms of several of our houses, and work continued when opportunities for relaxation beckoned. Fortunately, Henderson, Molly, Kiwi, and Keeper refused to play by the rules and demanded that I spend quality time with them. To my wife, Martha, I owe an incalculable debt. First, she has provided in her own work a continuing example of scholarly excellence that has been a constant source of inspiration. At the same time, she has shared her life with me in a way that has enriched everything I do—including finally moving Zeb and his notecards out of the house.

Zeb Vance

1 ❧ WHAT MANNER OF MAN?

The Senate galleries were packed, as was usually the case when Zebulon Baird Vance was the center of attention. Many of the better known personages in the nation's capital were present. They were unusually somber, acting as if there would be no clever remarks from the most popular speaker in Congress. Dressed in dark clothing, the crowd sat in resigned silence. Seated below them were the entire Senate and the House of Representatives, with the Speaker of the House and the vice president of the United States seated at the front. Slowly, the chief justice and the associate justices of the Supreme Court entered the chamber and took seats in the second row. They were soon followed by President Grover Cleveland and his cabinet. According to a contemporary account, this was only the president's second personal appearance at this type of ceremony during his tenure in office. Finally, the distinguished British ambassador Sir Julian Pauncefote and members of the diplomatic corps entered the hushed room and were seated in the front row.[1]

Then the Reverend Dr. Moses D. Hoge of Richmond, Virginia, began the funeral service for Zebulon Vance. Vance's second wife, Florence, and his son Charles joined the public officials in this impressive ceremony to the memory of the junior senator from North Carolina. Many seated on the Senate floor had clashed with Vance on public issues, but few bore any grudges, and most considered him their friend. In fact, many faces on the floor of the Senate and in the galleries bore smiles as Vance's remarks and actions were recalled, but soon thereafter these countenances reflected the sorrow of losing a valued colleague. Vance's journey from the mountains of western North Carolina to this seat of national power had not been an easy one, but most of the people in the room recognized that his presence among them was the result of his ability, ambition, and the needs of his state and nation. Even though Hoge's message emphasized that "there is nothing great but God," the ceremony and the assembled dignitaries signified that Vance had achieved a measure of greatness. After the brief service, the president and the ambassador personally comforted Vance's widow. The diplomat took several minutes to relate his personal feelings of loss as well as his official condolences.[2]

While the homage paid to Vance by the nation's political elite testified to one measure of his accomplishments, a more impressive display of his personal impact on his generation lay just ahead. Vance's body was removed from the Senate floor, and the casket, accompanied by many of the mourners, was taken to the Baltimore and Ohio Station, where it was transferred to a train bound for Raleigh, North Carolina. The Richmond and Danville Railroad had arranged for a special train, which included a private car, two Pullman sleepers, and a baggage car, to transport the body and funeral party. Joining the family on this difficult journey were a dozen members of Congress, who would represent the nation at later ceremonies. As the cars headed south, the train stopped briefly in Danville, Virginia. The early hour of 4 A.M. precluded a public ceremony, but many leading citizens and public officials paid their respects to their favorite senator.[3]

Waiting in Raleigh for the funeral train were the leading political, business, and social leaders of North Carolina. These men had been in touch with Florence Vance, trying to persuade her to allow her husband to be buried in the state capital. She gently refused, citing Vance's often expressed desire to be returned to his native mountains. Despite the rejection of their plan, the dignitaries organized an elaborate parade that accompanied the coffin to the Capitol Building. In six hours, more than eight thousand citizens filed past their former leader. Observers were quick to note that not only the elite of North Carolina visited the site, but that large numbers of poor whites and blacks paid their last respects as well. One of the most unusual mourners was an inmate from the state prison, who was accompanied by two prison guards. Vance had commuted the man's death sentence to life imprisonment more than a decade and a half earlier, and the grateful convict came to say farewell to his benefactor. The outpouring of public emotion was brought to an abrupt end late in the day when the state militia escorted the casket back to the train.[4]

At the same time that the ceremony was taking place in Raleigh, a large concourse of mourners gathered in Charlotte, North Carolina. In Vance's second hometown, thousands of people from all walks of life came together to honor their former neighbor. The highlight of the meeting was a speech given by Jewish businessman Samuel Wittkowsky. He spoke of how Vance's speeches about Jewish history had endeared him to this persecuted minority, and about how he in turn returned their affection. Other speakers mentioned the pleasure that reading brought Vance and reminisced about his remarkable memory, which allowed him to recall phrases from the Bible and great literature at a moment's notice. All of the statements praising the fallen leader were punctuated with sustained rounds of applause.[5]

Vance's final train ride from Raleigh to Asheville was a testament to his enduring connection with the people of his native state. The train, now carrying state officials, stopped briefly in the tobacco center of Durham, where thousands of people gathered to listen to spirituals sung by a choir of African American millworkers. Then the solemn cortege rolled on through the countryside, where small groups of men clad in gray stood at attention when their fallen leader passed them on the tracks. At Greensboro, the train stopped once again for formal ceremonies. The large crowd heard music performed by the Twenty-sixth Regiment band. This musical unit had been part of Vance's command during the Civil War, and its members had traveled from Winston-Salem to bid farewell to their old colonel.[6]

The deepening gloom of night prevented other elaborate ceremonies, but the *Asheville Citizen* reported that in "all towns along the route . . . there were demonstrations of grief and profound respect." As the distinguished mourners tried to sleep, the train traveled slowly westward and upward. In rural areas, their sleep was often disturbed by the light of large bonfires created by people along the tracks who wanted to be sure that they saw their leader pass. As the cars passed through small communities, the engineer tolled the locomotive bells to alert local residents to Vance's presence. Brief stops were made in Statesville, Hickory, Morganton, and Old Fort, and large crowds passed by the former governor and senator. Many of the exhausted riders recognized the appropriateness of the route that took Vance home. As the cars slowly made their way up the steep face of the Blue Ridge, the people inside recalled Vance's crucial role in the completion of the railroad line that opened the mountain counties to the modern world. Along the angled slopes, small groups of local people gathered by the tracks to welcome home one of their own for the last time. New Hampshire senator William E. Chandler remarked that the demonstrations of that day proved that Vance was the most popular state political leader in the country.[7]

The train finally arrived in Asheville at five thirty in the morning, and Vance's body was transferred to the First Presbyterian Church. It was escorted by a contingent of the Rough and Ready Guards, Vance's original Civil War unit. Accompanying that group were the members of the U.S. Congress from Washington and the representatives of the state government. For approximately three hours, thousands of Vance's fellow mountaineers slowly walked past the open coffin. Then, shortly after ten o'clock, the hearse left the church. Once again led by the Rough and Readys, the procession included 110 carriages that carried more than 700 dignitaries. As the funeral parade continued, other groups joined the marchers at designated intersections. These included not only the expected delegations from nearby communities, but also a contingent of Vance's former slaves and the Asheville chapter of the Grand Army of the Republic.[8]

By the time the funeral march reached Riverside Cemetery, the mourners numbered nearly ten thousand—approximately the total population of the city of Asheville. A large number of western North Carolinians also lined the route of march but did not join the procession. The final ceremony was conducted by the local Presbyterian minister. The traditional Protestant service left many of the mourners openly weeping, but they did not linger at its conclusion, since a driving rain started to fall at the close of the benediction. For months thereafter, groups of people appeared at Vance's grave to pay their respects and to share in the almost universal grief.[9]

The massive popular response to Vance's death and the presence of powerful men at every stop along the route of his funeral journey testified to the significance of Vance's life. To those who mourned in April 1894, the importance of his life was unambiguous and self-evident: Zebulon Vance was the most popular and greatest son of the Old North State. In North Carolina, that perception has been carefully nurtured and preserved. A closer examination of Vance's eventful life will reveal both the substantial basis for his historical renown and the numerous contemporary and scholarly controversies hidden behind the protective mantle of the selective popular memory.

ll of his life, Zebulon Baird Vance thought of himself as a mountaineer. It was his often expressed wish to be buried in the midst of the high peaks where he was born and reared. The meaning of Vance's highland heritage, however, has become clouded by the popular stereotypes associated with the term Appalachia. Starting in the 1870s, local color writers began drawing on stereotypes to create an enduring caricature of Southern mountain life that has appeared with regularity in novels, movies, and television programs ever since.[1] They depicted the Southern mountain region in the period before the Civil War as a heavily wooded area inhabited by pioneer farmers of small means. Travel in the region was difficult, and the inhabitants crude, parochial, and ignorant. Their social relations were said to be characterized by traditional neighborliness mixed with unpredictable outbreaks of violence. While Vance would occasionally act self-consciously in a manner that fit this stereotype, the fictionalized description of Southern mountain life sheds no light on his identity or career.

Fortunately, a much clearer picture of life in western North Carolina before the Civil War has emerged. Until 1776, North Carolina west of the Blue Ridge was the undisputed territory of the Cherokee Indians. In that year, an expeditionary force of 2,400 men under the leadership of General Griffith Rutherford destroyed dozens of Cherokee villages, farms, and orchards. While some warriors continued to resist, most members of the tribe accepted their political inclusion in the new American nation. With the end of the Revolutionary War, the state government of North Carolina awarded lands in the western part of the state to veterans of the conflict. Many of the grants were made in what would become the state of Tennessee. Disputes between the settlers and the Cherokees over boundaries escalated into violence on a number of occasions. In an attempt to resolve these difficulties, the federal government and the Cherokee Nation signed the Treaty of Holston in 1791. This agreement opened up western North Carolina to white settlement to the French Broad River. Zebulon Vance's grandparents moved into this region around the time of the treaty. Subsequent agreements opened substantial segments of western North Carolina to pioneers in 1802, 1819, and 1838, when the vast majority of the Cherokees were finally removed.[2] Thus, the mountain region of western North Carolina was a frontier area at a time when much of the rest of the eastern United States was becoming much more established and organized.

The people who settled in the western North Carolina mountains were a diverse group that defies easy description. The majority emigrated from Britain to American ports—primarily Philadelphia—and settled in the western Pennsylvania lands away from the port city. The emigrants and their descendants usually continued to move with the opening frontier until they found satisfactory land. For many who eventually settled in western North Carolina, the route they followed took them from southwestern Pennsylvania through the Shenandoah Valley of Virginia to the Piedmont of North Carolina. Along the way, they adapted to the land and their neighbors. Most of the settlers traveled with families and established homesteads in close proximity to people with whom they had previous associations. The migration also included a significant number of people of German heritage and, increasingly, African Americans.[3]

When the Cherokee lands opened across the Blue Ridge in the 1790s, the settlers in central North Carolina rushed to occupy them. Particularly fortunate were the veterans of the Revolutionary War who received relatively large land grants in compensation for payments owed to them by the government. The first settlers found that the lands around the French Broad River and the small streams that flowed into it were a part of a plateau surrounded by high peaks. While the high altitude precluded the planting of most of the staple commercial crops common to the lower South, the relatively flat land and abundant water meant that good crops could still be grown. In addition, the land itself became a source of wealth. Many of the earliest settlers were able to sell small plots to later families that sought to clear enough land to become self-sufficient in food.[4]

The society and economy of western North Carolina were not as simple as the above description might imply. No pioneer farming family could be truly self-sufficient, even if it raised all of the food it needed. The preservation of meat and other foods required salt, and this product and other necessities could only be obtained from a local merchant who had contacts outside of the mountains. At the same time, skilled craftsmen provided absolutely essential services to keep the agricultural economy working. The blacksmith shod horses, made nails, shaped implements, and fashioned tools that kept farms producing. Coopers made barrels that stored the produce, and millers ground corn and wheat into meal and flour. Wheelwrights built and repaired the wagons needed to transport goods, and joiners fashioned furniture and other necessary wood items. Professional men like ministers, teachers, and lawyers found a role to play in the small communities that developed soon after the pioneers arrived. They tended to cluster in the region's first small village, eventually named Asheville, which also served as the administrative and legal center of the newly formed county government.[5]

Recent scholarly investigations have reminded us that other social and economic groups existed in this frontier society. A significant minority of the population were settlers who did not own any land. Surviving documents indicate that this group consisted of farm workers, who lived with families unrelated to them, and tenant farmers, who usually worked with their own families on other people's land, paying a contracted rent for its use. At the opposite end of the social scale, the more successful farmers, craftsmen, merchants, and professional men in the region purchased a growing number of African American slaves as they became more established. The enslaved people did not work as members of gangs of agricultural workers, as they often did in the lowland South. Instead, they performed the same wide variety of tasks that their owners did. Significantly, the federal censuses also reveal that a small number of adult women owned farms and maintained themselves as independent economic operators. Thus the mountain economy and the society that it sustained were based on a complex system of interdependencies and relationships. In both economic and social terms, there was an identifiable elite and an underclass.[6]

In economic and social relationships, however, the family was the key unit for the inhabitants of the area. In this matter, Zebulon Vance was a most fortunate western North Carolinian. The Vances had migrated from the Ulster region of Ireland around 1715, when the Protestant Irish left the island in large numbers. Zebulon's direct ancestor Andrew Vance settled in the backcountry of Pennsylvania and farmed. His son Samuel, who was also born in Ireland, migrated to an area near Winchester, Virginia, in the Shenandoah Valley. Joined there by other Ulster immigrants, the Vances distinguished themselves as leading political figures at the county level. In the early 1770s, Andrew and his son David followed the traditional route of those seeking more and better land by moving to the foothills of the Blue Ridge in North Carolina. When the Revolutionary War broke out, David enlisted in the patriot army and served at the battles of Brandywine, Germantown, Monmouth, and King's Mountain. He was elected to the state legislature in 1786, 1790, and 1791 representing Burke County, the most western county in the state at the time. He married Priscilla Brank, a native of the North Carolina foothills whose family was largely German in heritage.

Around 1790, David and Priscilla moved to the area of Reems Creek on the plateau about ten miles north of the village of Asheville.[7]

There the Vance family prospered. David Vance was a surveyor by profession, and he found ample business in this newly settled region. He and Priscilla lived in a sturdy cabin surrounded by a landholding of 898 acres. David also served as the clerk of the court for the new county of Buncombe, an entity that he had helped to create while a member of the state legislature. He and Priscilla had eight children, including Zebulon's father, their second son, David. The younger David lived in the house built by his father and farmed the land. He also had an interest in business. After the completion of the Buncombe Turnpike in 1827, it was possible to travel from the eastern section of Tennessee through western North Carolina to upper South Carolina on a notably improved road system. Over this modest thoroughfare, people and livestock traveled with much greater speed than had been possible before. The rapidly expanding plantation economy of central South Carolina and Georgia needed the surplus food grown in Tennessee and North Carolina. The result was a series of animal drives south along the turnpike that included horses, cattle, swine, and even geese and other fowl. Since many of the animals could only travel short distances in any one day, inns and drovers' stands (enclosed stock lots) were built by enterprising farmers to provide shelter and feed for a fee. Around 1833, David Vance moved from Reems Creek to Lapland—present-day Marshall in Madison County—and ran one of these stands; he reported that in one month he provided services for ninety thousand swine. This traffic provided a steady source of revenue for the Vance family.[8]

David Vance married Mira Margaret Baird of Asheville, who came from another prominent and prosperous family. Her father was Zebulon Baird, a lowland Scot, who drove the first wagon into Buncombe County in 1793. The wagon was loaded with goods that Baird promptly used to open the first general store in the new village of Asheville. The venture was eminently successful, and Baird soon obtained title to virtually all of the land on which the growing community was sited. Representing Buncombe County, he served a number of terms in the state legislature. He married Hannah Erwin of Burke County, the daughter of a powerful political family that retained its prominence well into the twentieth century. Thus, Vance's mother was as well connected to the elite of the region as her husband.[9]

The younger David Vance's brother, Dr. Robert Vance, placed the only stain on the family's name. Robert suffered what contemporaries called "white swelling" as a child and remained physically challenged his entire life. This disease left him lame in one leg and apparently somewhat bitter about his fate. Following the family pattern, he entered politics and was

Vance's birthplace, Reems Creek, Buncombe County, North Carolina.
The porch and clapboards were probably added by later owners.
(North Carolina Division of Archives and History, Raleigh)

elected to Congress in 1824. He was challenged for his seat by Samuel T. Carson in 1826, and the two men became involved in a campaign notable for personal attacks. After Carson won the election, the two men sought vindication for the slights that they had suffered during the canvass. A duel was arranged across the border in South Carolina; the location prevented either man from breaking North Carolina's law against dueling. Carson's shot passed through Vance's belt and into his abdominal cavity. An abdominal gunshot wound was virtually always fatal in the early nineteenth century, and it proved to be so in this case. Although dueling was not regarded as shameful for people of the Vances' social class, the death of Dr. Vance cast a pall over all concerned in the matter.[10]

Just three years after this fateful confrontation, Mira Vance announced: "I have another son[.] He is a fine hearty child[.] I call him Zebulon Baird."

The infant was the third child in the family, having been preceded by a sister and a brother. Most of what we know about young Zeb during this period comes from a loving portrait drawn by his older brother Robert B. Vance after Zeb's death, a few surviving family letters, and a brief autobiographical sketch that Zeb wrote in the fall of 1865. If the episodes Robert recalled are accurate, Zeb was an energetic, daring, and willful person from the very beginning. When he was three, his mother had to bring a small hickory log in the house for him to chop to keep him occupied while he recovered from the measles. She apparently thought that if he was not provided with this entertainment, he would rush outside and expose himself to the elements. Zeb was constantly climbing trees and anything else close by, and in consequence he suffered two serious falls. In the first, he sustained a rupture that was repaired by a local doctor. A second fall from an apple tree left Zeb with a broken thighbone that was set by immobilizing his leg inside a box. The irrepressible young man amused himself while his leg healed by throwing stones at his playmates and siblings. The injury left Zeb with one leg shorter than the other, and he was forced to wear a built-up shoe and walk with a rolling gait for the remainder of his life.[11]

Young Vance attracted universal attention for more than just his physical vigor. His appearance was apparently arresting as well. He was bigger than most of his companions, with a great shock of black hair on his head. He never seemed to be able to keep his abundant hair under control, and this feature gave young Zeb a consistently unkempt look. Also, from the time he could talk, he stretched the limits of tolerance of those around him. Much like Huey Long and Theodore Roosevelt, Zeb Vance seemed unable to behave in a commonplace manner. When he drank water out of the French Broad River, he would not scoop the liquid with his hand or lower his head into the water. Instead, he insisted upon getting down on all fours and lapping up the water like a dog. What most provoked adults around him, however, was that Zeb had the command of a large vocabulary of profane language from an early age. Robert Vance surmised that his brother learned this vocabulary from the slaves owned by the Vance family. While that explanation is entirely plausible, it seems more likely that the young man was influenced by the stock drovers who passed by and stopped at the Vance place. The frustrations associated with driving hogs and geese to market undoubtedly elicited some pretty rough language from the provoked farmers. In any case, Zeb's family was greatly relieved when he said nothing colorful at the time of his baptism by a Presbyterian minister.[12]

Most efforts to curb Zeb's exuberance were apparently unsuccessful, and his antics continued when he started to attend school. Schools in western North Carolina in the 1830s were not centers of advanced learning. They were all of the stereotypical "one-room" variety, with a single teacher instructing students of all ages in the same setting. The school year rarely lasted longer than a couple of months, and most lessons involved the rote memorization of a few basic texts. Zeb was apparently bored by the routine on many occasions and was a regular discipline problem. He was a larger-than-average child who was constantly involved in youthful fights and scraps. His teacher, Mathew Woodson, once sought to break Zeb of his habitual use of profanity by using a most ingenious form of punishment. He forced Zeb to sit on the floor away from his schoolmates during the spelling competition—the only exciting part of class. Zeb could extricate himself from his position on the floor only by reforming or by catching a mouse with a pair of tongs that Woodson gave him. During the spelling contest, all of the other students forgot about Zeb, who was staring intently at a mouse hole. Suddenly Zeb, holding a mouse gripped in the tongs, interrupted the contest with a triumphant announcement that emphasized the futility of trying to harness his impetuosity: "Damned if I haven't got him."[13]

There is little evidence to suggest that Zeb had a difficult childhood, his challenges to adult authority notwithstanding. David Hackett Fischer asserts that the relative freedom from restraint enjoyed by young Vance was characteristic of childrearing among the Irish Protestant population. It is likely that the small number of adult female slaves owned by the Vances did much of the labor associated with the farm and the stock stand, and at least one member of that group had considerable responsibility for rearing the family's younger children. "Mammy" Venus was a large woman, estimated by Robert Vance to weigh 250 pounds. While Robert remembered her with obvious fondness, Zeb left no impressions of her or of any of the other enslaved persons who lived with his family.[14]

Zeb did not live a privileged childhood devoid of work responsibilities, however. Most of his chores probably related to meeting the public that journeyed along the Buncombe Turnpike that passed his home. He also worked at a nearby inn in Warm Springs as a hotel clerk. In this capacity, he met some of the notables who passed through the region, and he conversed with them in a very precocious manner. Family tradition maintains that one of the visitors most impressed by the young clerk was John C. Calhoun. Most of the time, however, Zeb probably worked with his father at the drovers' stand. This experience allowed Zeb to become familiar with people from all levels of mountain society and to learn how to communicate effectively with them. Later, when Zeb entered politics, he would put this knowledge to good use. The fairly unexciting work at the drovers' stand also gave Zeb plenty of time to find outlets for his seemingly endless energy. On one occasion, a couple of travelers asked for some liquor to take with them on their journey. What later would be called moonshine whiskey was a legally manufactured product at the time, often produced by mountain farmers as a convenient way of turning bulking grains into a saleable product that could be easily transported. Zeb agreed to get them "liquor" for their trip. When he returned with a container of liquid, he did not charge the men anything for the item. All he asked was that they not immediately consume it. Then he surreptitiously followed the men a short distance and laughed uproariously when they disgustedly threw the container down after tasting the "liquor." Zeb had substituted Mammy Venus's "pot liquor"—the liquid left in a pot after boiling meat and vegetables—for the expected alcoholic beverage.[15]

Despite his deserved reputation as a prankster, Zeb had another more serious characteristic that would become crucial to him as an adult. At some point in his childhood, perhaps when he broke his thighbone, he became an avid reader. The Vance family possessed a library of approximately five hundred volumes, a posthumous gift from Uncle Robert. Zeb read these books again and again, and using the skills inculcated in the local schools, he memorized short excerpts and the general themes of many of them. His later writings and speeches indicate that he read Shakespeare, Sir Walter Scott, and the Bible with considerable care and interest. Zeb imbibed the cultural landmarks of his time; these classic texts enjoyed widespread popularity throughout the nineteenth century. When he used quotations from these familiar sources to make points in his speeches, his audiences were able to follow his reasoning without difficulty. Zeb's unstructured reading was apparently a labor of love, and one that he continued to the very end of his life.[16]

Zeb's obvious intellectual abilities and personal ambition encouraged his father to send him away to a school where he could receive more rigorous training. At the age of twelve or thirteen, he was sent across the mountains to Jonesboro, Tennessee, to study at Washington College. During Zeb's lifetime, the name "college" was freely applied to any institution that offered instruction beyond the most elementary level. While Rev. Alexander Doak, the president of Washington College, was a trained scholar, Zeb received the equivalent of high school training at his institution. Nevertheless, a June 1843 letter from his brother, mother, and father indicated that Zeb thought that he was studying hard and learning a great deal at the school. The coursework included English grammar, Latin, geography, composition, and declamation. Zeb's intellectual pursuits were temporarily halted in January 1844. His father was severely injured while working on a building, and the young scholar was summoned home. He arrived just in time to be with his father when he died on January 14, 1844. Zeb returned to Washington College to finish the year despite the tragedy. His mother even found the resources to allow him to complete part of another year of study before the depleted family finances curtailed Zeb's schooling outside of Buncombe County.[17]

The death of David Vance left his widow with seven children—soon to be eight—and many debts. The family had plenty of land, but Mira needed cash to pay off her husband's creditors. First, she sold the family home in the country and moved onto land in Asheville previously owned by her father. She also sold all of the slaves that the family owned. Her creditors did allow her to buy back Mammy Venus for a dollar, and she provided sufficient childcare to keep the family together. Zeb and Robert both went to work to earn needed cash. Robert set up a separate household, leaving his younger brother with all of the head-of-household chores at the home place. Despite their new responsibilities, the two boys continued their educations on a sporadic basis at local academies in Asheville. While Asheville had become the largest community in western North Carolina, it was still nothing more than a small village of approximately five hundred permanent residents in the 1840s. Nevertheless, it was the center of social, economic, and political life west of the Blue Ridge. This new location put Zeb at the focal point of the region.[18]

Even before the family moved to Asheville, Zeb took part in his first political campaign. By 1844, the North Carolina political system that Zeb became involved in was well defined and understood by all of its participants. The second American party system had been organized in the late 1820s when followers and opponents of Andrew Jackson created national, state, and local structures to contest for offices at each level. The Jacksonians adopted the name of the Democratic Party, and the opposition coalition headed by Henry Clay and Daniel Webster took the name of Whigs. At the state level in North Carolina, the two parties developed distinctive personas. The Democrats came to be associated with the interests of the larger slaveowners of the eastern part of the state, and with agricultural interests in general. As the 1840s progressed, they became outspoken advocates of states' rights and the defense of slavery. The Whigs in North Carolina became the spokesmen for a more active state government and the sponsors of programs to expand state aid to railroads, particularly in the western part of the state.[19]

The two political coalitions were more complex than the above outline indicates. Harry Watson has demonstrated that ethnic identity played an important role in defining political allegiance. Other researchers have shown than eastern North Carolina Whigs and Democrats sometimes acted in concert to frustrate the efforts of western North Carolina political leaders of both parties. In addition, suffrage issues complicated the political system in the state. After the creation of the new constitution in 1835, all adult white males could vote to elect the governor and the members of the lower house of the legislature, but property requirements for voters restricted the electorate so that only approximately 50 percent of adult males could vote in elections for the state Senate. Another factor in the political equation was slaveowners' absolute domination of the political system. The leaders of both parties owned human chattel and were clearly members of the elite of the state. Thus, political philosophy, social and economic interests, and sectional identity all interacted to help to define partisan allegiance in North Carolina.[20]

For many North Carolinians, however, the most decisive factor in determining party alliance was family tradition. For Zebulon Vance, family tradition dictated that he be a member of the Whig party. Zeb's initial decision was reinforced by his perception of the Whigs as champions of the interests of the western section of the state. By the time that Zeb became personally involved in political canvasses, the candidates and their supporters had developed an elaborate array of activities to attract voters. In most electoral contests, the candidates for office spoke in open debates on a regular schedule, usually on court days in county seats. After the Whigs adopted more democratic appeals successfully in the 1840 presidential race, the party and its opponents began using all types of gimmicks to get people involved in their campaigns. Apparently Zeb was part of a Whig mobilization effort that is best described in his own words: "I headed a procession on mule back . . . [and] marched sixteen miles to the election precinct through the mountains of Madison County, filled with patriotism, zeal for the Whig cause, and hard cider. . . . Fifteen separate and distinct fights were then and there had, in part of which I participated and for all of which I might be set down as the proximate cause." Since the Whigs carried the state in 1844, Zeb's first political efforts were successful. If there had ever been any doubt about what career Zeb would pursue, this exciting introduction into politics may have been decisive in shaping his future.[21]

By the time that Zeb reached his late teens, the broad outline of his future could be discerned. He was an irrepressible and fun-loving extrovert who despite an incomplete education was widely read and had a good command of some significant pieces of classical literature. Zeb had also developed personal skills that allowed him to meet and converse with people from all segments of mountain society with great ease. He was the heir to a family tradition of political involvement; all branches of his family tree belonged to the relatively small number of families that formed the social, economic, and political elite of his native region. Finally, he had proven time and again that he was eager to play adult roles much earlier than many of his peers.

A s Zeb's teen years came to an end, his life took on more direction. Apparently he had a clear outline in mind of the way his life should unfold, and he worked toward the goals he set with considerable drive. It is clear from the surviving sources, however, that his clarity of vision did not cause him to move with single-minded commitment. As was true when he was a child, Zeb continued to be an ebullient person who rarely passed up an opportunity to have fun. Despite his seeming addiction to the light side of life, he gained public prominence at an unusually early age. The combination of political ambition, irrepressible wit, and the need to be the center of attention would characterize Zeb for his entire adult life.

Kemp P. Battle, a later adviser, provided a brief portrait of what Zeb was like as he approached manhood. Battle was the son of a distinguished lawyer who was a law professor at the University of North Carolina and an associate justice of the North Carolina Supreme Court. When he met Zeb, the younger Battle was in Asheville accompanying his father on his rounds of the state court system. Their brief meeting in the moonlight left a lasting impression on Battle. He was amazed to find in this small mountain village a young man who knew the classic literature of the period better than he did. Battle had to concede that Zeb's knowledge of Shakespeare put his to shame. The same was true for the Bible and the novels of Sir Walter Scott. Battle also noted, however, that Zeb's knowledge of the Scriptures was not accompanied by a corresponding piety. His conversation sparkled with good humor, but his manner was often somewhat crude and unpolished.[1]

Two years after he met Battle, Zeb began to study law with the expectation of passing the bar. He and his Asheville contemporary Augustus S. Merrimon studied under the guidance of Nicholas W. Woodfin. Fortunately, Merrimon kept a somewhat cryptic diary during this period, and a fairly detailed account of Zeb's activities emerges. It appears that Zeb and Merrimon were only two of several aspiring lawyers who studied with Woodfin, who was widely considered to be the leading attorney in the region at the time. Known both for his knowledge of the law and his excellent courtroom presentations, Woodfin carried a very heavy workload. Merrimon noted that he and Zeb could not be examined on the first evening they appeared before Woodfin because he was quizzing other students and quit at 11 P.M. before he got to the two newcomers. Four days later, on December 10, 1850, Merrimon reported: "Tonight for the first time we have had an examination upon the Law. Mr. Woodfin examined us about an hour and I believe we met his expectations." They continued these lessons for several months, often leaving Woodfin's office at close to midnight. They were being drilled on the content of the volumes of Blackstone. Apparently most of the work was rote memorization. Vance's progress was not as great as it might have been, however; Merrimon records several evenings when no examination was held because Zeb failed to appear.[2]

Vance later admitted that he had not been as diligent as he should have been at his law studies. One reason for this was that he was once again involved in politics. Both Zeb and his brother Robert (now often called Bob) were appointed to public office in early 1851. Bob, an officer in the Asheville division of the Sons of Temperance, was named clerk of the Board for Common Schools. This was a very responsible position for someone who was only twenty-two. At the same time, Zeb was appointed as one of eight members of the patrol for the county, a peacekeeping office. While this was not a major position, it signaled that Zeb was recognized as a significant member of the community. Several of the other appointees were older men from prominent Asheville families. Zeb thus held his first public position before he reached his twenty-first birthday. Participating in politics of a different type, during that same period he undoubtedly also attended a large Unionist meeting held at the courthouse, where participants reluctantly endorsed the Compromise of 1850. The exact wording of their statement is interesting to reflect upon in view of what would happen a decade later:

> 3. Resolved, That the fanaticism of the North on the subject of slavery is the chief cause of all the disturbances between the North and South.
>
>   . . .
>
> 5. Resolved, That as long as the Compromise acts of the last Session are carried out in good faith, we will remain in the Union.[3]

The Unionism of Asheville's residents in 1850 was decidedly conditional. But for Vance, the importance of the occasion was probably as much psychological as ideological. He seemed inexorably drawn to large crowds and political events. Even as he sought to train himself as a lawyer, he could not resist becoming involved in politics.

Another reason for Zeb's failure to study efficiently was his increasingly active social life. Merrimon noted in his diary on February 15, 1851, that Woodfin cut short their examination that evening. Having some unexpected free time, the two young men "enjoyed [themselves] . . . very much with the ladies." Exactly a month later, Zeb began corresponding with Harriett Newell Espy of Quaker Meadows in Burke County. She was a slight woman with striking red hair who was described as "erect and graceful in figure, with much vivacity and sweetness of manner, a musically modulated voice, and an unusual strength and quickness of mind." She lived with the Charles McDowell family after the death of her parents, who passed away before she was four. The McDowells were among the most prominent families in western North Carolina, and their home was one of the more imposing in the region. It was a very substantial two-story brick structure with columns in the front. Thus, Harriett was connected with a family that was equal in prestige to the Vances and vastly superior in financial status. The two young people apparently met on some occasion prior to beginning their correspondence, perhaps when Harriett visited her cousins at their Asheville home. According to a later letter, an Asheville woman had rejected Zeb's suit just before he started writing to Harriett. The awkwardness of the opening sentence in Zeb's first letter to her—"The object of this intrusive epistle is to beg to be allowed the favor of your correspondence"—may indicate that he feared being rejected a second time. When Harriett replied positively, Zeb was overjoyed. His second letter contained verse and hyperbolic pronouncements of devotion, among them: "I deem it preferable for my own peace to say directly and frankly, Miss Espy, that you have inspired me with a sentiment of love deep and lasting, and of the most sanguine and even enthusiastic character."[4]

The path of true love did not run smoothly for the young people, however. Illness delayed Harriett's return letter, and then she offered only friendship to the "bitterly crushed" Zeb. All of his ardent feelings returned in July when he visited Harriett briefly during his trip to Chapel Hill, where he would attend the University of North Carolina. Although Vance continued to assure Harriett of his love and devotion, it appears that he was also sizing up the romantic potential of other young women. In a letter to his cousin Martha E. Weaver, he reported: "I saw the two nieces of Mr. Norwood of our town, then, and all that kept me from falling desperately in love was because I couldn't for my life make a choice between them. They were so pretty!" But he asked Martha to assure another cousin that he had "*thought of somebody's bright eyes*, way up in the mountains, and that kept me from danger." As Glenn Tucker observed, this was probably not a reference to his relationship with Harriett, since Quaker Meadows was

*Quaker Meadows in Burke County. This substantial house was
the adopted home of Harriett Newell Espy, Vance's future wife.
(North Carolina Division of Archives and History, Raleigh)*

not located in the mountain region proper.[5] No hint of Zeb's interest in other young women made its way into his continuing correspondence with Harriett.

Whether due to his growing interest in Harriett or some other factor, Zeb suddenly seemed to seize control of his life for the first time. He made plans and followed through with them. He appeared to have distinct long-range goals and to recognize that he had to discipline himself to attain them. Once he had selected his goals, he moved purposefully toward them. His family could not afford to pay for the university training he desired. Thus, he was forced to write to the president of the University of North Carolina to request a loan of three hundred dollars. This seemingly improbable course of action was not as impractical as it seemed. The president, David L. Swain, was a native of Asheville and a friend of Vance's mother. Swain and the faculty quickly agreed to provide the loan, and Zeb was on his way to Chapel Hill.[6] While the exact catalyst for the change in Vance is impossible to pinpoint, the transformation is familiar to anyone who teaches young people. In such cases, a new depth of insight and poise appears almost overnight, without the young person having made any special effort to develop it. The youth's personal and intellectual development takes a giant stride forward, while doubts and uncertainties disappear. The new Zeb was still vigorous, irrepressible, and fun loving, but all of his energy was now directed toward achieving certain well-defined goals.

Vance's year at the University of North Carolina was crucial for his maturation. His impact on the quiet village of Chapel Hill and its small university was instantaneous and spectacular. More than four decades later, his former classmates could easily recall dozens of stories about Zeb's antics and humorous quips that they had laughed at and retold through the years. Vance's arrival itself was often remembered. When he descended from the coach that had brought him from Morganton, he looked like a hick. His pants were far too short, his shoes were obviously homemade, and the cut of his jacket was very unfashionable. Most of those who observed his arrival would have forgotten this fashion disaster if Vance had not thrust himself into the limelight immediately. He arrived on the stage with a number of other students, and he was apparently offended when these students were effusively greeted at the station by old college friends and he was not. Not to be outdone, Zeb rushed over to an elderly black man who was observing the coming of the stage and mimicked the enthusiastic reception given to the other arriving students. Within moments, he was the center of attention and making new friends easily.[7]

Zeb resided in West Hall, one of the three main buildings on campus. With no distractions besides the social life of the university, Zeb studied with uncommon fervor. As he told Harriett, he was up at five in the morning and did not go to bed until ten in the evening. This uncommonly hectic schedule was necessary because Zeb was taking a double course load. He took the law course, which was offered by the university on what today would be called a continuing education basis. The courses were not part of the university's regular offerings, and its faculty members were unpaid

David Lowry Swain, ca. 1850. A native of Buncombe County, Swain became a lawyer, governor of North Carolina, and president of the University of North Carolina. He served as a mentor to Vance during his stay at the university and during the Civil War. (North Carolina Division of Archives and History, Raleigh)

professionals who offered their services to the students. At the same time, Zeb was "studying the studies of the Senior Class entire, except, French & Greek." He noted that the senior course of study, which included two additional law classes, actually took more of his time than did his legal studies. His hard work paid off when he took "first honors" in one of his university classes; Vance noted, moreover, that he was "reading Law faster and learning more than when [he] was at home with nothing else to do."[8]

It would be completely misleading, however, to suggest that all of Vance's time at the university was spent on his studies. In fact, it was Zeb's antics in extracurricular activities that attracted the attention of most of his contemporaries. Apparently, he was not alone in being distracted from his work by the social life of the university. He remarked in a letter to Harriett that there was some kind of acting up going on every night. In fact, the situation had become so serious that President Swain and a member of the faculty were stationed in the dormitories at night to maintain order. Vance assured Harriett that he was not involved in any drunkenness or rowdy behavior. And in one sense, his disclaimer is credible. He was older than most of the other students on campus, and he was serious about his studies. But all of the stories that survived from Vance's university days indicate that he had an enjoyable social life. According to one such tale, he was hazed while joining an informal social organization, but he kept the situation from becoming too raucous by jesting with his assailants and keeping them in good humor.[9]

One of his favorite activities was taking part in the debates of the Dialectic Literary Society. The society taught the rules of formal debate, and knowledge of these rules would stand Vance in good stead for the remainder of his public life. His classmates noted that Vance was a poised speaker from the very beginning. This was probably the result of his experience working both as a hotel clerk and at his father's drovers' lot. These jobs required him to deal with the adult public, and in them he learned to converse with a broad cross section of Southern society. Because his exchanges with the public started when he was very young, Vance apparently never felt any anxiety when called upon to speak. This was even more the case at the university, where most of his fellow students were several years younger than he was. The meetings of the Dialectic Literary Society provided a more structured setting for him to speak in. The society forced him to defend his ideas in formal debate, extemporaneous speeches, and written compositions. His later writings and speeches show the imprint of this training.[10] Despite the occasional levity of his material and forms of expression, Vance's presentations were always well organized and logically argued.

Vance also received considerable training in legal argument and public speaking in moot court sessions conducted by the law professors. The sessions were relatively structured, as the students were required to discuss points of law chosen by the faculty. Apparently, Vance's greatest triumph using this format was his defense of the "College Bore." Vance was forced in his address to agree that the bore was a problem for those around him.

The poor unfortunate was not only uninteresting, but he kept other students from being able to study. Yet Vance contended that the bore was not to be found guilty of a crime. He was simply following the path laid out for him by his Creator, from which he could not deviate. Vance argued that the bore had been sent into their presence to teach them patience and fortitude.[11] This type of clever, if rather insubstantial, reasoning would mark many later courtroom presentations delivered by Vance.

Meanwhile, Zeb continued to correspond with Harriett, and their relationship deepened. By January 1852, Harriett's letters began with the salutation "My Beloved Zebulon." The subjects that couples contemplating marriage often discuss began to appear in their letters with greater regularity. One of these subjects, discussed briefly, was Zeb's religious beliefs. The significance of this topic to their future relationship would be difficult to underestimate. Harriett was an exceptionally pious person and was recognized as such by all who knew her, including Zeb. She wrote out a covenant of personal religious faith in 1848, which she periodically updated. An entry in Augustus S. Merrimon's diary that probably referred to Zeb, his most consistent discussion partner, captures Vance's religious ideas: "In conversation with many of my friends and associates I find a skeptical disposition. Many have not the courage to avow their principles openly, and perhaps this is better for them. Men at this day who profess themselves deists have little bearing in society."[12] Exactly what Zeb said and what Merrimon meant by Deism is not clear. Vance was widely read in the Scriptures and knew a great deal about Christian ideas and thought. Later events in his life indicate that he did believe in the existence of God. This sentiment might have been the basis for Merrimon's conclusion that his friend was Deist.

But Zeb was forced to acknowledge to Harriett that he was not as committed to the church as she was. In an October letter, he confessed: "As to any feeling, which might be termed, religious, I am frank enough to acknowledge, that I feel none whatever." This statement, which was rather upsetting to Harriett, was accompanied by others that may have reassured her. Zeb maintained, for example, that since he had moved to Chapel Hill he had "gained some important victories over [his] bad habits." In addition, he claimed that being in the presence of a person as devout as Harriett would be of great benefit to him.[13] She reluctantly accepted this assertion, and their later correspondence reveals no serious disagreements over religious matters.

Another matter of great significance that the couple mentioned in their correspondence was the rather precarious nature of Harriett's health. Her replies to Zeb's letters were frequently delayed, and when they arrived they would often contain an explanation like the following: "Although I am scarcely able to sit up, I cant allow another day [to] pass without informing My Dear Zebulon, of my illness. I have been quite sick for several days & still feel very unwell. . . . I have been suffering very much with a sore throat & and a most violent cough, but hope to be entirely relieved soon."[14] At no time in her adult life would Hattie (as she was now calling herself in her letters to Zeb) be free from the ravages of respiratory illnesses. Several times before she died of consumption in 1878, she suffered complete physical collapses that were followed by long periods of partial recovery and continuing weakness. Hattie's health would be the one consistent source of worry for Vance throughout their entire relationship. Despite his obvious devotion to her and his concern about her well-being, however, there is no indication that he ever made any changes in his own career plans to accommodate her health needs.

In the same letter in which she described her health problems, Hattie revealed a side of herself that undoubtedly attracted Zeb. She noted in passing that she had been forced by her illness to miss a meeting of the Reading Society of which she was president. In her letters, Hattie frequently mentioned books and magazines that she was reading. The broad context in which she discussed current events and other topics indicates that she had been reading fairly widely for a number of years. In acknowledgment of her abilities and interests, Zeb would send her current issues of magazines as an expression of love.[15] It seems quite clear that the couple shared a genuine interest in reading and in discussing issues raised by the material they read.

Although there was a long holiday break in December and January, the two lovers were unable to get together because Zeb had to be examined for his license to practice law in the lower courts. He reported to Hattie about the experience in a letter written on New Year's Day: "I have just returned from Raleigh where I obtained license without difficulty. Indeed I had been studying severely, and was conscious that I need not fear the result. From the manner in which the examination was conducted, I could not but infer a compliment to my preparation and that of several others, as the judges appeared satisfied with asking me but two or three questions." With this momentous point in his life passed, Vance relaxed by hunting and visiting with families in Chapel Hill. In less than two weeks, classes started again. He continued to carry a double load of courses, doing extra work to prepare for the examination that would allow him to practice law in the superior courts of North Carolina.[16]

Another reason that Zeb decided to stay in Chapel Hill during the holidays was that he had come to enjoy the company of many people in the university town. He found intellectual conversations stimulating and enjoyed talking with educated people about current events. Two families in particular offered Zeb a homelike atmosphere and conversation with young people near his own age. One was the Battle family. The patriarch of the family was Judge William H. Battle, the chief instructor in the law course. Battle had six sons, two of whom became lifelong friends of Vance. Kemp P. Battle, the older of the two, was an instructor at the university despite the fact that he was a year younger than Zeb. He would later be its president. Richard H. Battle was five years younger than Vance and a student at the college preparatory school at the university. Vance would later call upon Richard to be his private secretary during the crucial years of the Civil War.[17]

The other family that attracted a great deal of Vance's attention during this time was that of James Phillips, professor of mathematics at the university. Again, it was the presence of young adults in the family that served as Vance's incentive to spend time with the Phillipses. Because the two Phillips sons were older than Vance and already established as professionals, his closest relationship in the family was with Cornelia, the only daughter. Cornelia was five years older than Zeb and already recognized as a person of significant intellectual attainments. Born in New York, she had been educated largely by her father and had read voraciously within her family's extensive library. Vance mentioned her a number of times in his letters to Hattie as a remarkable person. The close friendship between Zeb and Cornelia, who married and left the state in the late 1850s, would result in the publication of an important history of the Civil War in 1866.[18] The presence of these two exciting families ensured that Zeb would continue to grow intellectually and socially while he lived in Chapel Hill, and his relationships with them probably left him less time for rowdy behavior than might otherwise have been the case.

As important as the Battle and Phillips families were to Zeb, two of his instructors seemed to affect him most: President David L. Swain and Professor Elisha Mitchell. Vance, who had lost his father seven years earlier, apparently adopted the two men as surrogates. Swain, in particular, became his mentor. Swain was a tall man of awkward gait and rather plain features who nonetheless was a convivial companion due to his courtesy and wit. Swain was attractive to Vance for a number of reasons. As a native of Asheville, Swain had known Vance's grandparents and had grown up with Zeb's parents. There were even hints that Swain had once thought of courting Zeb's mother. Thus, the student could be assured that the university president understood and appreciated his heritage. At the same time, Swain was an important role model in another way. The older man had come down out of the mountains and been elected governor of the state in the 1830s.

As a founder of the Whig Party in North Carolina, the same organization that Zeb joined, Swain offered an example to the young mountaineer of the possibilities open to him. As president for fifteen years of the major educational institution that trained the elite of North Carolina, Swain was also in a position to be able to connect Vance to other political leaders in the state.[19] Zeb took Swain's class in international law and benefited from the older man's extensive storehouse of practical legal knowledge. The friendship between the two men became quite close, if always unequal, and Vance would depend upon his mentor for sage advice throughout the trying days of the Civil War.

Elisha Mitchell addressed other needs for the young Vance. Much more scholarly than Swain, he nevertheless captured the imagination of the young mountain man with the incredible breadth of his learning. Mitchell was a graduate of Yale, and before coming to North Carolina he was a tutor at Yale and a student at the theological seminary at Andover, Massachusetts. He was licensed to preach by the Congregationalist Western Association in Connecticut. He arrived in Chapel Hill in 1818 and virtually became the university's entire science department by himself. By the time Zeb took classes from Mitchell, the scholar had been teaching chemistry, geology, and mineralogy for more than three decades. In addition, he conducted compulsory chapel services at the university six days a week. Given Zeb's personality, there would seem to have been little in Mitchell's background that would have appealed to him. But Mitchell had directed the geological survey of North Carolina and had become fascinated with the mountains near Asheville. He claimed to have located the highest mountain in the eastern half of the United States in the Black Mountains north of Asheville. Because he understood the topography of the region and the needs of its people, Mitchell became a champion of greater state funding for transportation systems into the mountains, an issue that would later be the centerpiece of Vance's own political platform for nearly two decades.[20] Although Mitchell apparently possessed a good sense of humor, Zeb never thought of getting as close to him as he did to Swain. Instead, he respected the scholar for his vast accumulation of knowledge. Vance later recognized his debts to the two men by delivering eulogies at their funeral services, two decades apart.

Although Zeb held Mitchell and Swain in the highest esteem, it did not prevent him from disrupting their classes. During a geological field trip with Mitchell, Vance apparently convulsed the class with a question about an antiquated gristmill, inquiring, "Doctor, do you think that old millhouse is worth a dam?" Since "damn" was considered to be an extremely indecent word at the time, Vance was not only making a pun but was skirting the edge of propriety as well. When Mitchell's questions during laboratory examination became too difficult, the class was always relieved when Zeb would ask some question about the geology of the mountains in the western part of the state. Mitchell would instantly change the topic and begin to discuss his research in the highland region. Swain's classes were often conducted in the recitation style that is common in law schools to the present day. Vance's retentive memory generally stood him in good stead, and he often sparred in a light vein with his professor and benefactor. During one class, Vance sat beside a classmate who had taken the precaution of writing a number of legal citations on his boot for reference. When Zeb was asked to give the authorities by Swain, he lifted his classmate's foot into his lap and read off the list. Swain, hoping to teach Zeb a lesson, called him to the front of the room and required him to recite the list without any assistance. Acting as if this was a simple task, Vance quickly repeated the citations without a mistake. The chagrined university president sent him back to his seat while the entire class chuckled.[21] The two older men recognized Vance's humor was good natured and did not penalize him for it.

Zeb expected to stay in Chapel Hill until June 1852 to fully prepare for the examination that would license him to practice in the superior courts, but he suddenly left campus and returned to Asheville in March. By that time, he and Hattie had become engaged to be married, although final approval from both of their families did not come until several weeks later. Zeb recognized that he had to establish himself in his profession before he could think about providing a home for Hattie. Thus, he hastened home in time to run for the office of solicitor of the Buncombe County Court. He stopped off briefly in Burke County to spend some time with Hattie, but he soon continued on to Asheville. He arrived just before the day that the magistrates were going to select the new solicitor. His exultation at the result is captured in his own words:

> On Monday morning early I went up to the village and announced myself a candidate and the vote coming off after dinner, I have the pleasure of informing you that I beat Mr Merrimon by a vote of 11 to 8. I laboured under many disadvantages, as he had been electioneering for three months and had obtained pledges from a great many magistrates who did not know that I was coming home to offer. Beside this there were only about half of them in town so that I stood quite a slim chance and my friends thought I would be defeated. . . . It seemed as if everybody I met wished me to succeed; my young friends and associates of the village especially were exceedingly warm and active in my favour I believe without an exception.[22]

Harriett Newell Espy, ca. 1862. Harriett was the first wife of Zebulon Vance, 1853–78.
(North Carolina Division of Archives and History, Raleigh)

Thus, before he turned twenty-two Vance was elected to his second public office. His success indicated that from the beginning he had a winning political style. It is also important to note that the voters in this contest were the county magistrates, members of the elite families of the county. The prominence of Vance's family connections undoubtedly contributed to his electoral success. It is also interesting to consider that his main competition for the office was Augustus Merrimon, a young man his own age. Obviously, more mature members of the bar were unwilling to give up their remunerative private practices to serve as the county lawyer. For lawyers like Merrimon and Vance who were just beginning their careers, however, the position offered the opportunity to gain experience while receiving a small but assured stipend.

Despite their fondest hopes, Zeb and Hattie were not married until August 2, 1853. Due to Hattie's ill health and the press of Zeb's business concerns, likely dates for the ceremony came and went with some regularity. On a number of occasions, Zeb managed to travel through the mountains to Quaker Meadows to visit briefly with Harriett. One of these trips nearly proved to be fatal. In late August 1852, Vance set off for Morganton with his friend Henry Dickson. Friends and relatives had asked them not to go, because a driving rain threatened to swell all of the rivers and streams along the way. Because Zeb was anxious to see Hattie after a long separation, however, he and his companion pushed on toward Burke County. When they entered a small creek at "Gen. Burgins lane," the two men, their horse, and their buggy were swept rapidly downstream. Dickson quickly jumped out of the vehicle, saving some of the baggage. Vance, who held the reins and had plunged into the torrent, stayed with the horse and buggy to try to preserve them. He recounted: "About fifty yards down the stream the buggy turned over, when I sprang out and [was] caught by a limb and thus narrowly saved a life which seems now scarcely worth saving." The extremity of the danger that Vance and Dickson faced was driven home when "the horse was dreadfully injured" and "the buggy broken into almost a thousand pieces."[23] This incident illustrates two of Vance's most important personal traits. First, he plunged directly after his objective, oblivious to the obstructions in his way. He would pursue a number of goals with similar single-mindedness in the future. Vance's lack of fear about his physical safety would also reappear when, a decade later, he led men on two Civil War battlefields.

The strong bonds that developed between Zeb and Hattie during the many trials of their courtship survived one last test. For a variety of reasons, a number of Hattie's Asheville relatives became convinced that Vance was a poor match for her. They went out of their way to snub him socially and to act hostile toward him in public. This was particularly true of Nicholas W. Woodfin, Zeb's first tutor in the law. Zeb returned the hostility of Hattie's relatives with civility for some time, but he eventually adopted the same tactics used by his opponents. This all took on a rather ridiculous cast, since everyone involved was part of a small elite in a village of five hundred people. Fortunately for Zeb and Hattie, the foolish behavior of their elders had no impact on their relationship. Their immediate families welcomed the long awaited wedding, and the young couple returned to Asheville to take up residence.

ebulon Vance's sudden reentry into Asheville's political and legal scene in the March 1852 solicitor's race was the prelude to several stormy years for him in both law and politics. Never one to avoid the limelight, Zeb thrust himself into the middle of several controversies and carefully kept his name before the people. His driving ambition led him to commit errors of excess that threatened his position, but his good humor and generally genial disposition helped him to retain the goodwill of most of the people with whom he came in contact. Nevertheless, he made powerful enemies among the elite who worked with considerable vigor to undercut his position. While both friends and relatives found him to be insufferable upon occasion, Vance's personality and public persona were attractive to many yeoman farmers from the mountains, and he began to build a powerful following that would last for the remainder of his life.

Writing to Hattie just three months before their wedding, Zeb offered the following assessment of himself: "To day I am just twenty three years old. . . . It seems but yesterday when I was a prattling mischievous school urchin, without any serious thought or anything else to indicate the man that was to be—, celebrated only for wickedness and wildness! And now I am in my twenty fourth year, at mature manhood, on the eve of matrimony and the duties and cares of life crowding upon me and driving sleep from my pillow! And what have I done in all this time to make myself admired or respected! Alas, little, *very little*." There is no doubt that his contemporaries shared the same opinion of the young lawyer-politician. Augustus S. Merrimon wrote a brief character sketch of Vance seven months later that confirmed Vance's own feeling that he had not accomplished enough with his life. Merrimon observed: "I consider him a sprightly man, though not talented. He is not an ordinary man however. He has had some advantages, some of which, he has not improved as he should." Merrimon went on to conjecture that Vance could become a "respectable" but not a "profound" lawyer.[1] Clearly, there was little indication early in his career that Zeb would achieve great things.

A scholarly study of lawyers in antebellum Virginia suggests that Zeb's

Asheville, North Carolina, in 1851. Asheville was a growing community when Vance began his career and brought his bride home. (North Carolina Division of Archives and History, Raleigh)

slow start in the profession was quite normal. In Virginia, the number of lawyers practicing may have doubled between 1830 and 1850; the same was probably true in North Carolina. The population increased at a much slower pace than the supply of lawyers, and thus competition among lawyers for cases intensified. In rural counties where the population was small and most lawyers were from local families, the established older lawyers were approached first by potential clients. Because professional ethics limited advertising appeals to notices of availability, young lawyers had little opportunity to attract the attention of the public through normal legal activities. For example, at the October 1853 court in Asheville there were eight lawyers from outside of Buncombe County present along with ten lawyers from around Asheville. About half of these men had practiced law for a decade or more. With all of these lawyers seeking work in a county of approximately six thousand people, only the cases that the older men rejected became available to the novices entering the profession.[2]

During the period between March 1852 and August 1853, Zeb faced an additional handicap: he had passed his initial law exam, but he had not obtained a license to practice in the superior courts of the state. In practical terms, this meant that he could help people prepare legal documents, but he could not appear in court to plead their cases. Despite this handicap, he joined the other lawyers as they traveled from one small county seat to another. He reported to Hattie the meager results of his first "trip on the circuit as an 'Attorney & Councellor at Law.'" He was forced to admit that there were few details for him to relate to her. He continued: "Suffice it to say, that as regards my success, as I did not expect much, I realized the blessing pronounced upon all such moderate spirits, for I was not disappointed. I made some Ciceronian displays, and also many acquaintances with some few friends, which is better."[3] These latter activities would be crucial for Zeb's future legal and political success. He, like most of his companions, would have to rely upon his personal contacts to create both business opportunities and a following for future political campaigns. His speeches provided the local population with an example of what they could expect to hear in the courtroom when he was allowed to enter it. They also gave Vance further training in the art of public persuasion.

The routine of traveling without much hope of financial reward was demoralizing for the young attorney from Asheville. Many years later, he described his trips to law students in Washington in humorous terms: "I went out to court on horseback, and carried a pair of saddlebags, with a change of shirts and the North Carolina Form-book in one end of the saddlebags, and it is none of your business what was in the other." What would seem amusing to him and his auditors later, however, was not funny at the time. In October 1852, Zeb told Hattie: "I am heartily tired of following the courts and am not going to attend any more this fall. With such a small share of the business as I have in the Superior Courts it becomes exceedingly tiresome to travel around the circuit and hang around the courts like a loafer." Two months later, he reported: "Alternate rain, snow & sleet characterised the weather during my absence, whilst the mud and bad roads will not admit of description. In consequence, the courts were rather poorly attended and very little business done." In the early spring of the following year, he complained to Hattie: "As I have no Superior Co[urt] license, I of course had nothing to do, but still I have been quite busy in attending to other business of a harassing and annoying kind, and am as glad as anyone to see the end of the week."[4] Recognizing the handicap that he would operate under if he failed to obtain his superior court license, Vance stopped traveling the circuit early in the spring of 1853 to prepare for his license examination, which would take place in Morganton in early August.

Travel around the circuit was very difficult for even the successful lawyers. While a novice attorney, Augustus S. Merrimon recorded a vivid picture of the travails of an 1853 journey that gives modern readers a feeling for the conditions that traveling lawyers endured. First, the county seats themselves were uninspiring. Merrimon described Waynesville, in Haywood County, as follows: "Waynesville is a dirty little village and there is no place of entertainment in it fit to stay at. One would suppose it a large negro quarter to see it at a distance. The buildings are poor and decayed. The

Court house is a verry bad one. The best building in the place is the Jail, a new building." Merrimon found the local inhabitants to be as unattractive as their villages. In several localities, he noted that some locals made the meeting of the court an occasion for substantial drunkenness, which often disrupted court proceedings. Merrimon also judged some of the people he met to be lacking in community spirit. He observed of Jackson County: "I think I can say with safety, that I have never been at a place, or in a County, where there seemed to be as much Mallice and diabolical revenge. Revenge seems to be in the bosom of everyone." The only recompense for the weary traveler was the occasional stop at "Mr. Jarrett's, a comfortable house on the Nantahala River." Like Merrimon, Vance deplored the difficulties of travel and the excesses associated with court days. He reported to Hattie that an enormous crowd had gathered for one man's hanging and, "not being of such a tender heart as most of the women there, [he] left and came back to keep from seeing him hung."[5] Even if Vance had been making a great deal of money, there would still have been many aspects of his new profession that he found disagreeable.

Although his success was limited, Zeb's correspondence reveals that the people of the small mountain county seats were slowly beginning to accept him. First, his public speaking began to attract attention. He reported that he made a "tall" speech in Franklin and that he was able to acquire a number of clients as a result. By the early spring of 1853, Vance's renown as a speaker was such that he was invited to Burnsville in Yancey County to deliver a prepared address on education. The obviously pleased Vance reported to Hattie: "I delivered my address at 12 O'clk to quite a large audience. I recd a great many compliments after its delivery from the appreciative citizens of Yancey, and have since recd. a written request from a committee on behalf of the school for a copy of the MSS. for publication." Zeb's success encouraged him to establish a regular program of public speaking. He informed Hattie: "I am going to make big speeches from one end of the circuit to the other and push myself along as much as the nature of the case and my native and *proverbial modesty* will permit." Zeb's ability to speak ironically about his personal investment in this program of advancement indicates his growing self-confidence. In addition, an act of family generosity gained Zeb a great measure of goodwill in Madison County. The North Carolina legislature had created the new county in 1851, and the county commissioners were trying to decide where to locate the county seat. Vance clinched the case for Lapland, where his father's stock drovers' stand had been located, by donating fifty acres to the county on behalf of his family on April 20, 1853. Renamed Marshall, the small community remained beholden to Vance for the remainder of his life.[6] Thus, even before Vance obtained his superior court license, he was making a positive impression on the people of western North Carolina.

Zeb's share of the legal work in the highland region began to expand consistently as his speaking brought him to public attention. After a swing through Madison and Yancey Counties, he announced that he had "numerous" clients who would be willing to retain his services when he earned his superior court license. He even began to obtain clients in the competitive Asheville court. He celebrated after securing his first two clients in the county, and he later claimed proudly, "at home I am getting on 'right down sharp' as the yankees would say." In addition, he secured a contract to manage the affairs of a mentally incompetent person—"My crazy ward"—in Buncombe County. This latter client provided little opportunity for Vance to display his abilities in public, but the arrangement probably supplied him with a small but steady income. In early August 1853, Vance left Asheville for Morganton. When he returned, he brought with him a new bride and his license to practice in the superior courts of North Carolina. He was now prepared to fulfill the prophecy that he had made earlier to Hattie: "Time and Perseverance can work wonders, and it is my candid opinion that you and I will make some noise in the world yet!"[7]

If Vance expected that obtaining his superior court license would suddenly make him a successful attorney, he must have been sorely disappointed. A biographer would later claim that Vance "at once took his place in the front rank of a very able bar." This conclusion appears to be entirely unwarranted. One of Zeb's contemporaries assessed the situation more accurately: "Well gintle*men*, I have noticed this little feller Vance, and if he kin git apast the jedge, he's about as good as any av 'em." The problem for Zeb was that it was very difficult to "get past" Judge David F. Caldwell. Merrimon described Caldwell as follows: "[He is] very stern in his commands, full of energy[,] and usually sees that the law is executed properly. He is quite sensitive and punishes any one, who infringes the least upon the dignity and privileges of the court."[8] Thus, Vance had to be prepared to present his cases according to a high standard of legal knowledge and decorum.

Nor was the judge the only officer of the court who held Zeb to high standards. The opposing lawyers were very competitive, and they took advantage of Vance's inexperience. When he was less than diligent, even his own contemporaries could severely punish him. In a case in Madison County, Vance cited an opinion delivered by the North Carolina Supreme Court to buttress his case. Augustus S. Merrimon, the opposing attorney, took great pleasure shortly thereafter in pointing out that the precedent was invalid. In its most recent session, the legislature had repealed the act upon which the Supreme Court had based its decision, and, therefore, the opinion Vance had cited no longer had the force of law. Trapped by his own negligence, Zeb resorted to verbal sophistry. He turned to the jury and asked: "Gentlemen of the jury, are you not amazed at the assurance of my friend, Mr. Merrimon, in citing an act of the legislature passed by such men as your good neighbor John Smith, who knows no more law than you do and Bill Jones of Yancey, who knows less, against the decision of our Supreme Court constituted of such men as Ruffin, Gaston, and Daniel?"[9] While the outcome of the case is unknown, Vance probably had to scramble to cover up many such blunders as he learned his profession.

If Zeb had confined himself to making clever verbal escapes from the situations in which his lack of experience and hard work placed him, he undoubtedly would have retained the goodwill of his fellow professionals. But even as a married man with greater responsibilities, he could not contain himself from acting like a schoolboy. One example of his childish behavior is so bizarre that an observer remembered it forty years later. Vance was arguing a case against his former teacher and personal enemy Nicholas W. Woodfin. Woodfin apparently had a very strong case and made a passionate presentation to the jury which he punctuated with a series of dramatic physical gestures. The court and the spectators waited anxiously for Vance's reply to this impressive performance. Drawing upon his considerable abilities as a mimic, Vance "walk[ed] boldly up to the jury, . . . struck a Woodfinian attitude and retained it. He turned himself into a kind of Nick Woodfin Kaleidoscope. He never opened his mouth, nor spoke a word, but continued to reproduce all of Col. Woodfin's distorted gestures. He sawed the air, he writhed, twisted, contorted and made grimaces for the space of five minutes or so, and then sat down." The inhabitants of the courtroom were convulsed with laughter at Woodfin's expense. One can well imagine that Woodfin and other members of the bar were furious with their young colleague for mocking a fellow member in public. As the observer of the incident concluded, "whether he gained a victory for his client or no, he gained one for himself."[10] This is the crucial point. Vance was using the law to advance himself rather than to serve the interests of his clients. And by using the immature tactics just described, he was alienating his fellow professionals.

Vance might have retained a fairly respectable reputation at the bar if he had confined his antics to the performance of his duties, but he seemed constitutionally unable to contain his abundant energy within appropriate bounds. During a session of the Buncombe County Court, Zeb became embroiled in an argument with another young attorney. A fight ensued. Vance, by now a large man just under six feet tall who weighed nearly two hundred pounds, had a significant advantage over his opponent. By the time the other members of the court reached the scene, the "belligerents were standing three feet apart, and Zeb was holding in his hand a wisp of his opponent's hair, jerked out in the fight." In addition, the man had a badly injured eye. It seemed likely to all concerned that a duel would result from this incident. Mediators discovered that the other lawyer was most provoked by what he considered to be Vance's deliberate attempt to gouge his eye out. Vance explained that he had struck the man in the eye accidentally and that he meant to do no permanent damage to him. His adversary accepted this explanation, and the two men did not repair to the field of honor.[11] But there is little doubt that the episode seriously damaged Vance's reputation among his fellow advocates.

During this same period, Vance's very aggressive activities in politics only served to confirm the reputation that he had created as a young man and as a lawyer. Whereas Vance's lack of decorum was a significant liability for his career in the law, it seemed to do him little harm as an aspiring politician. In fact, Vance's willingness to confront his adversaries directly stood him and his party in good stead in the midst of the rough-and-tumble political campaigns that characterized the second American party system. In that arena, his actions occasionally strayed beyond the hazy bounds of what was permissible, but his opponents proved quite adept at defending themselves and replied in kind. While no one involved gained a sterling reputation, Vance was apparently viewed by the broader public as a normal politician. Shortly after his return to the mountains in 1852, he became embroiled in a hotly contested campaign. He explained his behavior to Hattie in the following terms: "I intended keeping aloof from politics altogether and do nothing but vote silently, which course for a young man in my situation would have been far preferable to any other. But I could not, to save my life keep silent, when the crisis approached. When all around me became uproar and confusion, I became noisy too, and when I heard my friends being abused, I was affected like human nature generally on those occasions, and I defended them. Once embarked but in the slightest degree, I had to go the whole figure."[12] This statement is exceptionally revealing. Vance was incapable of keeping himself away from politics even "to save [his] life." As noted earlier, he had been an active participant in a political campaign at age fourteen, and he would continue to seek and use political power until the day he died. The compulsion to participate and to take part in a "noisy" way in politics would dominate his adult life.

Vance played a major role in the Whig Party campaign during the fall of 1852. Judging from later campaign materials produced by Vance, he was an aggressive critic of the opposition. In September, Zeb attended a grand

Buncombe County rally for Whig presidential candidate Winfield Scott. Unfortunately, the dinner that had been prepared for rally participants had to be served during a driving rainstorm. Zeb's hard work during the canvass for votes seemed to pay off when the Whigs did marginally better in Asheville than they had done in the previous election. This proved to be a rather remarkable performance, because the Whig Party was, in fact, disintegrating as a national organization, and Scott was badly defeated by Democratic candidate Franklin Pierce. Zeb reported to Hattie, "I have been mad, almost to the fighting point, ever since I heard it."[13] This time, he remained composed and retained his good standing with his fellow Whigs. Zeb was not totally consumed by partisanship during this election, because he did vote for David Coleman, a Democrat, for the legislature.

Despite the personal difficulties that Vance's behavior had inspired, the economic and political leaders of the county recognized that he was a person who could not be ignored. In June 1853, Zeb was selected as one of eleven delegates to represent Buncombe County at a railroad convention at Cumberland Gap, Tennessee. There were approximately two thousand people at the meeting from Tennessee, Kentucky, Virginia, and North Carolina. The delegates sought to persuade the Charleston and Cincinnati Railroad to select a route that led through the mountains. Vance did not speak at the gathering, but he was placed on a committee that reported back to the convention.[14] While nothing of any consequence resulted from the meeting, Vance's selection as a delegate signaled his increasing prominence.

Zeb's improved standing in the community was reflected during the next major campaign. As he told a relative, "I became seized with a hungering and thirsting after the equivocal honors of politics, and in due time yielded to the solicitations of a few (yes very few) friends, and became a Candidate for a seat in the house of Commons." His adversary was David Reynolds, a fellow Whig. Reynolds supported Thomas Lanier Clingman for the U.S. Senate, while Zeb supported the regular Whig Party candidate. Because each state legislature selected its senators in this period, the election in Buncombe County would affect the outcome of the Senate contest. The competition had even greater symbolic significance because Buncombe County was Clingman's home county. The campaign featured at least one debate between Reynolds and Vance, which produced an exchange that highlighted Zeb's quick thinking and good humor. In his opening remarks, Reynolds criticized Zeb for presuming to run for office when he was so young. As Zeb's older brother Robert remembered it, "Zeb apologized for his youth, and declared that he would have cheerfully been born at an earlier date if it had been in his power; that his father and mother gave him no chance whatever about the matter, and humbly begged pardon, and

Robert Brank Vance, ca. 1863. Zeb's older brother was a general in the Confederate army and a U.S. congressman for ten years. (North Carolina Division of Archives and History, Raleigh)

said he would try and do better next time."[15] This adroit reply caused a sensation and kept Reynolds on the defensive for much of the campaign. The substance of the issues discussed by the two candidates cannot be recovered, but there is general agreement that it was a hotly contested canvass.

The outcome was all that Zeb could have hoped for when he announced his candidacy. He exulted in a letter to his cousin, "I hope you will not think me vain for saying that my friends all agree in saying it was the greatest triumph that has been accomplished in this country for many years." In fact, the leading Democratic Party paper in North Carolina had predicted his defeat a week before the election. While there is no doubt that Vance's triumph was impressive for someone so young, an inspection of the election returns indicates that party discipline was largely responsible for his victory. Reynolds had been able to pull approximately 10 percent of the party vote away from Zeb, but it was not sufficient to win him the election. In nine of the eleven election precincts in Buncombe County, however, Vance ran significantly behind Whig gubernatorial candidate Alfred Dockery. Vance's good spirits were further bolstered by two events unrelated to politics. Just before the election, Harriett had presented him with their first child, a "large hale, blue-eyed little boy" named Robert Espy. Vance confided that he and Harriett doted on the child. In addition, the new parents were the proud owners of an *"extensive plantation* consisting of a *five acre lot"* in downtown Asheville.[16] It was a proud young man who headed off to take his seat in the North Carolina state legislature in December.

For the most part, Zeb was an active participant in the legislature, but his contributions were somewhat limited by his youth and inexperience. The first significant battle of the legislative session—the selection of a U.S. senator—placed Zeb in a position to play a crucial role in the contest. The Democrats held a majority of seats in the legislature and expected to nominate and elect their own candidates for the U.S. Senate. During the 1854 election campaign, Thomas Lanier Clingman, who represented the mountain district in Congress and was from Asheville, had supported the Democratic candidate for governor. Since Clingman was nominally a member of the Whig Party, he felt that the Democrats owed him their nomination. When the Democrats refused to support Clingman, his few followers appealed to Whig legislators like Zeb for support. Zeb joined with the other Whigs in completely rejecting Clingman's pleas. In this instance, Zeb placed party loyalty above the claims of his fellow townsman.[17]

In order to understand Vance's reluctance to support his fellow mountain Whig, it is necessary to know more about Thomas Lanier Clingman. According to his biographer, Clingman was a physically attractive man who was "uncharismatic, cerebral, egotistic, and pugnacious." He overcame his lack of social charms by means of driving ambition and iron will. Clingman was born in the foothill county of Surry in 1812. After graduating from the University of North Carolina and completing legal training with Whig Party leader William A. Graham, Clingman returned home and was elected to the state legislature. Having lost a bid for reelection, he moved to Asheville and tried his hand at national politics. He lost his first race for Congress in 1841, but he won election to the House in 1843. During the session that followed, Clingman followed the Whig Party line and voted against the continued imposition of the "gag" rule, which prevented the introduction of anti-slavery petitions into the House. Castigated as a traitor to the South for his vote, Clingman fought a duel with Alabama Democrat William L. Yancey. He next joined other Whigs in opposing the annexation of Texas, another vote that appeared to be against the interests of the South. Many members of the Whig Party in his district were angered by his votes and supported the candidacy of independent Whig James Graham. When Democrats did not nominate a candidate of their own and backed Graham, Clingman lost his seat.[18]

Clingman regained his seat in 1847 when Graham refused to run for re-election. Once back in office, Clingman tried to ensure that he would not be defeated again. In the controversies surrounding the end of the recent war with Mexico, Clingman spoke out forcefully in favor of the rights of slaveholders and the Southern states. When he failed to win a Senate seat in 1848, he became an independent Whig and built his own organization in the mountain counties. Despite the fact that the Whigs had a commanding majority in the North Carolina mountains, the regular Whig Party candidates lost to Clingman in 1849, 1851, and 1853. Further distancing himself from the regular Whigs, Clingman refused to support the Whig presidential candidate, Winfield Scott, in 1852. Drawing support from a solid base of Democrats and a segment of the Whig Party that was loyal to him personally, Clingman dominated the highland political scene.[19] For regular party men like Vance, Clingman was a menace. Even worse, he was a traitor to the party who could not be punished. Given Clingman's political history, it is not surprising that Vance did not vote for his hometown candidate.

For the remainder of the legislative term, Vance spent his time working hard on more mundane matters of interest to his Asheville constituents. For example, he introduced an amendment that would have forced the legislature to meet in Asheville, and he took the opportunity to praise the mountain region for its scenic beauty and its cool weather. On a more serious note, Vance supported a bill that would have added corporal punishment to the penalties for killing livestock found ranging on the western mountains. He defended mountain farmers' common-law practice of allowing their cattle to roam without restraint, and he contended that "the punishment of fine and imprisonment had no terrors for those who live better in jail than out of it." He also introduced legislation to incorporate the Asheville Mutual Insurance Company and the Holston Female College; to exempt certain people from working on the Asheville and Greenville plank road; to establish a public road in Yancey County; to authorize county and town subscriptions to the French Broad and Greenville Railroad; and to incorporate the Young Men's Literary Association in Asheville.[20] While none of this legislation was enacted, Vance did demonstrate his willingness to work for the benefit of Buncombe County and western North Carolina. It is clear from his record that Vance attended virtually every session of the legislature and was actively involved at all times.

There were several more substantive issues before the legislature in which Vance became deeply involved. The first was the extension of the Western North Carolina Railroad into the mountain region. This was not a new concern for the region's legislators, but success eluded them because they disagreed about the route that the extension would follow. Vance and Democratic senator David Coleman favored a bill that would bring the tracks to Asheville and swing them northwest through Madison County on the way to Knoxville. This was the route that had been favored by the North Carolina delegation to the Charleston and Cincinnati Railroad convention at Cumberland Gap in 1853. That route would effectively make Asheville the western North Carolina terminus of the railroad, cutting off the portion of the state that lay to the west of the city. Mountain legislators from the counties west of Asheville, led by Democratic senator William Holland Thomas, were understandably adamant that the line should continue due west of Asheville to Cherokee County and then on to Chattanooga.[21] The division among the western delegates prevented the resolution of the issue, but voters in Asheville must have been pleased with the stand that Vance had taken. The railroad lines would not actually reach the top of the Blue Ridge for another twenty-five years, and Vance, as governor of North Carolina, would be largely responsible for getting them there.

The second significant issue that Vance championed was the reform of the system by which state school funds were distributed. Once again, he was accurately reflecting the opinions and interests of his constituents. Federal surplus funds distributed to the states in the 1830s had been used in North Carolina to create a trust fund, and the interest from that fund was made available to support public education. Most of the children of the elite were able to attend private academies, and the public schools became avenues of opportunity for the children of yeoman farmers and poorer whites. However, public school funding was distributed by the state on "the federal basis"; that is, the formula that was used to determine how much money each county should receive was the same formula used to determine representation in the federal Congress. Under that system, each slave counted as three-fifths of a free person. The result was that schools in counties with large slave populations and small free populations received more dollars per white school child than did schools in counties with small slave populations.[22]

To Vance and other legislators from counties in the mountains, this system appeared to be discriminatory. Vance was serving on the Committee on Education in the Commons when he introduced an amendment to distribute public school funds based on the white population of each county. The committee rejected Vance's proposal, and he issued a minority report on December 15, 1854. He sent the report to the *Raleigh Register* to ensure that it would receive maximum publicity. Asserting that he spoke for three thousand Buncombe County school children, Vance maintained that the present funding system gave money to the "few" and withheld it from the "many." Committee chair T. H. Williams and the other members were from counties with large slave populations, and they quickly rejected Vance's arguments. On December 16, the full House of Commons rejected Vance's minority report.[23] While quite unsuccessful, Vance had done several notable things during this episode: he had claimed to speak for the common white North Carolinian on the matter of education; he had spoken in defense of the interests of the western counties and his constituents in Buncombe County; and, perhaps most significantly, Zeb had shown himself to be capable of constructive legislative work and able to work within the political system.

Unfortunately, some of Vance's other statements and votes were much less positive. Like many other Whigs across the United States, Vance was looking for a new political home as the party disintegrated in 1854 in the wake of the controversy over the Kansas-Nebraska Bill. This bill reopened the question of whether slavery would spread to the federal territories of the West, and it split the Southern and Northern Whigs into warring factions. Many Northern Whigs and some antislavery Democrats swarmed to the newly formed Republican Party, which took a strong stand against the spread of slavery into the West. The new party's antislavery stance ensured, however, that Southern Whigs like Vance could not contemplate joining it. Another party emerged at the same time in opposition to the Democrats and Republicans that seemed to offer a haven for homeless Whigs. This was the American Party, popularly known as the Know-Nothing Party. The Know-Nothings had emerged from a secret fraternal organization that refused to reveal anything about its internal workings. Not only was it a closed group, it was also openly nativist. Ever since the large Irish and German immigration of the late 1840s, some citizens of the United States—particularly those who lived in Northern urban centers or who feared the growing influence of the newly arrived Roman Catholic population—worked actively to reduce the influence of the most recent immigrants. The nativist Know-Nothing platform, then, called for restrictions to be placed on immigrants. At the same time, the party, made up largely of Whigs who were conservative on the slavery question, spoke in defense of the Union against the extreme proposals promoted by Republicans and Democrats.[24] It was this latter part of the Know-Nothing program that attracted many Southern Whigs.

It is not clear when Zeb joined the Know-Nothings, but he began to vote with the party on a number of measures in January 1855. On January 18, he voted in favor of a resolution that would extend the period of time that immigrants had to reside in the United States before they could gain citizen status—the major plank in the Know-Nothing platform. That same day, Zeb voted to defeat a resolution condemning the Know-Nothings. The closeness of the vote on this issue (fifty-nine against the Know-Nothings to forty-eight in favor) indicated that the majority of North Carolina Whigs had joined Vance in moving to the new party. Vance did not simply vote as a Know-Nothing; moreover, he also introduced a measure to restrict immigrant influence and spoke in favor of it on January 27. A Raleigh newspaper summarized the episode as follows: "Mr. Vance moved that a tax of ½ per cent be laid on ready-made clothing in addition to any other tax heretofore imposed. Mr. Vance made some very severe strictures on the foreigners engaged in that trade." While Vance's exact words have not been recorded, it seems clear that he had adopted part of the platform as well as the political identity of the Know-Nothings. Vance supported the other part of the Know-Nothing platform in the legislature as well. He voted against a resolution in favor of the Kansas-Nebraska Bill, a vote viewed at the time as a moderate and pro-Union stand.[25]

As soon as Vance returned to Asheville, he became embroiled in controversies surrounding his new political associations. By March 1855, he had become the partner of John D. Hyman in the *Asheville Spectator*, a formerly Whig newspaper that now supported the Know-Nothings. Within weeks, local Democrats were angered by what they viewed as the highly personal attacks that Vance made on them in the paper. In retaliation for his intemperate statements, a group of Democrats and Clingman loyalists convinced the local authorities to convene a grand jury to investigate the new political organization. The grand jury made a presentment against the Know-Nothings that was strengthened by the opinions of the presiding judge. Vance and Hyman maintained, with considerable justification, that this was a form of political persecution. Nothing of substance ever came of this legal action, and Vance's assertion that it was an attempt at political intimidation seems accurate.[26]

For later observers, what is most significant about this episode is the defense of the new party that Vance and Hyman made. On April 21, 1855, they printed the principal legislative goals and principles of the new party as they understood them. The Know-Nothings wished to extend the residence requirement for citizenship to twenty-one years; to prohibit paupers and criminals from entering the country; to forbid the election or appointment of foreign-born citizens to office; to dismiss the "higher law than the United States Constitution" doctrine of the abolitionists; to defend the "Constitution as it stands, the Union as it exists, and the Rights of the States, without diminution"; and to make no distinction within the party between former Whigs and former Democrats.[27] This is a fair summary of the Southern Know-Nothing position, and there is nothing exceptional in it.

There is, however, an interesting contradiction in this issue of the paper on the question of religion. In the Northern states, a fringe element of the Know-Nothings was ardently anti-Catholic. Know-Nothing mobs attacked Catholic people and Catholic buildings, destroying property and killing numerous individuals. A poisonous literature of hate and fear was manufactured to justify these attacks on Catholics. The virtual absence of Catholics in western North Carolina, however, ensured that no anti-Catholic rioting would take place in Asheville. The eighth principle on the *Spectator*'s list was a ringing endorsement of religious liberty: "We shall oppose and protest against all abridgment of religious liberty, holding it as a cardinal maxim, that religious faith is a question between each individual and his God, and over which no political government, or other human power can rightfully exercise any supervision or control, at any time, in any place, or in any form." In another column of the same issue, however, the editors admitted that the members of the party had pledged themselves not to vote for Roman Catholics.[28] It is difficult to find any consistency in these two statements. For Vance, this statement appears to have been aberrant. As he had admitted to Hattie, he was not concerned about matters of religion. Later in life, he became an advocate for Jewish Americans and married a Catholic woman. We will have to look elsewhere for the motive for this attack on the political rights of a religious minority.

Not surprisingly, Vance appears to have been driven by political ambition. The party supported Leander B. Charmichael as a candidate for Congress against Thomas Lanier Clingman. This action prompted a number of former Democrats to leave the organization. The most prominent of these individuals, James S. T. Baird, was a cousin of Zeb's from Asheville. Baird announced his defection in the June 21 issue of the *Asheville News*. In retaliation, Vance and Hyman charged that Baird had withdrawn from the party only after being promised that he would be the Democratic nominee for the House of Commons in 1856. Baird denied the charge. (He was the Democratic nominee in 1858.) He then went on to assert: "*To defeat Thomas L. Clingman for Congress was the substance of all of the speeches I ever heard in the walls of a council room, from the first night I first entered the order until I left it.*" Vance answered this attack by threatening Baird: "Take care, Doctor, we are loading our old American musket that played the very devil with the Hessians during the American Revolution."[29]

At this point, the war of words threatened to become much more than that. In a letter that appeared in the July 5 issue of the *Asheville News*, Baird denounced Vance and Hyman as "bullying blackguards." Later in the same letter, Baird described the two men as "fools and blackguards." Apparently Vance replied in kind. Baird asserted that Zeb had called him "a damned liar" in a private conversation immediately after his letter was published. On July 9, Baird sent a letter to Vance in which he challenged the young editor to a duel. According to Baird's later recollection, Zeb accepted the challenge. Apparently, only the intervention of family members prevented the two cousins from doing serious harm to each other. The episode illustrated two important points about Zeb's character at this point in his life. First, he was still quite impetuous, as he continued to stretch the bounds of acceptable behavior. This tendency toward outlandish behavior, moreover, was abetted by a driving political ambition. Vance sought to eliminate the one obstacle in his path to political power in the region: Thomas Lanier Clingman. Vance's partisan efforts were not successful, however, and Clingman rather easily defeated Charmichael in the August election.[30]

It is instructive to note, however, that Vance's seemingly destructive behavior did not impair his political fortunes. In early 1856, he was named to the Board of Directors of the Asheville Mutual Insurance Company. A month later, he was elected to a two-year term as a town commissioner for Asheville. Made incautious by these signs of esteem, Zeb decided to challenge David Coleman for the state Senate seat representing Buncombe, Yancey, Madison, and Henderson Counties. There was a certain irony in this situation, as Zeb had actually alienated some of his Whig friends in 1852 by voting for Coleman for the legislature. Now, all of the goodwill between the two young politicians had dissipated, and they went after each other with considerable zest. Vance faced a very difficult task. Coleman had carried the four counties by 114 votes in 1854, and the Know-Nothing candidate for governor had lost them by nearly 700 votes.[31] Because this was a race for the state Senate, Zeb also had to cope with a restricted electorate. The North Carolina Constitution restricted the right to vote for candidates for the state Senate to men who owned fifty acres of land or paid an equivalent tax. This requirement reduced the number of eligible voters in the

Senate race to approximately one-half that of the full electorate. Because Zeb had been involved in a number of episodes that might have damaged his reputation with the more refined members of local society, the more elite electorate for the Senate race posed a potential problem.

Zeb did not allow himself the luxury of worrying about his reputation; he plunged into the campaign with all of his considerable energy. Vance and Coleman adopted the practice, normal for North Carolina politics of that time, of directly debating each other in all of the small communities in the four-county district. Surviving newspaper accounts indicate that the two men faced each other at least a dozen times in Asheville and smaller towns like Flat Creek, Cathey's Mill, Mills River, and Whitson's Mill. Nor were the debates perfunctory exercises in public relations. The *Asheville News* wearily reported that "Messrs. Coleman and Vance, candidates for the Senate, addressed the people on Tuesday the 17th, for five mortal hours." During their long discussions, Vance and Coleman spent a good deal of time responsibly arguing about legitimate political issues. Vance's claim for voters' support was that he had more faithfully represented the western part of the state than had Coleman in the 1854–55 legislature. According to surviving accounts, Vance cited specific votes that Coleman had cast and substantiated his assertions with exact page numbers from the official records of the legislature.[32] While Zeb's careful claims seem a little tortured now, there is no doubt that he ran a responsible campaign on substantive issues of importance to the voters.

Unfortunately for Zeb, Coleman apparently spent most of his time discussing his opponent's most vulnerable point. While conceding that the platform adopted by the Know-Nothing convention that met in Buncombe County made a strong statement against religious intolerance, Coleman and the *Asheville News* attacked Vance as the candidate of a secret and dangerous political movement. As far as can be ascertained, Zeb made little defense of his political alliance with the Know-Nothings; rather, he simply returned to attacking Coleman's record of voting with his fellow Democrats against the interests of the western counties. Despite Vance's strenuous efforts, the *Asheville News* predicted that Coleman would easily win reelection. The prediction proved to be accurate, as Coleman carried three of the four counties by a margin of more than three hundred votes. Since this total represented a threefold increase over his margin of two years before, it is clear that Zeb suffered a very significant political defeat.[33] His affiliation with the Know-Nothings had proven to be a significant political liability. Furthermore, the crushing defeat of the national Know-Nothing candidate in the November presidential election and the party's subsequent disintegration left Zeb without a political home.

Vance's earliest sallies into western North Carolina law and politics achieved mixed results. He received his license to practice in the superior courts, but his own actions and an abundance of competition limited his financial rewards. While he achieved some notable successes in politics and appeared to be maturing into a more constructive public figure, his association with the Know-Nothings seemed to doom any future ventures into politics. Despite these somewhat discouraging signs, there seemed little likelihood that Zeb would abandon his pursuit of political office. His actions during the period between 1852 and 1856 demonstrated that he had a driving ambition that would not be stilled by an occasional setback. In addition, he had shown considerable talent as a public speaker who attracted a loyal following. The only question, then, was whether Vance's talents for reaching the public would be sufficient to overcome the obstacles that he placed in his own path.

L ess than two years after his political career seemed headed toward destruction, Zeb was elected to the Congress of the United States. An unlikely combination of fortuitous circumstances, tragedy, and dogged determination brought about this result. Throughout the period, the formidable form of Thomas Lanier Clingman towered over Vance and his ambitions. The hostility between the two men grew more public and more heated as both sought to fulfill their ambitions in a small arena. It surfaced openly just after the congressional election of 1855, when Clingman stated that the editors of the *Spectator*—Hyman and Vance—had printed "the meanest, dirtiest, and basest lie." When Vance remonstrated, Clingman announced that he declined "a verbal contest with one whose efforts are characterized only by imbecile scurrility."[1] Even controversies that were not remotely political became embroiled in their personal battle. While this was also a period of change in Zeb's private life, he seemed to ignore the private aspects of his existence, choosing instead to center his attention on his own political advancement.

The first major clash between Vance and Clingman began before Vance was defeated in the 1856 state Senate election. Clingman, who was a talented amateur scientist, became involved in a bitter controversy with Elisha Mitchell over the question of who had first discovered the highest mountain in the western counties of North Carolina. According to historian Thomas E. Jeffrey, the contest was a most unequal one. While it seems likely that Mitchell did in fact make the original discovery of the mountain, his recall of the events surrounding the discovery was faulty. Clingman was able to present much more persuasive evidence for his own claim and to dismiss Mitchell's assertions. An enraged Mitchell sought the assistance of Vance to prepare a public reply to Clingman. Vance, who had no scientific training except what he had learned in Mitchell's classroom, sought to secure evidence to sustain Mitchell's claim. Zeb did manage to locate the guide who had led Mitchell into the mountains in 1844, but since the man's testimony supported Clingman, Vance pursued the matter no further.[2] Although Vance was undoubtedly motivated to assist his former professor by his intense dislike of Clingman, he also must have felt in debt to

Mitchell, who had served as a surrogate father to the young mountaineer while he was studying in Chapel Hill. Thus, Vance's participation was probably as much due to his feelings for his mentor as it was to his desire for political advantage.

Prompted by his desire to reclaim the advantage in the controversy from Clingman, Mitchell decided to come to the mountains to establish the accuracy of his claim. In June 1857, the professor set out for the mountains with his family to revisit the region in question and to gather data to buttress his claim. In particular, Mitchell hoped to talk to a former guide by the name of William Wilson who had accompanied him on an 1835 expedition during which Mitchell probably identified the peak in question. Vance had located Wilson and another guide, Samuel Austin, for Mitchell prior to the older man's arrival in the mountains. On his way to Wilson's house, Mitchell left the trail in the mountains, stumbled over a precipice, and drowned in a pool of water at the bottom of a cliff. Vance was in the general vicinity at the time and was the leader of one of the search parties of "mountaineers and Towns-people" that finally located the body. At the time of his death, Mitchell had failed to substantiate his claim, and the highest mountain in western North Carolina seemed destined to retain its designation as Clingman's Peak.[3]

It was at this point that Vance politicized the dispute, rescued Mitchell's reputation, and rehabilitated his own political career. Thomas E. Jeffrey's explanation of the events that followed is convincing, although it does need to be supplemented somewhat. In a frenzy of activity, Vance sought to ensure that Mitchell received a proper memorial. First, he helped to organize a large public meeting in Asheville on July 8, 1857, where resolutions were passed that both called for Mitchell's burial "upon some eligible point of the Black Mountain" and recommended that a monument be erected on that point to his memory. Ironically, Clingman attended the Asheville meeting, and he "said he approved of the resolutions and hoped they would be adopted." Two committees were formed to take care of these matters, and Zeb was named a member of both. Finally, Zeb prepared a long essay describing the search for and discovery of Mitchell's body—probably a version of the account he delivered at the July 8 meeting—that was widely reprinted.[4] There can be little doubt that while all of this activity may have helped Vance politically, the intensity of his actions indicates that emotions deeper than simple political ambition motivated him. Zeb appeared to be genuinely grief stricken and angry. He blamed Clingman for Mitchell's death and seemed determined to avenge it, no matter what the political consequences might be.

Because Mitchell's death occurred in the midst of a political campaign,

*Thomas Lanier Clingman, ca. 1863. Congressman,
senator, and Confederate general, Clingman was Vance's
chief political opponent of the 1850s. (National Archives)*

the immediate impact of the events surrounding it on Vance's political
standing can be easily measured. Clingman was running for reelection, and
his opposition seemed dispirited and disorganized. William J. Wilson of
Haywood County offered himself as a candidate in opposition to the veteran
congressman. The nearly defunct Know-Nothing organization was dissatisfied with Wilson, who was apparently a political lightweight. A party con-

vention was called in Morganton in May, and only two delegates attended. Wilson once again announced himself as a candidate; thus it appeared that Clingman would have no effective opposition. Despite the disarray in the opposition ranks, he campaigned fairly strenuously, speaking at a number of communities across the district. After the death of Mitchell and the Asheville meeting at which Vance played a prominent role, a group of Clingman's opponents announced that they would vote for Zeb for Congress. There is no indication that Zeb engineered this movement. He failed to acknowledge the nomination and continued to do research to support Mitchell's claim. But, as Jeffrey notes, Zeb did not disavow the nomination either. When the votes were counted in the August election, Clingman won an overwhelming victory. He received 8,673 votes to 3,211 for Zeb and 446 for Wilson. Clingman carried every county, and in the four counties where Zeb had lost to Coleman by 318 votes in 1856, Clingman had a 1,800-vote plurality.[5] Thus, it is clear that Zeb gained no immediate political benefit from the Clingman-Mitchell controversy.

There is no doubt, however, that Vance was plotting to undermine Clingman's position in the controversy. He talked to Samuel Austin, one of Mitchell's guides on the 1835 expedition, and to Thomas Wilson, known as "Big Tom," who was a cousin of Mitchell's guide on his first visit to the top of Black Mountain. From both men, Zeb received confirmation that Mitchell had indeed reached the highest peak and made scientific measurements there. In addition, Zeb was able to learn that local people had called the peak Mount Mitchell until recently. Vance did not use this information himself. Instead, he turned it over to Professor Charles Phillips, a member of the Phillips family of Chapel Hill. Zeb showed a fine sense of timing in a letter to Phillips. Sensing that public opinion was swinging behind Mitchell as a result of the recent tragedy, he counseled Phillips to refrain from publishing the results of the interviews for the moment. In September, Zeb persuaded William Wilson, the original guide, to retrace the 1835 route to the top of the highest peak. In the presence of several witnesses, Wilson was able to do so without difficulty and was able to predict the appearance of certain geological features before the party came upon them. Not satisfied with this impressive evidence, Vance secured testimony from several other witnesses that laid the basis for the claim that Mitchell had climbed the mountain in 1844, an extremely dubious assertion.[6] Vance's part of the plan was now complete.

Phillips now swung into action against Clingman. In December 1857, the University of North Carolina mathematics professor recounted in newspaper articles all of the information that Vance had collected. Somewhat taken aback by the evidence massed against his position, Clingman fought back vigorously. He sought particularly to undermine the testimony of William Wilson, the key witness for Phillips and Vance, by claiming that Wilson had changed the story he had previously given to Clingman. Phillips replied with a twenty-six-page essay in the *North Carolina University Magazine*. Buttressing his argument with long extracts of the evidence collected by Vance, Phillips maintained that Mitchell's claim was irrefutable. Phillips also described Clingman as an ungrateful student, as Mitchell had taught the congressman at the university. Phillips urged Clingman to accept the designation of the highest peak in North Carolina as Mount Mitchell. Vance and Phillips persuaded the Mitchell family to allow for the reburial of the professor's body on the top of the mountain. Zeb made all of the arrangements, including the construction of a "road [that would] permit a lady to ride comfortably, to the very spot." Both the Episcopal bishop of Tennessee and David L. Swain, president of the University of North Carolina and part owner of the land on the summit, spoke at the service. They called upon the proper authorities to name the highest peak after the man who was now buried there.[7] The Vance-Phillips strategy worked, and Clingman's claim to have the mountain named after him was ignored.

For both Vance and Clingman, however, the battle over Mitchell's legacy was largely forgotten when the political situation in the mountains changed dramatically in May 1858. At that time, Clingman achieved his long thwarted ambition of election to the U.S. Senate by the North Carolina legislature. A special election was called in the mountain district to replace the popular congressman. Since Clingman had won so decisively against Vance a year before, Democrats expected to carry the district easily. Two Democratic candidates announced their intention to contest for the seat. The first was David Coleman, Zeb's opponent in the 1856 state Senate race. The other was William W. Avery of Burke County. The party leadership backed Avery's candidacy, which prompted Coleman to attack the *Asheville News* and the party. The *Asheville Spectator*, the Vance-Hyman paper, supported Coleman in this controversy. Coleman apparently became very bitter about the opposition to his candidacy, and he attacked Avery in very personal terms. Upon reviewing the situation, the *Asheville News* presciently predicted that the split in the Democratic ranks would lead to the appearance of an opposition candidate.[8]

Almost on cue, at a discussion between Avery and Coleman in Cherokee County, Zeb announced his candidacy. Coleman was outraged by what he viewed as Zeb's betrayal. In his speech that evening, he charged Vance with "deception." Coleman "said [Vance] had voluntarily approached him at Morganton and told him he would not be a candidate under any circumstances, but on the contrary promised that he, and the Know Nothing party as far as he could organize and influence them, would support him." This promise, Coleman asserted, had "since been reiterated again and again by Mr. Vance and his friends, both at Asheville and on the way to Cherokee, and even there."[9] There is no reason to doubt Coleman's account of these conversations. He was clearly outraged, and he consequently pledged to back Avery's candidacy with great enthusiasm. Why did Zeb change his mind and decide to run? As he had observed in his letter to Hattie in 1852, he could not stay out of politics once a campaign got started. He was drawn to the competition and to the opportunity to be in the spotlight. In addition, he probably sensed that a regular Democratic candidate might have trouble holding the Clingman coalition of Democrats and Whigs together.

Despite the heavy schedule that his association with the Mitchell ceremonies imposed on him, Vance energetically campaigned for Congress. A hostile report of a speech he gave in Cherokee County indicates that Zeb had already adopted the style of campaign speaking that would characterize his canvasses until his death. There were three elements that appeared in virtually every speech: discussion of topical issues, partisan appeals to his followers, and "anecdotes." In the Cherokee speech and others in the 1858 campaign, Vance attacked the Democrats and Avery as "Southern fanatics" who threatened the Union. The recent controversies over the Kansas-Nebraska Bill and the Dred Scott decision made the political issues affecting the future of the Union of paramount importance.[10] The Democrats had difficulty taking Vance seriously, however, because he constantly interjected humorous stories into the discussion of serious issues. If his later speeches provide a reliable guide to the content of those he gave in 1858, Vance's opponents seriously misjudged the impact of his anecdotes on audiences. Vance always used them to illustrate the important points he was making. In a society in which the majority of voters was either illiterate or semiliterate, this style of communication was remarkably effective. Some scholars would maintain that it was the usual style of folk communication, and that Vance was simply drawing on an existing tradition to communicate efficaciously.

Recalling the debacle of the previous year, however, Democrats were confident that Avery would easily defeat Vance. Unlike Clingman, Vance made no attempt to ally himself with the Democrats. In a letter written earlier in the year, in fact, he had made himself perfectly clear on that point. " 'I stand' therefore opposed to Democracy, & shall so stand till democracy amends or I grow corrupt," he wrote; Vance affirmed this stance despite being "completely shut off from advancement, by these opinions, which to a young man endowed with considerable ambition, is a gloomy enough prospect." Instead of forming an alliance with the Democratic Party, Vance claimed that he was running as a Whig, even though the party no longer existed. The Democrats gleefully reprinted the attacks on the Whigs as a party of corruption that Vance had made when he joined the Know-Nothings. They also attacked him for the manner in which he entered the race and compared his late entry in the canvass to his non-campaign for Congress of 1857.[11]

Unfortunately for Avery and the Democrats, there was an unspoken issue in the campaign that may have weakened their support. Avery was a successful lawyer in Burke County who had been elected to the state legislature in 1842 and 1850. He was a member of a local elite that prided itself on its position. In the 1850 election that sent Avery to the legislature, Burke County also elected Samuel Flemming. Flemming was a political opponent of Avery's, and Avery had been an opposing attorney in an acrimonious legal dispute in which Flemming was involved as counsel. Although both men were Democrats, they clashed in the legislature, using extremely harsh language to question each other's integrity. At the October term of the Burke County Court, personal relations between the two degenerated even further when Avery asserted that all of Flemming's business dealings were fraudulent. Flemming waited for Avery to leave the courthouse and then attacked him with a whip and a rock. For the next two weeks, Flemming boasted of his deed and tried to goad Avery into a duel. On November 11, when the two men were in the Burke County Courthouse, Avery shot and killed Flemming in open court. The affair was a sensation. Avery was tried for murder, but, claiming the novel defense of temporary insanity, he was acquitted by a jury that deliberated for only ten minutes. At the time, many observers thought that Avery had not received true justice. Vance, for example, wrote Hattie, "That Mr. Avery is one of the most estimable gentlemen in our state is not denied by any, and all are rejoiced that his life is spared to his friends and family, but many, very many shrink from the danger of establishing such a precedent as his triumphant acquittal."[12] Shrewdly, Zeb never mentioned the incident during his many debates with Avery, but the entire electorate was aware of the episode.

The campaign continued throughout the month of July, and there were indications that Zeb was gaining the allegiance of many of the former Whigs. When he arrived in the Whig stronghold of Wilkes County, the party faithful, who had never seen Vance before, were quite downcast because of his youthful appearance. But the aggressive and humorous speech he gave at Wilkesboro filled them with enthusiasm. Clingman attended one of the debates and offered the following assessment: "Well, Avery made but few points, and didn't make them very well, while Vance, with his jokes and nonsense, seemed to carry the crowd." Clingman noted, in particular, that

Vance had successfully defused the Know-Nothing issue. At one gathering, Zeb appealed to the voters in a new way: he led a group of followers in to the debate while playing traditional mountain tunes on his fiddle. Zeb's efforts to appeal to yeomen and tenant farmers by peppering his speeches with anecdotes and adopting popular culture, rather than by taking an intellectual approach, would become a staple of his future campaigns. To counter his growing popularity, the Democrats accused Vance of favoring a protective tariff, a stand that would have put Zeb in agreement with many Northern Republicans. Zeb denied the charge, but explained that he did feel that higher tariff rates would help to improve the economy.[13] While the tariff was a significant national issue, it was not the major point of contention between the two men.

As the campaign drew to a close, Democrats grew more concerned about the growing strength of Vance's support. They accused Vance's friends of running a secret campaign of character assassination against Avery. The *Asheville News* accused Zeb's friends in Cherokee County of making attacks on Avery of a very "personal" nature. Clearly this was a reference to the Avery-Flemming affair. The newspaper refused to go into details about Avery's difficulties, but there must have been some discussion of the episode to prompt the Democrats to acknowledge its existence. When the votes were counted in early August, the Democrats were mortified. Zeb was easily elected to replace Clingman by a vote of 8,321 to 6,272. The stunned Democrats searched for explanations. It was clearly either a personal victory for Vance or a repudiation of Avery, as the Democratic candidate for governor had carried the district handily during the same balloting. In Madison County, for example, the Democratic gubernatorial candidate swept to victory with 499 votes to his opponent's 231. Among the same voters, Zeb led Avery by a 384 to 239 count.[14] The Vance family's generosity in contributing land for the county seat helps to explain this result, but the same trend appeared in each jurisdiction. It should be noted, however, that the defeated candidate for governor was an independent Democrat who opposed internal improvements in the western counties. The contrast between his appeal to voters and that of Zeb, who had always been a spokesman for the western part of the state, was bound to be profound.

A number of factors contributed to the election's surprising result. Thomas E. Jeffrey is undoubtedly correct in arguing that much of the positive publicity from the reburial of Elisha Mitchell redounded to Zeb's benefit. The Democrats' claim that the whispering campaign about the Avery-Flemming affair was decisive may also be true. But there seems to be little doubt that Vance's own claim to be the spokesman for the Union appealed

Vance at the time of his election to Congress in 1858.
(North Carolina Division of Archives and History, Raleigh)

to voters. Perhaps Vance himself offered the most accurate analysis of the reasons for his victory in a speech that he gave at a postelection reconciliation meeting in Asheville. Both the style and the substance of the remarks capture the reasons for his success: "My opponent charged that I would be snowed under, but was vice versa. I remind myself of the Caldwell County 'possum, which an indignant mountaineer told me about. Said he, I stretched that 'possum's neck tell I thought he was dead; I skinned him and biled him for three hours, but don't you think when I took the lid off'n the pot, the cussed little devil was settin' up there on his hind legs, and had licked up the gravy."[15] There seems to be little reason to doubt that Zeb was correct in assuming that he was responsible for his own success. Although only twenty-eight, he had evolved a successful style of stump speaking that appealed to his constituents. In addition, he had selected a successful strategy of appealing to the former Whigs, including those who had supported Clingman. Other factors, including the Clingman-Mitchell and Avery-Flemming controversies, played a role in Zeb's victory, but he could justifiably claim most of the credit for himself.

Despite the demands of his schedule in 1858, Zeb tried to bring his personal life into focus. Surviving correspondence suggests that Vance's law practice continued to grow, if not exactly to prosper. None of the cases in which Vance was involved was significant enough to be recalled later, but he apparently worked more diligently for his clients than he had previously. The major comfort of his life was his family. Zeb and Hattie recovered slowly from the death of their firstborn son Robert Espy (called Espy), who succumbed to a gradual decline in strength in 1855. The episode was so painful that many years later Hattie still mourned her loss, but at the time there was little evidence of their feelings. In 1869, Hattie described her first son as "a most lovely little creature—better fitted to dwell with the Angels, around the throne of God in Heaven than with us, on earth." Because other sons appeared in short order, neither parent had time to brood. Charles Vance was born in 1856, and a third son, David, followed in 1857. The family was "increasing in a truly mountain ratio," as Vance noted, referring to the large families commonly found in the mountain counties. He confided to a relative: "Our dear little boys are quite hardy and stout, and are to us a source at once of unbounded pleasure & delight, amusement, anxiety and annoyance." Little David and Charles played outside with their father in good weather, and their existence undoubtedly contributed to the more mature demeanor he tended to show in public. Unfortunately, as Zeb had to admit to a correspondent, his wife was "still in delicate health."[16] This would continue to be the case for the next twenty years, as Hattie's health gradually deteriorated.

In early December, Zeb journeyed to Washington to attend Congress. He was sworn in with two other recently elected members on December 7, 1858. As a new member joining a Congress that had already met for one full session, Vance was at a distinct disadvantage. Because he was not a member of either of the two major parties, he was further restricted in the impact he could make. Even taking these limitations into account, however, Zeb's record in the second session of the Thirty-fifth Congress was not impressive. He spoke for the first time on January 26, 1859, when he filed two reports on behalf of the Committee on Revolutionary War Claims. Eight days later, Zeb made some short remarks. The first was a wry interjection into a debate about retrenchment. His observation was intended to be humorous, but it was brushed aside as irrelevant by those carrying on the debate. He made a more substantial statement on February 7 in regard to an amendment about a miscellaneous appropriation of forty thousand dollars. Vance attacked the measure, saying, "This whole bill reminds me very much of the bills I have seen of fast young men at fashionable hotels: For two days board, $5; sundries $50."[17] This was the first of literally hundreds of occasions on which Vance's comments provoked laughter in Congress. Once again, however, the matter discussed was not substantive.

On February 7, 1859, Zeb rose in the House and delivered his only significant address of the session. The long speech covered aspects of the tariff, public lands, and pensions for veterans of the War of 1812. While on the surface there was little internal coherence to the address, Zeb had a clear objective in mind that became apparent as he concluded. He had begun his speech with a somber appraisal of the national political landscape: "The late fury of the political heavens having spent itself in the fierce and bitter contests which raged in these Halls, we have now comparative quiet. But whether the winds merely pause to gather more wrath; whether it is merely a truce to enable the combatants to recruit and bury their dead, we cannot tell." During this lull in sectional hostilities, Vance asked the House to review tariff policy in order to improve the financial condition of the national government. He called for an increase in tariff rates to prevent the government from running a deficit—a position not particularly popular in the South. At the same time, Vance opposed a protective tariff that would greatly increase rates and hurt his constituents.[18] His remarks were essentially nonpartisan, practical, and moderate.

Vance continued his discussion of the state of the Union by turning to the topic of the distribution of public lands. He began by admitting that both sides of the tariff debate had valid points, but explained that he thought there was only one correct position on the distribution of public lands. Vance contrasted the policy of selling public lands to individuals with the policy of granting lands free of charge to corporations that used them to finance railroads and other internal improvements. He attacked the Democratic Party for being inconsistent on the issue and for not protecting the "older" states from the advantages given to the newer Midwestern states. He pointed out that the government was in great need of revenue and that the only appropriate policy for raising it was a consistent one. Either all states should share equally in the largesse—as the Morrill Bill to establish land grant colleges proposed—or the land should be sold to raise public revenues.[19] Vance was clearly trying to link two parts of the government revenue-raising process together.

He concluded his speech by pointing out that Congress should not deprive some Americans of government expenditures that they had earned, even to balance the budget. Specifically, Vance objected to a proposal to deny pensions to the veterans of the War of 1812. He ridiculed the assertion of an Ohio congressman that the old soldiers would be insulted to have their patriotism measured out in dollars and cents. Vance asked: "Can one of them walk into a market and buy a rump of beef or a leg of mutton, with glory? What merchant advertizes that he will take either glory, honor, or renown, in exchange for beef, pork, and cabbage? . . . You may talk of glory as much as you like, but these old soldiers want some more substantial testimonial of the country's gratitude." Vance then closed by asking that the old soldiers not be forced to make a sacrifice when the federal government had so many other fiscal options to exercise.[20] Vance's argument in this speech was logical and rhetorically persuasive. He presented viable alternative means of dealing with the budget problem, and he offered legitimate reasons for avoiding the proposed economies. The speech was dignified and entirely suited to the setting and audience. It was a measure of Vance's growing maturity and skill as a speaker that this generally impressive effort would be only his first major speech in Congress.

Apparently encouraged by the success of this address, Vance began to play a somewhat more active role in the routine work of the House. On February 15, he asked for unanimous consent to introduce an extension of a bill for bounties for "wagon-masters and teamsters." (In order to bypass the many rules governing how legislation came to the floor of the House, a member would ask that all other members give unanimous consent to waive the rules.) In this case, another member objected, and Zeb's proposal could not be debated. Apparently upset by this turn of events, he objected to the unanimous consent requests made by other congressmen the same day. Vance was later mollified when he was able to discuss his amendment briefly, and he subsequently withdrew it. The next day, he requested a separate vote on an amendment to the same legislation. When some other members yelled out "give it up," Zeb replied: "I cannot afford to give it up. It is for my constituents, and it is my duty to stand by their interests." Despite his tenacity, Vance's motion was easily defeated. He then sought to get the 1817 and 1819 treaties with the Cherokees implemented "by making provision for the reservations" that should have been established under the treaties. There was no further action on his request. The next day, Vance withdrew a motion on the post office appropriation bill and had another motion ruled out of order.[21] None of these efforts were of much substance, but collectively they demonstrated that Zeb was feeling more at home in Congress and was able to participate more fully in its activities.

Like congressmen in all other periods, Zeb found himself deluged with constituent requests. During his lifetime, congressmen and senators had no office staffs or, for that matter, offices. Zeb had to compose all of his own correspondence and travel to the federal agencies himself to solve problems. This type of work was time consuming and generally unrewarding. He wrote to one constituent after receiving a letter from her, "I sit down to answer it immediately, for I get so many letters, that if I lay one aside for future attention it loses its chance and I never catch up." This person, a cousin, had written about obtaining an appointment for her brother at the United States Naval Academy. Zeb gladly complied in arranging the appointment, but the young man was ultimately unsuccessful in passing the required entrance examination. Another cousin received a package of seeds available only from the Agriculture office. The only other constituent letter that survives from this period is a request for a new post office in Yancey County.[22] All of these requests were probably typical of the letters that filled Zeb's days and nights with work.

But not all of Zeb's time in Washington was spent at work. Although clearly not a prude, Zeb was apparently shocked by the open debauchery he saw in the nation's capital. He wrote to his cousin, Jane Smith, "I really believe, in point of wickedness and vice, that the cities at the bottom of the Dead Sea were holy places, compared to this." While not exactly Sodom and Gomorrah, Washington did offer opportunities that Asheville did not. Vance confided to Smith, "I had the honor of dining with the President and Swinging the accomplished Miss Lane to my arm; and of supping with Judge Douglas & his magnificent wife."[23] Since President James Buchanan and Senator Stephen A. Douglas were both Northerners and Democrats, it is clear that Zeb did not limit his social interactions to people with whom he agreed politically. This showed unusual liberality on Zeb's part in a city where political divisions often determined social relationships. When the session ended in early March, Zeb collected his belongings and returned to Asheville.

Zeb's reputation as a Unionist and spokesman for the former Whig Party earned him an invitation to speak at a Whig mass meeting in the eastern counties of Tennessee. This section of the South was strongly pro-Union and Whig, and Zeb had a receptive audience. Apparently, the major theme of his address was the corruption of the Buchanan administration, made evident in its attempt to purchase Cuba. He asserted that Daniel's biblical interpretation of the writing on Belshazzar's wall, "Mene, Mene, Tekel, Upharsin," applied to President Buchanan. But instead of using Daniel's interpretations—"God hath numbered thy kingdom and finished it," and "Thou art weighed in the balances, and art found wanting,"—Zeb supplied his own translation of the words. He asserted that the phrase meant, "Jeems, Jeems, you stole that money."[24] The crowd, which was probably familiar with the biblical account, roared its appreciation of Zeb's modernized version of the Scriptures. Vance meant no disrespect in this case; the connection between ancient and modern abuse of power was a clear one. Zeb was becoming a more polished performer as a speaker, and he now sought to use humor to make his points whenever possible.

No sooner had Zeb returned home than he found himself in the midst of a campaign for reelection to the House. His opponent was once again David Coleman. Coleman ran a very aggressive campaign and fully expected to defeat Zeb. This expectation was based upon two assumptions. First, Coleman had easily defeated Vance in the race for a seat in the state Senate in 1856. An impartial observer would have noted, however, that the electorate for that office was restricted, and that Zeb's style of campaigning was proving to be especially appealing to those excluded from voting for state senators. Coleman also drew solace from Avery's defeat in 1858. The Democrats, including Coleman, had convinced themselves that Vance's victory was an accident caused by popular revulsion at Avery's shooting of Flemming. Again, an outside observer might have noted that Zeb had attracted the old Whig majority in the district and predicted that he would be difficult to defeat.

Coleman was undoubtedly still angry with Zeb for forcing him out of the 1858 House race, and he attacked Zeb's record in the Thirty-fifth Congress with vigor. While his rhetoric was harsh, Zeb later judged that "from the relations that had hitherto existed between [them] and the latitude generally allowed to political discussions," the debates between the two men fell within the bounds of normal political language. In general terms, Coleman and the Democrats sought to tar Zeb with the Know-Nothing brush again. Zeb rejected the charge as irrelevant to the present canvass, and related the following imaginary conversation between Coleman and a mountain farmer: "'My friend, have you heard the news?'" Coleman asked. "The man dropped his plow in alarm, held up his hands and cried out: 'What in the world is it?' The Colonel [Coleman] said: 'The Know Nothings are rising.' 'Can it be possible,' cried the man; 'if so, just let them rise.'" Coleman also charged that Vance had voted to give himself a pay raise, had voted with Republicans on certain issues, had supported extravagant pensions for veterans of the War of 1812, and had been an ineffective congressman.[25]

Vance employed a particularly effective defense of his vote on the issue of veterans' pensions that apparently deeply affected an audience in Asheville. Other Vance replies were memorable for different reasons. Vance agreed that he had not been a particularly active congressman, but he was able to neutralize the effect of Coleman's point on their audience through his superior knowledge of the Scriptures. Coleman, using the parable of the barren fig tree, suggested as the owner of the tree that the barren tree— Vance—needed to "be cut down." Vance quickly pointed out that in the parable, the owner's gardener suggested that he "let [it] alone this year also, till I shall dig about it." Zeb then concluded that if he did not bear fruit in the next Congress he should be cut down. Coleman had no effective comeback to that observation. In another debate in Waynesville, Coleman implied that Vance's support for some Republican-sponsored resolutions indicated that he backed the Republican attempts to gain control of the House. This charge was so politically sensitive that Zeb felt compelled to challenge Coleman without waiting for his turn in the debate. He jumped to his feet and vehemently denied the charge, and his denials were accepted. The remainder of the campaign apparently came off without major incident. Later, Coleman would accuse Vance of having failed to contradict charges in Lenoir County that Coleman had been drunk at one of their debates.[26]

During the campaign itself, neither this rumor nor the debates between Vance and Coleman themselves had much effect; as Vance himself noted, the electorate seemed to be rather apathetic. The campaign centered on personalities rather than issues. As a result, fewer votes than usual were cast. Still, Vance won a decisive victory over Coleman. Coleman apparently brooded over the result for nearly two weeks, and then he sent an aggressively worded letter to Zeb that claimed Zeb had used ungentlemanly language, looks, and gestures during the campaign. Coleman cited the incident in Waynesville in particular. Zeb wrote conciliatory notes to this missive and another that followed. Finally sensing that Coleman would not be satisfied with words, Zeb agreed to a duel. All of the details were meticulously worked out in advance, and a tragic denouement seemed inevitable. Fortunately for all concerned, Dr. James F. E. Hardy, a prominent Asheville physician, intervened and persuaded Coleman and Vance to withdraw the offending correspondence.[27] In this episode, Zeb sought to be the responsible party. He made two efforts to reconcile himself with Coleman, and he readily accepted mediation and a peaceful settlement of the dispute. Yet despite his mature approach to the incident, Vance acted completely irresponsibly. As the father of two small children and the husband of a chronically ill wife, he threatened his family with catastrophe in order to satisfy the Southern code of honor. Even if we grant that his society provided him with few alternatives, we must nevertheless admit that Vance jeopardized the future of those closest to him.

Zeb's reelection to the House brought his early political career to an end. During the 1850s, he had proven himself to be a gifted public speaker and campaigner in the mountain region. The lure of politics was absolutely irresistible to him, and he leaped into the fray whenever an opportunity offered itself. He even used nonpolitical episodes, like the Clingman-Mitchell controversy, to win personal political advantage. Even Vance would have agreed, however, that he still had to prove that he could use the positions and power that he had obtained for constructive purposes. As the spring of 1859 came to an end and the United States faced the greatest crisis in its history, Zeb would not have the luxury of avoiding political responsibilities any longer.

s Zeb prepared to return to Washington for the opening of the first session of the Thirty-sixth Congress, the sectional peace that he had noted in his February 7 speech was shattered. On October 16, 1859, John Brown and his associates seized the federal armory in Harpers Ferry, Virginia, and tried to instigate a slave uprising. North Carolinians reacted with panic, their sense that slavery was a threatened institution having been renewed. Politicians in the state who favored splitting the Union and creating a new Southern nation used the incident to inflame public opinion in North Carolina against the abolitionist threat from the Northern states.[1] While Vance's personal reaction to Brown's raid has not been recorded, there is little doubt that he was outraged by it. At the same time, he must have recognized that North Carolinians' almost hysterical reaction to the raid would make it much more difficult to preserve the Union.

Unfortunately for Vance and the United States, the first order of business in the new Congress was the election of a Speaker. The membership of the House was so badly divided between Republicans, Democrats, and Whig–Know-Nothings that no party could command a majority. Adding even more difficulty to the selection of the Speaker, Republican candidate John Sherman had endorsed Hinton Rowan Helper's inflammatory book, *The Impending Crisis*. Helper, a North Carolinian, was a racist who challenged the institution of slavery. Using statistics from the 1850 census, he purported to show that the South had lost ground economically because of slavery. Helper was forced into exile in the Northern states, and Sherman's endorsement of his attack on slavery only further infuriated Southern congressmen already greatly upset by John Brown's raid. In this poisonous atmosphere, Vance occupied a very moderate position. When a Whig candidate for Speaker materialized, he voted for that candidate.[2]

But with a sure sense of where his own political future lay, Vance was willing to vote for only those Democratic candidates who took a national perspective on the dispute between the North and the South. A friend from Asheville warned Zeb that his course was alienating some of his friends. They apparently wanted him to vote more consistently with the Democrats to spite the Republicans. This correspondent warned Zeb that a group of men who supported the Democratic candidates "had a meeting a short time ago and formed a Vigilant Com[mittee]," and that this group "ran . . . out of town" one of Zeb's most loyal supporters. Feeling under some compulsion to explain himself after receiving this warning, Zeb took to the House floor on December 29. As he promised to vote for "any man upon a national and conservative basis," his remarks were punctuated with welcome laughter. He explained himself as follows: "I have voted for a Lecompton Democrat. I have voted for those who did not approve of the Lecompton bill. I have also voted for an administration Democrat. I have voted for an anti-administration Democrat. And if there is any other member of that great, prolific Democratic family that I have neglected, I hope they will trot him out and give me an opportunity to vote for him."[3] Unfortunately, few other members adopted Zeb's nonpartisan stance, and the dispute was not finally settled until the forty-fifth ballot in early February.

Zeb's moderate stance during the Speaker controversy also failed to please his Democratic opposition in western North Carolina. The *Asheville News* accused him of only voting for Democratic candidates who had no opportunity to win the balloting. Once again, Vance felt compelled to reply to his local critics. On January 31, he rose in the House to explain his vote for Illinois Democrat John A. McClernand for Speaker. He struck back at his partisan critics in the mountains in an emotional outburst:

> I do not consider myself as endorsing anything by this vote, save except alone my own opposition to Black Republicanism. I consider it an evidence of the degeneracy of the times that gentlemen here cannot sacrifice so small and insignificant thing as their party prejudices for the common good, when men may be sometime called upon, as our fathers were in times past, to sacrifice their lives, their fortunes, and their hearts best blood, to the cause of their country. . . . I only mean to say, that members of the Democracy refusing to vote for their own man, forms no sufficient reason why I should not meet the gentleman from Illinois on the high and conservative ground which he has occupied throughout this contest.[4]

While his critics were undoubtedly not mollified by Vance's speech, he probably felt that he had fully vindicated himself.

When the regular work of the Thirty-sixth Congress resumed, Vance once again played a minor role. He continued to be handicapped by his membership in the smallest of the three political groups in the House. He was reappointed to the Committee on Revolutionary War Claims, one of the least important committees in the House. On February 15, Zeb reintroduced his bill to execute the 1817 and 1819 treaties with the Cherokees by providing the stipulated reservations. But other matters occupied more of Zeb's attention; Hattie was nearing the end of another pregnancy. She presented Zeb with another son, Zebulon, in the middle of March. Zeb had remained in Washington during the delivery, and his brother reported later that Hattie had been "quite sick." She was slowly recovering, and Bob assured Zeb that he "need not feel special uneasiness."[5] Zeb's separation from his family during this critical time was difficult for him.

In late February, the loose coalition of former Whigs and Know-Nothings who made up the North Carolina opposition party met in convention to stake out its position for the coming campaign. The party platform adopted by those in attendance probably accurately reflected Zeb's political position at the time. The party affirmed the right of Southerners to own slaves and attacked the fugitive slave laws of the Northern states, but it maintained that slavery could best be protected within the Union rather than outside of it. At the same time, the party took the moderate position that new states should be admitted to the Union without reference to slavery. The platform went so far as to demand that "all further agitation of the [slavery] question be withdrawn from the arena of national politics." The opposition party also addressed a volatile state issue, arguing that slaves should be taxed equally with other property; at the time, slaves were taxed at a much lower rate than other property. The oppositionists were also careful to endorse religious freedom in an obvious effort to distance themselves from any association with the Know-Nothings.[6] On the basis of this moderate national platform and the accompanying fairly radical state platform, the party launched its campaign.

When Zeb returned to Congress in March, he delivered some remarks on slavery and abolition. These comments were not unexpected, because these topics were the most crucial issues of the day. Nor were Zeb's positions on the issue exceptional. William Freehling has demonstrated that some whites from the upper South recognized that the institution of slavery was growing weak in that region relative to the rest of the South. There was a discernable "slave drain" from the upper South to the new states of Alabama, Mississippi, and Texas. But as John C. Inscoe, Kenneth W. Noe, and Charles Dew have all pointed out, slavery was in fact expanding and flourishing in the mountain South. Inscoe has clearly shown that in western North Carolina, in particular, slavery was proving to be a remarkably adaptable labor system. A story in the *Asheville News* of January 1859 indicates that slave prices were at the same level in western North Carolina as in the plantation South. As the son of a slave owner and a slave owner himself, Vance was part of a mountain elite that had every reason to expect that the institution of slavery would flourish in its area. In fact, Zeb was able to enter politics and serve in Congress due, at least in part, to the presence of slaves in his household. Hattie informed Zeb, for example, that an enslaved man named Isaac would plant the potatoes and take care of the garden in the spring of 1860.[7] Thus, there was no reason to expect that Vance's views on the enslavement of African Americans would differ from those of most other elite Southerners.

The speech of March 16 was predictable in every way. Vance stated his conviction that African Americans were inferior to whites and that only the discipline of enslavement made productive workers out of blacks. While he would later accept the end of slavery as a necessity, there is nothing in any of his extant writings to indicate that he ever changed his mind about the inherent incapacity of African Americans. Vance went on to describe the imagined horrors that would accompany emancipation. Like many other whites, Vance found it hard to imagine a society in which the two socially defined racial groups could live together in harmony. He was particularly concerned about sexual contact between members of the two races, calling such mixing "odious" and claiming that "even the mind of a fanatic recoils in disgust and loathing from the prospect of intermingling the quick and jealous blood of the European with the putrid stream of African barbarism." Vance's ideas were similar to those of virtually all the other members of the western North Carolina elite. David W. Siler of Macon County, for example, wrote to Vance in 1862 making essentially the same point: "We have but little interest in the value of slaves, but there is one matter in this connection about which we feel a very deep interest. We are opposed to negro equality. To prevent this we are willing to spare the last man, down to the point where women and children begin to suffer."[8] Even if he had felt differently about African Americans, Vance would have felt constrained to recognize the prejudices of his constituents. But the evidence is clear: Vance fully shared their feelings. Pervasive racism would be a part of Vance's personal mental apparatus as the crisis of the Union approached, and it would help determine his future course.

While Vance dealt with issues of immense seriousness during this session, most of his colleagues probably remembered him for his humorous interjections into heated or dull debates. For example, during a debate on an appropriations bill on May 23, Vance offered the following amendment to a section authorizing funds for the extension of the Capitol: "Provided, That there shall not be paid for labor or material more than twice as much as the same could be obtained for by private individuals." His comment indicates that government contracts have been subject to abuse, and consequently to ridicule, during all periods of our history. On the evening of

June 5, Vance left the House during a debate and returned to his lodging for dinner and some sleep. At two o'clock the next morning, he was aroused from his sleep by someone from the sergeant at arms' office and placed under arrest. Vance was returned to the House, where he faced contempt charges and defended himself with a series of laughter-punctuated quips. After being forced to pay a small fine for his absence, Vance was delighted to discover that the Speaker of the House was also absent, and that he had been among those who forced Vance's arrest and return to the floor. When this worthy finally returned, Vance welcomed him with the comment, "I give the speaker the compliments of the morning and hope he had a good night's rest." At another point, he said he was paired—a practice by which absent members made an agreement with another member who planned to vote differently on a question to negate each other's votes—with another congressman "who had gone to Baltimore to witness the riot." The "riot" was the Northern Democratic Party's presidential nominating convention.[9] While none of these observations added much to the welfare of the nation, they did tend to reduce tensions in a volatile situation.

Although Vance provided some comic relief for the House, the tensions of the moment were apparently sufficient to cause him physical distress. In a letter to Hattie that has been lost, he complained of "inflamations of the Bowels" and "piles." A correspondent who had talked to Hattie offered the following medical advice: "I *repeat*, be *care*full of yourself & abstain from eating stimulants on account of the irritation of your bowels. use good olive oil freely in broken doses with occasionaly divers powder & Blue pill. At night, to stimulate the free action of the liver, avoid preparation with *aloes*." Part of the stress that Zeb felt during this period may have come from his work with the Committee on Revolutionary War Claims. While not one of the most crucial committees, it appears to have been one of the most active. On a number of occasions, Zeb introduced claims from multiple applicants that the committee had approved.[10] There seems to be little doubt, however, that Zeb was most happy to return home when the session ended in the early summer.

Zeb got little rest when he returned to Asheville, however, because the most critical presidential election campaign in American history to date had already begun. The campaigning efforts of four parties—Republicans, Northern Democrats, Southern Democrats, and Constitutional Unionists —were straining the political fabric of the nation. In North Carolina, William W. Holden, editor of Raleigh's *North Carolina Standard* and a leading Democratic spokesman, endorsed the presidential candidacy of Southern Democratic candidate John C. Breckinridge. But in a cautionary editorial, Holden warned against breaking up the Union. With unnerving accuracy, he predicted that "Disunion would be fraternal strife, civil and servile war, murder, arson and pillage, robbery, and fire and blood through long and cruel years."[11] Vance and the Constitutional Unionists, with whom he was now affiliated, agreed with Holden's prediction of what would happen if the Union was destroyed and worked fervently to prevent its being broken in two.

In the mountains, the voters were strongly attracted to the Unionist position. In the state Senate race in the Asheville district, the Unionists scored a major victory. Augustus S. Merrimon, running as a National Democratic Party candidate, defeated Democrat and Southern nationalist candidate David Coleman by twenty-five votes. While Merrimon's margin of victory was decidedly narrow, it must be remembered that Coleman had defeated Vance by over three hundred votes in the same district just four years before. Zeb spoke at a monstrous rally at Franklin in September where approximately five thousand people gathered in support of the extension of the Blue Ridge Railroad to Macon County. While Vance did not directly address the question of the Union on this occasion, he was involved in helping to cement sectional solidarity in western North Carolina. Unfortunately, all efforts to achieve political unity in the mountains failed. In early October, the Democrats held a large rally in Hendersonville at which fifteen hundred people listened as the vitality of the Union was questioned. In county seats, the leading political figures of the region debated each other ferociously. In Waynesville, for example, Senator Thomas Lanier Clingman argued about the future with John D. Hyman and Augustus S. Merrimon, both supporters of Stephen A. Douglas. Vance and Hyman, his former newspaper partner, squared off against each other in the Jackson County town of Webster.[12] Despite their disagreements, of course, no political figure in the mountains of any standing had anything but contempt for the eventual winner of the presidential election, Abraham Lincoln.

A Constitutional Union Party mass meeting at Salisbury in October 1860 produced a tremendous personal triumph for Vance; it would prove to be probably the most important single incident in his ascent to prominence during the coming war. The meeting was held in the open air, and throughout the day distinguished members of the party spoke to a mass audience of several thousand people. Among the speakers were George E. Badger and William A. Graham, both former U.S. senators and cabinet members as well as outstanding classical orators. Vance spoke for two full hours in the morning to an enthusiastic audience. After a full day of speeches, the increasingly fatigued crowd stayed for the concluding fireworks display. As this spectacular event concluded, several members of the crowd called upon Zeb for some final remarks. After climbing up on an informal platform of discarded boxes, Zeb launched into a highly partisan discussion that relied heavily upon anecdotes about his neighbors in the mountains. Forgetting their fatigue, by the end of Zeb's hour-long address the members of the audience had begun to cheer his every sentence. Several enthusiastic auditors lifted the new hero on their shoulders and paraded him around the town square as the cheering grew in volume. A torchlight parade followed, with Vance being called on for a few more words at every street corner. Not only were the rank and file of the party enthused, but party patriarch George E. Badger exclaimed, "There never lived such a stump speaker as he."[13] Vance's sudden rise to prominence as a leading figure in North Carolina's anti-Democratic coalition would have a dramatic impact on his career within two years.

The election of Abraham Lincoln to the presidency without the support of the Southern states cast an ominous shadow over western North Carolina and Vance's political career. In Cleveland County, which is located in the western Piedmont of North Carolina on the South Carolina border, a secession meeting was held as early as November 12. As his constituents tried to sort out their sentiments, Vance returned to Washington for the second session of the Thirty-sixth Congress. When he arrived in Raleigh on November 30, he discovered that South Carolina congressmen William W. Boyce and John D. Ashmore were to deliver secessionist speeches in the city that night. Waiting until the two secessionists had finished speaking, Vance made a reply in Raleigh's Wake County Courthouse. When he was introduced, the utmost excitement prevailed: "Canes rattled and banged—the tenure by which boot-heels were held was severely tested—strong lungs were exerted to the full extent of their powers—hats were swung in the air—white handkerchiefs were waved, and the gallery sent forth a full volume of bright eyes." Vance was equal to the occasion. He admitted that the South had legitimate grievances, but he denied that the solution was to be found in secession. He pointed out that Lincoln had promised to be a national president. Vance's support for the Union was not unconditional, however; he maintained that North Carolina needed to act in concert with other upper South states and that it should leave the Union if the others did.[14] The enthusiasm of the audience was overwhelming, and Vance was sent to Washington with cheers ringing in his ears.

The atmosphere in Washington was every bit as excited as it had been in Raleigh. Vance immediately established himself as one of the leading Southern Unionists. In mid-December, he ostentatiously refused to join twenty-eight other senators and congressmen in signing a manifesto that called for secession and independence for the Confederacy. He also met in conference with Senator John J. Crittenden and other upper South Unionists to plan strategy. Those at the meeting agreed "that the only earthly chance to save the Union [was] to gain time." Vance and the other Unionists were hopeful that if the first great surge of Southern nationalism could be withstood, the people of North Carolina and the other states of the upper South would have sober second thoughts about the developing situation. Vance hoped that it would be possible for the Northern and Southern border states to form a central confederation that would then confront the extremists in both the North and the South. Were such a confederation to be formed, Vance maintained that it "could dictate terms of compromise which Georgia would be compelled to accept, and the withdrawal of Georgia would break the back bone of the whole seceding Kingdom." This planned confederation would also eliminate other extremists by forcing New England out of the nation and not allowing it to return until it agreed to come back as one state.[15] There was an assumption in Vance's letters, however, that both he and his correspondents held in December 1860: if some compromise were not found, North Carolina would eventually join the Confederacy.

Vance's position on the question of whether to preserve the Union mirrored the views held by many of his constituents in western North Carolina, who truly believed in the greatness of the Union. One observer called it "the best government vouchsafed by God to man." Others were deeply concerned by the atmosphere of uncertainty. A Macon County man warned, "To take up the anchor in such a storm would be to commit ourselves to the mercy of the waves." Most of Zeb's constituents were more than willing to adopt his strategy of waiting to see what type of compromise could be arranged. As an Asheville man reported, "the great mass of the people [were] opposed to secession for existing causes." The final phrase was a crucial one, however, and it sheds light on the position of Vance and most of his western North Carolina neighbors during this troubled time. They were — in the contemporary parlance — "conditional" Unionists. Just as the resolutions adopted in 1850 in Asheville required Northern good faith to maintain the Union, many people in western North Carolina refused to support aggressive action against fellow Southerners. One Unionist declared, "it is the general feeling that if our sister States should secede that coercion or an attempt to coerce on the part of the north will be the signal for us to 'strike.'"[16] Thus, when Vance spoke out in defense of the Union during this period, he could be confident that he was speaking for the majority of his constituents.

On one matter of political strategy, however, Vance differed from many of his fellow Unionists. In November 1860, Governor John W. Ellis had recommended that the state legislature call for a state conference to consider the issues under discussion, with this meeting to be followed by a convention of the people. The majority of Unionists opposed the calling of the state convention from the beginning, because secessionists in other states had used meetings of this type to remove their states from the Union. But Vance thought differently. "Our friends ought to lead in the Convention movement," he wrote, "in order that they may as far as possible control it, and that its being called may not seem a disunion victory." There was much more to Vance's reasoning than the struggle for strategic advantage. Well before the war started, he sensed the tremendous toll on popular morale that the strife would take. He stressed that it was terribly important that the entire free population be involved in the discussion of the secession issue. "If after full and fair discussion, after hearing what our Northern brethren have to offer us, and after such mature and *decent* deliberation as becomes a great people about to do a great act," he explained, "if *they* choose to undo the work of their wise and heroic ancestors, if *they* choose to invite carnage to saturate their soil and desolation to waste their fields, they can not say their public servants *precipitated* them into it!"[17] Vance instinctively sensed that in order for the people of North Carolina to support the decision to leave the Union, they would have to be full participants in making that decision.

Vance's support for the convention movement in North Carolina almost led him into an alliance of convenience with his political enemies. On January 4, 1861, four pro-Confederate members of the North Carolina congressional delegation drew up a circular letter calling upon the state legislature to summon a state convention. The men, Thomas Lanier Clingman among them, visited Vance, who agreed to sign the letter and to secure the signature of another congressman. Later that evening, Vance went to the room of Senator Thomas Bragg and reported that the two congressmen he approached had refused to sign the letter. Bragg gave Vance a copy of the letter so that he could seek the signature of another congressman. When neither Vance nor the man he sought to speak to returned to see Bragg in the morning, Bragg concluded that Vance had changed his mind about signing the letter. It was issued with the signatures of six members of the delegation; Vance's was not among them. Apparently, other members of the congressional delegation had pointed out to Vance that he would be publicly associating himself with known secessionists if he endorsed the letter. The entire episode indicates that Vance was fully committed to the idea of a convention. In late January, the state legislature passed a bill that gave voters the opportunity to decide whether to hold a convention and to select delegates to send to it.[18] Vance's hope that the people of North Carolina would be directly involved in the decision-making process was fulfilled.

The Unionists' strategy of delay appeared to be working; there was a growing groundswell of support for giving the new president an opportunity to resolve the crisis. Letter after letter written to Vance by his constituents contained the same encouraging message: "All the Countys West of the Blue Ridge is union By a large majority." Letters written to the *North Carolina Standard*, often by Democrats who opposed Clingman and other mountain secessionists, confirmed the sentiments expressed by Vance's correspondents. Even when secessionists tried to act in the mountain counties, their Unionist neighbors intervened and prevented them from succeeding. In Jackson County, an attempt to pass a series of resolutions in favor of secession was tabled by a large Union majority. Much the same thing happened at a joint meeting in Polk and Rutherford Counties, and a conditional Unionist statement was overwhelmingly endorsed.[19] The secessionists' initial momentum had been destroyed, and the Unionists had an opportunity to seize control of the policy of the state.

In the midst of these revolutionary times, Vance continued his work as a member of Congress. In a letter discussing the crisis of the Union, Zeb was careful to inquire about sending seeds to the "Agricultural Society in Burke [County]." Reelection to the House would be the result of good constituent services as well as taking the correct stand on public issues. He also continued to make reports on behalf of the Committee on Revolutionary War Claims, becoming fairly involved in the case of Robert Stockton. He introduced resolutions from Buncombe and Caldwell Counties on the crisis of the Union, but the only extended remarks that Vance made during the session were to explain his vote on a revenue bill. Vance said that he opposed the bill because it held the seceded states responsible for paying federal taxes. Vance considered this policy to be "the greatest barrier to peaceful reconciliation," and he voted accordingly. The other element of normalcy in his life during this session was the presence of his family in Washington. He had arranged for Hattie and the three boys to accompany him to the nation's capital, although he was thinking of sending them home early if events warranted it.[20]

Like the other members of Congress from North Carolina, Vance's attention was more and more drawn to events in his own state. After the state legislature provided for a public referendum on the convention, most public men in the state began to address the people. They did so at some personal risk to themselves. One of Vance's correspondents wrote that secessionist David Coleman was nearly tarred and feathered in Madison County, and some unidentified person had hanged Zeb in effigy in Burnsville, Yancey County. Vance issued a circular to his constituents from Washington that condemned secession and called upon them to elect Unionists to the convention. Senator Bragg commented in his diary, "Surely it is a very different paper from what he would have issued a few weeks since, judging from his conversation."[21] It is not absolutely clear what Bragg was referring to; all other evidence indicates that Vance opposed immediate secession throughout this period. Perhaps Bragg thought that Vance's support for the convention was a commitment to secession. If that was Bragg's reasoning, then he clearly did not understand Vance's position. Vance recognized that his circular alone would not be sufficient to carry the Union message to the people in his absence, so he attempted—unsuccessfully—to start a Unionist newspaper in western North Carolina.

The short campaign on the convention question proved to be a startling success for the Unionists. Drawing upon the resources of the opposition party and the support of Unionist Democrats like the powerful newspaper editor William W. Holden, they ran a well-organized campaign. Their opponents, by contrast, ran a disorganized and ineffective canvass. Many secessionist candidates openly avowed their intention to take the state out of the Union. This open advocacy of disunion unnerved many Democrats who had voted for the Southern Democratic Party candidate for president in 1860, and they simply refused to vote. At the same time, many people who normally did not take part in elections in the western part of the state were motivated to go to the polls and vote in favor of Unionist candidates. The result was an overwhelming Unionist victory in which they captured 81 of the 120 contested seats. Unexpectedly, the enthusiasm of Unionist voters resulted in a 47,338 to 46,671 vote against holding the convention at all.[22] The Unionists were completely successful. There would be no convention, and the secessionist effort to take North Carolina out of the Union was completely stymied.

For Vance and many of his former Whig allies, this was a period of vindication. The people supported their position, and it seemed likely that their party would return to power at the state level. One major problem was that the Unionists had no concrete program to follow. Vance and others had put their faith in the Peace Conference of states that met throughout early 1861. The conference issued a report on February 27 that offered the South constitutional protection of slavery. Republicans opposed the adoption of such measures, and Congress refused to endorse them before the session ended on March 3. Despite this setback, the Unionists remained optimistic. Vance, for example, announced that he would be a candidate for reelection to the federal Congress in 1861. The Unionists' unflagging optimism was based on a guarantee extended to them by the incoming secretary of state, William H. Seward. Seward appeared to commit the Lincoln administration to a "let alone" policy that would avoid coercing the newly formed Confederacy. Specifically, North Carolina Unionists learned about and accepted his assurance that the Republican administration would abandon Fort Sumter in Charleston Harbor.[23]

This was certainly Vance's understanding of the arrangement. He recalled later that John A. Gilmer had told him that Lincoln had assured him and other Union congressmen from the upper South "that if possible he would avoid the attempt at coercion." Lincoln's own nationalism combined with pressure from other Republicans, particularly those who were most offended by the power of the slaveowners, to gradually move the new president away from this policy. As Vance and other Unionists waited for the fulfillment of the promises made by Seward and generally endorsed by Lincoln, they became uneasy. Lincoln was warned that if troops remained in Fort Sumter, the Confederates would attack the installation and the upper South would secede. On April 12, the Confederate attack on Fort Sumter came, just as the Unionists had predicted. They grew despondent and then outraged as Lincoln called for troops. Vance and others were particularly incensed when North Carolina was requested to supply troops. Using a logic that made sense only in the atmosphere of the time, William W. Holden admitted that the Confederacy fired the first shot, but nevertheless contended that Lincoln's response was unconstitutional.[24] Using this kind of reasoning, most of North Carolina's conditional Unionist leaders reluctantly swung around to support the Confederacy.

Vance remembered himself as greatly saddened by the turn of events. Many years later, he recalled: "For myself, I will say that I was canvassing for the Union with all my strength; I was addressing a large and excited crowd, large numbers of whom were armed, and literally had my arms extended upward in pleading for peace and the Union of our Fathers, when the telegraphic news was announced of the firing on Sumter and [the] President's call for seventy-five thousand volunteers. When my hand came down from that impassioned gesticulation, it fell slowly and sadly by the side of a Secessionist." This recollection may be entirely accurate, but there is no other evidence that Vance addressed a large crowd in favor of the Union in mid-April. If Vance did indeed feel regret, the emotion was only momentary, as he quickly expressed anger at what he felt to be Lincoln's betrayal of solemn commitments. Vance took part in a mass meeting in Asheville on April 18, where the participants called for an immediate session of the legislature, insisted that arms be provided for the military companies being formed in Buncombe County, and promised "to defend the honor and dignity of [their] State to the last extremity." This last statement was particularly revealing; it appears that the newly converted Confederates still felt little commitment to the new nation and were motivated largely by state patriotism. A state secession convention was called by the legislature. This body, composed largely of men who had long been secessionists, voted unanimously on May 20, 1861, to take North Carolina out of the Union.[25]

Zeb's bitterness at what he perceived as the betrayal of the Southern Unionists quickly prompted him to action. On May 3, 1861, he joined the second military unit raised in Buncombe County, which was known as the Rough and Ready Guards. The enthusiasm that filled this unit with slightly more than one hundred men was duplicated elsewhere in Buncombe County. Although volunteering in some parts of western North Carolina lagged, Asheville and its immediate surroundings contributed soldiers to the Confederacy in large numbers. By February 1862, nearly nine hundred men from Buncombe County had volunteered their services; a greater proportion of the county's total population volunteered than in all but four other counties of the state. Soon after the Rough and Ready Guards were organized, Zeb was selected by the men to be their captain.[1] In all likelihood, he had recruited the men with the understanding that he would assume the leadership role.

Several days later, the newest unit of the North Carolina state troops marched off to war. Zeb's brother Robert reported three decades later that "the streets were crowded with people, friends and admirers of the company." As the group of young men marched out of the city on South Main Street, they paused at the Swannanoa River and followed it for several miles before camping. That night Zeb returned home, and he rejoined his men the next day mounted on a horse from his own residence. On his way out of town, he paused at the top of Beaucatcher Gap and sorrowfully surveyed the beauties of the mountains for what might have been the last time. Then he rode on to rejoin his troops. They traveled by foot to reach the railroad in Burke County and then proceeded on to the small community of Statesville. The company remained there for several days while Zeb made a quick trip to Raleigh to learn about the future disposition of his men.[2]

Zeb wrote to Hattie on May 18 describing the reception that he and his men received in Statesville. For all concerned, the war was still a very romantic affair, and Vance's description captures the celebratory atmosphere well: "The people of Statesville have been Kind to us beyond description—My camp has been filled with cake & all sorts of good things ever since I came, and such piles of flowers, you never saw as grace my tent. I have a trunk full of bouquets to send home to you when I get an opportunity." But there was trouble in paradise. Zeb reported to Hattie that despite the rousing welcome he was "in rather low spirits at the way things [were] managed at Raleigh." He continued: "I see a pretty determined purpose there to carry on affairs under a strict party regimen; none but Locos and Secessionists will be appointed to the Offices: the old Union men will be made to take back Seats and do most of the hard work." Vance was not alone in perceiving discrimination against former Unionists; William W. Holden also noted in early June that former Unionists were being passed over for prominent places in the state military establishment.[3] But Zeb was determined not to let these slights distract him from his major task of getting his men prepared for combat.

The Rough and Ready Guards were transferred to Raleigh, and, after a brief stay in Weldon, were then sent on to a frontline position near Norfolk, Virginia. In this setting, Zeb learned all about the inefficiencies and bungling that were features of the management of the war effort at both the state and national levels. A letter from Augustus S. Merrimon to Vance indicates that Vance's men did not receive adequate food or any pay with which to purchase sustenance for themselves, but Vance himself seems to have suffered little direct deprivation since he received invitations from local families to dine with them on occasion. Although thoroughly committed to the army, Vance's interest in politics remained strong. He was very pleased when his cousin Allen T. Davidson was selected by the convention to be the Confederate congressman from the mountain district. But Zeb still had a personal grievance. Although he had informed convention members that he would not be a candidate for Congress, he had expected that they would ceremonially offer him the position so that he could decline it in a burst of patriotism.[4] The offer never came, and the mountain politician nursed a growing list of grievances against those who were directing the war effort.

Merrimon's letter conveyed other bad news as well. He had taken the time to travel along the coast of North Carolina to review the military situation, and he was appalled by what he found. He reported that there was only one fortification in good condition along the entire coastline and that an attacking force could easily outflank it. Reinforcing Vance's own dissatisfaction with the authorities, Merrimon concluded: "There are several exposed points totally unprotected. Our authorities are neglecting the coast defence most criminally." Like many others in the state, Vance would judge the success of the Confederacy on the basis of its performance defending his native state. North Carolina governor John W. Ellis was at least partially responsible for the failure to protect the coastline; his poor health made it difficult for him to devote attention to the state's defenses. His health continued to deteriorate, and he died in early July.[5] Henry T. Clark, president of the state Senate, replaced Ellis as the state's chief executive. While Clark appeared motivated to be an effective governor, his sudden elevation did little to improve the performance of the state government.

Like many of his fellow soldiers, Zeb found it difficult to be away from his family and home for such an extended period. First, the dull routine of camp life proved to be a lot less exciting than the men had imagined it would be when they left home. Zeb complained to Hattie in one letter, "I am again officer of the day and shall have to tramp all night around our lines and pickets." Much more difficult for Vance to cope with, however, was bad news from home. Hattie was apparently suffering both from physical maladies and deep depression. In addition, Zebbie, the newest member of the family, seemed constantly to be in poor health. Vance was frantic with worry about his family in Asheville. At the same time, he had to face up to his own mortality. Both the reality of combat and the illness of his Asheville comrades reminded him of his own vulnerability.[6] Vance would recall these lessons about the shared problems of all who served in the army many times in the next four years. His later efforts to assist common soldiers and their families can be traced to his own experiences with the Rough and Ready Guards.

Vance's ambitions, never far below the surface, led him to take a momentous step in August 1861. He was elected to and accepted the position of colonel of the Twenty-sixth Regiment of North Carolina Volunteers. This new regiment was formed in the camp of instruction near Raleigh in late August, and Vance became its first leader. The exact process by which his election took place is not clear, but many of the troops in the new regiment were from the western and central parts of the state, and they probably knew of Vance. The new position separated Zeb from the Rough and Ready Guards. He was assured that his soldiers would be allowed to join his new regiment, but the promise was never carried out. The change in command allowed Zeb to take a brief furlough and return to Asheville to see his family. When he rejoined his men, they were in a well-fortified position along the coast of North Carolina.[7]

Vance and his men had been placed there, despite the brevity of their training, because an Union army had finally taken full advantage of the deplorable Confederate preparations along the coast. In a nearby coastal area, General Benjamin F. Butler and Commodore Silas H. Stringham led a combined land-sea operation that forced the surrender of the small Confederate garrison at Fort Hatteras on the Outer Banks of North Carolina. After the garrison of North Carolinians was forced to surrender in what was viewed as the first major Confederate defeat of the war, many in the state began to look for scapegoats. The poor performance of both the state and the Confederate governments was duly noted. This seemingly minor affair was actually quite important. It opened the coastal region of North Carolina to future federal invasion and forced the Confederacy to lose control of a safe haven for its shipping. At the same time, many North Carolinians grew disillusioned with the lack of Confederate support for their territory, and they became much more critical of the conduct of the war.[8]

Vance joined the growing chorus of the dissatisfied. His immediate concern was the condition of his regiment, rather than the disaster at Fort Hatteras. He wrote to Governor Clark that his men were owed four months back pay and a group of them were "almost in a state of mutiny." He cataloged the problems faced by his men as follows: "Most of them are suffering for the most ordinary articles of everyday use, which they are unable to purchase. Whilst many others left behind them destitute and dependent families who are daily appealing to them for aid. Even such articles as fresh fish tho' plentiful & cheap here they are unable to buy."[9] Unfortunately for Vance and his men, the state government reacted slowly to his request for assistance. Vance never forgot this and other episodes of state government inefficiency, and he also noted that the Confederate government seemed to be in no position to help the state provide for his beleaguered regiment.

Zeb was very fortunate in his new command in one respect. After the officers of the Twenty-sixth Regiment selected him to be their colonel, they elected Harry K. Burgwyn Jr. as lieutenant colonel, the second-in-command. Burgwyn was the exact opposite of Vance as a military leader. First, he possessed the self-assurance and enthusiasm that often accompanies young people who have succeeded at everything they have tried. In addition, he appears from photographs and other evidence to have been physically well suited for military life: he was quite trim and very athletic. Burgwyn was born into considerable affluence, and he decided at a young age to prepare for a military career. He attended short courses in military matters at a preparatory school in New Jersey and then at West Point. Soon thereafter, he entered the University of North Carolina and graduated without difficulty. Burgwyn then entered the Virginia Military Institute, leaving just before the Civil War commenced. Burgwyn was exceptionally well trained in military matters, and despite his youth (he was twenty at the time), he commanded respect from all around him. It would be Burgwyn's job to train the regiment, since Vance was completely ignorant of all military science. The young man would prove to be quite intolerant of the failure of the men in the regiment to learn commands quickly. Vance often tempered Burgwyn's strictness with a more relaxed approach to discipline that sustained morale among men unused to military ways. Although the two leaders used radically different approaches to prepare the unit, their combined efforts paid dividends. The regiment was soon one of the most effective Confederate fighting units along the North Carolina coast.[10]

Burgwyn felt that he was able to train the men to accomplish all they did despite the presence of Vance. The well-trained subordinate officer found his superior to be a severe trial. A fellow member of the regiment remembered an apparently typical incident many years later: "One day after regimental drill, he informed Colonel Vance that he noticed a mistake that he, Vance, had made while on drill, and that was that he brought the regiment from present arms to order arms, and this, said Colonel Burgwin [sic] cannot be done. Vance at once replied, 'you are mistaken, Colonel, for I have just done that very thing.'" Distressed by the ineptitude of the men, Burgwyn drilled the unit incessantly until they reached an acceptable level of efficiency in the spring of 1862. Still dissatisfied with Vance's leadership, he sought to secure a position as brigadier general through the influence of his father.[11] This effort failed, however, and the young perfectionist remained under the command of a man he perceived to be a bumbler.

Burgwyn vented his anger and frustration about Vance in letters to his father. In January, he complained: "Col[.] Vance is however a man without any system or regularity whatever. . . . His abilities appear to me to be more overrated than those of any other person I know of. As an instance of his procrastinating habits: We have been in the service as an organized Reg. since the 27 of Aug. & until today we have not had a color bearer or general guides appointed. To day he appointed him. If I have mentioned the matter to him once I have done so 20 times." Vance was not only negligent about administrative details, but also, Burgwyn felt, far too lax with the officers and men. Apparently, Vance intuitively sensed that the Confederate soldier was not going to accept too harsh a regimen from his leaders. Still, Burgwyn's description of Vance indicates that Zeb was probably too casual as a commander: "As for discipline not the faintest idea of it has ever entered his head. One or two things of late occurrence I will Mention. I reported 27 officers absent from Reveille & he did not even ask them all why they did not go. I reported two or three absent from drill. Not a syllable did he say to them concerning it to my knowledge."[12] While it is possible to justify Vance's actions by arguing that they softened Burgwyn's zealousness enough to maintain morale, there is little doubt that Zeb was not a skilled military leader. He was probably no worse than the typical political officer found in great abundance in both armies. Burgwyn's critical attitude suggests that he was little better.

An incident that took place during this period illustrates how commanders of volunteer troops had to deal with exceptional situations. One mem-

Henry King Burgwyn Jr., ca. 1861. Burgwyn was a cadet at the Virginia Military Institute, lieutenant colonel of the Twenty-sixth Regiment under Vance, and colonel of the regiment when Vance resigned. He was killed at Gettysburg. (North Carolina Division of Archives and History, Raleigh)

ber of the Twenty-sixth Regiment was a mountain farmer by the name of Keith Blalock. After approximately one month in camp, Keith requested permission to return to his home county to recruit another soldier. Permission was granted, and Keith soon returned with his brother Sam, a boy who appeared to be a slight youth of eighteen. After about six more weeks in camp, Keith Blalock sought to leave the army. His strategy was to roll in some poison oak to develop a dangerous-looking rash. The Confederate medical authorities were deceived by Blalock's scheme. He was discharged from the service, whereupon Sam Blalock reported to Vance and said, "Col. Vance, my husband has been discharged from military service on account of disability, and is going home, now I want you to discharge me also." Vance quickly replied, "Your husband, the h[ell], you must be crazy, boy you are in for the war, my young man, I can't let you off." The soldier persisted, claiming that her name was not Sam, but Matilda. The unnerved Vance ordered the regimental medical officer to verify the claim. He quickly reported back that Matilda was indeed a woman, and Vance quickly issued a second set of discharge papers. The Blalocks went back to western North Carolina, where Keith became a Unionist guerrilla who plagued Vance and the state government for the remainder of the war.[13] Zeb, who was well known for telling stories, apparently never referred to this episode again.

There were also occasions when Zeb's concern about the morale of his men combined with his inattention to detail to put everyone in danger. In late January 1862, the regiment was ordered to the New Bern area. They were moved in response to the threat from a large expedition of federal forces under the leadership of General Ambrose Burnside. Vance selected the area where the regiment would camp before Burgwyn reached the site. When he did arrive, Burgwyn was quite upset, because the camp was located on clay soil that provided little drainage. It was, according to Burgwyn, a "mud hole." When the junior officer suggested that the troops be moved to another location, Vance replied, "The men have built chimneys to their tents & dont want to move." Despite suffering from ill health himself, and despite another officer's concurrence in Burgwyn's assessment of the location, Vance insisted on staying in the same place.[14] Clearly, it was not in the best interests of the men to leave them in an unhealthy environment, no matter what their short-term desires might have been. Vance had not yet learned the importance of making difficult decisions that traded momentary satisfaction for long-term gain.

Whatever difficulties the two commanders of the Twenty-sixth Regiment had disappeared momentarily when immediate danger threatened. Not only did the Burnside expedition land, but the federal army quickly gained its first objective by capturing Roanoke Island. This event was followed two days later, on February 10, with the destruction of the tiny Confederate fleet at Elizabeth City. The next objective for Burnside and his force was New Bern, the second largest city along the North Carolina coast. Fortunately for the Confederates, Burnside took his time organizing his relatively large army of thirteen thousand men, and the Confederates, including the Twenty-sixth Regiment, had an opportunity to prepare some fortifications near New Bern.[15] Unfortunately, the people in command of the Confederate defense were political generals, and their preparations did not to prove to be sufficient.

While waiting for the federal advance at New Bern, Zeb faced a serious crisis. The enlistment period for the members of his unit was about to expire. By law, every soldier would be free to return home without penalty. Apparently, some of the soldiers' fathers had shown up at camp to escort their sons home. It was in situations of this type that Zeb provided his greatest service to the Confederate military effort. Addressing the men, who had finally been paid and given new uniforms, Zeb was at his eloquent best. He drew a vivid picture with words of the desolation that invasion would bring to the soldiers' communities and families if they left the army at such a dangerous time. Vance's impassioned speech was made more effective by the position of the regiment. His appeal was masterful, and everyone in the unit signed up for an additional tour of duty.[16]

Zeb's achievement in this episode did not satisfy his still considerable ambition. Reporting his success in convincing his men to reenlist to his cousin, Congressman Allen T. Davidson, he also asked for a new command. Zeb reported: "I have the offer of some new companies from the mountains. In thirty days I could raise another regiment for the war, two companies of cavalry & one of artillery. This would make a handsome brigade with which I would like to take the field on active service."[17] Of course, the commander of a brigade would have to possess the rank of brigadier general. This was Zeb's immediate ambition, and it was one he would retain for as long as he remained in the army.

Zeb heard nothing from Richmond about his new plans before the approaching battle, but news of his successful reenlistment appeal reached other regimental commanders, and they asked him to address their units when their men's terms of service were about to expire. Around the same time, Zeb acquired assistance in making these appeals. Hearing that a Moravian band from Salem was in the area, he immediately got in touch with them. The bandleader remembered meeting Vance in a hotel: "A man wearing a colonel's uniform came in with a loaf of bread under each arm. This was Zeb Vance." The two men reached an agreement that the band would provide music for the regiment on ceremonial occasions.[18] Although the arrangement was entirely informal, the band was thenceforth always associated with the Twenty-sixth Regiment and Zeb. In fact, a fragment of the band would march in Vance's funeral procession more than three decades later. Wherever Vance went seeking to encourage reenlistment in the Confederate army, the band accompanied him. The combination of Vance's patriotic addresses and the band's stirring tunes prompted many to stay who had planned to leave the service. Shortly thereafter, all of this activity became moot, as the Confederate Congress passed a conscription law at Jefferson Davis's behest. This statute required all soldiers then in service to continue in the military for the duration of the war.

On March 10, Burnside received orders from Washington to advance, and Vance and his men had to turn their attention to the deadly business of combat. By Wednesday, March 12, the federal army of more than eleven thousand men disembarked from ships anchored inside the Neuse River near New Bern. The Confederate commander at New Bern, Lawrence O'Bryan Branch, found himself at a distinct disadvantage at this point. His defenses were not completed because the local population had been unwilling to assist his men. He reported to his superiors: "I then inserted in the newspaper an advertisement calling on slave owners to hire their slaves, with implements, for a few days, and I got a single Negro." Nevertheless, the Confederate commander did have a formidable defensive position in place between the Union army and New Bern: the recently constructed Croatan breastworks. This fortification was in a strong natural defensive position, bordered by a creek on one side and a swamp on the other. Although a small force could have held these works against a much larger army, Branch chose to abandon them. As he explained, the federal army could have easily circumvented his troops by ferrying men further down the Neuse toward New Bern and coming in behind the Confederate defenders at the Croatan breastworks. Branch maintained that his four-thousand-man army was not sufficient to hold the position and defend the river at the same time.[19]

Vance and the Twenty-sixth Regiment first became engaged in the battle at these Croatan works. Branch had sent the Thirty-fifth Regiment and other troops to contest the landing of federal soldiers below the breastworks. When it became obvious that the landing was being effected anyway, Branch ordered Vance and the Twenty-sixth Regiment into the Croatan position. Burgwyn actually led the troops into the works, because Vance was in temporary command of another unit. When the officer he was replacing returned to his command, Vance moved to rejoin his unit. Before he reached his men, however, their position had grown untenable, and the regiment had been ordered back to a second line of defense, which they were transported to by rail. Burgwyn had posted the men in their battle positions by the time Zeb finally caught up with his men. They spent the night of March 13 in a defensive position, enduring heavy rain that made military preparations difficult.[20]

Vance and the Twenty-sixth Regiment occupied a strong defensive position on the right wing of the Confederate line. On their extreme right, Bryce's Creek, a swift flowing stream about seventy-five yards wide that could be crossed only by boat, provided an anchor for the Confederate defense. Most of the troops were protected by felled trees and a swamp that limited the enemy forces' ability to maneuver. The Confederate left flank along the Neuse River was also strongly defended, with the troops occupying a naturally strong situation. Unfortunately, Branch had been unable to protect the center of the Confederate line completely. Partial defenses had been constructed around a brickyard and a railroad yard, but there were gaps where there were essentially no prepared fortifications. For reasons never adequately explained, Branch placed his least reliable troops—a militia unit that had been in the service only two weeks—in this vulnerable section of the battle line.[21]

The position occupied by the Twenty-sixth Regiment was quite strung out, and out of necessity the command was divided. On the left of the position, toward the center of the Confederate line, Vance placed Major Abner Charmichael in command. Vance himself took control of the troops in the center of the formation, and Burgwyn led the right wing. The initial attack on the morning of March 14 started on the other side of the Confederate position. Federal general John Gray Foster led an attack on the Confederate left at about 7:30. There was very stout resistance, and the two forces exchanged heavy fire. Starting about twenty minutes later, another wing of the Union army under the leadership of General Jesse Reno opened fire on Vance's regiment. The firing started on the extreme left of the position, where Charmichael had the command, and over the next forty minutes it gradually extended to the center of the regiment. At this point, Vance and the men under his immediate command came under direct fire.[22]

The fighting was especially fierce on the left part of the position. In fact, Branch was forced to send two companies from the Thirty-third Regiment to shore up that part of the line. Heavy fire continued until noon, with the regiment maintaining its position stubbornly. At eleven o'clock, Major Charmichael was killed by a shot through his skull. Shortly thereafter, another officer was felled on the right side of the line, but the discipline instilled by Burgwyn held, and the men kept their positions without wavering. Vance later reported that just one man in the entire regiment deserted his post. Zeb recalled being in continuous danger for five hours:

"Balls struck all around me, men were hit right at my feet." After making this gallant stand, Vance suddenly learned that he and his men were in even greater danger. Federal troops had bypassed their position and were preparing to attack them from the rear.[23]

This unexpected and unfortunate circumstance occurred because the Confederates had failed to hold the center of their line. As Reno's federal troops advanced, they not only engaged Vance's regiment but also came into direct contact with the militia troops in the center of the Confederate line. After some hard fighting, the federal troops were able to outflank the militiamen, who found themselves being attacked from the side as well as from the front. The unseasoned troops panicked and began to "flee in great disorder." Their confusion and panic then spread to the Thirty-fifth Regiment, which then retired rapidly to the rear, leaving a gaping hole in the center of the Confederate position. Reno's men, accompanied by the reserve troops that Burnside committed to battle at this point, swept forward and took complete control of the battlefield.[24]

This development left Vance and the Twenty-sixth Regiment dangerously exposed. General Branch sent couriers to warn Vance of the precarious situation, but they never reached the Twenty-sixth Regiment. Instead, Vance's quartermaster escaped from the regiment's campground, where federal troops were destroying the supplies, and warned Vance of his peril. Vance immediately ordered a retreat. Since he could not move to the rear because Union forces now occupied that area, he and his men had to move to the right of the contested field to find an escape route. He thought that the retreating Confederate forces had burned the bridge over the creek, leaving Vance and his men stranded. Several of the soldiers were determined to escape despite the fact that the waterway was more than two hundred feet wide at the point where they had to cross it. Several were able to make it to the other shore, but most found the task too daunting. Vance was determined to find some boats to transport the men under his command to the other side. As he reported to Hattie, "I jumped my horse in to swim him over but when a little way he refused to swim, sank two or three times with me, and I had to jump off and swim across with my sword, pistols, and cartridges box on." Zeb may have put the best face on an extremely dangerous situation; it appears that he was only saved from drowning by being pulled from the swift running current by some members of the regiment. Once he reached the opposite shore, Zeb rode about half a mile before a local man, Kit Foy, helped him to find three boats. By the time that Zeb returned to the creek, the evacuation of the regiment was already well under way.[25]

Soon after Zeb's impulsive plunge into the creek, Burgwyn and his force had arrived at the same location. Burgwyn's coolness and strict discipline saved the unit from capture. He located some boats, including one that would hold eighteen men. Burgwyn carefully limited the number of men who could enter each vessel at once. Because the boats were so small, the entire process of evacuating the regiment over the river took approximately four hours to complete. Apparently, a couple of the men had to be forced at sword point to wait for their turn to cross. The long hours Burgwyn had spent instilling discipline in the men paid enormous dividends, as only three men were lost during this dangerous operation. Upon reaching the other side of the creek, the exhausted men began a forced march to the town of Trenton, forty-eight miles away. Virtually all of the regiment's supplies had been destroyed or captured, and they had limited rations to eat and little clothing to cover them. Burgwyn and Vance pushed the men hard, allowing them to sleep only four hours at a time, and they covered the distance to Trenton in forty hours. In his official report, Vance paid tribute to his men for their exertions: "Drenched with rain, blistered feet, without sleep, many sick and wounded, and almost naked, they toiled on through the day [and] all of the weary watches of the night without murmuring."[26]

Although the battle had been a catastrophe for the Confederacy, Zeb emerged from the contest with a considerably enhanced reputation. First and foremost, he was exceedingly pleased with his own performance. He reported to Hattie, "[I] was surprised at my feelings, excitement and pleasure removed every other feeling and I could not resist cheering with might and main." Later in the same letter, he boasted: "I should like to dwell on the many instances of love and affection exhibited by the regiment toward me during the fight & the retreat—I believe they would follow me into the jaws of certain death if I lead the way."[27] Zeb was delighted to discover that he possessed courage and leadership abilities under extremely trying circumstances. He felt that he had proven himself to be a real man. If there had ever been any doubt about Vance's commitment to the Confederacy, this experience removed it for the duration of the war.

Vance's high opinion of his regiment's performance mirrored his feelings about his own achievements. Vance reported to General Branch that he was "scarcely willing to mention particular instances of gallantry where all did their duty." Using more informal language, Zeb told Hattie, "We feel quite proud of our good name we have obtained and are determined to maintain it." Seeking to find some positive news after the debacle, North Carolina newspapers seized upon the good performance of the Twenty-sixth Regiment. Both the *North Carolina Standard* and the *Fayetteville Observer* reported that the unit had performed with great gallantry. Vance was singled out for particular praise and was quoted by the *Observer* as having shouted, "Stand firm, my men—I am with you for victory or death!"

The *Standard* quoted Vance as having exclaimed, "Fight on, boys—we can die, but will never surrender!"[28] For the people of North Carolina, who had thus far experienced nothing but military humiliation on their own soil, the words attributed to Vance were a bracing tonic. The recent failures at Fort Hatteras, Roanoke Island, and New Bern had left the state starved for positive war news. The brave stand and escape of the Twenty-sixth Regiment, along with Vance's prominent role in it, might well have been largely overlooked later in the war, but their achievements were blown out of proportion by a public starved for good news. Thus, Vance quickly became a minor war hero.

Unfortunately, Vance's new status as a brave officer could not feed and clothe his men. Vance's quartermaster, J. J. Young, made a careful survey of existing supplies and discovered that the regiment had lost virtually all of its knapsacks and haversacks; approximately half of its guns, canteens, and cartridge boxes; a large number of tents; and a significant number of incidental items. Vance felt compelled to write to the *North Carolina Standard* to request assistance. He explained: "My regiment is here in a most destitute condition. Any persons that will send a coarse cotton shirt[,] drawers, or socks will be doing us a great kindness, as it will be weeks before the state can supply us." Two weeks later, another newspaper reported the accuracy of Vance's prediction about the performance of the state government: Vance's men were still without sufficient supplies.[29] Zeb would remember this period of neglect for the remainder of the war, and he would seek to prevent its recurrence when it was within his power to do so. Yet while the Confederate force had suffered a humiliating defeat, and supplies were slow in arriving, Vance's men maintained their fighting spirit.

Their ambitious commander began seeking more tangible rewards for his part in their recent stand against the enemy. North Carolina was scheduled to have a gubernatorial election in the summer of 1862, and Zeb's name was already appearing among the potential candidates in several state newspapers. This part of the story will be related in detail in the next chapter, but it is important to note here that while Zeb could not help but be influenced by the unsolicited political attention, his major concern appeared to be obtaining the rank of brigadier general. Vance seems to have felt that his actions at New Bern deserved a substantial reward. On April 3, he wrote a letter to the secretary of war requesting permission to raise a legion of soldiers. Apparently he obtained permission to try to organize this unit, because two weeks later he placed advertisements in North Carolina newspapers offering a bounty of one hundred dollars to anyone who would join him in his new unit.[30]

Vance's efforts to raise the troops proved to be quite unproductive, however. There is some evidence that neither state nor Confederate authorities were particularly anxious for Vance to succeed. A legion was an unwieldy organization of three regiments with some attached artillery and cavalry. Field commanders usually found legions to be too cumbersome to work with effectively, and the Confederate government no longer welcomed this type of unit. As a consequence of this attitude, the state government positively refused to sanction Vance's recruiting activities. Further, General Theophilus H. Holmes would not grant Vance permission to leave camp to recruit members for his legion. In the meantime, the Confederate Congress passed a statute that imposed conscription for the first time in American history. One of the provisions of the law limited the time that Vance had to secure his troops to thirty days after its passage.[31] Under the circumstances, it is not surprising that Vance failed to secure enough men to form the legion. Although his bitterness would be dissipated by later developments, there is little doubt that Vance felt that his efforts had not been properly appreciated.

At the same time that he was trying to form the legion and was being mentioned as a political candidate, a number of Vance's fellow soldiers began to complain about the hero status that he had begun to assume. Fortunately, the jealousy did not extend to the rank and file under his immediate command. Under the new conscription law, all men currently in the service were required to remain in the army until hostilities ceased. As a sop to the conscripted men, the Confederate Congress allowed the regiments to reorganize by selecting new officers. The Twenty-sixth Regiment used this discretionary power to reelect Vance unanimously as its colonel. Lieutenant Colonel Burgwyn, however, did not share the good opinion of Vance held by the men in the ranks. In his private correspondence, he complained, "You will see a great many accounts of the battle but they are all exaggerated." The exaggerations included "such expressions as a Col's rising in his stirrups & saying we can die but never surrender." Burgwyn went on to observe: "It is the easiest thing in the world to get up a reputation on that battle field: at least it appears to me from what I hear." He pointed out that he was the one responsible for laying out the defensive position at New Bern, for which he was receiving no credit, and he concluded his rant with the statement, "Col. V[ance] you know is no sort of commander."[32]

Several officers in the Thirty-third Regiment joined Burgwyn in criticizing the image of Zeb as a hero. The men of the Thirty-third had faced the full impact of the federal attack at New Bern and had sustained more than three times as many casualties as Vance's Twenty-sixth Regiment. While conceding that some men of the Twenty-sixth Regiment had fought bravely, these critics asserted that Vance himself had never faced hostile fire. While their claims appear to be inaccurate, their anger toward Vance is understandable. The soldiers of the Thirty-third did face the greater challenge during combat, and they were being denied the public recognition that Vance received. Since Vance was being mentioned as a possible gubernatorial candidate with increasing frequency, newspapers opposed to his possible candidacy picked up the sentiments of the officers of the Thirty-third Regiment and sought to deflate Vance's status as a hero. On June 15, Vance replied to his critics in a letter to the *North Carolina Standard*. In a very adroit move, Vance refused to comment on his own actions during the battle. Instead, he commended the bravery of the men under his command and prominently mentioned the two officers in the regiment who were killed during the battle.[33] While the issue had declined in importance by July, Vance's role in the battle at New Bern remained a matter of interest to the public.

The same day that he defended his regiment in print, Vance agreed to be drafted as a candidate for governor of North Carolina. In a letter to the *Fayetteville Observer*, he announced that he would not campaign for the position. Instead, he would remain with his men and share their fate. While this statement may have been made for political effect, Vance was soon required to live up to his brave words. On June 18, he and the regiment received word that they should be prepared to move quickly. Two days later, they boarded trains for a trip to Petersburg, Virginia. There they would join a growing Confederate force that was hastily being drawn together to defend Richmond against General George McClellan's large advancing army. After a difficult journey of thirty hours, Vance and his men reached their camp in Petersburg on June 22. Two days later, the Twenty-sixth Regiment traveled by train to Richmond and arrived early in the morning of June 25. Later that same day, the regiment was ordered forward to the Williamsburg Road, where they were held in reserve. Toward the end of the afternoon, they were engaged in a brief skirmish to recover some ground lost earlier in the day.[34]

The evening that followed was a nightmare for Vance and his men. At nightfall, they were ordered on picket duty to patrol the outer lines of the army's position. Their job was to ensure that the enemy would not make any advance without some warning being provided to the Confederate commanders. Unfortunately, neither Vance nor Burgwyn had any idea where the Confederate lines ended. The land they were to patrol was "full of bogs, swamps & bamboo briars," and the night was so dark that visibility was severely limited. Both officers and their men became hopelessly lost, and many of the men ended up stationed on land that was under the control of the federal army. The Union forces soon detected their presence, and a brief firefight took place. The regiment fell back to a safer position, where the men remained until daylight. At that time, the unit advanced to its proper position and discovered that its opponents had left. Vance and his men had been most fortunate; they could easily have been captured or killed. Burgwyn complained, with considerable justification, that General Robert Ransom was largely responsible for the debacle of the previous night.[35] The poor communication between regiments had placed the Twenty-sixth at considerable risk.

In the days that followed, a series of battles known as the Seven Days took place. The Army of Northern Virginia, under the leadership of Robert E. Lee for the first time, attacked McClellan's advancing columns. In a series of encounters, the Confederates stopped the federal advance and threatened to cut off McClellan's base from outside assistance. McClellan withdrew from his advanced positions and Lee sought, without success, to deliver a decisive blow against the retreating forces. While the overall result of the fighting was favorable to the Confederacy, Lee did not achieve everything that he had hoped to accomplish, in large part because many of his subordinates failed to carry out his orders effectively and in a timely manner. Vance's regiment was under the command of General Benjamin Huger. Huger appears to have been incapable of concerted and decisive action in this period, and the men under his command often found themselves out of position or unclear about their assigned tasks.[36]

Because the two armies were so large, individual units were rarely in action for long periods of time. The Twenty-sixth Regiment was fortunate enough to gain a little time to recover from their harrowing experience. The men continued on picket duty most of the day of June 26, exhausted by the strain of the previous night, many of them catching some sleep when they were able to. Relieved from that duty late in the afternoon, the soldiers returned to camp for a well-earned rest. Just as they fell asleep, an attack began on a nearby battlefront, and the crash of heavy artillery kept the men awake for part of the night. The next day, Vance and the regiment were ordered forward to an advanced position. Marching over the scene of the previous day's fighting, they received a sobering reminder of the reality of their situation. Burgwyn reported: "I saw many instances of the battle on Wednesday. Trees struck by balls & cut off by shells & solid shot, guns & equipments & bits of clothing, & finally unburied ghastly bodies of dead Yankees met our gaze at every step." The regiment advanced to a position at the front and came under artillery fire. An effective reply from Confederate guns eliminated that threat, and the unit saw no further action until it was relieved later that night.[37]

The next two days were a time of constant movement as McClellan retracted his lines and assumed a defensive stance. On June 29, the regiment was the first Confederate unit to enter an abandoned Union army position that had been left so hastily that most of the tents were still in place. On the evening of June 30, Vance's men bivouacked in White Oak Swamp and then moved forward with other units on the morning of July 1. About noon, they passed through a field that had been the scene of a battle the previous day. Burgwyn recorded that the bodies of Union soldiers remained on the field, while many of their wounded comrades lay unattended and suffering. After an extended march, the Twenty-sixth Regiment arrived at an advanced position near the base of Malvern Hill. As the men awaited orders under the pressure of an artillery barrage, Vance tried to relieve the tension. When a rabbit was scared into flight by the regiment's approach, Zeb shouted after it: "Go it, Mollie Cottontail. If I had no more reputation to lose than you have, I would run too."[38] The surviving members of the regiment would remember this comic episode long after the fighting was over.

The federal position at Malvern Hill was absolutely unassailable, but this did not prevent the Confederate leaders from testing their opponents. In the battles of the previous days, Lee had driven the federal army away from the outskirts of Richmond in a series of daring moves. Despite his impressive achievements, Lee was quite frustrated that his efforts to decisively defeat McClellan's large army had failed. Poor communications, unusually indecisive actions on the part of Stonewall Jackson, and the inept leadership of several other commanders had deprived Lee of the breakthrough he sought. As McClellan withdrew his forces toward a well-supplied and strategically impregnable base, Lee tried to lash out again. Malvern Hill would be the site of this last effort. Unfortunately for Vance and his comrades, everything militated against a successful attack. The federal forces were sheltered at the top of a long slope, with well-prepared bunkers to protect them, and they had had enough time to position a tremendous array of artillery to cover every part of the attack area.[39]

More important, the Confederate commanders at Malvern Hill handled their forces ineffectively. John B. Magruder and Benjamin Huger proved unable to coordinate the movement of the regiments at the base of Malvern Hill efficiently, and they ended up sending the unprotected regiments against the federal forces in a piecemeal fashion. As each individual unit advanced, the massed federal artillery was able to concentrate on it and smash it before it could reach the Union lines. Burgwyn described the scene accurately: "Magruder ordered the attack to be made in front & whole ranks were swept away by discharges which drove Magruder's men back with very heavy and useless slaughter." At seven o'clock in the evening, Vance and the Twenty-sixth Regiment received orders to advance. As had happened six days earlier, no one provided Vance with proper directions, and the regiment got lost. Burgwyn reacted to this calamity by forcing a "skulker" from another unit to take the soldiers to the battleground.[40]

By the time the Twenty-sixth Regiment arrived at the base of the attack area, it was quite dark. The troops had advanced quickly to within four hundred yards of the federal lines when they were told that there were Confederate units in front of them blocking access to enemy lines. They were then ordered to lie down until further orders were given. One company did not receive the new orders and charged to within a few paces of the federal lines before it absorbed a large number of casualties and was forced to seek shelter. The Twenty-sixth Regiment stayed pinned down until approximately ten o'clock, when it was ordered to withdraw. This the men did in good order. Unlike the battle of New Bern, there was no glory for anyone at Malvern Hill. Vance was careful to disclaim any special heroism on his part. In the ongoing gubernatorial election campaign, Vance's behavior once again came under attack. An anonymous letter to the *State Journal* in Raleigh claimed that Vance had not even been in the battle. This source stated that Vance had been separated from his troops and had not returned to them until the day after the battle. Like the critiques of Vance's performance at New Bern, this letter seems to have been a politically motivated attempt to deny Vance whatever honor was due to him.[41]

Vance's political allies stretched the truth in his favor, claiming that Vance led a charge on the federal position. A Confederate soldier who was present at the battle later recalled an incident that apparently fueled the critical article about Vance's nonparticipation at Malvern Hill. According to this man, who recalled the event many years after it occurred, Vance was missing when the regiment returned to its camp for the night. The assumption was that he had been killed. The next morning, this solder and another were detailed by General Robert Ransom to find Vance's body. While they were away on their search, Vance returned to camp completely unscathed. When the regiment had passed a badly shattered house on the battlefield during its late evening retreat, "Vance was accosted by the family, mostly women," who still lived there. When they "begged [him] to stay with them," he did so.[42] Because few people were aware of this action on Vance's part, his absence from the campsite apparently caused some people to conclude that he had died or been absent from the entire battle.

After Malvern Hill, neither of the two armies was able to gain a significant advantage. For the Twenty-sixth Regiment it was time for refitting and recovery. The close relationship Zeb had to his men at this point is illustrated in another anecdote that one of the members of the regiment recalled three decades later. As the soldiers left the battleground to return to

Petersburg, Vance noticed a private in considerable pain who was having difficulty carrying his gun and knapsack. Zeb dismounted from his horse and allowed the private to ride back to camp, while Zeb walked back with the rest of the regiment.[43] It was actions like these that endeared the colonel to his men. Vance saw no further military action. In early August, the voters of North Carolina elected him governor of the state by an overwhelming margin. He quickly returned home to Asheville for approximately three weeks of rest before assuming his new duties. The hardships that Zeb and his men had faced during the Seven Days could be read in Vance's enfeebled condition upon arriving home and in the length of time that it took him to fully recover.

Zeb left the army with full honors. He had raised troops for the Confederacy, helped to train a regiment, and fought in two battles without making a major mistake. In both battles, he had led his men with courage and looked after their material well-being with considerable skill. To a civilian population starved for positive news, Zeb appeared to be something of a hero. The truth was a lot less glamorous than it appeared. Zeb had succeeded in large part because of the skill of his second-in-command. Burgwyn trained the troops and taught Zeb; Burgwyn also bore most of the responsibility for engineering the successful retreat from New Bern. At the same time, Zeb had motivated his troops and persuaded them that their cause was worth their sacrifices. He had tempered the youthful perfectionism of Burgwyn and formed an indispensable part of their command team. Perhaps Zeb's most selfless moment came when he remained in the army after announcing his gubernatorial candidacy. He literally put his life on the line, placing the Confederacy before his own political advancement. For someone with Zeb's soaring ambitions, this act was a significant statement of commitment to the Confederate cause. While in the army, Zeb learned firsthand how inefficient the state and Confederate governments were in providing pay and supplies to North Carolina's troops. He left the army determined that a similar fate would not continue to befall them if it fell within his power to do something about it. Zeb's tenure in the army would prove to be excellent preparation for the important civilian position he was about to occupy.

When describing the development of the Confederate political system, George C. Rable called the system "the revolution against politics." Rable's point was that both the political leaders and the electorate felt strongly that to pursue politics as usual would be unpatriotic in the newly formed Confederacy. Political parties, they believed, should not be allowed to function—or even to be formed—as they had before the war. In many states, and at the national level, this revolution against partisanship appeared to be successful. Parties were not formed in most parts of the new nation, and President Davis had no organized opposition in the sessions of the Confederate Congress. These developments did not mean that there was no opposition to the new government. Opposition was particularly strong among a small group of people who had opposed the secession movement. In a number of locations along the coast, in the central Piedmont, and among the southern mountains, small groups of men actively opposed the disruption of the Union. Throughout the Confederacy there were also rough lines drawn between those who had openly supported secession early in the process and those who had left the Union with reluctance.[1]

Rable noted that developments in North Carolina were an exception to his rule. More than any other Confederate state, North Carolina retained most of the features of its antebellum political system during the war despite the fact that many of its political leaders and its voters endorsed the call for an end to politics. Marc W. Kruman documented consistent calls for an end to party alignment in the usually partisan state press. There was general agreement that parties should be abandoned until after Confederate independence was assured.[2] It is important to note, however, that there was a militant edge to this nonpartisanship. Those who adopted the new line of thinking were prepared to brand anyone who seemed to be pursuing personal or party advantage as traitors to the new nation. The result was a veneer of political unity that remained in place throughout the summer of 1861.

Despite the efforts of the state government's leaders to stand above partisan wrangling, their patronage policies betrayed them. Zeb complained—and William W. Holden echoed his criticism in early June in a series of articles in the *North Carolina Standard*—that all of the top military appointments went to men who had supported secession during the February referendum. While the men who had supported the Union until the federal attack on Fort Sumter claimed to be simply reacting to discrimination that was directed against them, they were being somewhat disingenuous. As early as the secession convention of May 20, 1861, the former Unionists had felt the need to hold a caucus at a private residence in order to maintain some sort of mutual support.[3] While this organization remained moribund throughout the summer months of 1861, it was there to be resurrected when conditions warranted it.

The chief spokesperson for the opposition to the secessionists, who dominated the new state government, was Holden. He was an average-sized man with dark, thinning hair who led his fellow North Carolinians with the words in his newspaper rather than through personal contact. Although Holden had been a member of the secession convention that took North Carolina out of the Union, he had supported the Union until Lincoln called for troops in April. Then, in his initial flush of anger at the Republican administration for using coercive measures, Holden pledged his "resistance to the last extremity [against] the usurpations and aggressions of the federal government." In a circular letter of late June, he maintained his support for "the present righteous war on the part of the people of the South in defence of their rights," but he went on to say that he would use his newspaper to ensure that the war effort was honestly run. Specifically, he asserted of the paper: "It will boldly expose all attempts to make mere party paramount to the public good; and it will expose and resist every tendency towards the concentration of power in the hands of the few at the expense of the many." Undoubtedly adding fuel to Holden's fury was the fact that the government had taken the lucrative state printing contract from him and given it to another publisher.[4] Holden's promise to be the watchdog of the state and Confederate administrations was one early indication that partisan differences would soon surface in North Carolina.

Matters were in this state of flux when the fall elections of 1861 took place. As Kruman notes, the traditional political system did not function during the campaign in most parts of the state. In most congressional districts, self-appointed candidates ran without any apparent partisan apparatus. In three districts, however, there were open contests between candidates who represented the different sides of the secession controversy. Partisan feeling was probably fueled by the disagreement surrounding the election of the first Confederate senators from North Carolina. In an effort to minimize partisan fighting, Augustus S. Merrimon proposed that the legislature elect one person from each of the two traditional parties to the Confederate Senate. This suggestion was rejected by a vote of forty-nine to forty-four. Several weeks later, the secessionists proceeded to elect an ardent secessionist to one seat: without giving any opportunity for their opposition to organize, they attempted to secure the immediate election of Zeb's nemesis, Thomas Lanier Clingman. Former Unionist Jonathan Worth reported that he and his compatriots then combined with a small number of supporters of former Democrat William T. Dortch. While Dortch had been an early supporter of secession, he had also expressed in strong terms his reluctance to leave the Union. Worth rejoiced in the defeat of Clingman, capturing the strong element of partisanship that remained in North Carolina politics in the following words: "We think that we have accomplished more than we expected and feel a kind of triumph over the bad men, whom we believe [were] governed only by selfish and wicked design."[5]

The congressional election in Vance's old district was distinguished by two developments important to Vance. The first remedied an earlier oversight that Vance felt had occurred when the convention selected Allen T. Davidson to replace him in the House. As noted, Vance felt that he should have been offered the position so that he could turn it down. Now the courtesy was extended. On September 2, N. G. Allman of Macon County wrote a letter to Robert Vance asking if Zeb wanted to be considered as a candidate for the Confederate House of Representatives. Zeb replied to Allman on September 18, declining the honor. He used the occasion to justify his course of action to date and to assert his loyalty to the Confederacy. He reviewed his commitment to the Union during the secession crisis and blamed the coming of the war on "the strong arm of Northern despotism." Noting that he had already received many honors from the voters in his district, he stated that he was "not a candidate for Congress, nor [would he] consent for [his] name to be run." Finally, he endorsed Allen T. Davidson's candidacy. Vance's letter was released to the press, and was reprinted with glowing comments.[6] For someone who was abandoning politics, Zeb had found a way to do so that would be widely appreciated and remembered by the voters.

Davidson's acknowledged Unionist past provoked William Holland Thomas, a secessionist Democrat, to challenge him. Thomas attacked Davidson, saying that the Unionist had once "openly declared that it was a bitter pill to vote for the ordinance of secession." The campaign that followed was very divisive, and it gave a clear signal that partisanship was not dead in North Carolina. Davidson maintained a facade of nonpartisan opposition by refusing to openly campaign for the seat. Instead, Thomas debated George W. Candler, his bitter political enemy, in several traditional open-air meetings. In these debates, Candler even stooped to racism, attacking Thomas's close association with the Cherokees. Thomas's record as an antebellum state legislator also became a major issue in the campaign. Thus, there was little to distinguish this canvass from any of those that preceded it. Davidson was easily elected to the seat in a vote that resembled the 1858 and 1859 results.[7] Voters in the Tenth Congressional District could probably be forgiven if they failed to detect the nonpartisan nature of Confederate politics.

An even clearer indication of the return of North Carolina's traditional partisan divisions came with the presidential election of 1861. In most states, the election of Jefferson Davis and Alexander Stephens was perfunctory; in many, it was performed by a legislative body. In North Carolina, however, there were two sets of electors. Both were pledged to vote for Davis and Stephens, but each obviously represented an organized group of either secessionists or former Unionists. The contest was muddled, because each ticket listed supporters of the other point of view, and four candidates were on both sets of tickets. Nevertheless, some newspapers made a distinction between the two slates. One paper accused the Unionist electors of not being committed to the Confederacy. The public seemed rather indifferent to the arguments, and approximately half of the normal electorate chose not to participate in the voting. The secessionists won 58 percent of the vote and proclaimed that the voters had endorsed their policies.[8] While the low turnout made that assertion somewhat dubious, no one could deny that the campaign had demonstrated that there were still two well-defined parties in the state.

Any doubt about the reemergence of partisan politics was eliminated with the onset of the 1862 gubernatorial campaign. This election, which normally would have occurred in 1863, was necessitated by the death of Governor Ellis in July 1861. The legislature decided that the term of Henry T. Clark, who had succeeded to the office from his position as president of the state Senate, should expire when the legislative term ended in the summer of 1862. As was often the case during this period, Holden took the initiative. Soon after the results of the presidential canvass were made known, he promised to take the issue of political dominance in the state "to the people." He maintained that "this course" had been "forced upon" the Unionists. He continued, "This is a war for Southern rights, and not for the exclusive benefit or advantage of a certain faction." (Holden apparently did not recognize the irony of attacking faction in this context.) According to Kruman, Holden and the Unionists spent the next few months organizing their forces for the coming campaign. Some members of the secessionist group echoed their call to let the people decide.[9]

Although the Unionists seemed to be making the greater effort to organize, the secessionists had a candidate in the field first. In February, the *Charlotte Democrat* nominated William Johnston of Charlotte for governor. Johnston represented something of a compromise candidate, and obviously the secessionists hoped that he would preempt other candidates and win without a contest. As a secessionist and a former Whig, Johnston was expected to draw support from all factions in the state. Within less than two weeks, however, former Unionists began to nominate members of their own group for the governor's position. In March, Holden attacked Johnston as "an ultra and bitter partisan secessionist." He called upon the people to hold public meetings and suggest possible Unionist candidates for governor. By this time, Holden had begun calling the antisecessionist group the "Conservatives." In late March, at one of the public meetings in Rutherford County, the attendants nominated Vance for the position of governor. The names of a variety of other former Whig leaders began to emerge as possible choices at other meetings. The clear favorite among all of the proposed candidates was former U.S. senator William A. Graham.[10]

Holden and the former Whig leaders recognized that without some sort of structure the public meetings would lead to confusion rather than to success. In April, approximately thirty men met in Raleigh to decide upon a single candidate. Most of them were former Whigs, and they were led by Graham. Holden is the only former Democrat identified as having been in attendance. There was general agreement among everyone assembled that Graham was the logical standard-bearer for the group. He refused the nomination for unstated personal reasons, however, and suggested John Pool, the most recent Whig gubernatorial candidate, for the position. Some of the men at the meeting felt that Pool would be viewed as too partisan a figure, and his name was rejected. At that point, former congressmen John A. Gilmer and James Madison Leach suggested Vance as a possible candidate. For the Whigs at the meeting, Vance's 1860 stump speeches at Salisbury were still a vivid memory. Everyone in attendance also recognized that Vance's status as a war hero would deflect much of the criticism that might be attached to any candidate who had avoided service. The entire group found Vance's credentials compelling, and he was designated as the nominee.[11]

The problem that these men now had to solve was how to make the call for Vance appear to be spontaneous. They first had to counteract the movement to make Graham the Conservative candidate. This was accomplished in mid-May, when Graham sent a letter to friendly newspapers in which he positively declined to run for the office. Then, accounts of public meetings, letters from prominent individuals, and expressions of support from members of the army that called for Vance to be the gubernatorial candidate were published. Exactly when Zeb was informed about the decision of the Raleigh caucus is not known, but by early June he had apparently decided to become a candidate. In a letter to George Little, Vance wrote that he was confident that Union men would support him. He also observed that Holden's advocacy of his candidacy was a problem; Zeb complained that the editor was too radical in his statements. This early evidence of differences between the two men is most intriguing.[12]

The next step was to make Zeb's decision public. An announcement of his candidacy was first published in the *Fayetteville Observer* on June 19. On June 15, Vance had sent his letter of intent to the editor of the *Observer*, Edward J. Hale, and asked that Hale and Holden review it. All three men viewed Zeb's decision to write to Hale rather than to Holden as a method of deflecting some of the controversy surrounding Holden from Vance. Although he had decided to run for office, Zeb indicated that he still shared much of the antiparty feeling that Rable has identified. In another letter dated that same day, Zeb deplored the appearance of political divisions in North Carolina. In his public letter of acceptance, he made the same point: "Sincerely deprecating the growing tendency toward party strife amongst our people, which every patriot should shun in the presence of common danger, I earnestly pray for that unity of sentiment and fraternity of feeling which alone, with the favor of God, can enable us to prosecute this war for Liberty and Independence, against all odds and under every adversity, to a glorious and triumphant issue."[13] Zeb kept his promise to avoid partisan bickering by making no further public statements during the two months remaining in the campaign.

Zeb's decision not to become involved in partisan politics was reflected in other parts of his statement as well. He began by noting that he was writing in response to public meetings, newspapers' endorsements, and private correspondence, rather than taking the initiative to nominate himself for the office of governor. He briefly reviewed his military record and asserted his willingness to remain in the army for the remainder of the conflict. Vance explained, however, that he recognized that service to the cause could take many forms, and he said that he would not decline the job of governor if the people chose to confer it upon him.[14] The letter was, in fact, a small masterpiece of the political art. Vance touched on all of the important themes that would appeal to a broad cross section of the public: patriotism, duty, and nonpartisanship. There is every reason to believe that he felt the sentiments expressed in the letter quite sincerely. While there is no doubt that Vance was frustrated by his inability to achieve military promotion, every piece of evidence available from this period indicates that he was fully committed to the cause of the Confederacy. Still, he welcomed the opportunity to return to politics without damaging his reputation as a patriot.

Because Vance—and Johnston for that matter—did not campaign personally, the canvass for votes was relatively quiet by the usual North Carolina standards. Most of the angry rhetoric and charges of partisanship came from the state's newspapers. This was not unexpected, since virtually all of the newspapers in the state were published by active politicians who were interested in little else but politics. Two weeks before Vance officially announced his candidacy, a Johnston newspaper published the key plank in his platform. It read: "An Unremitting Prosecution of the War—War to the Last Extremity—Complete Independence—Eternal Separation from the North—No Abridgement of Southern Territory—No Diminution of Southern Boundaries." Clearly, the secessionists sought to stake out the extreme patriot position; the Conservatives gladly conceded it. The Johnston supporters also made the point that their candidate was nonpartisan. First, they explained, he was a businessman who had stood above much of the angry rhetoric of the late antebellum period. In addition, he had supported the Whig Party and had cast his presidential ballot for Constitutional Unionist John Bell in 1860.[15] To the secessionists (or Confederates, as they now designated themselves), Johnston's candidacy appeared to be unassailable.

The Confederates apparently felt that Johnston's candidacy needed little justification, and they therefore concentrated on destroying the credibility of their opposition. One of their primary targets was Holden, the spokesperson for the Conservative coalition. The Confederates contrasted Johnston, the nonpartisan candidate, with Holden, the highly partisan editor. For example, the *Raleigh Register* sarcastically described Holden as "that patriotic individual [who is] dividing and distracting the people, and weakening the Southern cause in North Carolina." Later, the same paper accused Holden of subordinating the best interests of the state to his own personal concerns.[16] There can be little doubt that Holden still held a grudge against the secessionists for depriving him of the state printing contract, but there was obviously much more than personal animus driving the anti-Johnston campaign.

The Confederates found themselves in a difficult position when they sought to attack Vance, however. As noted in the previous chapter, they attempted to tarnish Vance's war record, but Vance's defenders successfully refuted both the charge that he was not under direct fire at New Bern and the charge that he was not on the battlefield at Malvern Hill. Letters from comrades who served with Vance in the two battles offered impressive testimony to his bravery.[17] Since Vance was actually putting his life on the line for the cause so fervently dear to the hearts of Confederates, their attacks on him were, of necessity, muted. While the stories of Vance's war heroism might have been somewhat inflated, Johnston had virtually no war record at all. He had obtained the title of colonel for his work providing transportation assistance to the Confederate commissary department. Not only was Johnston not risking his life, but it was possible to argue that he was enriching himself at the expense of soldiers and their families.

With somewhat more success, the Confederates also attacked Vance for seeking to leave the army. They pointed out that he was in the process of recruiting a legion, and they noted that the soldiers who were joining him expected to be led by Vance personally. The only problem with this particular criticism was that many of the people who faulted Zeb on this point were the very same men who had made it virtually impossible for Zeb to raise the legion. The more general charge—that Vance was leaving the army in the midst of a military emergency—had greater staying power. Many men who had joined the army in an early burst of enthusiasm were now having second thoughts. Some officers used the restructuring of the regiments as an excuse to give up their commissions and leave the army.[18] But Vance had anticipated that he would be criticized for leaving the service, and he had pointed out in his statement that he would leave the decision in this matter to the voters. He said he actually preferred to stay in the army, but that he would serve as governor if called upon by the people to do so. Since Vance made no further statements, the Confederate editors found it increasingly difficult to criticize him.

The Conservatives were not content to simply refute the charges made by their opponents. Instead, they took the offensive, accusing the Confederates of a variety of failures. In the Conservative platform, which was released at the same time that Vance's letter was published, there were two main criticisms of the opposition. One was directed at the Confederates' administration of the state government. The Conservatives asserted "that the partyism, favoritism, inefficiency, and misrule which [had] marked the administration of public affairs in the State, since the commencement of the present war, deserve[d] the stern and unqualified rebuke of the people." The Conservatives went on to charge that these failures of government were preventing North Carolina from marshaling a unified war effort.[19] What the Conservatives sought to do was to blame the incumbents for all of the problems that the people of the state faced. There were many North Carolinians, both civilians and soldiers, who could easily be convinced of the validity of one or more of the charges. The failure of the state government to provide pay and supplies to the North Carolina regiments was a matter of common knowledge. In addition, the unwillingness of the Ellis and Clark administrations to appoint Whigs and Unionists to responsible positions was obvious to all knowledgeable voters.

The Conservatives had another important grievance to air: they accused Jefferson Davis's Confederate government of not protecting the civil liberties of the people of North Carolina. The Conservative platform asserted "that the military power should always be subordinate to the civil power, whether in war or in peace; and that martial law should never be declared nor the writ of habeas corpus suspended, except when indispensable to the preservation of civil society."[20] Many North Carolinians had felt shock and dismay when the Confederate Congress granted Jefferson Davis the power to suspend habeas corpus and he did so for the first time on February 27, 1862. This suspension remained in force until February 13, 1863. While relatively few people in the state ever directly experienced the coercive power of the Confederate government under the new provisions of the law, many North Carolinians were concerned about the threat of government coercion. The institution of both conscription and taxes by the Confederate government already indicated that other government interventions might follow.

As the campaign progressed, the Confederates began to sense that Vance was a popular candidate, and they attempted to counteract his appeal. First, they portrayed Zeb as a mental lightweight who was incapable of running the state government. The *Raleigh Register* characterized Zeb as "the young stump-speaking, joke-telling, huzza-boying party politician." In contrast, Johnston was described as a solid, sound, experienced businessman who would understand how to run the state government during the present crisis.[21] The impact of this approach on voters appears to have been negligible. Vance's military record effectively quashed any criticism of his youth, inexperience, and reputation as a speaker who catered to the common man. He had clearly demonstrated admirable personal qualities in military service.

The Confederates also warned that a Vance victory could be misinterpreted in the North. One Confederate partisan observed, "The success of Vance can be regarded in no other light throughout the country both North and South than as counter-revolutionary in its tendency." The *State Journal* in Raleigh went even further, claiming that a Vance victory would be viewed as a pro-Union triumph.[22] This argument failed to persuade the voters of North Carolina. The idea that they should cast their ballots in order to prevent any misunderstanding outside of the state was found wanting. The Conservatives were so little concerned about this campaign tactic that they essentially ignored it.

They did not ignore the importance of campaign organization, however. One worried Confederate confided: "The 'Conservatives' or Holdenites — are thoroughly organized, they are working like beavers. The Southern-rights men have no party organization, they are comparatively supine and apathetic. Although they are in the decided majority, if that majority could be rallied, yet they are in danger of being beaten through their want of organization." The assertion that the Confederates represented the majority opinion is rather dubious, but the observer's description of the difference in organization and motivation between the two parties is apparently entirely accurate. Public meetings continued to be held around the state to endorse Zeb's candidacy. Since the soldiers could vote, some organized electioneering also went on in the army units.[23] Each side accused the other of trying to politicize the troops.

When the campaign drew to a close, most observers, including the candidate himself, expected Vance to emerge victorious. The soldiers voted a week earlier than the civilian population and foreshadowed Vance's sweep. Zeb carried all but seven of the votes in his own regiment, and he was the victor in his brigade of five North Carolina regiments by a similarly overwhelming margin. Johnston supporters sought to soften the impact of Vance's overwhelming support among the soldiers by selectively reporting returns from the few units that opposed Vance. This subterfuge fooled no one, because Holden and his editor allies published much more complete returns. A jubilant Holden predicted that Vance would win with an unprecedented majority of twenty to twenty-five thousand votes. In early August, the civilians went to the polls and ratified the soldiers' choice. The result was so decisive that Governor Clark declared Vance the victor long before the final tally was complete.[24]

An analysis of the returns reveals a number of interesting facts. First, Zeb's victory was the first true landslide in North Carolina history. He won nearly two-thirds of the army vote and almost three-quarters of the civilian vote for a final tally of 55,282 to 20,813. No one, including Holden, had anticipated such a complete victory. The Confederates reviewed the returns and pointed out that Vance had received fewer votes than either of the two gubernatorial candidates in 1860. But as Marc W. Kruman has noted, several North Carolina counties were under Union army control and their citizens did not vote; the adjoining counties often recorded a relatively light vote as well. Even taking the occupied counties into account, there is little doubt that approximately a third of the electorate failed to participate in the balloting. Many of those who sat out the election may have opposed politics in any form during the crisis period. Others who stayed away may have been former Democrats who would normally have voted for the Confederate candidate, but who could not bring themselves to support Johnston, a former Whig.[25]

By inspecting where Vance received his votes, historians have drawn some important conclusions. Kruman has demonstrated that the inhabitants of former Whig and Unionist areas tended to vote for Vance. Robin E. Baker uncovered an equally important fact: many voters who did not cast ballots in the election of 1860 were drawn back to the polls in 1862, and virtually all of them supported Vance. Former Democrats who refused to vote for Johnston and previous nonvoters who supported Vance both contributed to the wide margin of Vance's victory. Baker has also noted that Johnston received more votes in areas in which slaves were highly concentrated, while Vance did best in areas where yeoman farmers predominated. William T. Auman has identified another important group of Vance supporters. He analyzed the voting patterns in several central Piedmont counties where there was active resistance to both Confederate policies and the Confederacy itself, and he found that voters in those areas overwhelmingly supported Vance. Many of these voters may have been the same individuals who Baker identified as previous nonvoters.[26] In any case, the Conservative Party coalition that elected Vance contained a variety of groups, not all of them compatible. It included Whigs and Union Democrats, highly partisan politicians and recent nonparticipants in the political process, and soldiers and peace advocates. Vance's challenge would be to hold together this potentially explosive group and fashion policies that would satisfy all of his supporters.

Before he assumed his new responsibilities, Vance had to leave the army and return to North Carolina. This single action probably saved his life. If he had remained with the Twenty-sixth Regiment, he undoubtedly would have been killed at Gettysburg on July 1, 1863, as Colonel Henry K. Burgwyn Jr. and hundreds of other members of the regiment were. Instead, Zeb received a fancy ceremonial sword from Sergeant Major Leonidas L. Polk and the other officers of his command. He thanked the members of the regiment in a speech that the few survivors remembered, many years after the war had ended, as inspiring. From Virginia, Zeb traveled to Raleigh, where he stayed overnight at the Yarborough House. Although greatly fatigued by his journey and the rigors of camp life, he delivered a twenty-minute address to a large crowd that gave the first indication of the policies he would follow as governor. He started by saying that the election results demonstrated that the people of the state had rejected politics as usual and politicians. He also confronted the charge, leveled during the canvass, that he had not been involved in the battles of New Bern and Malvern Hill. After telling one of his illustrative stories, Vance concluded: "I thought . . . that I was in both of these fights; but after their efforts made to prove I was not, I am willing to admit that I was not there—though . . . I do retain an indistinct recollection of the bullets that whistled around my ears." The crowd laughed heartily, and Vance moved on to more substantial questions.[27]

Vance said that the first job of the governor of North Carolina was to "establish the independence of this glorious Confederation of States." He categorically rejected the charge that he and his fellow Conservatives desired to return to the Union. He said that the contention was "monstrous," and he highlighted the contributions that the entire population was making to the war effort. He described in some detail how one federal soldier had commented on the personal bravery of North Carolina troops by explaining that they always rushed their opponent's positions and fought at close quarters. Zeb also talked about the sacrifices that people were making on the home front. He noted "that many of these women and children, on hundreds and hundreds of farms, were toiling day by day in the burning sun, with bare feet, following the plow, handling the hoe and axe that they might produce and gather the harvests for sustenance." His concluding remarks included the following call to action: "I want you, and I want all the people of the State, to aid me with all their energies, all their means, all their confidence in this mighty struggle, until the Confederate States shall stand proudly among the nations free and independent."[28] Vance then retired to his room and proceeded soon thereafter to Asheville.

Significantly, the description of Vance's address in Holden's *North Carolina Standard* ended with the following observation: "His remarks, as we have stated, were most enthusiastically received, and we are glad to learn that they gave satisfaction to many of those present who had voted against him." Holden's insight into the thinking of the Confederates who listened to Vance's address was accurate. They were very pleased, in large part because Vance did not live up to his reputation as a person who favored reunion with the federal government. The irony, of course, was that these editors had been entirely responsible for Zeb's having that reputation. The *State Journal* of Raleigh even went so far as to conclude: "We believe . . . that the Confederate cause will have no more hearty, generous and fraternal co-operator than in the new Governor of North Carolina." Another Raleigh newspaper that had opposed Zeb's election expressed satisfaction when he defended conscription and threatened to search out deserters and return them to the ranks.[29]

These latter remarks were made shortly after Vance returned to Asheville to enjoy three weeks of rest before he assumed his new responsibilities.

In a note to William A. Graham, Zeb explained, "[The] state of my health renders it absolutely necessary that I should rest at home as long as possible before the inauguration." He went on to say that he was feeling "quite unwell" at the moment, but he hoped that a couple of weeks of breathing "mountain air" would restore him. The local newspaper, which had opposed his election, announced his arrival in Asheville and commented that he would be a good governor if he followed his own instincts and was not swayed by others. The paper observed that at age thirty-two, Zeb was the youngest man ever elected governor in North Carolina. Later, Zeb reported his own informal findings about how his recent elevation to chief executive had affected his old neighbors: "Between the stage office and my house I met with twenty men. Fifteen addressed me as *Zeb*, three called me *Colonel*, and two managed to get out *Governor*, with a leer, which partly intimated to me *that they considered it the grandest joke of the season*." While Vance was undoubtedly being modest for comic effect, there is little doubt that his neighbors were stunned that the local troublemaker and jokester was now the head of the state government. The mature Vance surfaced, however, when he gave an address to recently enrolled Confederate recruits who passed through Asheville. As noted, he came out in full support of the policy of conscription and promised vigorous enforcement of the measure.[30]

In early September, Zeb left Asheville on horseback to ride to Morganton, where he would catch the train to Raleigh. As he embarked on his new career, he faced a series of challenges likely to overwhelm any occupant of the governor's office. Enthusiasm for the war was waning in many parts of North Carolina. The federal government was bringing its greater resources to bear on the battlefields of the conflict. Neither the Confederate nor the North Carolina government was working effectively enough to supply Southern armies and feed and protect the civilian population at the same time. Despite these obvious difficulties, Zeb was in an ebullient mood as he reentered the political world once again.

Because the Confederate government failed, scholars have long sought to discover the reasons for its failure. This understandable impulse has led them to look for developments that appear to have weakened the Confederate cause. Both works of scholarship that deal with the government in Richmond and studies of events at the state level often share this common goal. Zeb had to cope with two of the major sources of internal weakness cited by many scholars: local opposition to Confederate authority and controversies involving differences in policy between states and the Confederate government. While both of these factors did weaken the Confederate war effort to some extent, the fact remains that the government of Confederate North Carolina functioned effectively throughout most of Zeb's gubernatorial tenure. That it did lends considerable credibility to Gary Gallagher's argument that military defeat, rather than the collapse of authority on the home front, doomed the incipient Southern nation.[1]

Zeb's administration did much more than merely maintain a strong state government, however. In the first year of the war, his predecessors had failed to put the state on a proper war footing, and Zeb inherited a state government unable to perform many of the most basic activities required of it. In part, this failure was structural. The state constitution had been framed in the heat of the revolt against Great Britain, and thus it was designed to limit executive authority. Until the 1830s, in fact, the governor was elected by the state legislature and had no independent political base of his own. Even in the 1860s the governor had no veto power, a limitation that further eroded whatever leverage he might have had with the state assembly. A veteran scholar of the state concluded that "the governor actually had very little power at all, as he was required to seek the advice and consent of his Council regarding any matter of importance."[2] Moreover, both Governor John W. Ellis and his successor Henry T. Clark served such short terms that little could be accomplished during their administrations.

By the summer of 1862, when Zeb was about to assume his duties as governor, North Carolina's soldiers were the worst provisioned in the Confederate army. This was not a failure of the state government alone. When the war began, the Richmond government had been unable to clothe and arm the army properly. As a result, it resorted to the commutation policy. This policy provided the states with payments for every soldier that they provisioned. By abdicating its responsibility to clothe and feed Confederate troops, the Confederate government attempted to force state governments to actively support regiments from their states. Zeb and many other North Carolina commanders knew from personal experience how poorly this had worked, as Ellis, Clark, and the North Carolina legislature had failed to fulfill their responsibilities. It is no wonder that Zeb would not trust the Confederate bureaucracy to supply North Carolina troops even after the commutation policy ended in October 1862.[3]

If the Ellis and Clark administrations had merely neglected their responsibilities, Zeb's task would have been difficult enough. In fact, the two Democratic and secessionist governors had also followed appointment policies that created a highly partisan atmosphere in both the state government and the military. The two men apparently distrusted anyone who had been a Whig or who had not been a proponent of secession before the firing on Fort Sumter. The result was that top government jobs, military appointments, and elected positions such as senator in the Confederate government went to men who were "original secessionists." Since those excluded from the government included the vast majority of the members of the former Whig Party as well as Democrats who followed popular newspaper editor William W. Holden, many ambitious men, including Zeb, felt slighted. John Connally later wrote to Zeb describing his experience with exclusion: "Gov Clark refused to commission me after I had been elected [colonel.] this I regarded as an assumption of authority and believed Gov Clark had been influenced by Gen' Martin to withhold the commission because my having been known as and raised a Whig." As noted earlier, the partisan behavior of the secession Democrats in office provoked a most unusual response during the meaningless popular vote for president in November 1861. The protesting slate of electors lost in a relatively close vote, but the results were significant in one important regard: the former Unionists had grown so dissatisfied with the partisanship of their opponents that they were willing to take a step in open opposition.[4] Vance's overwhelming victory in the 1862 election subsequently demonstrated that the secessionists were now a small minority of men who believed that their early commitment to the Confederacy entitled them to power.

There was a second crisis that Zeb needed to address when he came to office. The Union army had secured a firm foothold in many of the eastern counties of North Carolina, and neither the Confederate nor the state government seemed prepared to expel the invaders. Zeb, of course, knew firsthand from his experience at the battle of New Bern that the Confederate armies had been overmatched. Since that time, most of the Confederacy's limited military resources had been concentrated in Tennessee and Virginia. The small force deployed in North Carolina could do little more than ensure that the equally small federal force would not take more territory. The Ellis and Clark administrations had made no real effort to remedy the situation by taking initiative at the state level. The situation in eastern North Carolina was confusing, as some people pledged allegiance to both governments while irregular bands of soldiers threatened the social and economic stability of the region.

When Zeb took the oath of office as governor of North Carolina on September 8, 1862, there were reasons for him to despair as well as reasons for him to hope. The positive signs were on the military front. Robert E. Lee and his army had frustrated George McClellan's drive toward Richmond and had seized the initiative. The Army of Northern Virginia had swung to the offensive and had defeated John Pope's army at the second battle of Bull Run in late August. Then, Lee and his men moved north into Maryland and occupied Frederick just two days before Vance assumed his new duties. Both the Army of Tennessee under the leadership of Braxton Bragg and another force under Kirby Smith were simultaneously advancing into Kentucky. The city of Lexington had welcomed the gray-clad soldiers, and a Confederate governor of Kentucky had been sworn in in the state capital of Frankfort. In the far west the armies of Earl Van Dorn and Sterling Price were advancing along the Mississippi and challenging Union forces in Missouri. Thus, Zeb assumed office at a time when North Carolinians could logically hope that the new Confederacy would successfully defend its independence from the Union.[5]

At the same time, affairs in North Carolina were not in a state to make the new chief executive sanguine. Federal forces still held most of the coast with the exception of the area around the port city of Wilmington, and the Confederate government appeared to be indifferent to the plight of eastern North Carolina. At several places along the coast, many of the non-slaveowning residents of the state had rejected the Confederacy and begun working actively for federal success. North Carolina troops continued to be the worst clad in the Confederate army. Severe inflation was impoverishing many civilian families, and the feeble efforts of the Clark administration had done little to ameliorate the situation. The recent gubernatorial campaign had exacerbated political divisions in the state and made it unlikely that the political elite would be able to unify in the face of a common foe. Finally, in certain sections of central and western North Carolina, there were pockets of dissidents who either actively opposed conscription and the

Vance at the time he was inaugurated governor in 1862.
(North Carolina Division of Archives and History, Raleigh)

war or secretly supported the Union. While these groups were in the minority, they had been and would continue to be a major source of concern
for the state government.[6]

Facing all of these problems, Zeb sought the advice of veteran political
figures. Due to his ill health, Zeb worked on his inaugural address at home
in Asheville. After he produced a draft, he shared copies with William A.
Graham and William W. Holden. Their comments have not survived, but
apparently they suggested few changes. Three letters to Vance from promi-

nent state leaders do survive. The first came from David L. Swain, Vance's former professor and respected mentor at the University of North Carolina. Swain pointed out the interesting parallels between himself and Vance at the time that each man assumed the office of governor. Both Swain and Vance were members of pioneer families from Buncombe County, "nurtured under similar influences, physical, intellectual and moral." In addition, both men were elected by decisive majorities (Swain by the legislature) and were approximately thirty-two years of age when they were inaugurated. Swain advised Vance to declare himself unequivocally for Confederate independence so that his enemies in North Carolina and observers in states fighting the Confederacy could not misconstrue his message. The older man also counseled his former student to stay above partisan disputes and to unify the state.[7]

Many of the same ideas filled a letter from Jesse Shepherd. Vance had written to Shepherd, a former Democrat and conditional Unionist, in an effort to reach out to his recent political opponents. Shepherd was obviously flattered, and he recalled how well the two men had worked together in the House of Commons in 1854 despite their political differences. Shepherd called upon Zeb to avow "the most determined opposition to a reconstruction of the old Union." Shepherd also suggested that Zeb state positively that he would cooperate fully with the Confederate government. It is interesting that the question of how Zeb would relate to Jefferson Davis arose even before the new governor was inaugurated. Finally, Shepherd advised that Zeb mention his service in the army and make a statement of his determination not to be partisan in running the government of North Carolina.[8] There appears to have been nothing in this letter that Zeb was not already considering for inclusion in his maiden speech as governor.

The final surviving letter came from former Democratic governor David S. Reid. While admitting that he had not voted for Zeb during the recent election, Reid wrote that he was flattered by Zeb's request for advice, and he wished his young successor well. He cautioned that the chief executive should ignore state questions in his initial address. Instead, he advised Zeb to concentrate upon the larger questions of national independence and to "urge the vigorous prosecution of the War." Reid encouraged Zeb to call for a unity of spirit and action both among the people and between the Confederate and state governments. Undoubtedly thinking of his own financial interests, Reid also urged Zeb to retaliate against the federal government's policy of retaining control over escaped slaves.[9] Reid's comments are quite illuminating, as they demonstrate that when Zeb came into office, no active partisan opposition stood ready to undercut his administration. Apparently, his speeches in Raleigh and Asheville had assuaged his opponents' most pressing concerns.

In spite of the crisis, the inauguration on September 8 was full of pomp and celebration. For Hattie and Zeb, it was a time of double celebration. Just two days earlier, Hattie had given birth to their fifth child, Thomas Malvern, their fourth son who would survive to adulthood. Some of Zeb's opponents grumbled about the inauguration festivities, but the public reaction was generally quite positive. The Twenty-sixth Regiment band obtained permission to leave Virginia to provide music for the ceremonies. To a modern reader, Zeb's speech seems quite ornate, but his contemporaries apparently expected that type of oration, and it appears they were quite relieved when Zeb delivered a formal address. Several people noted that unlike his many other speeches, this address by the young governor included no jokes. Just as he had done in Asheville, Zeb embraced Confederate nationalism and defended conscription as a necessary war measure. The original secessionists, believing that this statement must have disappointed many of Vance's supporters, particularly welcomed the assertion.[10] Zeb's critics assumed, as they would throughout the war, that his supporters opposed the Confederacy. That was true in some cases, but most of Zeb's supporters disagreed with the secessionists and with some of the policies of the Davis administration, while favoring the new Southern nation's independence.

The majority of Zeb's address concerned the state government and its relationship to the public. First, Zeb committed himself to being an active governor. He stated, "I promise only that I bring a will and a determination to the performance of my duties which no one can surpass." He recognized that he could not alone do enough to ensure that North Carolina would win the war and that the state would have to do more than provide for the army in order to secure victory for the Confederacy. "To prosecute this war with success," he asserted, "there is quite as much for our people as for our soldiers to do." It would take a team effort to win the war, and Vance observed that "harmony" would be "one of the most vital elements of [the state's] success."[11] Zeb understood the importance of the civilian role in the war; this would make him both an effective wartime leader and a difficult colleague for many in the Richmond government. He considered virtually all policies, both military and civilian, in light of their potential impact on public opinion. Recognizing that most North Carolinians had adopted their Confederate identity late and reluctantly, Zeb sought ways to make the new nation seem like a desirable alternative to the old.

He recognized that there were two other concerns that had to be addressed. Since the Confederacy appeared to have been formed for the benefit of slaveowners, Zeb knew that the pressures of war might bring latent class antagonism to the surface. To forestall this eventuality, Zeb affirmed his intention to "let the law be executed impartially upon all, rich and poor, high and low." At the same time, the exigencies of war inevitably made the government increasingly visible in the everyday lives of the state's inhabitants, particularly after conscription was imposed. The enforcement of this radical innovation in American government policy had been crude, and conscription was widely resented. Zeb tried to reassure his fellow North Carolinians: "So far as I am concerned[,] next to the preservation of the State itself, I shall regard it my sacred paramount duty to protect the citizen in the enjoyment of all of his rights and liberties."[12] After all, the states that made up the Confederacy had left the Union in order to protect these rights.

While Zeb spoke about his administration largely in general terms, he did address some practical matters as well. Specifically, Zeb promised "to manage our increasing public liabilities—to search out the talent and worth of the country, and bring it into the service of the State—to clothe, equip and organize our troops, and to do justice to merit on the field." Without openly criticizing previous gubernatorial administrations, Zeb committed himself to doing what they had not done. In particular, he would properly equip the North Carolina regiments and give talented people who were not secessionists access to positions of power. Perceptive supporters of the Ellis and Clark administrations recognized Vance's implied criticism. About a week after the inauguration, William J. Yates submitted his resignation from the North Carolina Literary Board, which oversaw the state public school fund. Yates assumed that Zeb would want to appoint someone who shared his political views. In this case, Zeb asked Yates to remain in his position, and the surprised Yates was happy to do so.[13] It was clear, nevertheless, that a new day had come to North Carolina government.

Zeb quickly energized the moribund state government, first by setting a good example. Often, he worked at his office for sixteen to twenty hours a day. From the beginning, he set aside several of those hours to meet with members of the general public who brought their concerns to their accessible governor. Zeb, the supreme extrovert, loved these sessions with the people who sought him out. His earnestness and constant good humor charmed virtually all of his visitors. At the same time, these meetings gave him an opportunity to gather valuable information about the need to improve government services. Zeb's constant contact with the public enabled him to sense changes in the public's commitment to specific government policies much more rapidly than other public figures in the Confederacy could. Zeb then used the information he had gathered to argue his case for policy initiatives with Confederate officials. The sessions with the public also allowed Zeb to challenge both older political leaders in North Carolina and the received wisdom from Richmond. The result was that Zeb, despite his relative youth and inexperience, was a supremely self-confident leader from the beginning of his term in office.

Soon after he was inaugurated, Zeb began to solve the problems left by his predecessors. Drawing on his recent military experience, he addressed the growing resistance to conscription. Less than two weeks after assuming office, Zeb issued the first of dozens of proclamations that he would shower upon his constituents during the war. He started this document by stating the problem: "Information has reached me that certain persons, unmindful of the calls of patriotism & forgetful of the duties of good citizens, are using their influence to prevent obedience to the Congress, known as the Conscription Law, and that others are attempting to organize an open resistance to its execution." Zeb went on to assure the public that the law would be vigorously enforced as it had not been under Ellis and Clark. These were no idle words from Zeb. According to one scholar, North Carolina contributed more than twenty-one thousand conscripts to the Confederate war effort, approximately one-quarter of the total for the entire Confederacy. Virtually all of the newspapers in the state, including William W. Holden's *North Carolina Standard*, supported Zeb's plea.[14] Those who had voted for Zeb in the hope that he would not support the Confederate war effort must have been completely disabused by his quick action.

Working like a barely controlled dynamo, Zeb sought to energize state government in other ways. On September 18, he wrote to Weldon N. Edwards to request that the state convention be called into session. The convention had re-created the state's government when North Carolina joined the Confederacy, and Zeb hoped that it would be able to take some needed initiatives. Zeb apparently wished to call the convention into session primarily because the legislature was not then in session, and he wanted to move fast to blunt some of the sting of his conscription proclamation. Knowing that men refused induction into the army in part because they were concerned for their families' welfare, Zeb hoped that the convention would support conscripted soldiers by providing assistance to those they left behind. Vance reminded Edwards, "the cry of distress comes up from poor wives and children of our soldiers . . . from all parts of the State." Much to his chagrin, Edwards refused to act quickly, and he ultimately refused to call the convention back into session.[15] In retrospect, Edwards's caution was probably justified. It was not then necessary to circumvent the regular institutions of state government. Zeb was simply impatient to get things done.

Frustrated by his inability to get the legislative process going, Zeb turned with relief to the executive sphere. He immediately seized upon an idea submitted by Adjutant General James G. Martin to Governor Clark. Martin had suggested that the state use the port of Wilmington to secure the supplies needed by its soldiers. Specifically, he posited that the state could enter into agreements with shippers and British businessmen to trade North Carolina cotton for cloth, weapons, and medical supplies. Zeb instantly recognized that this initiative would help to solve several problems. It would not only provide needed military supplies, but also offer planters in eastern North Carolina an opportunity to salvage part of their investment in cotton. Zeb recognized that he could not carry out the full plan immediately, but he began to contact people in Wilmington to start it in motion.[16]

Wilmington was the focus of another of Zeb's efforts to invigorate state agencies. At the time, the only practical way for most North Carolinians to preserve meat was to store it in salt. With few inland sources of this precious commodity, the state became dependent on two primary sources— the large works at Saltville, Virginia, and others along North Carolina's coast—to supply it. Unfortunately for Zeb, because the federal army occupied a substantial portion of the state's coast, well-defended Wilmington, with its rail connections to the Piedmont, had to become a major source of this precious commodity. Equally unfortunately, yellow fever, which had been absent from the region for more than a decade, reappeared in September 1862. The impatient young governor would not allow increased demand and a deadly disease to excuse Wilmington's underperformance. In an October 1 letter to the director of the saltworks in Wilmington, Zeb wrote: "Your monthly report is recd. It is satisfactory in all respects except in the amount produced. In the present emergency it is desirable to have salt without regard to expense." Zeb went on to promise that, if necessary, he would provide "conscript labor" to boost production. Yet his zealous commitment could not overcome the realities of the situation. A week later, John M. Worth, the director of the saltworks, wrote to inform Vance that he had shut down the operation because of the health hazard. That Worth's own son had contracted yellow fever and had perished from it helped to confirm the seriousness of the threat. Zeb did not give up, however. In December, he journeyed to Wilmington and met with both the state salt workers and independent producers. He offered all of them a guaranteed price, a guaranteed purchase quantity, and an assured transportation rate, along with state-supplied labor. The independent salt makers' committee considered this proposal and ultimately worked out an agreement by which they would provide the state with an increased amount of the precious product.[17]

Zeb's attempts to jump-start the moribund North Carolina government during his first month in office were characteristic of his entire tenure as governor. Unwilling to wait for the fitful machinery of government to swing into action, he sought ways to get things done by intervening directly or by taking completely new initiatives. Too impatient to wait for more traditional methods to work, he forced both government officials and private businesspeople to conform to his accelerated pace. In his frenzy of activity, Zeb often bruised the feelings of those he addressed. Secretary of War George W. Randolph and President Jefferson Davis joined many others in North Carolina in finding Zeb's language disrespectful and unbecoming, but Zeb ignored their complaints and plunged ahead to solve the next crisis. At all times, he kept his ultimate objectives in mind: to provide for the army and soldiers' families; to unite the people of North Carolina behind the war; and to secure Confederate independence. Feeling secure in the righteousness of his goals, Zeb rushed eagerly from one encounter to the next.

There were certainly plenty of problems for Zeb to confront. One of the most vexing was how to prevent inflation and speculation from destroying the state's economy and undermining public support for the war. The cause of the inflation was twofold. First, the Confederate government chose to finance the war by printing money rather than raising taxes. This fiscal policy alone ensured that the level of inflation would be relatively high. Inflation tends to hurt those on fixed or low incomes, who find it difficult to make ends meet when the cost of necessities exceeds what their budgets allow them to pay. The withdrawal of a large segment of productive labor from the economy through enlistment in the army and conscription meant that there were fewer goods available for purchase. This fact invited individuals to buy scarce commodities at relatively low prices in rural areas and then ship them to urban areas, often outside of North Carolina, where prices were higher and profits consequently greater. These two factors combined made it hard for many of the yeoman and tenant farming families across the state to afford goods that they had become dependent upon.[18] Both the families themselves and their soldier husbands, sons, and fathers appealed to Zeb for assistance in this crisis.

Zeb recognized that the hardships caused by inflation could undermine most of the popular support that the Confederacy enjoyed in North Carolina, and he acted quickly on two fronts. First, he sought to persuade all

North Carolina businesses that had contracted with the state government to adhere to the 75 percent profit ceiling the state had previously put in place. An example of Zeb's technique has been preserved in his October letter to Francis L. and Henry W. Fries, the owners of a textile firm. Zeb began the letter by expressing surprise that the firm would not "comply with the provisions of the Exemption Law requiring manufacturers to furnish goods at 75 percent profit over the cost of production," and that the Fries brothers were in fact "declining to sell the State any more cloth for supplying the wants of [the] brave soldiers in the field." Zeb obviously got progressively angrier as he wrote, and several lines later he lamented, "If the Standard of patriotism was no higher in the great mass of the people, we might treat with the enemy tomorrow and consent to be slaves at once & forever." Zeb then turned aggressive. He informed the factory owners that he could easily deprive them of their business. "The Confederate authorities have desired my permission to seize the Mills of N.C. and work them for the benefit of the Army," he explained. "Should it be formally asked of me again I shall withdraw my objections & permit them to do as they wish, unless [businesses] make reasonable contracts with the State."[19]

The Fries brothers refused to be intimidated by the young governor's rhetoric. As soon as they received Vance's letter, they fired back a stiff reply in which they defended themselves in a well-argued discourse on the current economic conditions. They pointed out, quite correctly, that the scarcity of raw materials, unsettled business conditions, and inflation made estimating costs almost impossible. Thus, they maintained that they could not accurately determine what their true profit margin would be. As a result, they did not feel that they could in good conscience sign a document in which they pledged to hold to a 75 percent profit. Continuing, the brothers explained that they were more than willing to sell cloth to the state, but that they would not sign a contract with conditions they could not honestly adhere to. At the close of the letter, the obviously irritated businessmen complained to Vance, "the last part of your letter about extortion is entirely uncalled for."[20] Clearly, Zeb's impatience and bluntness had offended his fellow North Carolinians.

Zeb quickly learned that the pricing issue was a great deal more complex than he had initially thought. As the Fries brothers had pointed out, calculations of profit margin were open to considerable abuse. Some firms, especially those making woolen products, began to use replacement costs rather than purchase prices for their cost figures. During a period of inflation, this garnered them large profits and escalating prices. Zeb decided that under these circumstances, words were not enough. In January 1863, he judged that the owners of three mills were making excessive profits, and he removed their workers' exemption from conscription as a penalty. A month later, he removed the conscription exemption of workers in three shoe factories.[21] While these actions probably brought some restraint to mill owners' pricing strategies, Zeb eventually had to accept the fact that he could not control the pricing of goods. As he had pointed out in his letter to the salt commissioner, production was more important than price.

Zeb recognized that the rising cost of manufactured goods was only part of the problem. For many North Carolinians, the rapidly accelerating cost of agricultural products proved equally troubling. Many of the owners of large farms along railroad lines had quickly learned that they could make large profits by selling food and other supplies to urban markets. This practice quickly reduced supplies in rural areas and brought corresponding price increases. Country dwellers soon discovered that they could not afford to purchase many necessary items. Zeb's solution to this vexing problem was ingenious, but probably unconstitutional. As soon as the legislature met in November, he sought and received the power to impose an embargo to keep food and clothing from leaving the state of North Carolina.[22] While the rule could not be strictly enforced because some communities along the state's borders would have been seriously harmed, speculators found it a great deal more difficult to openly continue their search for profits. The impact of the embargo was rapid and beneficial. Goods that had been awaiting shipping were suddenly available within the state. Prices briefly declined, and necessary supplies became available again.

Zeb did not ignore developments on the military front; he was well aware that insufficient supplies were not the only problem North Carolina troops faced. From his own regiment's experience, Zeb understood that medical care for Confederate troops was inadequate, particularly at big battles like Malvern Hill. To remedy this problem, Zeb appointed Dr. Edward Warren to investigate the treatment of North Carolina troops in Virginia. In October, Warren reported back to Vance: "I then hastened to Charlottesville, where I found over 50 soldiers from our State, in a condition of great destitution. Their delight in seeing me, & learning that you had sent me to look after their wants cannot be expressed in words." After describing some of the conditions in detail, Warren concluded: "Taking all things together, the condition of these poor unfortunates is enough to wring tears from hearts of stone, and to stamp the authorities of the Confederacy with a brand of unutterable disgrace." Given his own experiences with the Confederate bureaucracy, Zeb needed little evidence to convince him of the problem. He quickly boarded a train and met Warren in Richmond. Together they toured the military hospitals in the region, and then Zeb met with Jefferson Davis to discuss ways to improve conditions for the wounded.[23]

This episode established a pattern by which Zeb took direct action whenever a battle seemed imminent. A short time after his visit to Richmond, he described to Davis a trip he had taken to eastern North Carolina to monitor a brief spurt of activity by the Union army. In December, Zeb traveled to the Goldsboro and Kinston area to be near some fighting provoked by a federal raid. The following February, the vigorous young governor made a quick trip to Wilmington with Dr. Warren to make sure that medical facilities in the area would be adequate in the event of a military engagement. A month later, the *Daily Progress* of Raleigh reported: "Gov. Vance, Dr. Warren and other surgeons who went below recently in anticipation of some heavy fighting, returned to the city yesterday." A few weeks later, Zeb joined the Confederate army near the coastal town of Washington, where a Confederate force was besieging a small federal force. This attempt to win back some territory ultimately failed, and the chagrined governor wrote to Secretary of War James A. Seddon: "From Roanoke Island to the late siege of Washington the history of the war has been a succession of calamities in North Carolina."[24] Zeb had done everything that he could do to promote the cause, but he could not prevent the Confederate bungling that he perceived to be a major cause of the state's problems. He and Dr. Warren had had to personally ensure that the wounded were cared for, and the military seemed incapable of driving opposing soldiers from the eastern counties.

Feeling that only more state action could resolve the crisis, Zeb sought to call the legislature into special session in October. The conservative men on the Council of State refused to give Zeb the authority to do so, and the young governor was forced to wait impatiently until the body met at its regularly scheduled time in November. On November 17, Zeb's message to the General Assembly contained requests to implement many of the programs that he had initiated or announced. He started the document with a sober observation: "The long continuance of the contest . . . [has] reduced us to straits and given rise to a class of evils in the presence of which ephemeral patriotism must perish and the tinsel enthusiasm of novelty give place to that stern and determined devotion to our cause which alone can sustain a revolution."[25] Zeb was attempting to guide his fellow North Carolinians to the point at which they would accept significant changes in their relationship with their government, and he pointed out that external circumstances, rather than personal desires, were forcing him to make these policy changes.

Then, in short order, Zeb proposed a series of initiatives that would have been revolutionary in any other context. First, he recommended that ten regiments of state reserves—approximately ten thousand men—be raised to supplement Confederate forces within the state. This unprecedented request demonstrated both Zeb's commitment to the Confederate cause and his wariness about the Richmond administration's ability to accomplish separation from the United States without independent assistance from the state of North Carolina. Zeb also requested the authority to "force" slaveowners to contribute their slaves when the new reserve regiments required their assistance. Zeb carefully avoided making any statement that could be construed to mean that these coerced laborers would be used to directly assist the Confederate government.[26] Thus, Zeb asked for extraordinary powers, but, in deference to the strong feeling against centralized government in the state, he limited their application to state programs.

Zeb then turned to the equally vexing problem of ensuring that the people living on the home front had adequate resources. He was undoubtedly motivated at least in part by humanitarian concerns; Zeb received many wrenching letters from women and men who lived throughout the state that provided him with detailed knowledge of the horrific suffering that was already taking place. Zeb also knew, however, that North Carolina soldiers were more likely to desert when they felt that their families were suffering. As noted, Zeb recommended that the state government place an embargo on "leather, shoes, woolen goods, cotton cloth, yarn, pork and bacon, flour and potatoes." In addition, he introduced the idea of the state's first large-scale welfare system to combat the problems of shortages and inflation. Under this plan, the state would purchase "200,000 bushels of corn and 500,000 pounds of pork" and store this produce in the interior. Counties would be able to draw on these supplies and sell the food to the needy at greatly reduced prices.[27] Zeb deserves full credit for initiating this needed innovation, which would expand considerably in the near future, in North Carolina.

The next major item on the new governor's agenda answered the question of how the state could pay for all of the radical new responsibilities that he proposed for it. The state's debt was growing rapidly under the stress of war, and Zeb asserted that the legislature had to find ways, at a minimum, to pay the interest on it. Zeb's predecessors had sought new sources of revenue as well, and one expedient the state had adopted was a tax on slave property. Zeb learned that differing local assessment policies had created a tax system with wide variations. This was a source of considerable discontent, and he therefore recommended "equalizing the tax on slaves." He further urged a 25 percent increase in all existing taxes and the imposition of a new tax, a 25 percent levy on the profits derived from the sale of necessities.[28] Zeb's bold program, if adopted, would have placed North Carolina on a firmer financial footing for the duration of the war.

Zeb also took the opportunity to vent his frustration with the Confederate government's war policies. First, he defended his decision to maintain contracts with North Carolina textile mills to clothe state troops. He justified his action by arguing that the Richmond government had violated the terms of the earlier commutation agreement, and thus North Carolina was now fully justified in taking her own course. Then he issued a protest against the Confederate suspension of the writ of habeas corpus. Finally, Zeb vented some additional anger by decrying the inability of gallant North Carolina officers to receive proper recognition from Confederate authorities.[29] There was nothing constructive in any of these remarks, but they did provide Zeb and his fellow citizens with the satisfaction of setting the record straight in regard to the injuries they believed that others in the Confederacy were causing them.

Finally, Zeb addressed problems that threatened the viability of the Confederacy. He supported previous efforts to discourage farmers from turning their grains into alcohol, hoping that by doing so the state could increase the amount of flour available to feed the civilian and military populations and to reduce the abuse of alcohol, which was widespread among all segments of the population.[30] During the war, farmers were forbidden to manufacture alcohol; the only exception allowed to this policy was the manufacture of alcohol for medicinal purposes for the Confederate army, and the Richmond authorities did have several large contracts for medicinal alcohol with North Carolina farmers. The policy of restricting alcohol production, however, ran counter to an important economic reality. In many remote parts of the state, particularly the mountain counties of the west, transporting bulky grains from remote fields to market was very difficult. Farmers often dealt with this problem by distilling their grain into alcohol and transporting the much more compact product to distant markets. Regardless of the advantages of this system, however, many North Carolina farmers followed the requirements of the law.

The second threat that Zeb drew attention to was the changing federal policy toward slavery. Near the end of his address, he attacked the Lincoln administration: "In the bitterness of their baffled rage they have shown a determination to re-enact the horrors of Saint Domingo, and to let loose the hellish passions of servile insurrection to revel in the desolation of our homes." Zeb, like many of the white elite in North Carolina, had been greatly angered when Lincoln issued his Preliminary Emancipation Proclamation a few weeks earlier. Equally disturbing was evidence that the federal government intended to enroll former slaves in the Union army. The idea that freed slaves might be armed and face their masters on the battlefield was an unthinkable nightmare. In February 1863, the editor of the *Daily Progress* in Raleigh captured the racist hysteria that the prospect of armed freedmen provoked: "The native Yankees assisted by the foreign element extracted from all of the sewers of Europe, failing in their attempts to subdue the South, now call to their aid the everlasting nigger."[31]

The presence of federal armies in the eastern counties of the state, where the heaviest concentrations of slaves existed, made it difficult to discipline slaves and relatively easy for them to escape to freedom. Thus, when two slaveowners were killed in the same week (probably by coincidence rather than conspiracy), the state's elite had to confront the reality of a new racial landscape. Many moved their slaves to relatively safe havens in the Piedmont and mountain counties, where the institution of slavery remained relatively stable until the end of the war. As the new year dawned, the racial situation became even more complex in North Carolina. Zeb began to get letters from his white constituents requesting that he exempt free African Americans from working on fortifications and other state and Confederate projects. The freedmen in question were skilled craftsmen and managers—millers and overseers—who were greatly needed in their communities.[32]

In the midst of invigorating the state government, Zeb took part in one of the most bizarre epistolary exchanges of the entire conflict. The Lincoln administration had appointed Edward Stanly the military governor of North Carolina. In Louisiana, Virginia, and Tennessee as well as North Carolina, the federal government created alternatives to the Confederate administration at the state level in an attempt to start the process of reconstructing the Union.[33] In the other three states, where the Union army controlled the majority of the territory, these military governments took formal actions. In Tennessee, former senator Andrew Johnson was appointed governor; he sought to protect Unionists, particularly in the eastern part of the state. The reorganized government of Virginia assisted in the creation of the new state of West Virginia. Stanly would play no such constructive role in North Carolina, where, unlike in the other three states, the federal forces controlled no major cities and only a small amount of territory. Stanly had no ready constituency, such as the businessmen of New Orleans or the Unionists in eastern Tennessee and West Virginia, to draw upon for support.

As a Whig, Stanly had been five times elected to the U.S. Congress from North Carolina between 1837 and 1851. After the collapse of the Whig Party in North Carolina, he moved to California and ran unsuccessfully for governor as a Republican in 1857. When the war began, he contacted President Lincoln and offered to return to North Carolina as a peace emissary. Lincoln appointed him in the spring of 1862, and Stanly arrived in North Carolina in May, when he found that he could not make contact with state officials to discuss peace proposals. Stanly sent his first letter to Vance on

October 21, 1862. He wrote, "My chief purpose is to see whether some measures cannot be adopted which may lead to an honorable peace." To that end, he requested an interview with Vance or some other appropriate official. Zeb bluntly replied soon after receiving this communication, "It is incompatible with my views of duty to grant you a personal interview." Zeb went on to explain that North Carolina could not and would not negotiate a separate peace with the federal government. He added that all further discussion on this and related issues would have to be conducted with the Confederate government in Richmond.[34]

From Zeb's perspective, the correspondence had ended, but Stanly persisted. Like many others who corresponded with Zeb, Stanly objected to some of his language. "I still think that this might have been done without the unbecoming language," Stanly wrote; he described some of Zeb's words as "entirely uncalled for, and especially ungracious in reply to a courteous letter." Far from being chastened, Zeb asked Stanly: "Do you Know sir, that your name is execrated and only pronounced with curses in North Carolina. Could any sane citizen believe in the 'blessings' which you propose to bestow upon the people whom you betrayed?"[35] That barrage apparently convinced Stanly not to send any further correspondence, and shortly thereafter he left the service of the Union. Stanly had never changed his views on the proper place of African Americans in Southern society. Thus, in January 1863, after the Emancipation Proclamation was made permanent, he resigned his position and returned to California. The exchange with Stanly draws attention to important aspects of Zeb's beliefs and character. First, he was unwilling to take any chance that might lead to questions about North Carolina's commitment to the Confederacy. Second, he was constitutionally unable to keep his enthusiasm and prose within the bounds of Victorian respectability. Stanly joined a list of individuals whom Vance had offended that stretched all the way back to his boyhood in Buncombe County.

The controversy with Stanly was quickly superseded by a much more significant disagreement. As earlier noted, Zeb and his fellow Conservative Party members had felt slighted by the original secessionists since the beginning of the war. Commissions in the army, state offices, and local appointments became the exclusive domain of those who had urged secession early and often. Soon after the legislature met in November 1862, it became clear that the Conservatives would exact their revenge. Zeb's role in this partisan scrap was hidden from the public, because the legislature retained the appointive power in most instances. The secessionists were enraged. One of them, Kenneth Rayner, wrote to a friend: "Well, the Legislature is in session here . . . turning out everybody, door-keepers, clerks, etc. that does not entertain opinions—or who did not vote for Governor—in accordance with the views of the majority." After former Whig William A. Graham was elected Confederate States senator with Zeb's open support, former governor Charles Manly erupted: "Not content with enemies abroad fierce, implacable and devilish; they must stir up strife and ill will and venom at home. No other state in the Confederacy is such a pack of Asses."[36] The original secessionists were politically helpless, however, because the Conservatives were in complete control of the legislature.

The political purge brought partisan conflict in North Carolina to the surface, and some significant consequences flowed from that. The *State Journal* in Raleigh dragged the dispute out of the realm of private correspondence and into print, attacking the Conservative Party for removing incumbents from office. Even a Conservative Party newspaper, the *Daily Progress* of Raleigh, called "the wisdom of some of the changes . . . questionable." But other Conservative Party newspapers defended the changes, downplaying the role of partisanship in the legislature's actions and suggesting that the new appointments were insignificant. In fact, there is no question that a new element had been introduced into state politics. Secessionists were particularly incensed when well-known former Unionists like Augustus S. Merrimon and Thomas Settle were appointed state's attorneys in the mountains and the Piedmont, respectively. They were even more distressed when the legislature chose Jonathan Worth as state treasurer. Worth came from a well-known dissenting family and had not accepted the legitimacy of the Confederacy until well after North Carolina seceded.[37] One result of all of these legislative appointments was an administrative structure more responsive to Zeb's direction. In general, the new appointees were also more likely than their predecessors to be concerned about the encroachment of the Richmond government into areas of authority that traditionally belonged to the states. Thus, Zeb began to receive even more reports of Confederate encroachments on the perceived rights of North Carolina citizens than he had before.

Another consequence of the political purge was that a small group of dedicated Confederate patriots in North Carolina began to work diligently to undermine Zeb's administration. For example, the *State Journal* attacked Zeb when he returned from a trip to eastern North Carolina, where he had sought to help North Carolina troops prepare for battle. The newspaper claimed that Zeb was not helping soldiers, but instead suppressing military news. Increasingly, however, criticism of Zeb and the North Carolina war effort came from outside of the state. In early January 1863, Richmond newspapers criticized the ten regiment bill, calling it a disloyal measure because it would drain troops from the Confederacy. When the story ran in Raleigh, an accompanying explanation refuted the charge, noting that Jefferson Davis supported North Carolina's effort to raise reserve troops and arguing that the regiments would attract only those men who were exempted from Confederate service. Nevertheless, it was difficult for Zeb and other North Carolinians to answer their critics directly. Indeed, shortly thereafter, other Virginia newspapers and some in South Carolina picked up the refrain of North Carolina's "disloyalty."[38]

As outside criticism mounted, the 1862–63 session of the state legislature became even more contentious. The small number of secessionists in the body asserted that Zeb and the people of North Carolina were not sufficiently committed to the Confederacy. Their anger was fueled by the ongoing partisan activities of the Conservatives, who kept up their efforts to gain full control of local governments by appointing sufficient magistrates to control local boards—fifty-two in the case of Forsyth County. Conservatives in the state legislature refused to back down or accept that their actions were unacceptable. Two of them introduced resolutions that affirmed their commitment to the Confederacy: "We hereby pledge ourselves most heartily and emphatically to the most vigorous Constitutional war policy, promising in the name of North Carolina the most liberal contribution of men and money to the support of it, and protesting against any settlement of the struggle which does not secure the entire independence of the Confederate States of America."[39] But such statements were not effective in silencing the continuing debate.

The frustrated secessionists decided to take their case to the public. A small caucus met in the state legislature on February 5, 1863, and adopted a statement framed by Kenneth Rayner. In part, the document read: "[We] protest against the bitter, proscriptive, partisan intolerance and tyranny which have marked the course of the present dominant faction in this State since they obtained power." Rayner justified his action to a sympathetic correspondent, writing, "The object I had in view was to present the salient points of grounds of opposition and resistance, to the most unprincipled faction (as I honestly believe) that ever had power in our country." The secessionists ridiculed the Conservatives' claim to be a "no-party" group. Vance supporters gleefully noted, however, that only three newspapers reprinted the secessionists' diatribe, and these papers did so without supporting the caucus's stand.[40]

In the winter and spring of 1863, the focus of the partisan debate began to switch from North Carolina to Richmond. The Conservatives took the offensive in this instance. Conservative newspapers began to contrast the "despotism" of the Davis administration with Zeb's defense of the rulings of Chief Justice Richmond M. Pearson on conscription. When the secessionists protested that criticism of the Confederate government would weaken the Confederate war effort, the editor of the *Daily Progress* replied, "As was predicted by us some days ago, a yell has started against Gov. Vance by a miserable little, factious, unscrupulous clique in this State, because he has dared to declare his determination to protect citizens of North Carolina from illegal arrests and false imprisonment by the agents of the Confederate Government."[41] This partisan debate, which grew much more complicated in the summer of 1863, presaged the coming demands for peace that would gain momentum throughout the state.

Despite the debilitating effects of partisan feuding, Zeb's efforts in the first nine months of his gubernatorial administration were quite successful. By June 1863, the state government was beginning to work with increasing effectiveness. Late that month, the state's blockade-runner *Advance* arrived in Wilmington for the first time with its valuable cargo, signaling that the state would be able to obtain some needed supplies through the port city. Furthermore, that same month Zeb persuaded the Council of State to call a special session of the legislature in to deal with some issues that had been neglected in the regular session. He also used his persuasive powers to take executive actions meant to strengthen the war effort. For example, he talked some factory owners into allowing their workers to go into the fields and help with the spring harvest, providing desperately needed labor. The net result of all of Zeb's initiatives was to bring virtually all of the resources of the state behind the Confederate government and its army. Zeb received full credit from most observers for bringing about this dramatic change in such a short time. With the exception of some bitter secessionists and committed Unionists, North Carolinians supported the young governor in his policies. Despite the friction between them and Zeb, moreover, Richmond authorities recognized that he was making an important contribution. In early January, Jefferson Davis praised Zeb in a Raleigh speech, saying, "the Governor had put his shoulders to the wheel, and had greatly aided [me] by swelling our regiments with conscripts."[42] Yet despite his successes, Zeb and other observers recognized that all was not well in North Carolina.

As Zeb sought to bring order to North Carolina society and government, he found himself enmeshed in a series of policy debates and implementation discussions with the leaders of the Confederacy. Clearly, this aspect of Zeb's administration was of great significance, but it has been difficult for scholars to interpret. The sheer volume of the surviving correspondence is partly to blame. There are, for example, 235 letters from Confederate secretary of war James A. Seddon to Zeb preserved in the surviving Vance manuscripts; there are 125 from Vance to Seddon.[1] In addition, Vance corresponded with Jefferson Davis as well as other military leaders, cabinet members, and Confederate officials. Nevertheless, a clear picture of the overall character of the relationship between Zeb and Confederate authorities does emerge from this mass of documentation. Everyone involved was working toward the goal of Confederate independence; Zeb almost always argued with the officials in Richmond and elsewhere about the best means to achieve this common objective.

It is important to keep in mind how few high-level personnel there were in the state and Confederate bureaucracies. Much of the correspondence between Vance and high-ranking Confederate officials would have been handled by department heads or lower-ranking staff members in a larger bureaucracy. Even where such officials existed, Zeb preferred to address his requests to the person most likely to approve his suggestions or requests. For example, early in Zeb's administration he wrote a letter to Davis that began, "Pardon me for addressing you in regard to a matter that should ordinarily come before the Quartermaster-General." In the letter, Zeb proposed that the Confederacy consider the possibility of using cotton harnesses for horses to save leather for shoes and boots that could be worn by soldiers and civilians. Replying through his aide, Burton N. Harrison, Davis took Zeb's question seriously and informed the young governor that the military leaders knew from experience that cotton harnesses would not hold up under the extreme conditions of combat and long-distance travel.[2]

Zeb appears to have had three principal assistants throughout most of the war. These relatively young men brought some important organizational skills—and much clearer handwriting—to Vance's aid, but they did not have sufficient standing to take independent action themselves. Jefferson Davis has been justifiably criticized by historians for micromanaging the Confederate government, but, like Vance, he had relatively few personal staff members to assist him with the many tasks that devolved upon him. Particularly in matters involving important officials or crucial policy decisions, either the president or a major cabinet officer had to take the initiative. Thus, some of the friction between Zeb and upper-level Confederate officials was simply the natural result of overburdened men struggling with details that could have been handled by others.

Of course, Zeb's attitude toward the Richmond government was primarily shaped by his experiences in military service. While in command of the Twenty-sixth Regiment, Zeb's basic commitment to the Confederacy was confirmed. The fact that he faced death, and led other men to face it, banished any doubts from Zeb's mind about his duty to his new country. At the same time, however, he was greatly frustrated by the inefficiency of the civil and military bureaucracy. He and his men were deployed under fire in circumstances in which they were doomed to fail. During part of Zeb's term of service, the government did not provide basic clothing and food to his regiment. Furthermore, Zeb deeply resented what he perceived as partisan discrimination directed against him, though this factor was not as significant as the other two experiences in determining his attitude towards the Confederate government. Zeb's inability to win promotion or to form a legion while his former political adversaries advanced steadily aggravated him and caused him to view the new government as little different from that of the United States. These experiences and attitudes led Zeb to take a seemingly confrontational approach to dealing with Confederate officials that often fostered misunderstandings.

While the great majority of Zeb's correspondence with Confederate officials dealt with particular incidents and offered no definitive discussion of his overall attitude toward the Confederacy, his exchanges with Jefferson Davis often addressed broader questions of policy. In their 116 extant letters, these two government leaders often addressed volatile questions about the basic nature of the Confederacy and how power should be divided between North Carolina and the Southern government. Some of the conflicts between Vance and Davis that emerged in their extended discussion were not, however, the result of policy differences. The two men possessed very different personalities, and the severity of some of their disagreements was fueled by the differences in their characters. Zeb, of course, was a voluble extrovert who often expressed himself in the heat of the moment with an asperity that offended his friends as well as those who opposed him. Davis, on the other hand, was a highly private man who found social intercourse difficult and who took offense easily when dealing with others. In further contrast to Zeb, he was a tall and painfully thin person who suffered from debilitating illnesses throughout the war. Only master diplomats like Robert E. Lee and Judah Benjamin or former colleagues who had proven themselves worthy of a special trust remained in good standing with the sensitive Confederate president for long.[3] The potential for difficult relations between Davis and Vance was, therefore, quite high.

For the first year of Zeb's gubernatorial administration, the relationship between the two chief executives remained correct, if not cordial. Davis was probably very pleased that the young and vigorous Vance had replaced his rather mediocre predecessor. Suddenly, North Carolina was a beehive of activity just when the Confederacy was in dire need of men, materiel, and good morale. In a letter dated October 17, 1862, Davis commented: "I gratefully acknowledge the earnest & patriotic manner in which your assumption of the Executive Authority in N. Car. [Y]ou have labored to fill her battle-thinned regiments and recruit her armies to the field. I am happy in the confidence that you will continue to afford this Government your valuable cooperation, & beg to assure you of the deep interest I feel in all that relates to the security & welfare of your state." Davis was responding to plans for securing more recruits from North Carolina that Zeb had laid before him and Confederate secretary of war George W. Randolph when Zeb traveled to Richmond in early October. Despite the president's praise, however, the new governor was not satisfied with Confederate policy, and he complained. In letters to both Randolph and Davis, Zeb pointed out that many of these new volunteers had come forward because he had promised, apparently with the support of Randolph and Davis, that the new soldiers would be able to choose their regiments. Zeb soon discovered that Confederate officials were not keeping that promise.[4]

Davis replied to Vance, and the tenor of his letter shows that he was willing to make allowances for his impetuous correspondent. First, Davis agreed with every essential point that Zeb had made: the Confederate government had agreed to allow North Carolina volunteers to join the regiments of their choice despite the fact that the legislation that had created that policy was no longer in force; many recruits had taken advantage of this offer when they joined the army; and their wishes had not been respected by Confederate authorities. Davis explained that he had not deliberately deceived Vance. Rather, the change in policy resulted from the renewed threat of federal army activity in North Carolina. Far from being an attack on North Carolina's sovereignty, the policy change was designed to contribute to the defense of the state. Trying to further mollify the angry governor, Davis added: "I feel grateful to you for the cordial manner in which you have sustained every proposition connected with the public defence and trust that there will always be such co-intelligence and accordance as will make us to cooperate for the public good."[5] While Zeb continued to grumble throughout the war about exceptions to the policy, this issue never became a major obstacle to cooperation between the state and the Confederate government.

The next significant controversy between the two executives was also settled without unusual acrimony. At the center of this incident was the Reverend Robert J. Graves of Orange County, North Carolina. Graves had secured a pass to go through Union lines in order to seek medical treatment in New York. When Union forces detained him, he refused to take an oath of allegiance. Despite this action, he was allowed to proceed and secure relief for his ailment. While in New York, Graves became impressed by the energy and commitment of the supporters of the federal effort. When he returned to North Carolina, he composed a letter to alert the Confederates to the determination of their foes. Apparently, some Confederate officials felt that his ideas were treasonous, and they sent an agent to North Carolina. The agent arrested Graves and spirited him away to Richmond, Virginia, where he was incarcerated. North Carolinians were outraged by the arrest, and Zeb sent a resolution of protest to Davis from the state legislature. Davis was absent from his office at the time, but James A. Seddon, the secretary of war, instantly recognized that a serious error had been made. In less than a week, Graves was returned to North Carolina's authorities, who eventually released him. Zeb was delighted with the result and wrote to Seddon: "Allow me Sir, to express my gratification not only at the prompt compliance with the wishes of our legislature, but also at the manner & spirit manifested in the deed. . . . Nothing tends more strongly to preserve harmony and cordial feeling, than for a state naturally & properly jealous of its rights, to perceive such a courteous disposition to respect and defend them, on the part of the General Government."[6] At this point, both sides were clearly making special efforts to maintain good relations with each other.

At the end of March 1863, Zeb wrote to Davis regarding a matter of constitutional interpretation. Zeb noted, "Heretofore I have not belonged to that class of politicians who made the 'night (and day) hideous' with cries for *States Rights* and was rather accused of Consolidationism." But he felt that he needed to protest vigorously the Confederate conscription of magistrates, constables, and local police officers. He pointed out that it seemed appropriate for the governor to decide which state officers were essential to the state and which could be spared under the Confederate Conscription Act. Authorities in Richmond had disputed Vance's interpretation and ordered the Confederate enrolling officers in North Carolina to draft the specified officials. Health problems prevented Davis from replying to Vance's letter until the middle of July, but Davis then stated that the commander of conscripts in North Carolina had been ordered to defer to Vance in every instance in which he could do so without breaking the law. Davis went on to say that the application of the law to specific types of officials was being thoroughly investigated.[7] While Zeb was not completely satisfied with his reply, Davis was generally conciliatory, and good relations were maintained.

One explanation for the good relations between Vance and Davis is that Zeb directed most of his ire about what he felt were wayward Confederate policies toward lower-level officials. Zeb's most frequent correspondents were the men who held the office of secretary of war. The man who held this position had multiple responsibilities that brought him in consistent contact—and often conflict—with Zeb. The secretary of war was responsible for the practical details of raising and equipping the manpower for the army. Disagreements on matters of policy, especially questions associated with the conscription law, led to contentious exchanges between Zeb and the men who served as secretary of war. In addition, matters involving the defense of North Carolina's eastern counties, military promotions, the quartering of troops, the suppression of Unionists, the treatment of deserters, and other difficult problems were standard elements of Zeb's correspondence with these men. Yet while there were instances of real friction between Zeb and individual secretaries of war that briefly undermined the war effort, for the most part Zeb managed to work quite effectively with these men.

When Zeb assumed the gubernatorial chair in September 1862, the incumbent secretary of war was George W. Randolph. This scion of several distinguished Virginia families was apparently appalled by the informality of the young governor. Their earliest correspondence took place in the spring of 1862, when Zeb was trying to raise his legion and Randolph and the military leadership were quite unenthusiastic. Their interactions at that time probably undermined any chance that the two men would later work together cordially. What was probably the most serious confrontation between the two men occurred in October 1862, when Zeb felt that Randolph and Davis had gone back on their promise to allow North Carolina recruits to choose their own regiments. Sensing that his honor and reputation were at stake, Zeb adopted the aggressive and sarcastic tone that sometimes characterized his correspondence with Confederate officials.

His letter to Randolph stated: "In regard to such political movements as secure most effectually the support of the execution of the conscript Law, I do claim that I ought to be heard. In this respect I might safely assert of myself . . . that I know more than all of the West Pointers in the service." Randolph refused to answer Zeb's letter "because it imputed 'bad faith' to the President and Secretary of War and could not be answered."[8] Clearly, Davis was not the only touchy Confederate leader.

But Zeb could be just as stubborn about carrying out policies developed by Randolph and the Confederate government. In mid-November, Randolph wrote to Zeb to request that the North Carolina governor supply laborers to complete a railroad line between Danville, Virginia, and Greensboro, North Carolina. The obvious objective behind this request was to build a much needed second rail line between the upper and lower South. Vance's reply showed his unwillingness to sacrifice the interests of his state for the needs of the Confederacy. Rather than answer the letter himself, Vance directed his aide David A. Barnes to reply. Barnes explained, "[Vance] hopes it will not be improper to remark that the government should at all hazards, and at all times, defend our present railroad connections at Weldon."[9] Vance balked at complying with Randolph's request because he feared that the existence of a second railroad line would encourage the Confederacy to abandon its military commitment to parts of eastern North Carolina.

If this episode had been an isolated incident, it would have been less significant. It was, however, part of Vance's ongoing effort to protect the state's public and private railroads against changes required by the war effort. Three months later, Secretary of War James A. Seddon wrote again to Vance to ask that the state of North Carolina assist construction by securing slave laborers to help build the connection to Danville. He also commended what he considered to be Vance's suggestion that the newly constructed lines be of standard width, which would allow trains carrying Confederate supplies to pass along them. This proved to be wishful thinking, because in his reply Vance objected to the change of track width. Vance noted his reservations about the new railroad in his reply of February 12, 1863, in which he stated that the railroad was "viewed with almost universal disfavor in the State . . . and that the charter never could have been obtained but as a pressing war necessity."[10] This point was important to Vance, who always remained aware of popular opinion and took it into account when he formulated policy.

Vance was also protecting the state government's financial interests in this episode. The state owned some of North Carolina's rail lines and was a part owner of many of the others. Most of the lines in North Carolina were built with a narrower-than-standard gauge, and it would have significantly inconvenienced the state's rail companies if the new line had been constructed in the standard width. Thus, when the construction was finally completed after a delay of two years, Vance had not forced the company that built it to adopt the standard gauge. As a result, all of the materials shipped to Danville had to be manually unloaded from one train and reloaded by hand onto another in order to proceed along tracks of a different width. As late as March 31, 1865, Secretary of War John C. Breckinridge had begged Zeb to reconstruct the rail line to Danville in the standard gauge. This Zeb and the North Carolina company refused to do.[11] In this instance, there is no question that Zeb sacrificed Confederate interests in favor of the interests of his state and its business constituents.

In other instances in which Vance disputed the sovereignty of the Confederacy, he had stronger arguments to defend. For example, the Confederate authorities objected to the young governor's plan for supplying North Carolina troops with equipment and clothing. Having personally been deprived of these necessities while a soldier, Zeb was determined to take action independent of the Confederate commissary department. His plan, already mentioned in brief, was both practically and constitutionally bold. Zeb decided to create a state assisted blockade-running operation centered at the well-defended port of Wilmington. He contracted with the British trading company Alexander Collie to secure swift sailing vessels that would ship cotton from Wilmington to Bermuda, where the cargo would be transferred to a British ship and taken to Britain for sale. Under this arrangement, half of the profits from the cotton sale would belong to the Collie Company and one-third would belong to the state. The remaining one-sixth of the financial returns would be available to other persons or groups, including the Confederate government. After the state's share of the cotton was sold in Britain, it had the right to fill all of the cargo space on the returning ships with uniforms, blankets, rifles, and medical supplies for North Carolina's troops.[12]

The Confederate authorities were unenthusiastic about Zeb's plan and appeared at first to be placing impediments in the way of its successful operation. The first confrontation took place over a minor personnel matter. North Carolina's agent in Britain was to be native Scot John White, a resident of Wilmington. White agreed to leave his business in Wilmington and to sail to Britain under one condition: that his son-in-law, S. P. Arrington, be discharged from the army to take care of White's business interests. For more than four months, successive secretaries of war refused to release Arrington from the Twelfth North Carolina Regiment for a variety of technical reasons. An exasperated Vance finally appealed directly to Jefferson Davis in March 1863, and Arrington was almost immediately furloughed.[13]

Zeb's efforts to secure ships and to maintain his contract with Collie generated much greater controversy. Initially, he had trouble securing funding from the Confederate government to purchase vessels. Zeb applied to the Richmond government for $250,000 in cotton bonds of the approximately $5 million owed North Carolina by the Confederate government. Zeb's agents were put off with a variety of bureaucratic excuses for at least six weeks. Once the bonds were secured and vessels purchased, the program proved to be extremely successful. North Carolina cotton commanded a premium in England, allowing the state to import a great many supplies and to purchase a fast British ship, which John White renamed the *Advance* in honor of the governor. From the beginning, however, there were serious objections within the Confederate bureaucracy to Zeb reserving all of the incoming materials for the use of North Carolina soldiers. One official explained why nothing was done to impede Zeb: "A full appreciation of the delicate relations of the States and Confederate Government, coupled with an earnest desire to avoid all perplexing questions between them, alone restrained the Bureau from protesting against the existing arrangement."[14]

As the war continued, however, virtually all of the Confederate ports were closed or rendered useless by the federal army's capture of the Mississippi River Valley. The Confederate government needed to ensure that all of the precious cargo space on board ships entering its remaining ports was devoted to carrying essential supplies. The Confederacy began claiming one-third of all space on private vessels. On January 6, 1864, Confederate officials made that claim on the *Don* despite the fact that the Collie Company had already claimed 75 percent of the space and the state of North Carolina the remaining 25 percent. The local Confederate official decided to hold the *Don* in port until the ensuing argument was settled. The next day, Zeb wrote a long letter to Seddon in which he explained how important the voyage of the *Don* was to the state. "I have now at Bermuda and on the way there eight or ten cargoes of supplies of the very first importance to the army and people," he wrote. "Knowing that one steamer could not bring these cargoes in before spring, at which time I anticipate the closing of the port, . . . I sold one-half of the State's steamer Advance, and purchased of Messrs. Collie & Co. one-fourth interest in four steamers—the Don and the Hansa, and two others now building—for the purpose of hurrying these supplies in." Local officials and Secretary of War Seddon recognized that no one would win by holding the *Don* in port, and the ship was finally allowed to go to sea. But in his letter of January 14, Seddon refused to back down. As he explained to Zeb: "The Don and the Hansa are upon a different footing. They are already engaged in carrying out one-third of the cargo for account of the [Confederate] Government. The owners made overtures to you in order to be relieved from what they regarded as an onerous obligation." Seddon correctly pointed out that the Collie Company sought greater profit for itself and that its agreement with North Carolina would result in fewer needed supplies reaching the South. On a more conciliatory note, Seddon agreed to allow Zeb to reduce the backlog of supplies in Bermuda without having one-third of the space on these ships claimed by the Confederacy. The secretary nevertheless took the opportunity to point out that the Confederate government was working for all of the states, and he reminded Zeb that North Carolina should recognize the primacy of the Richmond government. Subsequent correspondence between the two men settled nothing further.[15]

Seeking a final solution to this conflict, Zeb wrote a detailed letter to President Davis in March. In this rather tedious missive, the young North Carolina governor wrote like the lawyer he was. He dissected regulations and rules to demonstrate that vessels that were partly owned by the state should be free from regulation. His more sustained arguments were fairly persuasive. The first was that the Confederacy did not have a strong system of running the blockade in ships of its own. Secondly, Zeb argued that the government's regulation of blockade-running ships, by greatly reducing the profits of vessels' private owners, would thereby reduce these owners' incentive to bring in needed supplies. Zeb may well have been correct on this point, but his assertions did not fully justify his claim that North Carolina's blockade-runners should be exempted from regulation. Davis did not answer Zeb's letter directly, and the governor spent most of April 1864 trying to persuade lower-level officials to recognize North Carolina's right to exemption.[16]

This conflict resurfaced in the summer of 1864, when the Confederacy not only sent blockade-runners out from Wilmington but also sent out ships that preyed on Union shipping. This prompted the federal government to try to tighten its blockade of the North Carolina port. At one point, a Confederate privateer seized coal that had been purchased and saved for the North Carolina blockade-runners. When the *Advance* prepared to pass through the blockade again, it was able to find only inferior coal for fuel. This circumstance led to the capture of the pride of Zeb's fleet. Zeb was joined by Robert E. Lee in protesting the loss of the *Advance* and the Confederate policies that caused it. Davis shared Zeb's letter with Secretary of the Navy Stephen R. Mallory. Mallory asserted that the *Tallahassee*, one of the privateers blamed for the loss of the *Advance*, had destroyed thirty-one enemy vessels; he argued that its raiding activity weakened the enemy. Davis repeated most of Mallory's letter in his reply to Vance. This did not satisfy Vance, and he and Mallory engaged in an unbecoming correspondence that did nothing to assist their cause.[17]

Zeb is usually praised for his initiative in organizing North Carolina's blockade-runners, and it is clear that he did more to bring in European supplies than any other Confederate governor. He provided clothing and other resources that were badly needed to North Carolina troops, and these goods probably would not have been supplied by the Confederacy. With that said, however, it is also obvious that Zeb took too narrow a view of the situation in this instance. It was absolutely essential that the entire Confederate army be equipped as fully as possible, and this meant that it would have been better for Zeb to defer to the Richmond government in the supply emergency of 1864. It also seems clear, however, that Vance and Lee were correct in arguing that the Confederacy was in such dire need of supplies that it should not have been sacrificing blockade-runners for raiding vessels.

Zeb's zealous commitment to the state's foreign trade program was somewhat tainted by his financial stake in it. Surviving ship manifests and later newspaper articles document that Zeb had a personal financial interest in the trade. It is difficult to recover the precise details of the arrangement, but it appears that on several occasions the shipping company gave Zeb ownership of a small number of bales of cotton. This usually amounted to five or fewer bales out of a total of five to seven hundred bales.[18] It also appears that these bales were not part of the North Carolina state consignment, and thus that the state did not suffer directly from Vance's ownership of them. However, goods that were purchased with Zeb's share of the profit from the cotton sale did take up precious cargo room on the return voyage to Wilmington. Zeb apparently viewed these bales as a "gift" from his partner, and he therefore did not feel that there was anything illicit in the arrangement. When so many of his constituents were facing extreme hardship, both in the military and in civilian life, however, Zeb's acceptance of these gifts was ill considered at best, and covert bribery at worst.

Zeb also battled the Confederate leadership for control of the output of North Carolina's textile factories. Recognizing that the rebelling states would be most successful if each became more self-sufficient, Zeb purchased British textile equipment and brought it in through the blockade. This new machinery was quickly placed in the state's contract mills, and it greatly expanded North Carolina's cloth-making capacity. The products of these mills, of course, went to clothe and warm the soldiers and civilians of North Carolina. When the Confederate government sought to claim part of it, Zeb expressed outrage. He wrote to Seddon: "General Lawton has . . .

conceived the idea that the whole business of this State supplying her own troops must be broken up, no doubt for the reason that it is done better and cheaper that it could be done by him. Accordingly, details for hands in the factories have been refused and they are being sent to camp, unless they break their contract with the State and enter into others with General Lawton." Understandably, Lawton found Zeb's letter "extraordinary." Writing to Seddon, Lawton pointed out that North Carolina had one-third of all of the textile mills in the Confederacy, and he argued that it was not fair for the state's government to claim exclusive rights to its production. Lawton continued, complaining that Zeb had refused a request by the Confederate government for supplies in December 1863 and had contributed "only" twenty thousand uniforms to Richmond since that time. Lawton concluded his letter with a generous opinion: "Our cause is a common one, our soldiers struggle for it in common, and I submit what the country affords should be freely shared in common."[19]

Both men had made valid points in their letters. Zeb knew from personal experience that the Confederacy had not supplied its army well, and the letters he received from officers and men in the lower ranks of the military taught him that it had not markedly improved since he left the service. The situation called for bold and innovative action; this Zeb took. The Confederacy needed men like him to solve problems creatively, as Zeb had done when he contracted with the blockade-runners and imported textile machinery. The Davis administration did not have Zeb's imagination and drive. On the other hand, the Confederate government needed the states to unite behind it if it was going to succeed. The Richmond government could have simply commandeered the private ships and factories of the South, and while this expedient might well have done more harm than good, it was one alternative to wrangling with difficult state leaders like Vance. The other was for the Confederacy to encourage the kind of cooperation that depended upon trust and goodwill. Unfortunately for the Confederacy, these sentiments were often in short supply.

A series of disagreements between Zeb and Confederate authorities that dealt generally with civil liberties contributed to North Carolinians' distrust of the Confederacy. As Zeb and the Richmond government well knew, Confederate allegiance had come very late to most North Carolinians. For this reason, the Davis administration was constantly concerned about developments in North Carolina and suspicious of the motivations of many of the state's public leaders. Zeb was equally concerned about Confederate morale in his state; he recognized how fragile its loyalty to the cause was. He further recognized that most North Carolinians were more loyal to their state than to the broader cause of Southern independence. Thus, he knew that any violation of state sovereignty by the Richmond government would be greatly resented by many North Carolinians. If North Carolina was going to be a major contributor to the drive for Southern independence, its citizens would need to be assured that their state's sovereignty was being protected.

The first confrontation took place in the spring of 1863. Army enlistments were declining in North Carolina, and Zeb issued a proclamation that encouraged draft dodgers to enlist. The appeal was partially successful, but individual Confederate military officers were not satisfied with the situation near their commands. A cavalry squad from Georgia entered Cherokee County, North Carolina, and abducted eight accused Unionists, all of whom were over the conscription age. Although these North Carolina men were released, Zeb pledged that he would authorize county officials "to call out the Militia and shoot the first man who attempt[ed] to perpetrate a similar outrage." General Gideon Pillow, acting on his own, sent squads of his soldiers into western North Carolina from southwestern Virginia in an attempt to coerce men to join the Confederate army. Zeb protested this "invasion" of the state in strong terms, and the men who had been seized by Pillow's soldiers were released.[20]

The details of conscription policy also became a flash point between the two governments. Chief Justice Richmond Pearson of the North Carolina Supreme Court made a crucial ruling that governed a series of district court cases, including the case of John Irvin, which serves as an example. When drafted, Irvin had provided a substitute—a person not eligible for the draft who agreed to take his place—who was thirty-six years of age. When the Confederate government sought more soldiers to fill its depleted armies, it raised the upper age limit for conscripts from thirty-five to forty-five. As the Confederacy interpreted the law, it made Irvin's substitute eligible for conscription in his own right; thus Confederate authorities arrested Irvin for failing to report for duty, and Irvin applied to Chief Justice Pearson for a writ of habeas corpus. Pearson argued in his decision on the case that the legislation that had altered the conscription age had no impact on the status of those already in the army, and therefore that it made no change in the status of Irvin's substitute. Pearson concluded that Irvin still had a valid substitute in service, and he consequently discharged Irvin from Confederate authority. A number of other men who found themselves in the same position as Irvin applied for a writ from Pearson, and they were also freed from Confederate custody.[21]

Outraged, the Richmond authorities demanded that Zeb counteract the ruling of the chief justice. In the meantime, Confederate authorities ignored Pearson's rulings and continued to force men into the army whose substitutes had become eligible for conscription. On May 22, 1863, Zeb wrote an aggressive letter to Seddon. He warned the secretary of war that further Confederate decisions to ignore state courts "might lead to unpleasant and unprofitable consequences." The following February, Zeb agreed that the conscription issue had led to "a direct and unavoidable collision of State and Confederate authorities." He noted that he felt required by his oath to support the findings of Pearson in individual cases, but he also pointed out that the entire state supreme court would meet in June and that it might rule against the chief justice's district court verdicts. Zeb went on to propose that until the state supreme court ruled, the Confederacy should desist conscripting men who had hired substitutes. In December, the Confederacy removed the issue from the table by excising the substitute provision from the revised conscription law. While Zeb's stance may not have been completely sound legally, it was politically astute. The participants at a public meeting in Gaston County passed a resolution in favor of Vance's stand, stating, "Governor Vance, Judge Pearson, and others, who have taken a bold and independent stand to sustain the civil authorities of the State, are deserving of our lasting gratitude."[22]

In February 1864, the Confederate Congress again suspended the writ of habeas corpus, reigniting that controversy. Judge Pearson decided that the Confederate suspension of the writ did not apply in the conscription cases, but the Bureau of Conscription ignored his rulings. An angry Vance pointed out that he had no discretion as the executive officer of the state; he had to enforce the rulings of the state court. He protested: "If the process of the court is resisted I am forced by my oath of office to summon the military power of the State to enforce it. There is no escape from this conclusion." Zeb went on to point out that if the Richmond authorities would just wait, the entire North Carolina Supreme Court would decide the controversy in June. At that meeting of the court, the other two justices disagreed with Pearson and the controversy came to an end.[23] Zeb's extended battle with the Confederate government about the state courts' rulings showed Zeb to be an effective spokesman for his state. It was clear to Vance that Pearson had overstepped his bounds as a jurist, but the judge's decisions were binding until overruled. The inability of the Confederate government to handle this matter in the courts—the Confederate Congress had failed to create a supreme court to try cases like this—placed its administrators in a difficult position. Ignoring state courts was their only option, and when they exercised it in North Carolina they provoked a major controversy.

Related to this question of state sovereignty was the ongoing battle between Zeb and the Richmond government over the conscription of state government employees, which first surfaced late in the winter of 1863.

Vance wrote to Seddon at that time and requested that the Confederate army release a North Carolina officer who had just been elected solicitor of a judicial circuit by the state legislature. Vance "protest[ed] against this disrespect towards the civil government of N.C." The chief of the bureau of conscription, Gabriel J. Rains, a North Carolinian, wrote a conciliatory letter back to Zeb in which he explained that in the future, conscription agents in North Carolina would be ordered "that whenever the wishes of His Excellency the Governor can be accorded with without clear infraction of the law it is desirable to do so." Upon receipt of this letter, Zeb wrote back to Rains and then sent a second letter to Jefferson Davis. In the latter missive, Vance wrote: "In my letter to General Rains I assumed the position that the Confederate authorities should not conscribe any officers or agents of the State whose services were necessary to the due administration of her government, and that the State authorities (not the Confederacy) must judge of this necessity."[24] In his letter to Rains, Zeb assured the Confederate conscription director that he heartily supported conscription as a national policy. He went on to say that he was not one of those political leaders who had used states' rights as a slogan to obstruct Confederate policy; nevertheless, he was "not quite willing to see the State of North Carolina . . . blotted from the map and her government abolished by the conscription of her officers." It seems obvious with the benefit of hindsight that Zeb had a broader vision than Rains of the needs of the communities in his state. He and many others in North Carolina believed that it was absolutely essential for the state to retain sufficient personnel to keep both civil society and the economy functioning. If they were destroyed, then the army would have neither the morale nor the resources to carry on the war. Zeb's point was sustained by the state legislature when it passed resolutions exempting such skilled civilian operatives as millers and blacksmiths from conscription.[25]

Yet the executive's power to determine who would be exempt from the draft was open to potential abuse. In fact, a number of historians have condemned Zeb for shielding as many as 14,000 men from the operations of the conscription law. If this figure is accurate, it means that North Carolina claimed more exemptions for state officials than any other state in the Confederacy. One newspaper that supported Vance claimed that state records showed that "only" 5,153 state officials were exempted. A recent historical study concluded that the correct number is 5,589 out of a total of 18,843 for the entire Confederacy.[26] Even the lower figure makes it clear that Zeb's administration was particularly zealous in claiming protection for its officials. Zeb's contention that the state needed a bureaucracy to function was quite correct, but it nevertheless seems likely that many of those who were appointed to state office were looking for honorable ways to avoid being conscripted.

The most spectacular single case in the battle over the conscription of state officials involved Daniel L. Russell of Brunswick County. Russell, the son of a wealthy planter and slaveowner, was a student at the University of North Carolina when the conflict started. He returned home, raised a company of soldiers, and was commissioned as a captain when he was just sixteen years old. He proved, however, to be a source of trouble for his commanders. He opposed the imposition of the Conscription Act and encouraged members of the army who were small farmers to believe that there was class discrimination in the Confederate policies. In January 1864, he assaulted the conscript-enrolling officer for his unit. He then refused to apologize for assaulting a superior officer and was court-martialed. He was found guilty of the assault and discharged from the army rather than punished. His youth, obvious immaturity, and high social standing shielded him from the more drastic usual penalties.[27]

As soon as Russell was dismissed from the army, Zeb appointed him a commissioner to distribute money and provisions to soldiers' families. Seddon and the local Confederate commanders refused to acknowledge the legitimacy of the civilian appointment and sought to retain Russell in the service as a private. After arguing the law with Seddon, Zeb concluded: "Should I be in error upon the law of the case I must earnestly urge upon you not to wound the spirit of this gallant and promising young officer by sending him into the ranks." Zeb's letter had sufficient impact that Russell was not called into the service. That summer, Russell ran for a seat in the state legislature—even though he was not old enough to vote—and was elected.[28] In the 1880s he was elected to the U.S. Congress, and in 1896 he was elected governor of North Carolina. Russell's case illustrates that the power to protect state officials was a discretionary one that Zeb used on some occasions for political or personal reasons.

Other conflicts between Zeb and the Confederacy dealt with far more serious matters than the Russell case. Zeb was constantly contacting the Richmond authorities about the activities of Confederate soldiers in North Carolina. On one occasion, several units of cavalry that were stationed elsewhere were sent to forage in the state. Some of these units literally stripped individual farms and entire communities of their provisions. Recognizing that these depredations only added to the unrest that was growing throughout the state during the war, Zeb protested vehemently to Seddon and the responsible generals. He demanded the complete withdrawal of the offending troops, and he went on to assert: "If God Almighty had yet in store another plague worse than all others which he intended to let loose on the

Egyptians in case Pharaoh still hardened his heart[,] I am sure it must have been a regiment or so of half-armed, half-disciplined Confederate cavalry. Had they been turned loose among Pharaoh's subjects, with or without an impressment law, he would have been so sensible of the anger of God that he never would have followed the children of Israel to the Red Sea! No sir; not an inch!" The beleaguered Confederate officials claimed that they had no alternatives, and they did not withdraw the troops until after the soldiers had already done considerable damage.[29]

The most egregious incident of misconduct by Confederate troops occurred in the mountains of Madison County in the winter of 1863. In early January, a band of fifty deserters from the Sixty-fourth North Carolina Regiment—desperate Unionists, many of them from Shelton Laurel—organized a raid on the town of Marshall to secure the salt that would allow their needy families to preserve food. There was considerable animus in their motivation, because the Confederate partisans in Madison County had hoarded the prized commodity and refused to make it available to the Unionist families. When the band attacked the town of Marshall, they shot and wounded a Confederate officer on furlough, exposed the sick children of their regiment's colonel to the cold, and stole salt and other goods from the homes of the residents. This raid greatly angered the members of the Sixty-fourth North Carolina Regiment who had remained on duty in Tennessee. Zeb and other observers in the state capital shared their outrage. The normally unflappable editor of the *Raleigh Daily Progress* wrote of the Unionist raiders: "Let them be caught and hanged summarily." Zeb fired off a note to Henry Heth, the Confederate commanding general in eastern Tennessee, that read: "I hope you will not relax until the tories are crushed. But do not let our excited people deal too harshly with these misguided men. Please have the captured delivered to the proper authorities for trial."[30] This latter advice was not heeded, however, and a great tragedy began to unfold.

The remaining loyal Confederates in the Sixty-fourth North Carolina were sent from Saltville, Virginia, to Madison County under the leadership of James A. Keith to round up the Unionist raiders. As they reached the Laurel region, they learned that the two children who were exposed during the raid had just died. Barely able to contain their fury, they swept the area and apprehended fifteen men and boys. On the trip out of the small valley, two men escaped into the surrounding wilderness. The remaining thirteen—including a boy of thirteen, a boy of fifteen, and a fifty-six-year-old man—were then lined up, shot, and buried in a shallow grave. On January 31, Zeb's old comrade Augustus S. Merrimon wrote to him from Asheville about the incident. "I learn that a number of *prisoners* were *shot* without any trial or hearing whatever," he reported. "I hope that this is not true, but if so, the parties [who] are guilty of so dark a crime should be punished. Humanity revolts at so savage a crime."[31] Stunned by this revelation, Zeb sought to discover what had transpired in the mountain fastness.

Reacting with the decisiveness that characterized his wartime administration, Zeb immediately began to push for a full inquiry. As soon as he received letters from a Confederate officer and from Merrimon, he began a preliminary investigation. To General William G. M. Davis, Zeb stated: "I was fearful in the great excitement prevailing among our people that the misguided people of Laurel might be dealt too harshly with, and warned the officers to be civil and just. I was therefore sorry to learn this morning that Colonel Allen had hanged several of the captured prisoners." While Zeb had some of the details wrong, he was pursuing the reports vigorously. A week later, Zeb wrote to Merrimon, "I desire you also to make an investigation officially into the reported shooting of a number of these prisoners, with all of the circumstances, as I intend to look into the matter myself." In a letter of February 16, 1863, Merrimon supplied Vance with the full details of the incident and concluded, "I know not what you intend doing with the guilty parties, but I suggest that they are all guilty of murder." A week later, Merrimon named those killed and informed Vance that only five of them had been involved in the raid on Marshall. The irate governor wrote once again to General Davis and asserted, "I cannot reconcile it to my sense of duty to pass by in silence such cruel and barbarous conduct as is alleged to have characterized a portion of them, and more especially as the officers mentioned are citizens of this State."[32] Zeb was determined to bring the culprits to justice if it was within his power.

Zeb's efforts to bring Keith and his men to a civil trial failed due either to the obstruction or the extreme indifference of Confederate officials. When Zeb demanded action from Secretary of War James A. Seddon, an army investigation was launched and four junior officers of the Sixty-fourth North Carolina were placed under arrest. Further investigation yielded several affidavits that confirmed the details of the massacre. But neither the army nor Secretary Seddon made any public announcement about the fate of Keith and his four officers. Then, in May 1863, Merrimon broke the news to Zeb that Keith had been court-martialed and allowed to resign from the army. To the incredulous North Carolina governor, Seddon confirmed that Keith had not even been charged with the Laurel killings, and that he had indeed been allowed to resign. Furthermore, the army had not sought to keep him in custody, and Keith had escaped into the North Carolina mountains, where he would remain until the end of the war. The other four officers were also allowed to resign, and none of the participants in the massacre were ever brought to justice by the Confederate army.[33] Thus, Zeb's efforts were permanently frustrated, and his vigorous efforts were fruitless.

Zeb confronted another significant abuse perpetrated by the Confederate government in the winter of 1865. He received reports that the federal prisoners held in a prison camp in Salisbury, North Carolina, were in terrible condition. This subject was a matter of grave concern to Zeb for two reasons. First, his brother, General Robert Vance, was being held in the federal prison camp. Thanks to Bob's courteous handling of a prominent Unionist from eastern Tennessee whom he had imprisoned, he was well treated by his Unionist captors. Bob was even given a special assignment by the federal authorities to distribute clothing—much of which had been secured through Zeb's blockade-running program—that the Confederate authorities had purchased for Confederate prisoners of war. Zeb knew that if he were to be held accountable for the mistreatment of federal prisoners in North Carolina, however, the national government could retaliate against his brother.[34] In addition, it was becoming apparent by 1865 that those who mistreated federal prisoners of war would be held accountable when the fighting ended.

Given these motivations, Zeb reacted very strongly to the news about the bad conditions at Salisbury. An official at the prison camp informed Zeb of the particulars. The institution had been conceived of as a small prison to house Confederate soldiers detained by their own army. On November 5, 1864, however, approximately eight thousand federal prisoners of war were suddenly transferred to the inadequate facility. The officials at the prison believed they had done the best they could under the circumstances. They maintained that they had provided sufficient firewood to keep the captured soldiers warm during the cold winter, but very few prisoners were housed in any sort of shelter, and most were living in holes in the ground. The officials also asserted that adequate food supplies had been distributed. Unfortunately, there was not a reliable source of water at the prison. Considering how polluted the water sources at Andersonville and other Civil War prisons became, this may actually have been a blessing. Finally, the prison officials noted that the captured federal soldiers had an inadequate supply of clothing and blankets. Zeb quickly recognized that he could do something about the latter problem. He proposed to Robert Ould, the Confederate negotiator for prisoners of war, that North Carolina should supply clothing and blankets to the Salisbury soldiers in exchange for equivalent supplies to be given to a like number of Confederate prisoners in the North.[35] This bargain was apparently agreed to, and Zeb provided the Salisbury captives with clothing that had either been brought in through the blockade or made in

North Carolina. While Zeb's quick action prevented suffering at the camp from growing worse, the Salisbury camp was a death trap for many of its inmates, as were most other Civil War prison camps.

Much less important than the other controversies previously discussed, but nevertheless an important source of friction between Zeb and the Richmond government, were disagreements about questions of individual honor. One of the most persistent problems from Zeb's point of view was the unwillingness of the Confederate authorities to recognize worthy North Carolinians with promotions and positions in the army. Zeb was probably on the firmest ground with this grievance when he objected to the appointment of a Virginian to serve as director of conscription for the state of North Carolina in 1863, but there were other similar incidents. Zeb started one letter to Secretary Seddon by stating, "At Richmond a great portion of my complaint to President Davis was the presence of such a number of Virginians and Marylanders in our State filling the offices which were local and permanent in their character." He went on to demand the removal of five or six of the "most obnoxious" appointees from the state, noting that he had made this request a number of times before and no action had been taken. Zeb asserted that the matter involved more than state pride and honor. His missive was written in September 1863, when the first wave of public protest against the war had broken out in North Carolina. Zeb felt that the least the Confederacy could do in this hostile climate was make a small concession to public opinion. He concluded the letter, "I get disheartened at being so often foiled in my efforts to do something to quiet discontent."[36] While it is impossible to know how many of the appointed individuals from outside the state were eventually replaced with qualified North Carolinians, it is clear that Zeb's position was calculated to strengthen the war effort in North Carolina.

Of much less consequence to the Confederate war effort was Zeb's concern about appointment policy and promotion for officers in North Carolina regiments. Zeb maintained that he retained the authority to appoint the commanding officers to any North Carolina regiments formed before the passage of the Confederate Conscription Act. The Confederate authorities tried to placate the young governor in this matter, but the need for professional leadership in the Confederate army was their most pressing concern. The troops in the trenches also on occasion preferred to be led by a proven officer from outside of North Carolina than a less qualified man from their own state. Yet Zeb was galled by the fact that promotions in the Confederate army seemed to be based not on competence, but rather on political allegiance. He sarcastically noted that only 10 percent of the state's generals had been part of the large majority of North Carolinians who opposed secession in April 1861. Jefferson Davis took particular umbrage at this charge and wrote a detailed letter defending three promotions that Zeb had questioned.[37] From the present vantage point, the beleaguered president appears to have had the better argument; Zeb's problem was not actually with the Confederacy. The secessionist administrations that had dominated North Carolina's government for the first year of the war had made many political appointments. By the time that Zeb became governor, most of the important appointments had already been made. The brutality of the war, moreover, made combat skills rather than political connections the significant factor in most promotions.

While the aforementioned issues related directly to official business, the friction between Zeb and Confederate officials was caused in part by personality conflicts. As noted earlier, his correspondence with Randolph angered the aristocratic Virginian. Jefferson Davis, moreover, became incensed at Zeb on several occasions. Zeb's impatience with incompetence, combined with his frustration at the unwillingness of the Confederate government to acquiesce to all of his suggestions, irritated him and prompted him to write very sharp replies to letters from officials at all levels. Late in the winter of 1864, one of Zeb's letters sparked an open confrontation with the Confederate president. On February 9, Zeb had written a critical letter to Davis regarding certain activities of Confederate officials that the governor believed undermined public confidence. One sentence in the letter read, "I do not hold you responsible for all the petty annoyances, the insolence of office, under which our people lose heart and patience." This reasonably straightforward assertion—typical of Zeb—insulted the sensitive president.[38] On February 29, Davis penned a very stiff letter back to the youthful governor. In part he wrote, "I make no comment on this language, as I must suppose that you deem it becoming our mutual positions, and simply invite you to state what portion of these petty annoyances and this 'insolence of office' you do impute to me, and the facts on which the imputation rests." Davis declared that he would restrict all future contact with Zeb to strictly official correspondence. In reply, Zeb vigorously denied that he had included the president in his criticism of Confederate officials. He further stated, "I trust I am incapable of needlessly and wantonly insulting the Chief Magistrate of the Confederate States, and have ever endeavored in making unpleasant statements to you to avoid discourtesy, while expressing myself with candor." Refusing to back down, Zeb then cataloged a significant number of North Carolina's grievances against the Confederacy and the national government's failure to provide redress for them.[39] Correspondence between the two men continued after this exchange without any apparent acrimony. Apparently Davis was unused to being dealt with so brazenly, but Zeb's refusal to feel insulted when Davis became defensive made their continued relationship possible.

Zeb was not impervious to insult, however. There were a number of occasions when the actions of Confederate officials greatly angered him. The most sensational episode took place in Wilmington in early July 1863. Zeb made a special trip to meet the *Advance*, which had just returned to the North Carolina port. Realizing that all persons on board were subject to a fifteen-day quarantine, Zeb obtained permission from the military officials and the commissioners of navigation to board the ship and then immediately return to Raleigh. When he sought to leave the ship, however, a Lieutenant Colonel Thornburg refused to allow him to disembark. When Zeb showed Thornburg the documentation that gave him permission to circumvent the quarantine, the officer replied that he "did not care for Governor Vance nor Governor Jesus Christ." The officer then posted guards with orders to shoot anyone who tried to get off the ship. Once the fuming governor was freed, he wrote an indignant letter to Davis demanding that the offending soldier be instantly transferred.[40]

Despite unpleasant episodes such as this one, the relationship between Zeb and the Confederate government was usually productive. The young governor was a vigorous advocate of Southern independence and an energetic and imaginative administrator. Thus, he was often personally present at trouble spots to witness the inadequacies of the Confederate bureaucracy firsthand. Zeb's impatience with incompetence and the slow pace of bureaucracy led him to make aggressive statements in an attempt to solve problems. At the same time, Zeb was much more aware of popular dissatisfaction with Confederate policies than the Richmond government was. He knew that loyalty on the home front was fragile for both economic and social reasons in most parts of North Carolina. He also recognized that the growing problem of desertion among North Carolina troops was caused in large part by soldiers' concern for their families. The obtuseness of Davis, Seddon, and others to this reality caused many disagreements about policy implementation between the governor of North Carolina and Confederate officials. There were times, of course, when Zeb himself took the politically expedient route of protecting elite privilege in the state, such as when he refused to coerce slaveowners to provide laborers for the Danville line of the railroad or when he appointed local notables to conscription-proof public offices. This behavior was not unique during the war; the Confederate government itself had instituted a series of war policies that discriminated against the nonelite. All of the people involved in disagreements with Zeb were working with him toward one objective: Southern independence. Whatever conflicts occurred did so in that context. Zeb's efforts were primarily directed to speeding up and improving the Confederate war effort, not impeding it.

When Zeb presented his first message to the state legislature, North Carolinians had already begun to experience the hardships that would rule their lives during the remainder of the war. In many households in the state, a husband, son, nephew, uncle, or brother had been killed or dangerously wounded. The shock of these events to the families and communities directly affected was devastating. Not only did the deaths create a personal void that could never be completely filled, but they also removed needed producers from local economies. Because many North Carolinians had joined the Confederacy reluctantly and only at the last minute, their commitment to the new nation was often both tenuous and incomplete. Grief and financial hardship took their toll as the war progressed, increasingly causing discontent among certain segments of the state's population. Zeb and other leaders recognized that old policies would not suffice in this emergency.

At the same time, the leadership of North Carolina proved unwilling to make some of the sacrifices necessary for the state to make a maximum contribution to the war effort. Zeb and his allies felt, quite accurately, that because of their previous political affiliations or their positions on secession they had been systematically excluded from positions of responsibility and denied promotions. Now that they controlled the governor's office and the legislature, however, their decisions about patronage and electoral matters could not be blocked. Unlike Abraham Lincoln in the federal government, Zeb and his friends made little effort to reconcile with their political enemies. They turned both prominent and lesser-known secessionist leaders out of office and put their bitter opponents in place. While Zeb's policy initiatives were often in line with what the secessionists approved, these patriotic Confederates were marginalized in the country that they had founded, and such poor treatment alienated many people who might have been able to make significant contributions to the war effort. Zeb and his political allies may have found it personally satisfying to exact revenge, but their actions were partly responsible for splintering the political leadership of

North Carolina. While Zeb was often not the leader of these vendettas, he appointed the men who carried out this shortsighted policy.

Developments beyond the control of Zeb and his political allies, moreover, accentuated the divisions in North Carolina. The financial policies of the Confederate government had a particularly significant impact. The Confederate leadership, reflecting the financial self-interest of the elite, decided not to use taxes to finance a significant part of the war costs. Instead, the Confederacy had issued bonds and paper money. The result was a significant increase in the price of all goods. For those people involved in the cash economy, this development was not a disaster. They were able to charge higher prices for their products and services, and they often suffered little economic deprivation. However, for those North Carolinians who generated little cash in their normal economic transactions—the vast majority of white farmers and farmworkers in the state—the inflated prices of necessities caused tremendous hardship. Families that had been largely self-sufficient experienced great want.

It was in this atmosphere of growing crisis and division that Zeb had made his first address to the North Carolina legislature on November 15, 1862. Zeb began his long state paper with an analysis of the popular mood. He noted that the great mass of the white population had entered the contest with enthusiasm and was actually taking the lead in the uncharted course of secession. Zeb soberly observed, however, that the first, easy phase of the war had ended, and a new reality had to be faced. Zeb had called upon the General Assembly to set an example for the remainder of the state by showing a strong determination to sustain the Confederate cause. He had cautioned its members that they had to ensure that civil liberties were preserved despite the present emergency.[1]

Many of Zeb's efforts to unite the white population of North Carolina behind the war effort were undone by Zeb's political allies in the newly elected legislature. A leading secessionist complained: "The heart sickens at the sight of such doings. Never, never, in the worst days of party bitterness, did I witness any intolerance to be compared with it."[2] The wholesale changes made by the Conservative Party ensured that partisan battles would remain a significant factor in North Carolina politics throughout the remainder of the war. Of course, Vance and his allies argued that their actions were simply a normal reaction to the extreme partisanship shown by the secessionists after they had assumed power in the spring of 1861. If the North Carolina secessionists and the Confederate government had made active efforts to reconcile with their political opponents, the overreaction of Vance and his allies in the Conservative Party probably would not have taken place. Unfortunately for the Confederate cause in North Carolina, the Conservative counterrevolution was so complete and so ruthless that it ensured there would be a permanent and hostile opposition to the Vance administration.

The secessionists were infuriated not simply because they were turned out of office, but also because they objected to many of the people who took their places. The election of a Confederate States senator prompted the first test of strength between the two factions. The incumbent was George Davis, who, while a Whig like most of the Conservatives, was widely perceived to be a moderate. In February 1861, Davis had refused to call for separation from the United States as long as the Washington Peace Conference continued. Political leaders in North Carolina recognized, however, that Davis had worked behind the scenes with secessionists much earlier than that. Davis's Conservative opponent was William A. Graham, the leading former Whig in the state and Zeb's personal mentor. Graham's win by a vote of seventy to thirty-two confirmed the Conservatives' ascendancy. As dismayed as the secessionists were by Davis's defeat, however, they were thunderstruck by the results of the contest for state treasurer. The incumbent, D. W. Courts, was accused of using his office to benefit his friends and associates "in handing out 8 per cent Treasury notes and bonds." While the secessionists might have been willing to accept Courts' defeat with some equanimity because he had been charged with misusing state funds, they could not accept his replacement. As mentioned earlier, the Conservatives selected Jonathan Worth of Randolph County to run the finance office. Randolph County was the center of anti-Confederate feeling in central North Carolina, and other Worth family members had worked actively against slavery and the formation of the Confederacy.[3]

The Conservatives refused to recognize the legitimacy of their opponents' concerns. They defended the changes that they had made to the state bureaucracy without offering justifications much beyond political expediency. While an occasional Democrat was spared and some offices were left unfilled, the partisan nature of the purge was obvious to all. Former governor Charles Manly's critique of the Conservatives in the legislature, noted earlier, rings true.[4] For the remainder of the war, Zeb and his fellow Conservatives would have to deal with the hostility of the secessionists, a group that could have been conciliated fairly easily if greater efforts had been made to view the war effort as a common cause.

Zeb's calls to the general population to give greater efforts to sustain the Confederacy ran into growing opposition from the other side of the political spectrum, the Unionists. North Carolinians in such disparate regions as the coves of the western mountains, the central Piedmont, and the coastal plain began to work actively against the Confederate war effort. While some of these people were devoted loyalists to the Union, others simply opposed either the war or the Davis administration's policies. In response to the challenges to state and Confederate authority, Zeb used local militias and requested Confederate troops to round up the dissatisfied on a number of occasions. At other times, however, he issued proclamations offering amnesty to the disaffected and to those who had deserted from Confederate service. In addition, he sought to ameliorate the conditions that tempted some to leave their posts in an attempt to protect their families. While Zeb's efforts were quite energetic, they were never completely successful.

Hostility toward the Confederacy in North Carolina was concentrated most predictably in the eastern counties, where the Union army had established a permanent position. The presence of a safe haven for those opposed to the Confederacy emboldened many eastern North Carolinians to take up arms against Vance's government. Confederate General Samuel G. French made Vance's job in that part of the state no easier. French made a sweep of the eastern counties, arbitrarily arrested approximately forty men for disloyalty, and sent them to the Confederate prison at Salisbury. Eventually the men would be turned over to the state government and freed, but confidence in the impartiality of the Confederate authorities was sharply reduced due to the incident. This and similar episodes prompted the following comment from one of Vance's correspondents: "The people of Johnston County owe allegiance, first to *North Carolina*[,] Secondly to the Confederate States, and accordingly, to my Humble judgment *protection* is due from North Carolina to her Citizens even against the injustice of the Confederate Authorities."[5] Feelings like these made Vance's efforts to maintain the domestic peace in North Carolina very difficult.

The eastern counties quickly became a region where regular law enforcement was eroded, and irregular forces often controlled large portions of the countryside. The frequency with which slaves were able to escape from their masters became a major problem for the elite in the area. In the counties south of the rail center of Weldon and near the occupied town of Plymouth, scores of slaves escaped to Union lines. These slaves knew their former homes intimately, and they often acted as guides for raiding parties that ravaged their former owners' property. One distraught correspondent informed Zeb that "in a recent marauding expedition of the abolitionists, large quantities of . . . supplies were destroyed & horses necessary to save the crops were stolen & carried off." He went on to observe that the plantation owners were in a state of panic and were moving their families and enslaved workers to the interior part of the state for protection. He protested that the actions of the Confederate army were little better. In the name of denying the federal government access to the supplies of the region, the Confederate forces were burning cotton and other valuable products. He and his fellow planters protested "this singular method of *defending* a Country by burning up the sources of its wealth." While the correspondent was obviously motivated by self-interest to write his letter, Zeb had reasons to share his concerns.[6] The property that was being destroyed was essential to the financial well-being of the state and the welfare of its free population. Furthermore, the threat posed by the social revolution in eastern North Carolina was a challenge that Zeb and his government had to address.

Local Confederate sympathizers sought to protect themselves from the threats posed by local Unionists—known as Buffaloes—by taking the initiative. Herman Stilley wrote to Vance asking permission to raise an irregular company of approximately twenty men. Stilley assured Zeb that he and his men would supply themselves and would ask for no pay. They would be useful in "driving out the plunderers" and controlling "gangs of runaway & Starving negroes." There is no record of any reply from Vance to Stilley, and he did not immediately sanction the kind of retaliatory warfare suggested in the letter. But William T. Dortch, Confederate senator from North Carolina, did not match Zeb's reticence in the matter. Reacting to the implementation of President Lincoln's Emancipation Proclamation, which further unsettled social conditions in the eastern part of North Carolina, he encouraged Zeb to enforce all state laws about arming blacks by executing all blacks who were armed and any whites found in their company. Dortch thought, in fact, that there might be some need to strengthen the laws in this area.[7] There is no record that Zeb acted upon this suggestion, although he was as disturbed as Dortch and other slaveowners in the state were about the threat to slavery.

The only successful method of diminishing the threat posed by the Buffaloes and their African American allies appeared to be to use Confederate troops. A small Confederate band attacked an equally small Unionist contingent at Wingfield on November 17, 1862. While not successful, the assault forced the Buffaloes to strengthen their fortifications and limit their attacks on the local population. On December 10, a Confederate force of three hundred infantry and seventy-five cavalry attacked the federal forces in the town of Plymouth. The federals put up little effective resistance, despite their possession of a gunboat anchored in the harbor. The victorious Confederates were unable to dislodge the federal force from the customs house, but in the process they burned the majority of the dwellings in the community. They also killed or captured several dozen slaves, some of whom were owned by Unionists and some of whom had run away from

Confederate masters.[8] While these two attacks did not dislodge the threat posed by Union forces, they did curtail their activities in eastern North Carolina for the immediate future. Zeb had little direct influence, in any case, on events in the far eastern part of the state, where regular and irregular armed forces determined the direction the war would take.

In the Piedmont and mountain sections of North Carolina, Confederate authority was not challenged directly by the federal army. Despite this significant advantage, however, Vance and the state authorities were forced to expend considerable effort to try to counter anti-Confederate activities in both areas. While loyalty to the Union motivated many of the members of the opposition, some viewed the draft and other coercive Confederate policies as sufficient cause to resist. Still others began to turn against the Confederate cause due to the hardship that they and their families were forced to endure as the conflict grew longer and consumed the relatively scarce resources of rural North Carolina. A Raleigh newspaper reported that the wives and children of some soldiers had to receive state assistance or face starvation. Zeb wrote to Confederate officials begging that salt be provided to the state's civilian population. He warned, "The condition of every class of our people will be truly deplorable, unless salt is brought to them." Historian Paul Escott has noted that Confederate troops began to impress supplies in many areas, forcing local governments to provide assistance where they could.[9] The combination of scarcity, opposition to Confederate policies, and lingering Unionism ensured that Vance and the state authorities in North Carolina faced considerable, growing opposition throughout the state.

In the Piedmont, opposition to the Confederacy centered in Randolph, Chatham, and Moore Counties. Some of this opposition posed no direct threat to public order, but it was nevertheless indicative of the absence of consensus. For example, Bryan Tyson of Randolph County launched a quixotic peace campaign. Tyson was exempted from conscription because of his talents as a maker of agricultural implements. He used his time trying to convince Confederate leaders, including Vance, that the war should be ended and reunion with the federal government sought. He composed a reunion pamphlet in September 1862 and sent copies to Confederate political leaders. Later, he was arrested when he tried to distribute the same pamphlet to civilians riding a train between Raleigh and Richmond. Tyson was brought before Vance, who released him after three days. Zeb apparently judged Tyson to be mentally unstable, but the young governor did extract a promise from the Unionist that he would stop distributing his pamphlet. Tyson was unable to contain himself, however, and he soon sent copies of his publication to the members of the state legislature. Zeb was probably relieved when Tyson escaped across Union lines in eastern North Carolina and spent the remainder of the war in Washington, D.C.[10]

Although Tyson was no threat to the stability of Piedmont society, others were. As William T. Auman has demonstrated in a number of studies, the revolt against the Confederacy in the central Piedmont was persistent, often violent, and beyond the means of Vance and the Confederate government to fully suppress. Tyson indicated after the war that he had joined an anti-Confederate organization, the Heroes of America, in the fall of 1862. Whether or not his memory was accurate is not crucial, because events soon demonstrated that opposition to the state and Confederate governments was widespread and partially organized. When Zeb ordered militia officers in the Piedmont counties to suppress open dissent, they found it impossible. Some of those officials' attitudes toward the Confederacy were sufficiently similar to their neighbors' that they did not want to harass them. Other officials were threatened and visited with violence for carrying out their mandated assignments. For example, John A. Craven of Randolph County reported: "On Saturday night last an officer that lives within a mile of me arrested a conscript a neighbour of His. The Next Night the officers Barn with all its Contents Except His Horses was burned to the ground." Another incident in Yadkin County illustrated the difficulties facing law enforcement officials. An observer reported: "The Capt says he could have shot him down or at the risk of his life have attempted to arrest him but as he was a man of most desperate character and has 5 other brothers as bad as himself, the better plan he thought was to let him alone — It is the opinion of the well affected neighbors in order to avoid bloodshed that the best policy would be to send an officer with 12 or 15 armed men."[11] Clearly, local authorities were not strong enough to handle this situation.

Recognizing that fact, Vance began a systematic campaign to try to rid the central counties of overt opposition to the Confederacy. According to a regular army officer who tried to arrest a deserter in Iredell, the local militia captain's father was a notorious Tory who "curse[d] and abuse[d] the confederacy and declare[d] that all secessionists ought to be hung." As a result, the local population took the failure of the Tory's son to enforce the law as justification for not obeying it. When the regular army officer and another regular soldier tried to arrest a deserter, the deserter's family attacked them. Although the deserter was wounded, he escaped as his defenders — including four women — threw rocks at the soldiers. The exasperated officer, R. R. Crawford, warned the young governor, "if some step is not taken to put it down there will be many deserters in that neighborhood."[12] Zeb had little choice but to take that advice to heart.

A serious incident that took place in Yadkin County in mid-February

1863 indicated the limits of using the local militia against men who had deserted the army and understood military tactics. A local Confederate leader told Zeb, "There has been a strong feeling against the conscript law among the uninformed part of the citizens here ever since its passage." A group of deserters in the county had combined with approximately one hundred of these draft dodgers to create a formidable force. A squad of fourteen militia members came upon a group of deserters and conscript evaders numbering between twenty and thirty who were carefully protected by a school building. In the skirmish that followed, two on each side were killed and only four of the fugitives were captured. What made the situation even worse was that those who escaped remained "at large," and as one Yadkin County official explained, "the section of the County is so disloyal . . . it will be exceedingly difficult to find them."[13] This episode provided convincing evidence that local defense forces could never squelch anti-Confederates unless they had overwhelmingly superior numbers.

The militia in Robeson County also proved to be unable to handle local anti-Confederate forces. The militia had to deal with a group of twenty deserters from the regular army while spending most of its time watching a large free black population that was described as "very lawless." Furthermore, because most white males had volunteered for service, the militia had few members and virtually no ammunition. The result was that the families of soldiers were particularly vulnerable to attack, and several people had lost all of their property to the band of deserters. Even those persons who avoided choosing sides were coerced "by threats of burning their houses & destroying their effects." Because Robeson County bordered on South Carolina, moreover, another gang of forty to fifty deserters crossed the border at will.[14] Clearly, this was a situation in which local authorities were unable to bring order to their communities.

As difficult as matters were in these counties, the situation in the central Piedmont region that included Randolph, Moore, and Chatham Counties was viewed as more threatening. Dissenting groups in that region appeared to be organized across county lines and opposed to the Confederacy itself, rather than objecting to Confederate policies. The event that fostered anti-Confederate feeling in this region was the passage of the Conscription Act in April 1862. The act allowed owners of twenty or more slaves to be exempt from the workings of the law. One self-described "poor soldier" shared his view of the Conscription Act with Vance, a view that was pervasive in the central counties and elsewhere in the state: "The Govt. has made a distinction between the rich man (who has something to fight for) and the poor man who fights for that he will never have. The exemption of the owners of 20 negroes & the allowing of substitutes clearly proves it. Healthy and

active men who have furnished substitutes are grinding the poor by speculation while their substitutes have been discharged after a month's service
as being too old or as invalids. . . . Now Govr. do tell me how we soldiers who
are fighting for the 'rich mans negro' can support our families at $11 per
month?"[15] Zeb, of course, had no answer for the questions posed by this
soldier and others in the central counties. Nor did he have an answer for
the many Quakers and others who opposed the war on religious grounds.
He was forced to resort to coercion to ensure sufficient social order for the
war effort to continue.

Even before the Conscription Act was passed and implemented, there
were serious problems in the central counties. Before October 1862, 42
percent of the total wartime desertions in Randolph County for the entire war had already taken place. Many deserters, most likely in conjunction with Unionists, joined together in an organization called the Heroes
of America. The leader of this resistance group was William Owens, who
seized effective control of the rural parts of the county. The Heroes kid-
napped members of the militia, forced them to take an oath of allegiance
to the United States, and then set them free, threatening to kill them if
they turned against Owens and his followers. Confederate loyalists and the
Heroes of America took violent action against each other's followers. Barns
were burned; crops and smoked meat were stolen; civilians on both sides
were threatened with death. Even women and children were targets of violence as local partisans attacked the weak points of their opposition.[16]

When local and state militia forces proved unable to curb anti-Confederate resistance in the central Piedmont, Zeb ordered a regiment of Confederate troops into the region in January 1863. While the soldiers managed
to arrest several dozen deserters, the resistance was not broken. The Confederate officer in charge became particularly discouraged when he discovered that the men he had returned to the army quickly deserted again
and returned to their home areas. In February, the local militia was called
out again to try to eliminate deserters and Unionists, both thought to be
menaces to public order. This time the force included a cavalry unit that
provided far greater mobility to the militiamen.[17] In this instance, Zeb demonstrated considerable personal initiative in attempting to put down opposition to the Confederacy. He had no sympathy for Unionists and deserters,
and he was willing to use national forces to try to eliminate opposition to
the Confederate war effort.

Events in the mountain counties of eastern Tennessee proved to be the
catalyst for an outbreak of violence in western North Carolina. Although
Zeb was deeply concerned about his fellow mountaineers in North Carolina, he initially viewed the developments in eastern Tennessee as dis-

similar to what was happening in Piedmont North Carolina. Certainly, the Unionist revolt in east Tennessee found no other parallel in the Confederacy with the exception of that in what would become the state of West Virginia. The rebellion began during the night of November 18, 1861, when local Unionist vigilante groups burned five bridges over the Tennessee River to prevent Confederate reinforcements from reaching the area after the Union army invaded from Kentucky. When the federal invasion failed to materialize, a large number of Unionists were captured, and five were hanged along the route of the railroad. Following this striking incident, Confederate authorities arrested and imprisoned hundreds of Unionists, most without benefit of a trial. Many other Unionists sought to escape prosecution by leaving Tennessee. Most of them headed for Kentucky and joined the Union army, but a small number armed themselves and hid in the border counties of western North Carolina. The situation was exacerbated in the spring of 1862 when the Confederacy introduced conscription and imposed martial law on the beleaguered region. Conscripts who were forced into the army usually deserted; in fact, in December 1862 two companies of new recruits deserted to the mountains of western North Carolina.[18] The introduction of these embattled Unionists into western North Carolina sparked more violence in that region.

At the same time that guerrilla warfare was taking place in east Tennessee, the first direct military confrontation in western North Carolina took place. Part of the Forty-third Tennessee Regiment swept through the Laurel area of Madison County, killing fifteen men who resisted the advance in small groups. Although this effort seemed successful, the Confederate commander reported that the anti-Confederate partisans still controlled the area. Shortly thereafter, local militia organized by Marcus Erwin marched into Laurel. This local force, which was more familiar with the lay of the land than the Confederate troops had been, blocked all exits from the area. The militiamen then systematically swept through the area, forcing some Laurel men into the Confederate army and arresting the remainder, nearly forty in all. Most of the men rounded up in this operation quickly deserted, and they were soon joined by deserters from the regular army and those hiding out to avoid being conscripted.[19]

While local Unionists and deserters were slow to defy the Confederacy openly in the western highlands, in late 1862 there were already indications of the trouble to come. A large group of men broke into the Haywood County Jail to rescue a convicted murderer in November of that year. While many of the mob members were subsequently apprehended, the incident indicated that citizens were growing more willing to challenge traditional authority figures. The state government made the situation worse by labeling Unionists in the mountain counties as "enemy aliens" and confiscating their land in an attempt to coerce them into submission. Mountain residents became increasingly resentful, and they more and more often resorted to passive resistance. In one Macon County community, individuals facing conscription reached a private agreement as to which men would join the army and which ones would stay home and provide for the families. Those who remained behind were devastated when the Confederate government refused to honor their pact and forced them into the army. Others sought to secure jobs that would give them an exemption from conscription under Confederate legislation. In Rutherford and Polk Counties, a number of possible conscripts divided mail routes amongst themselves and claimed to be immune from military service.[20] The entire region was greatly unsettled and, if the right circumstances presented themselves, its people were ready to explode in opposition to the Confederacy.

Zeb's actions in the mountains were characteristic of his wartime policies involving civilian populations. Because Union soldiers were present in the town, he was not outraged when Confederate soldiers destroyed Plymouth. He did not seek to restrain the state troops in the Piedmont when they attacked their neighbors. But he did react angrily when Confederate soldiers killed civilians in the mountains. While his actions throughout the war were not absolutely consistent, it is clear that Zeb had developed a rough policy to follow in North Carolina's internecine battles. He became upset when Confederate troops were used to threaten or harm North Carolina's civilians. In virtually every other circumstance, Zeb tolerated official violence directed against deserters and Unionists. To many of those who actively or passively opposed the Confederacy, Zeb's policy was a distinction without a difference. But to Zeb, this policy of defending Confederate authority in North Carolina against encroachment proved to be useful for dealing with far more than the problem of civil unrest.

If desertion and disloyalty had been the only issues troubling current and potential deserters, then Zeb's job would have been relatively easy. Mily Barker wrote to Zeb that the relief committee in her county was "not doing justice to . . . soldiers wives." Another woman informed the governor, "My husband has been taken away from myself & family as a disloyalist whitch I think has been caused by desyning men that wont go into the army themselves but prefer to stay at home & speculate by selling the wives of soldiers good[s] at 500 per cent."[21] These women's problems did not stay confined at home, because their kinfolk in the army felt impelled to leave the service to assist them. Not only did many soldiers leave the army, but some of those who remained came to see the war in terms of class conflict within the Confederacy. Zeb recognized that he was dealing with a politically complex situation—a fact that the authorities in Richmond never seemed to appreciate.

A direct challenge to state and Confederate authority materialized in the western Piedmont city of Salisbury. In that place and in broad daylight, women not only seized food from government holdings, but claimed their right to do so. While their action was similar to developments in other states, it greatly concerned Zeb. He grew more troubled when women in the cities of Greensboro and Durham sought to emulate their sisters in Salisbury and were only prevented from doing so by the actions of local authorities. Rural women in Johnston County broke into a corncrib and carried away food to feed their starving families. Zeb issued an address in early April that reached most of the state through the pages of the *North Carolina Standard*. He noted that the state was facing the "calamities" of "scarcity of provisions and threatened famine." Since the legislature was not in session, Zeb announced that he was acting unilaterally. He called upon farmers to stop growing commercial crops like cotton and to concentrate instead upon food production. Showing the impact of the Salisbury, Greensboro, Durham, and Johnston County 'raids' on his thinking, he concluded his address: "Avoid, above all, mob violence. Broken laws will give you no bread, but much sorrow; and when forcible seizures have to be made to avert starvation, let it be done by your County or State agents."[22]

Zeb's address had contradictory effects. Apparently many people who had been hoarding food in the expectation that future supplies would be limited became convinced that Zeb's appeal to farmers would work. Reports came to Zeb that food was suddenly available to most citizens, and prices went into decline. On top of that, the spring harvest of 1863 was a good one. The situation improved so dramatically, in fact, that Zeb offered a delighted Seddon 250,000 pounds of bacon for the Confederate army in late April. At the same time that the civilian situation seemed under better control, however, desertions from North Carolina regiments continued without any reduction. An angry general reported that one of his regiments had lost two hundred men recently. This prompted Zeb once again to negotiate with the Confederate authorities to offer an amnesty to any North Carolina deserters who returned to their regiments. He issued this appeal in early May, and a reported two thousand men rejoined their units as a result.[23] Despite this limited success, Zeb knew that both civilian and military morale were still unstable.

Into this volatile situation, the increasingly desperate Confederate government sent an incendiary message. It introduced a new tax. The modified income tax required citizens to provide the government with 10 percent of the value of their production each year. For those who provided services or ran commercial establishments, this meant that they could pay their share in rapidly depreciating Confederate currency—usually not a hardship. The farmers who made up the vast majority of the state's population, however, had to pay the "tithe" in scarce produce. This tax in kind was to be collected by specially appointed county agents or, in the worst case, by Confederate troops seeking to feed their horses and themselves.[24] Quite a lot of these foodstuffs would eventually be used to feed the hungry and destitute, but the tax was nevertheless widely resented by the small farming and tenant farming population. The new tax, like conscription, was perceived as an unconscionable interference in the lives of the people of North Carolina. There was a growing feeling among many in the state that they had little to gain from their new government.

As the impact of the new tax law became clearer, resistance to the Confederacy began to surface in more menacing forms. In the central Piedmont region around Moore, Chatham, and Randolph Counties, attempts to restore order had only worsened the situation. Troops dealing with the recalcitrant civilian population began to threaten and to use violence to combat opposition to the Confederacy. According to historian William T. Auman, "Citizens charged that military authorities had illegally impressed horses and fodder, tortured and beat persons taken captive, fired into groups of unarmed outliers without giving them a chance to surrender, and tortured, plundered, and abused the wives and children of outliers' families." In light of these abuses, local authorities began to side with their neighbors against state and central government authorities.[25]

The people in the mountain counties to the west also expressed growing disenchantment with the Confederacy. The *North Carolina Standard* printed a letter from a resident of McDowell County on May 1, 1863, that stated, "We are all anxious for peace here, if we can have it honorably." Zeb received private correspondence that confirmed that the correspondent had assessed the situation accurately; about three weeks later, G. W. Dobson, also from McDowell County, informed Zeb, "There are a number of deserters lurking about in this county and the militia are maken no effort to arrest them and they are a doing a great deal of mischief." Many other mountaineers wrote to Zeb confirming that the developments in McDowell County were being duplicated all along the ridge.[26] Particularly worrisome was the fact that local government officials in the mountains seemed to be siding with their disaffected neighbors, just as their counterparts did in the Piedmont.

Increasingly, some of the state's newspapers began to reflect the growing disillusionment of their readers. Articles, editorials, and letters to the editor that appeared on a sporadic basis soon offered a consistent set of messages. One such message was that if the fighting continued, it would lead to greater centralization of power and consequently to the loss of liberty. The only way to avoid this undesirable outcome would be to seek peace as soon as possible. William W. Holden began to promote this theme starting as early as March 1863. Responses from readers quickly followed. One correspondent from Transylvania County stated, "We up this way, like yourself, desire peace, but are fearful that fighting will never bring it." Holden was joined by John L. Pennington of the *Daily Progress*, who wrote on April 3, "We ask for no dishonorable peace; we should accept no peace that would degrade our people, and would scorn any peace that refused the South her rights—but we want peace nevertheless." The editor of the *People's Press* of Salem also expressed his willingness to enter into peace negotiations.[27] These avowals of interest in finding a way to end the war were quite ambiguous. None of the editors was willing to accept reunion and the end to slavery, the Lincoln administration's two preconditions for negotiating for peace. Apparently, they hoped that those people devoted to ending the war in the North and South could work together and pressure or circumvent their existing governments.

In 1863, the peace forces pressured Zeb even further. Former state senator James Thomas Leach wrote a letter to the weekly *North Carolina Standard* in May in which he called for an end to the fighting and used the phrase "the Constitution as it is, the Union as it was." The phrase had become the political slogan of many Northern Democrats, and it represented a potential basis for peace negotiations. The problem for Zeb and others loyal to the Confederacy was that the slogan indicated that Leach would accept reunion if slavery was preserved. Since Leach owned a large plantation and more than forty slaves, this stance was a financial as well as a political position. On June 3, Holden editorialized, "North Carolina must be the equal of the other states of the Confederacy, or she will leave it, and endeavor to take care of herself." This threat was a rhetorical device Holden used to impress his readers with the seriousness of his concerns rather than a call for counterrevolution. Two weeks later, Holden offered the following observation: "The people of both sections are tired of war and desire peace. We desire it on terms honorable to our section, and we cannot expect it on terms dishonorable to the other section."[28] Like Leach, Holden appears to have been willing to accept a peace that would have been acceptable to peace-seeking Northerners. He refused to be more specific, contending that it was not the appropriate time to do so.

Holden and the others who spoke out during the spring of 1863 infuriated many North Carolinians; officers in the army were particularly incensed. Like Zeb, they were quite concerned about their state's reputation. D. H. Hill wrote to Zeb: "I learn that desertion is enormously on the increase in Lee's army & mainly & in fact almost entirely from North Carolina. This is very very mortifying. . . . this sorry state of things is due to the teachings at home. The blood of the poor deserter will rest upon the hearts of the Editors & the Politicians who fomented discontent for the sake of making capital." Hill's point was seconded by James J. Pettigrew in a May 22 letter to Zeb: "General Lee telegraphs me that men from our State are deserting every day. . . . We have watched for some months the course of certain newspapers, and a majority of the Legislature. I regret to say that I have not seen from either a single word calculated to aid us in our efforts."[29] It is clear from these letters that both their writers and people at the top of the Confederate military and political systems were concerned about the situation in North Carolina.

But Zeb knew better than to blame desertion solely on the editors and political figures. He recognized that Holden and others were reporting certain segments of popular opinion accurately. Zeb also thought that much of the unrest in North Carolina had been created by the shortsighted policies and ineptitude of the very Confederate officials who complained to him. Thus by June of 1863, Zeb found himself in a most difficult situation. Morale on the home front and among some North Carolina soldiers was beginning to deteriorate. The normal hardships of the war were being compounded by the failures of the central government. And popular discontent was being identified and partially shaped by his political allies in the press. The situation was not yet critical, but all that was required to make it so was some development that would focus people's attention on these issues.

Tragic events in early July provided just the fuel needed to light a fire of popular unrest. Confederate defeats at Vicksburg and Gettysburg destroyed all hope of a quick Confederate victory and an early end to the war. In fact, these decisive Union victories called into question the very viability of the Confederacy itself. Equally important, North Carolina regiments suffered catastrophic losses, particularly at Gettysburg. For Zeb, the fate of his former comrades in the Twenty-sixth North Carolina Regiment was particularly poignant. This unit fought desperate engagements on July 1 and July 3 and left the battlefield having suffered casualties of approximately 90 percent. Virtually all of Zeb's fellow officers were dead or seriously wounded, including Henry K. Burgwyn, who was killed on July 1. James J. Pettigrew informed Vance that his former regiment covered itself with glory, but the fact remained that there was virtually no regiment left. Since soldiers from specific counties formed companies together, the losses were magnified. Martin Crawford reports that one Ashe County unit suffered eleven killed and sixty-six wounded out of a total of ninety-two men during the July 1 battle alone.[30] Such losses were catastrophic for many communities across North Carolina. Many people in the state began to openly question the need to continue the conflict.

The news from Gettysburg was slow in reaching North Carolina. Zeb heard about the battle earlier than most of the people in the state. J. J. Young of the Twenty-sixth Regiment reported to his former commanding officer on the day after the battle, "It was a second Fredericksburg, only the wrong way." Letters from Samuel McDowell Tate, D. H. Hill, and James J. Pettigrew confirmed that North Carolinians had fought gallantly in a losing cause.[1] It would be more than a week before most of the state's residents would start to realize the enormity of the news from Vicksburg and Gettysburg. Even then many of the particulars remained unknown, but it was increasingly obvious that the Confederacy faced a crisis.

Fortunately for Zeb, he had called a special session of the legislature to meet on July 3. Two important initiatives came out of this session. The first was legislation that allowed Zeb to recruit the seven thousand militiamen requested by President Davis. As Zeb wrote to the Confederate president, this legislation was not as strong as it could have been. He explained: "I visited the Legislature in secret session and urged them to draft magistrates and militia officers. They declined to do so and adopted the exemption bill of Congress, which I fear will prevent me from raising the whole number required." On a more positive note from Zeb's perspective, the legislators in special session finally passed a law that would give state authorities some of the tools they felt they needed to deal with unrest. The bill was entitled "An Act to Punish Aiders and Abettors of Deserters."[2] Rather than rely on Confederate forces, who were often deeply resented, to keep the peace in North Carolina, this legislation allowed local law enforcement officers and the state militia to take the initiative.

Zeb also continued his efforts to remove North Carolinians' causes for resentment of Confederate treatment. On July 6, before he knew the full extent of the disaster in Pennsylvania, Zeb wrote a very plain letter to Jefferson Davis. He complained, "The last appointment by the Q. Master General, of a Col. [Edmund] Bradford of Norfolk Va., to the Chief Collectorship of the tax in kind for this State, have given almost universal offence, and I may be excused for saying, very justly." Zeb argued that his primary objective in asking for a North Carolinian to be appointed to the position was "to remove any cause so far as may be, for dissatisfaction."[3] Clearly Zeb recognized that the citizens of North Carolina had enough causes for complaint without the Confederacy adding more.

Davis apparently sought to placate Vance by first dealing with the vexatious conscription issue. On July 14, he wrote an apologetic letter to Vance about exemptions under the conscript law. He started the letter by observing, "In enforcing the enrolment of conscripts, it has been my desire to comply as far as possible with the views & wishes of the Governors of the several States, in all cases where there seemed to be any fair doubt as to the intention of Congress." He went on to concede virtually every point that Zeb had made about the necessity for North Carolina to exempt militia officers, state executive and judicial officials, policemen and constables, and justices of the peace. Davis noted that this policy had been in place for a number of months and that he hoped "all difficulties [had] been satisfactorily adjusted."[4] This would not be the case, as individual exemption cases would cause additional conflicts between the two governments.

Four days later, Davis wrote again to Zeb and addressed the matter of the new tax collector for North Carolina. First, the president explained that Bradford had for some time been a resident of North Carolina. In addition to this consideration, there was a need for a speedy appointment to get the new system of taxation underway, and North Carolina's political leaders had presented no other candidate. The tone of Davis's letter was conciliatory throughout, and by indicating that he had conferred with the secretary of war about the matter, the president hinted that a solution to the problem was being sought. Davis closed his letter with the following statement: "I am aware of the embarrassments you may have in carrying out your patriotic efforts to aid the Confederate government in this struggle and . . . would be very far from willingly allowing any additional obstruction to be thrown in your way."[5] This communication indicated that Davis recognized that Zeb faced a difficult task in maintaining civilian morale in North Carolina, and he knew that the Confederacy had inadvertently added to the governor's burden.

Around the same time, Zeb's task became immensely more difficult. John L. Pennington, editor of the *Daily Progress* in Raleigh, became the catalyst of the new development. Pennington's initial response to the losses at Vicksburg and Gettysburg was to call for greater effort from North Carolinians. In an editorial printed on July 11, he exhorted: "Nothing can be made by magnifying our disasters. Let us calmly and quietly look the worst in the face, and with the determination of a people that deserve to be free, set ourselves to work to repair the injuries we have sustained." After following his own advice briefly, however, Pennington concluded that perhaps the recent defeats did require a new Confederate policy. "Any peace that is honorable and that respects our rights," he now asserted, would find favor with the people of North Carolina. This statement was quite ambiguous, but elsewhere in the editorial he hinted at what "rights" needed to be respected. Pennington noted that "peace now would save slavery," but any prolongation of the struggle would "obliterate the last vestige of it."[6] Thus, Pennington sought a peace that would preserve slavery, and he was conspicuously silent about the fate of the Confederacy.

If Pennington's voice, which was largely heard in the immediate vicinity of Raleigh, had been the only one calling for a new policy, then Zeb would not have faced a formidable challenge. Two days later, however, William W. Holden picked up the theme that Pennington had introduced and spread it statewide through the *North Carolina Standard*. First, Holden critiqued Pennington's proposal and found it wanting. He pointed out that the people in the North, particularly the Lincoln administration, would require Southern concessions. Since both governments were unwilling to compromise, what was needed was "a cessation of hostilities and negotiations." Noting that federal soldiers fought bravely, he observed, "It is no disgrace to a people to be overpowered by mere brute force, if they resist manfully and desperately."[7] With this statement, Holden went a step further than any prominent North Carolinian had so far gone in a public statement: he mentioned the possibility of Confederate defeat.

If the situation was as serious as Pennington and Holden seemed to think that it was, then what was to be done? Holden quoted a letter from a reader who suggested that the fall elections for Confederate congressmen be waged on the issue of appointing commissioners to meet with representatives of the Lincoln administration. In addition, Holden asserted, "Our people . . . must remember *that they are sovereign*—that they are the masters of those who administer the government—that the government was established by them, for *their* benefit; and *they* must not be afraid to utter their opinions freely and boldly." This statement was interpreted by many at the time, both friends and foes of Holden, as a call for public meetings. In all probability, Holden knew that one such meeting had already been held at Snow Hill in Greene County on July 14. At that gathering of the Conservative Party, the citizens adopted resolutions that demanded an end to unfair Confederate treatment of North Carolinians and called "upon the people of North Carolina to hold meetings in their respective Counties and declare whether they shall be freemen or slaves."[8] Pennington printed the minutes of the Greene County meeting on July 21 in the *Daily Progress*, and the political landscape of Confederate North Carolina was forever changed.

There was an immediate reaction in Richmond. The newspapers in the Confederate capital seized on Holden's editorial and insisted that because he had advocated peace, his paper should be suppressed. Jefferson Davis picked up on the criticism and wrote a worried letter to Zeb on July 24. He noted, "This is not the first intimation I have received that Holden is engaged in the treasonable purpose of exciting the people of North Carolina to resistance against their government and cooperation with the enemy." Davis asked Zeb whether Holden had "gone so far as to render him[self] liable to criminal prosecution."[9] To Davis, what Holden had proposed appeared to be treason. The Confederate president did not understand that a political dialogue still existed in North Carolina, and that Holden was writing within that framework.

Zeb understood this, however, and he wrote a calming letter back to Davis two days later. He started with the most basic point. "I do not believe there is any reconstruction party in North Carolina," he wrote, "or that there exist any reason whatever to fear that this State will put herself in opposition to the Confederate Government." Zeb continued: "Neither does there exist any reason for taking steps against Holden, the editor of the Standard. On the contrary, it would be impolitic in the very highest degree to interfere with him or his paper."[10] The young governor recognized two important facts that the president either ignored or was unaware of. The first was that the people of North Carolina had joined the Confederacy to safeguard their liberties. If the Richmond government shut down a newspaper that suggested an alternative to government policy, it would once again be overriding the very liberties that it had promised to preserve.

Hasty action on the part of the Confederate government would, moreover, threaten all of the positive work that Zeb had accomplished. He cautioned the president, "I will not deny but there is a bad state of feeling here toward the Confederate Government, of which I have endeavored to make you sensible by various long communications, and which I have been unable to correct without your co-operation more cordially given than heretofore." Once again, Zeb was attempting to educate the Richmond government about the mistakes it had made in North Carolina. What Zeb did not say in his letter to Davis was that Holden was part of the Conservative coalition and that Zeb wanted to retain that coalition intact to support the active government he was in the process of creating. The worried governor closed the letter by suggesting that he visit Richmond to explain the situation to the president in detail.[11]

Davis was not the only person concerned about Holden's course. Edward J. Hale, another member of the Conservative leadership in North Carolina and the editor of the *Fayetteville Observer*, wrote to Zeb on the same day as Davis. Hale cautioned the governor: "There is a vast deal of feeling, very earnest & bitter, in various parts of the State against the course that the Standard is pursuing. It is regarded by calm & prudent men, dreadfully damaging to the cause." Hale went on to ask Vance if political allies of Vance and Holden in the Conservative Party could talk to Holden and Holden's newspaper opponents and secure a truce. If this were not possible, Hale recommended that Zeb alert the public that he disagreed with Holden's opinions. Looking further into the future, Hale also noted that if Zeb did break with Holden, the governor would have to arrange for an administration newspaper in Raleigh.[12]

As he had with Jefferson Davis, Zeb immediately replied to Hale. He tried to ease the editor's fears, writing, "I assure you I am deeply concerned at the turn that things have taken." The governor went on to admit that party leaders, including Confederate States senator William A. Graham and former governor David L. Swain, had tried and failed to persuade Holden to change his course. Holden continued to maintain that he was "only *following* the people not leading them." Zeb told Hale that he had had "a long talk with [Holden] yesterday and requested him to say in his paper that he was not [Vance's] organ in the matter and did not speak [Vance's] sentiments." Vance confided to Hale that he felt that a split was likely between himself and Holden but that he believed that he still retained more public support than the editor.[13] Zeb's confidence in his own standing in North Carolina would be sorely tested in the next six weeks.

True to his word, Holden inserted the following statement in the next issue of the paper: "It is due to Gov. Vance himself, as well as to the Standard, that we should state that he does not agree with us in our views on the subject of peace. . . . He regards peace movements among ourselves, with no overtures of any kind from the North, as premature and injudicious." Holden went on to explain his position in greater detail: "We are not in favor of 'reunion with our enemies' or of 'submission to them.'" Instead, Holden maintained, he was trying to provide a forum for the people to speak out against the failures of President Jefferson Davis and his administration.[14] If this was Holden's way of pointing out to Zeb and others that they shared common political foes, then the ploy was not successful.

Its failure was due to another article that appeared in the paper the same day. Holden reported the result of two public meetings held in Wake County. Since these gatherings were located near Raleigh, most observers assumed that either Holden had helped to organize them or his fervent local supporters had. At the time, Zeb and others called these events "peace" meetings. Looking closely at the resolutions adopted, however, it is more appropriate to define them as broad-based protest meetings at which peace was simply one of many issues under discussion. In fact, many of the resolutions adopted at the meetings reflected Zeb's own complaints about the Confederate government's treatment of North Carolina. At one of these Wake County meetings, the assembled citizens attacked the Richmond government for not appointing North Carolinians to offices in the state, for not appreciating contributions made by North Carolina, and for threatening civil liberties. They also resolved that they "would hail with joy any movement which might promise to lead to an honorable and lasting peace."[15] The ambiguity that characterized this statement was prominent in many peace resolutions. It appears as if those who attended the meeting wanted peace with few or no concessions on the part of the South. Realists like Vance and Davis—and even Holden—recognized that the Lincoln administration would not accept such terms.

The second meeting in Wake County was significantly different from the first. Ominously for Zeb's political future, the people at this gathering claimed to be meeting as members of the Conservative Party—the same party that had sponsored Zeb's gubernatorial candidacy. The citizens who attended this meeting did not mention peace or any related topics. Like their counterparts at the other meeting, they protested against the appointment of outsiders to positions of authority in North Carolina. But they also proposed that North Carolina send no more soldiers to the Confederate army until other states met their quotas. Resolutions like these would become the staples of many later meetings. The secessionists expressed outrage that the central government was being questioned. Their Raleigh paper, the *State Journal*, called upon Zeb "to discard the evil associations to which he is exposed, and set the people a proper example in this matter."[16] Thus, just as Vance and Hale had anticipated, as the protest movement began to take shape, Zeb found himself stuck in the middle of a battle between his political allies—Holden and his supporters—and the secessionists. The questions that remained unanswered were how significant the movement would become and what direction would it take.

The answer to the second question seemed to come almost immediately. Holden's last issue of July contained information that indicated that demands for peace would become a more significant part of the movement. At a Moore County meeting, attendees called "upon [their] representatives in the next Congress to use their utmost endeavors to obtain a cessation of hostilities and termination of [their] present struggle, in a just, honorable and lasting peace." This request for the Confederate Congress to bring about an armistice would also become standard fare at most protest meetings. Participants at a third Wake County meeting refined this proposal; assuming that the Lincoln and Davis administrations would never negotiate, they called for a convention of the states. Nevertheless, there were items on the agenda other than peace. At the Moore County meeting, North Carolina citizens also opposed the suspension of the writ of habeas corpus, objected to the imposition of the tax in kind, denounced the appointment of non–North Carolinians to office, condemned the call for seven thousand men for the state militia, and supported the state supreme court's defense of civil liberties.[17] It is probably accurate to say that many individuals viewed these latter issues as being just as important as the proposal for peace.

The item in the paper that caused the greatest sensation was not a meeting report, however. It was a letter to the editor from Lewis Hanes of Davidson County. Hanes first attacked the secessionists as promise breakers. He claimed that they had said that separation would be peaceful; that prosperity would follow independence; that states' rights would be protected; and that they would personally sacrifice for the cause. Hanes maintained that none of these things had come to pass. Due to the treachery of the secessionists, Hanes pointed out, the people of the Confederacy found themselves in a most difficult spot. Discussing the people's dilemma, he explained, "They may, perhaps, prefer that the independence of the South be acknowledged, but this they believe can not now be obtained, nor in viewing the situation of affairs, do they see much hope of it in the future." According to Hanes, the solution was to call a convention of states (bypassing the zealous Lincoln and Davis administrations) that would readmit the Southern states to the Union and pass a constitutional amendment guaranteeing slavery in the South.[18] To knowledgeable observers, Hanes appeared to be trying to resurrect the failed compromise of February 1861.

Hanes's letter, despite its lack of originality, became a very important impetus for the protest movement. Hanes had broached a forbidden topic: the end of the Confederacy, or reconstruction, as it was called at the time. Government leaders like Davis and Vance refused to countenance discussion of reconstruction, but the appearance of the Hanes letter opened the topic for public conversation. For many North Carolinians in the Confederate army, the discussion of reconstruction as a live issue was absolutely intolerable. Increasingly, civilian meetings in North Carolina provoked the passage of angry resolutions by soldiers who directed their anger at the most visible of targets: William W. Holden. Zeb's allies sought to protect the governor from getting caught in the crossfire between the two groups. First, admitting that it had once again erred, the Davis administration agreed to appoint a native North Carolinian to collect the despised tax in kind. Edward J. Hale started a campaign to ensure that Tar Heels remembered the important contributions that their governor had made. Hale asserted, "The people of North Carolina may rest assured that nothing that patriotism and firmness can effect will be wanting on the part of Gov. Vance to protect all of their rights." Then, in early August, Holden wrote that although he disagreed with Vance on the peace movement, he still supported the governor.[19] Clearly, Zeb was now at the center of a tug-of-war between factions that wished to take advantage of his still significant personal popularity.

Throughout the latter part of July and August, the protest meetings continued. As the number of gatherings increased rapidly, their participants echoed the themes of earlier meetings and brought new ideas to the forefront. The most significant new idea emerged from a meeting in Surry County. At that gathering, most of the resolutions adopted followed the pattern of earlier meetings. At the conclusion of the participants' petition, however, came this resolution: "That in our opinion, under the circumstances, the best thing that the people of North Carolina could do would be to go in for 'the Constitution as it is and the Union as it was.'"[20] This was an explosive choice of words. First, the phrase was the slogan of much of the Democratic Party in the North. Its use by North Carolinians clearly signified their attempt to make a political alliance across the battle lines in order to seek peace outside of regular channels of government. Like Hanes had in his letter, the resolution accepted reconstruction as a desirable end as long as slavery could be preserved. A popular meeting in North Carolina had spoken in favor of submitting to federal authority.

Nearly as influential as the Surry County resolution were the expressions of growing outrage about the tax in kind. Participants in a Davidson County meeting that was strongly in favor of peace—they nominated Lewis Hanes for Congress—insisted that they would vote for no one for Congress who would not agree to repeal the tax. At virtually all of the nearly one hundred meetings, attendees agreed that the "unjust and tyrannical tax" had to go.[21] The impost was widely disliked not simply because it was the first direct tax that most North Carolinians had experienced. The people who felt the full weight of the levy were the subsistence farm owners and tenants who generated only a small surplus in the best of times. In the conditions created by the war, many families and communities were barely surviving. The collection of 10 percent of their produce as a tax under these circumstances actually threatened their well-being. The pressure on farm families provided additional motivation for North Carolina troops to desert.

Probably the most surprising protests concerned foreign policy. Press reports from this period carried the news that the Davis administration was seeking the assistance of Great Britain and France. The participants at several meetings adopted resolutions that were actively hostile toward these initiatives. Attendees at a Forsyth County meeting strongly opposed any alliance with France in particular. The participants claimed that France was "a land of licentiousness and corruption, of guillotines and inquisitions, of infidelity and Roman Catholicism." At a Stanly County gathering, the assembled citizens asserted that North Carolinians would never "submit to be enslaved or annexed to any foreign or kingly government." In Iredell County, they pointed out that France had "abolished the institution of slavery throughout her dominions." Vance's associates became so concerned about the unexpected foreign policy protests that they arranged for an anonymous letter explaining the proposed alliances to be printed in the *Fayetteville Observer*.[22] Clearly, the meetings became opportunities for the dissatisfied citizens of the state to vent their hostility toward a government that seemed constantly to be imposing new requirements on its people.

Another striking innovation took place in the Pikeville community in Wayne County, where a planned protest meeting was squelched by the appearance of the county militia. The reaction of the community was to support a "meeting of the Ladies of Pikeville District of Wayne county." The meeting president was Elizabeth Winborn, who led the group in adopting a set of statements that challenged more than Confederate policy. The participants asserted: "The time is approaching we believe, when the wives, mothers and daughters of the soldiers of North Carolina, now in the service of their country, in prosecuting an unjust, unchristian and uncalled for war, will have to take care of themselves." In other resolutions, they encouraged enlisted men to serve honorably, called for the repeal of the tax in kind, condemned the militia leaders by name for breaking up the previous meeting, supported peace candidates for office, and encouraged other North Carolina women to follow their example. They concluded their meeting by declaring: "Should any man or woman in our country attempt to pass any insinuation that is lowering to the character and dignity of the female sex, in departing from the retired sphere of life usually assigned to them to hold this meeting under the exigencies of the case, and in the condition of our country, we treat and consider them as being unworthy of our regard."[23] The obvious militancy of these female protesters indicates that the protest movement was supported by a broad spectrum of the public, and that it drew into public life many people who were normally excluded from it.

The meeting that perhaps worried Zeb and his associates the most was held in August in Virginia. Company E of the Twenty-fourth North Carolina Regiment met and adopted resolutions that contrasted significantly with those passed at a gathering of officers at the Orange County Courthouse in Virginia. At the Virginia meeting, the officers, many of whom were secessionists, had condemned Holden and the peace movement and called for the suppression of the *Standard*. The men of Company E, by contrast, attacked the secessionists, demanding "that the blood and thunder men should practice what they preach, by going in the ranks and fighting, or forever hold their cowardly tongues." Then they took an even more radical step. They resolved: "That we are opposed to any more shedding of blood in this war, and that we are unanimously in favor of peace on the best terms it can be obtained."[24] These resolutions, which Holden published, constituted a direct challenge to Zeb and the Confederate leadership. Not only was there a clear indication of mutiny among the troops, but Holden, by publishing the resolutions, had informed the entire state and nation.

It soon became clear that the army officers' demand that Holden's paper be suppressed aroused deep resentment. At several subsequent meetings, the protection of civil liberties became one of the participants' paramount concerns. The army officers were specifically condemned for interfering in civil life. In addition, the citizens who attended increasing numbers of meetings began to vehemently protest the suspension of the writ of habeas corpus. At several meetings, Chief Justice Richmond Pearson and the North Carolina Supreme Court were praised for protecting the liberties of North Carolinians.[25] This development was a critical one. Most whites in North Carolina had initially supported the Confederacy because they believed that the Lincoln administration threatened the liberties of whites in the South. If these same people saw the Davis administration and the Confederate army as being guilty of the same thing, they had little reason to support the war effort.

As the month of August progressed, there were signs that the meetings had begun to threaten the legitimacy of both Zeb's administration and Confederate rule in North Carolina. The number of gatherings seemed to be increasing with no end in sight. Equally important, the number of people attending these events appeared to be growing. Reports came in that 200 people attended a Guilford County meeting, 600 to 700 gathered in Stanly County, and 1,200 to 1,500 participated in a Forsyth County event. Subscriptions to Holden's paper increased by approximately 25 percent, suggesting growing popular support for the antigovernment protest movement. Finally, a group of 300 people in Wilkes County marched to the courthouse and raised the U.S. flag.[26] Clearly, Zeb could no longer take a laissez-faire attitude toward Holden and the protesters.

One of the problems that Zeb faced was that many of the protesters were his political allies. The participants at a significant number of protest meetings adopted resolutions supporting and praising Zeb. As noted earlier, the secessionists recognized this fact, and their party paper called on Vance to distance himself from the peace advocates. Zeb, however, was not about to join forces with the people whom he blamed for most of the problems that

Confederate North Carolina faced. He described his political opponents to Edward J. Hale: "They are incapable of subordinating party prejudices for *any* purpose. I have talked to most of them and the only use they made of my information was to try to array Holden & myself against each other and write to Richmond urging Holdens arrest! I have no more faith in their patriotism than Holdens—not as much in fact."[27] Given his perception of the most vocal opposition to Holden and the protest meetings, Zeb tried to move carefully to prevent the secessionists from deriving any benefit from his actions.

The resolutions of the protesters also made it difficult for Vance to take decisive action, because many of them supported positions that Zeb himself had taken in letters to Confederate leaders. For example, a Moore County gathering affirmed "that Gov. Vance, Judge Pearson and others who have taken a bold and independent stand to sustain the civil authority of the State, are deserving of . . . lasting gratitude." The attendees at a second meeting in the same county asserted "that the patriotic course of Gov. Vance, in his devotion to the comfort and happiness of [the] soldiers" met their "entire approbation." In Johnston County, protesters resolved: "We do cordially and fully endorse his administration, and feel that every true North Carolinian can but be proud of the name of Z. B. Vance." When some of the protesters recognized that Zeb was not openly endorsing their efforts, they began to plead with him to join them. A group in Guilford County called "upon him *now* to take the lead in this great movement of the people for peace." Citizens who attended the large meeting in Forsyth County called on Zeb to resist the entreaties of the secessionists and to remain allied with his friends in the Conservative Party.[28] Obviously, if Zeb wanted to hold the coalition that had elected him together, he would have to move with great care.

But Zeb felt that he had a greater obligation than to maintain his political coalition; his primary responsibility was to assist the Confederacy in gaining its independence. He became convinced that the somewhat optimistic assessment he had made to Jefferson Davis on July 26 was no longer accurate. The protest campaign had gotten out of control, and it was threatening North Carolina's ability to contribute to the cause. In an effort to quiet the growing hostility to the Confederate government, Zeb resolved to correct some abuses immediately. In a July 28 letter to Secretary of War James A. Seddon, Zeb mentioned "the propriety of [Seddon's] forbidding positively the officers of the Government engaging in speculation on private account." Zeb went on to say that many officials' speculations were detrimental to the communities in which they resided. To the young governor, the request was yet another attempt to cope with one of a never ending series of blunders by the central government that undermined morale in North Carolina; worse, he had to deal with the problem while he struggled to keep public morale in the state from deteriorating. Seddon's reply—that regulations forbade speculating on private account and that his efforts to stop irregularities had failed—probably further confirmed Zeb's low opinion of the efforts of the Davis administration.[29]

In his letters to both Davis and Seddon, the energetic governor noted that he would soon make a trip to Richmond to explain the situation in North Carolina to the Confederate leaders. In a letter written to Edward J. Hale on August 11, Zeb recounted the results of the meeting with Davis: "I plainly told the President of . . . the injustice done by us by his appointments and gave him a fair and unvarnished statement of affairs here— He promised to remove all objectionable [men] and almost gave me carte blanche for the redress of grievances here."[30] One senses that Zeb finally felt that he had made Jefferson Davis fully aware of the failures of Confederate policies in North Carolina. Having achieved this, Zeb probably no longer felt threatened by the secessionists in North Carolina. He had the president behind him, and they would be powerless to harm him.

Freed from worrying about the opposing political faction, Zeb apparently felt much more secure about dealing with William W. Holden. The broader Confederate perspective that President Davis undoubtedly shared with him during their Richmond conference may also have impressed him. Whatever the factors, Zeb now took a much harder line in dealing with Holden. In the same letter to Hale in which he described the Davis meeting, Zeb explained, "I believe however the split with Holden is decreed of the gods," because Holden was "for submission, reconstruction or any thing else that will put him back under Lincoln & stop the war."[31] In just two weeks' time, Zeb had changed his opinion dramatically. Whether the change was the result of the meeting in Richmond or the growing number of protest meetings is not critical. What is important is that North Carolina's governor was now prepared to take on both a major ally and a portion of his own political following. Few politicians are willing to do this under any circumstances. That Zeb would consider it indicates how seriously concerned he was about the stability of North Carolina's commitment to the Confederacy.

The next question was what strategy to pursue. Zeb apparently determined early on to try to isolate Holden from the remainder of the leadership of the Conservative Party. In his letter to Hale, Vance concluded, "Pitch into them—Cry loud and spare not." Zeb sought to assure Hale that the editor would not be acting alone. He pledged: "My life[,] popularity and everything shall go into this contest." With the stakes that high, Zeb moved cautiously. Two days later, he wrote to William A. Graham, the leading former Whig in the state. Zeb explained the purpose of his letter: "I desire, as far as possible, to know how far, I will be sustained by my friends & former supporters—With this view I earnestly invite an expression of your opinion advice, fully, freely & confidentially given."[32] Zeb made contact with selected other political advisers with much the same request.

In the meantime, Zeb prepared to take action himself. He seized upon a letter addressed to him by Unionist John H. Haughton as a pretext for writing a public letter attacking the peace movement. In his long reply to Haughton, dated August 17, Vance made no effort to conceal his conclusion that the protests were both impractical and dishonorable. After reviewing how inflexible the federal government had been about negotiating with the Confederacy, he asserted: "I can only look upon propositions of peace coming from us, no matter how pure and patriotic the motive which induces them, as involving national dishonor, ruin and disgrace." Zeb painted a picture of the horrors of submission to the federal government. These included the end of slavery, the hanging of prominent Confederates, confiscation of property, heavy taxes, and a huge national debt. He dismissed the possibility of reuniting with Northerners "reeking with the slaughter of our people and the desolation of our country."[33]

Having given all of the reasons to not seek reunion, Zeb then sought to assure Haughton and his broader audience that the Confederacy could still achieve independence by continuing the war. Comparing the Confederate army favorably to those commanded by Washington and Napoleon, Vance concluded that the Army of Northern Virginia was an unsurpassed fighting organization. He quite correctly pointed out that there had been times during the Revolutionary War when the American patriot cause seemed more hopeless than the Confederate situation did in August 1863. He argued that internal division within the Confederacy would limit the effectiveness of Confederate military efforts and thus that it had to be avoided. He noted that the calls for peace in North Carolina were not having their desired effect in the North; instead of encouraging people there to press for a negotiated peace, Northerners were taking the protest meetings as a sign of weakness in the Confederacy, and they were consequently becoming less willing to consider any potential outcome besides total Confederate defeat. Zeb concluded his letter by appealing to Conservatives to make every effort to strengthen the army and to help the poor. He maintained that only by convincing the federal government that the Confederacy could not be conquered could the war be ended rapidly.[34]

Before he presented this rather aggressive reply to the public, Zeb sought the opinions of others. Most interestingly, he gave a copy to William W.

Holden to read. Holden thought the letter was too harsh, and he strongly suggested that Zeb share a copy with William A. Graham. Holden offered to abide by Graham's decision about whether to publish the letter. It is difficult to understand why Zeb decided to share the letter with Holden. Perhaps the governor hoped that the negative tone would bring Holden to his senses and that the letter would not have to be issued. In any case, Graham agreed with Holden that the letter was too plainly stated, and he suggested a series of modifications. Having decided not to edit the letter further, Zeb replied to Graham: "I had concluded before you returned my letter to Haughton to suspend its publication at least for the present."[35] Thus Zeb abandoned his first attempt to deal with the unrest in North Carolina while holding his political coalition together.

Zeb nevertheless recognized that it was essential to try to resolve the conflict. It was now clear to him that Holden would sacrifice the coalition to continue his support of the protesters. Writing to Graham, Zeb acknowledged that "the matter [was] one of great delicacy and a mistake might be fatal." Fearing that a split with Holden would divide the Conservative Party voters, allowing the incompetent and highly partisan secessionists back into power, Zeb sought the advice of many other political allies. He admitted to Graham that he was "really much distressed and harassed." He then went on to explain: "The crisis is fast approaching and hardly any two friends agree in their advice. I have some thirty or forty letters from different parts of the state." Zeb asked Graham to call together several party leaders to meet in Raleigh, where they would try to reach an agreement on strategy.[36]

Even before the meeting took place, however, Zeb had already made some decisions about the approach he would take. Those opposed to Holden and the protesters called for the suppression of the meetings and the possible arrest of some of those involved, and Zeb's public silence led some people to conclude that he was considering such measures. Concerned, one of Zeb's political allies wrote to the governor about the matter. Zeb's reply outlined the policy that he would eventually follow: "These *measures* are nothing more than persuasion, argument, & such moral force as my position may enable me to bring to bear on public opinion. . . . The idea of violence, possible arrests, proscription &c. never will find an advocate in me—I shall sustain the courts as heretofore."[37] Thus, Zeb had already decided upon the tactics he would use, and the major issue that remained to be decided was the strategic context within which these tactics would be employed.

Meanwhile, some of Zeb's friends sought to prepare public opinion for whatever decision the party leadership and the governor would make. Edward J. Hale published a comprehensive review of the situation in the *Fayetteville Observer*. Hale made three major points. First, he contended that there was a significant peace movement in North Carolina and that Holden was leading it. Second, Hale sought to absolve the Raleigh editor of part of the "blame" for his leadership of the movement. Hale maintained that unfair attacks by secessionists had embittered Holden and made him inclined to support the protesters. Finally, Hale concluded that the peace movement itself was fueled by deserters who sought public approval of their lawbreaking.[38] Hale's strategy was pretty transparent: he sought to remind Holden and his followers that their real enemies were the secessionists and not fellow Conservatives like Zeb. At the same time, Hale tried to convince the broader public that scheming men who had broken the law and betrayed their country were using the people for their own ends. While there is no indication that Holden or the protesters accepted Hale's reasoning, this editorial did provide support for Vance's position should he decide to break with Holden in the future.

Efforts to blunt the influence of the protest meetings were not confined to newspaper editorials, however. On August 28, the participants in a meeting at Love's Creek Church in embattled Chatham County issued a very different set of resolutions from those that had been appearing most frequently in North Carolina newspapers. The assembled citizens first expressed confidence in the soldiers and rulers of the Confederacy. They also expressed their sympathy for the suffering of the soldiers and the people, and they remarked that they understood the desire for peace. But the attendees went on to resolve that peace could only come with "national independence," and they averred that "reconstruction of the Union [was] impossible." Nor was this the only meeting that led to expressions of support for the continuation of the war until independence was achieved. Large gatherings in Charlotte and Salisbury endorsed the government's policies and rejected the peace resolutions passed in many other cities.[39] While there is no direct evidence, it seems likely that the Charlotte and Salisbury meetings were arranged by political leaders allied with Vance in an effort to provide the appearance of public support for the policies he was about to announce.

The efforts to provide counterdemonstrations in favor of Vance were aimed in part at persuading Holden to accept some sort of political compromise. On September 2, Holden agreed to meet with Zeb, William A. Graham, and other leaders of the Conservative Party. Zeb described the meeting for Hale: "Gov G[raham] talked to him earnestly for three hours. It would do no good—he would agree to nothing & insisted that the meetings should go on and I and no one else must say a word! Modest proposition truly. I offered to keep silent if he would discourage the meetings—would not agree to it. Gov Graham was clear that I should issue a proclamation, but insisted that it should be very mild and cautionary." According to William C. Harris, Holden's biographer, there was more to the final agreement than Zeb indicated to Hale. Apparently, Graham engineered a compromise: if Zeb issued a proclamation that did not attack or find fault with Holden, the editor agreed that he would not directly criticize it.[40]

On September 7, Zeb sent out copies of his proclamation to state newspapers. The first copies were available to the public on September 8. Zeb began by identifying his topic—the challenge that the protest meetings posed to state and Confederate authority—in his opening sentence: "A number of public meetings have recently been held in various portions of the State," he wrote, "in some of which threats have been made of combined resistance to the execution of the laws of Congress, in regard to conscription and the collection of taxes."[41] Zeb attacked behaviors that were clearly illegal and could be addressed within the existing legal system. It is important to notice, however, what he did not say. There is no mention anywhere in the proclamation of conventions, armistices, or peace negotiations. Zeb's compromise strategy appears to have been to avoid mentioning the issues that Holden and the Conservative leadership disagreed upon.

In the remainder of the document, Zeb alternately assured the protesters that their rights would be respected and asked them not to use those rights to threaten the Confederate war effort. For example, he promised that "the inalienable and invaluable right of the people to assemble together and consult for the common good" would "never find a disturber in [him]." But just a few lines later, Zeb warned: "Let no one be deceived. So long as these laws remain upon the Statute book, they shall be executed." He thereby confirmed that he would continue to enforce the unpopular conscription and tax laws. Alluding to the fact that the voters of North Carolina would soon be choosing Confederate congressmen, Zeb observed: "There is no grievance to redress and no proposition to be made, but can be most beneficially effected in the way our fathers marked out by the ballot box."[42] Thus, Zeb did not condemn and forbid the protest meetings, but instead sought to divert the protesters' energy into legitimate channels, including elective politics.

He closed the proclamation with a series of appeals that he hoped would unite the people of North Carolina. First, he called upon them to "abstain from assembling together for the purpose of denouncing each other, whether at home or in the Army." This attempt to be evenhanded was sincere. Zeb recognized that if the army was perceived to be intervening in the civilian debate, there could be a significant negative reaction against the Confederacy; he had already seen a similar reaction happen when cavalry units foraged and gathered conscripts. He closed out his address with appeals to the people to feed the hungry and to deserters to rejoin their regiments. Zeb characterized his proclamation as "mild and cautionary," and that seems to be a fair assessment.[43] He had let the people of North Carolina know that he felt that it would be unwise for them to hold further protest meetings, but he did not forbid them to assemble. He appealed most directly to those people who were part of the Conservative Party and asked them not to destroy the political coalition that they had created.

As Zeb recognized, his compromise approach entailed considerable risks. The protesters might not stop their meetings. In fact, on the day that the proclamation was published, a protest meeting was held in Leaksville in Rockingham County. The participants called for the end to the suspension of the writ of habeas corpus, for peace on honorable terms, for the repeal of the tithing law, and for an end to discrimination against North Carolina by the Confederate government.[44] These resolutions were typical of the protests that had been voiced throughout the summer. Although the Leaksville protesters were undoubtedly uninformed about Zeb's address, there was clearly no guarantee that his plea for understanding would be heeded. Zeb knew that the delicate balance that he had tried to create with his proclamation could be upset by extreme reactions on the part of any of several groups in the state.

13 ❧ CHALLENGES TO THE COMPROMISE

I n the immediate aftermath of his proclamation, Zeb waited to see what impact it would have. At the same time, he sought some rest. He had been feeling ill throughout this period of difficult negotiation, and he was worried because his brother had been furloughed from the army with typhoid fever. What remained of Zeb's attention was directed to a daring Confederate military maneuver. Sensing that the federal army at his front was not going to advance aggressively, General Robert E. Lee had detached a division of the Army of Northern Virginia under the leadership of General James Longstreet and sent it to reinforce the Army of Tennessee, which faced an advance from federal troops in the western theater. This transfer proved to be difficult due to the inadequacies of the Confederate rail system. Ironically, because Zeb had not provided much assistance to speed along the completion of the Danville to Greensboro rail link, which was still not complete in the autumn of 1863, all of Longstreet's troops would have to travel through Raleigh on their way west. This inconvenience would have grave consequences.

As the tired and ill governor prepared to go to bed on the evening of September 9, the day after his proclamation had been published, a local citizen aroused him and told him that Confederate troops were attacking Holden's newspaper office. Zeb ran out of the house, jumped on his horse, and rode down the street toward the rapidly developing riot. On the way, he stopped at a local hotel and persuaded Lieutenant Colonel Shepherd of a Georgia Regiment to accompany him to the scene. Once there, Zeb discovered a large number of troops from General Henry L. Benning's Georgia brigade—and perhaps some soldiers from North Carolina as well—destroying the supplies at Holden's office. Zeb arrived just in time to prevent the troops from damaging the presses. Acting quickly, he attracted the attention of the rioters and began to speak to them. He scolded the soldiers for taking part in such a disreputable exercise. He asserted that "a blow had been struck at the dearest rights of a private citizen—rights purchased by the richest blood of their patriotic fathers in defense of which every man among them should be ready to lay down his life."[1] Zeb's speech changed the atmosphere completely, and Shepherd was able to call the men to order and to march them back to camp.

The weary governor returned home to discover William W. Holden there. Apparently the troops had initially sought Holden at his home, he had escaped as they approached, and they had turned to looting his office as a secondary target. Holden justifiably believed that the soldiers had hoped to do him bodily harm. After reassuring the cowed editor, Zeb retired to sleep for what was left of the night. He was jolted out of his early morning routine at seven the next morning by the ringing of the town bell. Zeb once again mounted his horse and raced to the scene. There he found a group of Holden supporters systematically destroying the offices of the secessionist *State Journal*. Much better prepared than the soldiers had been the night before, these partisans actually destroyed the presses, which were virtually irreplaceable. Zeb was joined by Holden, who claimed to have had no fore-knowledge of the event. The governor once again quieted the crowd with an effective address on civil liberties. After Zeb's speech, the crowd went home and the streets returned to normal.[2]

The deeply concerned governor now tried to put all of the events of the previous evening and morning into some sort of perspective. Once again, he came to the conclusion that the incompetence of the Confederate government was wrecking one of his carefully constructed plans—this time, his strategy for placating dissatisfaction in North Carolina. He immediately telegraphed Davis, telling him of the events that had just transpired and requesting that the president divert all further troops from Raleigh. Davis wired back that he had instructed all commanders to keep their forces out of the city. After partially composing himself the next day, Zeb wrote an emotional letter to Jefferson Davis. He immediately got to the point: "I am now trembling to see its [the attack on Holden's office] effects upon the country, though I am greatly in hopes that the mob of citizens which destroyed the office of the State Journal will act as a counter-irritant and help to allay excitement, the damage being equal to both parties." Noting how delicate the balance between loyalty and opposition to the Confederacy was, Zeb continued, "I beg again to impress you with the importance of sustaining me in every essential particular . . . concerning which I spoke to you in Richmond."[3] Once again, Zeb felt insecure about the reliability of the government in Richmond.

After describing the actions of the troops during the events of the previous night in some detail, Zeb addressed the president directly. He mixed morose comments with threats. He started by sharing his own state of mind, writing, "I feel very sad in the contemplation of these outrages." He assured Davis that if any newspaper editors committed treason in North

Carolina, they would be arrested and tried in court. Zeb warned, however, that if there were any further outbreaks of violence he would "bring the North Carolina troops home to the defense of their own State and her institutions." This latter assertion was hyperbole, since Zeb had no authority over the North Carolina regiments and brigades in Confederate service. But he used the threat to underline the importance of the situation for Davis's benefit. Zeb closed the letter by thanking Davis for his telegram and observing that peace would be preserved if the president's orders were "rigidly obeyed."[4]

Shortly after sending the letter, Zeb discovered that in fact Davis's orders to the Confederate commanders were not being obeyed. In his second letter to Davis that day, Zeb related the events that followed: "This afternoon, in spite of your orders to Major Pierce, a large number of infuriated soldiers from an Alabama brigade . . . entered the city and spread terror in their path by threatening murder and conflagration. I rode with all speed to the depot and got a Colonel Scruggs to march a detachment into town and restrain them before they had done any damage. They even threatened my life if I interfered with them." The angry governor once again repeated his threat to withdraw North Carolina troops from the field. He elaborated, "For sixty hours I have traveled up and down making speeches alternately to citizens and soldiers, without rest or sleep almost, engaged in the humiliating task of trying to defend the laws and peace of the State against our own bayonets."[5] To the beleaguered governor, this latest incident appeared to be the final blow to the compromise between Holden and Vance, since Holden and his followers could use this incident to restart the anti-Confederate public meetings.

Upon receipt of the latest news from Vance, Davis acted decisively. He immediately ordered that troops should pass through Raleigh without being allowed to exit from their trains. The president then wrote to Zeb to assure him that this measure should "be sufficient to prevent further disorders." In fact, the crisis had passed. The troops were moving rapidly on their way to northern Georgia, where they would engage the federal army. A greatly relieved Zeb was able to telegraph Davis, "The troops are now passing quietly, and no further disturbance apprehended, Quiet is restored."[6] Although calm had been restored for the moment, Zeb knew that the disturbances caused by the Confederate soldiers could provide even greater fuel for the protest movement. After all, the events in Raleigh were precisely the type of developments that the participants in the protest meetings had denounced.

Much to Zeb's relief, the great explosion of protest did not take place. Apparently only one further public meeting was held after the events in

Raleigh. At a gathering in Davidson County on September 18, participants passed the standard resolutions protesting the mistreatment of the state by the Confederacy, stating their opposition to a foreign alliance and to the suspension of the writ of habeas corpus, and endorsing free speech and a free press. They made no specific mention of the assault on Holden's paper. Moreover, many newspapers praised Zeb for his role in keeping the peace. Edward J. Hale of the *Fayetteville Observer*, in particular, described Zeb's actions during the crisis in considerable detail.[7]

Even more important, newspapers that had openly supported the protest movement now praised Zeb. The *People's Press* of Salem strongly supported Zeb's proclamation, although it did stress the people's continued right to assemble and the importance of Zeb's commitment to the independence of North Carolina's courts. John L. Pennington of the *Daily Progress* in Raleigh, a close ally of Holden who had been a spectator during the events that took place on September 9–11, wrote in a lead editorial: "The experience of the last week in Raleigh though painful in the extreme has had at least one redeeming feature. The fact has been made patent that we have a *man* in the gubernatorial chair." When Holden resumed publication of the *Standard* on October 2, he recounted the events of early September on several occasions. Each time, he provided an account that gave Zeb full credit for his actions. Zeb noted in late September that Holden himself "seemed kindly disposed" toward him when they last spoke.[8] Ironically, the crisis that had seemed likely to destroy the compromise that Graham had crafted actually strengthened it.

Zeb discovered the absence of public outrage for himself. The harassed governor left Raleigh as soon as quiet returned for a quick trip to the mountains of the west. On September 4, Zeb had received a telegram from Jason Carson with alarming family news: Hattie was sick. A letter from Robert Vance had indicated this earlier, but he had said that her situation was not serious. The Carson telegram contained the additional distressing news that Zeb's son David had diphtheria. Because he received this telegram at a time when he could not leave Raleigh, Zeb had carried his worry with him through all of the events of the week that followed. Furthermore, Zeb had learned that federal soldiers under Ambrose Burnside had occupied Knoxville in early September, and that people in the mountains of North Carolina were deeply concerned about the impact that this development would have on them.[9]

As Zeb made his way to and from Asheville, he talked extensively with people along the way about the recent events in Raleigh. He jubilantly reported to Edward J. Hale: "The excitement about the stopping of Holden's paper is very small indeed. I met with hardly a man but was willing it should stay down if the [*State*] *Journal* was down with it." Just as Zeb had hoped, the violent activities of Holden's supporters had undermined the public sympathy that the destruction of his property might have elicited. Moreover, it seems that Holden's role in the protest movement was less significant than Zeb had thought. Zeb assured Hale, "*Holden has been weakened by the blow or I am vastly mistaken.*"[10] It seems more likely, however, that Holden's standing with the public had changed very little. Rather, Zeb and other Confederate nationalists had built up Holden's position to try to explain the protest movement, and they were elated to discover that Holden's hold on the public was weaker than they had thought.

Zeb and the Confederate authorities were taking no chances, however. In September, General Robert F. Hoke and a regiment of Confederate troops were detailed to the central and western counties of North Carolina at the governor's request. Zeb's instructions to Hoke were direct: "Use every effort to capture deserters and conscripts, and break up & disperse any organized bands of lawless men to be found there." The governor told Hoke that he should assist local civil authorities in arresting people who had helped to protect those hiding from the government. In particular, Hoke was ordered to arrest all local government officials who had either failed to do their duty or actively supported deserters and draft resisters and to force them into the army. Zeb was claiming that such officials had failed in their duties and had thereby lost their draft exemptions.[11] It is important to note that at no time in this letter did Zeb warn Hoke to respect the civil liberties of the civilian population.

Hoke performed his task with considerable thoroughness and with a lack of concern about the rights of the people in central and western North Carolina. He first moved his forces to Wilkes County, expecting an armed clash with hundreds of outliers. When this encounter did not materialize, he broke his forces into smaller contingents and, on some occasions, combined them with local Home Guard units. The result was entirely satisfactory from his perspective. The outliers made virtually no attempts to intimidate their neighbors during the approximately four months that Hoke's troops were stationed in North Carolina. According to Hoke, approximately three thousand deserters and conscripts were rounded up and forced into active service. Some of their leaders were arrested and placed in the notorious Castle Thunder in Richmond. Most of the men who were captured were persuaded to turn themselves in by a tactic that was deeply resented. The troops simply seized valuable farm property—often the family horse—and held it hostage until the male head of the household gave himself up. As Hoke himself admitted, this tactic often led to covert theft by his troops. Occasional violent confrontations between the troops and the outliers, moreover, left a significant number of men dead and wounded. Although Hoke's campaign led to abuses of the state's citizenry, Zeb was elated by its results. He wrote to Hale: "Deserters are pouring thro' in hundreds really, to their colors. About ten per day report to me at my office & beg for a letter to their officers asking for pardon for their offense—Near 2000 have returned this month, by far the greater part voluntarily."[12] As was often the case throughout the war, Zeb was concerned with strengthening the Confederacy above any other consideration.

When confronted with specific judicial cases, however, Zeb did seek to stay within the proper boundaries of the law. When justices of the peace in Yancey County arrested two men by the names of Edwards and Bailey under orders from military authorities, their cases were brought before Chief Justice Richmond M. Pearson. The sheriff involved in the case was "afraid to go into the county." Because the civilian law enforcement officer did not take part in the arrest, Pearson freed the prisoners and Zeb protested. Pearson explained the circumstances of the case and pointed out that he did not have to inform Confederate authorities of his decisions. Zeb wrote back, explaining that he understood the basis for the ruling but that he was anxious to prevent "two men alleged to have been found with arms in their hands in open resistance" who had been charged with the murder of two members of the militia from being freed. At the close of the letter, Zeb pledged to be patient with all of the restraints that Pearson had imposed upon him and to respect the independence of the law.[13] This Zeb did, but he was nevertheless determined to eliminate as much overt resistance to the Confederate war effort as possible.

In the meantime, the protest movement that had centered around Holden remained in eclipse. One explanation for this fact is that another avenue became available for those who sought redress of their grievances. At some of the protest meetings, participants had nominated delegates to conventions to select candidates for the Confederate Congress. The elections, scheduled for November 4, 1863, gave the dissatisfied and aggrieved an opportunity to legally and loyally register their protests. This congressional campaign was more unstructured than was traditionally the case, but in virtually every district the voters had a clear choice. Former Democrats who had been secessionists played a relatively small role in the canvass. Former Whigs and Holden Democrats who had created the Conservative Party were much more active, and they often divided over issues raised by the protesters. The result was that some of the ten contests were straight two-person ballots, particularly where the Democrats had been historically strong.[14] Other ballots featured as many as four men who represented a number of political perspectives. This sometimes confusing situation was partly the result of the relative absence of party discipline, but the divisions created by the war also played a significant role.

A classic example of the many currents at work during this election can be found in Zeb's old congressional district in the mountains. The incumbent, Zeb's cousin Allen T. Davidson, sought a second term. Although a certified Conservative, Davidson faced significant opposition from within his own party as well as from former Democrats. Davidson's problem was relatively easy to understand. Although he had been elected as a symbol of opposition to the Davis administration, Davidson had voted in favor of most of the measures submitted by the administration, including the widely hated tax in kind.[15] Nevertheless, Davidson retained his skepticism of the Richmond government and obviously strongly supported Zeb's efforts to energize the state government in Raleigh.

Even before the canvass opened, Davidson knew that he would face opposition to his reelection. Although there were fewer protest meetings in the mountains than in the Piedmont, there were enough of them to indicate that a peace candidate for Congress would emerge in Davidson's district. At two meetings, one in Henderson County and another in Rutherford County, participants made speeches and sponsored resolutions that promoted peace over independence. In fact, the attendees at the Rutherford County meeting nominated a local lawyer, George W. Logan, for Congress. At the same time, three men—former stalwarts of the Democratic Party and secessionists—maneuvered to present themselves to the public as viable candidates. After two of these candidates made serious political mistakes, Marcus Erwin, a longtime foe of the governor, emerged as the candidate of the secessionists.[16]

The greatest problem that Davidson faced was a split in his own party ranks. John D. Hyman, Zeb's former partner in the *Asheville Spectator*, opposed him. Very reluctantly, Zeb decided to intervene in this contest by trying to persuade Hyman not to split the Conservative vote. Hyman wrote a long letter justifying his course to Zeb and refused to step aside. Thus, there were three candidates in this contest who maintained that independence was a precondition for peace. Their case was not strengthened by a federal army raid into western North Carolina that took place in mid-September. A small Union force dashed through the Smokies and took control of Waynesville in Haywood County.[17] While this force quickly retreated, its appearance challenged the assertion that the Confederacy was holding its own militarily. Even the Confederate victory at Chickamauga did not seem to improve morale perceptibly, especially since many of the casualties in the battle hailed from western North Carolina.

The peace Conservatives met in Hendersonville on September 4 to select their candidate. A group of Confederate soldiers prevented that meeting from taking place and forced the newspaper sympathetic to the cause of peace—the *Hendersonville Times*—to shut down. William Dedman, the editor of the paper in question, agreed to print no more articles critical of the Davis or Vance administrations, and he was allowed to start publishing again. On September 28, the peace Conservatives held a small and quiet convention and nominated George W. Logan for Congress. Logan and his supporters ran a very quiet campaign. Their platform included a plank urging all deserters "to return to their proper commands till a permanent peace can be secured." Logan refused to make public appearances, and he made few statements. In his acceptance speech, however, he made his position absolutely clear. He asserted that peace was "the only practical issue now before the people, and upon which the election must turn." When the election was held in early November, Logan won a plurality of the vote, with Erwin finishing second. Rather ominously, Zeb's two candidates trailed badly, winning less than one-third of the vote between them.[18]

Nor was this result the only one that troubled Zeb and his allies. Due to the confusion of party labels, the exact result of the ten congressional elections was not clear. All contemporary observers and historians agree on two things. First, no secessionists won seats in the Confederate Congress. The party, which had been thoroughly defeated in the gubernatorial election of 1862, was now practically extinct as a political force. It is also clear that pro-Holden peace candidates won at least five seats. Beyond these facts, however, there is considerable disagreement. Holden claimed that seven of the winners were his supporters, but his biographer concluded that only six were. Historian Paul D. Escott has maintained that eight of the new congressmen were opponents of the Davis administration.[19] In any case, the result seemed to indicate that Zeb's position had been weakened by the returns. He, Holden, Davis, and everyone else now had proof that a substantial proportion of the voters in North Carolina favored some sort of peace initiative.

Zeb recognized that the voters had made an emphatic statement, and he sought to maintain the appearance of Conservative Party unity. He worked very carefully to maintain the compromise with William W. Holden that William A. Graham had engineered. Zeb had grown concerned during the campaign that Conservative Party newspapers were challenging the understanding reached in Raleigh. In a letter to his political ally Edward J. Hale, Zeb suggested that Hale refrain from supporting antipeace candidates openly in his paper so as not to alienate Holden. In a second letter, Zeb explained, "I not only refrained from quarrelling with [Holden] myself, but exerted myself to prevent a rupture between you & him." The strategy seemed to work during the campaign itself. John L. Pennington defended the personal loyalty of William A. Graham in the *Daily Progress* against attacks made by the secessionists. Then, in early November, Holden seemed to make an effort to move toward Zeb's position by calling on citizens to fight the war more vigorously and indicating his willingness to pay higher taxes to support new war measures. Zeb was not convinced, however, that Holden's editorial represented a significant change in policy. He told Hale in November that his opinion of Holden had not changed recently.[20]

Very concerned about recent developments in the mountain counties, Zeb journeyed to the west in early November. What he found was profoundly discouraging. He told Hale: "In my recent visit to the mountains I found an astonishing amount of disloyalty in the counties bordering on Tennessee. A regiment of 800 of the enemy, at Warm Springs was at least $^2/_3$ N.C. Tories! I blush to say it, but it is true. Several men who recently figured in 'peace meetings' have gone off and taken arms with the enemy— Great God what a disgrace to North Carolina!"[21] Despite his best efforts, it appeared as if a significant number of North Carolinians were abandoning their allegiance to the Confederacy. The Confederate defeat at Chattanooga in late November and Longstreet's failure to capture Knoxville several days later only added to the gloom that pervaded the mountain region.

When Zeb returned to Raleigh, his first task was to address the legislature, which had recently been called into session. Unlike many of his other wartime compositions, this address did not open with a description of the glorious future of the Confederacy. Instead, the governor outlined a series of proposals for dealing with many of the problems that had surfaced during the past year. He recommended that the legislature define Home Guard exemptions by law, give him the power to convene the Supreme Court of North Carolina in special session, restore the spring term of the superior courts, support a new system of graded schools, and double the previous year's appropriation of food for the poor. According to Zeb, the revenues generated by the state's blockade-running operation could finance this latter program. The proud governor asserted, "This enterprise of running the blockade and importing army supplies from abroad has proven a most *complete success*." The legislature demonstrated that its members had also been listening to the protest meetings. Each house quickly passed a resolution demanding that the Confederacy cease to impress food in North Carolina. Zeb forwarded the resolution along with his strong personal endorsement to Secretary of War James A. Seddon.[22]

Toward the end of his address to the legislature, Zeb sought to speak to the issue most often raised at the protest meetings: the question of securing peace. For the first time since the protest meetings began, Zeb outlined his full position in public. First, he claimed that the disloyal, though few in numbers, had grown "bold in the presence of national ills." According to Zeb, the great mass of people remained loyal to the Confederacy. This was certainly his hope, but his recent trip to the mountains must have caused him some doubt on this point. Then Zeb pointed out that the peace forces in the Northern states had been "trampled under the feet of reckless and blood-thirsty majorities." This left the people of the South with few options except continued military resistance. Zeb concluded: "We know at last precisely what we would get by submission, and therein has our enemy done us good service—abolition of slavery, confiscation of property, and territorial vassalage!" Zeb here adopted a strategy that, according to Paul D. Escott, Jefferson Davis originated around this time. Appeals to the public would no longer be couched in positive terms about the future of the Confederacy. Instead, the public would be invited to think about the horrors that would accompany federal success.[23]

Zeb's message to the legislature did not prevent protest leaders from acting on the popular desire for peace initiatives. In the House of Commons, leaders of the peace wing of the Conservative Party introduced resolutions in support of opening negotiations with the North. Once again William A. Graham acted as a mediator between the two wings of the party. In a long speech, he suggested that it was not the appropriate time or place to take action for peace. The peace leaders acquiesced, and the House voted to lay the resolutions on the table. Despite this success, however, Zeb recognized that the peace sentiment was still strong. In a letter to Edward J. Hale, he reported, "Mr. Graham was much depressed whilst here on the subject, for though we suppressed the revolution in the Caucus, yet there was much dissatisfaction among men of whom you would have thought better things."[24] Clearly, the political situation and public opinion were equally unstable in this time of crisis.

In the midst of Zeb's struggle to maintain stability and civilian morale, the Confederate bureaucracy struck again. In a letter to the secretary of war, Zeb pointed out that Seddon's department had contracted to make "spirits" at distilleries in Charlotte and Salisbury from thirty thousand bushels of grain that had been gathered under the tax in kind. As Zeb noted, these distilleries would be making alcohol from grain that could have been used to feed the starving civilian population. "I beg to inform you that the laws of this State positively forbid the distillation of any kind of grain within its borders under heavy penalties," Zeb told Seddon. He threatened: "It will, therefore, be my duty to interpose the arm of civil law to prevent and punish this violation thereof unless you order it to cease."[25] Technically Zeb had no power to influence what the Confederacy did with its collected taxes, but his threat indicated that the distilleries did pose a major law enforcement problem for him.

As food shortages developed early in the war, however, Governor Henry T. Clark secured legislation that forbade the distilling of foodstuffs into alcohol. Zeb continued supporting these laws when he assumed office. Of course, Zeb could not spare law enforcement officials to police these new policies. Enforcement, if it was to take place at all, would have to be done by county officials or by communities themselves. Reports of violations came in with some regularity, and specific violators were targeted. James Simmons of Rutherford County identified a significant problem in his area. Simmons even accompanied local magistrates as they made their rounds to ensure compliance with the laws. Simmons and the local officials discovered fifteen illegal stills, but they were unable to arrest the violators. The perpetrators apparently lived in South Carolina and did their distilling in North Carolina. E. R. Norton of Horse Cove in Transylvania County also found a still run by a man from South Carolina; the distiller's tools were hidden in a hollow tree. Norton personally seized the tools and wrote to Vance to find out what he should do.[26] In both of these cases, the moonshiners were not members of the local community, and local pressure could not be applied to them.

Even those people who recognized that some distilling had to be done were unwilling to do it without first obtaining permission from state authorities. Physicians in Rutherford and Jackson Counties petitioned Zeb for permission to produce twenty gallons of whisky; they assured him that "not one drop [would] be used as a beverage." By resisting the distillation of grain into alcohol, communities clearly indicated that they had accepted the state law as legitimate. A petition from Burke County captured all of the elements of this wartime ideology: "There are persons who claim to have authority from the Confederate Govt. to distill grain into whiskey, and said persons have bought & are now buying up grain for that purpose. We respectfully protest against this for the reason, that grain is scarce in the community and the families of soldiers and the poor & needy will require all the surplus which can be spared from the army, for their maintenance & support."[27] Given the absolutely crucial role that community support played in the implementation of the regulation of distilleries, it is easy to understand why Zeb perceived such a threat in the Confederacy's use of the large distilleries in Charlotte and Salisbury. Not only would much precious grain be converted to alcohol, but the community cohesion necessary to enforce the edicts that banned distillation would also be lost. This was something that Zeb understood and the Richmond government did not.

At the same time, Zeb faced a serious challenge within the state. While the peace resolutions had been tabled in the legislature, the peace Conservatives did not meekly disappear. Zeb observed to Edward J. Hale: "The Holdenites are making every effort to raise a row again. God help us. I fear we are on the eve of another revolution & civil war in the State." Soon thereafter, there were indications that Zeb's analysis was correct. The *Daily Progress* editorialized, "Our condition is desperate, and growing worse every day, and without a change of rulers, or management of some kind, the end is not far off." Three days later the same paper called for the end of conscription. Holden began to comment on the terms of reconstruction offered by Abraham Lincoln and the Democrats in Congress.[28] These editorials indicated that Zeb's intuition was accurate.

Holden's correspondence with his allies confirmed that a movement in open opposition to Zeb's reelection was taking shape during this period. In a letter to Thomas Settle, Holden wrote: "The future darkens, and I can see no ray of hope. It is now apparent that North Carolina must soon look to herself. The power that made the war can alone close it—the power of the sovereign states. Our next election will turn on the question of a State Convention. You will know where to find me on such a question."[29] While this letter and similar texts were not available to Zeb and his friends, the general direction that events were taking was nevertheless clear to them. The shaky compromises that William A. Graham had fashioned with Holden in September and with the legislators in December were about to come apart. All of the efforts to maintain the surface unity of the Conservative Party had failed.

In the midst of all of this political infighting, Zeb's health also failed momentarily. In the middle part of December he was confined to his bed. Part of the problem was a bad cold, probably brought on by simple exhaustion. As noted, he was constantly taking difficult trips to the mountains of the west and to the battlefronts in the eastern counties. In addition, his office door was always open during his sixteen-hour workdays. After the war, Zeb's aide Richard H. Battle remembered, "Into his office, day after day, streamed men and women of all conditions of life, with all sorts of schemes for his adoption, petitions for him to grant or refuse, and grievances, real and imaginary, for him to redress." The pace of his work would have worn anyone out, even a vigorous extrovert like Zeb. But there was more to his illness than simple exhaustion. In one letter, the governor described himself as being "sick and quite gloomy." Apparently, recent political developments and the difficult task facing the Confederacy had depressed the usually ebullient Zeb. In the same letter, Zeb also revealed that he had had other health problems, including "a large tumor which [he] had cut from [his] neck."[30] Although his physical and mental ailments were quite severe, Zeb started back to work approximately one week after being stricken.

He immediately faced a crisis in the eastern counties. The unsettled conditions created by the presence of federal troops led to guerrilla war that left civilians of all loyalties open to vicious attacks. Both the Union army and the state government sought to influence developments in eastern North Carolina. One of Zeb's strategies was to form irregular bodies of troops, or rangers, to operate where traditional forces could not. These forces, however, often slipped quickly out of his control. The citizens of Pasquotank County petitioned Vance and the legislature about the irregular forces: "We earnestly petition the Governor and Legislature of North Carolina, satisfied that you cannot protect us with the force at your command, to remove and disband these few rangers." Union general Edward A. Wild took direct action against some of these same marauders. Marching out of Elizabeth City with approximately sixteen hundred African American soldiers, Wild sought the rangers and guerrillas. He reported later: "Finding ordinary measures of little avail, I adopted a more rigorous style of warfare; burned their houses and barns, ate up their livestock, and took hostages from their families. This course we followed throughout the trip."[31] Wild's attacks were deeply resented by eastern North Carolinians, but Zeb was powerless to do anything more than protest.

One incident indicates that Zeb actively supported the guerrilla war in eastern North Carolina. In late January 1863, Jasper Spruill wrote to Zeb for permission to enlist men from Pitt and Martin Counties in his guerrilla band. This was not entirely an unusual request, and Spruill certainly acted as if he had Zeb's support. One of Spruill's promises was that he would "kill Buffaloes." This he proceeded to do, assassinating a leading Unionist by the name of John Giles. According to historian Wayne Durrill, Zeb inspired this deed. Durrill recounted: "Governor Vance reportedly replied: 'Go ahead and kill the king of them and then I will talk about it.'"[32] This piece of correspondence does not survive, however. Although the evidence is somewhat suspect, Zeb may have adopted some of the harsh tactics that he criticized General Wild for using.

As 1863 concluded, Zeb wrote two letters that indicated he had recovered sufficiently to be looking ahead. Each of them also proved that Zeb was already planning his campaign for reelection. One letter was to his close confidant Edward J. Hale. In this missive, Zeb stated that he intended to "make a record showing every desire for peace except at the expenses of [his] country's ruin and dishonor." He continued: "I want the question narrowed down to *Lincoln or no Lincoln*, and I don't intend to fritter away my strength on any minor issue."[33] Clearly Zeb saw the peace issue as paramount, and he was determined to force the opposition to face up to an inherent problem in its strategy. If no one in power in the federal government would negotiate with the South, then Southerners who favored peace would have to choose between reconstruction (Lincoln) and continuing the fight for independence (no Lincoln).

Zeb went on to speculate about whom his opponent would be. He thought it most likely that Alfred Dockery, Edward J. Warren, or Thomas Settle would be the candidate. William W. Holden's candidacy, he believed, was "out of the question." About a week earlier, Zeb had also outlined his basic tactical plan for Hale. He wrote: "I am going to Wilkes County to make a speech as soon as invited[,] preparations for which are going on, then I will go to the army if the enemy permits, and will speak wherever / & whenever / it may be thought prudent."[34] Thus, by the end of December, Zeb had a clear picture in mind of how he would approach the coming campaign, in terms of both strategy and tactics. Zeb's political instincts and knowledge of public sentiment were sure. With just a few modifications, he followed this plan through to election day in August 1864.

Zeb's second letter was to Jefferson Davis, and it figured in his strategy for launching his election campaign. In an effort to frame the peace question in an advantageous manner, Zeb sought the aid of the Confederate president. He explained, "After a careful consideration of all sources of discontent in North Carolina, I have concluded that it will be perhaps impossible to remove it except by making some effort at negotiation with the enemy." Zeb made it clear that he did not expect anything fruitful to come from Davis's attempt to reach an understanding with the Lincoln administration, but he knew that the people wanted the attempt made. Zeb told the president that many leading figures had assured him that when "fair terms" were rejected by the Lincoln administration, this action would "strengthen and intensify the war feeling, and [would] rally all classes to a more cordial support of the government." This last assertion was wishful thinking rather than tough-minded analysis. Even so, it would have been politically advantageous for Zeb to have the federal government's unwillingness to negotiate on record during the campaign, as it would have forced the opposition to either openly embrace reconstruction or drop the peace issue. Unfortunately for Zeb's election strategy, Davis's friendly return letter offered no real assistance. The Confederate chief executive pointed out that his administration had sought three times to negotiate with Lincoln, all to no avail. Davis gave Vance some political advice of his own: "If you would abandon a policy of conciliation and set them at defiance, In this course, frankly and firmly pursued, you would rally around you all that is best and noblest in your State."[35] While he was unable to be of direct assistance to Zeb's campaign, the Confederate president seemingly endorsed Zeb's intended strategy.

The compromises that William A. Graham had fashioned in September and December were obviously falling apart by the end of 1863. Federal military successes made the Confederacy's prospects in the fight for independence look exceedingly gloomy. The absence of open protest meetings in North Carolina did not mean that either the causes of the people's discontent or their feelings of growing hostility toward the Confederacy had disappeared. Some shrewd public figures and men worried about the social and economic revolution that emancipation promised sought a way to tie popular discontent to a program that would end the fighting while perpetuating the status quo. In retrospect, their quest was impossible, but they found the alternative so abhorrent that they refused to face reality. Zeb, on the other hand, recognized reality. He perceived the military weakness of the Confederacy, but he also saw that the only way to preserve the status quo was to continue the war. This would be the plan he offered the citizens of North Carolina in the political campaign of 1864.

The coming of the new year of 1864 brought North Carolina partisan politics out of the shadows and into the bright glare of the light. Zeb certainly expected this to happen. He wrote to William A. Graham on the first day of 1864 and told the author of the Conservative Party compromise that it was now dead. Zeb explained that he knew for certain that William W. Holden was sponsoring public meetings at which participants were calling for a state convention that would be used to seek peace. Zeb indicated that he would not allow such a program to be carried out. He asserted, "I will see the Conservative party blown into a thousand atoms and Holden and his understrappers in hell . . . before I will consent to a course which I think will bring dishonor and ruin upon both state & Confederacy."[1] From Vance's perspective, the compromise had come to an end and Graham needed to accept the changed situation and prepare for the coming political campaign.

The next day Zeb wrote an unusually introspective letter to David L. Swain. Toward the end of the letter, Zeb asked Swain if he thought Zeb should run for reelection. In fact, the query was more a request for Swain's blessing than for his advice. In the remainder of the letter, Zeb provided a detailed explanation of why he felt that he had to campaign against Holden and the convention movement. He informed Swain that Holden and others had already drawn up resolutions and sent them to Johnston County for presentation at an upcoming gathering of peace protesters. Zeb told Swain, as he had told Graham, that he would not accept this course of action, "believing," he said, "that it would be ruin alike to the State and Confederacy, producing war and devastation at home, and that it would steep the name [of North Carolina] in infamy and make her memory a reproach among the nations."[2] Zeb placed great emphasis upon the impossibility of compromising with Holden and his followers.

Then Zeb took the unusual step of taking a broad look at what the future held for North Carolina and the Confederacy. He told Swain that he thought that the American patriots had faced equally daunting odds during the Revolutionary War and yet had prevailed. Thus, it was possible that the Confederacy would succeed if it could manage to feed the families of soldiers and, by implication, keep the Confederate army together. However, he continued: "Liberty and independence can only be gathered of blood and misery sustained and fostered by devoted patriotism and heroic manhood. This requires a deep hold on the popular heart, *and our people will not pay this price*[,] I am satisfied[,] for their national independence." Having come to this conclusion, Zeb asserted: "But Sir, in tracing this sad story of the . . . self imposed degradation of a great people, the historian shall not say it was due to the weakness of their Governor."[3] He would never say any of these words in public or admit his own convictions in the political campaign that followed.

The significance of the frank observations Zeb made to Swain is enormous. Zeb admitted to Swain that he had reached the same conclusion that Holden had: the Confederacy would not be able to achieve independence. Unlike Holden, who sought to end the bloodshed, however, Zeb was willing for the fighting to continue. He thought that this was necessary for several reasons. First, North Carolina had no other real options. If the state tried to withdraw from the Confederacy, it would find itself fighting fellow Southerners. Zeb foresaw, probably accurately, that such internecine warfare would devastate the state physically and fiscally. A second reason was of equal importance to Zeb: the withdrawal of North Carolina from the Confederacy would be completely dishonorable. North Carolina would be disgraced, and so would Vance as the governor of the traitor state. Thus, Zeb was determined that North Carolina would fulfill completely its obligations to the threatened Southern nation. This was particularly important because outsiders, especially Virginians, had already branded North Carolina's soldiers as ineffective and its civilians as Unionists.

Zeb waited impatiently for Holden and his allies to give him an opportunity to both attack them as threats to the state's honor and expose the flaws in their peace plan. Unwilling to give the opposition the initiative, Zeb and his allies tried to prepare the public for the battle to come. Edward J. Hale published a story about Holden on January 4 that anticipated the coming call for a state peace convention and accused Holden of proposing to "go out of the Confederacy." A letter sent to Zeb the next day seemingly provided confirmation of the radical nature of the convention movement. The correspondent reported that he had talked to a proconvention person in Greensboro and asked the man what would happen if the Lincoln administration refused the North Carolina convention's peace overtures. The man replied that "he would have N.C. secede from the Confederacy, & then make the very best terms with Lincoln & the Congress of the U.S. that she could." This was exactly the kind of statement that Zeb hoped his opponents would proclaim in the Johnston County resolutions. That same day the *Daily Progress*, a proconvention paper, accused the Confederate Congress of military despotism.[4] It was clear that an open break within the Conservative Party was just a few days away.

At the meeting in Johnston County on January 7, a large assembly did adopt a series of resolutions, just as Zeb had expected. Unexpectedly, however, they were extremely adroitly drawn, and they left Zeb with little room to criticize them publicly. The participants at the Johnston County meeting protested the conscription of men who had legally paid substitutes to take their places in the army; opposed the proposed suspension of the writ of habeas corpus; called for a state convention that would secure state sovereignty and protect North Carolinians' civil liberties; and endorsed the newspapers that supported a negotiated peace.[5] These resolutions were much what Zeb had expected, but they were phrased in such a way that it would have been difficult for him to criticize them. They emphasized the protection of civil liberties rather than the need for North Carolina to negotiate for peace.

Still, Zeb might have attacked the protesters for previous resolutions that were disloyal to the Confederacy. But Holden and his allies had very cleverly minimized this possibility by sponsoring other resolutions at the Johnston County meeting that were agreeable to Vance. One stated: "The prompt and decided course of Gov. Vance in maintaining the rights of the people, and the supremacy of the civil over the military law, meets our unqualified approbation." The document also encouraged the assembly to make sure that soldiers' families would be fed, and it asked the soldiers not to "desert their comrades in arms." Finally, the participants at the rally contributed two hundred dollars to the Stonewall Jackson monument fund. Obviously Zeb could not object to these sentiments. In fact, he remarked in a letter to Hale that the Johnston County resolutions "were not particularly objectionable." The mildness of the resolutions caught even the secessionists off guard and made them suspicious. Kenneth Rayner wrote to a friend, "I hear the proceedings of the Johnston meeting are covert, and therefore the more dangerous."[6] Zeb's original campaign plan was based on assumptions about the protest movement that appeared at first to be too simplistic. His opponents were going to launch a sophisticated campaign that would require a flexible response from Zeb.

The proconvention forces continued their aggressive, indirect campaign after the Johnston County meeting. The *Daily Progress* denied that any plan to take North Carolina out of the Confederacy existed, while at the same time it denounced the proposal to give President Davis power to suspend the writ of habeas corpus. Holden claimed that there was no organized opposition to Vance's reelection. On January 20, Holden decried what he saw as an effort to defame the convention movement. He asserted that the movement was not designed to undercut the Confederacy and that it was not treasonable. Rather, he argued, achieving a peace settlement would prevent unnecessary bloodshed and preserve the institution of slavery. In the same issue, however, Holden published two letters that may have reflected his position more accurately. One correspondent urged Vance to call the state legislature into session for the purpose of summoning a convention, and the other wrote that he would accept peace without Confederate independence if the people approved.[7] While Holden did not generate the latter plan, the fact that he printed the letter indicates the direction of his thinking.

As everyone expected, the Johnston County meeting provoked further reactions. The first was a potential disaster for Zeb. As Holden and his allies had expected, Jefferson Davis asked the Confederate Congress for the power to suspend the writ of habeas corpus. This request was soon granted by the Congress with provisions that seemed to be—and in fact were—aimed at eradicating the protest movement in North Carolina. One clause appeared to have been designed to suppress peace protests, which occurred with more frequency in North Carolina than elsewhere in the Confederacy. It suspended the writ for any person arrested for "advising or inciting others to abandon the Confederate cause, or to resist the Confederate States, or to adhere to the enemy."[8] Since the convention advocates had already stressed the importance of preserving civil liberties, this provision alone ensured that the issue of civil liberties would become a significant one in the campaign.

The public meetings anticipated by most astute political observers soon began. Participants at two of the first, which occurred in Greene and Granville Counties, employed the compromise strategy of both calling for a convention and endorsing Zeb's civil liberties record. At other meetings in Guilford and Moore Counties, North Carolina's citizens continued the trend. Approximately a thousand people attended a Greensboro meeting, where they were addressed by prominent leaders of the community. The Moore County meeting at Carthage was also directed by some of the proconvention local elite. The participants at the Carthage meeting praised the state supreme court for protecting civil liberties and protested the suspension of the writ, but they also mentioned the hated tax in kind.[9] Thus, the meetings took on the broad coloration of protest that the meetings of the previous summer had displayed.

The proconvention forces also introduced new strategies to mobilize public opinion in favor of their cause. In Forsyth, Henderson, and Rutherford Counties, men began to sign petitions and send them directly to Zeb.

This method of expressing support for the convention proposal had a number of advantages. The first was that Zeb was made to feel the full weight of public opinion unmediated by the newspapers. Second, and probably more important, Zeb's opponents used petitions to generate expressions of support for a convention without running the risk of making public addresses, which could lead to arrest and incarceration without benefit of habeas corpus. Proconvention forces also sponsored a letter-writing campaign; a form letter from the campaign is preserved in the papers of Thomas Settle.[10]

Finally, Holden took the offensive by printing a series of relatively nonpartisan editorials. First, he complained that the convention movement had been unfairly branded as an unpatriotic movement that favored the reconstruction of the Union. Holden denied the accuracy of this characterization emphatically. On February 5, Holden brought his pro-Confederate offensive to a climax by writing the following: "We must fight and talk for peace at the same time; and the effectiveness of the latter, whether by public meetings, or public journals, or of members of Congress or of State Legislatures, or Conventions of the States, depends on the vigor of the former. *We must treat with arms in our hands*."[11] There was nothing in this statement to which Zeb could object. The proconvention forces appeared to have seized the political initiative and outmaneuvered the governor and his allies.

The variety of strategies used by Zeb's opponents threw him and his allies off balance for a short period. Edward J. Hale wrote to William A. Graham, "We are on the verge of ruin, and I verily believe that unless the purposes of a treasonable party in this State can be arrested, in some way, & at once, all is lost." Graham felt that Hale had overreacted, and he saw a greater threat to North Carolina's internal peace lurking in his ally's words. In his reply to Hale, Graham observed "that any attempt to introduce military force to control freedom of opinion or discussion, would have a most unfortunate operation." A community leader in Greensboro wrote to the secretary of war and reported that the proconvention leaders of a public meeting in their community included "some of [their] most prominent citizens." Although the meeting itself was "harmless," disaffection was rapidly increasing in that part of North Carolina.[12] The Vance forces were on the defensive, and they believed that the state faced a great crisis.

Zeb agreed with their assessment, and once again he saw the bungling government in Richmond as the greatest threat to the success of the Confederate revolution. The political stability of North Carolina was tenuous, and it looked as though the actions of the Confederate government might upset the balance with potentially devastating consequences. As Holden

William Woods Holden, ca. 1865. Holden was the editor of the Standard, *Vance's opponent in the 1864 gubernatorial election, provisional governor in 1865, and governor of North Carolina from 1869 to 1871, when he was impeached. (North Carolina Division of Archives and History, Raleigh)*

and his allies had anticipated, Jefferson Davis sent a formal request to the Confederate Congress asking for legislation that would allow him to suspend the writ of habeas corpus. The Congress readily agreed, and in less than a week the bill had become law. On February 9, Zeb addressed an argumentative letter to the Confederate president. He urged Davis not to use the powers granted to him under the new legislation. "If our citizens are left untouched by the arm of military violence," he wrote, "I do not despair of an appeal to reason and the patriotism of the people at the ballot box." Zeb informed Davis that he would begin his campaign for reelection in the very near future, and he stated that he was confident he would succeed if Davis refrained from using "bayonets and dungeons." The governor pointed out that it was essential for Confederate success that North Carolinians be zealous supporters of the Confederacy, and he argued that their enthusiasm could only be won through persuasion.[13]

Zeb then turned his attention to practicalities. He pointed out to the Confederate president that it would take two-thirds of the state legislators' votes to create a state convention. Zeb assured Davis that the votes to make that happen were simply not there. The only other way for the legislature to call a convention was to allow a referendum on the issue; if a referendum was submitted to the voters, a majority of the electorate would have to favor a convention in order for the measure to pass. Again Zeb assured Davis that such a result was "impossible." He concluded his analysis by observing, "The approaching State elections will afford an opportunity for a full and complete discussion of all issues, the result of which I do not fear, if left to ourselves." This last phrase was the key to Zeb's position. If Davis and the rest of the Confederate leadership would just not meddle in North Carolina's affairs, Zeb believed that he could take care of Holden and the convention movement through normal political channels. Davis was outraged by Zeb's words, which he called "discourteous," "untrue," and "slander."[14]

Showing little of the concern of his allies, Zeb prepared for the coming campaign. He contacted the Twenty-sixth Regiment band and arranged for them to play at his speech in Wilkesboro. He corresponded with Calvin Cowles in Wilkes County about travel and local arrangements and agreed to give the speech on February 22, Washington's birthday. In a letter to Edward J. Hale, Zeb analyzed the strength of his position at that moment. He concluded that he did not need to worry about the secessionists. They would not run a candidate, because "they [were] as dead as a door nail." He expected to capture their votes, as well as some from the different factions found among the people who supported peace, by arguing in favor of a vigorous war and opposing the convention movement. After Vance wrote this letter, one of his supporters accused Holden of starting the convention movement for the purpose of defeating Vance for the governorship. Holden retorted: "This charge is utterly without foundation."[15] Zeb refused to be cowed by the initiatives and unexpected maneuvers of the opposition, and he prepared confidently for the coming campaign.

The Confederate Congress passed two pieces of legislation on February 17 that would have an impact on the campaign that followed. The first amended the conscription law by extending the age of maximum eligibility for the draft from forty-five to fifty. This amendment was an attempt to place the state militias under the Richmond government's control. Those over forty-five were expected to remain at home, but they became militarily subject to the authority of the Confederacy, rather than their state governments. The Congress added a requirement that any planter who employed an exempted overseer on his plantation had to agree to contribute two hundred pounds of meat to his local government for distribution to soldiers' families and the poor. Zeb assumed that the expansion of conscription would have a significant impact on popular opinion, and he requested that western North Carolina be exempted from the amended act. The Davis administration turned down his request.[16] In fact, however, there seems to have been little additional protest about these changes in the conscription law. Virtually everyone in North Carolina had already chosen a side on this issue, and these relatively minor changes made little difference.

The other law had a significant effect that few people noticed either at the time or later. The Congress passed the Currency Reform Act in an attempt to deal with the rapid increase in the rate of inflation. The Confederate government had insufficient revenues to cover even a small proportion of the costs of the war, and it made up for this deficit by printing vast sums of paper money, an inflationary practice. Since this money would have value only if the Confederacy won its independence, moreover, growing pessimism about the viability of the Confederacy fed the inflation. These two pressures pushed the general price index for the eastern section of the Confederacy to over four thousand in March 1864 from a base of one hundred in the spring of 1861. This fortyfold increase in prices was a disaster for North Carolina's small landowning farmers. The Currency Reform Act was designed to counter the inflationary trend. It mandated that by April 1, 1864, people in the Confederacy would have to use new currency. Anyone could receive two new dollars by trading in three of the existing dollars. The legislation was designed to remove approximately 33 percent of the inflated paper currency from circulation. The economic policy actually worked. Between March 1864, when the gubernatorial campaign started in earnest, and August 1864, when the voting took place, the general price index declined slightly.[17] This development was a significant political bonus for Zeb. Throughout the entire campaign, the voters enjoyed more economic stability than they had had at any other time during the war. Because prices were already extremely high and declined only slightly, no one noticed their good fortune at the time, but Zeb nevertheless benefited from the decline in the rate of inflation and its effect on the voters.

Zeb traveled to Wilkesboro, where he had long planned to give the opening speech of his reelection campaign. The weather on February 22 was clear and cold; there had been a snowstorm in the region less than a week before. The Twenty-sixth Regiment band starting playing about an hour before Zeb spoke, and it warmed up the crowd with many favorites, including "The Old North State." A large crowd—estimated at eight hundred to two thousand people—came to hear the governor speak to the assemblage for approximately three hours. To ensure that the speech reached the widest possible audience, Zeb employed G. Clinton Stedman of the *Richmond Enquirer* to take the speech down in shorthand for later publication. He started his speech with a humorous observation: "I do not know [if] it is possible for me to make myself heard by this large audience, unless I adopt the plan of the one[-]armed soldier who could not hug his sweetheart all the way around, and so he was forced to chalk the distance he could reach on one side, and then turn and hug as far on the other." Stedman recorded that the audience laughed at this remark. In his opening statement, Zeb went on to say that he was going to be doing something unusual for a politician in his speech: "telling the truth."[18] He mocked himself, to the amusement of the crowd, by suggesting that he was a political speaker who had not always been completely straightforward.

Quickly Zeb moved on to weightier topics. The first was the question of whether North Carolina should call a convention. Zeb pointed out that the people of Wilkes County were in their present straits because of secession. He then asked if the solution was another dose of the same medicine. To illustrate his point, he asked, "Suppose you were sick of typhoid fever and had been close to death's door; and becoming convalescent the physician should gravely inform you that the only plan to affect your entire recovery would be to take another spell of the infernal fever? Would you not think him a fool?" Then Zeb went on to point out that North Carolina's secession from the United States had been brought about by popularly elected officials and that the action had represented the will of the people at that time.[19]

Seeking positive reasons for citizens to support the Confederacy, Zeb argued that loyalty to country was part of a series of bonds that also included loyalty to family, community, state, and nation. He maintained that loyalty to the Confederacy mandated supporting its Constitution. Zeb then read several articles from the Confederate Constitution that stated that no state or group that belonged to the Confederacy could legally negotiate with other governments. He speculated about what would happen if a convention were called and it decided, despite the Constitution, to secede from the Confederacy. He concluded that the Confederacy would declare war on North Carolina, and that all of the horrors of combat would consequently be directly visited upon the state. "Old Abraham," Zeb explained further, "is fighting us not because we are a part of the Southern Confederacy, but because we are in rebellion to the old Union; and so long as we refused obedience to him he would continue to fight us." This meant, he argued, that if North Carolina left the Confederacy it would become involved in a war with two enemies. Or, Zeb continued, if the state rejoined the Union, the men who were now loyal soldiers of the Confederacy would be required to become Union soldiers. Upon consideration of this possibility, Zeb concluded "that any step" toward leaving the Confederacy would "involve" North Carolina "in a deeper and bloodier war."[20]

Then, Zeb painted a picture of what would happen in the future if North Carolina returned to the Union. He played on the racism of his audience by emphasizing the effects of African American freedom. He noted, accurately, the hypocrisy of many Northern states that forbade blacks from entering them, and he informed his auditors that there would be no escape from the problems of racial readjustment. He mentioned that the federal government was already confiscating land from its white owners in the Sea Islands and making it available to black farmers. He said that he would no more trust Lincoln on slavery than a shepherd should trust a wolf. He warned his audience that those people who thought they could work with the federal government on racial issues made the same type of proposition as the lunatic who wanted "to purchase Mount Aetna for a powder house."[21]

Zeb then confronted the desire of many in the peace movement to restore the old Union with slavery intact. His response to their desire is a classic: "I tell you candidly, there is no more possibility of reconstructing the old Union and reinstating things as they were four years ago, than exists for you to gather up the scattered bones of your sons who have fallen in this struggle from one end of the country to the other, recloth them with flesh, fill their veins with the blood they have so generously shed, and their lungs with the same breath with which they breathed out their last prayer for their country's triumph and independence." Zeb went on for several minutes explaining why national reconciliation with "the murderer of his father, the outrager of his sister" was impossible. He asserted that even if the South were overwhelmed in this conflict, the people of the section would later rise again in revolt and eventually achieve their independence.[22]

Then Zeb turned to his favorite target: the secessionists. He did this in the context of discussing the rights of men who had hired substitutes who were now subject to conscription. Justice Richmond Pearson was still providing these men with protection, and Zeb vowed to continue to support him as long as Pearson's rulings were sustained by the state supreme court. However, Zeb satirized the individuals who had hired substitutes as rich men who "were for giving the last man and the last dollar (provided they didn't happen to be the final individual, and the dollar came out of the pocket of any other man)." Stedman recorded considerable audience support for Zeb's attacks on the upper classes and the secessionists. Zeb also defended the suspension of the writ of habeas corpus and quoted a lawyer's opinion defending the suspension of the writ from a recent news-paper. Finally, Zeb compared North Carolina's situation to that of Kentucky, where General Ambrose Burnside had imposed harsh martial law. Vance concluded that North Carolinians were much better off than the people of Kentucky, and that they should therefore accept the temporary inconve-niences that were natural in their present situation.[23]

Finally, Zeb turned to the military prospects of the Confederacy. First, he asserted, "There never was a war upon the face of the earth, that has been, in my opinion, so badly managed." As we have seen, that observation was not a rhetorical exaggeration; much of Zeb's interaction with the Confed-erate government involved his dissatisfaction with its management of the war. Zeb compared the Confederate position with those of the Americans during the Revolution and the Scottish in their struggles with the English. He maintained that the Confederacy had greater resources available to it than either of these historical combatants. While admitting that the Con-federacy had suffered losses near the coast and along rivers, — "We have never been much with water affairs. Indeed, I believe most of our people prefer whiskey," he quipped — Zeb argued that the Southern forces were still strong, and he noted they were led by "the greatest general of modern times, who nearest approaches Washington in all that is noble and true." Thus, Zeb concluded, the Confederacy could and would achieve indepen-dence if only his auditors would put up with the small annoyances that war produced and continue to support their family members and neighbors in the army.[24]

Seizing upon an episode in the New Testament Book of Ephesians, Zeb made one final point in a rousing conclusion: "Do nothing rash." He con-tinued, "I have come among you, to beg you in the name of reason, of humanity, to obey the law; to recognize order and authority; to do nothing except in the manner prescribed by the Constitution." He then thanked the members of his audience for their patience with his "rambling remarks."[25] This last statement was, of course, a form of false modesty on Zeb's part. It is clear from reading the speech today that it was carefully and artfully crafted. Zeb dealt with the major issues in the campaign directly, but he framed them in such a way that his opponents were placed at an immediate disadvantage. He also used many cleverly phrased anecdotes and humor-ous stories to allow the most unsophisticated of his auditors to understand the points that he was making exactly. From a political point of view, the speech was a very effective opening to the campaign.

Zeb quickly followed his opening speech with additional thrusts against the convention movement. On successive days, he spoke at Statesville, Taylorsville, and Salisbury. The crowds were large at all stops, and according to one source the governor spoke to three thousand people at Salisbury. Reactions to the Wilkesboro speech within the political establishment were generally positive. One of Zeb's friends admitted that the majority of the crowd in Wilkesboro probably disagreed with Zeb on the convention question, but he thought that they still enjoyed the speech. It was first printed in a North Carolina newspaper on March 1. Calvin Cowles, who was present at the Wilkesboro speech, asserted that the published report had been altered. He claimed that Zeb had been much harder on the secessionists in his talk than the published version of the speech indicated. There is some evidence that Cowles's claim is accurate, although Zeb's published statements about the secessionists seem quite severe.[26] In any case, after March 1 the governor's point of view became available to the public.

Zeb's early campaign efforts had to share public attention with other political developments. First, William W. Holden, claiming that the suspension of the writ of habeas corpus made the attempt to publish freely a perilous action, announced that he was suspending publication of his newspaper. The editor of the *Daily Progress* in Raleigh also sought to distance his paper from the extreme peace position that Zeb had described in his speech. On March 2, John L. Pennington editorialized, "No peace sentiment that *we* have ever uttered was intended to look to re-construction or secession from the Confederacy." The next day, Holden dropped a political bombshell. In a special issue of the *Standard*, he announced that he would oppose Vance for governor. Maintaining that the governor had joined the "Destructives," Holden argued that peace was the major issue in the campaign. He proclaimed, "If the people of North Carolina are for perpetual conscription, impressments, and seizures to keep up a perpetual, devastating, and exhausting war, let them vote for Governor Vance." Holden went on to say that he would not campaign directly before the people.[27] This latter decision probably had a decisive effect on the outcome of the election. Since Holden would not have access to the public through his newspaper and would not speak in public during the campaign, he left the stage entirely open for the energetic governor to shape the campaign as he pleased.

Many individuals who supported the peace initiative were immediately dubious about Holden's candidacy. Confederate congressman James T. Leach wrote a confidential letter to Zeb. In it, Leach pleaded with the governor to say something to satisfy the peace men. "You would beat Holden and all comers to death!" he wrote. "The people like you personally, and don't like your present competition Holden personally." University of North Carolina Professor Samuel F. Phillips remarked: "I can hardly anticipate the state of things which would make it proper that Mr. Holden should be governor of North Carolina, at a time when spirit, coolness, singleness of purpose, & statesmanship, are so much required as now. Vance may lack the latter qualification, but I attribute the others to him. I do not regard Holden as possessing any of them." Holden's Wilkes County political ally Calvin Cowles was surprised by Holden's announcement, and he observed, "Vance has been as good a Conservative as possible under 'trying circumstances.'" Zeb's own reaction was rather resigned. In a letter to William A. Graham, Zeb wrote, "The man who has borne deepest on my confidence and whom my friends have persisted in apologizing for, has at length shown his purpose."[28]

Zeb did not let the appearance of a formal opponent deter him. Instead, he began to map out a vigorous speaking schedule, ignoring his own illness and the illness in his family. He soon received an invitation—undoubtedly arranged by some military friends at his request—to address a North Carolina brigade on winter duty in Virginia. This became the first address in a very successful series of speeches Zeb delivered to brigades between March 26 and April 3; the speeches later became legendary when the Confederate cause was celebrated and sentimentalized in the post-Reconstruction period. There was widespread testimony that the officers were delighted by what Zeb had to say. Jeb Stuart apparently followed Zeb around, trying to listen to each of his addresses. Robert E. Lee was so pleased that he attended two of the talks and honored Zeb with a review of the entire army. Zeb was "the only civilian so honored." Colonel Joseph E. Webb reported, "I don't think I ever saw a more attentive or enthusiastic audience than he had here, not withstanding that the men had to stand in mud and water all the time he was speaking." Apparently when he addressed the first brigades, he sought to identify himself with them by addressing them as "fellow soldiers." But Zeb quickly recognized that the salutation might be resented, and from that point on he admitted that he had "skulked out of service by being elected to a little office down in North Carolina."[29] This self-deprecating humor served Zeb very well with the officers, and he appears to have aroused considerable enthusiasm among the rank and file as well.

Only one detailed description of any one of these addresses exists. It was published in the *Fayetteville Observer* and was apparently authored by Edward J. Hale's son. According to young Hale, the speech he described was the final one of the tour. Zeb spoke for about an hour and forty minutes despite having a hoarse voice from "continual speaking and exposure in bad weather." He simplified his address to cover three major points. First, he argued that North Carolina could not take action outside of the confines of the Confederate Constitution without suffering disastrous consequences. Next, Zeb assured the soldiers that the people of North Carolina supported them, and he pointed to the supplies that the state government supplied to them and to their families at home as evidence. Finally, he praised the soldiers for their great record in battle, saying that they had defeated every general that had faced them. He concluded by stating that "if the army but fought as well as it had done, the end of the summer would see the end of the war."[30] Zeb had obviously tailored his message to his audience, but he nevertheless said things that were consistent with the positions he took in his address to the people in Wilkesboro.

Zeb's political opponents painted a somewhat different picture of the reception of the army speeches. According to the *Daily Progress* of Raleigh, the officers supported Zeb but the common soldiers were for Holden. There has been little evidence to support this assertion, and most historians have concluded that it was simply wishful thinking. However, a privately held letter written by Jesse M. Frank backs up the claim of the *Daily Progress*. Frank described one of Vance's speeches: "I will say to you that Gov- Vance has been threw the army making stump speeches[.] that is a[ ]thing near all of the soldiers in regular service dispise to here[.]" Frank's comments indicate that enthusiasm for Zeb's candidacy was far from universal. Frank continued: "Some of the officers[,] the onley vance men we have in our part of the army[,] cuse him [Holden] saying he wanted peace on any terms."[31] It would be incautious to draw any conclusions from this single piece of evidence, but it does seem reasonable to expect that there were differences of political opinion within the ranks and that some—or even many—soldiers did not agree with Zeb's positions.

Upon his return to Raleigh, Zeb found that the political situation was still unstable. On April 6, Holden brought out a special issue of the *Standard* that presented his platform for the campaign. It was quite general, but he used the common phrase "honorable peace" to describe his ultimate objective. Five days later, Holden assured the electorate that he was opposed to both the reconstruction of the Union and submission to federal authority. In addition to Holden's burst of activity, there was further evidence that the convention movement was still alive. After Zeb had returned from giving his speeches in late February, he had exultantly told Edward J. Hale, "the Convention is dead, *dead*, *dead*, if our public men will only be a little bold." According to historian William T. Auman, Zeb was partially correct. There were only thirty-two public meetings during this period, twelve of them in Wake and Johnston Counties, and this figure was only one-third as many meetings as were held the previous summer.[32] Still, some meetings did take place, and they were duly publicized by Vance's opponents.

Zeb recognized the strategy that Holden and his supporters were pursuing. In a letter to William A. Graham, Zeb observed, "The only damage [that they are] doing to me is by making the impression that I have 'gone over' to the secessionists." This was precisely the tactic that his opponents used. The *Daily Progress* claimed that by opposing the convention movement Zeb had betrayed the Conservative Party and the people of North Carolina. Later, the same paper noted that the people who most bitterly opposed Vance in 1862—the secessionists—now supported the governor. The most virulent attack against Vance came at a public meeting in Wake County. The participants at this gathering attacked Vance's Wilkesboro speech for being "*all war, and no propositions for peace.*"[33] While Zeb made light of the issue in his letter to Graham, both citizens' desire for peace and their hatred of the secessionists were still potent forces in North Carolina politics.

Proof of their power was provided in a special election for Congress held in the Seventh District in April. The incumbent, who had the support of Holden in the fall of 1863, had died soon after he was elected. The major candidates who vied to replace him were James M. Leach and Alfred G. Foster. Leach was the peace candidate, but he refused to directly connect himself with Holden. Foster was "staunchly for independence," and he actively sided with Zeb. Following a campaign in which the issues were clearly delineated, the voters elected Leach by a clear majority; even a majority of soldiers voted for the peace candidate.[34] Clearly there was substantial support for peace, even if the convention issue was not as potent as Zeb's opponents had hoped.

They had one more issue to introduce into the campaign. This was a defense of civil liberties. The decision of the Confederate Congress to give Jefferson Davis the power to suspend the writ of habeas corpus was widely deplored. The strongest reaction to the legislation came in Georgia, however, rather than North Carolina. Georgia governor Joseph E. Brown and Confederate vice president Alexander Stephens made vitriolic statements condemning the suspension legislation. The Holden partisans quickly picked up on the development in Georgia. The *Daily Progress* praised both Stephens and Brown for their defense of civil liberties and announced that Holden was running on the "Georgia Platform." A proconvention public meeting in Wake County concluded its indictment of Zeb with the following statement: "We had a right to expect that the Governor, like Gov. Brown, would properly characterize the law suspending the *habeas corpus*, and boldly demand its repeal. When Gov. Vance deserts civil liberty and the rights of the State and throws himself into the embraces of his former enemies, he cannot be surprised at our deserting him." This last assertion was potentially very dangerous for Zeb, and he knew it. As a result, he eagerly accepted an invitation to speak on April 22 at Fayetteville, where he knew that he would get full and friendly newspaper coverage.[35]

Two days before Zeb spoke in Fayetteville, he received very valuable campaign assistance from the Confederate army. A substantial force made up primarily of North Carolina soldiers commanded by North Carolina general Robert F. Hoke attacked a federal garrison at Plymouth. Through the innovative use of a locally based ironclad, the Confederate force cut off the federal troops from reinforcement. Following a fierce bombardment and a courageous advance by the Confederate army, the federal forces surrendered. The Confederates secured approximately twenty-five hundred prisoners and a great deal of needed materiel, and they also regained control over a section of eastern North Carolina. This victory helped to shore up morale throughout the state. As the primary historian of the battle noted, "The battle of Plymouth created a constituency in North Carolina for continuing the war."[36] If the Confederate army in the main theaters of the war could hold their own against the great armies arrayed against them, the victory at Plymouth would be particularly helpful to Zeb's campaign.

A new responsibility fell to Zeb in the immediate aftermath of the victory at Plymouth. General Braxton Bragg, now Jefferson Davis's military adviser, reported to Zeb: "The President directs that the Negroes captured by our forces be turned over to you for the present." African American prisoners of war were going to be treated differently from other soldiers. Zeb was instructed to find out if any of them had been enslaved in North Carolina; those persons were to be returned to their former owners. The Richmond government would try to locate the former owners of the other African American prisoners, at which point Zeb would also be responsible for returning these former slaves to their owners. Bragg further instructed Zeb "to take the necessary steps to have such disposition kept out of the newspapers" in order to avoid "complications with the military authorities of the United States."[37] What Bragg was asking Zeb to do contravened the prisoner of war agreement that the Confederacy had agreed to with the Union. Zeb followed this order very effectively. No further reference to the policy or to the actual disposition of the African American prisoners of war can be found.

By the end of the third week in April, the election campaign was well under way. Several features of the campaign were relatively clear by this point. First, Zeb's opposition had run a relatively subtle campaign that forced him to focus on new issues. Second, two relatively long-term developments that were beyond Zeb's control were working in his favor. Starting with the overwhelming victory at Plymouth, Confederate military fortunes did not significantly decline throughout the remainder of the election campaign. This meant that the defeatism that Zeb noted in his January letter to Swain did not become as decisive a factor in the voting as it could have been. In addition, the hyperinflation of the Confederate currency ceased, and the civilian population enjoyed a period of monetary stability. Finally, William W. Holden was not the most effective opponent that Zeb could have faced. Holden refused to campaign before the public in joint debates of the traditional North Carolina style. He also chose to silence his foremost weapon, the *Standard*, during the early part of the campaign. Furthermore, Holden had spent the better part of fifteen years alienating the former Whigs in North Carolina as the editor of the major Democratic paper in the state. The result was that many of the political leaders who agreed with Holden on policy matters simply could not bring themselves to support him for governor. Thus, Zeb was well positioned to run a strong campaign. It was clear, nevertheless, that the citizens of the state were committed to minimal government and opposed to the invasion of their lives by the Confederacy. Zeb still had some battles to fight before he could be reelected.

Zeb was eager to confront the new challenges posed by the Holden campaign. As a true extrovert, Zeb thrived in public settings in which he was the center of attention. He now recognized that his opponents had finally hit upon a position that could prove to be broadly popular among the electorate. From the beginning of the war, the political leadership of North Carolina had justified its defiance of the Lincoln administration by claiming that the call for troops after Fort Sumter was a violation of civil liberties. However, the imposition of conscription, the tax in kind, and the suspension of the writ of habeas corpus had made the Confederate government seem to be little different from the Lincoln administration. Obviously, Holden and his allies sought to tie Zeb to the highly unpopular Davis administration and to the despised secessionists in North Carolina.

Zeb's task at Fayetteville was to make sure that he publicly distanced himself from the president and his local supporters. As was the case with the Wilkesboro speech, he left little to chance. Zeb left Raleigh on a train on Thursday afternoon, April 21. During the trip, he stopped to speak at several locations for a total of two hours; during these impromptu speeches, he apparently encouraged people to join him in Fayetteville. When he arrived at his destination, he was greeted by the mayor and a large crowd. After giving a brief speech, Zeb retired to the Fayetteville Hotel, where he met with local groups throughout the evening. Friday was an unofficial holiday in town, and all business was suspended. Throngs of people showed up from neighboring counties throughout the morning. By the time that Zeb reached the speaker's platform at half past eleven, a military band was entertaining the crowd. The local newspaper estimated its size at approximately three thousand people, an extraordinary audience for that time.[1]

The early part of Vance's speech was quite similar to what he had said in Wilkesboro. He told the audience that he had come to tell the truth, no matter how painful. He went on to say that the most critical time in the life of the Confederacy had been reached, and that its fate would be determined by the end of the summer. He acknowledged that everyone wanted peace, but he stated that removing the state from the Confederacy by means of a convention would not bring peace. As he had at Wilkesboro, Zeb considered the possible results if North Carolina acted on its own and predicted disaster. He pointed out that the popularly elected legislature could do anything that a convention could do within the confines of the Confederate Constitution, and he recommended that it should be the body that people looked to for action.[2]

The first innovation in the address was Zeb's acknowledgment of Holden's candidacy. Since Holden had not formally announced it until after the Wilkesboro speech, Zeb had been careful to avoid alienating the editor in February. Now he took his gloves off and went to work. He mocked Holden for refusing to debate in public, saying that he had sent a personal invitation to Holden to meet him in Fayetteville. Then Zeb accused his competitor of espousing many different positions on issues and never being consistent: "One may know what principles he professed ten years ago, what different principles he professed five years ago, and what principles he professed six weeks ago." Zeb went on to declare, "I am for prosecuting the war which Mr. Holden helped to bring on." Zeb described in inelegant detail Holden's terror during the attack on the *Standard* office in September.[3] While this may have been entertaining for the crowd, Zeb was using personal information in a crudely political way. This portion of the speech was an important indicator: Zeb was signaling that he intended to conduct a total campaign and that he would hold nothing back to achieve victory. Holden, who was a partisan politician effective with words, had never experienced this kind of competition before.

In the latter part of his speech, Zeb turned to Holden's claim that he stood on Governor Brown's "Georgia Platform." Zeb pointed to the contradiction inherent in Holden's claim: "Gov. Brown and the Georgia Legislature do not propose any Convention, any separate State action, any new secession, as Mr. Holden does." Then Zeb began sharing part of his official correspondence with the public, a tactic that would become a central feature of his campaign from this point forward. In this case, he read his December 30, 1863, letter to Jefferson Davis in which he had asked the Confederate president to seek to negotiate with the federal government. He also read a letter that he had sent to Brown urging the Georgia governor to protest against the suspension of the writ of habeas corpus. Zeb then asserted that while Holden was embracing Brown, Brown had followed Vance's lead. "As to the pretence that [Vance] was for the suspension of the habeas corpus," he explained that "he had an armful of Standards in which he was praised by Mr. Holden for his firmness in upholding the rights and liberties of the citizen and the supremacy of the civil law." Having met his major challenger head on, Zeb then briefly discussed the high morale of the army and sent the crowd home with a burst of patriotic sentiments.[4]

The energetic governor then continued his hectic schedule for the next twenty-four hours. Immediately after giving the Fayetteville speech, he visited the Fayetteville Armory and took an intensive tour of the important facility. He concluded his afternoon with a review of the workers at the establishment. The next morning, Zeb took a train to the town of Egypt for another major public address. The military band was with him, and apparently the train stopped every few miles so that the band could play to alert people to the coming festivities. When he arrived in Egypt, he found a crowd of approximately two thousand people in attendance. While no full record of his Egypt speech survives, it appears to have been a close copy of the one he had delivered the day before.[5] The campaign was totally under way at this point. In the Fayetteville and Egypt speeches, Zeb had made a significant addition to his campaign tactics. He had begun to directly assail Holden's record and to defend his own. This was particularly true regarding the issue of civil liberties.

Around the same time, Zeb seized the initiative in another part of the campaign. He sponsored a newspaper in Raleigh to provide a direct outlet for his views. Named the *Daily Conservative*—a reminder that Zeb still considered himself a member of that party—it first appeared as a special issue on April 16 and then began regular publication four days later. Among the first things that the editor, Zeb's old partner John D. Hyman, did was to print Zeb's new platform in an attempt to minimize distortion. It read in full:

> The True Conservative Platform
> The supremacy of the civil over military law.
> A speedy repeal of the act suspending the writ of habeas corpus.
> A quiet submission to all laws, whether good or bad, while they remain upon our statute books.
> No reconstruction, or submission, but perpetual independence.
> An unbroken front to the common enemy; but timely and repeated negotiations for *peace* by the proper authorities.
> No separate State action through a Convention; no counter revolution; no combined resistance to the government.
> Opposition to despotism in every form, and the preservation of our Republican institutions in all their purity.[6]

There are two rather striking things about this otherwise predictable list. The first is its obvious promotion of civil liberties over the convention issue as a campaign priority. The second is that it suggests some concern that groups were combining in opposition to the Confederate government. Zeb may have had in his possession at this point some information about organizations that actively sought to return North Carolina to the Union.

The counterattack by the Holden forces was reactive but not particularly innovative. The *Daily Progress*, for example, attacked Vance for his unwillingness to listen to the voice of the people as expressed in a convention, but its editor appeared to be on the defensive when he assured readers in the same editorial that the convention would not remove North Carolina from the Confederacy. The next day, the same paper claimed that Zeb's new emphasis on civil liberties would persuade no one; the statement held little water, as it was itself an attempt to counter the strategy. Zeb's personal attacks on Holden prompted some attacks of the same type from the other side. At a public meeting, Holden supporters in Wake County charged, "His wretched jokes at a time like this when our people are almost literally bathed in blood and tears . . . will neither add to the dignity of his office nor convince the judgment of his hearers."[7] None of these attacks were likely to harm Zeb in the least. Much more significant was the fact that the Holden forces had begun reacting to Zeb's initiatives. Zeb was in control of the campaign once again.

He quickly demonstrated that he was determined to maintain this control. He arranged to speak before large crowds in Asheboro on May 3, Carthage on May 7, and Pittsboro on May 9. Shortly thereafter, he spoke to a gathering of approximately fifteen hundred people at Snow Camp in Guilford County. Speaking for two and a half hours, Zeb once again attacked the convention movement as unpatriotic and argued that it would make it even more likely that combat would come to North Carolina. As had become his custom by this point, he read his letters to Joseph E. Brown and Jefferson Davis to establish his credentials as a true supporter of civil liberties. He laid particular emphasis on his opposition to the suspension of the writ of habeas corpus. He concluded his address with a humorous attack on Holden's political inconsistency. Most significantly, the newsman at the scene reported, "Many of the Society of Friends were there and went away satisfied that Gov. Vance is . . . a staunch friend of immediate and continued efforts for peace, and the right man in the right place."[8] This statement had considerable importance. The Quakers had refused to participate in the military side of the conflict and were critical of government war efforts. For Zeb to convince them of his commitment to peace was a significant accomplishment.

Nor did Zeb shrink from directly confronting the people in Holden's strongholds. In mid-May, he spoke to a large public gathering in Wake

County, both the home of the city of Raleigh and the county where Zeb had been roundly criticized at another meeting just a few nights before. He started off with his now familiar criticism of Holden for failing to appear at the meeting to debate the issues. Then he discussed the convention, peace negotiations, and the suspension of the writ of habeas corpus. There was nothing new either in these remarks or in his criticism of Holden's political inconsistencies.[9] What is obvious from the accounts of this meeting is that Zeb felt secure that he had finally found the right mix of issues to attract the largest amount of public support. He also clearly felt that going directly to the public was the correct strategy, especially since Holden refused to participate in a debate.

While Zeb's speeches were having a profound impact on the people who attended them, his new newspaper kept up the attack on Holden and reached other voters. Starting in the April 27 edition, the paper began posing a series of questions about Holden. These included: "Who voted for Breckinridge, the secession candidate for the Presidency, in 1860?" and "Who was the father of secession in North Carolina?" Two weeks later, the paper started reprinting Holden's 1856 editorials in which he had called for secession if the Republicans won the presidency.[10] The paper continued to print similar explorations of Holden's political history until the vote in August.

Zeb's counterattack was so overwhelming that some members of the Conservative Party sought to convince Holden that he should consider withdrawing from the contest. For example, North Carolina state treasurer Jonathan Worth wrote to Holden in the hope of finding a way to heal the "breach" that had opened between Holden and Vance. From Worth's perspective, Zeb had "put himself right on the peace and Habeas Corpus questions by the publication of his correspondence with the president." Worth thought that Vance's "rectified position" offered Holden an opportunity to retreat.[11] The combination of Vance's aggressive political assault and the governor's friends' effort to get Holden to withdraw caused him to realize that his campaign was losing its momentum.

Holden's recognition that Zeb had seized the initiative prompted the editor to change his campaign strategy. Starting on May 18, he began to publish his paper on a regular basis again. Two days later, he wrote yet another long editorial that justified his candidacy. Holden traced his differences with Vance back to the summer of 1863, when they first disagreed about the peace movement. In this, his recollection was entirely accurate, but in what followed it probably was not. Holden charged: "[In] a conversation I had with [Vance] on the 22d of September, thirteen days after the mob, of a public official character, he declared to me . . . so fixed and bitter was his repugnance to the peace movement, that if I persisted in publishing the peace meetings and encouraging the peace movement in the South, my property would be laid in ashes by an armed mob, and I would meet a violent death."[12] This type of threat would have been out of character for Zeb; he simply did not threaten people with physical harm. In late September, moreover, Zeb had been making every effort to limit the public relations damage caused by the destruction of the *Standard* office. It would have been very counterproductive for him to have the scene repeated, with the addition of Holden's death.

Holden was on much more solid ground when he compared Zeb's early campaign with the governor's more recent speeches. He noted that Zeb was now in favor of repealing the suspension of the writ of habeas corpus. Holden, quite reasonably, asked whether the public could believe that Zeb's "conversion" was sincere. Holden then asserted that he was a candidate at the request of the people and the common soldiers who felt that Zeb had allied himself with the secessionists. Holden also revealed that he felt greatly insulted by Zeb's description of the editor's actions on the night the mob had destroyed his newspaper. He had every right to feel badly treated; Zeb's decision to publicize Holden's cowardice showed extremely poor judgment. Finally, Holden charged that Zeb was using the patronage available to the governor to make political alliances that would further his candidacy.[13] This was true, but most voters accepted that it was part of the regular political process. Holden apparently hoped that the voters would punish Zeb for following what amounted to a political tradition.

At the end of the editorial, Holden claimed that he was certain of victory. Holden's biographer attributes this belief, which was apparently genuine, to Holden's conviction that the differences between his own position on both peace and the convention and Zeb's were distinctive enough for the voters to see the difference. According to Holden, virtually all of the voters sided with him on these issues, and he, therefore, could not lose. Holden also felt that his attacks on the corruption of Zeb's administration were justified and would sway the public. Holden had concluded that the public knew that "those who may vote for Vance and the Destructives will vote for War and Despotism."[14] Despite all indications to the contrary, Holden persisted in this view through the entire campaign.

Around the same time that Holden issued his lengthy attack on Zeb, the evidence was mounting that Vance's campaign image as the defender of North Carolina was very popular. On the day that Holden denounced him, the Conservative Party caucus in the legislature endorsed Zeb's administration with only a small number of dissenters. Two days later, the state Senate voted thirty-three to two to endorse the Vance administration. The next day, the House of Commons did the same, with only three negative votes.[15] Obviously Zeb had virtually all of the popularly elected officials backing his candidacy. As the Conservative Party dominated the General Assembly, it is clear that Zeb, rather than Holden, was the choice of the party's leadership. Undoubtedly for better reasons, Zeb felt as confident as Holden did about the outcome of the election.

A new tactic that encouraged the voters to revisit North Carolina politics of the past two decades also made Zeb feel confident. Reading the *Daily Conservative*'s list of all of the notables who supported Vance, any reasonably well-informed North Carolina voter would have instantly realized that everyone on the list was a former member of the Whig Party. Then, to make the point even more obvious, the papers began to print some of Holden's editorials from the 1840s in which he had attacked Henry Clay and William A. Graham.[16] These reprints were reminders to Conservative Party voters who were former Whigs that Holden had been strongly anti-Whig in the years before the Civil War. While virtually all of the secessionists had been Democrats, the vast majority of Conservatives were former Whigs. Zeb and his allies sought to convince these voters that they could not trust Holden to direct the state government. Apparently Holden either did not recognize this strategy or had no answer for it, because he made little effort to counter it.

The only counterattack that Holden fashioned was to assert that the Vance administration was corrupt. There were two thrusts to this approach. First, Holden maintained that many of the men around Zeb were profiting from the war. The accused individuals included the owners of shipping companies involved in blockade-running as well as state officials who took advantage of their positions to enrich themselves. Holden even accused Zeb of trading cotton by shipping it out on the *Advance*, a charge that was, as we have already noted, entirely accurate. Zeb sought to minimize the damage this revelation caused to his reputation by underreporting the amount of cotton he had sent and claiming that the supplies he had purchased were primarily medicinal.[17] Holden was understandably skeptical. For reasons that are not clear, however, he failed to pursue this legitimate issue very vigorously.

Holden also attacked Zeb for using vulgar language in his public addresses, particularly in his speeches to the soldiers in Virginia. Holden accused Vance of promising to buy the soldiers whiskey after they defeated the federal army, of using the phrase "till hell freezes over," and of making disrespectful remarks about Holden. There is no question that Zeb did all of these things and more.[18] To the modern reader, Zeb's choice of words is not particularly shocking. But to the people of his time, Zeb's public language apparently skirted close to the edge of acceptability on many occasions. The fact that he had been challenged to two duels suggests that he crossed the line in his personal communications as well. While Holden was undoubtedly correct that Zeb's speech could be offensive, there is little indication that it did the governor any particular harm in the campaign.

Zeb was able to counter Holden's attacks by going directly to the people. Starting on June 4 at Greensboro and ending on August 1 in Wilmington, Zeb spoke virtually every day (except Sundays) for two months at some location in the state. He usually attracted large crowds, and reports suggest that he gave his by now standard speech. He always opened with an attack on the convention movement; then, he contrasted the variety of stands Holden had taken on public issues; finally, he defended himself from any attacks made by Holden and his allies. Zeb showed considerable courage in going to some locations where he knew that audiences might be quite hostile. He spent most of his time in the central Piedmont and the mountain counties trying to persuade those who had deserted or who were supporting men who had that all deserters should return to the army. For example, he visited the Trap Hill community in Wilkes County, where there was an active pro-Union group that had raised the U.S. flag at some of its meetings.[19]

Zeb also pursued a strategy of carefully distancing himself from Jefferson Davis. This move was dictated by the continuing hostility of many North Carolinians to both the secessionists—and Davis as their leader—and the impositions made upon them by the Confederate government. The state legislature reflected the people's continued resentment of the secessionists and Davis. The same body that overwhelmingly endorsed Zeb's administration voted to endorse the Davis government by a vote of forty-five to forty-two.[20] Thus, Zeb was careful to quote letters he had written to Davis that not only protested the Richmond government's policies but did so in the most insulting way possible. These were the same letters that Davis himself had found to be offensive. This approach put off the secessionists in North Carolina, but Zeb knew that they would never vote for Holden. By emphasizing his rudeness to Davis, Zeb made certain that Holden's efforts to tie him to the widely disliked Confederate president would be unsuccessful.

Zeb's candidacy also got a significant boost late in the campaign from some of his political opponents. Unionists and those most thoroughly disaffected with the Confederacy formed a secret society known as the Heroes of America. Because this group organized itself in local cells and kept virtually no records, it is difficult to ascertain exactly how many people joined it. Some observers have estimated that as many as ten thousand men joined the organization, which ultimately sought to reunite the country. This action was, of course, treason to the Confederacy. Apparently the organization's central objective was not made plain to the initiates at first, and some of the people who were members in the summer of 1864 may have joined not because they were committed Unionists, but simply to express their dissatisfaction with the Confederacy.[21]

The most careful investigators of the Heroes of America conclude that its opponents carefully timed their public exposure of the society to have the maximum political effect. It is possible that state and Confederate authorities were aware of the existence of the secret organization in the early spring. Certainly by early June they had identified the Reverend Orrin Churchill as one of its leaders. At about the same time, the Confederate military became aware of the organization and requested permission from the government in Richmond to start making arrests. Zeb and his allies held off making a formal announcement of the group's existence throughout June. Instead, the *Raleigh Confederate*, a secessionist paper that worked very closely with Zeb in this instance, published a series of articles about the existence of an unnamed organization and urged citizens to come forward and expose the group. The *Confederate* also sought to tie Holden directly to the Heroes. This campaign was so aggressive that Holden felt constrained to deny both that he belonged and that the organization actually existed. Then, on July 2, Zeb's newspaper printed a full exposé of the Heroes of America, including Churchill's confession. The paper kept the organization in the news for the remaining weeks of the campaign, providing new revelations on a regular basis. While the paper accepted Holden's claim that he was not a member, Zeb's editor asserted that all of the members of the Heroes would vote for Holden.[22] To many North Carolina voters, these charges made Holden appear to be a traitor.

At this point, only the intervention of outside forces could have prevented a Holden defeat. And fortunately for Zeb, the developments in the economy and the war tended to work in his favor. Perceptive Virginia diarist Edmund Ruffin reported on July 14, "The financial measures & especially reducing the amount of depreciated C.S. money in circulation, has had a general effect in reducing prices of provisions considerably."[23] The general improvement in the Confederate economic situation continued through election day. This did not mean that all North Carolinians were in good shape financially. For those on fixed incomes, including privates and noncommissioned officers in the military, the situation was still desperate. The same was true for families in communities that lacked the skilled craftspeople and farmers needed to keep their local economies functioning. At the time of the balloting, however, the people of North Carolina faced fewer economic problems than they had in several years.

Zeb was equally fortunate in the crucial area of the military. The campaigns of the late spring and the summer of 1864 had been very frustrating for the federal forces. Starting with the battles in the Wilderness in early May and carrying on through the slaughter at Cold Harbor and the stalemate near Petersburg, the Army of Northern Virginia repulsed attack after attack sent by General Ulysses S. Grant. The Union army's casualties in these battles were their heaviest of the entire war. While Robert E. Lee was clearly no longer able to assume the offensive, it seemed equally clear that the massive Union army could not break through his stout defensive lines. The appalling Union casualties depressed civilian morale in the North and conversely elevated morale throughout the Confederacy. Since most North Carolina soldiers were in Lee's army, this turnabout in sentiment was particularly strong among Tar Heel soldiers.[24]

Nor was this the only good military news available to North Carolina voters in the summer of 1864. In the western theater, Union general William T. Sherman's massive army moved slowly south as it sought to capture its Confederate opponents. While the Confederates under Joseph E. Johnston steadily lost ground, they were able to repulse several direct attacks and keep the army intact. When Jefferson Davis replaced Johnston on July 17 with John Bell Hood, the new commander of the army immediately took the offensive. He fought three aggressive battles in the next ten days. In retrospect these battles were failures, but at the time of North Carolina's gubernatorial election they did not look that way. Hood's Confederate troops appeared to be as successful as Lee's army when the voters went to the polls.[25]

The least important of the military developments from a strategic point of view may have had the greatest impact on the morale of the voters. The fighting that took place in the Shenandoah Valley in the spring and summer of 1864 did a great deal to boost Confederate morale. In that location, where Union general after Union general had proved to be a failure, Jubal Early won a string of victories. His most spectacular exploit was his raid of July 6–12, which brought him from the valley to the outskirts of Washington. While the raid served no useful military purpose, the civilian populations of the North and the South saw this exploit as a significant demonstration of Confederate military resilience. The Democratic Party of the North seemed poised to win the presidency on a platform that might lead to Confederate independence. Lincoln was so despondent that he had his cabinet sign a document that outlined a strategy to save the Union after the Democrats won the presidency.[26] It was in this atmosphere that North Carolina's citizens voted, first the soldiers in late July and then the civilians in early August.

Despite all of these developments, Holden still expected to win. In a July letter to a supporter, Holden proclaimed: "The intelligence I receive continues to be of the most cheering character. I feel sure of a decided majority in the army. The minds of the people and soldiers are made up, and nothing will change them." The day before the soldiers began voting, another correspondent reported that Holden's son was confident of his father's victory. But other observers recognized that the voters had rejected Holden. In mid-July, secessionist Kenneth Rayner returned home from an extended tour of the state. He reported to a friend: "I did not see, nor could I hear of any Holden Men. I am now inclined to think the talk about Holden's strength is all fallacious; and I do not think he will obtain a respectable vote in the whole state. You may rely on it, Vance's majority will be overwhelming." Zeb's newspaper confidently predicted that the governor would win by a margin of thirty-five thousand votes at the polls. Many previously neutral people began to announce their support for the incumbent.[27]

Even before the voting began, Holden complained about illegal and coercive tactics used by the Vance forces. The first had to do with the ballots themselves. In this period, ballots were provided by the parties or the candidates, not by the state or local governments. By a sort of gentleman's agreement, all candidates and parties agreed to provide white ballots so that no one could identify the supporters of a particular candidate by the ballots they cast. Without any explanation or warning, however, the Vance forces sent out their ballots in 1864 on yellow paper. This meant that the white Holden ballots could be instantly recognized, and the people holding them could be identified as opponents of the war effort. When Holden tried to counter with yellow ballots of his own, they proved to be of a different shade than Vance's, and therefore easily detected. Furthermore, Holden claimed that the postmaster at Weldon had burned the Holden ballots. The postmaster indignantly replied that he had delivered the ballots to the addressee unharmed, and that the addressee had burned the ballots.[28] The result of the machinations against him, Holden complained, was that many of his supporters either would have no ballots to cast or would be required to identify themselves publicly as his supporters at the polls.

Holden and his allies also asserted that Zeb planned to overawe Holden supporters by placing a military presence at the polls. Zeb's newspaper claimed that deserters and members of the Heroes of America planned to seize the ballot boxes in selected locations. Calvin Cowles in Wilkes County wrote to Holden to assure him that no such plot existed in his area. Cowles assumed, rather, that Vance was using the threat of the militia as a pretext to frighten people away from the polls. Zeb did call out the militia in selected areas, but armed men did not actually appear at the polling places.

Nevertheless, Holden people felt intimidated by the display of force. In the occupied town of Plymouth, moreover, regular Confederate troops apparently prevented Holden supporters from voting.[29] Zeb's objective in calling out the militia was apparently to prevent deserters from voting or taking control of the electoral process in selected areas, and in this he succeeded. While his tactic was somewhat heavy-handed, it stopped short of direct coercion.

What happened in the army, however, was coercion. There is no question that many Holden supporters in the military were denied their right to vote. Holden reported what happened in the military establishments near Raleigh: "Never before in the annals of American history did such voting take place. The Provost Guard of this place march up and voted under orders, and beneath the supervision of Confederate officials. All Holden's men were summarily disposed of, in guarding the bridges in the vicinity and those who did vote have been sent forward to the Army in many instances. The Hospitals were filled with Secesh women, who, in some instances, 'maligned' the soldiers bitterly, snatching the tickets from their hands, tearing them up and stamping upon the remnants. They then gave them Vance tickets." This incident could be dismissed as an isolated case or partisan hyperbole, but there is abundant additional evidence that many, if not most, Holden supporters in the military faced similar pressures. A soldier wrote to the *Daily Progress* and related the following election incident. Two companies, apparently identified as largely pro-Holden, were drawn into formation by their commanding officer and told to vote for Vance or not at all. The officer then threatened to send them "to the hottest battlefield in Virginia or the West" if they disobeyed his orders. The officers numbered the ballots to make sure that they could identify how each soldier voted. The correspondent reported that out of approximately two hundred soldiers, Zeb got 70 votes and Holden only a small number. The remainder of the soldiers refused to vote. The Holden forces noted that approximately two-thirds of all North Carolina soldiers failed to vote in the election.[30]

Nor were these the only incidents that were reported. In other outfits, the names of the soldiers were placed on their ballots to make sure that they voted in the approved manner. In Lynchburg, Virginia, Holden supporters had their ballots destroyed before they could be counted. The most conclusive evidence of the coercion used to limit soldiers' votes for Holden comes from an unexpected source. Federal general Winfield S. Hancock reported: "Two soldiers from Heth's division just come in . . . They deserted because they were not allowed to vote yesterday. They say that in very few cases, and those depended on the character of the officers, were any allowed to vote who did not vote for Vance." Under these circumstances, it is little wonder that Zeb swept the soldiers' vote by 13,209 to 1,824.[31] There is no question that Holden was deprived of a substantial number of votes, but the conclusion of his biographer that Zeb would have won a fair contest seems accurate.

When the civilians voted on August 4, the result was much more clear-cut. Although some Holden voters had felt intimidated at the polls, the results of the contest favored Vance so overwhelmingly that there is little question that Zeb was the people's choice for governor. The final civilian vote total was Vance 44,664, Holden 12,608. Holden was able to carry only three counties (Johnston, Randolph, and Wilkes), and in twenty counties he received fewer than 50 votes. After the tallies came in, no one except Holden doubted that Zeb had won a landslide. Holden labeled the result a "farce," and he later contended that he would have won if it had been a fair election. But Holden was virtually alone in this opinion. Robert P. Dick, his close ally, exclaimed, "I can not account for so universal and so sudden revulsion in public sentiment."[32] Yet unlike the defeated candidate, Dick accepted the fact that Zeb had won the election.

A statistical analysis of the voting patterns reveals some interesting insights into who supported Zeb. One of the first things that an observer notices is that approximately 49 percent of the electorate did not cast ballots. Since approximately two-thirds of the soldiers did not vote, this is not a surprise. Paul D. Escott has pointed out, moreover, that voter turnout in many counties had been low in the 1850s and that the low turnout in this election was part of that pattern. Not surprisingly, virtually all of the secessionists supported Zeb; they made up approximately one-third of his supporters. Another third of Vance's voters were people who had not voted in the gubernatorial election of 1862, but who had cast ballots for the Constitutional Union presidential candidate in 1860. They most likely viewed themselves as Whigs. The final third of Zeb's backers were drawn from those who had voted for him in 1862. Holden apparently drew all of his votes from this group, but he attracted a smaller number of them than Zeb. Approximately 40 percent of those who had voted for Zeb in 1862 failed to vote in the 1864 election.[33] This would seem to indicate that many of these citizens were conflicted. Perhaps they favored Holden's platform but were unwilling to vote for a candidate they did not trust.

In sifting through all of the evidence, it seems that Zeb's reelection was a personal triumph. As we have shown, Holden and his allies were able to force Zeb to change his strategy and to deal with issues of their choosing, such as civil liberties and the unpopularity of Jefferson Davis. Furthermore, they managed to persuade nearly two-thirds of those who had voted for Zeb in 1862 not to do so in 1864. They forced Zeb to adopt their platform and to campaign on it. Despite this handicap, Zeb won a very convincing victory due to a combination of factors. The most important was his personal contact and popularity with the voters. He worked tirelessly to meet with the public and to present his case directly to the voters. He shrewdly positioned himself to attract former Whigs, enemies of Jefferson Davis, and those who loathed Holden. After his opponents took his issues away, Zeb adapted brilliantly. He deserves full credit for his victory.

Many observers, probably including Zeb himself, credited the governor with securing North Carolina's allegiance to the Confederacy. In the eight months after his reelection, Zeb would seek to ensure that his state maintained its tie to the dying rebellion even when discretion might have suggested another course. Fully aware of the Southern code of honor even if he did not always observe it himself, Zeb was determined that he and his state would not be accused of violating it. Further, Zeb was aware that people in other Confederate states, especially Virginia and South Carolina, were already blaming North Carolina for many of the failings of the rebellion. Zeb's gubernatorial campaign had been framed in part to assure the rest of the South of his state's commitment to the Confederacy.

In the immediate aftermath of the election, there seemed to be little reason for Zeb to be concerned about the future of the Confederacy and the honor of his state. His electoral victory was so complete that the Davis administration finally conceded that North Carolina posed no immediate threat to the Confederacy. Davis allowed the suspension of the writ of habeas corpus to lapse. Once this major thorn in Zeb's side was removed, it ceased to be a matter of contention between the two governments. Moreover, William W. Holden wrote a generous concession editorial that promised a measure of political peace in North Carolina. Holden pledged his continued loyalty to the Confederacy and expressed his desire to avoid political discussions for the immediate future.[1] With these two major challenges to his authority out of the way, Zeb seemed poised to continue his constructive efforts to achieve Confederate independence.

Along with his new status as a stalwart for Southern independence came an unwelcome dose of reality. Late in August, Zeb received a letter directly from General Robert E. Lee. Prior to the late summer of 1864, the two had usually communicated through the Richmond offices of the secretary of war or the president. Apparently Lee had been much taken with Zeb's commitment to the cause and his ability to inspire the troops during his March and April tour of North Carolina regiments, and the general had recognized that Zeb was someone who could get things done. Perhaps Lee was as impatient as Zeb was with the inefficiencies and ineptitude of the Confederate administration, and he sought out someone who had proven himself to be competent. In any case, Lee's communication brought the welcome news that North Carolina troops had performed very well in recent battles against the massive federal army at their front. However, the tremendous pressure at the front made it impossible for Lee to send any regular forces to assist with the defense of Wilmington, the only major Confederate seaport left after the recent closing of Mobile Bay. Thus, the general asked the governor's help to defend the port city with "local and reserve forces."[2] This Zeb would attempt to do, but he must have realized how few resources the Confederacy had available to it if it had to call on him to defend its only link with the outside world without assistance from regular Confederate troops.

This letter actually opened the second collaboration between Lee and Vance in the aftermath of the election. The two had worked together earlier in an attempt to deal with a significant internal disturbance within North Carolina. While Holden accepted his defeat with outward calm, not all of his supporters did. Although the Heroes of America had apparently been disrupted by their exposure, there was still organized opposition to the Confederacy within North Carolina. In the central counties of the state, disappointed Holden supporters and Unionists attacked local defense forces. Almost immediately after the election, deserters attacked a loyal force, killing three and mortally wounding another near Carthage in Moore County, and a military picket line was put up around the town to protect it from threatened arson. Four senior reserves were killed in an attack on Franklinville in Randolph County. No longer constrained by the need to take public reactions that might register at the ballot box into account, Zeb fought back with force. He ordered the militia into the area and instructed the soldiers to deal harshly with those in revolt.[3]

Zeb also sought to cope with the evident dissension in a more constructive way. Working closely with Lee, he issued a proclamation on August 24 offering amnesty to the many deserters hiding out in North Carolina. This part of the proclamation was not unusual; it promised no penalties or the lightest possible sentences to those who voluntarily returned to the ranks within thirty days. From that point forward, however, Zeb's proclamation had a hardness to it not found in his previous addresses to deserters. He asserted "that the utmost powers of this State [would] be exerted to capture them or drive them from the borders of a country . . . they disgrace[d] by refusing to defend, and that the extremest penalties of the law [would] be enforced without exception when caught, as well as against their aiders and abettors in the civil courts." Zeb closed his appeal to the deserters by calling on local citizens and government officials to take part in this effort to return deserters to the army.[4]

Just as the hopes for domestic peace within North Carolina seemed to dissipate soon after the election, the general outlook for the future of the Confederacy also went into rapid decline. At first, the signs were more positive. The Northern Democrats met in convention in late August and adopted a platform plank that called for an armistice and negotiations with the Confederacy. This "peace" plank was exactly what Holden and his supporters had called for during the North Carolina campaign. For it to be realized, the Democrats had only to win control of the government and implement it. The possibility of a Democratic victory quickly disappeared beneath a succession of Union army victories, however. In early September, General William T. Sherman's army forced Confederate General John Bell Hood and his army to evacuate Atlanta. This success electrified the North and appeared to ensure Abraham Lincoln's reelection. About three weeks later, General Phillip Sheridan and his Union army won the first major victory by a federal force in the Shenandoah Valley. This success further strengthened the Republican position in the election. Finally, George McClellan, the Democratic Party's presidential nominee, announced that no matter what the party platform said, he would not accept anything less than the full reunion of all of the states.[5] In less than two months after Zeb's reelection, the future of the Confederacy had begun to look very bleak again.

Zeb recognized the change in the Confederacy's position and unburdened himself in another introspective letter to David L. Swain. He started by observing, "I never before have been so gloomy about the condition of affairs." He went on to explain why: "Early's defeat in the valley I consider as the turning point in this campaign; and, confidentially, I fear it seals the fate of Richmond, though not immediately." Furthermore, "The army in Georgia is utterly demoralized; and by the time President Davis, who has gone there, displays again his obstinacy in defying public sentiment, and his ignorance of men in the change of commanders, its ruin will be complete." The badly shaken governor conceded that if the federal forces pushed their advantage, they might be able to finish off the Confederacy by the end of the year.[6] At no time over the next seven months would Zeb give such a frank and realistic picture of the future of the Confederacy in his public utterances.

Zeb went on in his letter to Swain to lament that it was evident that popular support for the Confederacy was fast ebbing. He noted that Sherman's army in Georgia was meeting no resistance from the local population.

"What does this show, my dear sir?" he asked. "It shows what I have always believed, that the great popular heart is not now, and never has been in this war. It was a revolution of the Politicians; not the People."[7] This statement is very similar to one that Zeb made in his letter to Swain of January 2, 1864. In a sense, he was in the same position that he had been nine months before. During the gubernatorial campaign and the military stalemate of the summer of 1864, Zeb had apparently hoped that the Confederacy could survive as an independent nation. Now, as earlier, he knew better.

Under these difficult circumstances, what was he to do? Asserting, accurately, that he had a "buoyant and hopeful temperament," Zeb resolved to support General Robert E. Lee and the Confederate army. He would continue to try to help his fellow North Carolinians "through the tangled and bloody pathway" that lay ahead. This would mean that he would have to continue to take an active role in the defense of North Carolina and the Confederacy. He told Swain that he had one consolation in this situation: "The beginning was bad; I had no hand in it. Should the end be bad, I shall, with God's help, be equally blameless."[8] This last sentence is significant for two reasons. First, Zeb began to mention the deity much more frequently in his private and public statements in this period. He seems not to have had a profound religious experience that produced this mode of expression. Instead, this phraseology appears to have expressed his resignation to the idea that the outcome of the war was beyond human control. Abraham Lincoln reached a similar conclusion much more eloquently in his writing and speeches of this same period.

But Zeb's statement to Swain is also significant because it provides the motivation for Zeb's actions in the remaining months of the war. He had resolved to act in a way that would leave him "blameless." This meant that he would make sure that no one, either a contemporary or a later biographer or historian, could accuse him of being responsible for Confederate defeat. Zeb, of course, was not alone in making this determination. His actions throughout the entire war had been predicated upon his understanding of honor. Now he was determined that no misstep would deprive him of his reputation. In some cases, this decision prompted him to ask the public and officials around him to make unrealistic exertions and sacrifices. He was determined that he and North Carolina would be vindicated.

The day after he sent the introspective letter to Swain, Zeb swung back into action. He wrote letters to the governors of the Confederate states east of the Mississippi River and suggested a meeting to coordinate state actions during the coming crisis. In particular, he wanted to make sure that the states adopted uniform procedures both for making state workers available to the military and for arresting the spread of desertion. The response from the governors was quite favorable, and Georgia governor Joseph E. Brown agreed to act as host of the meeting, which would be held on October 17 in Augusta, Georgia.[9] The idea for the meeting was a significant innovation on Zeb's part. Few, if any, precedents existed for this type of gathering. It was an inspired response to the desperate straits in which the Confederacy found itself.

Three days before the meeting began, Zeb took the train out of Raleigh and navigated his way through the collapsing Southern railway system to Augusta. Once there, Zeb and the governors from Virginia, South Carolina, Georgia, Alabama, and Mississippi worked diligently to complete their task. The resolutions they adopted combined the expected with the unexpected. The governors announced: "There is nothing in the present aspect of public affairs to cause any abatement in our zeal in the prosecution of the war to the accomplishment of peace based on the independence of the Confederate States." With this end in mind, the governors adopted resolutions encouraging states to send local forces beyond state boundaries, requesting that Confederate bureaucrats be sent into the army, recommending stringent state efforts to arrest deserters, and asking the Richmond Congress to remove all restrictions on state trading with foreign nations.[10] All of these measures were ones that Zeb was either already pursuing or in favor of.

But the governors added one more suggestion to their list that was much more controversial. The governors asserted: "The course of the enemy in appropriating our slaves who happen to fall into their hands to purposes of war, seems to justify a change of policy on our part." The new policy that they recommended was, "under proper regulations, to appropriate such part of them [the slaves] to the public service as may be required."[11] Exactly what this language was supposed to mean is not clear. The reason may well be that the resolution represented a compromise. At the very least, the governors' resolution said that slaves could be used for noncombat roles. This was not a controversial decision, as it did not represent a change of policy. The Confederacy had been appropriating slaves for noncombat work for quite some time. The resolution would have been a real change in policy if it suggested that slaves should be considered as potential Confederate soldiers. Zeb's role in the framing of the resolution's language is not clear.

When Zeb returned to Raleigh, he quickly recognized that the resolution on slaves would be controversial. His newspaper immediately published an article that asserted that the statement did not endorse the use of slave soldiers. Holden disagreed with this assessment of the resolution, claiming that it did indeed open the way for slaves to serve in the Confederate military. He went on to assert that the meeting had been under the control of the Davis administration, and the administration had not allowed any criticism of its policy to surface in the final document. Zeb refuted that charge through his own paper and claimed that the policies were sound ones.[12] He never deviated from his interpretation of the language on slave service in the Confederacy, but there is little doubt that the resolution tested public opinion on this volatile issue.

The campaign against the deserter uprising in the central counties also caused controversy. Zeb's orders to the local defense forces were broad enough to allow significant abuses of civil liberties. The forces started to round up the families of those thought to be in opposition to the government. The women and children were all taken to a central location where they were forced to remain until the deserters in their families turned themselves in. This policy led to appalling abuses, but it also had the effect of stopping the overt rebellion. Approximately three hundred deserters returned to the army, and armed bands made up of deserters and those avoiding the draft withdrew from the public eye.[13] The uneasy calm fooled no one, however. All it would take for disorder to spread again would be the relaxation of the state's repressive efforts.

In the meantime, Zeb became fully aware of the Confederacy's perilous military situation. General W. H. C. Whiting, the commanding officer of Confederate forces near Wilmington, told Zeb that the defense of Fort Fisher and the coastal region would depend upon state forces. Zeb said that if Whiting was correct, "the place might as well be surrendered on the first summons of the enemy." Zeb continued, "The entire force I could send you for three months would not exceed 5,000 men, raw and untrained." He explained, moreover, that as it was now the harvest season, these men were much more valuable on their farms than in the army.[14] While Zeb was right on all points, Whiting was also correct. The resources of the Confederacy were spread so thin that the defense of the Confederacy's last major seaport would indeed fall to local troops.

Zeb, in the meantime, discovered that in its desperation the Confederate government was threatening the state programs that the military and civilian populations of the state needed to continue the war. Desperate military commanders began to conscript workers who were under state contract. These included laborers in textile factories as well as workers from saltworks near Wilmington and at Saltville, Virginia. In an effort to protect these essential civilian workers, Zeb prepared a list of needed workers organized by category and sent them to a military officer. The needs of the Confederacy were so great, however, that even Zeb's protests, which had achieved significant results in previous years, no longer had any impact. In December, the exasperated governor wrote to the secretary of war: "Having broken up my salt-works at Wilmington, you have now conscripted my hands at Saltville and stopped those there. Please inform me where North Carolina is to get salt, or how her people can do without it."[15] There was no good answer for Zeb, but the Confederacy had no choice.

Hoping to find a way to use state resources to aid the struggling Richmond government, Zeb sought to call the state legislature into special session. He was stymied, however, by the Council of State, which refused to agree to his proposal. Apparently, Zeb had hoped that the militia might be sent to assist Robert E. Lee and, in return, some of Lee's veteran troops would be stationed in Wilmington to defend the port. Zeb's concern about the weakness of Confederate forces in North Carolina was confirmed in late October when a federal force recaptured Plymouth and forced the Confederates to evacuate Washington. About a week later, Zeb journeyed with Braxton Bragg to Wilmington and inspected Forts Fisher, Caswell, Campbell, and Holmes. He reported to Jefferson Davis: "I have just returned from a visit to the works below that City [Wilmington] and find them all in excellent condition; so far as I am able to judge there seems to be nothing wanting except troops." On November 30, Robert E. Lee informed the secretary of war that he could spare no troops from his forces to send to Wilmington.[16] The strategic importance of the port was emphasized by the continuing success of the blockade-running ships, which managed to slip in and out of Wilmington despite a heavy federal naval presence. Since the port at Wilmington was the only place where the Confederacy could receive absolutely essential goods from Europe, the fact that the Southern military could not send troops there illustrated the Confederacy's untenable position.

Shortly thereafter, the legislature met in regular session. Zeb's message to that body was somber, but he made a number of suggestions that he thought might help to remedy the situation in North Carolina. He reported the recent loss of Plymouth and Washington, the growing lawlessness in the western counties of the state, and the failure of the effort to return deserters to the army. Zeb went on to defend his system of trading in Europe to gain supplies needed by North Carolina troops and civilians, probably in response to newspaper attacks that claimed considerable corruption attended this trade. He further requested the power to reorganize the militia to meet the current military emergency.[17]

Zeb also devoted a considerable amount of his speech to a discussion of the resolutions adopted by the governor's conference, and he requested that the legislature officially approve them. This request, of course, raised the issue of whether African Americans should be used as Confederate soldiers. Zeb made his opposition absolutely clear: "Under no circumstances would I consent to see them armed. . . . This course would, it seems to me, surrender the entire question which has ever separated the North from the South, would . . . render our whole revolution nugatory—a mere objectless waste of human life."[18] While the issue would continue to be publicly debated throughout the remaining months of the war and many Southerners would reluctantly accept the necessity of this previously unthinkable act, Zeb never budged. Throughout his life his estimate of African Americans' potential would never change, and his overt racism would remain a part of his public persona.

Once Zeb delivered his message to the legislature, the initiative passed out of his hands. National developments undermined whatever optimism most Southerners had for the future of their new nation. First, General Phillip Sheridan and his army virtually eliminated the Confederate army of Jubal Early in the Shenandoah Valley. Abraham Lincoln was easily re-elected to another four-year term as president, ensuring that the federal military advantage would be pressed relentlessly. General William T. Sherman then began his punitive raid through middle and south Georgia. In the middle of December, a Union army under the leadership of George Thomas virtually annihilated the Confederate army of John Bell Hood at the battle of Nashville. And to top it off, Sherman and his army captured Savannah just before Christmas.[19] All of these events left little doubt in the minds of most Southerners, including Zeb, that the Confederacy would soon be crushed unless something totally unanticipated took place.

The first reaction to these developments by a North Carolina legislator actually took place in the Confederate Congress in Richmond. Congressman James T. Leach offered a resolution: "That whenever the Government of the United States shall signify its willingness to recognize the reserved rights of the States and guarantee to the citizens of the States their rights of property . . . we will agree to treat for peace." Leach rejected the charge that he was creating dissension with this statement. He claimed that Davis's plan to put slaves in the army—which the governors seemed to endorse at Augusta—had undermined public confidence. Leach's fellow congressmen found his reasoning unacceptable, and they defeated the resolution. (It received only three affirmative votes, all of them from North Carolina's representatives.)[20]

Leach's initiative was picked up by North Carolina state legislators, who introduced peace initiatives into the Senate and House of Commons. Senator John Pool proposed that "five commissioners be elected by the General Assembly, to act with commissioners from the other States of the Confederacy, as a medium for negotiating peace with the United States." This initiative was tabled and not acted upon by a close vote of twenty-four to twenty. A month later, a bill was introduced into the House of Commons that called for a state convention. This proposal was also voted down by fifty-eight votes to thirty-nine.[21] While Zeb and his allies were able to keep the legislature from taking unilateral action to remove North Carolina from the Confederacy, these votes indicated that a growing number of public figures no longer had any confidence in its survival.

Their confidence was not bolstered when it became obvious that the federal government intended to seize Fort Fisher and close the port of Wilmington. Zeb and the Confederate authorities were in the midst of arguing over whether it was desirable to have Confederate raiding ships using Wilmington as a port. Confederate intelligence was still impressive, and as early as December 8, Lee had notified the authorities in Richmond that a large federal force was headed for North Carolina. Whiting warned Zeb on the eighteenth that large forces were headed to North Carolina in the immediate future. Almost in a panic, Zeb issued a proclamation on December 20 asking "all good people . . . who may be able to stand behind breastworks and fire a musket, of all ages and conditions, to rally at once to the defense of their country and hurry to Wilmington." Zeb melodramatically ended his address with the following statement: "Your Governor will meet you at the front and will share the worst with you."[22] Fortunately for all concerned, neither the citizens nor the governor made it to Wilmington in time for the coming battle.

The battle turned out to be something of a farce in any case. The Union army commander was the incompetent Benjamin F. Butler. Butler persuaded the authorities to try a new tactic, and they in turn convinced Admiral David Porter. Butler's idea was to fill a ship with explosives and detonate it near the fort with the intention of causing massive destruction. Observers ever since have mocked Butler for this idea, because the explosion that took place had virtually no impact on the sand fort. Some historians now recognize, however, that Butler's device would have worked if the defense works had been built of solid material. After the failure of the explosive ship, Porter's ships bombarded the fort on December 24 and did considerable damage. Butler landed his troops, who greatly outnumbered the defenders, but on Christmas Day he lost his nerve, failed to attack, and withdrew his forces to the waiting naval vessels.[23] Fort Fisher and Wilmington had been spared.

Zeb had not been at Fort Fisher to see these events unfold, because he was delivering his second inaugural address. In many ways, this speech may have been the least effective one he ever gave. The published version of the address indicates that it was no more than ten minutes long. As Zeb admitted, he had no new initiatives to suggest; the "darkness which obscures the Statesman's path," he said, was "even blacker than before." Approximately one-third of the speech dwelled on the question of how the public would perceive the job that he was doing. Zeb's concern about his place both in history and in the public's esteem was clearly weighing upon him. Finally, he called for an end to North Carolina's internal civil war. If this occurred, Zeb concluded, "victory" would be "not only doubly assured but thrice glorious, and defeat [would] be robbed of half its calamities."[24] Zeb's speech was hardly the kind of appeal that would drive men into the last ditch brimming with enthusiasm for the Confederate cause.

Zeb's foreboding was not misplaced. The federal desire to close the port of Wilmington had not been quenched by Butler's failure. The Lincoln administration realized that with the presidential election over, it did not have to worry about Butler's political appeal. Butler was sent home, and veteran general Alfred H. Terry took over as the army commander. The federal forces returned in mid-January for another engagement. Terry's army landed near Fort Fisher and placed itself between a small army directed by Braxton Bragg and the fort. The federal naval forces unloosed a tremendous barrage of shells, which Admiral Porter thought was the most sustained attack of its kind that he had witnessed during the war. Then, a group of sailors, marines, and soldiers gained entry into the fort. During this period the Confederate commanders in the fort called upon Bragg to assist them. Bragg's force did not make any aggressive moves, however, and the small force defending Fort Fisher was overwhelmed despite putting up a stout defense.[25] This federal victory sealed the fate of the Confederacy. With no outlet to the outside world, the Southern government was in no position to resist the armies of Grant and Sherman.

As if the Wilmington catastrophe were not enough, Zeb found himself facing disasters elsewhere in the state as well. The internal civil war in the central counties burst out into the open again. The state treasurer, Jonathan Worth, reported, "Theft, robbery and almost every other crime are common in almost all the rural districts, and are lately becoming more common." With all of the pressure being applied to the state's defense system by the renewed federal aggression along the coast, Zeb no longer had the resources to send reinforcements. Making a bad situation even worse, Zeb and his fellow Tar Heels also faced a natural disaster. An observer reported that a quick-rising flood had "washed low grounds, carried off fences, bridges, mills and tore up railroads all through the central part of the state." Apparently this event caused considerable panic, and the price of food nearly doubled in the region. The price rise was also fueled by a fire in Charlotte that destroyed seventy thousand bushels of grain and large amounts of sugar and molasses in a warehouse under the control of the army quartermaster.[26] Any of these developments would have been a cause for concern at any time during the war, but coming as they did at about the same time as the defeat at Fort Fisher, they only added to the existing despondency.

In this atmosphere, observers sought to fix blame for the Confederate failure at Fort Fisher. A Wilmington newspaper claimed that Zeb had undermined General Whiting. Zeb's paper fired back that Whiting's drinking habits had made him unreliable during the crisis; there appears to have been no basis for that assertion. Zeb's editor was on much more solid ground when he noted that the governor had not assigned Bragg to the Wilmington command and could not be held responsible for Bragg's decisions. The *Daily Progress* of Raleigh picked up the anti-Vance theme and published a broader attack on Zeb's leadership. It read, in part, "Gov. Vance, who seems to desire nothing but ruin, entire and complete for his State and people, is rapidly losing the influence his quackery and the tricks of the mountebank had achieved over the people."[27] As the shadows lengthened over the Confederacy, this type of fault finding became a public pastime.

A number of North Carolinians in public life sought to find a way to bring the war to a close; they were willing even to forfeit Confederate independence. Josiah Turner, a Confederate congressman from North Carolina, called for the thirteen Confederate states to appoint peace commissioners who would initiate a peace conference without the participation of the Confederate government. On January 23, the *Daily Progress* stated that it would support a convention in the hope that it would remove North Carolina from the Confederacy. The same day, Lewis Hanes from Davidson County introduced a resolution into the House of Commons calling for a state convention, which would be followed by a Southern convention. That resolution was tabled by a vote of fifty-nine to forty. A week later, four members of the North Carolina legislature formed themselves into an informal delegation and traveled to Richmond to urge President Davis to open peace negotiations.[28] None of these initiatives resulted in any action, but they were a barometer of the declining faith in the Confederate war effort.

In early February, the Richmond government took a step that seemed to open the door to the type of settlement that many North Carolinians sought. Abraham Lincoln had allowed Francis P. Blair to travel to Richmond to see if Blair could find a way to secure a peaceful solution to the conflict. Blair met with Jefferson Davis and proposed that the Union and the Confederacy cease fighting and work together to drive the French out of Mexico. Davis seized the opportunity to demonstrate that it was not his intransigence that blocked the way to peace. He appointed three commissioners to meet with Secretary of State William H. Seward. These appointees were all men thought to favor a negotiated end to the war. They were

Alexander Stephens, the vice president of the Confederate States; John A. Campbell, assistant secretary of war; and R. M. T. Hunter, a Confederate States senator from Virginia. After a slight delay that allowed Lincoln to join Seward, the representatives of the two governments met. As Davis had anticipated, however, they could reach no agreement. Lincoln and Seward would not negotiate on any terms other than reunion, slave emancipation, and a total end to hostilities. The three Confederate representatives offered the alliance against the French and an armistice as alternatives, but their proposals were summarily rejected.[29] When the commissioners returned from their unsuccessful mission, Davis gave a major public address that called on the people of the South to fight to the bitter end.

Zeb followed the president's example. On February 14, he issued a proclamation that sought to use the negative outcome of the peace conference to rally North Carolinians to the cause of Confederate independence. This state paper began by once again pointing out that North Carolina was not responsible for starting the conflict, but that the state had contributed more than its fair share to support the Confederacy. Zeb then described several of the Richmond government's peacemaking efforts, including its recent meeting with Lincoln and Seward. Zeb printed the full commissioners' report in his proclamation to demonstrate the inflexibility of the Lincoln administration's conditions for peace. Zeb summed up the results of the conference by explaining that the Union required the complete surrender of the Confederacy and that it would not honor separate action by any state.[30] In a sense, Zeb was saying to his adversaries within North Carolina, "I told you so."

Zeb then turned his attention to imagining the consequences of surrendering to the Lincoln administration. These included freedom for the slaves, the confiscation of land and its redistribution to the former slaves, poverty for most Southerners, and the cutting off of wounded and diseased veterans of the Confederate army from assistance. Zeb continued: "Great God! Is there a man in all this honorable, high spirited, and noble Commonwealth so steeped in every conceivable meanness, so blackened with all the guilt of treason, or so damned with all of the leprosy of cowardice as to say: Yes, we will submit to all this." One scholar asserted that Zeb seemed to reach the point of near hysteria at this time.[31] That is something of an overstatement, but there is little question that Zeb was very much on edge and determined to try to make sure that North Carolinians did not betray the Confederacy.

Zeb made two suggestions that he said would help restore the fighting power of the Confederacy. The first was to return the many thousands of deserters to the ranks of the Confederate army. This would only be possible if the public persuaded deserters to return to the army, and the people could best do this, he then suggested, by demonstrating that they still supported the Confederacy. Zeb recommended that they express this sentiment in "primary meetings in every county in the State." Zeb had to know that his strategy for attracting deserters was a forlorn hope at best. The proponents of peace reacted to the proclamation with ridicule. The *Daily Progress* pointed out that Zeb was now resorting to encouraging public meetings after he had worked so hard to suppress them in September of 1863. The previous day, the paper had ironically named Zeb the "Model Governor" and reminded readers that he had "no plan, no suggestion, [and] no counsel [for peace] to lay before the people's representatives."[32] This type of open criticism would grow as the crisis deepened.

The Confederate military situation in North Carolina was becoming more desperate with each passing day. General William T. Sherman left Savannah on the first of February and started north through South Carolina. Confederate military strategists were convinced that the flooded South Carolina low country was impassible. Sherman's veterans, however, made makeshift bridges and trails through the swamps and continued their rapid march toward the North Carolina border. With more than sixty thousand men and no appreciable force in its way, the federal army looked very menacing. It looked even more so because of the destruction it left in its path. Sherman's army destroyed virtually every building it passed, along with many supplies. The state capital of Columbia was not spared; many of the public buildings in the city were utterly destroyed.[33] Confederate civilians feared not simply that Sherman's men were coming, but also that they seemed bent on destroying everything in their path.

Nor was this the only military threat that the Confederacy faced in North Carolina. General John M. Schofield sought to move from Fort Fisher to capture Wilmington. His initial efforts on February 11–14 were unsuccessful, as Confederate General Robert F. Hoke kept the Union forces bottled up on a slim peninsula east of the city. The arrival of additional troops allowed Schofield to send another force across the Cape Fear River to advance on Wilmington. The federal forces captured Fort Anderson on February 18 and immediately pressed the retreating Confederates as they sought safety near Wilmington. A determined federal push persuaded Braxton Bragg that he could no longer defend the city, and the Confederate forces withdrew on February 22.[34] The federal army was now in position to move inland with a secure line of communication and supplies protected by the powerful Union Navy.

It was while this distressing military news was becoming known that Zeb called for public meetings. He sought to arouse the public by personally attending as many of these meetings as possible. At a meeting in Golds-boro, Zeb spoke for an hour and a half to a large crowd. He assured his audience that if the deserters would just return to their units, the Confederacy would obtain its independence. It was up to the civilian population, he explained, to encourage those who had left the ranks to return. Then Zeb considered the alternative to Confederate independence. He conjured an image of General Lee begging for his life before President Lincoln. He claimed that slaves would dominate Southern society and would be given whites' land. He also asserted that Southern whites would be ruined financially and that the leaders of the Confederacy would be executed. Zeb used a wide variety of images to ensure that his audience was emotionally involved in the outcome of the war, and the reporter who recorded his speech noted that Zeb's auditors responded enthusiastically. Even this late in the conflict, Zeb was able to reach his fellow North Carolinians. Still, he recognized that these meetings were having a limited impact. In a letter to Robert E. Lee, he admitted that the rapidly approaching military crisis had distracted most citizens from acting upon his proposals.[35]

The unity that Zeb sought to create among North Carolina's civilian population was forged between its public figures on a policy issue. As the Confederacy tried to find a way to redress the growing military imbalance between the Southern and Northern armies, Robert E. Lee and Jefferson Davis asked the Congress in Richmond to allow slaves to assume combat roles in the Confederate army. North Carolina spokesmen from all points on the political spectrum actively opposed this proposal. Zeb was among those who strongly condemned the innovation. Ironically, William W. Holden and John L. Pennington joined him in this opinion. North Carolina Confederate senator William A. Graham worked assiduously in the Confederate Senate to defeat the legislation. When Samuel F. Phillips of Chapel Hill introduced a resolution in the state legislature that declared slavery dead and called for slaves to be armed, there was virtually no support for his measure.[36] The underlying reasons that most North Carolina politicians resisted arming the slaves seem to have been that they had supported the Confederacy to safeguard slavery and that they could not imagine African Americans in the role of soldiers. This was particularly true for Zeb, who had portrayed the black Union soldier as a threat to Southern society in so many of his speeches.

Despite all of the distractions and pressures on him, Zeb continued to maintain his composure and to work effectively as governor. One observer visited Zeb in early March, 1865, and found the governor hard at work in his Raleigh office. Among the matters he dealt with were "hunting up deserters, arranging transport, impressing houses, wagon horses,

& niggers, raising provisions, organizing committees & superintending his Home Guard." There is every indication that Zeb continued to administer his office effectively until he was driven from it by the federal advance. His final administrative task was to arrange for all of the state papers to be boxed up and moved to keep them out of the way of advancing armies.[37] In this endeavor, Zeb and other state officials were largely successful.

The military situation in the state continued to deteriorate rapidly despite Zeb's efforts to arouse the civilian population. Sherman and his army entered North Carolina on March 6 and marched toward Goldsboro. On their way there, they seized Fayetteville and destroyed the armory and some public buildings, including Edward J. Hale's *Observer* office. Schofield and his army moved out of Wilmington and reached Goldsboro, where the men waited for Sherman's army. In the meantime, Confederate general Joseph E. Johnston attempted to attack wings of Sherman's forces at the battles of Averasboro and Bentonville before they reached their destination. The Confederate forces fought effectively on both occasions, but they were unable to overcome the massive federal advantage in manpower. On March 23, 1865, the two federal armies united at Goldsboro and created an unstoppable force. Five days later, a federal raid led by General George Stoneman from east Tennessee into western North Carolina disrupted communications in that part of the state.[38] From that point forward, the military future of Confederate North Carolina was clear.

The Confederates sought to stop the inevitable with desperate measures. Knowing that he would soon have to retreat, Robert E. Lee attempted to secure his route. Recognizing that the large number of deserters in the central counties of North Carolina threatened the Danville to Greensboro link of the railroad, Lee sent a force of five hundred regular soldiers to make sure that the deserters did not rise against his army. As Lee wrote to Zeb, this force was "instructed to take no prisoners among . . . deserters who resist with arms civil or military authorities." The troops stayed in the region for the last three weeks of March and rounded up about one hundred deserters. It appears that several of these deserters were indeed killed during the period.[39] Of course, Lee's army never reached North Carolina, and the presence of the Confederate troops only served to further destabilize the region.

Although the world around him was collapsing, Zeb had a clear plan of action. He was going to make sure that everyone understood that North Carolina and its governor had not undermined the Confederacy. First, through his newspaper, he sought to assign blame where he felt it deserved to be placed. The *Daily Conservative* editorialized, "The utter incompetency of the government or its blindness and obstinacy in the management

of public affairs, daily loses it friends and weakens the public confidence."
The attack on Jefferson Davis and the Richmond government continued,
"What might be done at this crisis, is seriously retarded and hampered
by the mismanagement of those in authority."[40] There was nothing new in
these statements. Zeb had been saying the same things to Confederate authorities in his correspondence with them for nearly three years. But now
he wanted the wider world to understand the difficulties he had faced in
working with them.

The *Daily Conservative* editorial closed with a call to the people to make
Robert E. Lee the head of the government.[41] This appeal reflected both
Zeb's anger with the Davis administration and the strength of the growing
relationship between the governor and the general. The men had grown
to enjoy each other's company when Zeb visited Virginia to speak to the
troops. Zeb greatly admired Lee and eagerly sought to establish a relationship with the older man, much as he had done with David L. Swain and
William A. Graham. Lee, who was normally very careful to route all of
his communications through the proper civilian channels, began to correspond directly with Vance, who responded in kind. Lee apparently recognized many of the same shortcomings in the Davis administration that
Zeb did, and he welcomed the opportunity to communicate with someone
who made every effort to assist his army. For Zeb, the contrast between the
high level of competence and broad vision that he found in Lee and what
he perceived to be the bumbling and narrow vision of Davis and the other
civilians he had to work with was a sharp one.

There were limits, however, to the deference he would show to his older
advisers in this crisis. Zeb was in constant contact with Swain and Graham
as the Confederacy collapsed. Graham, in particular, offered Zeb inside information from his position in the Confederate Senate. In a March 26 letter
to Swain, Graham remarked about how surprised Zeb was to learn of the
Confederacy's precarious situation.[42] Armed with more information than
the governor, Graham sought to influence Zeb to follow the plan of action
that he favored. Apparently Graham had concluded that the Confederacy
was doomed, an assessment that Zeb agreed with. For Graham, however,
this fact meant that the legitimate policy to follow was to sacrifice the Confederacy to rescue slavery. Zeb disagreed. While the governor embraced
slavery, he was more concerned about his personal honor and that of North
Carolina. He was determined not to undermine the Confederacy in such
a way that he or his state could be accused of failing to give everything to
sustain it.

Zeb's conviction that this course was the right one meant that he ultimately could not follow Graham's suggestions. For example, when Graham

brought Zeb a message from unidentified members of the Confederate establishment that asked Zeb to withdraw North Carolina troops from the Confederate army, Zeb exploded. "No! I would see the last one in perdition before I would do it," he reportedly replied. "Were I to do that . . . . [It] would be charged that the Confederacy might have succeeded but for the treachery of North Carolina. So far as the honor of the state is in my keeping it shall be untarnished. She must stand or fall with her sisters." As the war was winding down, Graham persuaded a reluctant Vance to call the legislature into special session to give the state an opportunity to reach an agreement with General Sherman. It is clear from the record that Zeb did not really desire to do so and that he used the Council of State as a means to delay calling the legislature into session.[43]

On April 4, Zeb enjoyed one last instance of Confederate glory. On that day, he watched Joseph E. Johnston's Army of Tennessee march in review in Raleigh. This was the Confederacy's last gasp in North Carolina. By that time, Lee's army was in retreat from its trenches around Richmond and Petersburg. Jefferson Davis and his government were in flight in southern Virginia. Grant pursued Lee vigorously and forced the Army of Northern Virginia to capitulate on April 9. By the next day, part of Stoneman's force had entered Winston and Salem and there was no escape to the west. As news of these events reached Zeb, he rushed to save as many of the supplies that he had accumulated through his blockade-running activities as possible. It is estimated that these items included sufficient cloth to make one hundred thousand uniforms, forty thousand blankets, leathers to make ten thousand shoes, and forty thousand bushels of corn.[44] Sherman's great army was now advancing toward Raleigh, and the end of the Confederacy was visible for all to see.

T he last three weeks of April would be the most difficult of Zeb's life. The Confederacy was falling apart, and he had to find a way to reconcile his duty to the people of North Carolina with his loyalty to the Confederate government. This task would ultimately prove to be impossible, and Zeb would remain sensitive about the events of these weeks to the end of his life. It was distressing to Zeb to find that he was no longer in control of events. There were two large armies in the vicinity of Raleigh, and neither was likely to be persuaded that Zeb needed to be consulted. In addition, there were civilians who sought to influence Zeb's actions. Several times during the ordeals of April 1865, Zeb was accused of committing treason against the Confederacy, and he rejected the charges as false. But as he would note later, the Confederacy had virtually ceased to exist at the time he was supposed to have betrayed it.

On April 9, David L. Swain traveled to Hillsborough and met with William A. Graham to discuss whether there was a way for North Carolina to escape the fate of South Carolina. Graham proposed that North Carolina should seek a separate peace, and Swain agreed. Graham suggested, among other things, that Zeb should send a commission to General William T. Sherman to request an armistice. The next day, Swain brought Graham's proposals to Zeb for consideration. Zeb refused to act on the ideas, saying that he needed to consult with General Joseph E. Johnston. When Zeb asked the Confederate general his opinion, Johnston replied that he thought Zeb should obtain the best terms that he could. As soon as he received this message, Zeb sent for Graham. In the meantime, he contacted General Sherman in an attempt to shield Raleigh from the ravages that had been visited on Columbia, South Carolina. He pleaded for protection for the "Charitable Institutions" and the "Capitol of the State with its Libraries, Museum and much of the public records."[1]

Graham arrived before the sun was up on April 12 and soon met with Swain and Vance. The three of them composed a letter to Sherman that followed the formula developed earlier by Graham. It said, in part, "I have to request, under proper safe-conduct, a personal interview, at such time as may be agreeable to you, for the purpose of conferring upon the subject of a suspension of hostilities, with a view to further communications with the authorities of the United States, touching the final termination of the existing war." This letter went out over Zeb's signature. Zeb then requested that Graham and Swain act as commissioners for the state and meet with Sherman. They agreed and took a train to Sherman's lines. Later that same day, newspaper editor Duncan K. McRae visited Zeb's office and accused the governor of trying to make a separate peace for North Carolina. Zeb denied the charge and convinced McRae that he was not doing so.[2] How Zeb could have justified this claim is unclear. Perhaps he had convinced himself that the message he had signed was Graham's and not his own. In any case, Zeb's denial to McRae would be the first in a lifelong series of statements by which he attempted to obscure the obvious meaning of the words he had just sent.

The events of April 12 battered Zeb without mercy. The first rumors of Lee's surrender reached the area, and the weary governor tried to ascertain the accuracy of the reports. He later heard that Swain and Graham had been captured and would not return to Raleigh that day. In the meantime, the fleeing Jefferson Davis had reached Greensboro and sought a meeting with the beleaguered North Carolina governor. Unwilling to subject either himself or North Carolina to the charge that they had deserted the Confederacy, Zeb replied to Davis. He assured the now powerless president, "It is not my intention to do anything subversive of your prerogative or without consultation with yourself." Like his denial to McRae, Zeb's answer to Davis was evasive at best. All of the day's events weighed heavily on the governor as he rode slowly out of Raleigh toward Cary in the company of two Confederate officers who had offered to protect him. The usually jovial Zeb was confused and embittered. As he observed later, his friends had deserted him in his hour of greatest trial. He wrote, "I rode out of Raleigh at midnight without a single officer of my staff with me! Not one."[3]

Zeb reached Graham's home in Hillsborough and awaited developments. After meeting with Sherman and suffering many adventures on their return trip, Swain and Graham had arrived back in Raleigh. When he learned Zeb's whereabouts, Graham continued to his home. He delivered Sherman's offer, which was to allow Zeb to return to his office in Raleigh. Zeb stated that he could not do that, because he had agreed to go to Greensboro to meet with Davis. The next day, Zeb started for Greensboro to meet with the Confederate leader. Unfortunately, Davis and his cabinet had decided to move on to Charlotte. Thus, Zeb was unable to discuss the situation with these Confederate officials. Instead, he attended a meeting called by General Johnston in Greensboro. Present at the meeting were Vance, Johnston, General Wade Hampton, Secretary of War John C. Breckinridge, and Postmaster General John H. Reagan. After a sumptuous dinner, Hampton confronted Zeb about the letter he had sent to Sherman. Zeb was humiliated by the accusation of treason and mortified when none of the other men in attendance contradicted Hampton's indictment. Then, Zeb was ingloriously dismissed while the cabinet officers and generals drafted a reply to Sherman's peace offer.[4]

After a fitful sleep, Zeb sought to explain himself to a Confederate officer who was an aide to Hampton. Major William J. Saunders provided an account of Vance's conduct at the meeting: "'I came here to explain the Sherman letter,' he said, the tears rolling down his face, 'and they wouldn't hear me. Me in communication with the enemy, me making terms for my State unknown to the authorities! Of all men, sir, I am the last man they can accuse of such infamy!'" Apparently, Zeb made a distinction between attempting to make a separate peace for the state of North Carolina, which he had not directly attempted to do in the letter to Sherman, and attempting to secure a general cessation of hostilities. Zeb would continue to make this distinction and stress his innocence for the remainder of his life. Shortly after he met with Hampton's assistant, Breckinridge informed Zeb of Lincoln's assassination. The stunned governor left Greensboro and returned to Graham's house to await developments.[5]

Sensing Zeb's impotence and the powerful position of federal forces, several of Zeb's wartime opponents sought to make him the scapegoat for North Carolina's Confederate adventure. William W. Holden claimed that by fleeing to Greensboro and Charlotte, Zeb had left the governor's office vacant, and Holden maintained that a new governor should be elected. The next day, Holden argued that Zeb had been elected in 1864 through the use of force and fraud, and that he was not the legal governor of the state in any case. Holden did not demand punishment for Zeb, however, feeling that depriving him of his office would have been sufficient retribution. John L. Pennington of the *Raleigh Daily Progress* was not as moderate in his attacks on Vance. Pennington wrote, "Vance, more than any other man, is responsible for whatever may seem to be hostile to the National Authority in North Carolina." He followed that attack with the claim that "Vance said . . . he had rather live under the King of Dahomy, and eat fried negro babies for breakfast every morning than to live again under the same government with the people of the North."[6]

This outpouring of abuse was prompted by the terms of surrender agreed to by Sherman and Johnston. The extremely generous terms required the surrender of all Confederate troops east of the Mississippi River and the restoration of full federal authority. But, as the jubilant Zeb wrote to Graham, the terms related to the state government would have allowed the recognition of the existing state government after Zeb took the oath of allegiance, with the ultimate fate of Zeb's administration to be determined by the United States Supreme Court. This agreement would have restored Vance to his office until controversies were settled at a later date. Although Zeb would spend the next three decades attacking Sherman's military policies, he would always acknowledge that the victorious general had proposed humane surrender terms. Unfortunately for Zeb, Sherman's offer was politically naive, and the federal authorities repudiated the pact immediately.[7]

After meeting with Sherman and agreeing to surrender his army, Johnston boarded a train for Greensboro. The train stopped in Hillsborough to pick up Zeb, but the governor had waited four hours for the train and then returned to Graham's house just before it arrived. No great effort was made to contact Zeb, and the train continued on without him. He was able to reach Greensboro within hours, however, thanks to a specially commissioned train. Upon arriving in Greensboro, Zeb exchanged two sets of angry letters with Johnston in which he complained about Hampton's conduct, his exclusion from the discussion about Sherman's offer, and the failure of those on the train to contact him in Hillsborough. A conciliatory Johnston managed to soothe the beleaguered governor's feelings with the assurance that no disrespect had been intended. Reports reached Zeb, however, that Johnston's disintegrating army was pillaging state warehouses and the surrounding civilian population. This development spawned another series of letters between the general and the governor.[8]

When Johnston went to Charlotte to confer with Jefferson Davis about Sherman's generous peace terms, Zeb followed. Davis was delighted to see Vance and assumed that the North Carolina governor had come to join in a last ditch stand against the Union. The Confederate president quickly outlined a plan to escape to the western Confederacy, where resistance could be sustained. Fortunately for Zeb, Breckinridge intervened and scolded Davis for not being realistic with Zeb. Davis was forced to accept this point, and it was agreed that Zeb should return to Greensboro with no obligations to the Confederate government. Acknowledging the tremendous efforts that Zeb had made, Davis thanked Vance and North Carolina for their contributions to the failed revolution. Zeb then returned to Greensboro and tried to make contact with General Sherman. Sherman had left the state by that time, so Zeb sought to surrender to General John M. Schofield. Schofield stated that he had no authority to arrest Zeb, and Zeb consequently informed the general that he planned to join his family in Statesville. As his last official act, Zeb issued a proclamation calling for a return to social peace and an end to the strife generated by the war.[9]

Zeb was deeply needed by his family. Hattie's mental and physical health had deteriorated under the pressures caused by the end of the war. Not only was she concerned for her husband's safety, but she had been forced to flee to protect herself and the four boys. A Union cavalry force had reached Statesville, and Hattie and the boys had fled to Lincolnton to seek safety. Forced to leave on short notice, the family left its possessions, including two thousand dollars in gold currency, in the care of friends in a neighboring community. Union soldiers liberated these possessions, but a strict officer forced them to return the property. Zeb's own trip from Greensboro to Statesville was difficult, especially because he had brought his horse and two mules with him on the train. At each stop, recently discharged Confederate soldiers crowded into the cars and pressed the people and animals to the point of discomfort. Getting tired of the crush of bodies, Zeb finally used his pistol to threaten a soldier who was attempting to enter the car. The battle-hardened veteran took one look at Zeb and observed, "You don't look like you'd shoot." Amidst the laughter of the onlookers and Zeb himself, the man climbed into the car.[10]

Zeb arrived home on May 4 and enjoyed only a short stay with his family. On that same day, Holden editorialized, "It is this man *Zebulon B. Vance*, that has done more to protract the war and bring ruin and desolation upon the people of North Carolina who had honored him." Federal officials apparently drew similar conclusions, and on May 8 General Grant ordered Schofield to arrest Zeb. The chaos of the state's transportation system delayed the arrival of Union troops in Statesville until May 13, when Major John M. Porter and his company surrounded the Vance house. At nine o'clock the next morning, Zeb left Statesville under guard, riding in a buggy driven by local businessman Samuel Wittkowsky. Uncharacteristically, but not surprisingly, Zeb was quite depressed, and he wept as they began their journey. He explained to Wittkowsky, "I am not so much concerned about what may be in store for me, but my poor wife and little children—they have not a cent to live on." Presently Zeb regained his composure, and by lunchtime he was regaling his captors with colorful stories that gained their sympathy. Wittkowsky made the courageous decision to assist the disgraced former governor, and by doing so the Jewish merchant left Zeb forever in his debt. This incident may well have been the most important single factor in Zeb's appreciation of and later support for the Jewish community.[11]

The remainder of Zeb's journey to Washington was handled with considerable humanity, and every effort was made to allow Zeb to maintain some of his dignity. He and Wittkowsky were permitted to ride into Salisbury, where Zeb stayed at the home of Charles E. Shober. The next morning, Zeb borrowed money for the expenses he would incur during his incarceration, and he was taken by train to Raleigh. There he stayed for two days. He met with old friends, including Kemp P. Battle, and shared meals with them. On May 17, he boarded a train for Washington, where he arrived on May 20. A reporter for the *Philadelphia Inquirer* described Zeb as he arrived: "He wore a clean linen shirt, with a black neck tie carelessly arranged, his collar turned down around his neck, and gave him a rather eccentric look; his hair is very long and combed backward from his forehead . . . . While he was awaiting an audience with the Secretary of War, Mr. Aiken, one of the counsel for Mrs. Surratt, came in, and recognized him as an old friend. They seemed glad to see each other, and had quite a chat together." There is no record of the conversation between Zeb and Secretary of War Edwin M. Stanton; Zeb was quickly taken away. Nevertheless, he seemed buoyed by his meetings with friends along the route, and he entered prison in a much better frame of mind than he had been in when he left Statesville.[12]

Although Zeb felt considerable stress during the forty-seven days of his confinement, the experience was not as devastating as it might have been. Still, it was a time of considerable anxiety. Since no charges were ever preferred against him, Zeb had no idea how long he would remain in Washington. In addition, he faced the remote possibility that he might be tried for treason and executed. Despite these significant concerns, however, Zeb seems to have had a relatively easy stay in jail. For a gregarious person like Zeb, the location and accommodations of the prison were the best that could have been imagined. He was kept in a large first-floor cell in the Old Capitol—or Carroll—Prison on First Street. The building was located directly across from the Capitol on the site of the present Supreme Court Building. Access to the building was so uncontrolled and the location so central to official Washington that Zeb and other prisoners had a constant stream of visitors with whom to converse. Zeb quickly made friends with the jailer in his section, Newton T. Colby, and this friendship assured that Zeb would have every advantage possible under the circumstances.[13]

What eased the pain of separation from his family the most, however, was the fact that he shared a cell with five other people. Zeb's fellow prisoners included former governors Joseph E. Brown of Georgia and John Letcher of Virginia; Savannah, Georgia, banker Gazeway B. Lamar; army general Edward Johnson from Virginia; and a physician from King George County, Virginia, by the name of Stewart. Although Brown thought himself improperly imprisoned and was often morose, the others seemed to enjoy the company. They played cards with some regularity, shared stories about the war, and watched events from their window, including the parade of Sherman's army on May 21 and a massive Fourth of July fireworks display. They had meals which they paid for themselves provided from local restaurants, and Zeb and Letcher kept an ample supply of liquor on hand. On occasion, the suffocating Washington heat and humidity forced the prisoners to disrobe to their underwear, but generally they suffered little discomfort.[14]

Zeb kept in constant contact with the outside world. Hattie and his brother Robert kept him informed about family matters and developments in North Carolina. While this information was a solace, their letters also reminded Zeb of Hattie's delicate health. One prominent visitor to the prison was Thomas Corwin, a former cabinet officer and U.S. senator. According to one account, Corwin asked Zeb, "Vance, what are you doing in prison?" Showing his ability to see the lighter side of any situation, Zeb replied: "Holden pledged the last man and the last dollar for the Confederacy. I stood his security and am imprisoned for the pledge." But Zeb's sense of humor often deserted him, as the following exchange with an unidentified group of Northern visitors indicates:

> "Why is the Confederacy like Lazarus?" asked Vance.
> "Because it is poor," said someone.
> "No, that's not the reason," said Zeb.
> "We give up," said another. "You tell us why."
> "Because," Vance said, looking them over, "it was licked by a pack of dogs."[15]

Zeb's hostility and frustration were fueled by his inability to obtain a hearing on his request for a pardon. His anxiety only increased on June 2 when Brown obtained parole and was allowed to return to Georgia. On the next day, Zeb drafted a twelve-hundred-word petition for a pardon and sent it to President Andrew Johnson. Zeb noted that the Amnesty Proclamation that Johnson had issued on May 29th did not cover him and that he was therefore making the special application for pardon required by the president. Zeb explained that since Johnson had "in a great measure, knowledge of the facts of the case, touching the participation of the undersigned in the National troubles," he would touch only briefly on the facts. Zeb reminded Johnson that as "a member of the Congress of the United States, he had the honor, during the session of 1860–61 of co-operating with [Johnson] in earnest efforts to save the Union and avert civil war." After the firing on Fort Sumter, Zeb asserted that "with great sorrow, [he] saw, that he could do nothing more, except to stir up domestic strife." While this reasoning might have persuaded other people in the national government, President

Johnson, of course, had faced the same choice and had chosen the Union and "domestic Strife."[16]

Zeb then recounted his career within the Confederacy. He acknowledged in two short sentences that he had served in the Confederate army, and he noted his election as governor. To historians, the next sentence is a major disappointment. Rather than explain his actions as governor, Zeb stated, "Since the assumption of that office, his public acts are of course, matters of official notoriety and need not be further alluded to here." An attorney may have suggested this strategy, since Zeb faced potential legal action for his wartime activities and did not want to incriminate himself. Zeb made no effort to hide his disloyalty to the United States, however. He stated: "It is due to truth, in order that all the 'facts of the case' may be understood, to say however reluctantly he felt compelled to yield to circumstances in the beginning his feelings became in time thoroughly and earnestly enlisted in behalf of the cause his state espoused." He went on to say that he contemplated "no further resistance whatever to the authority of the United States" and that he accepted the abolition of slavery.[17]

On July 6, Johnson gave Zeb parole so that he could return to Statesville to be with his sick wife. Hattie's condition had worsened when a squad of soldiers took all of the furniture in the house, claiming that it belonged in the executive mansion in Raleigh. The esteem in which Zeb's neighbors still held the former governor and his family was demonstrated by the fact that the house was completely refurnished with donations in less than a day. This incident, however, may have triggered the lung hemorrhage that nearly killed Hattie. Zeb hurried home as quickly as the wrecked Southern transportation system would allow. He arrived in Salisbury on July 11 and reached Statesville the next day. Within a short period of time, he was able to report that Hattie was much better. Although he was pleased to be out of prison and to see Hattie improved, Zeb was still frustrated with his situation. Since he had been paroled rather than pardoned, he was greatly restricted in his movements. As he explained, "So I am here, a prisoner still. . . . We are living very poorly and quietly, as I can do no business until I am pardoned or released from my parole."[18]

Zeb's dissatisfaction manifested itself in virtually every letter he wrote. After being in the center of great events and in the public eye, Zeb found exile in Statesville to be unbearable. In a letter to John Evans Brown in Australia, Zeb explored the options that seemed open to him. He explained that "the state of society" in the mountains was "not pleasant," and he continued: "I don't think I shall ever return there to live. Murder and outrages are frequent and the absence of civil law encourages the wickedly inclined." If he decided to stay in the state, Zeb thought that he would move to Wilmington and practice law again. The depth of his depression was revealed when he concluded: "Many thought have I directed towards the distant Orient where you are. . . . What would it cost me and how would I get there? What could I do there? Either in Australia or New Zealand?"[19] Although there is no evidence that Zeb ever seriously planned to leave the United States, his request for information from Brown makes the depth of his desperation and confusion clear.

Zeb did apparently investigate a number of options for his future, including relocation to Baltimore. A letter from William A. Graham indicates that Zeb had asked him about the possibility of pursuing a business opportunity in that city. Graham encouraged Zeb, saying that everyone would understand his need to earn money to support his family. Graham did observe that he thought that Zeb was better suited for the law, but he acknowledged that the profession offered few economic advantages. But Zeb was trapped in Statesville. In a September letter to Kemp P. Battle, he vented his frustrations. He wrote, "The genius of dullness & stupidity may apply to y[ou]r agency for a location, & if he does you will scarcely deal honestly by him unless you recommend him to Statesville." He went on to describe his typical day in that small community: "I try to read law. Most of my time is however employed in delivering imaginary stump speeches in favor of civil liberty, habeas corpus and the freedom of the Press as gloriously illustrated in our escape from Jeff Davis' military despotism and our return to the 'land of the free' et cet., or else calculating how long I can escape death by starvation or inaction, at the rate I am going on."[20] As North Carolina's social, economic, and political life slowly began to resume, Zeb's dissatisfaction with the limitations of his parole only increased.

Zeb was particularly upset when he was excluded from the revived political system. Andrew Johnson appointed William W. Holden provisional governor of North Carolina and held elections to select members of a convention to end slavery and to repudiate both the Confederate debt and secession. It was the first election in two decades for which Zeb was unable to take to the campaign trail. The result of the election disgusted Zeb: "The election for delegates in this section indicates the intention of Holden to set up a menagerie . . . in Raleigh. This region will contribute largely to the ass line. Such a set you never saw in Raleigh in y[ou]r life. Judge Pearson's defeat took everyone by surprise except myself. They proved on him that he changed shirts once a week, and very properly beat him—served him right—the sweet-scented aristocrat!" Zeb's own sense—usually well concealed from the general population—of being part of the elite began to emerge during Reconstruction as people from the lower reaches of North

Carolina society took prominent public offices. Zeb's anger with these developments was probably further fueled by the fact that only one person among his correspondents even hinted that there might be a role for him to play in the new order.[21]

In desperation to be freed from his imprisonment, Zeb played his most personal card: he asked Hattie to go to Washington to present his case to Johnson. She left Statesville in mid-October and arrived in Greensboro on October 21. She reported to Zeb that she had received a very warm welcome in Greensboro and would soon be proceeding to Washington. That part of the trip never took place, however, because Hattie collapsed and remained seriously ill. Former peace advocate Robert P. Dick contacted both Johnson and Vance about the crisis. Dick's intercession was effective, and Zeb's parole was modified to allow him to visit Greensboro and to take Hattie back to Statesville. Zeb's guilt about sending Hattie to Washington was now compounded by his anger at not having been able to go to her aid without permission from Washington. He suspected that Holden was responsible for his continued political disabilities. Although Zeb did not have direct evidence, the president's correspondence reveals that Zeb's hunch was correct. In a July 24, 1865, letter, Holden advised Johnson: "By the way, it would not be good policy to extend a pardon to Vance for sometime to come. . . . There are indications on the part of some of the oligarchs and the old Whig leaders to concoct opposition. A firm, discreet use of the pardoning power and the patronage of the government will contribute greatly to keep them down, and thus preserve tranquility and order in the state."[22]

Two very different developments helped to lift Zeb's spirits despite his recent setbacks. The first indication that Zeb's fortunes were improving was manifest in the election campaign in the fall of 1865. Jonathan Worth, treasurer of North Carolina during the Civil War, challenged Holden for the governor's seat. Holden's initial expectation of victory was soon replaced by fear that the election would be close. Recognizing that Zeb's name still had political potency, Holden claimed to have been kind to Vance immediately after the war. Unwilling to allow that statement to pass unchallenged, Worth's backers charged that Holden was in fact responsible for Zeb's arrest. When Worth and his allies won control of the state government, there was considerable speculation that Zeb would be elected by the state legislature to the U.S. Senate. Although the members of the legislature did not elect Vance due to their concern that he could not obtain a pardon and would therefore be ineligible to serve, they did pass a resolution asserting that Zeb was completely loyal to the U.S. government. There was one other fact about the election that gave Zeb a psychological lift: he received 247 votes, scattered throughout the state, for governor. Since he had not been a candidate, these votes represented his loyal supporters' protest against his enforced absence from the political process.[23]

During this brief political campaign and the subsequent constitutional convention, an issue came to the fore that would dominate North Carolina politics for the remainder of Zeb's lifetime. That was the question of what legal and moral rights African Americans should possess in the state's political system. Among whites in North Carolina in 1865 there was little disagreement. Not only did those who led the secession movement oppose any role for blacks in the electoral process, but so did those who had most actively opposed the Davis administration. Even before Holden was appointed provisional governor, his allies had contended that the freedmen should be "excluded" from suffrage until they were "deemed qualified to enjoy said privilege." Holden himself confirmed in August that he was opposed to the idea of allowing blacks to vote, and though Zeb made no public statements on the matter, there can be no doubt that he agreed with his contemporaries on this point. North Carolina's African Americans refused to accept that they would be denied suffrage, and they began to demand their political rights in public meetings held in New Bern and Raleigh.[24] With no pressure from President Andrew Johnson to address this issue, however, North Carolina's established leadership simply ignored it for the time being.

Vance's partial political rehabilitation was accompanied by a simultaneous intellectual revival. On October 30, he received a most welcome letter from Cornelia Phillips Spencer. Spencer reported that she was writing a series of articles that would explain Zeb's role in the end of the war in North Carolina. She told Vance that she had conferred with David L. Swain about the manuscript, but that she wanted Zeb's assistance as well. Having received her letter after he returned from Greensboro with Hattie, Zeb replied immediately. His elation about the project was evident in the gush of his first paragraph: "I am truly gratified, not so much at the handsome things said about myself, but at the fact that in my checkered career I have been able notwithstanding my follies & short-comings, to inspire such disinterested and sincere friendship." Zeb's psychological vulnerability led him to share this important personal insight. He continued: "Notwithstanding my years & my ambition, I retain so much of the simplicity of the boy as to still prefer the gratification of my affections rather than my pride. Mrs. V. expresses the opinion that I never will be a *full grown* man tho' my head is already gray."[25] Zeb's recent behavior had indeed shown the volatility of youth, and now that his fortunes seemed to be about to improve, his natural optimism returned in a flood. The fact that he was now reestablishing contact with someone who had acted as an intellectual sister when he was in college only encouraged him to think in terms of his life as a youth.

Zeb's specific comments on Spencer's manuscript showed a mature understanding of past events. He corrected the romantic idea that the *Advance* had been named for Hattie and pointed out that the federal prisoners at Salisbury had not received any clothing from North Carolina's supplies. He also agreed to allow Spencer to quote from his personal letters to ensure accuracy. He did have one reservation, however: "I must confess however that I feel some repugnance to making public my remarks on Mr. Davis in the letter you copy. When they were written he was in power, and backed by mighty armies: now he is in chains and a mean mob clamoring for his blood." Apparently everything else met with his approval. The obviously exhilarated Zeb confided: "I too am writing—not a history of the war, but of the adventures, opinions, &c. of 'the undersigned' during the war. It is not for publication, and I am so unsettled that it progresses slowly. If finished, revised & published I hardly believe it would survive more than forty editions." Two weeks later, he was happily discussing Spencer's manuscript with her in a lengthy and spirited letter.[26]

For 130 years, Zeb's own written account remained unavailable and apparently lost. But it has recently come to light, and it suggests that his attitude during this period was much darker than his correspondence with Spencer indicates. The first part of the manuscript gave a short and breezy account of his life before the war. As he described the coming of the sectional crisis, however, Zeb's tone shifted rapidly. First, he became very defensive about his reasons for turning against the Union, using justifications that he had previously made to Swain and others. In a lengthy apologia, he wrote:

Could I, or any true son of hers [North Carolina] refuse to go with her or sustain her action? Was she wrong, was she embarking on a course that would lead to ruin? There was, in my opinion, the greater necessity for the faithful adherence of her children, a more chivalrous call *for the manhood* of *her true sons*.

Besides I did not believe she was wrong. There were great errors and great crimes committed for the production of this, as of all other wars; but I submit to the opinion of the candid world that they were not committed by North Carolina. The great crime of unnatural strife belongs to those who, by long course of aggression upon *chartered* rights on the one hand and of injudicious agitation on the other, produced an "irrepressible conflict" naturally resulting in bloodshed: and it was the misfortune of North Carolina to be placed in such a position as to render action unavoidable.[27]

This self-justification remained a standard part of Zeb's internal defenses against the conflict that he felt about his abandonment of the Union in 1861.

In the manuscript, Zeb did not remain on the defensive for very long. Instead, he turned in bitterness and rage on those he felt were most responsible for his situation. He still had not reconciled himself to the destruction of slavery, and he blamed the abolitionists for his and his state's conditions. He cited chapter and verse from the Scriptures to justify the institution of slavery, his own activities, and the activities of his social class. Slashing at his opponents, he exploded: "How much wiser and holier are the New England Saints! Christ—the Son of God—equal in power and glory with the Father—comes upon earth and dwells in bodily flesh to teach sinners the 'way of salvation,' yet omits an important part of his mission—the denunciation of slavery—Happily however for sinful man, the Superior Sanctity, or wisdom, of the Beachers [sic], the John Browns and the Sumners, has supplied this omission!"[28] Zeb's harsh denunciation continued on for several pages, at which point the document abruptly ends. Perhaps Zeb had sufficiently vented his frustration and anger and no longer felt the need to continue the tirade. Equally likely, he may have recognized that any opportunity that he had to obtain a full pardon would be greatly damaged if his sentiments about slavery surfaced.

In his second letter to Spencer, Zeb stated his concern that he would not receive his pardon for quite some time. At around the same time, he wrote to Swain, indicating that he was making every effort to obtain a pardon. Prompted by Zeb's letter, Swain traveled to Washington to talk to Johnson about Zeb's case. Apparently Swain's intervention had some impact, because Zeb received notification that the conditions of his parole had been modified and he was now free to travel throughout the state. Swain had not been the first to approach the president on Vance's behalf; Johnson complained that at least fifty people had spoken to him about the Vance case. The altered conditions of his parole allowed Zeb to pursue plans to move his family to Wilmington. By the end of January, he had already located a rental house in the coastal city, and he was being offered legal business by local businessmen. Without warning, however, Zeb suffered a slight stroke in February and was temporarily paralyzed. His recovery from the attack was rapid, but the episode apparently caused him to reassess whether it was wise to move to Wilmington. He had been concerned about the potential effects of the move on Hattie's health, and now the condition of his own health also argued strongly in favor of a city with a healthier climate.[29]

By the end of February, Zeb had decided to move to Charlotte, and he was seeking a rental house in that city. He agreed to form a law partnership with Clement Dowd, his former wartime aide. By April 3, the two men and a third partner, R. D. Johnson, were advertising their new firm. As Dowd later recounted, Zeb was not prepared to take full responsibility for all parts of the practice of law. He explained to his former aide: "Every law office contains one working man and one gentleman. In this partnership, I propose to be the gentleman." But even this new arrangement did not satisfy his need for larger projects and a bigger stage. He actively sought an appointment from Governor Worth as the president of the North Carolina Railroad. While he was not appointed, the episode indicates how restless Zeb had become and how determined he was to restore his economic and public standing.[30]

Zeb's reemergence—as limited as it was—into the public arena prompted William W. Holden to attack his 1864 opponent in print. Holden was quite embittered by his loss to Worth, and all of the favorable articles being written about Vance in the state's newspapers increasingly angered him. (All of these favorable essays were apparently written to persuade President Johnson to issue Zeb a pardon.) On January 10, 1866, Holden wrote a long editorial in which he claimed credit for securing Zeb's release from prison. Holden asserted that in return for this favor, he had been met by "abuse at the hands of Gov. Vance's partisans and by profound silence . . . on the part of Gov. Vance." Unwilling to endure these slights any longer, Holden warned, "We now give notice that if these laudations of Gov. Vance should be continued, coupled with disparaging allusions to Mr. Holden, we shall appeal in the most earnest terms to the President of the United States to cause Gov. Vance to be returned to the Old Capitol prison to be tried with Jefferson Davis for the crime of treason."[31] This fate, of course, was the cloud that hung over Zeb throughout this period. At any time, he could have been returned to prison. The controversy demonstrated, on the other hand, that he was still a significant public figure. Even when he lived under severe limitations, Zeb remained prominent in the public life of the state.

As his public world expanded, Zeb remained in close contact with Cornelia Phillips Spencer, who continued to write articles about the end of the war. Zeb's letters provided her with careful justifications of his actions. Ironically, Zeb's most notable disagreement at this time was with his wartime mentor and ally William A. Graham. Graham had written a letter to Spencer in which he criticized Zeb for not taking a more active part in ending the war in North Carolina. Zeb, requesting that his reply be kept a secret from Graham, replied to Spencer and stated that Graham had wanted him to take an initiative that his mentor was unwilling to take himself. Zeb revealed that in early 1865, Graham had brought Zeb a request from some members of the Confederate Congress to lead North Carolina out of the Confederacy and thereby to stop the war. Zeb had refused to do so unless Graham joined him in the effort, and the older man would not. Spencer accepted Zeb's account of the events and protected his reputation in her article.[32]

Spencer protected Zeb in another way as well. Her work was immediately valuable to the former governor because she used it to publish many of the original documents from the war for the first time. Since the federal government had confiscated all of the state government records, Spencer had to rely upon copies of materials in the hands of private individuals. She often chose to print the full text of these documents in order to allow Zeb and his allies to explain themselves. This was a very valuable service at the time, and it gave her work great credibility. A close examination of the documents indicates, however, that either Spencer or her sources had made some modifications to the documents that benefited Zeb. The clearest example of this editorial handiwork is in the reproduction of Zeb's letter to David L. Swain of January 2, 1864. In that letter, Zeb wrote, "Our people will not pay this price [in blood and misery]. I am satisfied for their national independence." Spencer's wording of the same passage was different: "whether our people are willing to pay this price for Southern independence, I am somewhat inclined to doubt."[33] Clearly the Spencer version is a much less harsh statement, and one that would be likely to do Zeb much less harm in postwar political contests.

In this period of expanded activity, Zeb was offered his first postwar opportunity to play a public role. As a man who needed to be in the center of public awareness, Zeb welcomed the chance to address the people of North Carolina as a tonic for his mental and physical health. The two debating societies at the university in Chapel Hill invited him to address their membership during the 1866 commencement festivities. Despite the fact that Zeb's presence in Chapel Hill caused some embarrassment to his friends, who thought his appearance was premature, he was determined to speak. He confessed to David L. Swain, his host for the occasion, that he had experienced great difficulty composing his address. This was partly because Zeb was still on parole, and he therefore had to be very careful about the language that he used. To ensure that he would not harm his reputation further, he carefully wrote out his speech, a fairly rare practice for Zeb up to this point in his life.[34]

Addressing the future leaders of North Carolina in an address entitled "The Duties of Defeat," Zeb urged his auditors to look forward and accept the results of the war. He exhorted them: "It is *our* country still, and if it cannot be governed as *we* wish it, it must be governed in some other way; and it is still our duty to labor for its prosperity and glory with ardor and sincerity." Zeb was quick to point out that there were other equally important duties, including the duties of returning economic prosperity to the state and providing free public education to the children of dead soldiers. While most of the speech was quite sober and relatively straightforward, Zeb's natural tendency to romanticize rural North Carolina was evident in several passages of the speech. In describing the need for the revitalization of the state's agricultural system, Zeb lost all control of his syntax: "The noblest soldier now, is he that with ax and plough pitches his tent against the waste places of his fire-blasted home and swears that from its ruins there shall arise another like unto it, and from the gladdening sheen of dew-gemmed meadows, in the rising and golden waves of ripening harvests, in the setting sun."[35]

The speech marked a major turning point in Zeb's recovery from the depression and anxiety that had plagued him after the war. Despondency had made him a mental prisoner to match his restricted physical mobility. Since that time, however, there had been some encouraging developments. Cornelia Phillips Spencer's history of Zeb's efforts at the end of the war promised to help to restore his reputation in North Carolina. He had relocated his family and formed a law partnership that gave him the opportunity to try cases. There appeared to be palpable evidence of the public's regard for him, and even of his personal popularity, that indicated that his political career might soon be resuscitated. Finally, Vance could return to a public speaking career with confidence in his ability to influence his auditors. The essentially positive tone of his June 7 speech in Chapel Hill reflected his growing self-confidence and marked the end of Zeb's personal reconstruction.

Reconstruction was a difficult period in North Carolina, and it was a period of frustration for Zebulon Vance. Predictably, the effort to repair the economic, political, and social fabric of the United States following a conflict that had killed 625,000 people in the military and tens of thousands of civilians did not go smoothly. There was uncertainty, miscalculation, and malfeasance at the national, state, and local levels. For those caught in the midst of this turmoil, and particularly for those in the South, the lack of certainty was often debilitating. The question of what role African Americans would play in the reunited nation remained particularly contentious. Many of the elite who dominated Southern society, including those in North Carolina, were strongly determined to retain their traditional position in the world to the greatest extent possible.

Between June 1865 and March 1867, Andrew Johnson's lenient policy toward the Southerners gave North Carolinians an opportunity to shape Reconstruction in their state. Under William W. Holden's provisional governorship, local administration was restored to most of the counties. The state's convention only partially accepted the results of the war; it ended slavery and accepted reunion but rejected the president's demands that the Southerners allow African Americans to testify in court and that they repudiate the Confederate debt. When Jonathan Worth defeated Holden in the November 1865 gubernatorial contest, the government returned to the control of the old elite. In the same election, North Carolina also selected congressmen and state legislators. The legislature in turn chose William A. Graham and John Pool as U.S. senators. Other states in the former Confederacy were less restrained in returning Confederate statesmen to power than North Carolina was, and an indignant U.S. Congress refused to accept the congressmen and senators from the South.[1]

Within North Carolina, the new legislature attempted to deal with the consequences of the social revolution created by the war. Its major responsibility was to create a code of laws that would integrate African Americans into the existing legal system of the state. According to the leading scholar of Southern self-reconstruction, the work of Bartholomew Moore and the

North Carolina Commission on the Freedmen showed less overt racism in dealing with this problem than did that of any other former Confederate state. Moore and his colleagues suggested that all references to race in the state's statutes should be eliminated except in laws relating to suffrage, service on juries, and marriage across racial lines. The legislature generally followed the commission's recommendations. However, it did restrict black testimony to cases in which African Americans alone were involved, and it made the rape of white women by black men a capital offense. The legislators' relatively moderate stance was governed by their recognition that if North Carolina did not treat African Americans fairly, Congress was prepared to act by imposing legislation that would provide even more rights to blacks. As state senator Leander Gash explained to his wife, "All know that we got to meet it in its present form or have it forced on us in a far worse one."[2]

Although North Carolina's effort to provide African Americans with some measure of legal rights was relatively moderate, it was not matched in other Southern states. Throughout the South, both state and local ordinances were passed to keep black residents legally subservient. Understandably, Northern observers viewed such ordinances as evidence of the South's unwillingness to accept the results of the war. A split grew between President Johnson and the Republican majority in the U.S. Congress. As the Republicans in Congress came to recognize that the Southern gentry had allied themselves with the president, they began to seek ways to force the South to accept the social changes that they believed were a necessary outcome of the war. One product of their efforts was the passage of the Fourteenth Amendment and its submission to the states for ratification. By reducing a state's representation in Congress in proportion to the number of male citizens who could not vote, this compromise initiative encouraged Southern states to offer African Americans the right to vote.[3]

By the summer of 1866, North Carolinians had begun to align themselves with national groups and to form political parties on the basis of their allegiances. It was at this point that Zeb resumed his participation in the political process. In July, he attended at meeting in Charlotte that had been organized to name delegates to a district convention in Salisbury. This convention would then name delegates to a state convention in Raleigh, and the state convention would in turn send delegates to a National Union convention in Philadelphia, where they would support President Andrew Johnson against congressional Republicans. These meetings were the genesis of the post–Civil War Democratic Party in North Carolina. Zeb played a very active role at the Charlotte meeting. He addressed the assembled delegates and probably endorsed the president's opposition to the plans of the

Republicans. He was named to the Resolutions Committee and as a delegate to the Salisbury meeting. At Salisbury, Zeb was again a major speaker, and he was selected as a delegate to the state convention in Raleigh. He was not selected as a district or state delegate to the Philadelphia meeting, however; his failure to obtain a pardon prevented him from leaving the state.[4] Zeb's political activities placed him in the forefront of those who organized the opposition to Republican Reconstruction in North Carolina. In addition, they allowed Zeb to make important political contacts in his new home of Charlotte.

The political opponents of Vance and his allies, led by William W. Holden, recognized that they needed to reassess their relationship to national political developments. Holden came to recognize that President Johnson's Reconstruction policies had failed to win Holden the support that he needed to challenge the political establishment in the state. Worth's victory in the fall 1865 election had once again placed Holden outside of North Carolina's political mainstream. This forced Holden and his allies to look to the Republican Party as an alternative to the Democrats who dominated the Worth administration. In early June 1866, Holden endorsed the Fourteenth Amendment as the best deal that the South could expect to get under the circumstances. By August, many of those who supported Holden were joining the Union League. This organization, which quickly evolved into the Republican Party in North Carolina, was especially strong in the central and western counties of the state.[5] Its alliance with the national Republican Party was not immediately acknowledged, but Holden and his allies had nevertheless clearly committed themselves to seeking outside support to challenge the entrenched political leadership in North Carolina.

While Zeb was very pleased to be involved in politics once again, he still had to depend on his law practice to earn a living. Most of his cases were adjudicated in the small county seat communities of Piedmont North Carolina. Zeb's strength as a lawyer was his ability to give a convincing address to the jury at the close of each case, and large crowds used to congregate at the local courthouses when Zeb delivered one of these summations. County courts did not take verbatim transcriptions of proceedings during Zeb's lifetime, so it is difficult to recreate the magic that he performed in the courtroom. Fortunately, however, one of his local cases gained some notoriety, and the surviving record shows that Zeb had greatly improved as an attorney since his early prewar performances in the mountain counties.

In reminiscences written thirty years later, Zeb's law partner Clement Dowd captured an impression of Zeb's approach to the law in this period. Dowd admitted that Zeb "was not always diligent in the preparation of cases." This was not because Zeb was lazy, but because the lingering effects

Vance in the immediate aftermath of the war in 1866.
(North Carolina Division of Archives and History, Raleigh)

of his recent stroke caused "the muscles of the left cheek and eye to occasionally jerk and twitch, so that he was at times nervous, and could not well undergo continuous labor in a sitting position." Dowd remembered the case of *Maxwell v. McDowell* as an excellent example of Zeb's strengths as a lawyer. The controversy was over the ownership of a valuable piece of land, and both sides had hired very talented attorneys. At first, Zeb played little role in the proceedings, but he "literally absorbed the testimony of the witness, even the smallest details, and very soon became posted as to the law points involved." After the testimony closed each day, Dowd recalled, "Vance would take the [law] books home with him . . . and it was astonishing to see . . . the next morning . . . [with] what freshness, lucidity, ease and originality he discussed the various points of law arising from the case."[6] Dowd's description captures the essence of Zeb as a lawyer. His great strengths were his quick intelligence and his use of language in the courtroom, skills that he had carefully honed as a political debater in his campaigns in western North Carolina.

A more typical case for Zeb was the murder trial of Thomas Dula, for which he acted as the lead defense attorney. Dula, a former Confederate soldier, was accused of killing his girlfriend Laura Foster after she gave him a venereal disease. According to the indictment, Dula had lured Foster to his home with the promise of marriage. As she traveled a mountain path to get there, Dula and another girlfriend—Ann Melton, a married woman— stabbed Foster to death and buried her in shallow grave, which Dula had recently dug with a tool he borrowed from a neighbor. Soon thereafter, Dula fled to Tennessee. A local posse crossed the state line, captured him, and placed him in the jail in Wilkesboro. After Laura Foster's body was discovered, Dula and Melton were indicted and brought to trial in early October. Claiming that "the Public mind [had] been prejudiced against" his clients, Zeb and two other attorneys appointed by the court to defend Dula asked for a change of venue. The court agreed with Zeb's assessment of public opinion and moved the case to Statesville in Iredell County. In addition, Zeb asked the court to separate the Dula and Melton cases, claiming that it would weaken Dula's case to try the two of them together. The judge agreed to try Dula alone.[7]

On October 19, 1866, the trial began. Together, the prosecution and the defense called eighty-three witnesses to support their arguments. The court remained in session all day on the nineteenth, a Friday, and all through Saturday. When the witnesses were finished testifying, Zeb addressed the jury members; he had been careful to make sure that most of them had served in the Confederate army. Zeb called upon the members of the jury to free Dula, whom he portrayed as a former Confederate soldier who had been unjustly accused of attacking a wanton woman. Then, Zeb offered five stipulations that he asked the judge to include in his charge to the jury. The judge did so, and the jury retired after midnight to consider the case. By early the next morning, the jury brought back a guilty verdict. The judge sentenced Dula to be hanged on November 9.[8]

Zeb immediately appealed the verdict to the North Carolina Supreme Court on a writ of error. In this document, Zeb asserted that the trial judge had committed several errors; he had, for instance, allowed a major prosecution witness to provide some hearsay evidence. Dula's execution was stayed during the appeal, and the Supreme Court ultimately agreed with two of Zeb's assertions and ordered a new trial. This took place in Statesville on January 21, 1868. The trial was apparently very similar to the previous one, but the testimony that Zeb had objected to was not given. One of Zeb's questions during the trial was ruled out of order by the judge. Zeb, apparently trying to play on the racism of the jurors, had asked a white woman if she "was related to John Anderson—John Anderson was a man of color." Although Zeb again appealed to the jurors to save the life of a fellow Confederate soldier, the second jury reached the same verdict as the first one had. Zeb once again appealed to the Supreme Court, but the court rejected the appeal. On May 1, 1868, Dula was hanged before an enormous crowd in Statesville. The night before his execution, he wrote a short note in which he accepted full responsibility for the murder and exonerated Ann Melton.[9]

This case reveals a great deal about Zeb's performance as a lead trial lawyer during this period. He appears to have been well prepared for the trial, and his technical motions and appeals were very professionally made. It is interesting to note that at least in this instance, Zeb's famed appeal to the jury failed twice to sway its members. It is also notable that Zeb worked hard for a client who could not pay any fees. Whatever compensation he received from the state for defending Dula could not have come close to covering his expenses. Unfortunately for Zeb, many of his rural clients were in similar economic straits, and he and his associates probably did not make a great deal of money from criminal trials.

The absence of money was not a problem in the Johnston will case of 1867. James C. Johnston was one of the wealthiest men in eastern North Carolina when he made out his will in 1863. A bachelor, Johnston had become estranged from his family, and he left the bulk of his estate to three men who had proven themselves capable of administering his three plantations. After Johnston died in 1865, some of his relatives predictably challenged the validity of the will. They employed a number of distinguished lawyers, including William A. Graham, who acted as lead attorney, former governor Thomas Bragg, and Zeb. Ironically, the presiding judge in the case was Augustus S. Merrimon, Zeb's former fellow Asheville law student. Johnston's relatives sought to prove that Johnston was not mentally competent to create a will in 1863, a novel legal strategy for the time. The trial lasted for six days, and Zeb took turns with Graham and Bragg in examining the witnesses. One of the witnesses remembered Zeb as "equal to any occasion." The witness recalled: "Up to the time of my departure, he had not spoken often, but, whenever he stood up, every body seemed to prepare for something good, or, at any rate, something amusing. He was evidently the popular idol."[10] Like the two juries in the Dula case, the Johnston jury was not persuaded by the points that Zeb and his associates made, and it found for the other side. Numerous appeals were made to the North Carolina Supreme Court, but the verdict was sustained through the eight years it took to finally settle the case.

The likelihood of failure in high-profile cases undoubtedly gave Zeb an additional motivation to find a way to reenter public life. One safe way to do so was to give public addresses that dealt with noncontroversial topics. On December 8, Zeb spoke to a large crowd in Raleigh at a benefit for the poor sponsored by the Young Men's Christian Association. One member of the audience reported that Zeb "said many rich things in a small way in regular Zeb style, to the delight of the audience." He continued, "He is the most popular man in the state and knew well how to talk to the crowd before him and did so greatly to their edification." Later that same month, Zeb spoke at a tournament in New Bern and to the Ladies' Philanthropic Society in Charlotte. While these addresses were essentially nonpartisan, Zeb did touch on contemporary political issues in his New Bern talk. He observed: "Reconstruction would take place . . . when the North made us willing, and that would be by doing us justice."[11] Clearly Zeb was anxious to get back into the political arena again if he could only obtain a pardon.

Since that document was not immediately forthcoming, Zeb continued his nonpartisan public speaking. In January 1867, he gave a talk to the Young Men of Raleigh about the future of the South. In this address, Zeb urged the young people in the South to match the North's "physical energy, mechanical genius, and immigration policy." He claimed that the old ways had to be dropped and new challenges met. He asserted that in the future, the South would cease to be a land of large plantations and would instead feature the small family farm as its chief unit of production. He further hypothesized that African Americans would be unable to adjust to the changes brought by freedom and would become "extinct."[12] This flawed analysis was safe from partisan criticism, while public speaking allowed Zeb to remain in the public eye.

During this same period, national and state politics were undergoing dramatic changes. The break between President Johnson and the Republicans in Congress became irreconcilable. Under these circumstances, the congressional Republicans sought ways to protect both African Americans and former Unionists from the retaliation of former Confederates. Many people in North Carolina who viewed themselves as Unionists had aligned themselves with William W. Holden, and they perceived men like Zeb as their enemies. However, when the congressional Republicans first rejected the Southern men who were elected to Congress in 1865 and then began to demand more rights for blacks, the former Unionists began to join with men like Vance and ally themselves with Andrew Johnson against the radical congressional Republicans.[13]

The defining issue in the restructuring of political alignments in North Carolina was the Fourteenth Amendment. As early as September 18, 1866, Holden had endorsed the amendment and blamed Southern leaders for provoking this response from the Republicans with their actions. Once he became committed to the national Republican program, he attempted to run a candidate for governor in the fall of 1866. The convention that named Alfred Dockery was a farce, however, and Dockery refused the nomination. In the letter in which he declined to run, Dockery endorsed federal intervention in the South. In November, Jonathan Worth won reelection over Dockery, who remained on the ballot despite his refusal to run, with a majority 23,496 out of 44,994 votes cast. After holding a number of conferences with Republicans in Washington, Holden endorsed black suffrage in January. On March 27, 1867, he and his allies, including approximately forty-five African American delegates, formed the Republican Party of North Carolina at a convention in Raleigh.[14] By doing so, Holden and his supporters placed themselves outside of what most whites perceived as the accepted boundaries of political life.

Holden's political opponents were unified only by their rejection of the Republican program. State senator Leander Gash of Transylvania County left behind a voluminous record of North Carolina's political transformation. Gash, who corresponded with Zeb during the war, had embraced the peace movement in 1863. He had disagreed with Zeb on public policy for most of the next three years, and because of his strong commitment to the Union he was a potential postwar Republican. In a letter to his wife, however, Gash labeled the Reconstruction Bill introduced by congressional Republican Thaddeus Stevens as "the worst bill of the season." Gash's transformation from a potential recruit for the Republican Party into an open opponent was one that many North Carolinians experienced. In December, the state legislature rejected the Fourteenth Amendment by votes of ninety-three to ten in the House of Commons and forty-four to one in the Senate.[15] The opposition of many self-proclaimed Unionists to the Republican Party only grew stronger when the Republican-controlled Congress passed the Reconstruction Acts over Andrew Johnson's veto.

The restructuring of state and national politics worked to bring Zeb back into the political arena once again. In a show of defiance, the state legislature nearly named a new county after Zeb in January 1867. He was appointed to the board of directors of the Eastern Division of the Western Extension of the North Carolina Railroad. Zeb even received a token vote when the legislature appointed a U.S. senator, though the legislators recognized that he could not serve. On March 11, Andrew Johnson officially recognized the changing political loyalties in the South by pardoning many people who had previously been excluded from pardon as extreme Confederates. Zeb was among the people pardoned, although he did not receive official notification until more than a month later.[16] The great irony in the situation was that while the pardon gave Zeb the right to participate in politics once again, the Reconstruction Act that had been passed a week earlier had taken that right away. Under the Reconstruction Act, Zeb was still excluded from voting and holding office, but at least he could campaign and take partisan positions. Still, he was exceedingly upset by his exclusion from the political process, particularly when the new legislation gave African Americans full political rights. Zeb's resentment of this development was fed by his lifelong belief in the inferiority of African Americans; he never fully accepted African American citizenship.

Holden was irate that Vance no longer faced punishment for his wartime activities. On April 13, 1867, he asserted that Johnson's March pardons of former extreme Confederates would only encourage the "rebels" to continue to resist the coming changes. Three days later, Holden published a highly personal attack on Vance: "Gov. Vance issued with his own hand the orders under which scores of Union men were hanged and shot, and women and children arrested, imprisoned and outraged, only because they were true to their fathers, sons, and brothers. Every bullet that crashed through the brain of the poor Unionist was substantially directed by his hand. He is still unrepentant and defiant. In our opinion he will always be so. To pardon such a man is to offer a premium for treason." A newspaper in Zeb's adopted hometown countered this attack with the observation that Zeb's application for pardon was endorsed by twelve U.S. senators and twenty-eight congressmen.[17] This rebuttal probably did little to diminish the deep concern of Holden and the Republicans that Zeb would be a leading member of the opposition in the future.

That the public continued to approve of Zeb was demonstrated by its demand for his services as a speaker. Vance complained to David L. Swain, "I am beset on all sides to make speeches, or write papers, etc." While he declined some invitations, he agreed to speak at the installation of Masonic lodge officers in Charlotte. His speech, according to the *Charlotte Democrat*, "was appropriate to the occasion, in good taste, and was well received by the audience." There seems to have been a note of relief in this report that Zeb did not resort to funny stories and coarse language. Zeb also spoke at the Davidson College commencement, where he was awarded an honorary doctorate.[18] These nonpolitical speeches kept Zeb in the public eye and gave him the visibility he would need when he actively pursued politics again.

In the meantime, the Republicans were forging ahead with their plans. Across the state, the party leadership encouraged the rank and file to join the Union League, a support organization that sought to protect poor blacks and whites from the sanctions imposed on them by the elites who opposed Reconstruction. The party had a convention in August to organize itself for the coming battles over the changes that the Reconstruction Acts required in the state government. Notably, Northern whites and local blacks managed to seize control of the meeting. Unionists like Daniel R. Goodloe, John Pool, Thomas Settle, and Robert P. Dick protested their exclusion from the party's leadership to no avail. The resolutions that the convention adopted stressed the rights of African Americans, yet William W. Holden, recognizing the racism of the white electorate, went to great lengths to deny that Republicans favored "social equality" between the races.[19]

The Republican organization then swung into action as it prepared for a November 20, 1867, election in which voters would decide whether there should be a state constitutional convention—as specified in the Reconstruction Acts—and elect delegates to it. The Republicans' first task was to register all of the eligible voters—that is, to make sure that all adult black males were registered and that anyone who, like Zeb, was excluded from voting by the Reconstruction Acts was not registered. When registration rolls were closed in mid-October, there were 106,721 white voters listed and 72,932 black voters. The Republicans quickly identified their supporters and made sure that they went to the polls. The result was that the convention was approved by a vote of 93,006 to 32,961.[20] Virtually all of the delegates to the convention were Republicans, and approximately 70 percent of them were white.

By contrast, the opponents of the convention were in disarray. Calling themselves the Conservative Party after the Civil War party, they pursued two contradictory strategies. Governor Jonathan Worth urged those opposed to the convention to stay away from the polls. He hoped that fewer than half of the registered voters would vote in favor of the convention. If this happened, then there could be no convention according to the terms of the Reconstruction Acts. Zeb and other Conservatives argued that the opposite policy should be pursued; they thought that the Conservatives should go to the polls and try to defeat the convention. If this strategy failed, they could at least elect Conservative delegates to it. In early November,

Zeb spoke against the convention in Raleigh. Holden refused to publish the speech, claiming that it contained "treason, profanity, and blackguardism."[21] The campaign against the convention brought Zeb back into direct contact with politics once again. He and his allies were defeated, but he was clearly recognized as a leading member of the party by friend and foe alike.

On January 14, 1868, the North Carolina Constitutional Convention met to draft a reformed constitution for the state. Having managed to send few delegates to the convention, the Conservatives countered by holding a state convention of their own on February 5 and 6 in Raleigh. Zeb's messages to the assembled politicians were clear. The first was that the party had to contest the approaching elections and not let them go by "default" as they had just done in November. The second message was equally unambiguous: the Conservatives had to run on the issue of race. A newspaper correspondent summarized one of Zeb's statements as follows: "If there is any man in the state, outside of the Insane Asylum, who needed any argument to convince him that the white man must rule this country, life was too short for him to waste his breath on him."[22] With his second suggestion, Zeb had framed the strategy that the Conservative Party would follow for the remainder of the Reconstruction period.

There were several reasons that Zeb urged the party to focus its attention on race. He and most other Conservatives were well aware that their coalition of antebellum Whigs and Democrats could not agree on many other issues. Some Conservatives favored state support for railroads and other internal improvements, while others wanted to keep taxes low. Some, like Zeb, were anxious to reestablish the public school system, but others did not want to pursue a policy that would provide educational opportunities for the poor of both races. The elite wanted to reclaim its control of the government, while many from the underclass, including poorer whites, applauded the democratic features of the Republican constitution that was in the process of being created. Zeb and the other political leaders who had strongly supported the Confederacy and sought to limit public dissent during the war knew that there were many thousands of men in the central and western counties who wanted revenge on their perceived oppressors. The Conservative leadership understood that the only thing that could unite their disparate coalition was racial prejudice.

The Conservative Party convention agreed with Zeb's assessment of the situation. The convention named Zeb and Lewis Hanes as the members of the Resolutions Committee from the Sixth District. The move indicated how difficult it must have been to attempt to unite the party; during the war, Hanes had written the famous "Davidson" letter in which he made the first public call for North Carolinians to accept peace without Confederate independence. Now Zeb and Hanes had to try to put a party platform together. They concentrated on the race issue. The Conservative convention protested against the Reconstruction Acts, opposed African American claims for equal political and social rights, and offered black North Carolinians only those "privileges" that could be given "consistently with the safety and welfare of both races." The Conservatives also stated that they would vigorously contest the next state election and that they would work closely with the national Democratic Party.[23] While Zeb may not have been the primary author of these statements, there is little doubt that he felt very comfortable with the platform.

Political observers in both parties now recognized Zeb as the leading Conservative. This was clearly demonstrated when the Executive Committee of the Conservative Party voted unanimously to make Zeb the party's gubernatorial candidate; he would face William W. Holden, the recently announced Republican nominee. The Republican press immediately attacked Zeb on his weakest point among white voters. The *North Carolina Standard* indicated that, as in 1864, Holden would not debate Vance. Instead, the paper asserted, "the most eloquent orators would be the women whose fingers he had put under rails. . . . These together with the ghosts of Laurel Valley and the men who were murdered under his authority will be present whenever Vance speaks." Leading Democrats agreed that Zeb's record made him a politically dangerous gubernatorial candidate for the Conservative Party. On February 27, Jonathan Worth wrote to William A. Graham and pointed out that the party's primary objective was to defeat the proposed Republican constitution. Worth argued that if Vance were their candidate, the Conservatives would lose the votes they needed in the central counties due to the fresh memories in that region of the campaigns that Vance had supported against deserters and draft dodgers.[24]

Zeb reached the same conclusion. In a letter to Graham, he acknowledged that without the support of these voters in the central counties, he "would incur almost certain defeat." Zeb assured Graham, however, that he would continue to work for the cause: "I shall abate nothing of my zeal, but intend to canvass earnestly until election day." On March 6, 1868, Zeb sent a letter to the chair of the Executive Committee in which he declined to run for governor. He kept his word to Graham by traveling across the state delivering passionate addresses in which he stressed the need to establish white supremacy. A committee in Rutherford County reported, "On Tuesday, the 17th inst. Gov. Vance addressed not less than two thousand of the citizens of this County, in a speech regarded by those who have often heard him, as the greatest effort of his life." Holden's newspaper drew a different conclusion about Zeb's campaign speeches: "Vance is raving like a mad wolf. . . .

He is doing devil work; fomenting sedition, stirring up strife between the races and inciting another WAR."[25]

Despite Zeb's efforts and the sensational racism of the Conservative campaign, the Republicans swept the April elections. The Constitution was adopted by a vote of 94,084 to 74,015; Holden was elected as governor by a somewhat smaller margin. The Republicans had gained an overwhelming advantage in the legislature. Their success was due in large part to their careful organization of their voters. Through the Union League, which had approximately seventy thousand members, the party protected its supporters from the political, social, and economic pressures that the elite sought to bring to bear on the people—mostly poor men—who voted Republican. The Conservatives had recognized that traditional electioneering methods might not give them sufficient leverage to defeat the Republicans, and unfortunately for democracy in North Carolina, they began to adopt terrorist methods already in use by anti-Republican groups in other states. Less than three weeks before the election, the Ku Klux Klan attempted to intimidate voters in Chapel Hill.[26] The Klan played a relatively small role during the April election, but the Conservatives would begin to use the organization more and more during the next two years.

Shaking off the Conservative Party's defeat in the spring election, Zeb began eagerly participating in the presidential campaign of 1868. He was selected as a delegate from the Sixth District to the Democratic National Convention. Delighted with the presidential nomination of New York governor Horatio Seymour, he spoke to a partisan crowd after the nomination. He attacked the Republicans for forcing black suffrage on the South while some Northern states still denied the ballot to African Americans. A Republican newspaper in New York quoted Vance as saying that secession was more alive than ever in the South, but he vehemently denied that he had ever "on any occasion" promoted secession, saying: "I never was a secessionist."[27] While the distinction Vance made was probably lost on a Northern audience, he distinguished between his own views and those of the original secessionists, and he knew that many North Carolinians did as well.

Zeb was as active in the fall campaign as he had been in the spring. When the Conservative Party nominated its candidate for a U.S. congressman from the Sixth District he received some votes, but Zeb's political disabilities under the Fourteenth Amendment still precluded him being an active candidate. Instead, he worked hard to bring white voters who supported the Republicans into the Conservative fold. According to some political leaders who were troubled by the extremism of the times, one way to do this would have been to revive the Whig Party. Zeb dismissed that strategy with a typical quip: "I used to believe the old Whigs were the salt of the earth, and I'm sorter of that notion yet. But the party is dead and buried and the tombstone placed over it, and I don't care about spending the balance of my days mourning at its grave." Instead, Zeb told the voters that they had to choose between the "wooly head of the negro" and the "straight hair of the white man." One Republican leader confirmed that Zeb's call "to the white people to stand up for their race" was quite effective in the mountain county where he lived.[28] Zeb remained active, and he used the same language that he had used in the spring campaign.

He did so with a heavy heart, however. His mentor David L. Swain was thrown from his carriage in mid-August, and he sustained serious injuries. He declined rapidly and died before the end of the month.[29] About a decade later, Zeb paid his respects to his friend by publishing a carefully prepared biographical sketch that outlined the important civic and educational contributions made by this man who had offered him comfort and advice. Swain's death was of critical importance to Zeb for reasons beyond the personal. Swain had often been a restraining influence on Zeb, and the essential element of restraint went missing from Zeb's life at a time when he could have benefited from it.

Zeb stayed active after Swain's death; one task that occupied his attention was the protection of his image as a participant in the Confederate cause. Within the state, the Republicans sought to tar him by reminding voters of Zeb's staunch support of the Confederacy; from outside North Carolina, however, a challenge to Zeb's image came from Union general Hugh J. Kilpatrick. Kilpatrick claimed to have captured Vance and forced him to ride two hundred miles on a mule. Zeb disputed the claim and provided an accurate account of his capture, noting Major John M. Porter's kindness toward him. Unable to contain his anger completely, Zeb ended his defense with the following riposte: "I saw no mule on the trip, yet I thought I saw an ass at the general's headquarters; this impression has since been confirmed."[30] Although this episode did not seriously challenge Zeb's status in North Carolina, it demonstrated that he took his image as a Civil War figure very seriously.

Despite Zeb's strenuous campaigning, the Republicans outpolled the Conservatives in the North Carolina presidential election. Yet while the Republican vote had increased slightly from the spring, the resurgent Conservatives gained approximately eleven thousand votes. This increase confirmed for Zeb and his allies that they were pursuing the right strategy, but both nineteenth-century and modern observers have noted what a sterile approach it was. One of Zeb's contemporaries commented, "Vance suffered the disadvantage common to many others, of not being able to link his name . . . with great positive progressive measures devised and put into operation for the advancement and glory of the State and her people; but his fame must rest rather upon what he did to rescue and shield them from injury." Historian Paul D. Escott has explained that the "angry and beleaguered elite determined to regain its privileges by attacking racial equality as the weakest point in the Republican program of social reform."[31]

Both of these explanations for the political behavior of most elite North Carolinians are accurate. Zeb was part of an upper-class group that deeply resented its exclusion from the state's power structure; its members were determined to regain their former position of preeminence by any means. They did not consider appealing to the underclass with positive programs. Instead, these leaders decided that the surest way to return to power was to divide the poor along racial lines and to use "slander, falsehoods, and violence" to achieve their ends.[32] Since Zeb was identified by friend and foe alike as the leading figure in the Conservative Party, he bears the greatest responsibility for this baneful development. The contrast between the generally positive approaches he took to solve problems during the war and the essentially negative approach that he took during Reconstruction is significant, and his negative approach had unfortunate consequences for race relations in North Carolina. Given the difficult adjustment that North Carolina had to make during these years, the politics of the period were bound to be turbulent. But some talented members of the establishment like Thomas Settle and Samuel F. Phillips made positive attempts to bring various social groups in the state together to benefit as many people as possible. Zeb did not. He appears to have been intent on securing a major public office, and he used the means that he thought were necessary to ensure that he would achieve that goal.

The following year was one of intensifying tensions, and Zeb was in the middle of the fray. In a move that attracted a great deal of attention, Conservative Party lawyers charged the North Carolina Supreme Court with basing decisions along partisan lines. Chief Justice Richmond M. Pearson found that the individuals, including Zeb, who accused the court had overstepped the bounds of advocacy, and he verbally chastised them. Pearson did not exact any penalties from the protesting lawyers, however, and the controversy ended rapidly. This episode was of little consequence, but it demonstrates that the Conservatives were keeping the pressure on the Republicans in every conceivable way. The Republicans returned fire: using patronage effectively, for example, Holden dismissed Zeb from his position as a director of the Eastern Division of the Western Extension of the North Carolina Railroad. This action proved to be beneficial to Zeb in the long run. The directors were mismanaging the railroad system, and the reputations of several leading political figures were later badly tarnished when their mismanagement caused a public scandal. Despite his setback, Zeb still believed in the importance of railroad expansion. He canvassed Mecklenburg County to secure money to extend the South Carolina Railroad to Charlotte. The next year, he spoke in eight different locations to secure subscriptions that would assist the Airline and Statesville Railroad in making a connection to Charlotte.[33]

Unfortunately, 1869 was a year in which the Conservative Party in North Carolina expanded the reach of the Ku Klux Klan. The most prominent Conservative Party leaders in approximately fifteen counties assumed the leadership of this organization. While there is no official tally of the terrorist incidents committed by the Klan that year, one scholar counted "at least fifteen murders and hundreds of lesser atrocities." Ironically, as governor, William W. Holden was forced to resort to the same type of tactics that he had so vehemently protested during the Civil War. He employed detectives to investigate the crimes, and by the end of the year thirty-one men had been indicted, ten of them for murder. By October 1869, Holden had asked President Grant to use force to suppress the Klan. In addition, he warned in a proclamation that he would create and use a state militia to confront Klan violence if necessary.[34] The escalating Klan violence suggested that the election of 1870 might be an extremely violent one.

As this crucial election year opened, the Republicans were on the defensive. In January, the Conservatives won a special state Senate election for a seat in western North Carolina that had previously been held by a Republican. Recognizing that the Conservatives planned to use force and terror to try to regain power, William W. Holden reluctantly accepted the challenge and asked the legislature to give him the power to declare a state of insurrection in individual counties. The legislature complied, giving the political campaign of 1870 ominous overtones from the very beginning. All that was needed for the expected confrontation to occur was an incident to precipitate it. That incident took place on February 26, 1870, in Graham, the county seat of Alamance County. In the middle of the night, a mob of Klansmen dressed in robes and hoods seized Wyatt Outlaw from his home and hanged him in the public square.[35] Outlaw, an African American, had been a leading Republican in the county, the president of the Union League, and a prominent community leader. Significantly, none of the Conservative Party's leaders, including Zeb, spoke out against this outrage.

The often indecisive Holden reacted quickly, however. In a proclamation that was moderate in tone, he declared Alamance County to be in a state of insurrection. He explained to a fellow Republican why he had decided to take a hard line against the Klan: "I concur with you that the Klan of Ku

Klux is very formidable and warlike, but I fear it will grow with indulgence."
Holden also contacted President Ulysses S. Grant and requested that he
make federal troops available in North Carolina. "I cannot rely upon the
militia to repress these outrages," Holden told him. What Holden apparently hoped to do was not to catch and prosecute the Klan leaders, but to
create an atmosphere in which Republicans felt safe enough to vote. Any
illusion of safety they had was destroyed on May 24, however. That evening,
state senator and Republican John W. Stevens was murdered by assailants
outside the courthouse in Yanceyville.[36]

This atrocity prompted the Republican leadership to take decisive action. Holden created a state militia and called for volunteers. Unable to
secure sufficient numbers of men of reliable loyalty in the Piedmont counties, he contacted George W. Kirk and contracted with him to raise a force
of mountaineers. The Conservatives reacted with outrage, claiming that
Kirk was not a North Carolinian, which was inaccurate. As noted earlier,
Holden then contacted President Grant, who promised that federal troops
would be made available. In mid-July, Kirk and his militia began to arrest
Klan members in Alamance and Caswell Counties. They apprehended approximately one hundred men, and many others apparently fled to avoid
incarceration.[37] Under these extraordinary conditions, the election campaign continued throughout the state.

Zeb's role in the campaign was relatively small. He made an attempt to
conciliate black voters and to soothe the racial divisions brought on by the
electoral canvass. In April, he addressed a meeting of African Americans in
Statesville on the topic of education. He pointed out that the state's literary (educational) fund was depleted, and he claimed that the Republicans
had done nothing to restore public education in the state. Zeb made this
same point on other occasions, and Holden refuted it with statistics that
demonstrated that Zeb was misinforming the public for partisan advantage. At a Conservative rally in Wake County in June, Zeb also attacked the
Republicans for their railroad policies. He claimed that they had sold and
stolen large numbers of state bonds without laying any track. While this
was an exaggeration, Zeb was making a legitimate political point. There had
been misuse of state funds, —a bipartisan legislative investigating committee had uncovered some of it in the winter of 1870—and the Republican
building program was behind schedule.[38] Thus, not all of Zeb's activities
were racially based, nor was the entirety of the Conservative campaign. The
Republicans had not enacted a positive program to attract voters, and the
Conservatives justifiably attacked them for it.

In the midst of all of this turmoil, Zeb was nominated as a candidate for
the state Senate from Mecklenburg County. The nomination was made in

spite of Zeb's efforts to decline it through proxies at the convention. This time, the nomination was not honorific in nature. The Conservatives had determined that one way to recapture the legislature would be to run their strongest candidates in each district. Apparently Zeb recognized the legitimacy of this strategy, because he did not formally decline the nomination until four weeks after it was made. Using language that he would probably later regret, Zeb stated that he could not run; "[After] consultation with some of the most eminent legal minds in the State," he explained, "I became satisfied that I was not eligible for a seat in the legislature."[39] Zeb recognized that the Fourteenth Amendment still barred him from legally holding public office.

Zeb's final contribution to the campaign came in its closing days. The Conservatives reacted swiftly to the arrests of their Klan allies. They went to state courts to try to free them under writs of habeas corpus. Ironically, the judge who would decide the writ cases was Richmond M. Pearson, who had upheld habeas corpus to the dismay of so many Conservatives during the war. Pearson remained consistent and issued the writs. Holden, who had been a champion of civil liberties during the war, refused to honor them. The Conservatives then went to the federal judiciary and sought writs. The federal courts ordered the prisoners to be released, and President Grant refused to interfere. The Klan members were freed, and the Conservatives felt free to attack the Republicans for violating the rights of the prisoners. Even the last-minute public confessions by many Klansmen of the partisan nature of their activities did not nullify the tactical advantage held by the Conservatives. Sensing that the Conservatives had a winning issue, Democratic chairman Thomas Bragg issued orders to end all violent activities.[40]

Zeb joined the chorus of Conservatives who blamed the Republicans for the "outrage" against the prisoners. Recognizing that the African American vote in the eastern counties was well organized and that both the presence of federal troops in Raleigh and other tactical considerations made further terrorist activities in the Piedmont untenable, the Conservatives decided to concentrate their efforts on the mountain counties in the west. Zeb was sent there to energize the Conservative forces and to appeal to the voters in his old congressional district. Although he was still a controversial figure in many mountain counties, he did not suffer from some of the disabilities there that he did in the central counties. He had never sent Confederate troops into the mountains, and the inner civil war had taken place there without much intervention from the state government. Equally important, Zeb appealed to the mountain residents on the race issue in terms that they appreciated. He remembered that the major racial disturbance during the 1868 election had taken place in Asheville, not in the lowland section of the state, and he knew that there had been considerable Klan activity in the mountains as well.[41]

The Conservative strategy was quite successful. The party gained control of the legislature by a wide margin in the August 4 election. An examination of the returns shows how the Conservatives achieved this impressive result. Apparently Zeb's work—along with that of many others—in the western counties was critical. The Conservatives swept this contested region and gained most of their winning margin from that part of the state. They did not win by attracting a surge of new voters; the Conservatives only increased their vote by three thousand for the state as a whole from the previous election. Rather, their victory was due to a 15 percent decline in votes cast by Republicans since the previous legislative election.[42] The obvious conclusion, therefore, is that the primary reason for their triumph was the terror campaign that they conducted. The Conservatives had coerced enough Republicans to absent themselves from the polls to allow them to seize power. The question that now confronted them was how they would use their victory.

The Conservative party's victory in the 1870 legislative election placed Zeb back into a prominent position in North Carolina politics. The acknowledged leading figure in the party, he had been selected by the party leadership as the organization's standard-bearer two years earlier. The fact that Zeb had felt constrained to turn down that honor indicated that the situation was much more complicated than it appeared to be at first sight. The old elite had been pushed to the sidelines, and there were many men who viewed themselves as deserving of party support for high offices. This caused the Conservative Party, which had been so united when the Republicans assumed power, to begin to splinter into a variety of personal followings and interest groups. In addition, the Republicans still controlled the governor's office and state patronage, which guaranteed that they would continue to play a significant role in state politics.

For Zeb, this uncertain political landscape was a place of both opportunity and danger. As the most popular and visible leader of the Conservative Party, he drew ambitious men to him who expected to further their careers by attaching themselves to the former governor. Other political leaders saw Zeb as a giant roadblock in the path to their aspirations. Still other local Conservative leaders either resented the harsh measures that Zeb had sanctioned to round up deserters and draft evaders or had been elected by constituents who still remembered the inner civil war vividly. Zeb hoped and expected to negotiate this difficult political terrain to become one of North Carolina's U.S. senators. Equally important, he wanted to reshape the political landscape to give the Conservative Party a secure enough hold on power that he could count on returning to the Senate.

No sooner had the election results become known than Zeb started on his twin missions. Almost immediately, friendly newspapers began to publish editorials that endorsed Zeb for the Conservative Party's Senate nomination. Zeb's plans were hidden from the public during this period, but a letter from George W. Swepson to Matt W. Ransom reveals the essence of his thoughts and tactics. According to Swepson, Zeb was determined to restore the former political elite to its dominant position again. Swepson told

Ransom, "Vance says the plan will be for the Legislature to be very moderate and after the present Congress shall come to a close [we will call] a convention, [and] go back to the old Constitution & laws as near as possible."[1] Zeb's plan called for a subtle approach to the national authority; however, such an approach would have required the kind of discipline that only a well-organized party could muster.

There was no such subtlety in Zeb's plan to secure the Senate seat. According to Swepson, Zeb thought that there were three main claimants for the position: Augustus S. Merrimon, Matt W. Ransom, and himself. Zeb said that many Conservative Party leaders thought that Ransom was "too easy on the Radicals," and the leaders "wanted to come down very hard on the Radicals." Swepson further reported that Zeb and Merrimon had reached a deal. He recounted the terms as follows: "If it was determined to elect no one who has not been 'relieved' of the political disabilities imposed by the Fourteenth Amendment, Vance is to support Merrimon. But if it is thought prudent to elect one who was not 'relieved' M is to go for Vance."[2]

Although he had struck a deal with one of his major opponents, Zeb recognized that his election was not assured. He began to make contacts with prominent party leaders and legislators throughout the state. Apparently he tried to meet as many of these individuals in person as possible in order to persuade them with his presence. One letter from this campaign has fortunately survived, and it undoubtedly captures the essence of Zeb's appeal. He wrote it to Kemp P. Battle, who served as state treasurer during the Worth administration and was the brother of one of Zeb's wartime office staff members. Apparently the question that stood between Zeb and his election to the Senate was whether his disabilities under the Fourteenth Amendment would prevent him from either winning votes or being seated. Zeb began his letter to Kemp by asserting, "I found that the idea of voting for no man under disabilities was not so general as I supposed, or had been led to believe by the papers." Under these circumstances, he explained, he had decided to run—a disingenuous argument, since Zeb had obviously sought to run before he could have made this determination. He reported, furthermore, that he had received "many assurances from high Radical sources that [his] disabilities would be removed if [he] would apply." This meant that Zeb had good reason to believe that he would be seated if he were elected. To clinch the case, however, Zeb promised, "If I cant get my seat I'll resign to the Legislature next Novr, or in March should it be then in session."[3]

Zeb's plan to secure the Senate seat eventually became public knowledge. After the legislature met in November, Holden's paper revealed it in detail—and with commendable accuracy.[4] It is impossible now to determine whether the revelation had any impact on the Conservative Party caucus as it met to select a U.S. senator. The fate of Zeb and the other candidates was ruled in part by a tradition that North Carolina's political parties had developed over the years as a means to maintain harmony within both the parties and the state. There was an unwritten agreement that one of the two senators would come from the eastern counties and the other would be selected from the Piedmont or mountain counties. Since the other senator from North Carolina, John Pool, was from the eastern part of the state, tradition required a western man to be selected during this balloting. Thus Zeb and Augustus S. Merrimon, both from western North Carolina, were most likely to win the support of the Conservative Party.

When the balloting started in the caucus, the issue of Zeb's eligibility greatly weakened his chances of winning the nomination. For more than a dozen ballots Merrimon was the leader, with Zeb within five to ten votes. Trailing both of them was Matt W. Ransom, a resident of eastern North Carolina. Zeb and his partisans finally broke the deadlock by promising that if Zeb were elected senator he would seek to have his disabilities removed quickly. If he did not succeed, then he would resign his position and allow the caucus to select another candidate. This strategy appealed to the followers of Ransom, who was unlikely to be elected this time and who may have anticipated Zeb's support when the "eastern seat" became available. On succeeding ballots, Ransom began to lose votes to Zeb, who thereby gained a majority and the nomination.[5] Apparently relatively little animosity attended this result, since each of the losing candidates still had a chance of benefiting from it.

Once he had achieved his goal and a form of vindication, Zeb sought to allay congressional Republicans' concerns about his loyalty to the nation. In a public speech that he delivered in Raleigh soon after his election, Zeb attempted to conciliate his opponents. He argued that "bitterness and vituperation should cease" and that North Carolinians should "strive to engender kindly feelings among all classes of citizens."[6] If Zeb could manage to present the picture of a civil North Carolina to Northerners, then he had a good chance of being seated in the Senate. At the same time, he recognized that for the health of his political future he needed to keep peace within the Conservative Party. Although Merrimon made no outward display of disappointment about his defeat, Zeb recognized that his fellow mountaineer had a claim on the party for future preference.

Zeb's plan of action started to fall apart almost immediately. On December 9, a state legislator introduced a resolution to impeach Governor William W. Holden for misusing the powers of his office. Ten days later, the members of the North Carolina General Assembly's lower house—now renamed the House of Representatives—voted sixty to forty-six to support the resolution. Zeb was deeply concerned about this initiative. He understood the animosity that most Conservatives had toward Holden, but he also knew that an impeachment controversy would raise questions about the commitment of the North Carolina Conservatives to political peace. In an attempt to distance himself politically from the vengeful people who had just elected him to the Senate, Zeb publicly opposed the impeachment proceedings against Holden. This did him little good. His example was ignored in North Carolina, and Northern Republicans associated Zeb with the proceedings taking place in North Carolina despite his efforts. Zeb observed to Cornelia Phillips Spencer: "I had no apprehension at all about my seat until the impeachment trouble began—now I think my chances doubtful."[7]

At the same time, Zeb was forced to answer charges directed at him by Northern critics. The most serious of these came from the editor of the *Washington Chronicle*, the spokesman for the Grant administration. The editor accused Zeb of refusing to change his opinions and feelings since the war, of neglecting the Union prisoners of war at Salisbury, and of seeking to destroy the Union during the war. Zeb recognized that he could not avoid confronting an attack that came from such a prominent Republican source. In his written reply, he stressed that he fully accepted the outcome of the war, and he promised that he would be a loyal American in the future. He also pointed out that the Confederate government, not the state of North Carolina, had been responsible for the prison at Salisbury, and he explained that he had sought to provide assistance to the prisoners as a humanitarian gesture. Zeb understood that his letter would be read in North Carolina as well as in Washington, and he knew that there were limits to what he could say in it without doing serious damage to his political future. He admitted to his correspondent, "If you mean that my abstract opinions as to what was right have not been changed by the result of the war, you are correct."[8] Thus, as the new year began, Zeb's Senate seat was imperiled on two fronts.

Early in the new year, Zeb took a train from Charlotte to Raleigh and conferred briefly with political leaders. He then went to Washington to lobby for the removal of his political disabilities. Vance submitted a memorial in which he requested that the Fourteenth Amendment restrictions on his freedoms be removed and that he be seated in the Senate. He was observed on the floor of the House of Representatives talking to leading Republicans about his case. But prevailing opinion was that the Republican-controlled Senate would refuse to seat him. In an effort to convince Senate Republicans of his loyalty to the United States, Zeb prevailed upon some moderate Republicans from North Carolina to sign petitions in support of his claim to the Senate seat. Lieutenant Governor Tod R. Caldwell, Chief Justice

Richmond Pearson, Robert P. Dick, and Thomas Settle signed the most impressive of these documents, which recommended that Vance be granted a seat.[9] While Vance would remember this generous gesture by his political opponents, the document apparently had little impact in Washington.

It was ineffective at least in part because other petitions were arriving in Washington from different Republicans who attacked Zeb's position. More than one hundred Republicans in the Third Congressional District vigorously protested the idea of seating Vance. In denying that the sanctions against Zeb and another congressional claimant should be lifted, the petitioners explained their objection to the two Southern politicians: "Their election has been brought about by systematic violence and bloodshed, for which they themselves are responsible, and by which they seek to profit."[10] This kind of appeal must have weakened Zeb's case with those Republicans who were concerned about the resurgence of the old elite throughout the South.

An unexpected complication arose when North Carolina state senator and Republican Joseph C. Abbott contested Zeb's right to the seat. In the state legislature, Abbott had been the Republican Party's nominee for the senate seat. Abbott contended that because Zeb was not eligible to be seated, Abbott—as the legal candidate who had received the largest number of votes—deserved the seat. Fortunately for Zeb, Abbott was a carpetbagger from New Hampshire. The wing of the North Carolina Republican Party that supported him had been discredited by the railroad scandals, and Abbott commanded little respect in either North Carolina or Washington. Although it was irritating to Zeb, Abbott's claim to the seat was more of a nuisance than a genuine threat to Zeb's position. A year after Abbott lodged his appeal, the overwhelmingly Republican Senate rejected it by a vote of forty-four to ten.[11]

A much more serious threat to Zeb's claim was the continuing controversy surrounding Ku Klux Klan activities in North Carolina. Just as Zeb arrived in Washington, President Grant's newspaper lashed out at the Klan for its outrages in North Carolina and demanded an investigation. That same day, a correspondent sent evidence to William W. Holden about thirty Klan incidents in Orange County alone; this material was undoubtedly headed for Washington. An investigation was launched, and it generated considerable publicity. The investigative committee issued a report in March 1871 that described many of the worst abuses that took place during the 1870 election. In an effort to distance himself from the unfavorable publicity generated by the investigation and report, Zeb issued a statement. He claimed: "I opposed the Ku Klux from the start[.] Refusing to have anything to do with such an organization on the ground that it was a secret society. . . . I not only refused to approve of it but made a speech in a certain county against such organizations." Zeb was not willing to acknowledge the violence and racism of the Klan, which would have offended some party members in North Carolina; rather, his stated objection to the Klan was that it was a secret organization.[12] This explanation was disingenuous at best, and it did Zeb no good in his effort to persuade the Republicans to seat him.

Just as Zeb tried to shake off the controversy about the Klan, Democrats in the North Carolina legislature—the Conservatives were more and more frequently calling themselves by the national party name—started impeachment proceedings against Governor William W. Holden. The trial was another public relations disaster for Zeb. To ensure Holden's conviction, the Democrats challenged the credentials of several Republican senators, seated their Democratic opponents, and thereby achieved the two-thirds majority needed to convict Holden. Richmond Pearson presided at the trial and made a crucial ruling that favored Holden and greatly damaged Zeb's standing in Washington: he allowed Holden's lawyers to introduce evidence related to Klan violence. The Republicans brought more than one hundred witnesses to testify about the outrages committed against them. Zeb continued to try to distance himself from the proceedings. He was consistent in this, having opposed the impeachment from the beginning. His efforts did him little good, however, as the state Senate convicted Holden and removed him from office.[13] Since Northern Republicans had no other way to strike back at North Carolina Democrats except through Zeb, his claim to the Senate seat looked weaker with each passing day.

In addition to his problems at the national level, Zeb faced trouble in his home state from some of his fellow party members. When Zeb had discussed his situation with the state legislators in the fall, he had promised to give up his claim in March 1871 if he had not yet been seated and the state legislature was in session. That had seemed a safe promise, because in a normal year the state legislative session would have ended in February. The impeachment proceedings against Holden had extended the session, however, and Zeb suddenly faced pressure to take some kind of action on his promise. A number of Democratic newspapers in the eastern part of the state began calling upon Zeb to live up to his part of the bargain. The legislature, probably at Zeb's covert request, defeated a motion that would have requested his resignation. Fortunately for Zeb, that same week the U.S. Senate's Select Committee on Removal of Political Disabilities reported a bill to end Zeb's disabilities under the Fourteenth Amendment. North Carolina Republican senator John Pool made it known that he thought the bill would pass in December, and this information bought Zeb some time to wait for a decision.[14]

Unfortunately for Zeb, the news from North Carolina continued to undermine his case. In early May, Klan violence broke out once again in Rutherford and Cleveland Counties in the western part of the state. Klansmen viciously beat several prominent Republicans and destroyed the office of the *Rutherford Star*, a Republican paper. Horrified state Democratic leaders, including Augustus S. Merrimon, met with new Republican governor Tod R. Caldwell to devise a strategy for ending the violence, but the state and local authorities could not contain the outbreak, and the federal government was forced to act. President Grant declared martial law in both Rutherford and Cleveland Counties and in neighboring counties in South Carolina. Dozens of Klansmen were arrested and federal forces besieged two hundred Klansmen on a mountaintop. Once arrested, these Klan members—along with Randolph A. Shotwell, their apparent leader—were tried in federal court in Raleigh and sentenced to imprisonment in federal penitentiaries. Abashed Democratic Party leaders, including Matt W. Ransom, assured the federal judge in the case that any future outbreaks of violence would be suppressed by local authorities.[15]

For Zeb, these events could not have come at a worse time. The Klan violence, which served no useful political purpose, kept the charge that Klansmen had been involved in political intimidation in the 1870 election fresh in the minds of the senators who would decide his fate. While Zeb gave every outward indication that he was upset by the Klan violence in North Carolina, he did not directly condemn the perpetrators. Moreover, he attacked the federal prosecution of the Klan members, calling the trials "political" and disparaging the "infamous unconstitutional Kuklux act." He also corresponded with convicted Klan leader Randolph A. Shotwell. He assured Shotwell that despite being a convicted felon, he would be able to return to public life in North Carolina after serving his prison term; most people would forget his deeds, Zeb assured Shotwell, and remember instead the "infamy" of his arrest and trial.[16] These sentiments were not what the Republican leadership in the Senate expected to hear from a man who wanted to be relieved of his political disabilities.

Making matters worse for Zeb, the Democrats also suffered a humiliating defeat in a statewide referendum held in the summer of 1871. Following the plan outlined by Zeb immediately after the election of 1870, the state legislature passed a measure that gave the voters an opportunity to call a constitutional convention. The Democratic Party, however, was not united behind this initiative. The party leadership was only able to force the legislature to act in the waning moments of the session. Almost immediately, some Democrats began to protest the decision and to call for the measure's defeat. Even Zeb refused to support his own strategy publicly. In contrast to the divided Democrats, the Republicans were thoroughly united behind a strong message. They appealed to the poor of both races to preserve the homestead exemption—a constitutional provision that protected a debtor's home from seizure by creditors—that existed under the current constitution. They also warned African Americans that they could lose their newly acquired rights, and they asserted that if that happened the state might be returned to federal control. The result was a defeat by nine thousand votes for the convention forces.[17] This result indicated that the Republican Party was still a threat to the Democrats in statewide races, a reality that would upset Zeb's plans in the future.

When the Congress met again late in the fall of 1871, Zeb came under renewed pressure to settle the controversy about his Senate seat. In the middle of November, the Republican paper in Asheville, Zeb's hometown, reported that some legislators wanted to demand Zeb's resignation. It was later revealed that Zeb actually wrote out a resignation letter in this period; he gave it to a state legislator and instructed him to make it public if it became clear that the legislature was about to adjourn before the U.S. Senate had agreed to seat Zeb. On January 20, Zeb finally decided that the appropriate time had come for him to give up the fight, and his resignation as senator-elect was made official. In his resignation letter, Zeb returned his certificate of election to the legislature. He went on to thank the legislators for selecting him in the previous year and to assure them that his greatest disappointment was his inability to serve his state at the national level.[18] This last statement was probably not entirely accurate. If he had been entirely candid, Zeb would probably have said that his inability to occupy center stage in the political arena was his greatest disappointment.

Immediately after receiving Zeb's letter, the legislature moved to select another person to occupy the Senate seat. The selection process posed a dilemma for Zeb. If the tradition of selecting senators from different sections of the state were followed, then Augustus S. Merrimon would be the logical candidate. If Merrimon were elected, however, the Senate seat that would next come open in 1872 would belong to the east, and Matt W. Ransom would be the favored candidate. Thus, it would be 1876 before Zeb could expect another opportunity to be elected to the Senate. Such a result would not have been acceptable to Zeb. He was the most popular man in his party, and—to his way of thinking—only the obstinacy of Northern Republicans had caused him to be denied what was rightfully his. Reasoning in this manner, Zeb and some of his supporters in the western counties backed

Augustus Summerfield Merrimon, ca. 1879. Merrimon studied the law with Vance as a youth, ran as the Democratic candidate for governor in 1872, and defeated Vance for the Senate in the legislative balloting of 1873. (North Carolina Division of Archives and History, Raleigh)

Ransom for the Senate, and Ransom prevailed by the slimmest of margins.[19] This result meant that Zeb could anticipate running for the Senate again within the calendar year.

Many Merrimon supporters, however, felt betrayed by Zeb and the party. The *Asheville Citizen*, the party's paper in Zeb's former hometown, was particularly critical of the election result. Zeb saw Merrimon as a competitor for the Senate seat he coveted. His solution was to offer Merrimon an office that would eliminate him from the competition. Ransom recognized that if Merrimon were selected as a senator in 1872, Zeb would become a candidate for Ransom's seat in 1876. It was thus in the best interests of both Ransom and Vance that Merrimon be placated. Both men, along with Merrimon's friends, worked hard to secure Merrimon the Democratic Party's gubernatorial nomination for 1872. It was a good strategy for the party for other reasons as well. The Republicans had nominated incumbent governor Tod R. Caldwell as their candidate.[20] Since Caldwell was from the western part of the state and that section was very competitive, the Democrats had to match the Republicans with a western candidate of their own in order not to lose important western votes to their competitors.

For the strategy for placating Merrimon to work, however, the Democrats had to win the election. The recent vote on the constitutional convention indicated that it was far from certain that the party could win a majority of votes. One development, however, looked quite promising for the Democrats. Moderate Republicans across the nation were upset by their party's continued concentration on black civil rights and war-related issues. They started a "liberal" movement outside of the discipline of the party that challenged the Republican leadership. The movement caught on in North Carolina. Hardie H. Helper issued a call for liberal Republicans in the state to form an anti-Grant coalition for the 1872 elections.[21] This development looked as though it would offer Democrats an opportunity to sweep the state and place Merrimon in the governor's chair.

The campaign did not develop the way that the Democrats had hoped it would. At the Republican state convention, the party adopted a very conciliatory platform that called for federal amnesty both for those with political disabilities and for those who had been jailed for political terrorist activities. The Democrats allied with liberal Republicans at both the state and national levels. Zeb was selected as a delegate to the Democratic National Convention, where he supported the party's nomination of liberal Republican Horace Greeley for president.[22] While Zeb hoped that the alliance with the liberal Republicans would provide his party with a way to overcome the Republican majorities in Northern states, he was more interested in achieving the same results in North Carolina.

Ironically, the Democrats' alliance with the liberal Republicans placed some significant limits on their campaign in North Carolina. With a well-known abolitionist at the head of their national ticket, North Carolina Democrats found it politically impossible to make race the defining issue in the campaign. Instead, Zeb focused his attention on the proven corruption of the Republican governments in Raleigh and Washington. During a speech in Statesville, Zeb used figures from a congressional report to demonstrate that Republican administrations throughout the South had flagrantly misused public funds. He charged: "They have become so sly and skillful in their thefts they would steal a chew of tobacco from between your teeth. . . . They would steal the nails out of the hind feet of a kicking mule." He also disparaged the Republicans for their deplorable lack of progress on the state's railroad system; his comments no doubt reminded his listeners that much of the corruption in the state Republican administration had involved the railroad.[23]

Zeb made note of other issues in his presentations, moreover. He attacked the federal law enforcement efforts directed at the Klan and asserted, "If there had been no damnable union leagues, there would have been no damnable kuklux." He also attacked the Holden administration's use of the militia during the confrontations in 1870. Zeb claimed that "aged and virtuous citizens [were] seized by rude soldiery without warrant, at the instigation of vagabond negroes, and placed in dungeons without bail." At no time did Zeb acknowledge the role that his party's clandestine allies had played in the violence of 1870. Finally, he sought to counter a Republican claim that their party was the true heir of the Whig Party of North Carolina. He ridiculed this claim by asking his audience to imagine "Henry Clay wallowing in the same bed with Billy Holden."[24] Throughout the campaign, Zeb concentrated on these themes in the speeches he delivered to large and enthusiastic audiences.

While making appearances around the state, however, Zeb did much more than make campaign speeches. Drawing on the organizing experiences that he had acquired in the military and as governor, Zeb began to create a personal organization within the Democratic Party. This was a significant innovation on Zeb's part. In traditional antebellum North Carolina politics, the office sought the man, particularly the office of U.S. senator. State legislators held on to the illusion that they or their party made the decisions about who would receive a particular office. The tradition had prevailed during the 1870 party caucus, when Zeb—with little leverage beyond his broad popularity with the public—had to bargain with the party for his nomination.

Determined to exercise more control over the process in the future, Zeb and trusted local party members began to actively intervene in the party's candidate selection process. Zeb's allies sought out his supporters in each county and strongly urged them to attend county party conventions. At these meetings, the Vance forces nominated and voted for legislative candidates who had pledged to vote for Zeb for the Senate in the party caucus. When Zeb failed to place his own candidate in an office, he resorted to other tactics. According to members of an opposing faction, Zeb or one of his associates would approach the successful candidate and threaten to withhold votes from him during the election if he did not pledge to support Zeb for the Senate.[25] Methods similar to Zeb's were being used in many other states at this time, but they were new in North Carolina. Given Zeb's personal popularity, many legislative candidates were more than willing to pledge their support to him without coercion. But others were offended by Zeb's strong-arm tactics, and these individuals became more likely to support a candidate who would help them express their displeasure.

One major obstacle to Zeb's political plans was finally removed during the campaign. Ransom went to Washington soon after he was elected in January to take his seat in the Senate. In an effort either to punish North Carolina for Klan excesses or to gain partisan advantage, the Senate Republicans did not seat Ransom until April. Once seated, Ransom seemed intimidated by his surroundings and did not address the Senate until June. On the occasion of his maiden address to the Senate, however, he offered an amendment that added Zeb's name to those covered by a special amnesty bill. The Senate accepted Ransom's amendment, and after the bill was passed by both houses of Congress, President Grant signed it into law. For the first time in seven years, Zeb was free from any federal restrictions. He could run for the Senate seat without fear of any impediments. Ransom also offered Zeb $2,500, a portion of the back pay due to the unoccupied Senate seat, and Zeb accepted it.[26] The two men both understood that it was in their best interests to work together and acted accordingly.

They had only one more task to accomplish to assure that Zeb would win his long sought Senate seat: to get Merrimon elected governor. It proved to be a more difficult task than Zeb anticipated. Reading partisan news accounts carefully, it becomes clear that Merrimon was not an effective campaigner. Unlike many of his contemporaries, the judge was more a scholarly speaker than someone who easily conveyed his empathy for the common man. The party leadership apparently recognized this weakness early, and they sent Zeb into every convenient county seat to make a major address on Merrimon's behalf. Zeb's tour started with a crowded schedule in the eastern part of the state and concluded with a swing through the mountains and the Piedmont. When the voters went to the polls on August 4, they rendered a split decision. The Democrats won small but safe majorities in both houses of the legislature. Much to their dismay, however, Caldwell won a two-thousand-vote victory over Merrimon in the governor's race. Aggressive party leaders demanded that Merrimon request a recount so that they could fraudulently reverse the result, but Merrimon insisted that he would not do so unless obvious fraud had occurred.[27] Since the Democrats had been the polling officials during the balloting, there had been no incidents of fraud that fulfilled Merrimon's requirement. The Democrats were forced to accept Caldwell's election as irreversible.

This unexpected turn of events prompted Zeb to attempt to head off any attempt by Merrimon to secure the Senate nomination. The Democrats had named Zeb as one of their two statewide electors in the fall presidential campaign with the expectation that he would tour the state on behalf of the Greeley ticket. With his own future suddenly uncertain, however, Zeb declined the position and did not participate in the campaign. Instead, he spent a great deal of time writing to Democratic state legislators who had not previously committed themselves on the U.S. senator question. In these letters, which do not survive, Zeb apparently attacked Merrimon personally.[28] This tactic offended a minority of the Democratic state legislators sufficiently that they either became or continued to be ardent Merrimon supporters.

The stridency of Zeb's opposition to Merrimon was apparently prompted by articles that had appeared in Republican newspapers. The *Asheville Pioneer*, a Republican paper in Merrimon's and Vance's shared hometown, hinted that Republicans might vote for Merrimon if there was a contest within Democratic ranks. After the Republicans swept the presidential balloting in North Carolina in early November, the state legislature met in regular session. Apparently Zeb and the party leadership had decided to eliminate the challenge from Merrimon before he made it. The party press ran articles that suggested that any Democrat who did not support the party caucus's nominee would be someone who had received payoffs from the Republicans. Zeb told Merrimon and his supporters that the majority of the Democratic members of the legislature were pledged to vote for Zeb—forty-nine out of ninety-six. This heavy-handed tactic failed because the Merrimon supporters felt that the "pledging" of legislators to a particular candidate went against North Carolina's political traditions. As a result, at least nineteen Democratic legislators refused either to join the party caucus or to be bound by its choice of candidate.[29]

The result of all of this maneuvering was a tense series of ballots in late November. The votes on the first five days were as follows:

Dates	26th	27th	28th	29th	30th
Zebulon Vance	78	78	73	74	72
Augustus Merrimon	18	20	22	22	31
John Pool	73	72	71	71	58

The developments of November 30 were a clear sign that Zeb's candidacy was in serious trouble. Republican legislators were apparently beginning to drift in the direction of Merrimon. In a move of desperation, Zeb proposed to withdraw his name from the balloting if Merrimon would agree to do the same thing. The next ballot was total chaos; more than sixty men received at least one vote.[30]

Fearing that they were losing control of the situation, Zeb and the Democratic leadership reconvened the party caucus. Zeb was once again named the party's choice for the position, and, as before, the group of Merrimon supporters refused either to attend the meeting or to abide by its result. In the meantime, the Republicans apparently also met and made a decisive decision. They agreed to switch their votes from their own candidate, John Pool, to Merrimon. There is no indication that the Republicans made any type of deal with Merrimon to bring this change about. The Republicans simply saw an opportunity to embarrass the Democratic leadership and to cause hard feelings within the Democratic Party. When the next ballot took place, Merrimon had eighty-seven votes, one more than a majority, and he was elected to the Senate instead of Zeb, who had eighty votes.[31]

Zeb was outraged by the result. He charged the Merrimon supporters with committing "treachery" against the party and the people. He further implied that there had been an alliance between Merrimon's supporters and the Republicans. Zeb undoubtedly needed to vent his anger in this manner, but his public display of emotion did not enhance his reputation. Nor did it change the result. Zeb could not run for the Senate again until 1876, and at that time he would have to run against Ransom for the seat that normally belonged to the eastern part of the state. Unable to occupy public office, Zeb once again had to rely on his law practice to earn a living. His law partner Clement Dowd reported: "He returned to the practice of law with manifest reluctance. His depression was conspicuous and was the subject of anxiety and remark among his friends." According to Dowd, Zeb's natural ebullience and optimism eventually returned, but there is no question that he felt grievously wounded by the turn of events.[32]

With no alternative, Zeb returned to the two activities that could provide him with an adequate income: law and public speaking. The most important case he took on during this period included several people from his youth. It involved a charge of criminal libel brought by Zeb's old law teacher Nicholas W. Woodfin against newspaper editor Thomas D. Carter. Carter had accused Woodfin of fraud, corruption, and conspiracy; Woodfin swore out a criminal complaint against Carter for libel. Zeb, along with his former political opponents David Coleman and Augustus S. Merrimon, was a lawyer for Carter. The essence of Carter's defense was the argument that the press was free to criticize public officials. After all of the testimony had been given, Zeb arranged a compromise solution to the case with Woodfin's lawyers which was accepted by the judge. Carter was declared not guilty, but the accusations against Woodfin of fraud or conspiracy were cleared.[33]

Zeb usually found delivering public addresses to be much more congenial than working as an attorney. It was in this period that he began to achieve a national reputation as a public speaker. Moreover, the study and exposition of history became a minor but significant part of his career in the next two decades. Zeb identified himself as a historian, and he joined several of the leading organizations of his time. He was the vice president of the Southern Historical Society for North Carolina, a committee member of the Historical Society of North Carolina, and a member of the American Social Sciences Association.[34] He also assumed many of the roles of a serious student of the past, including editor, interpreter, document seeker, biographer, and book reviewer. While he chose some untraditional venues in which to present his findings, including newspaper articles and addresses both at veterans' reunions and on the floor of the U.S. Senate, Zeb used history to inform, educate, and persuade.

Zeb's made his only formal address to a historical group in the summer of 1875. In a speech before the Southern Historical Society at White Sulphur Springs, West Virginia, he analyzed North Carolina's contribution to the Confederate war effort. Zeb's rather relaxed standards of historical documentation were captured in his introductory statement: "I regret exceedingly that many of the facts and figures that I shall give you are reproduced from memory, though I am quite sure they will approximate exactitude." The exposition that followed was similar to public utterances that Zeb had made during and immediately following the war. He asserted that despite its Unionism prior to the firing on Fort Sumter, North Carolina had contributed more men and materiel to the Confederacy than any other state. In fact, it had conducted a foreign trade that supplied part of Lee's army. Refusing to accept personal or state responsibility for the Confederate defeat, Zeb claimed that it was due entirely to the failures of the Davis administration. He maintained that the Confederacy's early optimism had been unrealistic, and that it had made it necessary for the government to impose the disastrous conscription policy. At the same time, Zeb claimed that Davis and others had failed to develop an ideology in support of the Confederate cause that appealed to the common people.[35] Thus, Zeb placed the blame for Confederate defeat squarely in Richmond, not in Raleigh.

By the time his speech was published, Zeb found himself embroiled in a controversy about its content. His description of his March 20, 1865, meeting with William A. Graham contradicted Graham's own account of the occasion. In Vance's speech, he had accused Graham of carrying messages from the Confederate Congress that proposed that North Carolina surrender to the Union. While there is little doubt that Zeb's memory of the event was essentially accurate, both Graham's relatives—Graham had died in August 1875—and former members of the Confederate Congress sharply disputed Zeb's version. In a footnote to the published text of his speech, Zeb attempted to placate his attackers by explaining that he did not regard Graham's proposal as treasonous; in fact, he believed that it would have been the logical plan to follow given the unbending commitment of Davis to continuing a hopeless war. Amplifying his explanation, Zeb wrote: "I was only indignant that those, who were so lively in the beginning of the fight and who reflected so severely on North Carolina for her tardiness, should undertake to make her the scape-goat of defeat."[36] It is important to note that Zeb was much more moderate in his assessment of Graham in 1875 than he had been in his letter to Cornelia Phillips Spencer nine years earlier.

Zeb also spoke on matters beyond his own immediate experience. In the winter of 1874, he delivered one such address in Baltimore entitled "The Scattered Nation." Faced with uncertain income as an attorney, Zeb delivered this address—an overview of the history of the Jewish people—for significant fees many times on a national speaking circuit. It was probably his finest effort as an interpreter of the past. Zeb did considerable research for the article in secondary sources, and he showed an openness to new information that scholars were providing from the Middle East. For example, he conceded that monotheism may have originated in Babylon, rather than with the Hebrew patriarchs.[37] While he quoted extensively from Middle Eastern authorities, Zeb's organization and interpretation of the material was entirely original.

Squeezed by the temporal limitations of a public address and by the ornateness of his style, Zeb devoted little attention in "The Scattered Nation" to specific episodes, assuming, perhaps, that his audience was familiar with the Old Testament. Instead, he concentrated on the origins of the ancient Hebrew government and on the Jewish people's economic and legal systems, their postexile adaptations, and the discrimination they faced in the modern world. What was particularly striking about the address was Zeb's call, at a time when anti-Semitism was on the rise in Europe and America, for an end to the restrictions placed on American Jews. Selections from the speech capture the liberality of Zeb's position: "I agree with Lord McCauley that the Jew is what we have made him," he wrote. "If he is a bad job, in all honesty we should contemplate him as the handiwork of our own civilization." In a passage about anti-Semitism, Zeb declared:

"Let us judge the Jew as we judge other men—*by his merits*. And above all, let us cease the abominable injustice of holding the *class* responsible for the sins of the *individual*. We apply this to no other people." Unfortunately, Zeb proved himself to be a man of his own time and place when he compared African Americans unfavorably to Jews: "The African Negro, the descendants of barbarian tribes," he wrote, "for 4000 years have contributed nothing to, though in close contact with civilization." In the United States, Zeb averred, "laws and partisan courts alike have been used to force him into an equality with those he could not equal."[38] Apparently neither Zeb nor the members of his predominantly white audiences noticed the obvious inconsistency in his reasoning.

Another project that kept Zeb busy was the restoration of the University of North Carolina. This venerable institution had been one of the victims of Reconstruction. Upon assuming office, the Republicans had appointed their own competent instructors and administration for the university. Since most of the students came from families that supported the Republicans' opponents, however, student attendance fell dramatically until the university, having accumulated large debts, closed its doors. Zeb joined with other members of the elite to raise more than eighteen thousand dollars in donations that were used to repay the debt and reopen the campus. Zeb was a prominent figure in the ceremonies that celebrated the happy event in the fall of 1875. As a reward for his services, and to ensure the high profile of the university, Zeb was offered the position of president. He recognized that holding the office would have made it difficult for him to return to politics, however, and he refused it. But rather than hurt anyone's feelings, he explained his decision as follows: "Say to my friends that it would kill me in a few weeks to be obliged to behave as is required of a college president in order to furnish an example to the boys."[39]

Part of the reason for Zeb's reluctance to remove himself from politics was that recent events seemed to promise unusual opportunities for Democratic candidates. The economic downturn of 1873–74 and revelations of corruption among national Republican officials led to dramatic Democratic victories in the 1874 congressional elections. In an effort to focus the campaign on issues that favored them and to ensure that their Reconstruction legacy would be preserved, Republicans had introduced a sweeping Civil Rights Bill into Congress. In North Carolina, the bill was extremely unpopular with white voters. North Carolina Republicans recognized that it would be politically disastrous for them to defend the measure. They immediately came out against it, and they were greatly angered when a somewhat more moderate bill passed in early 1875. By raising the issue of race, the Republicans had handed Southern Democrats a legitimate reason to make racism the key to winning the campaign. The congressional elections of 1874 demonstrated how unpopular the Republicans were at the time. Republican candidates won only one race, and that was in the Second District, where black voters were in the majority. Zeb's brother Robert was easily re-elected to Congress from the district that Zeb had represented before the Civil War.[40]

The elite leadership of the Democratic Party decided to take advantage of this opportunity to secure their dominant position in state politics. They decided to hold a constitutional convention. Unwilling to take a chance that the public would vote down the meeting again, the legislature simply called the convention into being and asked the voters to choose delegates. There was considerable opposition to the initiative within Democratic ranks, however, and the party leadership was forced to limit the topics that the convention could address. Zeb turned down his nomination to be a delegate to the meeting, but he willingly campaigned for other candidates. One of the most effective tactics of the convention's opponents was to claim that the homestead exemption would be eliminated. Zeb replied to that claim with this biblical-sounding pronouncement: "He who sayeth so is a fool or a liar. For would we destroy the law that gives us our home, where our children have been born and reared—where they have died and been carried forth to their last resting place? I say no, we will not."[41]

Despite the Democrats' best efforts, the voters delivered a split result. The Republican candidates actually received slightly more votes than the Democrats, and enough Republican candidates were elected to adjourn the convention before it started. However, the Democrats fraudulently elected two delegates from Robeson County and thereby gained sufficient votes in the convention to accomplish some of their agenda. The Democrat-controlled convention gave the legislature the power to determine how local officials would be selected, thereby allowing the Democrat-controlled legislature to appoint officials rather than allow them to be elected. The convention also prohibited interracial schooling and marriage, reduced the number of state judges, lengthened the residence requirement for voters, created a bureau of agriculture, and restricted the powers of the governor.[42] While these changes would make political life somewhat harder for Republicans, particularly African Americans, they did not ensure that the Democrats could control a balanced electorate.

The gubernatorial election of 1876 now became even more important to Democrats. The convention vote had indicated that the Republicans were still a powerful force in the state, able to win an election even while laboring under the disadvantages posed by the civil rights legislation and the economic downturn. For the Democrats to regain control of the executive branch of the government, they would have to unite behind a strong candidate and run a campaign that unified the party. In early December, the *Charlotte Democrat* suggested that Zeb would be the best Democratic candidate.[43] As more and more party members looked over the field, they reached a similar conclusion.

The gubernatorial campaign of 1876 has assumed mythical status in North Carolina's history. The two protagonists have been portrayed as the outstanding leaders of their respective parties; their open-air debates became legendary episodes of intellectual warfare. The election is also remembered as a turning point in the state's political history: in 1876, the Democratic Party seized control of the state's political machinery and held it for the next century, during which time the "right" people ruled for the good of the entire society; the party also brought to an end the "corrupt" government by blacks, carpetbaggers, and scalawags that had disgraced North Carolina during Reconstruction. Like many other myths, this one contains historically accurate elements combined with misinformation and self-serving distortion. Yet when the inaccuracies and distortions are removed, it remains clear that the campaign was a crucial one for determining the state's future.

The great battle almost failed to take place. While Zeb was the most obvious Democratic gubernatorial candidate, there are a number of indications that he was not enthusiastic about serving another term as governor. In addition, several of his fellow Democrats were convinced that he would be a divisive candidate who might fail to oust the Republicans from the governor's office. Probably the person most anxious for Zeb to receive the gubernatorial nomination was Democratic senator Matt W. Ransom. Ransom had been elected to take the Senate seat Zeb was denied in 1871 and 1872, and he was aware that Zeb could have legitimately laid claim to the seat following the 1876 election. Surviving correspondence indicates that Ransom worked diligently to secure support among his operatives to nominate Zeb for governor.[1]

Before the gubernatorial nominating convention took place, Democrats in the Sixth District of North Carolina were called on to nominate a candidate for Congress. Although there was a Democratic incumbent in place, Thomas S. Ashe, Zeb was apparently interested in securing his position. Zeb, his law partner Clement Dowd, and prominent local politician Walter L. Steele worked together quietly to send delegates to the congressional nominating convention who opposed Ashe. Zeb apparently hoped to claim the nomination without openly declaring his candidacy. One local leader observed that Zeb seemed to prefer "the certainty of Congress to the chance of the governorship." When the congressional nominating convention met in early June, the result of the first ballot was 3,735 for Ashe, 2,619 for Vance, 2,618 for Steele, and 3,772 for others. (Representatives from each county could cast as many votes as the number of Democratic votes they had recorded in the previous election.) It was a very confused situation, and it was not clear whether the anti-Ashe forces were in control of the meeting. At this crucial junction, one of Zeb's supporters withdrew his name from consideration. When the balloting continued, Steele was eventually nominated by the narrow margin of 228 votes on the fifth ballot. Zeb subsequently claimed that he had never seriously contemplated being a congressional candidate and that he had tried to discourage people from voting for him.[2] That may have been true, but he may also have sought to secure the nomination through stealth and then decided, when the convention ended up being closely divided, not to take the chance of weakening his political stature by risking defeat.

With the congressional nomination settled on Steele, Zeb turned his attention to the gubernatorial nominating convention. Given the political practices of the time, he could not appear to be actively pursuing the nomination. In an open letter to the party, he promised: "I am willing to do anything that is best, and propose to leave the whole matter to the convention without exerting the slightest influence over it. I have no ambition to gratify at the expense of the general good. I will work anywhere I am hitched, in the off wheel, off lead, under the saddle or I will take to the woods and hide out if it is thought best."[3] Despite this disclaimer, Zeb was clearly interested in getting the nomination, and he apparently reached some understanding with Ransom that the senator would support him. There is no indication that Zeb promised not to run against Ransom for the Senate seat, but it would certainly have been difficult for him to do so if he had just been elected governor.

While Zeb's understanding with Ransom smoothed the way for his nomination, there were still many within the Democratic Party who were not enthusiastic about his candidacy. The *Warrenton Gazette* maintained that between one and ten thousand voters who had supported Conservative Party candidate Augustus S. Merrimon in the 1872 election would not vote for Zeb. The paper claimed that these voters were deserters and former Unionists who would never vote for Zeb because of the repressive measures he had taken against them during the war. Another party worker predicted in a letter to Ransom that Zeb could cost the party the opportunity to win the gubernatorial race. Despite these reservations, however, popular support for Zeb was very strong, and he traveled from Charlotte to Raleigh to attend the convention in high spirits.[4]

The convention took on all of the aspects of a coronation after the initial ceremonies were completed. Zeb and six other candidates were nominated and the roll was called. It became obvious early in the proceedings that Zeb had the support of a large majority of the delegates. After the counties had finished announcing their preferences, Zeb had 767 votes, his nearest competitor 116, and all others 83. Soon the other candidates began to withdraw from the contest, and in the end Zeb was officially nominated by 962 votes to 4. The convention then completed its work by nominating candidates for the other state offices and electing a state committee to run the campaign. The party platform it adopted was a very aggressive document that chastised the Republican Party for its "disregard for constitutional limitations, its unequal and oppressive taxations, its extravagant and wasteful expenditure, its unwise and mischievous financial policy, and its unexampled official corruption." The Democrats also called for an end to campaigns that emphasized the issues of the past, namely, the divisions of the Civil War period.[5]

The excited delegates called upon Zeb for a speech, which he delivered in front of the National Hotel. In his opening, he touched squarely on one of the points that he and the Democrats would turn into a major appeal during the 1876 campaign: he praised the convention that had just nominated him as representative of "the worth and intelligence of the white people of the State." Zeb and his Democratic compatriots would claim throughout the canvass to be the sole representatives of North Carolina whites, and they would emphasize racial differences at every opportunity. Zeb then went on to define what he believed were the major goals for which the party should campaign:

1. Retrenchment of the public expenditures, State and National;
2. The restoration of the government and its administration to the hands of honest men; and
3. A return to constitutional government in the maintenance of our laws.

"Briefer still," he continued, "we desire to administer the government more nearly upon the basis of the American constitution and the Ten Commandments." He then proceeded to enumerate the extensive incidents of corruption that had taken place during the administration of President Ulysses S. Grant. He called on honest Republicans to repudiate their party and to join the Democrats in cleaning up the country. He concluded by defending his Civil War administration and claiming that he had been a friend of the common people in that conflict.[6]

On his return trip from Raleigh to Charlotte, huge crowds greeted Zeb in Durham, Greensboro, Salisbury, and Concord. In Concord, there was a spectacular fireworks display and considerable celebrating by the party faithful. When Zeb finally arrived in Charlotte, another large crowd awaited him. The night was illuminated with bonfires, and a local band provided the music. A tired Vance limited his remarks to fifteen minutes and kept the atmosphere light and entertaining. He delighted the crowd by deprecating his recent success, observing that he "had been spoilt by popular applause to the extent that his clothes had become too small for him." On that note of levity, he retired to plan the remainder of his campaign. Zeb decided that he would not formally begin campaigning until July because he had some court cases that he had to complete. This did not mean that the party organization lay dormant in this period. The party began to organize Tilden and Vance clubs across the state to ensure that its local organizations were strong. (Samuel Tilden was the Democratic presidential candidate.) At the same time, the state committee asked Matt W. Ransom to secure money from the Democratic National Committee to aid the party in North Carolina.[7]

As Zeb cleared out his remaining court cases, an incident took place in the small city of Tarboro that allowed him to begin his campaign in a blaze of excitement. During a Fourth of July celebration, there was a violent confrontation between a white policeman and an African American. The Democratic press quickly began calling this incident a "negro riot." Zeb, who had already been planning to start his canvass of the state in Concord, quickly scheduled a speech in Tarboro. When he arrived there, he was greeted by a large group of Tilden and Vance Club members and a brass band. He spoke to approximately thirty-five hundred people in the Tarboro town square. Never mentioning the racial incident, Zeb attacked Republican corruption and called for reform of the state and national governments. As was his usual strategy, he told a considerable number of funny stories and made observations that entertained the crowd. For example, a local newspaper recounted how Zeb explained his rapid change of allegiance from the Union to the Confederacy as follows: His course reminded him of a marriage notice he had once seen of John R. Rush to Mrs. Julia Canter.

> When Cupid first did this maiden banter
> O'er Hyman's course to take a brush.
> At first she went at it with a Canter,
> But now she goes it with a Rush.

The combination of an excited white audience, a partisan attack on the corruption of the opposition, and general good humor brought an enthusiastic response from the crowd. Zeb continued his tour of the eastern counties that had large African American populations and was greeted everywhere by large and ardent crowds.[8] Little more seemed to be required of Zeb to assure his victory than for him to repeat his successful performances several dozen times between July and election day in November.

Zeb and the Democrats apparently expected to run a campaign that centered on the political situation in the South in 1876. While Zeb himself was relatively restrained on racial questions, the remainder of the party was not. Commenting on the Republican gubernatorial convention in North Carolina, one Democratic newspaper reported, "The African slave trade has been literally revived and niggers are now bought and sold by the leaders of the contending radical factions, at lower figures and greater profit than in the days of our forefathers." Heavy-handed racism such as this became the central feature of the Democratic campaign to retain control of the legislature. Matt W. Ransom, the informal Democratic Party candidate for the position of U.S. senator, was particularly violent in denouncing African American political power. Some Democratic papers even partially justified the recent racial massacre in Hamburg, South Carolina.[9] It seemed that all Zeb had to do was to let the party organization split the electorate along racial lines.

Zeb apparently assumed that he would conduct his campaign much as he had conducted the campaign against Holden in 1864. He and his managers expected him to tour the state and to ignore his Republican opponent. Zeb was startled to receive a challenge to engage in a statewide series of debates with Republican standard-bearer Thomas Settle. Born in Rockingham County in 1831, Settle was the son of a prominent political figure who served as a congressman and a superior court judge. Settle grew into a tall, attractive adult who was personally charming in both small and large group settings. The combination of family prominence and physical and social grace with which Settle was blessed ensured that he would be a success in North Carolina public life. Entering politics as a Democrat, Settle was first elected to the North Carolina House of Commons in 1854, the same term that Zeb served. During the 1858–59 session, Settle was elected Speaker. A few years earlier, he had introduced a series of nine resolutions on the recently passed Kansas-Nebraska Act that Zeb would cite often during the 1876 campaign. One read: "That in the event the Federal Government repeal or i[m]pair the efficiency of the provisions of the Fugitive Slave law, or refuse its execution in good faith, that it will amount to a[n] initial dissolution of the Union, and that it will become the duty of the State to take

Thomas Settle Jr., ca. 1870. Settle was a leader in the Republican Party in North Carolina and opposed Vance in the 1876 gubernatorial election. (North Carolina Division of Archives and History, Raleigh)

such measures as may be required for her safety and security." Settle was the owner of twenty-six slaves; this statement undoubtedly represented his opinion at the time.[10]

When the secession crisis came in 1860, Settle found himself occupying about the same position that Zeb did. He supported Stephen A. Douglas, the Unionist, Democratic candidate for president. Settle won election as a

Unionist candidate in February 1861 for the state convention that was voted down by the electorate. After that, he supported the Union in a series of public debates, much like Zeb did. When Settle learned about Lincoln's call for troops, he, again like Zeb, became an officer in a North Carolina Confederate regiment. His path diverged from Zeb's, however, from that point forward. Settle resigned his commission in April 1862 to assume the position of solicitor of the Fourth Judicial District. In that position, he worked with William W. Holden to promote the meeting of a peace convention in North Carolina. In the immediate aftermath of the war, Settle was an important member of the North Carolina Constitutional Convention of 1865. By 1867, he had become one of the founders of the Republican Party in North Carolina and as such was one who supported greater rights for African Americans. Elected associate justice of the North Carolina Supreme Court in 1868, Settle became an active opponent of the Ku Klux Klan and of racial and economic injustice. He stepped down from the court to serve as the U.S. minister to Peru for one year.[11]

When he returned to North Carolina in 1872, Settle ran for Congress; in his campaign, he developed many of the themes that he would later use in the 1876 gubernatorial campaign. Settle reminded white voters of the excesses and suffering that had taken place during the war, and he blamed the Conservative Party for these events. Challenging congressman James M. Leach to a joint canvass, Settle asserted that the militiamen Zeb had ordered out in the Piedmont counties had behaved with "barbarity and savageness." He defended the Republican Party for supporting African American rights and publicly attacked the Ku Klux Klan. The campaign that followed was punctuated by several violent incidents in which Settle was threatened with severe bodily harm. Despite his opponents' attempts to counter his appeals with undemocratic methods, Settle nearly won the election. His defeat did him little harm within the Republican Party, and Republican governor Tod R. Caldwell reappointed Settle to the state supreme court.[12]

At first Zeb tried to avoid Settle's challenge. His campaign managers sought every avenue open to them, including proposing rules of debate that would have put Settle at a severe disadvantage, to keep Vance from having to face Settle directly. But the weight of tradition—virtually all gubernatorial campaigns in antebellum North Carolina had featured direct debates—forced Zeb to reconsider his position and to agree to participate in more than fifty meetings.[13] It apparently went unnoticed at the time that Zeb had refused to take part in any discussion in an area where African Americans formed the majority of the population. Settle's strategy during the campaign was very simple: he tried to retain the support of virtually all of North

Carolina's African American voters while splitting the white vote. Zeb's plan was equally simple: he conceded the African American vote to Settle and attempted to gain the entire white vote. Throughout the campaign, the candidates discussed issues from both the present and the past. Settle sought to avoid discussing the recently exposed Republican corruption in Washington and the poor economic conditions. Instead, he concentrated on the festering hatreds that the Civil War had created within North Carolina society. Zeb tried to avoid talking about the contentious war-related issues, focusing instead on national issues that were often not directly related to North Carolina.

Settle began the campaign in the western counties by taking the initiative. Concentrating on Zeb's two Civil War administrations in an area where Unionism and anti-Confederate feeling had been strong during the war, Settle accused Zeb of having been a persecutor of deserters and Unionists. Specifically, he charged that Vance had run as a peace candidate during the 1862 gubernatorial election and had then failed to carry out the peace platform later in the war. Settle further contended that Vance had vigorously enforced the Confederate Conscription Act, punishing those who had opposed the Confederacy and torturing women to find out where their male relatives were hiding. When Zeb denied that he had been personally responsible for these actions, Settle pointed out that the governor had allowed the men who perpetrated such outrages to remain in office long after their abuses of power had been exposed. Settle also charged Zeb with sending underage youths to their deaths by forcing them into the army.[14]

Settle and the Republican newspaper editors who backed him supported their attack on Zeb with his war letters and other official documents. Zeb complained, with some justification, that Settle and his backers in the press were not providing voters with complete and accurate documents. In fact, the Republican press was remarkably careful to attack Vance with his own words. While it is true that Settle did substitute words when he read from some documents, his major editorial change was to substitute the word "Unionists" for "deserters" in several passages. To Settle's mind, this change was legitimate; because virtually all deserters opposed the Confederacy, they could fairly be called Unionists. Zeb believed, however, that the distinction he had made in his correspondence between deserters and Unionists was crucial. He felt that many men had left the Confederate service to look after their families, rather than because they opposed the war effort. In any case, Settle was able to demonstrate convincingly that Zeb had sought to use state and Confederate military forces to suppress desertion and that he had worked closely with Robert E. Lee and Jefferson Davis.[15]

Not content with Settle's direct attack on Zeb's war record, Republicans produced an extended version of it that was more than eighty pages long. This detailed examination of the Vance administration did not shy away from insulting the former governor personally. The early pages claimed that in 1862 Zeb would not have been a suitable gubernatorial candidate under normal circumstances because he was not "a man of the finest culture and the highest social rank," as all previous governors had been. Yet Zeb had been chosen by William W. Holden to be his candidate. The anonymous author of the tract claimed that Holden, and therefore Vance, had run a veiled campaign on the platform that North Carolina should secede from the Confederacy and bring an early end to the war. Therefore, the tract argued, Zeb had been elected as a peace candidate. The author went on to assert that Zeb's commitment to peace had ended when he had a conference with Jefferson Davis in Richmond, after which he "threw himself body and soul into the arms of the war party and turned on his former friends with inconceivable rage and fury." The essay concluded with the text of documents relating to the Shelton Laurel massacre and with the May 11, 1863, proclamation on desertion.[16] The anonymous tract was designed to appeal directly to anyone who had opposed the Confederacy at any time during the war.

Having established that Vance had directed violence toward individual deserters and Unionists, Settle and his allies then accused Zeb of cupidity and ambition, and they held him personally responsible for ruining the state. Specifically, they charged him with shipping goods on the state blockade-runners for his personal profit and comfort, seeking to become Jefferson Davis's successor as president of the Confederacy, ruining the credit of the state education fund by investing it in Confederate bonds, prolonging the war unnecessarily and thereby killing many North Carolinians, and deserting his post in Raleigh when William T. Sherman's army approached. Portions of the personal attack on Zeb are contained in this piece of Republican campaign verse:

> Z. B. V. thought he'd be in clover
> To see us fight till Hell froze over
> And then he said it would be nice
> To see us fight the Yanks on the ice
> But when Sherman came this way
> He mounted a mule and rode away.[17]

This was precisely the kind of ridicule that Zeb had sought to avoid when he had consciously programmed his actions at the end of the war. While Settle's portrait of Zeb was somewhat overdrawn, many members of the audiences the two men addressed would have recognized that the Republican candidate's assertions were basically accurate.

Zeb's strategy for the opening debates in the western mountain counties was to avoid answering Settle directly and to counterattack with his own charges. The debates began on July 25 in Rutherfordton before a crowd of four thousand people. Zeb opened with a speech of an hour and a half. Settle replied for the same length of time, and then they each had thirty minutes for rebuttal arguments. Zeb spent most of his time attacking Republican corruption, which he blamed on a few party leaders, completely absolving the mass of the party. He also stated that "he could forgive many of the crimes of the Radicals, but he never could forgive [their] attempt to degrade [the] good old Anglo-Saxon race beneath the African race." Zeb also secured considerable sympathy from his own supporters by demonstrating that Settle was providing only partial quotes from Zeb's Civil War correspondence.[18] The debate was conducted in general good humor, and no threat of violence marred the proceedings.

As the campaign proceeded to the mountain communities of Marshall, Burnsville, Bakersville, Asheville, Boone, Jefferson, Wilkesboro, and Hendersonville, Settle pressed his attack on Zeb's wartime administration. Acknowledging that the federal and state governments were currently spending more than they had in the past, Settle laid the blame on Zeb and the Confederacy for causing both the destruction of property and the dislocation that had followed the repudiation of Confederate money. In these mountain communities, Zeb unexpectedly found himself at a disadvantage when he became quite hoarse and was unable to project his voice to reach the entire audience. Despite Settle's initial advantage in the debates, however, the Democratic campaign was gathering momentum. When the two men met in Asheville, the members of the Tilden and Vance Club put on a much more impressive parade than their Republican counterparts. In fact, the Democrats felt safe enough from retribution to deface the Republican campaign paraphernalia. These signs of growing Democratic strength would prove to be significant. The Democrats, who had recently been well organized only during the state campaign of 1870, were concentrating on local arrangements in 1876. A Cabarrus County Republican reported the result of the Democrats' efforts to Republican presidential candidate Rutherford B. Hayes: "It is true our noble state standard bearer, Judge Settle, and other candidates, are making a splendid canvass as far as it goes, but they can only visit the larger towns and not one half of the people ever see or hear them. The Democrats are forming Tilden & Vance clubs in all the Townships so as to bring out their full strength and to make converts. We ought to do the same, but alas: we lack the men and means and the organization and the concert of action that alone can ensure success." The Democrats recognized how effective their local organizing was, and they were jubilant when local clubs took root quickly. Remarkably, there were five Tilden and Vance clubs in Alamance County alone.[19] Thus, it was becoming clear that the spectacular debates which captured public attention were not going to be the decisive factor in the election.

For Zeb, however, the debates with Settle remained the central concern of his campaign. Zeb sensed that Settle had gained an initial advantage, and he sought to place his Republican opponent on the defensive. In the small mountain community of Burnsville, Zeb first posed a series of questions designed to force Settle to confront some of the contradictions in his addresses. These included:

1. Did Settle endorse Holden's suspension of the writ of *habeas corpus* during the 1870 political crisis?
2. Which of the state constitutional amendments did Settle endorse?
3. How did the South get out of the Union?
4. Was giving "colored men" the right to vote constitutional?
5. Was it right to evict five members of the Louisiana legislature with the bayonet?
6. Was he in favor of the 1874 civil rights bill as it originally left the house that called for racially integrated schools and cemeteries?
7. Did he approve the Grant administration?
8. Was Settle not elected to the Supreme Court by fraud?
9. Was desertion from the Confederate army right?
10. Was the election under the Canby [1868] Constitution constitutional?[20]

According to the news account that listed these along with Zeb's other questions, Settle was surprised by them and made no immediate reply. Zeb's strategy was patently clear. If Settle was going to dwell on the past, then Zeb would do so, too. But instead of centering his attention on the war, where Settle appeared to have an advantage, Zeb focused on Reconstruction, where the evidence of Republican excesses gave the Democrats an advantage.

Perhaps the most crucial of the questions that Zeb posed were the two that dealt with the state constitutional amendments and the federal Civil Rights Bill. Zeb asked these questions in order to ensure that racial issues would remain at the center of the North Carolina campaign. Like Wade Hampton of South Carolina, who was also running for governor in 1876, he was very careful to distance himself from the type of violence that had attracted federal troops and law enforcement officials in the past. For example, in the debate in Marshall, Zeb denounced the Ku Klux Klan and said that "he never belonged to it, and was always opposed to it, and if it had been in his power he would have stopped it before it even budded." Nevertheless, Zeb and the Democrats ran a strongly racist campaign. They emphasized that Sumner's Civil Rights Bill had originally included provisions for social racial integration. Zeb's question about the state constitutional amendments has a more complicated history. The state constitutional convention of 1875 had passed several constitutional amendments that would be voted upon during the 1876 balloting. One of these amendments proposed that county officials be appointed by the state legislature. If passed, this amendment would prevent African Americans from dominating county governments in the areas of eastern North Carolina where they formed the majority of the population. The Democrats had insisted that the voters be required either to vote for all of the amendments together or to vote against all of them. As Republicans had voted for the vast majority of the amendments that were on the ballot, the Democrats hoped that this strategy would help pass the few controversial provisions. For many Democrats in the eastern part of the state, passing the amendments was more important than winning the gubernatorial election.[21]

The most effective racist Democratic strategy was pursued on a very local basis without reference to the candidates or their campaigns. The Republican operative in Cabarrus County described the essence of the Democratic effort. He claimed that the Democrats reduced white Republican voting "not so much by intimidation as by sneering, and by twitting the republicans because they vote with negroes." As a result, he complained, "many of the whites of our party in this section appear to be ashamed or afraid to acknowledge that they are republicans, and all the canvassing that has been done in many of the counties of this state . . . has been done in a kind of clandestine way, as if our party were an infamous or dishonorable one."[22] To retain the support of those who had opposed the Confederacy, Settle would have to provide his voters with a way to overcome the pressure to conform to the racial prejudices of their communities.

Settle refused to back away from the racist challenge that Zeb and the Democrats posed to Republican voters. He called upon Zeb to repudiate the Klan and the killing of Republican partisans during the campaign of 1870, which Zeb willingly did, as noted above. Settle ridiculed the Democratic Party's assertions that African Americans in North Carolina posed a threat. He concluded one section of a speech by deriding the notion "that forty millions of the great Anglo-Saxon race should not be willing to give to four millions of poor, ignorant, slave-ridden Africans an equal and fair race in the contest of life; [and] accord to them protection before the law, and the exercise of the ballot as citizens." He proposed that "instead of raising prejudices of passion against them," white North Carolinians should allow African Americans "to become better citizens, and a useful as they are an industrious people."[23] While Settle's speech contained its own form of paternalistic racism, the Republican gubernatorial candidate showed considerable courage in espousing what was clearly an unpopular point of view with many of the white voters he was trying to reach.

Settle, while not replying directly to Zeb's questions, did address some of the issues that Zeb had raised. For example, he and his Republican allies were more than willing to identify the proposed amendments to the state Constitution to which they objected. They equated those who had suffered at the hands of the Confederacy during the war with the group that would be denied rights by the Democratic amendments. Settle questioned the legitimacy of the convention that had passed the amendments; as noted previously, he had excellent reasons to do so. Settle and the Republicans emphasized that African Americans were not the only targets of the amendments. They ridiculed the amendment that prohibited interracial marriages, pointing out that the state supreme court had already held these unions illegal. Refusing to back down from Zeb's attack, Settle asserted the Republican state constitution of 1868 was the finest in North Carolina's history. He pointed out that it provided each landowner with a homestead exemption from state taxes and debts that allowed many farmers, both small and large, to retain control of their property.[24] Settle thought (and Zeb probably would have agreed) that many of the men who received homestead exemptions were the same men who had opposed the Confederacy at some time during the war.

Settle also criticized Zeb and the Democrats for seeking to change the structure of local governments. Settle pointed out that the amendments would abolish townships and "uproot . . . present county governments." They would also, he noted, "take away the election of the Justices of the Peace from the people." Settle predicted, moreover, that county government in the state would eventually differ greatly from one county to another. He anticipated that townships would be abolished and county courts— dominated by the local elite—would be restored.[25] There is no doubt that Settle was appealing to the nonelite is his addresses, men whom he knew had often opposed the Confederacy during the war. Zeb and the Democrats decried Settle's class-based appeals and hid behind the rationale that the amendments were necessary to deny local governing power to African Americans in the eastern counties of the state.

Feeling threatened by the apparent effectiveness of Settle's appeals to whites in the western and Piedmont sections of the state, Democratic Party leaders sought to intimidate the candidate and his followers. They used this tactic, to give only the most pronounced example, in Jonesboro on August 25. On that occasion, Democratic partisans from Fayetteville traveled to Jonesboro in large numbers and heckled Settle as he tried to speak. They shouted and hissed and thoroughly disrupted the Republican nominee's address. Losing his composure for the only time during the campaign, Settle shouted at his tormentors, calling them "Fiends of Hell" and "Ku Klux." Zeb apparently recognized that the situation could deteriorate to a point at which it would damage his campaign, and he stepped forward and quieted the boisterous crowd. Democratic newspapers attacked Settle for using such harsh language against his hecklers, but Republican journals replied, "If the democrats think that they are making anything by filling up railroad trains with noisy town chaps, to take the front seats and yell all the time, they are greatly mistaken."[26] The Republican bravado aside, there seems to be little question that the Democrats' attempts to intimidate their opponents were partially successful.

Although Settle and Vance were fighting for the white vote during the canvass, Republican speakers and newspapers did not ignore African American voters. In late August, the *New North State* of Greensboro ran an article that highlighted a number of statements Zeb had made early in the campaign that appeared to threaten the civil status of blacks in North Carolina. The paper quoted Zeb as saying that the Reconstruction amendments to the national Constitution were fraudulent and had been illegally ratified. According to the paper, Zeb concluded, "I would not give one cent for the flag or the Union, unless it be administered under the old constitution of our fathers." He was further quoted as having said that "the abolition of slavery was a palpable violation of the Constitution." Leaving nothing to chance, the editor of the paper also claimed that Zeb thought the abolition of slavery was as void as was the right of African Americans to vote.[27] Zeb never took specific notice of these charges and never directly replied to them. They may or may not have been accurate, but they certainly conveyed the essence of Zeb's position on the rights of blacks in North Carolina.

Zeb sought to direct the focus of the campaign onto issues that demonstrated the corrupt nature of the Republican administration of the national government. Choosing an example that he hoped would appeal to many voters in western and central North Carolina, he called for an end to the federal enforcement of the revenue laws that placed a tax on liquor made by distillers and farmers in North Carolina. The first excise on liquor was passed as a war measure in 1862 and was continued after the war to help reduce the national debt. Federal officials who collected the tax were political appointees and were expected to assist the Settle campaign in 1876. Calling the enforcement agents "red-legged grasshoppers," he claimed that they unfairly arrested many honest distillers and misused the revenue they collected. Zeb claimed, with acknowledged exaggeration, that revenue officers could "take a drink from a branch 5 miles below a still house, and tell whether whiskey was being made above them; [they] could look at a fellow's track in the sand, or smell a man's breath and tell whether his whiskey was tax-paid."[28] While Zeb was making an exaggerated point rather than reporting on actual behavior, he knew that the agents had abused their power and that many of the members of his audiences would agree with his basic claim.

As the campaign entered the late summer and fall, the candidates swung back to the mountain counties to stage the remaining twenty-seven debates while making another full tour of the state. All evidence indicates that the two men continued to use the same basic speeches that they had used earlier in the campaign. The only detailed existing accounts of the speeches given by both men that have survived are of two long addresses they delivered at Oxford on October 9. Settle started his address by trying to defuse Zeb's charges of Republican malfeasance. In particular, he attempted to show that the average federal tax burden in the country was actually less than it had been in 1860, when the Democrats were last in power. Settle also cited charges by Josiah Turner, a maverick Democrat, of Democratic mismanagement. He specifically noted Democrat Stephen D. Pool's misuse of education funds and Democratic county law enforcement officials' default on personal bonds. Finally, Settle asserted that Zeb was driving Northern capital from North Carolina by constantly abusing carpetbaggers; Zeb, he charged, had "kept thousands of energetic, enterprising men out of the State and millions in treasure."[29]

As he had done in his earlier speeches, however, Settle concentrated primarily on Zeb's record as a Civil War governor. He charged that in Wilkes County, "seventeen Union men were hanged to one pole, and house after house was burned, and man after man was shot down." Settle read from a letter that Zeb had written to Confederate secretary of war James A. Seddon in which he had recommended that a military court be established in western North Carolina in place of existing civilian courts. Settle concluded his arraignment of Zeb and Confederate policy in North Carolina by quoting from a letter from Robert E. Lee in which the general instructed the Confederate troops in Chatham and Moore Counties "to take no prisoners among [the] deserters who resist with arms the civil or military authorities." Settle claimed that Zeb had known about this letter and had endorsed its "black flag" policy against his own people.[30] Clearly, Settle had not backed away from his initial strategy of placing a critique of Zeb's wartime administration at the center of his campaign.

Likewise, Zeb's speech in Oxford also included the themes that he had made central throughout his campaign. He maintained that the Republicans had remained in power much too long and had become hopelessly corrupt. Zeb observed: "Reforms never begin in the penitentiary. The devil never takes the lead in revivals of religion, and the only way to reform the Republican party is to serve it like the Dutchman did his worthless dog — cut off a small piece of his tail right behind the ears." Zeb claimed that Republican presidential candidate Rutherford B. Hayes would simply leave the same corrupt people in office who had been appointed by the Grant administration. Appealing to the experience of his rural listeners, Zeb related the following adage: "When an old hen has set her time on a nest of rotten eggs you do not put a new hen on the same eggs with the hope of hatching them; you take a new nest and fresh eggs." After briefly mentioning the Civil War, Zeb moved on to discuss what he felt were the Republican excesses of Reconstruction in the South. He spent a great deal of time denouncing Republican governor William W. Holden's use of the militia during the 1870 election in North Carolina. Zeb even claimed that the Republicans were responsible for one of the Klan murders that had provoked the calling of the militia; Settle and other Republicans vigorously denied the charge, however, and evidence suggests that Zeb's accusation was entirely false. Continuing his assault on the Republicans, Zeb introduced national budget figures that clearly contradicted Settle's statements and demonstrated that the government was taxing and spending much more than it had in the past. He described frauds at the Bureau of Internal Revenue that had been traced directly to Republican leaders. Finally, Zeb reassured African Americans that they would prosper under Democratic rule in the South.[31]

While Zeb's speech contained plenty of specifics and dealt with legitimate campaign issues, many in the audience remembered his points not because they were particularly brilliant but because they remembered the stories he used to illustrate them. For example, Republican efforts to shift blame onto the Democrats for the misuse of public funds reminded Zeb of the following vignette: "My competitor's reply to all this is like the fellow who was put to watching a cornfield when the fence was down. After a while the owner of the field went out to see how things were getting on and he found the field full of hungry hogs wasting and devouring the crops. Hello! said he to the fellow. Didn't I send you here to watch the field and keep these hogs out and here you turned the whole of'em in & let 'em destroy everything. Well yes so you did says the fellow, but then Mister some of them hogs in thar are your'n."

Ridiculing Republican efforts at self-reform, Zeb was apparently fond of telling the following story: "A gentleman, who once had a drunken servant [John] and wanted to reform him from his ways, read him an account of a man who had been drinking until every vein was full of whiskey and his breath was [so] strongly impregnated with the alcohol that when he went to blow out the candle, the flames ignited with his breath and there wasn't enough of the man left to make a decent funeral. John by this time was greatly scared and called for the Bible and wanted to swear off right away. The Bible was brought and John took a most solemn oath never to blow out a candle as long as he lived."[32] These stories became legendary, and they sustained Zeb's reputation as an outstanding campaigner.

Many of Zeb's shorter anecdotes depended for their humor upon his white listeners' willingness to find negative stereotypes of African Americans humorous. In Lenoir, he sought to warn blacks about the false promises of Republicans by relating the story "of the man who gave his hands watermelon to fill them up before the meal to save meat and bread." While it is doubtful that this narrative convinced many blacks to vote for him, it apparently got an appreciative laugh from white Democrats. To reassure blacks that they would have a prosperous future under a Democratic administration, Zeb told "of the little Guinea nigger he met in Yadkin who had, 'taken notice that the Democratic niggers always wore the best breeches.'"[33] Again, it is hard to believe that African Americans were anything but deeply offended by these remarks, but Zeb and many of his white auditors apparently found this kind of story both funny and appropriate.

Zeb's appeals for black support were more than matched by Republican efforts. A Republican newspaper in Raleigh wrote: "Colored men, have you all registered? *This is your last chance for freedom in North Carolina.* If the Democrats succeed, you will be worse off than when you were slaves." That same paper also accused the Democratic Party of organizing the Ku Klux Klan to kill North Carolina Republicans. Some African Americans apparently took the Republican assertions quite literally and used intimidation against other blacks who had indicated that they would support Democratic candidates. Democratic newspapers reported incidents of this type of intimidation in Charlotte and Monroe in September.[34] While these reports could have been manufactured, the fact that Republicans did not deny that they happened indicates that the violent episodes probably took place. Thus, any slim chance that Zeb might have had to pick up blacks' votes probably disappeared under the pressure brought by the African American community.

Settle and the Republicans did not limit their appeals to underclass voters simply to recalling the abuses visited on wartime Unionists and African Americans. They also appealed to small property holders and to the poor of both races. They charged that the Democrats had tried "through the amendments to abolish the homestead" by replacing "the present Supreme Court." The accusation continued: "They want to abolish the township system and restore the old county courts. They favor the imposition of a poll tax as a pre-requisite to voting. They are against the education of the poor man's children." The Republicans further charged that the "Democratic party, by its passing the oppressive Landlord and Tenant act, prove[d] itself the enemy of the poor laboring man." Finally, they appealed to poor parents by arguing that the Democrats had voted "a large sum to educate rich men's children but refused to appropriate a cent for the education of poor children."[35] Such appeals to class were clearly aimed at uniting the potential Republican constituencies across racial lines.

The response of the Democrats was to try to divide the poor along racial lines and to turn poor whites against the Republicans. For example, the *Warrenton Gazette* ran a story on September 1 in which the writer claimed that some poor white paupers, unable to pay their legal debts, had been farmed out by the Republican government to African American landowners in Jones County, where they became "white slaves." The assertion proved to be so effective that the Democratic state committee reprinted the article under the title "White Slavery in North Carolina" and distributed it widely throughout the eastern part of the state. A Democratic newspaper in Elizabeth City, not content to allow white voters to draw their own conclusions, editorialized, "Men of Pasquotank, of Perquimans, and other counties who have a Board of county commissioners composed of low whites and ignorant gizzard footed negroes, look and tremble." Writers for other Democratic papers asserted that only by voting for the amendments could whites maintain racially segregated schools. This was an inaccurate statement; the Republican state supreme court had already accepted the legality of segregated schools under the existing North Carolina Constitution. Finally, the Democrats charged that Republicans were prepared to import black voters from Virginia and Maryland to steal the election.[36]

The accusations made by both parties greatly inflamed the electorate, and the campaign debates became subject to increasing rowdiness and violence. The worst incident of violence took place in early October near Fayetteville. According to a local paper, the trouble was not inspired by partisan differences. Apparently, the excitement of the campaign itself was enough to encourage the crowd to get "uproariously drunk." Settle started the discussion and delivered his address without incident. During Zeb's speech, however, everything got out of hand, and the two candidates were forced to abandon the platform and leave town without finishing their debate. The reporter who was present stated that after the candidates left, "fisticuffs soon grew contemptible, and pistols, knives, fence-rails, sticks, rocks, and everything else that could be found to injure a man was called into play." One man emerged with broken ribs, someone else had a finger bitten off, and, according to the reporter, gouged-out eyes were "strewn around like muscadines."[37] While no similar riots occurred during the two remaining weeks of the campaign, it is clear that the passions of the entire electorate had been thoroughly aroused.

Despite the increasing tension within the entire North Carolina electoral system, Vance and Settle concluded their joint debates on October 21 at Swift Creek on a very amicable note. According to a contemporary account, "they parted friends with reciprocal words of kindness and goodwill." Zeb praised Settle for his honorable conduct and asserted that the state of North Carolina would benefit from the civil tenor of the campaign. Settle said in reply that he was pleased that he and Vance had debated fifty-seven times and had left no lasting wounds.[38] Both men's observations were accurate. When the events in North Carolina are compared with similar election campaigns that took place in South Carolina and Louisiana in 1876, the Settle-Vance debates appear to have been a model of democratic practice. The fact that other members of their parties in North Carolina would resort to illegal tactics should not obscure the constructive nature of this battle between two well-matched foes.

As election day approached, the two party organizations sought to strengthen their positions as much as possible. The Republicans, sensing that the tide was running against them, tried to defend themselves against defeat with several different tactics. A local leader contacted Republican presidential candidate Rutherford B. Hayes and asked him to promise some patronage to North Carolina Republicans to encourage them to remain in the party. One beneficiary of patronage was persuaded to give up his position and to run against Zeb's brother Robert in the mountain district for a seat in Congress. The Republicans felt that this officeholder's candidacy would add at least a thousand votes to Settle's total. In Charlotte, Republican activists were on the alert for any Democratic frauds, and they were preparing to challenge a number of Jewish immigrants who had not secured their citizenship at the polls.[39] Although somewhat beleaguered and without the resources of their opponents, the Republicans were using every political weapon available to them.

As the campaign closed, Republicans made one last appeal to former Unionists and those who had been disaffected with the Confederacy. They brought to prominence a charge that had been made rather incidentally earlier in the campaign: that Zeb had used his position as governor and obtained space on the *Advance* to have luxury goods shipped to him while other North Carolinians suffered. Democratic papers had quoted Zeb's categorical denials of the charge early in the campaign, but Republican access to Zeb's wartime correspondence allowed them to corroborate it. Unable to refute this Republican attack, Democrats persuaded A. M. McPheeters, one of Zeb's former wartime secretaries, to confirm the Republican charges while attempting to minimize their effects. McPheeters asserted that Zeb had not taken space on the ship claimed by the state. Rather, he had accepted free space from the shipping firm, Power, Low, and Company.[40] Why McPheeters and the Democrats thought that this admission would be less damaging to Zeb than some other interpretation of the evidence is not clear. In any case, if voters were going to be persuaded to cast their ballots against Zeb on the basis of his Civil War record, this revelation gave them another cogent reason to reject the war governor.

The Democrats were much better organized than the Republicans, and they had more resources available to draw upon. Despite these advantages, however, Democratic Party strategists apparently decided that it was important to emphasize the race issue at the end of the campaign. The leading Democratic paper in Raleigh called upon individual party members to support Zeb in terms that stressed the desirability of racial solidarity: "Be a white man, in deed as well as the color of your skin." On the night before the election, Democrats in Raleigh claimed that when a Democratic torchlight parade had been disrupted by a group of black Republicans an altercation had ensued. A similar incident may have been planned in Charlotte as well, but a local Republican leader reported that all had grown quiet there after the Grant administration sent troops to South Carolina to deal with election violence in that state: "Since the troops have gone to S.C. the rebel element have subsided. You know how partri[d]ges squat when the hawk is about." Elsewhere in the state, Democratic organizations resorted to scare tactics to try to ensure racial solidarity at the polls.[41]

The result of the election seemed to indicate that Zeb's campaign was a great success. Early reports pointed to a sweeping victory; Zeb even won some black votes in selected areas. He carried the state by a margin of nearly 14,000 votes of approximately 223,000 cast. A closer look at the election returns suggests, however, that Zeb's personal triumph may have been less impressive than it first appeared. Republicans claimed that Democrats allowed fraudulent returns to be made in at least two counties. In Stokes County, 2,300 votes were counted although there were only 1,800 registered voters, and Zeb received 1,100 more votes in his adopted home county of Mecklenburg than there were registered voters. While the Republican complaints of electoral fraud seem to have been legitimate, these two incidents alone would not have reduced the margin of Zeb's victory enough to elect Settle. However, one Republican charged that there was significant fraud on a smaller scale in many counties. He reported to Settle, "In every county where the Democrats had control of the Registrar who was the umpire as to challenged voters and was a rampart partisan of their side."[42] Thus, it is entirely possible that in a completely fair and free election the vote might have been a great deal closer.

Comparison of the existing presidential and gubernatorial returns also suggests that Zeb's campaign may not have been as effective as most observers have thought. Samuel Tilden, the Democratic presidential candidate, actually received seven thousand more votes than Zeb and had a margin of victory larger than Zeb's by three thousand votes. It seems obvious that Settle's attack on Zeb's war record had a significant effect on voters in selected areas. A review of the returns in individual counties where Unionism was strongest and desertion greatest during the war—Mitchell, Wilkes, Henderson, Randolph, and Moore—shows that a substantial number of white voters, in some cases a majority, supported Settle. In Henderson and Mitchell Counties, for example, Tilden won the presidential contest, but Settle received a majority of the gubernatorial votes.[43] Thus, the voters who felt that the wartime activities of Zeb's administration were of paramount importance showed their willingness to vote against the Democratic candidate for governor.

Nevertheless, Zeb probably served a very important purpose for the Democratic Party. His rousing campaign encouraged many people who had avoided taking part in elections since the end of the war to participate in 1876. James Heaton reported to Settle that "the 'poor decrepid souls that had not voted in any election since the war.' . . . finally came out of 'their hiding places' and, in a 'gross act of ingratitude,' voted for Vance." The result was that Zeb received twenty-two thousand more votes than Democratic candidate Augustus S. Merrimon had just four years before. The formerly inactive voters also supported the constitutional amendments, which passed by about the same number of votes that Zeb won by. The Democratic newspapers were ecstatic that local government would now be firmly in the party's hands. One reported that North Carolina was "now a white man's state and white men intend[ed] to govern it hereafter."[44] The spectacular Democratic campaign, which had combined Zeb and racism, had succeeded in drawing people to the polls who might otherwise have stayed at home and allowed Settle and the Republicans to win.

The long-term impact of the election was as clear as its immediate result. Republican A. V. Dockery of Rockingham wrote to embattled Republican presidential candidate Rutherford B. Hayes to encourage him and other

Northern Republicans to be as partisan as they could be in the dispute over who won the presidential election of 1876 that was evolving. He used the following assessment of the recent North Carolina campaign to justify his recommendation: "Republicanism henceforth is dead [in the] South. We will not, as such, be permitted to exist. The South must hereafter be counted solid. Democrats have revived sectionalism here."[45] Dockery was quite correct in his assessment. Zeb and the Democrats had revived sectionalism in North Carolina, and they expected to use it in the future to retain secure control of the state and local government. There is absolutely no evidence to suggest that Zeb thought that the undemocratic measures taken by the Democrats were unacceptable. As we will see, he would support the status quo created by the 1876 campaign until his death. For Zeb at least, this "settlement" of the controversies surrounding the Civil War and Reconstruction would prove to be a great personal boon.

Settle's defeat pointed to another important development in the lives of the people of North Carolina. The vast majority of the white population of the state had rejected—or chosen to ignore—the criticism of Zeb's wartime administration. From that point on, North Carolina whites began to view the war as a positive experience in which they took pride. Memories of desertion, deprivation, and government oppression began to fade in all but the most abused areas, and the history of the Confederacy took on a romantic aura. Never again would Zeb or any other North Carolina Democrat be challenged to defend the Confederacy and its policies. The romantic vision of the conflict would eventually be publicized by organizations that plastered the South with memorials to the Confederate dead, rehabilitated Jefferson Davis, and elevated Robert E. Lee to secular sainthood.[46] Zeb would take advantage of the public's changed feelings about the war to consolidate his own political power during the next fifteen years.

Z eb was understandably exhilarated by the outcome of the election. After the result became clear, he traveled to Raleigh to address a monster rally of joyous Democrats. One journalist estimated the size of the crowd that attended Zeb's speech to be ten thousand, a gigantic audience for the time, especially considering the limits of North Carolina's transportation system. The address was apparently even more informal than Zeb's usual impromptu efforts. He related a number of incidents that had indicated to him that the white population of the state was beginning to heal the wounds created by the war. For example, he recounted a story that had occurred in the heavily Republican Mitchell County in the western mountains. There he had spotted a large number of horsemen on the road carrying the flag of the United States. Zeb said that he had become quite downhearted, assuming that they were Settle supporters. But when the men saw Zeb in the distance, "they raised a shout and it was the old familiar cry for Vance and Tilden."[1] That Zeb told this story indicates that he felt completely vindicated by the campaign and believed that he and the state could now focus on the future instead of reexamining the painful past.

Unfortunately for Zeb, there was little time to enjoy the fruits of victory. The Democratic Party faithful had been kept out of public offices for nearly a decade, and many of them were impatient to be appointed to some appropriate place. Since the party had been out of office for so long and so many people had made major contributions to Zeb's victory, there were an unusually large number of applicants for every position in state government. Mountain politicians were particularly ardent in pursuit of places on the Board of Commissioners of the Western North Carolina Railroad. The most persistent of these applicants was William W. Stringfield of Waynesville. Stringfield had been a lieutenant colonel during the war in Walker's battalion of Thomas's legion in western North Carolina. After the war, he returned to his home in eastern Tennessee, but he was forced to move; his neighbors were hostile toward him because he had supported the Confederacy during the conflict. Stringfield then went to Haywood County, North Carolina, where his wife's family lived. After Zeb's brother Robert was elected to Congress in 1872, Stringfield moved with him to Washington to act as his clerk for a time. Afterward, although Stringfield was establishing himself as a successful hotel owner in Waynesville, he still desired a government position.[2] For a period of five weeks in late 1876, he and his friends inundated Zeb with requests that the governor appoint Springfield as a commissioner.

While Stringfield was the most persistent of the applicants, Zeb was soon overwhelmed with many other requests for positions. Applicants from Jackson and McDowell Counties also asked to be named to the position that Stringfield coveted. Others pleaded to be made members of the state judiciary, and one petition supported a candidate for the position of state librarian. Making a claim on Vance that would become more insistent as the patronage fight continued, places were sought for and by wounded veterans of Confederate service.[3] These claimants were undoubtedly prompted to write to Zeb by the praise that he had heaped upon Confederate soldiers during the course of the fall campaign. Most of the state positions sought by the party faithful were not Zeb's to bestow. In an effort to maintain some semblance of order, most positions were assigned to a specific geographical area, and only applicants from that location were considered for appointment. Many in the party were unaware of this arrangement, however, and Zeb continued to receive an outpouring of patronage requests.

Business interests in the state also tried to influence the new governor and to persuade him that their particular concerns needed immediate attention. Several of those interested in the state's railroad system urged Zeb to appoint members of the commission carefully in order to ensure the rapid completion of the desirable network. The president of the company responsible for the construction of the Albemarle and Chesapeake Canal (or the Great Dismal Swamp Canal, as it was more commonly known) sought to encourage the new governor to continue state support. Finally, another businessman reported that a compromise had been reached between the state and its creditors on the status of bonds on which the state had been forced to default.[4] Virtually all governors of the late nineteenth century wrestled with problems of this nature, and it was becoming clear that Zeb would be no exception.

Some of Zeb's correspondence during this period was more personal, and it brought its own unique pressures to bear upon him. Cornelia Phillips Spencer resumed her correspondence with Zeb, and the two friends rejoiced in the outcome in North Carolina. Able to express himself without fear of being compromised in public, Zeb boasted: "There are many delightful memories connected with the campaign. It was fought avowedly on my 'war record'—in the vilest and bitterest style. . . . [Y]et my vote exceeds by near 20,000 that ever cast for any man in N.C. before. I was met by the largest crowds, the most intense enthusiasm, and by the evidences of the warmest personal regards not to say devotion—that I reckon any man ever received in our state." This private comment probably captures Zeb's frame of mind better than any of his other correspondence from this period does. In other correspondence, all of which arrived in a single month, an Asheville businessman wrote twice to alert Zeb to some problems associated with Hattie's rental property in that city. A relative wrote from western North Carolina to request a state patronage position and to announce that despite his interest in Zeb's success, he could not attend his cousin's inaugural; needless to say, he did not receive his desired appointment. Finally, Thomas Settle wrote Zeb a short letter to explain some of his published remarks that he felt were open to misinterpretation. Settle told Vance that he did not want to appear to be initiating hostilities, because he felt that the recent canvass had increased the friendship between the two men.[5] These matters pressed for Zeb's attention, but the enthusiasm that he had expressed in his letter to Cornelia Phillips Spencer enabled him to carry his new responsibilities without any major problems.

As Zeb sought to bring some order to his life amid its many pressures, others prepared for his inaugural address with great enthusiasm. The owner of the largest hotel in Raleigh announced that he could accept no more reservations. He said that he could not accommodate all who had already contacted him "if he were to put ten to twenty in a room and three and four in every bed." North Carolina railroads, anticipating large crowds for the inauguration, scheduled many special trains to and from Raleigh. To make sure that everyone who wanted to could see and hear the new governor deliver his address, a private contractor built a huge platform to hold Zeb and all of the dignitaries who wanted to sit on the stage with him. While all of these preparations were made, however, no one took into account that the ceremony would take place in the middle of the winter season. January 1 dawned "dark and dismal." By ten o'clock it had started to snow, and the flakes were very large and falling fast. A call went out to the state prison, and a large number of prisoners were detailed to remove all of the snow from the inaugural grounds. As the hour of Zeb's speech approached, however, prudence prevailed and the ceremony was moved inside.[6] Thus, many who had come long distances were denied the opportunity to hear the address, and the festivities that followed it were muted.

This unpleasant turn of events did not dampen Zeb's spirits, however. The hall was very crowded, so much so that it appeared at first that Zeb would have great difficulty reaching the stage to take his oath. After the other officers had sworn to uphold the state constitution, Zeb stepped for-

Vance after his third election to the governorship in 1876.
(North Carolina Division of Archives and History, Raleigh)

ward and repeated the simple phrases to the delight of the multitude. Then he delivered his address with considerable enthusiasm despite the change of venue. He started with an observation: "There is retribution in history. For all of the wrongs and inequalities of individual and national life there is compensation, provided we do but patiently await its coming." For the next hour, Zeb delivered an address that was essentially a rehash of his standard campaign speech minus the humor, which must have seemed unsuitable for the state occasion. He unfortunately did not eliminate the remarks from the speech that demonstrated his hostility toward his political opponents. For example, he attacked the Republicans in the following terms:

"North Carolina was placed in the hands of [the] designing and ignorant of our people, organized and led by unscrupulous and disreputable adventurers from the slums of Northern politics; a base . . . tribe of reptiles which seem to spring like fungi from the rottenness and corruption of revolutionary times." In a much more positive line, Zeb stated that Reconstruction had demonstrated the problems an ignorant electorate could cause, and he called for a much more comprehensive state educational system.[7] After the speech concluded, the large concourse celebrated as much as the weather would allow.

In addition to the state issues he addressed, Zeb spoke out on the great national crisis that threatened the political stability of the United States. The presidential election of 1876 had ended in confusion, with both Democrats and Republicans claiming the electoral votes of Florida, Louisiana, and South Carolina. Since having these electoral votes meant the difference between victory and defeat in the national contest, both parties were threatening to disrupt the government in Washington. All Democrats were convinced that Tilden had won at least one of the states and thereby earned a majority in the Electoral College, and they therefore felt that Tilden should be the next president. Some hotheads in the South threatened to restart the Civil War again to seat Tilden. Zeb, however, had already concluded in November that the Republicans would find a way to reclaim the presidency. Thus, he counseled moderation and restraint in a period when others thought the situation was uncertain and foreboding. He pointed out that the people of North Carolina had been "blasted . . . by the devastation of war: purged of rashness by the fires of revolution and sobered both by public calamity and private sorrow." He further observed, "more than all things else, except good government, we need peace." Because of this need for peace, Zeb urged the people of North Carolina to support Tilden within the political process and not "embark in revolution."[8] In the overheated atmosphere of the time, Zeb was a highly responsible guide to the people of North Carolina and the South.

Perhaps recognizing that his inaugural address had not been sufficiently conciliatory, Zeb made another address the next day to a very different audience. For more than an hour, he spoke without notes to African Americans gathered to celebrate the anniversary of the Emancipation Proclamation. Zeb began his discussion at Raleigh's Metropolitan Hall by trying to establish some credibility with an audience made up of people who rightfully resented much of his recent campaign rhetoric about African Americans. He started out by assuring his auditors that he was bound by his oath to respect the rights of all citizens. He reiterated his commitment, announced in his inaugural address, to providing improved and equal education for all North Carolinians. Zeb then endorsed the idea of celebrating the Emancipation Proclamation, stating that he understood the reason for African Americans' joy. Finally, he delivered political advice that demonstrated that he truly did not understand the problems faced by his audience. He encouraged all of his auditors to become free men politically and to cease voting as a group. He maintained that only when they exercised individual judgment would they be fully integrated into the political system.[9] While most of the African Americans at the meeting must have recognized the self-serving nature of Zeb's advice, they appreciated that he made the gesture of appearing before them. At several points during the speech, they applauded Vance with some enthusiasm.

On January 13, Zeb sent a message to the recently assembled legislature outlining the program that he felt needed to be followed in order for the Democrats to carry out the pledges they had made in the recent campaign. Many of the items he addressed were priorities established by one or more of the amendments to the state constitution the voters had approved less than two months before. He began with a diatribe against corrupt local government; this served as his justification for making the changes in county governance that the Democrats had called for during the 1876 campaign. Zeb's recommendations sounded a cautionary note, however. He suggested: "1st. That whatever system of county government you adopt shall be uniform. 2d. That you violate the elective principle in the selection of county officers as slightly as possible." Zeb continued, "I would not recommend any change greatly radical, for my opinion is that public sentiment will rapidly cure the evils complained of without departure from the principles of elective representation."[10] These words of caution were widely ignored—the governor of North Carolina did not possess veto power—and the Democratic legislature placed control of local government in its own hands. This policy created an oligarchic structure in state and local government that later encouraged the rise of a powerful Populist Party in the state in the 1890s.

The next major initiative that Zeb recommended was the establishment of a Department of Agriculture, Immigration, and Statistics. He explained, "[The] farmer alone has been left without any public aid to enable him to grasp the improvements and advances which science has been evolving for his benefit." He also encouraged the legislature to establish a board to gather detailed economic statistics from all parts of the state. Zeb maintained that this action would be absolutely essential if North Carolina was to prosper. He also spoke in support of establishing an "Experiment Station" in agriculture at the University of North Carolina. In a related comment, the new governor urged the legislature to provide the means for restocking the state's rivers with fish and for removing obstacles from the coastal rivers so that some species could return to their spawning grounds. This new initiative, he hoped, would also be the responsibility of the Department of Agriculture.[11]

Along the same lines, Zeb supported the expansion of the role of the state university. First, he suggested that the state geologist be made part of the faculty so that important geological work would continue and others would be trained in the important area of inquiry. The new governor also made a plea for a "normal," or teacher education, department to be added to the university. He deplored the low level of preparedness among public school teachers and urged the legislators to provide funding for a professorship in this field. Following up on the pledges he had made two weeks before, Zeb also called for the creation of a separate normal school for African Americans. He asserted, "It is our plain duty to make no discrimination in the matter of public education." He justified the departure from Democratic Party policy by explaining that better education would provide North Carolina blacks with an incentive to remain in the state.[12]

On other matters, Zeb called for small changes in existing policies. He recommended that the administration of the Western Insane Asylum and the Board of Public Charities be improved. He applauded the decision of past legislators to force convicts to work on public projects across the state and, demonstrating his ongoing interest in his native region, he recommended that all convicts not assigned to a particular project be sent to the Western North Carolina Railroad construction crew in McDowell County. Zeb, like most of the people beyond the Blue Ridge escarpment, felt that western North Carolina had waited too long for rail connections. He promised that with sufficient labor, the tracks would be completed from "the present terminus of the road to the French Broad River" before the legislature assembled again. Like most of North Carolina's political leaders, Zeb saw no urgent reason to pay off the state debt. He called for the legislature to initiate further negotiations with the bondholders with an eye to the eventual settlement of this difficult issue. Having outlined the responsibilities that he believed the legislature should assume, Zeb ended his message by predicting future prosperity for the state.[13]

After months of making speeches, Zeb was forced to deal with the practical problems of administering the state government. One of his first actions, perhaps the most important to his political future, was to distribute government offices to deserving Democrats. The proper accomplishment of this task was crucial to the new governor for several reasons. The distribution of patronage gave him an opportunity to reward his friends and to create a statewide network of men who had a personal interest in his future political success. Zeb's ultimate objective, even this early in his gubernatorial administration, was to be elected to the U.S. Senate. In early January, he sent a large number of nominees to the state Senate for confirmation. Apparently these nominations had already been cleared with state and local party officials, because they were confirmed without dissent within three days. The new officials soon discovered, however, that the institutions they had inherited were not the sinecures that they may have hoped for. The new state librarian reported that his facility in Raleigh was in poor condition and that he needed immediate assistance. Likewise, the new director of the yellow fever quarantine hospital in Wilmington reported that he had inherited a depleted inventory and a facility in great need of repair.[14] Thus, the new Vance administration could claim to be acting as a reform administration, providing greatly improved services and making expeditious appointments of more qualified individuals to public offices.

Despite the early indications that the distribution of patronage was going well, difficulties and controversies soon developed for Zeb and his Democratic colleagues. Most predictably, the appointment of county-level officials brought difficulties where large numbers of potential appointees had high expectations. In one instance, Zeb wrote to William S. Carter: "Mr. Geo. W. Swindell has tendered his resignation as Commissioner of your County, which has been accepted. He recommends W. P. Burns or Henry Jones as his successor. Please advise me as to the proper man." As Vance's letter indicates, he and his party were concerned about the quality of the people they placed in office; they apparently wished to appoint men who would offer a contrast to the "unqualified" Republicans who had preceded them. After Carter indicated the proper person, he was forced to write to Zeb to announce that the nominee had refused to accept the position. In most instances, however, local political activists were grateful for the patronage, and confirmation of their nominations was speedily granted by the state Senate.[15]

Filling state offices also presented some unanticipated difficulties. For example, Zeb nominated a new slate of board members for the insane asylum, and the state Senate promptly approved his nominees. The Republican incumbents refused to leave their positions, however. Zeb was forced to ask for a formal opinion from the attorney general of North Carolina on whether the Republican officials could be replaced. Not unexpectedly, that official, Democrat Thomas S. Kenan, informed the governor that the sitting members of the asylum's board could be replaced. Unlike the appointed employees of virtually every other agency in the state government, however, the incumbents were able to resist replacement for a considerable period of time. Even when other attorneys confirmed the attorney general's opinion, Zeb found himself facing a national crusader with a political power he could not ignore. The incumbent director, Dr. Eugene Grissom, was a nationally recognized expert in the treatment of the mentally ill. One of Grissom's supporters who wrote directly to Zeb was Dorothea L. Dix, the person who had led the campaign to create the asylum in Raleigh in the first place. A cautious Zeb had to inform the Democratic applicants for Grissom's position that they would have to wait until the situation was fully resolved before requesting it. There were a wide variety of official positions available for Zeb's friends; he also sent nominations to the senate for the directors of the Western North Carolina Railroad and the board members of the North Carolina Institution for the Deaf, Dumb, and Blind.[16] It was particularly important to Zeb to fill these state positions with the right men, because these appointees could become future state legislators who would play a significant role in the selection of U.S. senators.

Although Zeb seemed to possess sweeping patronage power, he found that there were limitations on it, particularly in the field of education. When two teachers wrote to Zeb demanding that they be reinstated in their positions as political appointees, Zeb, probably with considerable relief, informed the pair that he had no power over the employment of teachers. When the North Carolina legislature followed Zeb's recommendation and created a normal school for African American teachers, Zeb felt constrained to pass over white Democrats for the position of director. Instead, Zeb named Robert Harris, an African American, to that position. Significantly, there was no hue and cry from Democrats about the appointment. This may have been due in part to the fact that Harris was not an "offensive" partisan; his letter of acceptance showed what Zeb and other white Democrats would have regarded as appropriate deference.[17] Moreover, Zeb and his fellow Democrats had committed themselves to providing equal educational opportunities, and Harris's symbolic appointment relieved them of further responsibility in the area of African American education.

One omission of the legislature, however, allowed Zeb and other Democratic leaders to reap political benefit from the new normal school for African Americans: the legislators had failed to designate a site for the new institution. They had also failed to designate a site for the new asylum for the insane that they had created for black North Carolinians. A virtual frenzy of activity swept the state as communities sought to attract the normal school. Residents of Fayetteville, Charlotte, Goldsboro, Weldon, New Bern, Salisbury, Greensboro, Raleigh, and Iredell County all tried to persuade Zeb's administration that their community would be an ideal place to house the school. Significantly, the local white leadership often worked closely with African American communities in these campaigns. Fayetteville mounted a particularly impressive petition drive and was chosen as the host city. Whether the Vance administration was impressed with the local support for the normal school or whether a secret political deal was responsible for the decision to award the school to Fayetteville is difficult to reconstruct. The asylum, in contrast, provoked only mild interest; Wilmington, Goldsboro, and Edgecombe County bid to host the institution.[18] In both cases, however, the ability to distribute patronage of this magnitude allowed Zeb to strengthen his political standing within the state.

As important as these new institutions were as public projects, Zeb's interest in them was dwarfed by his commitment to completing the Western North Carolina Railroad. His single-minded devotion to bringing the railroad to Asheville before he left office led Zeb to make two of his least reputable decisions. The first involved a large number of railroad bonds that had been issued by the Republican legislature during Reconstruction. Carpetbagger Milton S. Littlefield and native North Carolinian George W. Swepson had bribed the legislature to issue excess securities for the Western North Carolina Railroad. The two men subsequently misappropriated bonds worth approximately $4 million. After the Democrats returned to power in the legislature, they repudiated much of this debt without specifically admitting that they were doing so. The situation demanded a solution, and the bondholders were constantly contacting Zeb and suggesting alternative policies. Zeb apparently decided simply to prevent any constructive action from being taken. Certainly he suspected many of the bondholders of being guilty of "general villainy," and he believed that the out-of-state bondholders were undercutting the state's interests. Still, he recognized that something would eventually have to be done, and he exclaimed to one correspondent, "For Gods sake lets break this company out of its old ruts if we can."[19] Nevertheless, Zeb took no definitive action before he left office in January 1879.

The second decision involved the use of convict labor to construct the railroad. By the time that Zeb became governor in 1877, the railroad line had reached the base of the Blue Ridge in McDowell County. The engineering problem that faced the state there was one of the most significant east of the Rocky Mountains. The road would have to ascend nearly a thousand feet in a distance of three and one-third miles. To accomplish this difficult task, the final route would contain the equivalent of eight complete circles in the nine miles of track up the cliffs and sharp rises. As noted earlier, Zeb, in his first message to the legislature, had recommended that all available state convicts be sent to the Western North Carolina Railroad camp in McDowell County. He also requested that county prisoners who would have been transferred to the state penitentiary be sent directly to this same camp.[20] The use of convict labor was becoming standard throughout the South during this period. By placing convicts at work sites, the Southern states eliminated many of the costs of maintaining the prisoners in prison buildings. The use of convict labor also allowed the state to make investments in projects through labor without having to raise taxes.[21] Since the vast majority of prisoners were African Americans, the convict labor system differed very little from the coerced industrial labor system of slavery.

Zeb's plan to complete the railroad quickly ran into immediate problems. First, the members of the Board of Directors at the state penitentiary offered an alternative plan for the prison population. They requested that 250 prisoners be retained in Raleigh to construct a modern facility that would eventually house prisoners. Since their request required an additional outlay of ten thousand dollars and offered none of the savings of Zeb's plan, he was able to reject it as economically impractical. The problem was that Zeb did not have enough money to carry out his own plan. The meager state appropriations for the prison system and the railroad did not provide enough money to transport the prisoners to Old Fort and provide them with sufficient equipment to do the required work. With that fact in mind, Zeb wrote a letter to the chairman of the Buncombe County Commission in which he asked the local elite to raise twenty-five thousand dollars to be used to acquire needed construction equipment. J. E. Rankin's reply stated that he had shown the governor's letter to some of Buncombe County's "most prominent citizens" and he had discovered "that no subscription either private or public could be obtained for the W.N.C.R Road." The outraged chief executive fired back a scorching reply. He began by informing Rankin that his letter had "caused [Zeb] great surprise and mortification." Zeb explained that he had assumed that most of the people of his home county were eagerly awaiting the coming of the railroad. He could only conclude, he wrote, that the leading men of Asheville were upset because Zeb had not appointed them to prominent state offices. He ended his diatribe with a most revealing observation: "I intend to finish the Road to Asheville in less than two years whether Buncombe County helps me or not."[22] Zeb's use of the personal pronoun in this sentence indicates that the construction of the line up the Blue Ridge had become a personal crusade for him that would brook no challenges.

Zeb was assisted in his drive to complete the construction by James W. Wilson of the Western North Carolina Railroad. Shortly after receiving the "mortifying" letter from the chairman of the Buncombe County Commission, Zeb got a note from Wilson with the following promise: "If our quota [of convicts] is furnished and my plans are not obstructed by the Penitentiary Board I will reach Asheville in 12 months." This was precisely the kind of positive and confident talk that the governor wanted to hear, and by using it Wilson ensured that Zeb would firmly back him. From Wilson's perspective, however, the penitentiary board was blocking his efforts to expedite construction. In June 1877, Zeb leaned on the board to try to get its members to assist Wilson. Vance reported to the board members that Wilson and his associate Ephraim Clayton "complain[ed] that the Railroad authorities are retarded in their operations by conflicting opinions [with penitentiary officials] as to time and manner of working, excusing from work, &c." He continued, "I think it would greatly promote the efficiency of the force if Mr Clayton should be allowed to control the convicts in all matters except the guarding, care of them &c." Apparently this system was agreed to, and in December 1877 the penitentiary board announced that it had provided its quota of five hundred convicts for the Western North Carolina Railroad.[23]

Clearly, the situation was open to abuse. Wilson and Clayton recognized that Zeb was primarily interested in results. The restraining hand of the penitentiary board had been removed, and construction was begun in earnest. Although Zeb was physically removed from the day-to-day events at the site, he was fully aware that abuses might occur there. In July 1877, he wrote a strong letter to the penitentiary board about the abuse of prisoners at other locations. It read in part: "Information has reached me from sources entirely reliable that the convicts on the Chester & Lenoir Narrow Gauge Railroad have been treated with considerable cruelty both by whipping and overwork. The same reports reach me from the convicts on the Spartanburg and Asheville Railroad. This state of things is not to be tolerated for a moment and I beg you to take immediate steps to . . . punish the guilty parties and to provide against the reoccurrence of such disgraceful conduct."[24] Thus, Zeb had both created conditions for the Western North Carolina Railroad workers that could lead to substantial abuse and attempted to mitigate similar abuse in other locations. The question that he would soon face was whether his desire to build the railroad to Asheville was stronger than his concerns about convict safety.

Unfortunately, it was. Zeb's insistence on completing the railroad line was responsible for terrible suffering and many workers' deaths. By 1878, the majority of the state's convicts (558) were working in dangerous conditions and in inclement weather on the line. Wilson reported on March 4 that there had been an "unusual fall of snow and rain" during the winter of 1877–78. Wilson's report indicated that despite the bad weather, convicts had worked on the railroad for eighty-eight of the ninety days of December 1877–February 1878. The prisoners got only Christmas Day and one day in February off during the entire period; Sundays were just another workday for them. Later that year, Wilson reported that the state and the company

The Swannanoa Tunnel under construction in 1878 and 1879. Vance's push to complete the Western North Carolina Railroad led to deaths of many convicts. (North Carolina Division of Archives and History, Raleigh)

were spending only thirty cents a day to maintain the prisoners, seven cents of which went to food.[25] This level of support was totally inadequate. Many of the deaths that occurred during the construction project were caused by the demanding work schedule and the inadequate food and care provided to the prisoners.

Wilson's report did not cause Zeb to back away from his goal. In 1878, the North Carolina legislature approved funding for the continuation of the work on the western line provided that the Western North Carolina Railroad reroute some of its tracks near Newton in the Piedmont. In order to do so, Wilson would have had to take convicts from the McDowell County site; this action would have slowed the pace of the work in the mountains. Zeb intervened and persuaded the directors of the Chester and Lenoir Railroad—the same officials he had earlier criticized for being cruel to their workers—to move prisoners from their line to Newton who could make the required changes. In his letter to the company directors, Zeb wrote, "It would break my heart to take hands from the mountains to work this road."[26] Once again Zeb had personalized the completion of the Western North Carolina Railroad in a way that left state officials little discretion in their use of state laborers.

The consequence of the unrelenting schedule that Zeb dictated was that approximately 125 convicts died during the construction of the Western North Carolina Railroad. It thereby qualifies as one of the most egregious industrial construction disasters in North Carolina history. The official explanation for the slaughter was that many of those who died were African Americans from the eastern part of the state who were unprepared for the cold winter weather. While the weather was undoubtedly a factor in many prisoners' deaths, there were at least two other significant causes of death. The construction work itself was extremely dangerous; at least 21 convicts died in cave-ins and accidents in the Swannanoa Tunnel alone. In addition, guards shot and killed prisoners who sought to escape. Zeb was not unaware of the harsh treatment doled out to the convicts. While Wilson did not provide full details, he and his associates did inform Vance when prisoners perished. Zeb's usual response was to demand that the work continue at the same rigorous pace despite the toll that it was taking on the prisoners. While he acknowledged some of the problems associated with the convict labor system in his address to the legislature in January 1879, he never accepted responsibility for the tragedy that he had helped to create.[27]

The extent of the convict laborers' suffering is not adequately expressed in the death count from the construction site. Local color writer Rebecca Harding Davis observed the work and reported: "The gorge swarmed with hundreds of wretched blacks in the striped yellow convict garb. After their supper was cooked (over campfires) and eaten, they were driven into a row of prison cars, where they were tightly boxed for the night, with no possible chance to obtain either air or light." In a report to the state made in 1884, a physician acknowledged that exceedingly high numbers of deaths resulted from such conditions, but he made no recommendations for remediation. The warden of the state penitentiary pointed to the ongoing horror of the convicts' situation in his report: "[Many convicts had] taken their regular shifts for several years in the Swannanoa and other tunnels on the Western North Carolina Railway [and] were finally returned to the prisons with shattered constitutions and their physical strength entirely gone, so that [with even] the most skillful medical treatment and the best nursing, it was impossible for them to recuperate."[28] Thus, the actual number of people killed by their work on the Western North Carolina Railroad probably numbered many dozens more than the figure reported in the official documents of the company. Although Zeb never acknowledged the full extent of the suffering he imposed, he did fulfill his political commitment to extend the railroad to Asheville.

While Zeb was coping with a demanding schedule of official duties, he was also burdened with personal and family obligations. To fulfill one such obligation, Zeb delivered a memorial address on the life of his mentor David L. Swain at the University of North Carolina in 1877. Zeb was, of course, extremely sympathetic toward his subject. He painted a very positive portrait of a man that he had deeply admired. The address was also carefully researched. It was the only one of Zeb's historical expositions for which he provided precisely accurate dates, locations, and names. In the address, Zeb was careful to use stories that demonstrated Swain's humanity, the characteristic that made him a much loved teacher and person, including one that stressed the former governor's mania for family history. The portrait was generally laudatory, but Zeb did make a seemingly disparaging remark: "In many senses of the term Gov. Swain was not a great man. As an author, though a man of letters, he neither achieved nor attempted anything lasting. As a politician, though he rose rapidly to the highest honors of his native State, he did not strikingly impress himself upon his times by any great speech, or by any grand stroke of policy. . . . As a lawyer and a judge, he occupied comparatively about the same position; and as a scholar he was not to be distinguished, being inferior to several of his co-laborers in the University." Zeb then concluded that Swain's greatness was personal rather than public.[29] In the address, Zeb gave the impression that he was a biographer and a historian in complete command of his material. He had set aside precious time from his official duties willingly in order to prepare the tribute to Swain.

Likewise, there is no reason to think that Zeb resented his family obligations, but they did present him with emotional jolts that eventually brought him close to a complete collapse. His four sons were all beginning to reach adulthood, and they collectively presented quite a challenge to their father. Due to Hattie's ill health, Zeb had to assume most of the responsibility for their care. Zebbie secured an appointment to West Point through his father's influence. While he apparently applied himself to the demanding regimen of the service academy, he was at best a mediocre student, and he was a worry to his father. Thomas, the youngest, was a student at the Bingham School in Asheville; he did not excel there, and the principal characterized him as "lazy." David had left North Carolina for eastern Tennessee, where he was apparently living the life of an irresponsible youth. He frequently asked his father for money and even managed to lose his train ticket in Memphis, consequently stranding himself for nearly a week. Zeb brought this prodigal back to Charlotte and placed him in a law firm where some friends could watch him. They reported that he partied a great deal, and there were early signs that he already had an alcohol problem.[30] Apparently only Charlie, who worked for his father in the governor's office in Raleigh, was reliable.

The fairly predictable problems with his sons were not Zeb's major family concerns, however. Throughout his second gubernatorial administration, both his mother's and Hattie's health declined steadily. In a business letter in April 1878, Zeb mentioned his mother's serious illness as a cause of the delay in his reply to Cornelia Phillips Spencer. At the end of the same letter he commented that Hattie had "been quite unwell," but he hoped that she was "growing better." Throughout the summer and early fall, however, the two women's health continued to decline. On October 4, Zeb's mother apparently suffered a final stroke. She lost the ability to speak and died late in the day. Zeb was not present at the time of her death, but he was assured by his family that she spoke her last words—"Give my love to Zebulon"—in response to a telegram he sent her. In late October, Zeb wrote to one correspondent, "I solemnly assert that I would exchange the feeling that those blessed assurances of my mother's love and approbation inspired for all the honors I ever received or may receive in this world."[31] His other comments indicated that he was greatly shaken by the events surrounding her death and the funeral.

At the end of the letter to Spencer, Zeb commented on Hattie's condition. He sadly reported, "If the physicians are to be relied on, we can not shut our eyes to the fact that she is slowly but surely sinking away." Equally distressing to Zeb was the fact that "her sufferings [were] simply inexpressible." Two weeks later, Hattie died. While her death was expected, its rapidity unnerved Zeb, particularly given that his mother had died so recently. He had asked Hattie's doctor to give him at least two days' notice when she was about to die so that he could bring his sons to their mother's bedside in Raleigh. The doctor informed Zeb that the end was near at 10 A.M. on Sunday November 3, but by 3 P.M. she had died. Because he had such short notice, Zebulon Jr. could not get a leave of absence to attend his mother's funeral. Zebulon Sr. and his other three sons left Raleigh on Monday and accompanied Hattie's body on the long train ride back to Asheville. The funeral was held on Wednesday, and more than two thousand people attended the burial ceremony. Hattie was laid to rest beside her infant son Espy, who had died more than two decades before.[32]

A distraught Zeb wrote to Cornelia Phillips Spencer a week after Hattie's death and tried to make sense of all of the tragedy that had so recently visited him. He sought refuge in "God—her [Hattie's] God," he told Spencer, so that the "influence" of the tragedies would not "be lost on himself or her children." He continued: "I fear to face the world which lies before me without her help. How can I do my duty to my boys, now at so dangerous an age, without that firm moral hand to aid me, without that courageous & upright heart to sustain me! If such a mother as mine was, and such a wife could barely prevent my being a castaway, what am I to do now that I have lost both[?]" As Zeb had hinted, he found the answer to his last question in religion. The exact nature of the religious experience Zeb had following Hattie's death is unclear, but it induced him to formally join a church for the first time in his life. He became a member of the Second Presbyterian Church of Raleigh, and many of his friends were delighted by his action.[33] Zeb was basically not an introspective person; his conversion was a reaction to the deaths of the two most important women in his life.

Mixed in with the letters of condolence were reminders that Zeb was about to reach the climax of his postwar political career. Fortunately for Zeb, his campaign to secure a seat in the U.S. Senate had been well underway long before the tragic autumn of 1878. As early as December 1877, leading Democrats in the state had been corresponding with the new governor about his chances of succeeding Augustus S. Merrimon in the Senate. As Democrats started to hold county conventions to select the legislative candidates who would elect the next U.S. senator, Vance's supporters kept him very well informed about developments in all parts of the state. While they generally reported good news, they did warn Zeb of some potential problems. For example, one ally mentioned that there was considerable dissatisfaction with Zeb's appointments in western Carteret County. Another correspondent warned that the future distribution of patronage in the state railroad system posed a potential danger. Zeb was also cautioned about growing divisions among Democrats in several parts of the state.[34]

The Republicans and some former Whigs who had joined the Democrats during Reconstruction sought to take advantage of the dissatisfaction of some Democratic constituencies. Former Whig leader James M. Leach tried to create an opposition party made up of former Whigs and current Republicans in the spring of 1877. Apparently accepting the invitation extended by President Rutherford B. Hayes to conservatives in the South during his tour of the region in the fall of 1877, Leach, formerly both a U.S. congressman and an antiwar Confederate congressman, was looking for a way to gain enough support to be elected to the U.S. Senate. His attempts did not amount to much, but they indicated the presence of disaffection with the Democrats among the white electorate. This unease was reflected in the defection of enough Democrats in the state legislature from the party line to prevent a poll tax, which would have denied many poor whites and blacks the right to vote, from being imposed.[35] Thus it is clear that the Republicans still retained considerable strength as the state elections of 1878 approached.

Unexpectedly, the North Carolina Republicans adopted a most unorthodox strategy in the 1878 campaign. Meeting in Raleigh in July, the state executive committee "decided that it was 'inexpedient' to put up a ticket for state offices, and due to a lack of funds, and the apathy of Republicans generally over administration policies, [concluded] it would be best to disband the party." This bombshell was directed at several targets. One of the objectives of the party leadership was to protest President Hayes's decision to appoint conservative Democrats to important patronage positions in the South. At the local level, moreover, the decision was not defeatist, but tactical. The absence of a formal Republican canvass encouraged dissatisfied Democrats to announce themselves as candidates, and many did, running against regular Democrats who had endorsed Zeb's Senate candidacy. The shrewd Republican policy had an immediate impact. One Democratic paper reported: "The pledging of candidates for seats in the Legislature in favor of some particular man, is having a disastrous effect on the Democratic party—it has already caused several County Conventions to break up in a row—and unless discontinued will; we fear, divide, weaken and ultimately ruin the Democratic party in North Carolina. . . . and the bad feeling is spreading in other counties, so that we hear of 'bolters' and 'independents' in all directions." The party regulars were completely powerless to prevent the spread of political factionalism. As a result, independent Democratic and Republican candidates made a significant showing in the legislative elections.[36] While the regular Democrats retained a majority of the seats in the legislature, their position was not strong. It now seemed possible that some sort of political deal like the one that had denied Zeb his election to the Senate in 1872 would once again be struck.

The same person who had benefited from the previous split in Democratic ranks positioned himself to take advantage of the now fluid electoral situation. On June 1, Senator Augustus S. Merrimon issued a long statement designed to stake out his position for the coming battle for the U.S. Senate seat. Significantly, he addressed himself to the outcome of the 1872 caucus and subsequent events in the state legislature. He once again denied that he had made any deal with the Republicans to obtain election six years before. He also again attacked Zeb for undermining the caucus process during that election by obtaining pledges of support from legislators before the caucus began. As noted earlier, Zeb had used political tactics that were increasingly coming into vogue in the post–Civil War world. Merrimon's statement indicated that he had not adapted to such political changes in the intervening period. He protested, "Such a practice has never prevailed in North Carolina before; it is novel and contravenes the free spirit that animates our conservative people." Most of Zeb's political supporters judged Merrimon's attack to be feeble and ineffective, and Zeb made little effort to answer Merrimon's charges directly.[37]

The Senate election remained a matter of interest throughout the fall of

1878 as elections were held to fill North Carolina's seats in the U.S. Congress. The Republicans once again declined to run official candidates for most of the seats, but they supported a variety of unofficial nominees, including candidates who were affiliated with the party as well as independent nominees. Because of the crises in his family life, Zeb played no active role in the campaign. Despite both the somewhat untraditional nature of the campaign and Zeb's absence, he continued to gain support as a candidate for the Senate. When the election was over and one Republican and one independent candidate had defeated the Democratic congressional candidates, the battle for the Senate seat began in earnest. Shedding his Olympian attitude of a few months earlier, Merrimon became a whirlwind of activity. He began to circulate literature to party leaders, including a letter from a "maimed soldier" who attacked Zeb for his actions during the Civil War. Despite his feverish activity, however, Merrimon was unable to make a dent in Zeb's support. In fact, surviving documents appear to indicate that Merrimon's campaigning convinced many legislators to support Zeb in the coming crisis.[38]

Before the Senate election would take place, however, Zeb had responsibilities as governor to discharge. The most important of these was to prepare his recommendations and assessment of state programs for the incoming legislature. He was very pleased to be able to announce that the construction of the Western North Carolina Railroad was proceeding well and that trains would soon be able to travel into Asheville. He mentioned some of the problems associated with the convict labor system, but he offered legislators no viable alternative to the existing system. While acknowledging that the state faced a debt crisis, moreover, Zeb had no specific solution to it to suggest to the incoming lawmakers. He congratulated the legislature for providing the state with a Board of Agriculture and praised that organization for assisting the state's beleaguered farmers. He said that he was particularly pleased to describe the excellent work of the normal programs for black and white teachers. Zeb announced that the school for African Americans at Fayetteville had been an "unexpected success." In a report that broke little new ground in general, Zeb did recommend an interesting innovation for the normal schools. Funding for these schools had been earmarked by law for the training of male teachers. Zeb argued that this policy was "ungallant" at best and that it should be remedied to allow women to receive state-funded teacher training.[39] In the document generally, Zeb looked back rather than forward, since he anticipated that he would not be governor much longer.

When Zeb delivered his message to the state legislature, it looked as though the battle to elect a U.S. senator might be a bitter one. The organization of the legislature seemed to bode ill for Zeb, because a Democrat who had bolted the party to support Merrimon in 1872 had recently been elected Speaker. Some newspapers began to forecast a very bitter contest. When the Democratic caucus met on the evening of January 13, however, "a letter was read from Senator Merrimon withdrawing his name from consideration as a candidate." A newspaper report described the scene that followed: "Gov. Vance was nominated by the Democratic caucus . . . amid great enthusiasm, and responded to the call of a committee with an address on the triumph of party organization." On January 21, the election was held in the two houses of the state legislature. Zeb won 110 votes, Republican R. P. Buxton 51, Merrimon 2, and another candidate received 1 vote. Reports indicated that some Republicans would have been willing to support Vance if they had thought that Merrimon posed a real threat.[40] Little official business remained for Zeb to do. He announced his resignation as governor, effective at the beginning of February, and he began to prepare to take his seat in Washington on March 4.

Thus, Zeb's gubernatorial tenure came to an end, and many of the objectives that he had worked so hard to achieve had been partially or fully realized. His third term was much less exciting than either of his war terms, but it was still an important one in the history of North Carolina. The transition in North Carolina from Reconstruction to what has been called the period of Southern "redemption" was handled with less coercion and violence than in many other states. Zeb supported and championed programs during his term and brought about concrete results. He was personally most gratified by the state's completion of the Western North Carolina Railroad, which finally connected the entire mountain region to the outside world in 1892. His recommendation that teacher education be improved had been implemented, and the results were even more positive than the most hopeful observers had anticipated. Many among the white elite and the middle class thought that the state government had been more effectively administered while Zeb was in office as well.

At the same time, however, Zeb and his fellow Democrats had ignored or exacerbated some conditions and problems. The most glaring example of their disregard for the general welfare was their use of the convict lease system for public construction projects. On the Western North Carolina Railroad alone, more than a hundred petty larcenists and vagrants gave their lives in the inhumane conditions created by the state and its agents. The gross neglect of human life was actually made worse by Zeb's insistence that the difficult construction between Old Fort and Asheville be continued under dangerous conditions; the speed of completion was the only consideration that mattered to him. Zeb and his fellow Democrats also neglected to deal with the state debt. While the state was not in a position to pay its obligations, the governor and the legislature should still have sought to bring closure to the situation. As we will see, the debt would plague Zeb and his party in one form or another for more than two decades. Finally, the Democratic legislature ignored Zeb's advice to retain as many elective offices as possible at the local level while ensuring white supremacy at the county level. Instead, the Democrats made virtually every local office an appointive one and denied African Americans, Republicans, and poor whites any significant voice in the local government of the state. As local oligarchies came to dominate cities and counties in the next fifteen years, resentment against Zeb and the Democrats would reach politically dangerous levels. Despite these significant failures, however, Zeb and his associates looked upon his term as a major success. He would never publicly express regret about any aspect of his gubernatorial tenure of the 1870s.

Zeb's election to the U.S. Senate fulfilled many needs for him. It provided him with an opportunity to start life anew after the deaths of his mother and his wife had caused him great pain. It also allowed him to escape the daily pressure to bestow patronage that was associated with being governor of North Carolina. It meant that Zeb was no longer responsible for the detailed administration of the many state programs that his office directed. By giving up the office of governor, moreover, he also escaped the frustration of being a chief executive without a veto who was unable to influence the course of legislation. But Zeb's return to Washington gave him much more than simply a way to escape. It vindicated him. The Senate seat was his reward for accepting his defeats in 1870 and 1872. Zeb must have been deeply satisfied to serve as an honored official across the street from the prison where he had been ingloriously housed in the summer of 1865. Many former Confederates, when they returned to Congress during and after Reconstruction, felt the same vindication as Zeb did. Perhaps they had failed to create and sustain an independent nation, but their subsequent election to the Congress of the United States indicated that they had spoken and acted with the backing of popular support during the crisis of 1861 and the war that followed it. While Zeb rarely articulated his feelings about having been elected to the Senate, brief comments in his letters and public addresses indicate that all of these sentiments were present when he was sworn in as senator in March 1879.

Like the good practical politician that he was, Zeb did not evade the opportunities and obligations that his new responsibilities brought. One of his first accomplishments was to get his son Charles, formerly his secretary in the governor's office, appointed clerk of the U.S. Senate Committee on Enrolled Bills. Not coincidently, Zeb was the newly appointed chairman of that committee. Zeb soon discovered that the life of a U.S. senator was not all glamour. In September 1879, he traveled to Kansas to hear three weeks of testimony in a disputed Senate election case. The work was apparently very tedious, and as soon as the hearings ended Zeb traveled further west to the Rockies for some badly needed rest. When he returned to Charlotte after the trip, the local newspaper referred to Zeb as looking "weary and travel-stained."[1]

As might have been expected given the character of his early career, Zeb made his mark in the Senate as a speaker in highly partisan debates. In a short discussion with Republican leader James G. Blaine, Zeb defended Southern history textbooks to the delight of his constituents back home. His first major speech addressed the broader issue of sectional relations, and in it Zeb gave his colleagues a preview of the role he would play in the Senate for the next decade and a half. He ridiculed the Republican claim that their party addressed timeless issues by observing of one Republican speech, "In the above it is assumed axiomatically that the terms 'liberty' and 'purity of elections' are synonymous with the term 'Republican party.'" He also poked fun at himself by describing how two members of the Senate, in their former capacities as Union generals during the Civil War, had "persuaded" him to return his loyalty to the Union: "I have a distinct recollection that the Senator from Illinois (Mr. Logan) and the Senator from Rhode Island (Mr. Burnside) came all the way down to North Carolina to invite that State to send Senators here, and they came attended with such a numerous retinue, and were urgent in their solicitation, that I, for one, found it impossible to resist so weighty an invitation." Zeb also took the opportunity, when he found it, to tell timely and humorous stories that made his point without injuring anyone's sensibilities.[2]

But Zeb also had a serious message that he would continue to deliver to people in the North for the remainder of his political career: The war was over. The South only asked to be left alone. He concluded his address: "Restoration is nature's law; let us imitate her; God of all mercy and grace, may not these gaping wounds of civil war be permitted to heal, if they will."[3] What Zeb did not mention—and his Republican adversaries did—was that if the North did choose to leave the South alone, it would be leaving whites in complete control of the Southern political, economic, and social systems. According to Zeb's opponents, it was only the threat, as weak as it was, of federal intervention that allowed African Americans to retain a few rights. After 1890, when this threat was removed, the disfranchisement movement would indeed eliminate blacks from the Southern political system and allow legal segregation to become a way of life in the South. The immediate result of Zeb's defense of the white South, however, was that he became more popular with his fellow Democrats both throughout the South and in North Carolina.

Zeb did not manage to escape entirely from his responsibilities in North Carolina. He continued to have an obligation to bring the Western North Carolina Railroad to completion even after he had left the governor's office.

The railroad had made it to Asheville, but the state did not have the resources to complete the line that would connect the city with Knoxville and Chattanooga. Without this line, the railroad would neither serve the interests of western North Carolina nor make money. Zeb was among those who suggested that the solution to this problem would be to sell the line to a private group headed by William J. Best. While many people in the western part of the state endorsed this suggestion, a number of other North Carolinians thought that such a sale would violate the public trust. In a letter written in the midst of this controversy, Zeb complained, "It is mortifying to hear that any one should intimate that my motives were improper in this thing." The legislature agreed to the sale and appointed Zeb, Governor Thomas Jarvis, and state treasurer John Worth to be commissioners to look out for the state's interests.[4]

The sale and completion of the line soon became embroiled in controversy due to the business ambitions of the Richmond and Danville Railroad. The owners of this railroad came to recognize that the route between Asheville and Knoxville was critical to their entire network. They joined Best as part of his purchase group and then outmaneuvered him and seized control of the lease. The lease required work upon a segment of the Asheville to Knoxville line to be completed in a matter of months. Zeb sided with Best in the controversy over the lease and sought to force the Richmond and Danville to either forfeit or sell its claim. The company's owners refused to do so, and they pressured Jarvis and Worth into authorizing an extension of the construction time under the lease. Zeb was outraged by this turn of events, and he fumed helplessly as the Richmond and Danville completed its construction agreements.[5] Ironically, then, the completion of one of Zeb's most cherished projects brought him little joy and no immediate political advantage.

The most important event in Zeb's first year in Washington came without warning. Despite having a very sore throat that continued to plague him for several weeks, Zeb attended a party in the Blue Parlor of the Riggs Hotel in Washington on the evening of January 27. At that time, he was introduced to Florence Steele Martin, a widow from Louisville, Kentucky. He was immediately infatuated with the forty-year-old woman, who was in Washington for a short vacation. Like Hattie, Florence was small in stature. But unlike Zeb's first wife, Florence dressed in the latest fashions and moved easily in sophisticated social circles. While not a person of great physical beauty, she was attractive and possessed a lively mind and manner. Six days after meeting her, Zeb sent Florence flowers and a note that he signed, "Your impatient patient, who is holding on to a sore throat with yet a sorer heart." By February 3, the North Carolina senator was completely head over heels. He related the following observation about his condition to Florence: "I have been at work all this forenoon disposing of a neglected pile of letters. In glancing at the tenth answer I was surprised to find that I had concluded every one with a fervent 'God bless you,' including one to a man in California whom I have never seen! . . . overflowing with happiness myself I let some of it *slop* over on the poor fellow who I fear has *no sweetheart*!" On February 11, Florence left Washington and returned to Louisville.[6] Because of their social obligations, Zeb and Florence would not see each other again until Zeb traveled to Louisville in June for their wedding.

Able to contain himself for only two hours after her departure, Zeb wrote to Florence about his sense of loss: "Oh my darling! How feeble are our tongues to express the feelings of the heart. You have been so good and so kind to me. You have blessed me with your love and promised to be my wife. The fountain of youth is once more opened within my heart." Clearly Zeb had been completely swept off his feet. Within the space of three weeks, he had met, wooed, and proposed to a woman while ignoring everything else around him. Eight days after Florence left Washington, Zeb confessed that he was perhaps overdoing it a little when he wrote his third letter of the day. He was probably making up for the fact that he had just returned from Baltimore and had sent no letters during that time.[7] Zeb's effusions of love continued for the next three months unabated.

Inevitably, reality began to insinuate its way into the fevered correspondence. Zeb apparently recognized that Florence came from the highest levels of Louisville society and was used to having substantial financial resources at her disposal. In a February 29 letter, Zeb confessed, "I never before regretted being a poor man." Zeb's financial woes were all relative, of course. He was not in fact destitute, but like many Southerners after the Civil War, his assets were not very liquid. He explained his situation more fully in a March 8 letter:

> One of the great secrets of my success has been this very thing; from my first entrance into public life I have been placed in the very trying situation of occupying high political positions without the money to live in a style commensurate with their supposed dignity. Instead of trying to cut a swell at the expense of my friends and by going into debt to everybody I lived scrupulously within my means and paid every man the last cent due him. When we (my wife and I) had the money to keep a carriage we rode in it, when we didn't we walked. . . . What we lost in display I found we more than made up in respect of all sensible people and in the comfort of a good conscience.[8]

While Zeb exaggerated his situation somewhat, there is much evidence to indicate that this description was essentially accurate.

Although financial matters could have caused friction between the two lovers, they managed to work them out to their own satisfaction. Zeb attempted to sell his house and property in Charlotte to provide ready cash to finance their activities as newlyweds. Unfortunately, his agent in Charlotte reported that he could not sell the senator's property, and the next day Zeb had to inform his future bride that they could not honeymoon in Europe. Before they married, however, Florence talked with a lawyer and apparently arranged to retain control over her own estate. This action did not signal that she would not share her largess with her new husband. According to surviving records, Florence's holdings totaled $87,586 in May 1881. She later made money available to Zeb when he purchased a house in Charlotte for the two of them for $13,500 in cash. In addition to this significant expenditure, Florence also spent large sums on paintings and furnishings for the new home. In 1882, one of Zeb's relatives was able to sell some family land near Asheville, and Zeb finally acquired some cash beyond his salary to contribute to the family budget.[9]

Although financial matters caused no problems for Zeb and Florence, religious differences did. As Michael Fellman has shown in his character study of William T. Sherman, there was significant potential for misunderstanding between a public man of Protestant heritage and his Roman Catholic wife during this period. Zeb and Florence were most concerned about the effect that the news of their engagement would have in North Carolina. While it did cause a momentary sensation in the press, Zeb's brother Bob assured him that there would be no problem with the family. Zeb reported to Florence, "My kinfolk—that innumerable mountain tribe —will receive you kindly from the start and will be your sworn admirers and fighting partisans in six months, and so will the great bulk of my neighbors and associates at home." In early March he was happy to be able to inform her that many of his friends in Raleigh already knew about the unannounced engagement, and that her Catholicism seemed to pose no major problem. The next day, however, Zeb sent a frantic letter to Florence in which he expressed his own concerns about the religion issue. He wrote, "It then occurred to me that my brother's doctor . . . had married a Catholic and I had heard the Doctor say the priest had made him promise that he should bring up all his children in the Catholic church." An overwrought Zeb raved on: "For Jesus' sake make me do nothing to be with you that would separate me forever from my self respect. You could not love me, Precious darling, if my manhood was humiliated and my proud integrity of principle was wounded unto death."[10]

The next day, a much more composed Zeb wrote to Florence and apologized for his lack of control. He then announced that he would be visiting the archbishop of Baltimore the next day to discuss the situation. Archbishop James Gibbons and Zeb apparently had a very cordial conversation and reached an understanding about the matter. Quite understandably, Florence had become extremely concerned about the excesses in her future husband's behavior. Zeb recognized that he had stepped beyond all proper bounds, and he sought to make amends. He assured Florence that he had absolutely no objection to her practicing her religious beliefs fully and that he would have no objections if Catholic clergymen wished to visit their home. He happily explained, "On the contrary I have already invited the Archbishop to visit us when we go housekeeping and he has promised to come on the first notice of that interesting fact!" While there was further mention of religious differences in their correspondence, there are no other indications that religion continued to create problems between Florence and Zeb.[11]

The agreement they reached about religion did not stop another major problem from developing, however. The individual who caused the hard feelings that arose between the couple was Cornelia Phillips Spencer. On May 17, Zeb sent Florence a letter in which he enclosed a letter that Spencer had written him. Zeb told his future bride that he had noted "a touch — just a touch of disapprobation" in Spencer's letter, and he asked Florence if the letter struck her the same way. Zeb, who often missed nuances in social correspondence, definitely underestimated the impact that this missive would have on Florence. Her reply was as emotional as his earlier letter about her Catholicism had been. Florence began, "Do you know that Mrs. Spencer's letter made me *so* mad I just couldn't see[?]" She continued, "Oh, I just went to pieces — so cool — so audacious — inasmuch as it was written to you — She would uphold you in your hour of misfortune &c &c." Having finally recognized when he received this letter that Spencer's words had deeply wounded his bride-to-be, Zeb wrote two long letters to Florence. He assured her that nothing that he had said to Spencer would have led her to think that he was in any way upset by Florence's religious beliefs.[12]

Zeb went on to say that he felt certain that Florence had misunderstood Spencer's sentiments and that he believed the two women would be friends. Florence replied that she thought that outcome was unlikely. She told Zeb: "[Spencer] would never know from my manners but the day will come when she will understand that I understand the cool impertinence of the letter!" Zeb sought to assure Florence of Spencer's good wishes, but

Florence Steele Martin, ca. 1880. Florence was the second wife of Zebulon Vance,
1880–94. (North Carolina Division of Archives and History, Raleigh)

his future bride remained unconvinced. It turns out that her interpretation of Spencer's letter was in fact quite correct. In a letter to her sister-in-law, Spencer unburdened herself: "I do believe I would not have felt as deeply hurt if he had told me she was a Mahometan or a heathen. There would be some hope for her conversion then. . . . Isn't it unspeakable, all things considered?"[13] From this point forward, the long friendship and interesting correspondence between Spencer and Vance began to ebb and slowly die. Zeb, who remained devoted to Florence for the remainder of his life, seems not to have noticed or to have been particularly concerned about the rupture in this important relationship.

Despite these significant bumps in the road, the two mature lovers were married in Louisville, Kentucky, on June 16, 1880. In a letter that he wrote to Florence less than a week before the event, Zeb noted that many of his fellow senators were teasing him in a good-natured way. Zeb's good humor was strained, however, when only one of his sons made it to Louisville to join about one hundred fifty guests for the outdoor ceremony. According to the *Louisville Courier-Journal*, the wedding was the social event of the year. The ceremony, a Catholic one, was held in a grove of trees outside of the plantation mansion that Florence had called home as a child. Chinese lanterns illuminated the grove, and Eichorn's Orchestra provided the music for the occasion. After the ceremony, there was bountiful food and drink and dancing until dawn.[14]

The *Courier-Journal* contained interesting descriptions of the bride and groom. The new Mrs. Vance was described as "a lady possessing all of the accomplishments and graces that adorn any station in life." Physically "petite and delicate in form, a brunette, with frank eyes and an intellectual face," she was, according to the piece, "exceedingly attractive." The reporter was even more interested in Zeb, who was new to the Louisville community. He was presented to the readers as follows: "Senator Vance, who just entered his fiftieth year, looks fully ten years younger; a man of magnificent presence, tall, impressive, and handsome. His hair and mustache, both luxuriant, are iron gray, but the color of his face, the quick light in his eyes, speak of physical and mental prime." The reporter noted that Zeb made the reception line—usually a "solemn" occasion—full of good cheer; not unexpectedly, Zeb "was soon the center of an admiring group of persons."[15] Florence received the first lesson of her new marriage: even at their wedding, Zeb was the center of attention.

The newly married couple remained in Louisville for several days, staying at the Galt House on the Ohio River. The couple honeymooned for about three weeks in Canada and at a resort in White Sulphur Springs, West Virginia. Then they returned to the new home in Washington that

Zeb had purchased in the late spring. Florence eagerly decorated the house with paintings, fine furniture, carpets, and curtains of a much finer quality and in a much greater quantity than Zeb and Hattie had ever had in their homes. The house was located on Massachusetts Avenue and was judged by a reporter to be "a rather modest residence, as residences go in this luxurious city." This observer went on to explain, "There is a modest lawn in front, and the house is one part of a double house."[16] Zeb and Florence set up a comfortable lifestyle that gave Zeb relief from the pressures of state and national politics.

According to historian Anne C. Rose, Zeb and Florence's domestic arrangements were characteristic of America's Victorian society and culture. Rose has asserted that the emphasis the two of them placed on mutual affection was a hallmark of the middle class in this period. Zeb shared other attributes with his contemporary Victorians, including his commitment to improving the secular world, his need for greater regularity and professionalism in life, and his desire to render public service. In one of Rose's most important insights, she argued that the experience of the Civil War did little to change the basic outlook of most of the people she examined. She was particularly struck by the elements of continuity in Zeb's life. Zeb's affectionate marriages, his assumptions of gender and racial superiority, and his commitment to his political career remained essentially unchanged despite his significant wartime experiences.[17]

In the midst of his courtship of Florence, Zeb did occasionally take time out to be a politician and a U.S. senator. For example, he served as a member of a select committee of the Senate that had been appointed in 1879 to investigate the migration of African Americans from the South to the Midwest. The meetings of the select committee were highly partisan, with Republicans seeking every opportunity to attack Southern Democrats for their mistreatment of blacks. Zeb sought to blunt the Republican forays, to portray the South as a reasonably hospitable place in which blacks could work and enjoy basic rights, and to expose the political motivations behind the Republicans' attacks. On March 9, for example, Zeb was able to force one witness to agree that one of the migration leaders had expressed his desire to bring African Americans north in the hope that they could assist Northern Republicans. At another point, Zeb elicited the observation from an African American witness that although black politicians wanted their followers to migrate, the movement was opposed by black ministers and other community leaders. Later, Zeb tried to persuade a witness that whites were not the only ones who intimidated black voters. The witness grudgingly agreed that some members of the black community also sought to physically intimidate any blacks who tried to vote for the Democrats.

Finally, Zeb impugned the motives of the leaders of the migration by implying that they received kickbacks from the railroads for the extra passengers they supplied.[18]

At the same time, Zeb acted as the defender of Southern whites' honor. For example, he tried to convince one witness that post-Reconstruction elections were both free of violence and fair. Refusing to agree with Zeb, the witness said that the threat of violence was still quite sufficient to restrict black political rights. When another witness maintained that blacks were denied equal educational opportunities, however, Zeb refused to concede an inch. The witness claimed that only twelve thousand blacks attended schools in North Carolina, and Zeb would not allow this reflection on his own record to pass unchallenged. Citing recent statistics provided by the state government, Zeb accurately pointed out that there were in fact eighty-one thousand African Americans in the state's public schools.[19] While Zeb was unable to prevent Republicans from proving that blacks were suffering in the South, he was able to blunt some of their most significant thrusts with aggressive rebuttals of his own.

These sessions also provided a stage upon which Zeb began to perform some of his characteristic verbal games for the amusement of both his fellow senators and the public. In the midst of turgid testimony, the following exchange took place:

Q: Do you think Reuben White is a Democrat?
A: I think he is a Whig.
Q: O, you have Whigs down there?
MR. VANCE: I protest in the name of the Whig Party.

To the modern observer, this exchange does not seem to be particularly humorous, but his contemporaries thought otherwise. Like any good humorist, Zeb refused to let a good thing go. A short time later, the following dialogue occurred:

Q: Well you colored people voted for him didn't you?
A: Yes; we voted for him because he said he would see that we got our rights.
Q: And he took away your turkeys?
A: Yes; and our other goods and property.
MR. VANCE: That is Whig profession and Democratic practice.[20]

While these remarks added nothing substantial to the committee's work, the comic relief that Vance offered his colleagues was welcomed. Virtually all of them recognized that most of his observations were made neither maliciously nor in an effort to gain political advantage. The result was that

Zeb found it easy to make friends of men who were often opposed to him ideologically and politically.

Zeb recognized that if he wanted to remain in the Senate, the Democratic Party would have to retain control of the legislature in North Carolina. While his victory in 1876 had given the party full control of the state government, the Republicans remained competitive in several parts of the state. Events outside of North Carolina indicated that Tar Heel Democrats needed to be alert for potential threats to their hegemony. In the late 1870s, an independent political group that called itself the Readjusters had challenged the dominant wing of the Democratic Party in Virginia. When the Readjusters found their path blocked within the party, they decided to run a separate slate of candidates in the state elections of 1879. The Readjusters, in alliance with much of the Virginia Republican Party, swept to victory in that election. Readjuster leader William Mahone was elected by the legislature to the U.S. Senate, where his vote gave the Republicans control of that body. Two years later, the Readjuster-Republican coalition carried the state again and elected both another U.S. senator and Virginia's governor. Democrats in the neighboring state of North Carolina were stunned by these developments, and they were on guard for any indication that a similar type of independent movement would appear there.[21]

The state legislature, controlled by the Democratic Party, became vulnerable to the development of just such an independent movement in March 1881. At that time, pressure from church groups and other reformers induced the legislature to hold a referendum on the question of whether the state should prohibit the sale and consumption of alcoholic beverages. This initiative was a direct threat to the livelihood of several hundred Republicans who held positions in the Internal Revenue Service. Republican leader John J. Mott sensed, moreover, that the issue might be used to divide the Democratic Party much as the debt issue had in Virginia. First, Mott engineered a coup within the Republican Party that put him in control as chairman of the state Executive Committee. Because prohibition was not popular in many parts of the state, some Democratic politicians joined with Mott in a nonpartisan liberal movement against prohibition. This opposition movement proved to be effective, and the referendum was voted down by a margin of more than two to one.[22] Despite the opposition of prominent African American leaders, moreover, Mott was able to maintain his leadership position after the referendum. If Mott and his allies had managed to keep their coalition together, the traditional Democratic leadership could well have been swept from power in North Carolina.

Zeb was alert to the threat posed by Mott's strategy. As noted, Zeb had sought to regulate the production of alcohol during the Civil War, and he knew from experience that the issue could be very divisive. Zeb recognized that not only did attempts to ban the production and use of alcohol create social controversy, they also threatened the Internal Revenue patronage that was sustaining the Republicans' organization. The Internal Revenue Service's primary responsibility during this period was to collect the tax on alcohol. Local officials, called assessors, were stationed in many North Carolina communities to enforce the law and collect the tax. As early as the 1876 gubernatorial campaign, Zeb had made the federal revenue agents the objects of special scorn, calling them "red-legged grasshoppers" and attacking the entire system of revenue collection as politically corrupt. Nor was Zeb alone in his opposition to the law enforcement officials; they were widely disliked, particularly in the mountains of western North Carolina. One official warned a correspondent that stills in Ashe County could not "be seized without a small force," and he predicted that "one or two men [would] be resisted." His warning was on target; large numbers of men confronted federal revenue officials on a number of occasions. In one Burke County incident, sixty men fired upon a group of federal officials when the agents sought to extradite a notorious moonshiner to South Carolina. Revenue agent Jacob Wagner reported that a gang of moonshiners had attacked a courtroom in Henderson County and killed a deputy U.S. marshal. Federal officials faced personal sabotage as well. In 1879, buildings on two agents' farms were destroyed by irate blockaders, as the small liquor producers who resisted the tax were called, who had lost property as a result of federal raids.[23] Clearly Zeb would have significant support in some locations in his crusade against revenue officials.

In an effort to undermine the alliance of Republicans and antiprohibition Democrats, Zeb sought to highlight federal revenue officials' political abuses. He encouraged Allen T. Davidson, an Asheville attorney and his relative, to point out in testimony before the committee that the agency had been the subject of much bitter debate during political campaigns; that debate alone, Davidson claimed, had reduced partisanship in the service. In addition, Davidson noted that many of the officials in the service were active Republican leaders. Finally, Davidson indicated that many people felt that Democratic moonshiners received harsher treatment from the courts than did their Republican counterparts. Mott, himself a revenue collector, actively defended himself and his associates and accused the Democrats of unfairly demeaning the agency. Mott charged: "The purpose of the Democratic party, as I understood it and felt it, was to make capital by traduction of the Revenue laws and officers. This was done by the public speakers and newspapers throughout the State. That system of abuse and traduction grew, and was taken from the speakers and the press by the populace." Davidson partially refuted Mott's charge that the Democrats were responsible for the poor reputation of the agency. No one disputed Mott, however, when he claimed that he had reduced partisanship in the service in western North Carolina by appointing a small number of highly qualified Democrats.[24]

Recognizing that the Davidson-Mott exchange was not sufficient to discredit both the Republicans and the liberal Democrats in the western counties, Zeb persuaded the Senate in April 1882 to allow him to investigate the Internal Revenue Service in western North Carolina. Even before he formally asked for an investigation, he had been gathering evidence against Mott and the Republicans. Apparently Zeb had been led to believe that a number of Republicans might be willing to testify against their party leader. His decision to call for the investigation was motivated in large part by his awareness that the liberal movement to weaken Democratic Party loyalties in the mountain counties was succeeding; prominent western North Carolina Democrat Tyre York, for example, was running as a liberal candidate for Congress. The hearings were held in Washington in July 1882, and they generated more than 450 pages of testimony and another 200 pages of official data related to the operation of the Internal Revenue Service in North Carolina. The entire proceeding had a strongly partisan flavor to it. Not only did Zeb focus most of his attention on the political activities of Republican appointees, but the witnesses were partially protected by John Pool, a former Republican U.S. senator from North Carolina, who acted as their attorney.[25]

The two most important witnesses at the hearing were Commissioner of Internal Revenue Green B. Raum and Collector John J. Mott. After several minutes of verbal fencing, Zeb was able to induce Raum to state that the revenue officers in North Carolina had not been very competent before 1876, but Raum was lavish in his praise of Mott, and he rated the current agents in western North Carolina very highly. Zeb's questioning of Mott was a classic confrontation between two crafty political veterans who shared many of the same values and understood how political organizations functioned. Zeb finally secured an admission from Mott that the collector had solicited money from revenue agency workers in North Carolina to fund the 1880 state Republican campaign. Mott stated that he had raised fourteen thousand dollars, but he maintained that the donations had been voluntary and that no one had been disciplined for not contributing.[26] Mott was being a little disingenuous here, since many revenue agents understood that they had received their positions in return for their commitment to the party, broadly understood. While Zeb did not manage to dig up any sensational revelations of malfeasance, he apparently felt that he had clearly demonstrated the partisan nature of the revenue service under Mott's administration. This information, Zeb hoped, would allow him and other spokesmen for the Democratic Party to attack the alliance of Republicans and liberals in the fall and accuse their opponents of being part of the corrupt internal revenue machine.

Apparently not convinced that he had done a thorough enough job, however, Zeb reconvened the committee after the 1882 fall elections. This action necessitated his first extended absence from Florence since their marriage, and his numerous letters to her indicate that the grueling pace of the investigation did not prevent him from missing his wife. The committee traveled from Morganton to Asheville—using the new railroad connection that Governor Vance had pushed—and on to the small Gaston County community of Dallas. While he and his staff had some difficulty securing testimony from reluctant witnesses, Zeb was quite satisfied with the results of the committee's work.[27] Despite Zeb's belief in the importance of the committee's work, however, it had little impact. The committee provided the people of North Carolina with little information that was not already widely known or suspected. In fact, the argument can be made that the hearings gave men like Raum and Mott an opportunity to distinguish themselves from those who had clearly abused the system before them.

Zeb was determined to do more than simply expose fraud, however. On February 19, 1883, he attempted to persuade the Senate to vote on a series of amendments to the revenue laws that were designed to curb the abuses of authority he felt he had detected in the Sixth District of North Carolina. The amendments would have created a separate category of organization for small distillers, the type of distiller most often found in western North Carolina; greatly reduced the reporting requirements for these small businessmen in order to limit the pressure that federal officials could place on them; limited the fees that these small distillers could be charged; and finally (and most important politically), reduced significantly the salaries for revenue agents and the size of their staffs in the regions in which most of the distillers were small producers. Zeb pointed out that there were more than eight hundred distillers in the Third District and only four of them produced a significant volume of whiskey. Yet each of the eight hundred stills had a federal worker attached to it. Zeb explained the result: "During the fiscal year ending June 30, 1881, there was collected in that collection district $499,455.80 and the expenses attending the collection were $268,324, being a little more than 54 per cent." He went on to demonstrate that staff costs rose during election years and fell during off years, which seemed to indicate that many revenue employees were hired for purely political reasons. Zeb charged that the federal revenue workers often worked in conjunction with bootleggers and that much revenue remained uncollected. He even accused Commissioner Raum of sanctioning the existence of the small bootleggers' stills.[28]

The Republicans immediately responded to Zeb's attack on the revenue workers. They charged that Zeb had obtained indirect evidence and that he had no absolute proof to back up his accusations. Zeb maintained that some of the witnesses he had interviewed testified that they had taken part in the disputed practices. He offered James H. Harris, an African American Republican leader who lived outside of the mountain district, as an example. He quoted one Republican official, who had written in a letter to Commissioner Raum, "There is no record in the collector's office showing that he [Harris] has accomplished anything during the seven months he has been on this duty." Zeb pointed out that Harris's period of employment coincided with the entire 1880 political campaign, and that Harris "had a splendid record rallying the colored people to the support of the Republican ticket in 1872." Harris's appointment as a revenue agent, Zeb insinuated, was a reward for his service to the Republican Party. Citing another example, Zeb mentioned that although one Republican revenue worker had abandoned his revenue post to run a Republican newspaper during the 1880 campaign, he had continued to draw his government pay. When challenged about the veracity of this story, Zeb simply introduced another example of a Republican editor who had been supported with federal money during that same election. Finally, Zeb defended his constituents against the charge that they had unnecessarily used force to defend themselves against revenue officers. Using rather disingenuous reasoning, he exonerated the moonshiners by claiming that revenue officers had actually killed more distillers than the reverse.[29] Unfortunately, this explanation only served to reinforce the picture of the Southern mountain people as violent, and it did not address their motivation for using violence against the federal agents. The entire discussion was essentially useless from Zeb's perspective, because no vote was taken on his amendments, and the Republican control of the revenue bureaucracy remained firm throughout western North Carolina.

While he remained quite concerned about local political matters, Zeb began to address national policy issues as well. Perhaps the most important of these in the 1880s was the issue of American tariff policy. From the earliest years of the republic, this system of taxation had inspired much debate. Followers of Thomas Jefferson and Alexander Hamilton had argued vehemently about forms of taxation and their costs to consumers. During the period of the second American party system, the partisans of Henry Clay, John C. Calhoun, and Andrew Jackson had argued about tariff policy with great passion. As a Whig and a Know-Nothing, Zeb had supported the parties that favored higher tariffs, but the issue had never fully engaged his interest during that time. The inability of the Confederacy to carry on viable trade during the Civil War stifled any Southern debate about the issue until after 1865. After the war, the ascendancy of the Republican Party, which favored high tariffs, led to a long period in which import taxes were so high that the U.S. government ran an annual budget surplus. The taxes were placed primarily on manufactured goods that competed with products made in the Northeast and in parts of the urban Midwest. Rural areas in the West and the South received virtually no economic benefit from the tariff system. Residents of these areas were forced to buy manufactured goods at inflated prices, while the overproduction of agricultural goods in the United States meant that they received low prices for the goods that they produced.

After Zeb became a member of the Senate in 1879, he became a consistent opponent of any tariff that reduced economic competition in the manufacturing sector of the economy. His position, which he held without significant deviation throughout the remainder of his career, put him at odds with virtually all Republicans and some Democrats as well. Zeb was not opposed to the tariff in principle, and he preferred it to some other taxes, particularly the internal revenue taxes. His position was somewhat similar to that of a modern free trade advocate who wishes to retain some tariffs but who generally encourages international competition in most parts of the economy. Zeb refined his position in a January 19, 1883, Senate speech: "So far as the fact goes that we are compelled to levy a tariff duty to some extent for the support of the Government of the United States which we can do under the Constitution, as a matter of course, I am willing for them to derive all protection that arises from it."[30] Thus he would allow industrialists to receive some benefit from the need to raise revenue for the government as long as the businessmen received no special consideration from the tax. Zeb's attitude toward the tariff was clearly not an extreme one, but it seemed to threaten many of his contemporaries in the Senate. At no time did Zeb encourage increases in the tariff, and he often ridiculed both his Republican and Democratic colleagues for using it to openly protect the interests of their constituents.

Because Democrats, particularly those who opposed the tariff, were in a minority in the Senate at that time, Zeb often turned to barbed humor as his only effective weapon against the policy he opposed. On one occasion, Zeb cited testimony from manufacturers who had claimed they needed no further increases in taxes to protect them from foreign competition only to have the Republicans propose to increase the tax anyway. In another instance, he resorted to rephrasing a well-known poem:

Oh, men with sisters dear!
   Oh, men with mothers and wives,
It is not linen you're wearing out,
   But human creatures lives.

Stitch—stitch—stitch,
   In poverty, hunger, and dirt,
Serving at once with a double (taxed) thread
   A shroud as well as a shirt.[31]

Zeb's comments of this kind angered the pro-tariff senators but left them with few ways to attack Vance except by making unsupported assertions of their own.

Zeb also sallied forth to attack a 100 percent tariff on foreign-made fire-crackers, noting that the young men who sought to purchase them could not afford the high prices. His remarks brought a retort from Senator William B. Allison of Iowa, who observed that the taxes on firecrackers and rice—a Southern agricultural product—were essentially the same. Zeb pounced quickly, asking, "Does the Senator think that fire-crackers are as absolutely necessary to this people as rice is?"[32] This was precisely the kind of question that most angered his opponents. Zeb took great delight in pointing out the practical inconsistencies that surfaced during these debates about the protective tariff. The pro-tariff forces, in fact, did not follow any consistent policy, and they thus left themselves open to attacks from opponents like Zeb who had no particular industries to protect.

With no viable defense against Zeb's increasingly pointed attacks, his opponents sought to nullify them by demeaning them. One of his colleagues chided Zeb for being "often witty at the expense of justice." The *Washington Post* had previously made a similar point about Zeb: "Since he has been in the Senate he has aspired only to be the *wit* or 'king's fool' or 'clown' of that body of statesmen, even having made a speech on the tariff, inspired by the notion that his *wit* and ridicule could humbug the people." Thus, Zeb's opponents sought to blunt the effectiveness of his attacks by portraying them as attention-seeking jokes, rather than comments with substance. The barrage of personal criticism had some impact on Zeb. He prefaced his remarks a year later with the cautionary comment, "If I may be permitted to disturb the dignified solemnities of this body for one moment, I will state what it reminds me of."[33] He followed this statement, however, with a story that highlighted the absurdity of his opponents' opinions. The attempt to silence Zeb through peer pressure had failed, and the public and the press continued to eagerly await his addresses to the Senate.

His opponents sought to impugn Zeb's motives by claiming that he was seeking to protect products from his own state. In reply to one such accusation from Democratic senator Arthur P. Gorman of Maryland, Zeb playfully asked, "Would the Senator have me get up when there is a general divide of the plunder and refuse the share which is equitably due to my state?" Amid the laughter that followed that quip, Gorman had to admit that he would not. Then Zeb turned the tables and announced that he would happily forfeit any benefit that North Carolina received from the tariff protection of rice, turpentine, or any other product in order to have a tariff that raised enough money to run the government without protecting industry. Another Democratic senator, Daniel Voorhees of Indiana, also attacked Zeb directly, accusing his North Carolina colleague of being doctrinaire. Voorhees, known as "the tall sycamore of the Wabash," stood six and a half feet tall; he was a striking figure who often invited gentle ridicule from his colleagues. Voorhees also claimed that his North Carolina colleague had not been present during part of the debate in which he had decided to take part. Zeb made a classic response: "I had the pleasure of hearing every word he said, and I always listen to him with pleasure. I beg to assure him, in the language of an old constituent of mine that 'I shirk no responsibility and shrink from no refreshments.'"[34] The laughter that followed this exchange only served to anger Zeb's opponents further.

The exchanges with fellow Democrats Gorman and Voorhees greatly upset Zeb. He accepted that the Republicans had campaigned in support of high tariffs and that the voters had elected them on that basis. Zeb disagreed with the policy, but he recognized that its implementation by the Republicans was politically legitimate. The Democrats, on the other hand, had campaigned as the party opposed to the protective tariff. Zeb lashed out at his Democratic colleagues who supported the tariff: "I do not blame a Senator for advocating the local interests of his State if he thinks that is proper; but I do not think he ought to call himself a constitutional Democrat if he goes back on the professed principles of his party and helps all other interests to plunder the people provided his own people can share in the plunder. This is not Democracy, whatever else it may be. I am tired of being stabbed daily by professed Democrats, and it is time the country understood this method of looking one way and rowing another."[35] This was unusually strong criticism for the Senate floor, particularly from someone who had so recently joined the Senate. Zeb's belief that the party platform should mean something was not shared by many of his colleagues.

In discussing the effects of the tariff on laborers, Zeb used offensive language and cultural stereotypes to defend the interests of American workers against their foreign-born competitors. He chided his opponents for supporting industrialists who often hired immigrant laborers at wages comparable to those found in sweatshops abroad. He spoke particularly disparagingly about Franco-American workers in New England and Chinese workers in the West. While describing a letter from a man from New Hampshire, Zeb claimed that the "kanucks" and the "off-clippings of the fungus growth" of Chinese society came to the United States as temporary workers but were not "American" workers in any true sense. Thus, he argued, the manufacturers who claimed that they needed protection from "low-wage foreign labor" nevertheless used foreign-born workers in their American plants. Zeb's opponents understandably attacked him for the racist tenor of his remarks, and they brought up his former membership in the nativist Know-Nothing Party. Zeb openly repudiated the party and stated that he was simply trying to point out the inconsistency of those who made the cheapness of foreign labor an argument for high tariffs. In his defense, Zeb also pointed out that he strenuously objected to the proposed tariff on non-English language books. Books written in English were to be allowed into the country duty-free, and Zeb could not see the logic of the discriminatory tax.[36]

As the debate wound down, Zeb's patience wore thin. In an exchange with Voorhees, Zeb denied that his stance on the tariff was "foolish" and observed, "the foolish things of this world are selected, so the Scriptures say, to confound the wise and the mighty." He pointed out once again that it was grossly unfair for his farming constituents to receive no assistance from the tariff while paying high prices for most of their consumer goods due to it. Thoroughly worked up and exasperated, Vance concluded that his opponents were not simply opportunistic. Rather, their policy stance "border[ed] on dishonesty." These words were unusually strong for the Senate debates of that time, and Voorhees claimed in response that Zeb was being "shamelessly" inconsistent in his stand against the protective tariff. Zeb ably defended his record, explaining that he supported import taxes that would raise revenue without raising the price of consumer goods.[37]

The tariff bills approved by the Senate and the House of Representatives conflicted with each other, and they were sent to a conference committee of the two chambers so that their differences could be resolved. The resulting compromise bill was introduced in early March just as the Forty-seventh Congress was concluding. From Zeb's perspective, the final bill was even more objectionable than the original Senate version had been. He attacked the whole notion of a conference committee in the following volley of words: "They set out in the only practicable way [to pass the bill], and that is, to avoid the publicity and to resort to a secret conclave, a Venetian Council of Ten, a kind of political star-chamber, called a conference committee, whose proceedings are hidden, and . . . the light of publicity could not be poured in upon them."[38] Ignoring Zeb's vocal opposition, the Senate passed the tariff bill. Although he was defeated in this instance, Zeb had clearly managed to define himself for a national audience. He was the most outspoken proponent of the Democratic Party's tariff position. Soon he began to receive invitations to speak to both partisan and nonpartisan organizations that supported his position on the tariff.

Zeb did not define himself solely as an opponent of proposed legislation. In March 1884, he entered the ongoing debate about the Blair Education Bill. This bill proposed to distribute the federal budget surplus to the states over a ten-year period for their use in funding public education. The proportion of the money that would go to each state was to be based on the percentage of the state's citizens who were illiterate. As a result, most of the money would go to Southern states with large African American populations. This was certainly Senator William H. Blair's intention.[39] The legislation did not fit neatly into traditional partisan categories. Many Republicans supported the idea of aiding blacks in theory, but they were upset that such a large proportion of the money would be going to the Southern states. Many Democrats recognized that the spending bill would require tariff rates to remain unacceptably high, and those in the North also objected to the apparent Southern bias of the proposed law.

Zeb, who had shown great interest in improving education in North Carolina as governor, did not let the fact that the bill was a Republican proposal deter him from supporting it. He announced his support in an extended speech in which he explained why he supported the measure. Zeb noted that the bill would allow Southern states to retain racially segregated schools while for the first time providing adequate revenues to pay for both white and black education. When a Northern Republican accused Zeb of wanting the money to educate the many illiterate whites in the state, Zeb replied, "I asked for it for the benefit of the colored people whom the white tax-payers were not able to properly educate, and, notwithstanding that this bill is irrespective of race, we all know that the colored man is the meritorious cause of action in this bill and that it is chiefly intended for his benefit."[40] The extended debate on the tariff doomed the Blair Bill during the session that it was introduced in Congress, but by supporting it Zeb had clearly demonstrated his willingness to take positive action while in office. Not only was he willing to do so, in fact, but he was willing to do so on behalf of people who were his political opponents when he believed in the cause.

By March 1884, Zeb had created a widely recognized position for himself in the U.S. Senate. He was known, of course, as the chamber's chief humorist. While he did not reject this designation, Zeb argued that he only used his humorous stories to make complex matters clear to the voting public. At the same time, the debates on the tariff and on the Blair Bill had demonstrated that Zeb could hold his own against any member of the Senate. In the tariff debates in particular, he showed a willingness to do research and to become acquainted with the arcane details that dominated that discussion. At the same time, he consistently espoused a position that defended the national platform of the Democratic Party. There were few well-informed Americans in the early 1880s who did not know about Zeb and his positions on some major issues. To have achieved such public recognition was a significant accomplishment for a man just beginning his congressional career.

Z eb's success in establishing himself as an active member of the Senate obligated him to assume a leadership role in the Democratic Party, particularly in the South. Although the party had regained control of all of the states that had allowed slavery in 1861, its hold on power was constantly being challenged during the 1880s in the upper South. Zeb recognized the precarious nature of the Democratic advantage and worked with considerable determination to make the party's position more secure. All of his efforts had the added advantage of making his own position more secure. From Zeb's perspective, however, the Democrats needed to do more than simply defeat the Republicans in order to maintain hegemony. The Democrats of the South were truly a coalition party in this period. The party's elite leadership, which frequently sought to bring the region's economy into the national mainstream, often found itself at odds with its predominant constituency of small farmers. In addition, communities, counties, and regions within states felt neglected by the party on many occasions. The only glue that held the party together was its racist commitment to white political, economic, and social dominance.

As the last chapter noted, the greatest challenge to the Democratic coalition, and thus to Zeb's position, occurred in the state of Virginia.[1] To Southern Democrats, the Readjusters posed a potent threat. First, their strategy provided an example that could be used successfully to split the Democratic Party in other states. Several attempts to duplicate the Readjuster experiment were in fact made in other states. In North Carolina, the coalition of antiprohibition and independent politicians attempted to duplicate the Virginia example. Zeb recognized as soon as the new party appeared that the situation in Virginia was dangerous to Southern Democrats like himself. He campaigned in Virginia for the Democrats during the 1880 presidential canvass and had his first personal contact with the Readjusters. During a September speech in Virginia, Zeb claimed that William Mahone's allies were attempting to break up the address and that they had shown weapons in the crowd. The next year, Zeb attacked the Readjusters in a Senate speech that was apparently part of a broader Democratic campaign to weaken the Virginia coalition.[2] Thus, it is clear that Zeb viewed the Virginia situation with great concern throughout the early 1880s.

The Virginia Democrats conceded to readjusting the state debt, and they reorganized themselves. In the 1883 spring elections for local offices, the Democratic strategy had sufficient impact to provide them with the margin of victory. In the fall election of legislators, the Democrats were equally well prepared. Still not completely sure of their position, however, they resorted to playing the Southern Democratic trump card: race. About ten days before the election, they sent out an inflammatory pamphlet entitled "Coalition Rule in Danville." This circular described—inaccurately—African American domination of local government in the southern Virginia city of Danville. This document was spread throughout the rural counties in the mountains in an effort to persuade the white majorities in those areas to support the Democrats. On November 3, the whites in Danville precipitated a race riot in which many blacks were shot. The impact of this incident on the election four days later was predictable: the Democrats once again seized control of the Virginia state government.[3]

The Readjusters and their Republican allies in the U.S. Senate—the two Readjuster members gave the Republicans control of that body—cried foul. The result was a Senate investigation into the Danville riot. Zeb was named as a member of the investigative committee, and he acted as the Virginia Democrats' chief advocate. In that capacity, he sought to deflect all blame from his allies and to place it on African Americans. He came to view the investigation as another effort on the part of the Republicans to raise Civil War and Reconstruction issues during the 1884 presidential campaign. In June 1884, he issued his minority report on the results of the committee's investigation. In it, he attacked the Republicans for making a partisan spectacle out of the committee proceedings. He also dismissed the idea that the Democrats were culpable for the riot despite the abundant evidence of his party's guilt.[4]

Unfortunately, Zeb took the lead on behalf of his Virginia allies and invoked racial slurs in their defense. He described a key African American witness as the "most worthless, dangerous, unprincipled, cowardly, lying negro, a disgrace and injury to the whole race." In other instances in his report, he rejected testimony simply because the witnesses were African American. In his conclusion, he asserted that the Republican members of the investigative committee had been unfair to Southern Democrats, who had simply "appeal[ed] in turn to their own race in the desperate attempt to preserve their institutions, their property, their every interest, and civilization itself." Not surprisingly, Virginia Democrats were delighted with Zeb's defense of their activities, and he became their contact in the U.S. Senate until the two Readjuster members were replaced by Virginia Democrats in the Senate after the 1886 election.[5] Zeb's performance on the committee revealed a great deal about his own perception of his party's mission. He felt that he was justified in attacking the Republicans for raising old issues, but he refused to recognize that his—and his party's—use of race was equally illegitimate. His assumption that whites were racially superior to blacks was so deeply ingrained that he often found himself unable to express his point in any other terms.

Zeb did not neglect the political situation in North Carolina as he worked to help Virginia Democrats. The election of 1884 was not merely a presidential election; the state legislature selected in that year would choose Zeb's successor. To ensure that he had no viable opponent within his own party, Zeb and other party leaders arranged for Augustus S. Merrimon to be appointed to the state supreme court, an appointment he very much wanted. Zeb toured the state throughout September and October speaking to large crowds in the mountain, Piedmont, and eastern counties. This tour was not a leisurely and triumphant one for Zeb. The *Wilmington Star* captured the rather frenzied nature of Zeb's appearances in its description of his speaking schedule: "We told Gov. Vance that he was a cast-iron man. He spoke at Burgaw for two and a half hours, and then taking an extra train for Wilmington and with only a few hours intermission, he again in the open air . . . spoke for two and a half hours. One hour thereafter he was on a riverboat for his appointment at Point Caswell, where he spoke yesterday." All of this hard work had a significant impact. The Democrats swept virtually every race in North Carolina. The Republicans won only 30 of 160 seats in the legislature, and no viable Democratic opponent to Zeb surfaced after the election. As a result, Zeb was easily reelected to the Senate for another six-year term in January 1885.[6]

Grover Cleveland's election to the presidency as the first Democratic president since 1861 was an equally important development for Zeb. As a delegate to the national convention, he had not supported Cleveland for the nomination, preferring border state senator Thomas Bayard. In fact, immediately after the Democratic convention Zeb predicted Cleveland's defeat. Once Cleveland had been elected, the exultant Democrats expected to take full advantage of the national patronage opportunities that became available to them for the first time in more than two decades. Within ten days of the election, Zeb reported to another party member "that he [had] received fifty letters asking for places" already. It turned out that virtually every party leader in North Carolina expected to be appointed to a suitable position by the president, and the volume of mail Zeb received only increased with each passing day. Nor did the requests come to him only from North Carolina Democrats. Since Virginia had no Democratic senators, applicants from that state often wrote to Zeb as well. Zeb's old friend Edward J. Hale, former editor of the *Fayetteville Observer* and now a resident of New York, asked Zeb to obtain a foreign mission for him.[7]

In the midst of this frenzy of activity, General William T. Sherman assaulted Zeb's reputation in a description of events that had taken place at the close of the Civil War. Sherman maintained that Zeb had chosen not to take North Carolina out of the Confederacy only because Jefferson Davis had threatened to send Lee's army to North Carolina to prevent it. He went on to claim that he had seen a letter stating as much in Vance's office when his army entered Raleigh. Finally, Sherman claimed that the commissioners Zeb had sent to meet him had stated that Zeb "wanted to make separate terms for the state, but was afraid of 'Jeff Davis.'" Sherman's assertions threatened both Zeb's perception of his own role in the events at the end of the war and his public reputation as a former participant in the war. The latter was of considerable importance, particularly at a time when the divisiveness of the war years was being glossed over and the legend of the Confederacy had begun to replace the reality of the conflict in the public memory.[8]

Zeb immediately answered Sherman's slander with an extended speech on the floor of the Senate on January 13, 1885. First, he attacked Sherman's claim that he had seen the threatening letter from Davis in Vance's office. Zeb asserted, "I aver most positively, on the honor of a gentleman and an American Senator, that no letter containing such a threat was ever received by me from Mr. Jefferson Davis." A thorough review of all of the Vance correspondence and the extensive literature on Davis's life confirms the truth of Zeb's statement. On the second charge, Zeb quite accurately noted that the Confederacy had been virtually extinguished by the time Sherman reached North Carolina, and thus that Davis could not have threatened anyone.[9] There is no question that Sherman erred on this point.

As Zeb continued his discussion of the incident, however, he too distorted the events of April 1865. He concluded his argument by saying: "True it is that I sent a commissioner to him under a flag of truce to ask protection, not separate terms for the people of my State, but at that moment the war was virtually ended."[10] Zeb had apparently forgotten that the letter Swain and Graham had carried to Sherman over Zeb's signature had included a phrase that indicated his desire to bring the hostilities to a close. Sherman's memory that Zeb had wanted to remove North Carolina from the Confederacy may well have been based on this phrase. In the two decades that followed the end of the war,—a traumatic event in Zeb's life—perhaps he had managed to suppress his memory of this part of the message he had sent to the Union general. Such an outcome could have been the result of a normal process by which people select memories that conform to their need to square remembered actions with their preferred interpretations of events. On the other hand, perhaps because Zeb did not approve of the phrase about ending hostilities at the time, he later refused to acknowledge it as his own.

Zeb's extreme sensitivity on this point of honor was captured in a letter he wrote to S. A. Ashe three days after making his Senate speech. Ashe was the editor of the *Charlotte Observer*, which was generally recognized as the flagship Democratic newspaper for the state. Zeb was very upset that Ashe had published Sherman's speech in full and had not done the same with Zeb's address. He admitted that Ashe had criticized Sherman in his article about the controversy, but in doing so, Ashe had used an explanation that Zeb found unacceptable. He charged, "You revive the old slander of Holdens that I had in a speech advised the people 'to fight until hell froze over' which I have denied a hundred times at least."[11] The problem with Zeb's complaint, however, is that there is considerable evidence that when he addressed the troops in Virginia in 1864, he did use phrases very much like the one Ashe quoted. Once again, his memory had apparently selected one interpretation of the past and held fast to it as he tried to reconcile his actions during the war with the image he had created for himself in its aftermath.

The Sherman controversy was only a brief diversion from the more pressing business of distributing patronage to deserving North Carolina Democrats. Zeb's problem—one that he shared with every major political figure in both parties during the Gilded Age—was that there were not nearly enough jobs available to satisfy those party workers who viewed themselves as particularly worthy. Nor were the applicants particularly shy about stating their desire for positions. One correspondent admitted that he wanted "a small share of the spoils." Another announced boldly, "I am an *Office Seeker*." These fairly brazen admissions were subtle in contrast to the statement of James W. Forbes, who was pursuing the position of postmaster of Greensboro. He informed Zeb, "I want it, and I want it bad."[12] Unfortunately for Zeb and other party leaders, Cleveland would not be inaugurated until March 4, 1885, and none of the requests could be processed until after that. The result was that the ardent office seekers had to be placated for months.

In the meantime, Zeb and other party leaders had some matters that they needed to attend to. Both Zeb and Matt W. Ransom were concerned about the ambitions of Thomas Jarvis, the recent governor of North Carolina. Jarvis had demonstrated some real empathy for the white underclass in North Carolina, and he had a substantial following in the party as a result. Both incumbent senators recognized that Jarvis might well be a formidable challenger for one of their seats. Their strategy was to recommend that Jarvis be appointed to Cleveland's cabinet. This would have put Jarvis in their debt and taken him out of the state and away from the party structure. Their plan failed in a way that worked greatly to their advantage. Cleveland refused to consider Jarvis for the post they suggested, but he offered Jarvis a mission in Brazil as a consolation prize. Rather stunned by the offer, Jarvis eventually took it.[13] From Vance and Ransom's perspective, this appointment provided an ideal solution to their dilemma. Jarvis was beholden to them for his position; furthermore, he was thousands of miles away from North Carolina, and he could not meddle in state politics from that distance.

Most other patronage controversies did not work out as well. In an effort to keep peace in the party, some informal agreements were negotiated between North Carolina's senators and its congressmen. The avid office seekers soon knew about these arrangements. Within three weeks of Cleveland's inauguration, one correspondent wrote to Ransom, "The papers state that North Carolina is divided between you & Senator Vance, he taking the western half." Office seekers soon became quite dissatisfied with the division of influence in patronage decisions. One applicant in Charlotte was willing to grant that Zeb had the authority to name the postmaster, but he was deeply upset that Vance opposed his nomination to become assayer of the mint in Charlotte. One of Zeb's first recommendations for high office in North Carolina, which the president accepted, was that his former law partner Clement Dowd be made the collector of internal revenue for the western district. According to one party worker, this nomination "caused great indignation" in the region.[14] Virtually every time he selected a candidate, Zeb left a number of other people dissatisfied.

Perhaps the most contentious appointment controversy in western North Carolina involved the naming of the Asheville postmaster. The Democratic congressman for the district, Thomas D. Johnston, claimed the right to name the person who would assume this position. Zeb claimed the same right. It soon became obvious that the fight was as much personal as it was political. An observer wrote to Ransom: "The contest seems confined to Capt. W. T. Weaver who is soon to be a brother in law of Hon T. D. Johnston and who has lived in town 2 years. And the other is one Elisha Baird a cousin of Gov Vance who is wholly unfit for any such position." A third candidate emerged quite by accident: when James M. Gudger was crushed by the collapse of his porch in the summer of 1885, several prominent Democrats suggested that he would make a good compromise candidate. Gudger wrote to Ransom and explained his other qualifications as follows: "Gov. Vance is my friend. T. D. Johnston is my relative and friend."[15] There were simply too many able and willing candidates for Zeb and other political leaders to satisfy them all.

This fact of political life convinced Zeb to lead a crusade against one of the major political reform campaigns of the Gilded Age: civil service reform. The patronage or "spoils" system of nominating people to positions in the federal bureaucracy as a reward for their partisan allegiance became accepted policy during the administration of Andrew Jackson during the 1830s, although it had been used in some form from the earliest days of the national government. By the 1840s, both Whigs and Democrats turned out virtually every federal office holder in the United States and replaced them with their supporters when their party's presidential candidate was elected. During the political battles of the 1850s, President James Buchanan even removed loyal Democrats from office if they supported his rival within the party, Stephen A. Douglas. The spoils system prevailed in the federal government during the Civil War and continued to operate without any discernible change through Reconstruction and after.[16]

But there were pressures building within parties and in society at large that challenged this political tradition. Between 1861 and 1885, the Republicans controlled the presidency, and party leaders used the patronage system to further their own ambitions. John Sherman, a senator from Ohio and secretary of the treasury, was particularly adept at using patronage as a form of political infighting. A perennial presidential hopeful, he attempted to use the spoils system to lure Southern Republican votes away from his competitors within the party. The infighting became so vicious that the two wings of the party had epic battles at the presidential nominating conventions about who would control the national patronage. The climax came in June of 1881 when a disappointed office seeker shot President James Garfield. Garfield was badly wounded, but he survived throughout the summer before finally passing away in September. The nation was horrified, and many political leaders began to recognize the limitations of the spoils system.[17]

Partisan self-interest joined public disgust as a motive for reforming the civil service after the 1882 elections. The Republicans suffered a major defeat in that contest. Since the party had barely won the last two presidential elections, it seemed probable that they would lose in 1884. Thus, it was the Republicans who supported and passed the Pendleton Civil Service Reform Act in 1883. The new law had several provisions that infuriated Zeb and many other Southern Democrats. First, it dictated specific terms of employment for those already in office; that is, it protected many Republican placeholders from immediate dismissal. The law also required many of the new appointees to pass written examinations in order to qualify for federal jobs, a provision that tended to favor candidates from the Northeast and the Midwest, where literacy rates were much higher than in the South. Both reformers and business leaders had sought this change. An illiterate mail worker cost businesses money, and the same principle applied to many other federal jobs as well.[18]

None of this reasoning was persuasive either to Zeb or to most other North Carolina Democrats. It was, however, to Grover Cleveland. Cleveland accepted the civil service reforms and generally followed the letter of the law in making appointments. He removed people at the highest levels of office as well as those who could be proven to be "offensive" partisans, but he left many Republican office holders undisturbed until their terms of office expired. Cleveland's policy had very predictable results. By early June 1885, there was growing discontent among North Carolina Democrats. The next month, Clement Dowd, the new collector in the western district, reported that he had recommended fifty men for positions in the Internal Revenue Service in his district, but only one had been appointed. Zeb expressed his frustration with the situation in a newspaper interview published in October. He summed up his perspective, asserting: "Politics, in great measure, depends upon the civil service branch of the government. Separate the two and politics will be robbed of its impulses; of its ambitions. I believe in parties, and the good of the people depends upon such conditions." Zeb went on to say that he planned to introduce legislation to repeal or modify the civil service reforms when Congress resumed its deliberations. These remarks were interpreted as a criticism of Grover Cleveland, and Zeb was later forced to "clarify" them. He stated that he was not making "war" on the president and that he would continue to back the party no matter what happened with patronage.[19]

But, in fact, Zeb was growing increasingly disenchanted with the Democratic president. The problem was not simply that the two men disagreed on patronage policy. Zeb found the chief executive to be a very different type of person than the people he usually associated with in politics. When a senator mentioned that Cleveland was indifferent and even disrespectful toward him to Zeb, he replied, "Oh . . . you need not complain of that, it is his way. He treats me so, he treats everybody so." When Zeb introduced legislation to place a new federal building in the now rapidly growing city of Asheville, he was able to secure its passage. He was outraged when Cleveland vetoed the bill, saying that Asheville did not need the building. As a result of these developments, Zeb found himself consistently at odds with the leader of his own party.[20]

True to his promise, Zeb rose in the Senate on March 31, 1886, to speak in favor of his bill to modify the Civil Service Reform Act. He attacked the new system as one that defeated "the will of the people as expressed at popular elections." Throughout his extended speech, Zeb harped on this theme. He offered a strong defense of the role of political parties, claiming "that a government by party is the only way in which there can be government by the people." His assertions about the importance of party and the sanctity of popular access to government positions allowed Zeb to claim that the new system was undemocratic. While his bill would have modified the law that regulated the civil service, his rhetoric demanded the total destruction of that law.[21]

Perhaps recognizing that the civil service reformers were working with a different definition of the function of public service than the one he embraced, Zeb also attacked the reformers personally. Using the language common to many critics of the new system, Zeb observed that the reformers and the civil servants appointed since the passage of the reform act were not true men like the political warriors whom he wanted to appoint to office. Attacking the newcomers by calling them "our mock philosophers, our sentimental women, and our effeminate men," Zeb claimed that these people had been unable to gain public office by means of honest political work. He divided the reformers into two categories: they were either "political old maids whose blood [had] been turned to vinegar by a failure to secure lovers before their unappreciated charms had fled, or . . . grass widows who had failed to retain the lovers they had won by artifice and fraud." His effort to deny the masculinity of his opponents and to insult the female applicants for public offices, whose numbers were increasing, clearly demonstrated Zeb's unwillingness to recognize the middle-class ethos that was beginning to reshape political and social ideas, particularly in the urban North. Zeb's crusade to save the old patronage system was a complete failure. The Senate rejected his amendment by an overwhelming majority, and virtually no senators from outside of the South voted for his initiative.[22]

Although he was very concerned about the problems created by the patronage controversies, Zeb did not neglect other legislative topics. The stand he took that was most popular among his constituents again brought him in conflict with Grover Cleveland. In December 1885, Cleveland had urged the Congress to suspend the Silver Coinage Act. He took this action in response to concerns expressed by businesses and banks in urban areas, particularly in the Northeast, that an inflationary spiral would cause people to lose confidence in the currency. He asked Congress to require all money to consist of gold coinage. Such a law would have had negative consequences, however; it would have limited the amount of capital available to farmers and small-town businessmen, especially those located in the western and southern states. About a month after Cleveland delivered his message, the Senate considered his recommendation in an emotional debate. Zeb eagerly joined the fray. In his opening remarks, he stated his view of the issue in stark terms: "The effort which is now making in different parts of the world to demonetize and degrade silver coins is one of the grandest conspiracies against the rights of the people ever inaugurated by human greed."[23] Zeb had obviously embraced the conspiracy theories that many historians have noted were in common circulation among the political supporters of silver coinage.

But Zeb's critique of Cleveland's actions had much more substance to it than a simple, shadowy conspiracy theory. He quite correctly pointed out that given the rapid expansion of the U.S. and the world populations, as well as the consequent expansion of economic production, both the national and the international economies needed more money to facilitate trade and commerce, not less. Zeb also asserted that scarcity of money made it much more difficult for debtors to pay off loans and facilitated the destruction of small businesses to the benefit of "the combinations of capital." As was common in his addresses to the Senate, Zeb could not refrain from using very aggressive language. He referred to his opponents' arguments as examples of "the national platitudes which fill the pages of the Congressional Record," and he described them as an "abuse of logic" and a "feebler attempt to outrage common sense." Needless to say, this rhetoric did not persuade his colleagues, but Zeb's constituents in North Carolina appreciated it that he had voiced their anger and frustration. Letters from home poured into Zeb's office which praised his speech and assured him that he had the support of the people of North Carolina.[24]

Although he participated consistently in Senate debates, Zeb spent a considerable amount of time in North Carolina as well. He returned on one occasion when a most unusual honor was paid to him by the North Carolina legislature. The legislature had carved out a new county in the Piedmont on the Virginia state line in 1881, and the legislators decided to name it Vance County after Zeb. It was one of the rare instances in American history when a living person was so honored. In November 1885, Zeb and Florence journeyed to Henderson, the new county's seat, for a public celebration. Zeb was greeted at the train station with a formal address and then taken to the home of Colonel W. H. S. Burgwyn, his host on this occasion. In the afternoon, Zeb and Florence met hundreds of people from the county at a formal reception in the largest hall in town. Zeb returned to the hall that evening and delivered a talk entitled "North Carolina and Her People."[25] This address appears to have been largely derivative, but his audience did not seem to mind. They were simply happy to be able to honor Zeb, and he was happy to accept.

Zeb was even happier to begin a project in North Carolina that would give him more pleasure and satisfaction than any other during the last decade of his life: he started work on his dream house in the mountains of western North Carolina. He purchased a thousand-acre tract near the small community of Black Mountain in Buncombe County. This cost him $3,000, his first purchase in a long and expensive process of construction. Zeb helped to finance this extravagance, in part, by selling family land that he had inherited from his mother. The sale of lots in Asheville netted him about $8,500 during one auction. Zeb's efforts to realize a profit from family holdings led to a major local controversy in Asheville. One of the potential purchasers of Zeb's land in what is present-day Pack Square in Asheville was the First Baptist Church. For reasons that are not clear, Zeb did not want to sell his land to the Baptists. His friends chided him for his close-minded approach to this matter, and Zeb was eventually forced to grudgingly make the sale.[26]

Despite all of the difficulties Zeb had raising money (Florence also contributed), he enjoyed the construction of his new home. The house, named Gombroon by Zeb, was located on the top of a small hill about eight miles north of the Black Mountain railway station. Zeb hired local men to cut a road to the house's remote location; the road was so long and the house was so remote that visitors often remarked as much about the trip to the house as they did about the structure itself. Zeb employed local craftsmen to do much of the work, and the project began to contribute to the community's identity. A newspaper recounted an event during the construction in the summer of 1885: "Gov. Vance had an old-fashioned 'log-rolling' at his residence, 'Gombroon,' near Black Mountain, on Thursday. There was a large crowd of old and young men present from the surrounding country. Two cooks were kept at work several days before the time preparing food for the occasion."[27] Apparently, Zeb turned his need to move many of the large native trees to the house site so that the carpenters could begin construction into a community occasion.

The work on the house continued for at least three years. The slow pace was due in part to Zeb's desire to supervise most of the construction himself. During the long stretches in which he was in Washington attending Senate sessions, very little work was done on the house. When he was in North Carolina, he lived in a small log cabin on the property so that he would not have to make the long trip back and forth to the site in order to keep an eye on the construction. The pace of construction was also slow because Zeb and Florence were very particular about some details. For example, they wanted all thirteen rooms in the three-story house to be paneled with native woods, and they wanted the grain of the wood panels to have pleasing designs in it. This meant that only trees with a curly pattern in the grain of their wood could be used for the panels. One of the lumberman remembered that his crew cut down a giant poplar—almost eighteen feet in circumference—to obtain paneling for the living room. The library was finished in wild cherry, and the dining room was done in black walnut and oak. All of the halls, alcoves, and stairways were finished in oak timbers.[28]

While the basic construction was done with local products, many of the accessories were brought in from the outside. "Mantels, windows and decorations were ordered from New York" and were shipped to Black Mountain. Most of the furniture was purchased in exclusive stores in Washington, and it made the long rail trip to western North Carolina as well. The workmen vividly remembered having to carry "case after case of books" for Zeb's library. The final touch came when Florence's piano arrived, apparently causing quite a sensation among the immediate neighbors. While Zeb and Florence moved into their new home in 1887, the house and grounds remained unfinished until 1890. Gombroon was clearly designed to impress visitors from outside the region, and it did. Local people remembered that an endless stream of visitors arrived in Black Mountain during the summer and fall when the Vances entertained the political elite at their mountain estate.[29]

As impressive as they found the house to be, most were even more impressed by the grounds and the landscape in which the house was situated. Gombroon faced into the Craggy and Black Mountains, where several peaks topped out at more than a mile high. Since Zeb owned most of the land in the immediate foreground and made sure that it was not cut over, the scene that greeted visitors was one of unspoiled wilderness. Nearer the house, however, much human labor—quite a bit of it Zeb's—went into the creation of carefully structured grounds. A spring-fed brook flowed to a small lake that was surrounded by a spacious lawn "fully adorned with majestic oaks, chestnuts, black gums, poplars, dogwoods, and several other varieties of native trees." In addition, the estate contained a vineyard, several orchards and gardens, a greenhouse, a dairy and several barns, and a springhouse with ice for cooling and preserving food.[30] It was at Gombroon that Zeb felt most at ease, and he and Florence returned to this well-appointed house at every opportunity in the years that followed.

As much as Zeb might have wanted to ignore the outside world now that he had his dream home, the world—and politics, in particular—demanded his constant attention. Of greatest concern to Zeb was the health of the

Democratic Party in North Carolina. One minor incident illustrates the strains that plagued the party. In the midst of a national tour, the president and the first lady decided to visit Asheville. The leaders of the growing city were very pleased, and they invited Zeb and fellow senator Matt W. Ransom to join the first couple in a parade and welcome ceremony. Zeb seriously considered boycotting the ceremony because of his differences with the president on patronage, but wiser counsels prevailed. Zeb was very pleased to report to Florence that he received louder cheers than Cleveland did from the western North Carolina crowd.[31]

On a much more serious level, North Carolina Democrats faced a crisis in the 1886 elections. The patronage battles within the party had sapped the enthusiasm of many party workers, and reports indicated that there was widespread apathy among local Democratic leaders. Even more significant, some of the legislative policies pursued by the party had prompted adverse reactions. The county government law adopted during Reconstruction by the Democrats, for example, increasingly caused dissatisfaction. This legislation had taken the selection of local government officials out of the hands of voters and placed the responsibility with the legislature. The ostensible justification for the law was that it prevented African American majorities in eastern North Carolina from electing blacks to local offices. However, Republican counties with overwhelmingly white populations like Randolph, Wilkes, and Mitchell had also been saddled with Democratic administrations. Equally significant, some factions in the Democratic Party were shut off from local patronage because they were not part of the dominant faction of the party. Throughout the state, older incumbents tended to control the offices, shutting out ambitious younger Democrats from holding government posts.[32]

Another piece of legislation passed in 1885 brought dissatisfaction to a boiling point. Known as both the stock law and the fence law, it was passed at the request of larger commercial farmers throughout the state. The law allowed counties to pass local ordinances that did away with the concept of the commons. Before this law had been passed, landowners were expected to fence in their garden areas only. Small landowners and the landless had the right both to let their livestock run free on anyone's land and to use the products of the forest, like ginseng, for their own profit. The new fence law enabled counties to permit landowners to fence their entire property and to prohibit both their neighbors and their neighbors' animals from trespassing on the enclosed lands. Needless to say, the changes created great hardship for people in the lower economic classes in rural parts of the state. Buncombe County was one of the first in the state to put the fence law into effect, and the action was deeply resented.[33]

The combination of all of the factors mentioned above led to a wide-spread revolt against the Democrats in 1886. Particularly in the western Piedmont and mountain counties, Democrats competed against a large number of independent candidates for seats in the state legislature. The most prominent of these candidates was Richmond Pearson of Asheville. Pearson, the son of the Civil War chief justice, was a Democrat who announced that he was opposed both to the way in which the legislature controlled the county governments and to the fence law. He attacked the regular party leaders, and he won the support of local Republicans. The party leadership recognized that a crisis was brewing and called upon Zeb to tour the western part of the state in order to arouse the faithful. He complied. In his speeches, Zeb attacked the national Republican Party; this part of his message was warmly received. But when he spoke about local questions, his appeals often did not satisfy his auditors. Zeb called upon all Democrats to vote for the party's regular candidates whether either the party or the candidates were "right or wrong." He maintained that it was absolutely essential for the party to remain in power. Zeb's call for party regularity failed to rally the voters; the Republicans and the independent Democrats won a majority in the House and twenty-four out of fifty seats in the North Carolina Senate. One result of this political reversal was that many new men, including large numbers of Republicans, were appointed by the legislature to local offices throughout the state. In Zeb's own Buncombe County, Pearson won election to the legislature by 2,783 votes to 1,696.[34] If Zeb had been running for reelection to the Senate in 1886, it was a sobering fact that this legislature would not have selected him. The outcome of the election encouraged Zeb and other party leaders to redouble their efforts to organize the state.

Zeb did his part in support of the party's attempt to attract voters by attempting to redress problems that plagued his constituents. One such problem was rate discrimination by the railroads. Railroads tended to favor people who lived in major trading centers like Chicago and New York and to force people in rural areas to pay higher rates. It struck Zeb and many rural people as manifestly unfair that it was often cheaper to send goods long distances between major cities than it was to send them short distances between two rural points, and the senator protested. Zeb also attacked the railroads for using predatory pricing to destroy the viability of their rivals.[35] Zeb criticized the nation's railroads in an effort to ease the economic distress that North Carolina farmers faced during this period.

Zeb was convinced, however, that he could do the greatest good for the farmers if he could reduce the cost of the goods they had to purchase by getting the tariff rates lowered. In January 1888, Zeb opposed a bill to reduce federal internal revenue taxes. While many of his mountain constituents might have favored the bill, Zeb detected a conspiracy in the measure. If the flow of government revenue from internal sources were reduced, then he believed that the government would become even more dependent for revenue on taxes on goods entering the country. For that reason, Zeb refused to support the bill. He explained that his constituents were more upset by the method of collecting the tax than by the tax itself. He ended his statement of protest in the Senate by once again attacking the high tariff rates, even though they were not under discussion.[36]

Zeb's consistent opposition to the protective tariff caused him to receive an unusual opportunity to reach the public. The *Baltimore Sun*, a Democratic paper, decided to run a series of front-page articles on the protective tariff. The paper selected Zeb, the best-known spokesman for the Democrats on this issue, to represent his party's views. The seven long articles that appeared between March 19 and April 27, 1888, were used as campaign literature in the presidential election of that year. While there were few new facts in the articles, Zeb took great care to spell out how particular segments of the population were harmed by high protective tariffs. He singled out farmers, industrial workers, and the merchant marine for special attention. Focusing on the positive, Zeb maintained that the United States would enjoy even greater prosperity if the nation followed a free trade policy. Using language that would enjoy much greater public support a century later, Zeb observed, "There is no country on earth prepared to become so rich by foreign trade as these United States, because there is none so abundantly supplied with all the material and all the conditions of production—absolutely none."[37] With the publication of these articles, Zeb's status as the most consistent opponent of the protective tariff in the U.S. Senate was confirmed.

Zeb's concern about the impact of the tariff on farmers was not simply a theoretical problem; impoverished farmers were increasingly becoming a personal political threat, as well. Starting late in the spring of 1887, North Carolina farmers began to join sub-alliances (as the local chapters were called) of the National Farmers' Alliance. By October of that year, a state organization had been formed, with Leonidas L. Polk as the secretary and spokesman. In the spring and summer of 1888, the Alliance moved into local and state politics and sought to nominate its own candidates on the Democratic ticket. Strongest in the eastern and Piedmont counties that specialized in cotton and tobacco production, the organization challenged the established hierarchy of the party. Its members backed their state president, Sydenham B. Alexander, for the Democratic gubernatorial nomination against the party regulars' nominee. Alexander was denied the nomination only after twenty-three contentious ballots.[38]

This result left the Democrats in a vulnerable position during the 1888 campaign. They had actively opposed some reform measures introduced by the independents and the Republicans in the legislature, including the ten-hour workday and the creation of a state railroad commission. Thus, the Democrats found themselves on the defensive during the state campaign. As they often had in the past, they resorted to racist appeals to firm up their support among white voters. This campaign tactic was not as effective during this canvass as usual, however, and the racist speeches that William H. "Buck" Kitchin gave in the western counties were actually thought to be harming the party's chances. Once again, the Democrats called upon Zeb to arouse and unite the party members. This time Zeb ignored local issues, a relatively easy task in a presidential election year. Instead of focusing directly on state or regional issues, he denounced the Republican tariff policies in "a masterly manner." As usual, Zeb spoke for more than two hours each time he gave an address, and he drew thousands of spectators at each stop on his tour.[39]

North Carolina Democrats achieved a victory, but Grover Cleveland was defeated in the national election. Under the intense party pressure imposed during the presidential campaign, there had been virtually no independent Democratic candidates for the state legislature. The result was a sweeping Democratic victory. When the legislature met, however, the party's surface unity cracked. Incumbent U.S. senator Matt W. Ransom was challenged for his seat by Alliance president Sydenham B. Alexander and other ambitious party leaders. For the first time in more than a decade, the leading candidate did not achieve a victory on the first ballot. Ransom did win on the second ballot, but the incident forewarned Zeb that his reelection in 1890 was not assured.[40]

The Democrats' defeat in the presidential election did Zeb very little harm. Since he had had little success in placing his own people in patronage positions, he did not lose much by his party's defeat. Cleveland's failure to win reelection also gave Zeb the opportunity to claim that the president had lost because he had refused to follow Zeb's lead. In the immediate aftermath of the election, Zeb declared, "Twas this confounded Civil Service humbug that fixed us." More mature reflection produced a more balanced assessment. By March 1889, Zeb had concluded that both the tariff issue and civil service reform had played a major role in the Democratic president's defeat. Zeb also noted that Cleveland had conscientiously examined the many special Civil War pension bills that Congress had passed to assist Union army veterans, and that he had vetoed many of the most questionable. By doing so, he had allowed the Republicans to revive Civil War issues, a strategy that aided them considerably in Northern states where the election was closely contested.[41]

By the time that Zeb made the latter assessment, he had participated in the debate over the Mills Tariff Bill. This legislation originated in the House of Representatives, which was controlled by the Democrats. It proposed slight reductions in some tax rates, but it was hardly a revolutionary measure. Senate Republicans took advantage of their majority status by proposing an entirely new bill as an amendment to the Mills bill. They used tactics to protect their version of the bill that infuriated Zeb and the Democrats. The Republicans had drafted their bill in a committee that included no members of the opposition party. They then tried to push the bill through their chamber as quickly as possible. At one point, Zeb complained, "We are forced in this way, without an opportunity even at night to acquire the information that is necessary for us to dispose of the bill properly, without even a Christmas holiday." Despite these handicaps, Zeb did participate in the debates extensively. He sought, in particular, to remove the tax placed on the metal ties that bound cotton bales. Zeb pointed out that the bill created problems for farmers whose products sold in the free trade markets of the world but who were forced to buy their consumer and business goods in a protected home market.[42] Zeb's efforts availed little, however.

Zeb's inability to persuade his fellow senators of the problems associated with the Republican bill was due in part to his own failing health. Zeb's intense study of the Republican proposal caused inflammation in one of his eyes. (Remember that Zeb and the other senators had virtually no staff.) The situation worsened rapidly, and in late January 1889, Dr. J. J. Chilton removed the eye. This radical approach seemed to have been the best one to take to Zeb's chronic eye troubles. Florence wrote to Matt W. Ransom soon after the surgery that the doctor could not save the eye and its removal would improve Zeb's general health. Florence went on to say that Zeb had slept well the night after the operation without using any drugs. Zeb's recovery from this trauma was indeed quite quick. Two weeks later, he replied to a sympathy card from William W. Holden, saying, "I am happy to say that I daily grow better & that all things indicate that my remaining eye will be preserved intact." The Senate recognized that the physical change would pose special challenges for Zeb, and its members voted to grant him an additional staff member to assist him with his work.[43]

The eye operation marked the conclusion of Zeb's most successful period as a national legislator. During this period he had established a national reputation as a speaker and as a party leader. He was probably the Senate member who had most consistently supported the reduction of trade barriers during a period when protective tariffs were predominant. He had also proved to be the mainstay of the Democratic Party in North Carolina and Virginia for most of these years. Still an effective campaigner in an unsettled political period, he acted as the chief spokesman for the established leadership of North Carolina's Democratic Party. He also spoke for the broader South on many economic and political issues. While he championed the common man at the national level, however, Zeb seemed to have lost touch with the immediate concerns of nonelite whites in North Carolina. Nevertheless, he still retained much of his enormous personal popularity among the public at large.

Zeb faced a difficult battle to win a third term in the Senate. The small farmers of North Carolina were in financial distress and were looking for political solutions to their problems. Through the Farmers' Alliance, they had challenged the leadership of the Democratic Party in 1888 and had nearly succeeded in seizing control of the Democratic organization. Since the farmers' difficulties had only grown worse in the intervening years, it was plain that they would seek to gain redress for their grievances from the state and federal governments in the 1890 election. Zeb recognized that this situation was fraught with danger for him. Viewing himself as a consistent friend of nonelite whites, however, he assumed that he would be able to survive the challenge through traditional political means by making his now standard addresses and appeals to the voters. He followed this plan as much as his health would allow, but he discovered that a new generation of voters did not respond to the appeals that had protected Zeb and the older leaders of the Democratic Party since 1865.

Zeb recovered slowly from his eye operation. In March he was in Black Mountain, and he reported to Florence that he was feeling fine. Less than two weeks later, however, he had to admit that his strength was only returning slowly. Zeb's weakness was emphasized when Florence's mother died in Louisville in April and Zeb was unable to accompany his wife to the funeral. Finally, in May, Zeb had recovered sufficiently to be able to resume some more strenuous physical activities. He traveled to Greensboro and gave a major address. Then he returned to Black Mountain and began to work around the estate. He also began writing a chapter on Reconstruction in North Carolina for Hilary A. Herbert, which is described in detail later in this chapter. By the late fall he seemed fully mended. He spoke to a large gathering in Carthage, North Carolina, and he delivered some campaign speeches in Virginia during the fall elections of that year. As late as October 1889, however, he still had to reassure his family and friends that he was "getting quite strong."[1]

He made his first major public appearance in the spring of 1889 to deliver a speech at the Guilford Battle Ground before a crowd that he estimated numbered ten thousand people. This speech, which commemorated one of the major battles of the Revolutionary War, gave Zeb a chance to discuss two matters that would become increasingly important to the elder statesman. First, he celebrated the forefathers of the now united country. This, of course, gave him an opportunity to explore the contributions made by his own family. Second, he noted the failure of North Carolina to properly recognize those people who had made important contributions to its history and development. The usually friendly *Charlotte Democrat* criticized this part of the speech, saying that the state did not need to build historical monuments, but to spend money on the living. But in this matter, Zeb once again understood popular sentiment much better than his critics. The nostalgic commemoration of the Civil War had grown popular in the South, and monuments soon began to appear throughout both the state and the region dedicated to the heroes of the past.[2]

While Zeb slowly recovered from his surgery, the Democratic Party of North Carolina sought to find ways to defend itself against both the still viable Republican Party and the threat posed by the growing unrest among farmers, particularly those in the eastern and Piedmont counties of the state. The legislature passed the Payne Election Law, which was designed to discriminate against those voters who most directly threatened the position of the Democratic Party leadership. It gave local registrars considerable discretion in determining whether voters were qualified. Since the Democratic legislature had appointed all of these officials, the registrars would naturally be expected to eliminate as many Republican voters, particularly African Americans, as possible. Another feature of the law was less partisan, but it was directed against the poor of both races and parties. In counties where officials chose to implement this section of the law, voters had to deposit multiple ballots, placing the correct ballot for each elective office in a separate box. Since a voter could know that he was casting his votes correctly only by reading the designations on the boxes, illiterate voters were put at a significant disadvantage. They either had to ask for assistance from the local election official and thereby reveal themselves as illiterate or cast their ballots incorrectly. Democratic Party leaders assumed that most poorly educated voters either would not risk public humiliation in order to vote or would become so confused that they would cast their ballots in the wrong boxes, in which case their votes could be nullified. Republicans were quick to protest these electoral changes.[3]

The eventful election year of 1890 quickly demonstrated that in the changing electoral climate, traditional expectations did not apply. Zeb, like many Southern Democrats, assumed that racial animosity would still be a powerful motivating force among the electorate in 1890. Thus, he took the opportunity to speak extensively on a bill that proposed to return African Americans to Africa. He used the occasion not only to disparage blacks, but also to attack the election reform bill introduced into the federal House of Representatives by Republican Henry Cabot Lodge. In this debate, his justification for denying blacks the right to vote was a classic example of blaming the victim: "If it be true that in States where they largely outnumber the whites they are intimidated from voting or are defrauded in the counting of their votes, is not that a strong argument against their supposed capacity for self government? Are a people fit to govern themselves and others who would suffer themselves thus to be treated?" Then, anticlimactically, Zeb announced that he could not support the legislation to send blacks back to Africa because there was no economical way to accomplish this objective.[4]

Zeb did not limit his attack on Lodge's bill to the halls of Congress, however. Working with Alabama Democratic congressman Hilary A. Herbert, Zeb wrote an essay on Reconstruction in North Carolina that was designed to reveal the shortcomings of African Americans' political actions between 1868 and 1877. Joining Zeb in the enterprise of writing a history of Reconstruction were eight past or present members of Congress and four other "experts." Zeb's contribution to the book, which was published in 1890, can best be described as a diatribe. He relentlessly distorted his descriptions of the developments of the Reconstruction era for partisan effect. He emphasized those episodes that supported his argument, including the railroad bond fraud perpetrated by Milton S. Littlefield and George W. Swepson, the failure of the state to build railroad lines, and the collapse of both educational and welfare institutions between 1868 and 1870.[5] While Zeb's description of these developments was selective, his decision to emphasize these episodes can be accepted as a matter of historical judgment.

The remainder of Zeb's essay, however, fell outside the pale of acceptable historical scholarship, even by the less stringent standards of his day. His discussion of the militia raised by George W. Kirk and William W. Holden was marred by his failure to mention the Ku Klux Klan. This omission was matched by his failure to describe either the undemocratic system of local government that the redeemers fastened on the state in 1875 or the frauds committed that same year to elect a majority to the constitutional convention. Moreover, Zeb used openly racist language to discuss African American participation in the events of the Reconstruction era. The following excerpt from his article, in which he tells a story about the political corruption of a fictional African American man named Uncle Cuffy, is only one of many examples that could have been selected: "A friend going to see him one night at his rooms found him sitting at a table, by the dim light of a tallow dip, laboriously counting a pile of money and chuckling to himself.

'Why,' said his visitor, 'What amuses you so Uncle Cuffy?' 'Well boss,' he replied, grinning ear to ear, 'I's been sold in my life 'leven times an' fo' de Lord, dis is de fust time I eber got de money!'"[6] This account is not historical, and its use in this essay suggests that Zeb did not write the piece for intellectual reasons. Rather, he used his talents for political advantage in a way that was demeaning to his fellow citizens.

In late February, Zeb introduced two bills in the Senate. The bills would change his political world; in his future, race would no longer be the major issue in North Carolina politics. Zeb introduced the bills at the request of the National Farmers' Alliance. They would have established "a system of agricultural depositories" and "a system of Government storehouses for agricultural products." Together, the bills would have created the subtreasury system that the Farmers' Alliance advocated. The subtreasury plan was designed to solve the farmers' most pressing problem: they were losing money because they were all forced to market their products at harvest time. Because farmers had to bring their products to market at roughly the same time, the market for the products became oversupplied, which drove down the prices that farmers could obtain. The Alliance wanted to create a series of agricultural warehouses where farmers could store their non-perishable products, borrow money on the products' expected value, and then sell the goods at an advantageous time. With the proceeds of their sales, the farmers could pay off their loans and still realize a profit.[7]

Zeb's willingness to introduce these two bills led to a series of misunderstandings that threatened both the stability of the Democratic Party in North Carolina and his own reelection. The leader of the Farmers' Alliance, Leonidas L. Polk, who had been an officer with Zeb in the Twenty-sixth Regiment, asked Zeb to request that he be invited to address both houses of Congress on the plight of the farmer. When Zeb made the rather unique request and it was immediately turned down, he arranged for Polk and other Alliance officials to testify before the Senate Agriculture Committee. Despite all of this activity on behalf of the Alliance, however, Zeb had not actually endorsed the bills that he introduced. This fact prompted Eugene C. Beddingfield, secretary of the Farmers' Alliance of North Carolina, to write to Zeb on May 16. Beddingfield posed eight questions to Zeb that covered the full range of issues identified by the Alliance as critical to the problems of the farmer.[8]

Zeb's reply was quick and direct. On May 18, he wrote to Beddingfield and answered each question without making the usual political qualifications. On a number of issues, including silver coinage, railroad landholding, ownership of land by foreign corporations, and the issue of paper money by the government, he fully agreed with the Alliance's stand. On other points, however, Zeb was at odds with the farmers' organization. He indicated that he opposed congressional regulation of the trading of future contracts on agricultural commodities, government control of the railroads and telegraphs, the immediate abolition of national banks, and the substitution of local bank notes for a national currency.[9] These planks were all part of the national platform of the Alliance, and Zeb was unwilling to bend his principles to agree with them simply because it would have been politically expedient.

But in many respects, all of these were side issues. Beddingfield's final question had been about Zeb's position on the subtreasury. Zeb's reply in this case was much more artful than his others. He said in part: "I am in favor not of this particular bill (for it is crude and imperfect) but of the principles of the bill, provided it not be established as unconstitutional. . . . If it were once reported from the Committee it would receive thorough discussion and the country could see for itself. My hope and earnest wish is that the discussion will result in some practical scheme for the relief of farmers in this direction."[10] This was as far as Zeb would go toward satisfying the Alliance on this issue. He had agreed to work for some type of legislation, but he would not support the Alliance's bills. There was no immediate public reaction to Zeb's reply, because Beddingfield chose not to have Zeb's letter published at that time.

Zeb was clearly troubled by the growing resistance of the Alliance to the discipline of the Democratic Party. On May 20, 1890, he participated in the 115th anniversary celebration of the Mecklenburg Declaration of Independence. Zeb was not listed on the program, but, as often happened at events he attended, the audience called for him to speak. He stated that he had not expected to speak and that he was unprepared to do so. As was usually the case on these occasions, however, he did speak. It is interesting to note that rather than deliver a few meaningless platitudes about the Revolutionary forefathers, he discussed the contemporary political situation. He observed that farmers and laborers were organizing to defend themselves, but, he cautioned, "if those who seek redress of wrongs, let it go into seeking vengeance, there are ominous times ahead of us."[11] This is a rather revealing statement. Zeb was clearly worried that he would be the object of a vengeful campaign against the establishment. Developments in North Carolina politics soon proved that he had reason to be concerned.

All across the South, the Alliance urged its members to attend the county nominating conventions of the Democratic Party. Members were encouraged to vote for state legislative candidates who would support the Alliance program, particularly those who would support the subtreasury proposals. Zeb knew that his efforts and those of his allies in the Democratic Party around the state to elect state legislators committed to Zeb's reelection might conflict with the Alliance strategy. He apparently decided that he could not allow this potential conflict to simmer beneath the surface. Thus, on June 29, he addressed a letter to Elias Carr, president of the Farmers' Alliance of North Carolina. Zeb made two major points in the letter. First, he commented, "I cannot gain my consent to vote for this subtreasury bill which provides for the loaning of money to the people by the government, and which, in my opinion, is without constitutional authority." Then, Zeb warned that if the Alliance formed a third party, this maneuver "could only destroy the Democratic party" in the South.[12]

Zeb was anxious to place this issue before the public as soon as possible. He not only requested that Carr share his letter with the public, he also instructed Democratic editors to reprint the letter. In his reply to Vance, Carr was quite conciliatory. He assured Zeb that the farmers were intent only on improving their lot in the world, and that they had no intention of "going into politics." He went on to state that the Alliance would operate within the confines of the Democratic Party. Carr's perspective was not shared, however, by many of the most militant of the Alliance's members. J. L. Ramsey, the editor of the movement's statewide newspaper, the *Progressive Farmer*, attacked Zeb and his position on the subtreasury in a July 8 editorial. Ramsey wrote: "If he is not willing to serve the people we want to know it. We can't afford to pay men $8,000 per annum and then allow them to put up their brains against the entire State." It is little wonder that on that same day, Zeb wrote to Florence and lamented that the Alliance had "declared war" on him.[13]

Zeb sought to soften the acrimony surrounding the subtreasury issue by actively championing the Alliance position on the expansion of the coinage of silver currency. On June 12, he gave an extended address in the Senate in which he pointed out the impact that the failure to expand the national currency had had on the farmer. He asserted, "a very large portion of that class of our fellow citizens are doomed to bankruptcy and ruin." Calling silver coins the "money of the people," Zeb claimed that the government's currency policy was a great "crime against the American people." On July 10, Zeb indicated that he would support what he considered to be an imperfect silver coinage bill. It provided for the expansion in the number of silver coins, but it failed to ensure that they would be placed in circulation. Zeb commented about this compromise legislation, "I find that under the operation of this bill the lion and the lamb have lain down together, and, as usual, the lamb is inside the lion."[14] In any case, Zeb sought to direct the Alliance's attention away from the subtreasury bill and onto another one of its major issues.

Perhaps this strategy succeeded, or perhaps Zeb's popularity was such that many Alliance members refused to accept Ramsey's criticism. Whatever the reason, Warren County Democrats passed resolutions endorsing Zeb's course in the Senate and supporting him for reelection. Other Democrats followed suit at their county nominating conventions, and Zeb was able to report to Florence two weeks later that many conventions had endorsed him for another Senate term. In the most explicit break from the recommendations of the Alliance's state newspaper, the Alliance members in Wilson County specifically endorsed Zeb's letter to Carr in full. Still, there were instances in which Zeb's efforts to secure the backing of county conventions failed. In Wake and Granville Counties, resolutions to endorse his reelection were not carried.[15] Thus, when this first battle between the Alliance and the party regulars, who lined up solidly behind Zeb, came to a close, Zeb had accrued a slight advantage.

The controversy did not die, however. Democratic newspapers and the *Progressive Farmer* continued to attack each other and to fight about Zeb. When the state Democratic nominating convention met in August, the party leadership once again asserted itself in Zeb's favor. While the party refused to endorse the subtreasury bill in Congress as part of its platform, it did recommend that a measure that supported the same principles be passed. The convention also supported Zeb for reelection, an unusual move that encroached on the sovereignty of the party's legislative caucus, which would select the party's next Senate candidate. Ironically, the push by the party regulars to reduce the influence of the Alliance probably cost Zeb's brother Robert a congressional nomination. He was the Alliance candidate in the Ninth District, and he had secured the votes of more delegates than any other candidate. However, he was unable to win over a majority of the delegates, and the nomination went to William T. Crawford, who had strong support both from party regulars and from the Alliance.[16]

Shortly after all of the excitement surrounding the conventions had subsided, another sensation occurred that kept the controversy alive. Eugene C. Beddingfield released Zeb's letter of May 18 for publication in Alliance newspapers. Leonidas L. Polk and the editor of the *Progressive Farmer* unleashed another attack on Zeb on September 1, in which they accused Zeb of acting in bad faith on the subtreasury issue. Regular Democratic papers answered in kind, and open warfare between the two wings of the Democratic Party seemed imminent. Many of those involved in the controversy, however, remembered the results of the 1886 elections in North Carolina and acted to keep the party from offering the Republicans an opening. Apparently Matt W. Ransom was able to reach an agreement with Polk that each side would desist from making further attacks.[17] The result was that a partially united Democratic Party faced the opposition.

Ironically, North Carolina Republicans were as badly shattered as were the state's Democrats. The debate over the Lodge election reform bill was particularly bitter. Congressman Hamilton G. Ewart strongly opposed the legislation, calling it "damnable, illogical, inequitable, and vicious." He prophesied that the elections bill would solidify the white voters of the South behind the Democrats and lead to crushing Republican defeats. Many Republicans agreed with Ewart and left the party during the subsequent campaign. The Republicans were also badly divided over the distribution of patronage, particularly those positions involved with the collection of internal revenue.[18] The result was that the Republican opposition was in no condition to challenge the fractured Democrats.

Zeb sought to make the debate on the McKinley Tariff Bill of 1890 a centerpiece of the campaign. This bill proposed to enact the highest tax rates of the period, but the Democrats were the minority party in both houses of Congress and could not hope to defeat it. Instead, Zeb and his fellow Democrats sought to use what they predicted would be the worst effects of the bill for ammunition in the 1890 congressional elections. Aiming many of his remarks at the dissatisfied farmers in the South generally, and at North Carolina's farmers particularly, Zeb made many statements like the following: "An American laborer, a man in the field, may be a native-born American citizen, and his forefathers for generations may have been American citizens, yet when it comes to the question of protecting his labor he is not an American, and he is not a laborer either." As noted earlier, Zeb was especially angered that the bill proposed a substantial increase in the tax on the metal ties that bound cotton bales together. Southern farmers who gained no protection from the bill would now be forced to pay higher prices to purchase a necessary product. Zeb warned the Republicans that enormous resentment was building against their policies, and if relief was not offered soon, the dam holding back the public's anger would burst and sweep away "everything that stands in its reach below."[19]

Zeb spent a good part of the early fall trying to amend specific parts of the McKinley bill. Virtually all of the changes he sought would have assisted farmers in their capacity as consumers of necessities. Although the debates on the bill were partisan in nature and took place during an election year, the Republicans' confidence that the bill would pass reduced the acrimony of the discussions somewhat. The following exchange illustrates both how Zeb played to the public beyond the walls of Congress and the good humor of the replies he often provoked:

MR. VANCE: That is not right, sir, it is not just, sir; it is almost, I was going to say, impiety itself to thus oppress men who, as the instruments of the Almighty, answer for us the prayer He taught us to utter: 'Give us this day our daily bread.' (Applause in the galleries.)

MR. EDMUNDS: Mr. President, I believe the county of Buncombe is still in the State of North Carolina.

Another politician from western North Carolina had earlier been responsible for bringing the word "buncombe" into common usage to signify overblown speech, but Zeb's fellow legislators clearly felt that his speeches fit into the regional tradition on occasion.[20]

Zeb and the Democrats recognized that he would be most useful if he spoke directly to the voters in North Carolina. He started his direct campaign for the party and for his own reelection with a major speech in Goldsboro in mid-September. Since the speech incorporated most of the elements of the speeches he gave throughout that fall, it is worth examining in detail. He first attempted to bind the voters to the Democratic Party as Southerners. Zeb attacked the sectionalism that he perceived to be evident in both the Lodge bill and the McKinley Tariff Bill. He went on to provide a detailed account of how he had supported the increased coinage of silver currency. Then Zeb returned to the subject of the tariff and the tremendous hardships that tariffs had placed on the farmers of North Carolina. Finally, he addressed the issue of the subtreasury bills. He explained once again why he had opposed the particular bills pending in Congress, but he assured his audience that he was seeking alternative means to assist the farmers.[21]

In the conclusion of his speech, Zeb turned to a topic that he had never addressed before. According to a reporter who was present, Zeb "reviewed his 36 years of political life, at times reaching the topmost heights of pathetic eloquence that moved the hearts almost to worship of the man." Earlier in the summer, Zeb had written to Florence and told her that he felt unappreciated by his fellow North Carolinians and that he was considering withdrawing from politics.[22] This self-pitying statement was undoubtedly prompted in part by the physical challenges that Zeb faced, but there seems to have been more to it than that. Many of the people who participated in politics in the early 1890s belonged to a younger generation that had little memory of the searing experiences of the Civil War. The same was true of the voters, and Zeb found that the language he had long used to rouse and rally voters no longer had the potency that it once had. In addition, people who in the past would have deferred to him no longer did. Zeb spoke of his past achievements as a way of repairing his damaged self-esteem and explaining to the younger voters why he deserved another Senate term.

Two weeks later, he spoke before the Young Men's Democratic Convention in Raleigh. In this speech and in others that followed, Zeb sought to further defuse the hostility between regular party members and Alliance Democrats. Zeb claimed, "There is not a single demand of the Farmer's Alliance that is not a cardinal doctrine of the Democratic party." Later in the speech, Zeb acknowledged the difference between the two groups over the subtreasury. But, interestingly, he framed that difference not as one that existed between the wings of the party, but as one that had largely been fabricated in order to criticize him. He also spent time telling the young men about his "36 years of service" to North Carolina; it is clear that Zeb had increasingly personalized the campaign.[23]

As the campaign came to a close, the uneasy truce between the regular Democrats and Alliance leaders held together. Zeb helped to keep it together by finally agreeing to support the subtreasury bill if it was "demonstrated to be constitutional by any decision of the Supreme Court." This was a rather disingenuous statement on his part, however, because Zeb was convinced that no such decision had been made or was forthcoming. With the Republicans in complete disarray, the Democrats swept to an overwhelming victory in November. They won control of the state Senate by a vote of 43 to 7 and carried the House by a majority of 102 to 18.[24] This meant that all Zeb had to do to be reelected to the Senate was to win the Democratic caucus nomination and hold the Democratic majority together.

That task proved to be difficult, because approximately two-thirds of the state legislators were also members of the Farmers' Alliance; probably three-quarters of the Democrats belonged to the farmers' organization. Fortunately for Zeb, the Republicans were such a small minority in the legislature that there was little likelihood that a faction of the Democratic Party would split off and form a coalition with the rival party. Recognizing this reality, the Alliance adopted a strategy that put pressure on Zeb. Since U.S. senators were elected by the legislature during this period, a tradition had developed that the legislature could "instruct" a senator,—directing him to vote for a particular piece of legislation—and the senator would be honor bound to vote as the legislature demanded. Two weeks after the election, Elias Carr wrote to Zeb on behalf of the Alliance and asked if he would agree to accept instructions "to advocate and vote for the sub-Treasury plan of financial reform."[25]

Zeb took nearly three weeks to reply to Carr's inquiry. Tensions began to build during that time, and the Democrats seemed to be on the verge of a major split. When Zeb's reply of December 6 was made public, however, the simmering controversy settled down. Zeb acknowledged the existence and legitimacy of the instruction tradition. He continued, "I hold that the will of the people clearly and unequivocally expressed must be obeyed unless compliance would involve the representative in a moral wrong, in which case it would be his duty to resign and give place to a representative who would obey." Once this statement became public, most of the legislators confirmed that they would support Zeb for reelection.[26]

Before the legislature met, however, Zeb returned to Washington to participate in the final debates on the Lodge election bill. The atmosphere in the Senate had changed rather dramatically since the earlier discussions of the tariff bill. The Republicans had suffered severe reversals in virtually every state; their losses had been particularly bad in the South. It seemed likely that the Democrats would control Congress in the next session and would win the presidency in 1892. Thus, it would almost certainly be the Democrats who would administer the new election law if it was passed, not the Republicans. Under these circumstances, the Republicans did not push the bill with any enthusiasm. Zeb participated extensively in the debates. He attacked the hypocrisy of the Republicans for seeking to ensure that African Americans had the right to vote in the South while failing to provide them with the same right in the District of Columbia. Showing his own perspective on African Americans' participation in politics, Zeb claimed, "The policy of subjecting the intelligence and property of the South to the control of ignorance and poverty is not a new one."[27] Zeb did not make these efforts to defeat the bill in vain; the Lodge bill failed to pass. Through his speeches on the Senate floor, moreover, Zeb had reminded the North Carolina legislature, which was about to decide his fate, that the power he had in Washington could be used for their benefit.

Alliance leaders were not impressed by Zeb's performance in Washington. They wanted to ensure that he would support the subtreasury bills. Polk and other Alliance leaders were determined to get the legislature to pass instructions for the newly elected senator before the Democratic caucus met. That way, the candidate would have to commit himself to the instructions before he was elected. Following this plan of action, the legislature passed a resolution directing the North Carolina senators and congressmen to use "all honorable means to secure the financial reforms" contained in the Alliance platform of the last two years. This resolution would have required Zeb to support the existing subtreasury bill. Zeb refused to accept this instruction, just as Polk and other Alliance leaders had suspected he would. It appeared as if the Democratic caucus was about to become a major battleground; Zeb felt confident that he could secure reelection despite the opposition of the Alliance leaders.[28]

As the crisis loomed, a Democratic member of the House introduced a compromise set of instructions that passed easily. These requested that the senators and congressmen "secure the objects of the financial reforms." This meant that Zeb would not have to vote for the current bills, but that he would be obligated to try to put the subtreasury system in place by means of other legislation. Since this had been Zeb's plan all along, he happily accepted the modified instructions. Although some of the Alliance leaders grumbled, Zeb was renominated by the Democratic caucus by acclamation. Significantly, about twenty-five Alliance members chose to absent themselves from that meeting. Considering how small the Republican contingent was in the legislature, however, the dissatisfied Democrats could not challenge Zeb's reelection. Zeb himself was delighted with the outcome, and he sought to make light of the controversy surrounding his election. In his acceptance address to the Democratic caucus, he quipped, "In fact on a cloudy day I cannot tell an Alliance man from a Democrat."[29]

Zeb returned to the Senate and tried to concentrate on national issues. This session of the Congress, however, was largely barren of accomplishment. The Republicans apparently recognized that they had been discredited by the recent elections, and the Democrats decided to wait until they had their new majorities before addressing national issues. The only question that Zeb felt compelled to speak on at length during the session was whether the United States should recognize the international copyright convention. At the beginning of his talk, Zeb admitted that it "require[d] some considerable degree of courage for a Representative or a senator to stand up in his place and object to what is apparently and upon the surface so fair, and so reasonable, and so desirable a thing as is claimed to be aimed at in this bill." However, Zeb asserted, the copyright was a form of monopoly, a relic of the medieval period. He would prefer, he said, that books be made available to the poor than that the giant publishers make great profits.[30] For Zeb, the rights of authors were a secondary consideration. Once again, he took a stand that squared with his view of himself as the champion of the underclass.

The campaign for reelection had been a painful one for Zeb. His physical limitations had made the effort difficult. Even more painful, the aging political warrior had to face voters' seeming unwillingness to recognize the contributions he had made in public service. Political issues related to the war and Reconstruction no longer had the potency that they had once had in North Carolina, and unpalatable new issues seemed to dominate the political discourse. Zeb had survived the ordeal of the campaign, but he now felt that he and his party were under siege. This placed a consistent pressure on him that a younger and healthier man would have found difficult to handle, and it was especially problematic for someone in Zeb's condition. The question that Zeb now faced was how he could serve the people of North Carolina effectively in this new political world.

During the last three years of his life, Zeb entered a period of gradual political and physical decline. While evidence of his slow loss of influence and energy was obvious at various times, the fact that his health was declining was masked by bursts of accomplishment. It is important to recognize that at this time there was a fundamental historical shift that would have undermined Zeb's political position whether he had been in good health or not. At times, Zeb seemed to recognize the changes happening both around him and to him and to accept them with some grace. At other times, he resisted the new forces of change with a ferocity that brought his youth to mind. Throughout this entire period, however, he remained in the public eye, and that fact was of enormous importance to this extroverted political figure.

Toward the end of the 1891 congressional session, his health began to deteriorate once again. There is very little direct evidence as to what his physical problems were, but the best existing evidence indicates that all of the pressure associated with his reelection campaign caused a recurrence of the symptoms that had plagued him two years earlier. He apparently became quite weak and tired, and he was unable to carry out his duties as a senator.[1] Florence decided that the only cure for Zeb's condition would be an extended vacation. Apparently recognizing that taking time away at Gombroon would not be enough of a break, she arranged for Zeb to take an extended foreign tour for the first time in his life.

Zeb, Florence, and her son Harry Martin set sail for Europe on May 27, 1891. The crossing took eight days, and the ride was smooth for the first four days, but the ocean became quite rough after that. Zeb admitted that he had experienced enough seasickness on the journey "to satisfy any curiosity that I may have felt." He told another correspondent that he had thrown "up everything except my seat in the Senate!" The party landed at Queenstown in Ireland and traveled rapidly through Cork, Killarney, Dublin, and Belfast. When they reached Ulster, Florence and Harry continued on to the west coast, where the family home of Florence's first husband was located. Florence proved to be an avid tourist, and she loved Ireland. Apparently she suffered a number of scrapes and falls during the trip, but she was not daunted by any of them. While she and Harry traveled in western Ireland, Zeb went on to London, where he attended a Sunday worship service at Saint Paul's. After the group reunited, the three travelers spent nearly a month in London seeing the sights, shopping, doing business with Zeb's London banker, and visiting the American minister to Great Britain. According to Zeb, the trip up to this point seemed to have helped his health, and he felt much more rested.[2]

After their extended stay in London, they headed for Scotland and the continent. They made Edinburgh their headquarters and spent quite a few days exploring the northern kingdom. They traveled through the highlands and the lochs and journeyed as far north as Inverness. They also went to Glasgow, where Zeb was able to visit the site where the Civil War blockade-runner *Advance* had been constructed. From Scotland, they went to Germany, where they took in the Wagner festival in Bayreuth. While there, they saw performances of *Parsifal* and *Tristan und Isolde*. Then, in rapid succession, the intrepid three saw the sights in Berlin, Dresden, Prague, and Vienna before traveling through the Alps to Venice, Milan, Zurich, Bern, Geneva, and on to Paris. Once in the French capital, they stayed for a month and saw all the great buildings there. One thing that struck Zeb in his travels was the large number of American tourists, "many of them," he complained, "so loud and vulgar" that he was "ashamed."[3]

From Paris, Zeb, Florence, and Harry headed back to Italy. They traveled to Turin, Genoa, Pisa, Florence, Rome, and Naples. They spent a month in Rome seeing all of the Roman ruins and visiting the Vatican. They sailed from Italy to Egypt, where Zeb saw the pyramids. From there, they planned to go to Jerusalem, but the ports of Palestine were quarantined due to the outbreak of some kind of fever. They sailed to Athens and saw the many historic buildings there. Finally, they traveled to Constantinople, where they visited a number of imposing edifices. They took a train—probably the fabled Orient Express—across Europe and reached London in late November. Then they sailed home in time for Zeb to attend the opening session of the Fifty-second Congress.[4]

While Zeb found the trip to be very interesting, there is considerable doubt that it really improved his health. He reported to one son, "My general health is good but have had some little spells, one in Venice (diarrhea) a bad boil in Paris and a terrible cold here (Rome)." Writing to another correspondent from Cairo near the end of the trip, he complained that he was "worn out." He also said in the same letter that he would "rejoice exceedingly to get home again."[5] Though the trip probably did not have a salutary effect on Zeb's health, the travels certainly did take him away from the day-to-day pressures that he experienced in Washington. There is no doubt that seeing and visiting so many new and interesting places took Zeb's attention off many of his problems at home. But some refused to wait for his return, and he was forced to try to deal with land sales in Asheville from half a world away.

Nor could Zeb fully escape from the constantly evolving political situation in North Carolina while he was away. The legislature that had elected Vance went on to enact a series of progressive laws which indicated that the Alliance Democrats felt that the Democratic Party had not been as responsive to voters' concerns in the previous decade as it should have been. The Democratic majority chartered a state railway commission and gave it the power to set rates; created a state college for women and a second college for African Americans; allocated more tax money to public education; and provided many communities with much needed new banks. The contrast between these lawmakers' solid accomplishments and the record of the regular Democrats who had preceded them in office was obvious to all. At the same time, North Carolina Republicans sought to reinvent themselves as well. Led by Jeter C. Pritchard from the western mountains, the party sought to distance itself from the Lodge bill and from African American voters. Instead, the party's core issue became its support of the protective tariff. The Republicans hoped that their stand on the tariff issue would make them less vulnerable to a racist Democratic campaign.[6]

Recognizing that the Farmers' Alliance was more than a momentary phenomenon, Zeb sought to neutralize its impact from Europe. In October, the *Raleigh News and Observer* published an anonymous article that Zeb had written. In it, he once again addressed the issue of the subtreasury. He answered the proponents of the legislation by demonstrating that their interpretation of the precedents they cited to prove the constitutionality of the pending bill was erroneous. He characterized the legislation as "flagrantly unconstitutional" and concluded his essay with a rhetorical question that supported his own position. It is doubtful that the essay convinced anyone who disagreed with Vance, but the remarks did provide a justification for his actions and those of his supporters.[7] Ironically, Polk and other Alliance leaders were beginning to play down the subtreasury bill and to emphasize the free coinage of silver as their major issue.

With the dawn of the new year, Zeb returned to the Senate. He seemed to be in improved health and able to carry on a busy schedule of regular Senate duties. In February, he made a long argument in the Senate about a forgettable election case from Idaho. He argument was quite technical and able, if ultimately unpersuasive to his fellow senators. In April, however, he was forced to return to North Carolina for an extended period of rest. A friendly newspaper reported, "Some of his friends fear his days of great usefulness are about ended."[8] In retrospect, Zeb's health problems were to be expected. He had developed a lifestyle that practically ensured that his body would eventually begin to break down. He had been overweight, weighing at least 230 pounds and standing five feet eleven inches tall, since he was a youth. He preferred to eat fatty and sweet foods, and in great quantities. He chewed tobacco all of his adult life and drank liquor regularly, although the amount of his intake is unknown. While he did quite a bit of work around the house and grounds at Gombroon, he did not exercise consistently. Given that this lifestyle was coupled with the constant stress of political life, and considering that Zeb had suffered a stroke in 1865, it seems unsurprising that his body began to fail.

By the summer of 1892, it was clear that Zeb was not going to be able to play a major role in the political campaign of that year. For the second year in a row, Zeb was unable to attend the ceremony marking the anniversary of the Mecklenburg Declaration of Independence. In July, Zeb and Florence went to an oceanfront resort for additional relaxation and rest. The following "positive" report from that period indicates that Zeb failed to bounce back quickly: "He suffers but little pain, sleeps pretty well without opiates of any kind, walks with comparative ease, and on the whole is doing splendidly." The last sentiment appears to have been wishful thinking. In August, Zeb declined an invitation to attend the annual meeting of the North Carolina Press Association.[9] Clearly, it would be beyond his abilities to carry a heavy load in the upcoming campaign.

This was most unfortunate for North Carolina's Democrats, because all observers agreed that they faced a challenging task during that campaign. A significant minority of Farmers' Alliance members had broken away from the Democratic Party and formed the People's Party, more commonly known as the Populists. The Republicans decided to run a full campaign themselves, and they were particularly active in the western counties of the state. Moreover, the Democrats of North Carolina were once again saddled with Grover Cleveland as their presidential candidate. Virtually none of the North Carolina Democrats, including Zeb, had favored the former president's renomination. Since Cleveland had already announced his opposition to the free coinage of silver—the most salient issue in North Carolina that year—the state's Democrats faced a potential disaster.[10]

The task of organizing and directing the Democrats during the campaign fell to campaign chairman Furnifold M. Simmons, a young political operative from the eastern part of the state. Simmons decided that the Democrats needed Zeb's influence even if they could not have his presence. Simmons wrote to Zeb in September requesting that he issue a campaign letter. Zeb willingly complied. In his letter, Zeb used most of his space to attempt to convince farmers that they should not support the Populists. He acknowledged that Cleveland was not popular in North Carolina, but he said that the Democrats needed to support their party to prevent a Republican victory. He asserted that by voting for the Populists, Democrats would put their political opponents in office. He then went on to claim that the new party's leaders were not farmers and that their programs were not constitutional.[11] The Democratic Party leadership was pleased with the letter and sent it to voters across the state.

Zeb's rather passive role in the campaign did not satisfy him. As the contest neared its climax, Zeb sought to participate. He traveled to Morganton, Lincolnton, and Charlotte and appeared at campaign rallies. At the first two stops, he was greeted with great enthusiasm. When he got to Charlotte, the city of his former residence, however, his welcome was overwhelming. A local reporter captured the moment: "Vance! Vance! was the sound which burst spontaneously from the immense audience . . . and as the noble loved 'Zeb' rose, the people went wild. Old men, young men, women and children jumped to their feet, waving handkerchiefs and hats, and cheering until the very building seemed to rock. Not a person in the house remained seated; many stood on benches, hats were thrown up. . . . On the rostrum every man rose, and following Mr. Ham's lead all waved their handkerchiefs and cheered for fully ten minutes."[12] Most of the people present must have recognized that this might be Zeb's last public appearance in his adopted home, as indeed it was, and they wanted to share their feelings with their former neighbor and friend.

Caught up in the emotion of the moment, Zeb decided to give a short address. He began, "To-night I speak against the advice of my physician, but you know when we begin to get well we think less of the doctor than when we are sick." The euphoria of speaking before an audience again provided Zeb with sufficient strength to speak for fifteen minutes. His message to his auditors was that those who became Populists were likely to "land right in the Republican party." After the meeting, Zeb wrote to Florence to tell her about the evening and to assure her that he was feeling fine.[13] Nevertheless, his extraordinary appearance in Charlotte was the last campaign appearance that Zeb would ever make. The special outpouring of popular affection that Zeb met with on that occasion was most appropriate. Zeb had lived his life since the age of fourteen for events like these, where he could be the center of attention. He had used them to judge how well his messages were being received by the public. After November 1892, unfortunately, Zeb was no longer capable of meeting the public, and he lost the ability to avail himself of the valuable interactions with voters that had made him such an effective spokesman for an important segment of North Carolina's population.

Thanks to the hard work of Simmons, Zeb and the Democrats swept to victory in North Carolina in 1892. Foreshadowing the strategy the party would adopt later in the decade, Simmons had encouraged Democratic election officials to use the latitude given them by the election laws to discourage many poor black and white citizens from voting. Despite the use of these tactics, however, the Republicans and Populists combined received several thousand more votes than the Democrats.[14] If the two opposition parties found a way to combine in 1894, it seemed likely that North Carolina Democrats would lose control of the state. Matt W. Ransom believed that it was absolutely critical to keep this from happening. The legislature elected in 1894 would select his successor, and if he were going to have any chance to return to Washington, he needed the Democratic Party to be as well organized and energetic as possible. This meant that the party had to recognize the contributions of many of its younger members, including party chair Furnifold M. Simmons. Ransom's attempt to carry out this plan quickly brought him into open conflict with Zeb.

This conflict also grew out of the Democrats' national victory in 1892. Grover Cleveland was once again elected the president of the United States. This meant that Democratic leaders once again had to wrestle with patronage problems. Vance and Ransom agreed to divide the patronage of the state along geographical lines, with Zeb taking the major offices in the western part of the state. He nominated his cousin, H. A. Gudger of Asheville, to be collector of internal revenue for the western district.[15] This was the most important appointment the party could make in the western part of the state, because the collector had the power to name more than four hundred subordinates, several in each county. The Republicans had demonstrated over the years how these workers could be used as partisan organizers. Ransom nominated Furnifold M. Simmons to be collector in the eastern internal revenue district. If this arrangement had been implemented by Cleveland and the appointees approved by the Congress, there would have been relatively little conflict in North Carolina over patronage.

Ransom felt that he could not afford to accept Gudger as the western collector, however. He recognized that Gudger had little influence outside of Asheville and that he had not proven himself to be a capable party worker. While Zeb was recuperating at Gombroon, Ransom was able to abrogate his agreement with Zeb without informing him. Ransom persuaded President Cleveland to appoint Kope Elias, a legislator from Macon County, to be the collector rather than Gudger. This action greatly angered Zeb. He would have been even more upset had he been able to read the correspondence between Elias and Ransom. A letter written in July captured the situation well. Elias informed Ransom, "I appoint none but the brightest characters and active and influential Ransom men." This was in line with what Ransom needed and wanted. But Elias went one step further when he reported: "L. H. Smith is a splendid friend of yours. . . . He despises Senator Vance his own cousin and has no use for his brother-in-law Gudger but the public does not know it nor Vance."[16] Elias's covert hostility to Zeb would soon become publicly apparent, and this development would in turn ensure that Zeb would defend his right to name the holder of the office.

Zeb launched his counterattack against Ransom with his most powerful weapon: his access to the voting majority of North Carolina Democrats. In July, Zeb sent an open letter to R. W. Elliott, president of the Farmers' Alliance of Mecklenburg County. Elliott had addressed a letter to the state's congressmen and senators requesting that they support the Sherman Silver Purchase Bill, which President Cleveland had asked Congress to repeal. Zeb replied with a letter of his own in which he agreed completely with the Alliance position. Since Zeb knew that Ransom was going to vote with the president against the wishes of the Alliance and most Democrats in the state, his letter was designed to undermine public support for Ransom. For anyone who missed the import of what he was trying accomplish, Zeb explained, "I hope it is unnecessary for me to say that the hope of ingratiating myself with the administration in order to secure patronage at its hands has in no sense affected my opinion of right in the premises."[17] Vance's letter not only emphasized that Ransom was taking an unpopular position, but it also suggested that he was doing so merely to enhance his power over patronage in North Carolina.

On September 1, Zeb used another forum to make the same point. He addressed the Senate on the Sherman bill for an hour and forty-five minutes. This would be his only major speech of the session and the last long address of his career. He tried to demonstrate that Cleveland and Ransom were not living up to the promises that the Democratic Party had made its platform of 1892. While Zeb spoke with even greater emotional fervor than he had in most of his Senate speeches, he still used humor to great effect. Discussing the failure of some Democrats to honor the party's commitments, he said: "It shall not be said of me, 'Greater love hath no man than this, that a man killed his friend that he might save his life.'" Near the end of this address, he once again implied a contrast between Ransom and himself: "I speak plainly upon this subject, Mr. President, because I feel deeply. I am too old—I have been too long in public life. I have been greatly trusted and honored by the people of my State—to make myself a party now to anything which appears to me may be construed as a want of faith in public professions."[18]

The effort left Zeb physically drained. He thought that the result was worth it, however. He wrote to Florence and informed her that in his estimation this address was his "greatest" speech. If Zeb meant that in it he had made his greatest emotional investment, then he was probably correct. In all other regards, however, the oration was inferior to many of his others. It contained no new facts, it persuaded no one to adopt his point of view, and it was not particularly well organized. In addition, the chief purpose of the address appears to have been to take vengeance against Ransom and Cleveland. Zeb continued to take part in the day-to-day business of the Senate for several weeks thereafter. He introduced several bills of interest to his constituents and made brief comments during debates.[19] But he would make no further contributions to the difficult Senate discussions that were taking place about the stock market collapse and the distress caused by the depression that followed it.

Instead, Zeb sought to block confirmation of the Elias and Simmons nominations. Requesting one of the courtesies that all senators extend to each other, he persuaded Indiana senator Daniel Voorhees to keep the two nominations in committee and not to permit a vote on them by the full Senate. This tactic worked, and the Senate session ended in November with neither man having been confirmed. Zeb was severely criticized by many North Carolina Democrats for taking this action. In an effort to explain it, he returned to North Carolina in October and spoke at the state fair in Raleigh. Finally, the impasse was broken when Elias withdrew his name from further consideration and a compromise candidate acceptable to both Vance and Ransom was named.[20]

By the time that understanding had been reached, Zeb had suffered another physical collapse. He once again had to decline speaking engagements in North Carolina. In late January, Florence and Zeb took the train to Florida in the hope that the warmer weather would help Zeb. His absence and his continued opposition to Furnifold M. Simmons's confirmation caused ongoing conflict between him and Ransom. The hoped-for improvement in Zeb's health did not materialize. By the middle of February he had declined further and was confined to his bed. Two weeks later, the *Charlotte Democrat* reported that a private letter from Tampa said that his health was "not satisfactory." About a week later, another report characterized his condition as "precarious." Democrats both in the Senate and in North Carolina felt that it was unfair to Simmons and to the party to hold up Simmons's nomination any further. Under pressure from the party, Zeb and Florence left Florida and traveled back to their residence in Washington.[21]

The trip was apparently a difficult one for Zeb, and it took him several days to recover sufficiently to meet people in Washington. Sensing that he could no longer delay the Simmons nomination, Zeb asked the Senate to vote on the matter. While he could not make it to the chamber, he paired with another member against Simmons; that is, another member who would have voted for Simmons agreed not to cast his vote. When visitors were able to see Zeb during the first week in April, they reported, "He cannot live very long unless he improves speedily." Either seated or in bed (his legs could no longer support his weight), Zeb met the many people who came to see him and chatted pleasantly about the past. On the morning of April 14th, a barber from the Senate came to the residence to shave Zeb at about ten o'clock. Zeb suffered a stroke shortly thereafter, and the barber ran to the Senate and informed Zeb's son Charles. Zeb was still conscious when Charles returned, and he asked his son to sit near him. Zeb then lapsed into a coma and died later that evening surrounded by his family and friends.[22]

H istorian David W. Blight has examined the way that Americans have remembered and commemorated the Civil War. He has maintained that three competing memorial traditions emerged in America after the war. These were the African American tradition, the Northern celebration of victory, and the Lost Cause movement in the South. In his detailed study of literature, historical writing, and public celebrations, Blight has shown how the Southerners who commemorated the Lost Cause came to dominate discussions of the Civil War and Reconstruction in the South. He has demonstrated how the effort to reconcile the North and the South virtually eliminated the black presence in the historical narratives of the time. Men like Robert E. Lee and Jefferson Davis became virtual cult figures, and organizations like the Southern Historical Society and the United Daughters of the Confederacy (UDC) sought to provide a "correct" view of the war. One manifestation of the growing strength of the Lost Cause idea was the widespread dedication of monuments to selected heroes of the Confederacy.[1]

Zeb's death came during a period in which the Confederate heroes were being honored all over the South. Since there were no great military leaders from North Carolina for him to compete with, Zeb became the symbolic leader of the Lost Cause in his home state. Within two weeks of his death, there were plans to provide a suitable memorial to the fallen hero. Ironically, the first attempt to do so was fiercely resisted by his family. Zeb was laid to rest in the Riverside Cemetery in Asheville beside Hattie and their infant son Espy. Florence felt that no adequate memorial could be placed in that location. She had Zeb's body removed from the site to a place where a more appropriate monument could be constructed and where she could be buried next to Zeb. Zeb's son Charles was angered by this action, and he took her to court. Charles also arranged for Zeb's body to be disinterred and moved back to its original location. Florence eventually decided not to contest the case further; in the future, North Carolinians would have to remember Zeb at locations other than his burial site.[2]

While the unpleasant rivalry within the family was taking place, Zeb's

Vance monument in Pack Square, Asheville, North Carolina, ca. 1930.
(North Carolina Division of Archives and History, Raleigh)

friends and neighbors in Asheville began the process of providing the first
public monument to him. They formed the Vance Monument Association,
which attempted to find an appropriate way to remember Zeb. The effort
languished until May 30, 1896, when local philanthropist George W. Pack
offered the Buncombe County Commission two thousand dollars to erect a
monument to Vance in front of the courthouse. The commissioners agreed,
and they raised the remaining funds needed for the monument relatively
quickly through a public subscription. An architect was secured, and the
commissioners agreed to his plan of building an obelisk to Vance's memory. On December 22, 1897, the cornerstone was laid in a public ceremony.
The monument committee selected a number of items to place inside the
cornerstone, including several that Zeb would most likely have found appropriate. Among these were some silver coins and the muster roll of the
Rough and Ready Guards.[3]

The orator on the occasion was Rev. H. H. Swope, who delivered an address in the classic Lost Cause vein. He portrayed Zeb as a great soldier and
a selfless patriot who had risked everything during and after the Civil War
for the people of his state. Swope could not claim to have known Zeb well,

so he quoted Zeb's colleagues Dr. Edward Warren and Senator Matt W. Ransom. The material that he presented from both men stressed that Zeb's contemporaries had recognized him as a great man from the beginning. Furthermore, Swope offered no evidence to suggest that anyone had ever opposed any of Zeb's ideas or disagreed with any action he took. The speech was one aspect of a larger celebration that included music by the Asheville Concert Band. When the band began to play "Dixie," "there came a shout (from the Zebulon Vance Camp of the United Confederate Veterans) that rattled the leaves of the trees."[4] Three months later, the obelisk was completed, and it has stood in what is today Pack Square for over a century.

Unwilling to be outdone, the state government in Raleigh commissioned a monument to Zeb as well. The eight-and-a-half-foot likeness of Vance, which was placed on an equally high pedestal, was dedicated on August 22, 1900. Family members, including Florence and Zebulon Jr., participated in the official celebration. The organizers invited Confederate veterans to attend, including members of the Twenty-sixth Regiment band and the Rough and Ready Guards. The orator for the occasion was Richard H. Battle, who had been a member of Zeb's staff in the governor's office during the Civil War. Battle gave a relatively balanced speech about his mentor. Noting that Zeb's humor was often both ironic and sarcastic, Battle portrayed Zeb as a man who had enjoyed political combat. Most of the address, however, focused on Zeb's contributions as a soldier and a wartime governor. Rather than offer his audience the vague generalities that were the usual fare in Lost Cause speeches, Battle mentioned Zeb's visits to the troops, discussed how he had found provisions for soldiers and civilians, and lauded his innovative blockade-running plan. Like the Lost Cause orator he was, however, he failed to mention the origins of the war, Zeb's conflicts with Jefferson Davis, or the protests that the state's citizens had made against Confederate policies in North Carolina.[5]

Battle ended his speech with the following observation: "There are two niches in statuary hall in the capitol at Washington reserved for North Carolina to fill with two of her sons. . . . We may not be agreed as to whose statue shall fill one of those niches, but I think that in one of them shall stand a statue . . . of Zebulon B. Vance. Let us see to it, my friends, that this duty we owe to ourselves and to him is no longer deferred." Battle's suggestion was carried out only after a considerable delay, but as World War I raged, the state of North Carolina did designate Zeb as one of its two honorees. An imposing bronze study by the distinguished American sculptor Gutzon Borglum was unveiled in Washington on June 22, 1916, by Zeb's great-granddaughter, Dorothy Espy Pillow. Locke Craig, the governor of North Carolina, presented the statue of his fellow Buncombe County resident with an uncritical biographical sketch. Vice President Thomas R. Marshall accepted the sculpture on behalf of the nation and made comments of his own that were based on personal knowledge of Zeb and his career.[6]

That same day, several members of the Senate spoke in support of a resolution concerning the acceptance of the statue. North Carolina senator Lee S. Overman shared his vivid personal memories of Zeb's 1876 campaign against Settle, and he pointed out that Zeb's native region had already raised an appropriate monument to Zeb in Asheville. Henry Cabot Lodge, not known for his generosity towards Democrats or informal Southerners, mentioned some of the attributes that he felt had made Zeb a special person. The Massachusetts senator observed, "He had a strong personality; . . . but unlike some strong personalities, his carried with it nothing but a sense of kindliness and humor." Lodge went on to laud Zeb as a man of "principle and conviction" for whom "there were higher ideals to be followed than living in comfort and safety with opportunity to accumulate money." Lodge concluded that Zeb was the equal of the men who had started and sustained the revolution that created the United States; the comparison, which would have gratified Zeb, was probably the greatest compliment that Lodge could have bestowed.[7]

On July 25, 1916, North Carolina congressmen spoke briefly as the House of Representatives also accepted the statue of Vance. Ironically, a Republican, James J. Britt, now represented Zeb's old mountain district. Britt was not the least bit embarrassed by the difference of party, and he made several telling points about his predecessor. He described Zeb as having had "no patience with shams and pretenses." Britt explained: "With him life was an open book. His heart was always open, his words frank, and his manner firm. He was warm and responsive. His handclasp was magnetic. No one ever forgot its thrill." Britt came as close as any of the later speakers did to adequately describing the charisma that Zeb had projected to his contemporaries. Congressman Claude Kitchen explained why Zeb had been selected as North Carolina's first honoree in the Capitol. He asserted: "Of all the distinguished men, living and dead, he stands out in the admiration and esteem in the confidence and affection of her people, the central figure. None other approaches him." By 1916, there was no disagreement on this point in the state of North Carolina.[8] The controversies of his youth, the harsh policies of the Civil War, and the partisan battles that followed the war had been forgotten. Instead, Zeb's qualities as a person and as a public speaker defined him for the succeeding generations.

Twelve years later, another memorial to Vance was unveiled that testified to the important contribution that he had made in constructing the

Statue of Vance in the U.S. Capitol. (North Carolina Division of Archives and History, Raleigh)

popular understanding of the Jewish past. A memorial tablet was placed in his honor at Calvary Episcopal Church in Fletcher, North Carolina. At this particular site, where other outstanding Southerners including Sidney Lanier and Robert E. Lee had been honored, Zeb was remembered as the author of the "Scattered Nation" address. Already, the Jewish community of Asheville had begun honoring Zeb with an annual ceremony that took place downtown. Each year, a wreath was laid at the base of the Vance monument; it was paid for with money from an endowed fund created by Nathan Strauss. The annual ceremony had particular significance in the 1920s, when the Ku Klux Klan gained great national popularity with its virulently anti-Semitic message. In the ceremony, Zeb was honored as a Southern political leader who had challenged the bigotry inherent in his own society. The Calvary Episcopal Church ceremony took place on Sunday, October 14, 1928. The dedication of the tablet was preceded by a worship service that was conducted jointly by Rabbi Moses P. Jacobson of Synagogue Beth Ha Tehilla in Asheville, Dr. Leland Cook, pastor of the First Christian Church in Asheville, and Rev. Clarence Stuart McClellan of Calvary Episcopal Church.[9]

The dedication ceremonies were completed in a style that would have been heartily approved by Zeb. Approximately two thousand people saw the tablet unveiled by his grandniece, Rosa May Vance of Cedarton, Georgia. Harry Millard Roberts, Zeb's third cousin and a member of Calvary Episcopal Church, accepted the plaque for the Vance family. The ceremony concluded with a ringing address delivered by Rabbi Stephen S. Wise, who had traveled from New York City to deliver his remarks. Wise was the rabbi of the Free Synagogue in New York and one of the leading Zionists in the United States. He compared Vance's contributions in helping to promote the acceptance of the Jewish presence in American society to those made by King Cyrus of Persia, Alexander the Great, Arthur Balfour, and Woodrow Wilson, a comparison that Zeb would have welcomed. Wise went on to laud Zeb as a man who had been "under the compulsion of the ideal of true religion, the spirit of religion pure and undefiled who ought to move every human being who professes the religion of Jesus of Nazareth to be utterly and undeviating[ly] just to his people."[10] On this point, even Zeb might have concluded that Wise was overstating the case. Nevertheless, Wise and the Jewish community of Asheville were not wrong to celebrate Zeb's contribution to the dialogue between Christians and Jews in the South. He had indeed championed acceptance and understanding at a time when it provided him no political advantage. For the last two decades of his life, as a Christian figure who openly supported Jewish causes, he had been a model for his fellow citizens. If no other monuments to Zeb had been built, this one in Fletcher would have given him glory enough.

Another ceremony that took place in Asheville on Zeb's birthday in 1938 indicated that even fame as great as his was not impervious to the passage of time. Several organizations, including the B'nai B'rith, the United Daughters of the Confederacy, and the American Legion, worked together to place a bronze tablet on the Vance obelisk. It contained Zeb's name, his birth and death dates, and a brief description of his life. The orator on the occasion was a distant relative, Zebulon Baird Weaver Jr. Weaver, a former Democratic congressman from the mountain district, delivered a short address in the UDC building after the ceremony. That the ceremony was attended by fewer than one hundred people indicated the relative insignificance this event had for the community at large.[11] The simple fact that Zeb's monument now had to identify him to a public that no longer recalled his life in any detail also indicates that the importance of his memory in North Carolina had diminished.

Other communities sought to find fitting ways to honor Zeb as his legacy dimmed. The small city of Statesville was one of the first to act. Residents in the area formed a commission to purchase and save the home where Hattie had stayed at the end of the war and in which Zeb was captured and taken to Washington. The United Daughters of the Confederacy sponsored a twenty-five thousand dollar subscription to purchase the home. Sufficient funds for the purchase were raised, and the building was removed from its original setting and placed in a public park near the center of town. It was opened to the public on September 1, 1951, and was maintained by the UDC. Part of the building was used for the Vance House Museum.[12] While the building was preserved by this effort and Zeb's name honored, the setting was not historically appropriate, and the structure was only loosely connected with Zeb's life.

The descendants of Zeb's neighbors in Buncombe County got into the act next. They persuaded the North Carolina legislature to pass a bill to authorize a commission that would investigate the possibility of preserving the home in which Zeb was born in 1830. Governor J. Melville Broughton appointed a commission of eight people from the Asheville area to investigate the matter. The members recommended to the governor "that the birthplace of Governor Zebulon Vance be acquired and preserved as a state shrine." Their recommendation was presented to the General Assembly in 1945. The language they used in their report is significant for several reasons. First, Zeb is referred to as a "governor," rather than by any of the other titles he won. Clearly, his lasting legacy in North Carolina grew out of his three gubernatorial administrations rather than any of his other life works. The use of the word "shrine" to describe Zeb's birthplace also indicates how serious his fellow Tar Heels were about commemorating his life. The state followed through on the committee's recommendation, and Zeb's birthplace was carefully reconstructed around the original chimney, which had survived the ravages of time.[13] The home is open to the public today and is maintained by the state government.

Blight's contention that the Lost Cause emerged victorious in the battle over the interpretation of the Civil War is borne out by these monuments to the life of Zebulon Vance. There is a significant irony in this fact, however. As it does for many important figures in the Confederate leadership, the Lost Cause stereotype actually undervalues the significance of Zeb's role in the Civil War and the achievements of his political career. For nearly a century, one narrative of the Civil War held sway in the South: a united South had fought valiantly during the war, led by exemplary leaders like Robert E. Lee and Jefferson Davis; during Reconstruction, the virtually united white South was the victim of federal interference and the rapacity of Northern carpetbaggers, unscrupulous Southern scalawags, and incompetent blacks; after Reconstruction, the South's true leaders returned to power, redeemed their people, and tranquility reigned.

A substantial number of scholarly studies have destroyed the credibility of this carefully constructed narrative, but the real role that men like Zebulon Vance played in Southern history has only recently begun to be appreciated by scholars and discerning readers. In 1925, Frank Owsley maintained that Zeb, along with Georgia governor Joseph E. Brown, was responsible for the defeat of the Confederacy. Owsley asserted that Vance and Brown used states' rights arguments to oppose the Confederate government and weaken the war effort. Recent studies by George C. Rable and Joe A. Mobley have completely demolished Owsley's line of argument. Both of these scholars correctly point out that Zeb was a Confederate nationalist who fought for Confederate independence throughout the war years.[14] But Owsley had nevertheless made an important point: there was friction between Vance and Davis, and their disputes centered on developments in North Carolina. Zeb opposed some of Davis's policies and personnel decisions based on the impact that he believed Davis's choices would have both on civilian morale in North Carolina and on the Confederate armed forces.

The Lost Cause narrative, by ignoring the conflicts within the Confederacy, undervalued the contribution that Zeb made to the Southern war effort. He sought to provide logistical support to state troops when the Confederacy failed to do so. He tried to stem desertion by providing soldiers' families with food, seeking out deserters and outliers and forcing them into the army, and confronting the opposition to the Davis administration in open political debates before the public. These initiatives were only partially successful, and they were resented by many in North Carolina. Often Zeb's best efforts were neutralized both by the insensitive policies of the Richmond government and by the incompetent Confederate officials who administered them. But despite the obstacles placed in his path by the growing disillusionment of the public and the inability of the Davis administration to understand the situation in North Carolina, Zeb was able to ensure that his state maintained its status as a contributing member of the Confederacy until April 1865. It is doubtful that any other person in the state could have accomplished as much under the existing circumstances.

The legends of Reconstruction and of the "redeemers" who reclaimed the South from federal tyranny also diminished the public's appreciation of both the difficulties that Zeb faced and of his accomplishments. When the Conservatives seized control of the state in 1870, their opponents refused to disappear. In the 1872 gubernatorial election and the legislative elections of 1886 and 1894, the Republicans and their allies won statewide contests in North Carolina. Zeb's battle against Thomas Settle in 1876 was strongly contested. Moreover, the Democrats themselves were never as united as the traditional narratives would suggest. Zeb had to play the roles of party leader, conciliator, and emergency campaigner in an effort to maintain the narrow Democratic advantage in North Carolina. He was successful in doing so in part because he was a very effective public speaker. But on numerous occasions his appeals failed, and when they did his opponents from both inside and outside the party triumphed.

With a more accurate picture of the challenges that the Confederacy and the redeemers faced, scholars have recently been able to reassess Zeb as a historical figure. It now seems clear that Zeb was indeed one of those larger-than-life people who tend to dominate any situation in which they are placed. He had a great ability to reach out to nonelite audiences and to persuade his listeners that he understood their needs and concerns. In many instances, he was able to sense their feelings and articulate them in a way they found persuasive. This skill gave him a solid base upon which to build a highly successful political career in a turbulent and unsettled period of American history. Zeb also seems to have had genuine executive ability that allowed him to understand problems clearly and to find creative solutions to them. The combination of these gifts made him an extremely effective governor of North Carolina during the Civil War and a good executive after the Reconstruction period came to an end. Like many successful leaders, Zeb was also willing to make hard decisions and to use coercive means to accomplish his ends when he felt the situation required it. His effort to round up deserters and outliers during the Civil War and his drive to complete the Western North Carolina Railroad both testify to the presence of this aspect of his personality. He also had the courage to present his side of a controversial argument directly before potentially critical audiences. In his speech at Wilkesboro in 1864, in the addresses he made to African American audiences after 1876, and in his appearances at agricultural fairs during the subtreasury controversy, Zeb demonstrated that he had real fortitude.

That he possessed these very real strengths should not blind us to the other, less attractive sides of his personality or to his personal failings. All of his life, he assumed that African Americans were intellectually and morally inferior to whites. While he did have good relationships with those blacks who worked for and with him, he was an avowed racist who used the racism of other whites for personal advantage and political purposes. Despite his empathy for nonelite whites, moreover, he was a confirmed member of an elite, and he believed that as such he had a right to direct the economy and government of the state. He was very ambitious, and he seemed to view the opportunity to hold public office as his birthright. He was an indifferent military leader who was fortunate to have done the men under his command little harm. He appears to have been a mediocre lawyer at best, poorly prepared and often ineffective. When he faced competent opponents at the bar, he failed to win the verdict in many cases. He was not a creative legislator, and he was most effective as a spokesman when his party was in opposition. He was also an advocate of the old-fashioned spoils system at a time when that system had outlived its usefulness. While he was highly intelligent and a quick study, he rarely tried to organize information into complex patterns or to analyze material in depth.

To most of his contemporaries, however, few of these failings mattered. Zeb was fun to be around. He was genuinely good-humored, and he apparently took a real interest when he conversed with people. In his willingness to interact with people, he made it appear as if social class and economic status were unimportant to him. He appears to have been as comfortable communicating with women as with men, which would have been a fairly unusual characteristic for a man of his time. He was a devoted husband to two very different women, and he was a concerned parent, although often an absent one. He appears to have been personally and professionally honest in virtually all of his dealings. He appreciated the importance of education and thought that all persons—men and women, black and white—could be improved through greater access to learning. In sum, he appears to have liked to be with people, and he liked for them to enjoy the experience of being with him. For this, and for his creative leadership during the greatest crisis in North Carolina's history, the people of the state have honored him as one of their greatest sons.

NOTES ✳

PREFACE

1. Glenn Tucker, *Zeb Vance: Champion of Personal Freedom* (Indianapolis: Bobbs-Merrill, 1965).

2. J. G. de Roulhac Hamilton, *Reconstruction in North Carolina* (Gloucester, Mass.: Peter Smith, 1964); Frank L. Owsley, *State Rights in the Confederacy* (Chicago: University of Chicago Press, 1925).

3. John G. Barrett, *The Civil War in North Carolina* (Chapel Hill: University of North Carolina Press, 1963).

4. William T. Auman, "Neighbor against Neighbor: The Inner Civil War in the Randolph County Area of Confederate North Carolina," *North Carolina Historical Review* 61 (January 1984): 59-92; William T. Auman and David D. Scarboro, "The Heroes of America in Civil War North Carolina," *North Carolina Historical Review* 58 (October 1981): 327-63; William T. Auman, "Neighbor against Neighbor: The Inner Civil War in the Central Counties of Confederate North Carolina" (Ph.D. diss., University of North Carolina, 1988); Paul D. Escott, *After Secession: Jefferson Davis and the Failure of Confederate Nationalism* (Baton Rouge: Louisiana State University Press, 1978); Gordon B. McKinney, *Southern Mountain Republicans, 1865-1900: Politics and the Appalachian Community* (Chapel Hill: University of North Carolina Press, 1978).

5. Max R. Williams, ed., *The Papers of William Alexander Graham*, vol. 5, *1857-1863*, vol. 6, *1864-1865*, vol. 7, *1866-1868* (Raleigh: North Carolina Division of Archives and History, 1957-92); Archie K. Davis, *Boy Colonel of the Confederacy: The Life and Times of Henry King Burgwyn, Jr.* (Chapel Hill: University of North Carolina Press, 1985); William C. Harris, *William Woods Holden: Firebrand of North Carolina Politics* (Baton Rouge: Louisiana State University Press, 1987); Horace Raper and Thornton W. Mitchell, eds., *The Papers of William Woods Holden*, vol. 1, *1841-1868* (Raleigh: North Carolina Division of Archives and History, 2000); E. Stanly Godbold and Mattie U. Russell, *Confederate Colonel and Cherokee Chief: The Life of William Holland Thomas* (Knoxville: University of Tennessee Press, 1990); Jeffrey J. Crow, "Thomas Settle Jr., Reconstruction, and the Memory of the Civil War," *Journal of Southern History* 62 (November 1996): 689-726; Thomas E. Jeffrey, *Thomas Lanier Clingman: Fire Eater from the Carolina Mountains* (Athens: University of Georgia Press, 1998).

6. Phillip Shaw Paludan, *Victims: A True Story of the Civil War* (Knoxville: University of Tennessee Press, 1981); John C. Inscoe, *Mountain Masters, Slavery, and the Sectional Crisis in Western North Carolina* (Knoxville: University of Tennessee Press, 1989); John C. Inscoe and Gordon B. McKinney, *The Heart of Confederate Appalachia: Western North Carolina in the Civil War* (Chapel Hill: University of North Carolina Press, 2000); Kenneth W. Noe and Shannon H. Wilson, eds., *The Civil War in Appalachia: Collected Essays* (Knoxville: University of Tennessee Press, 1997); Martin Crawford, *Ashe County's Civil War: Community and Society in the Appalachian South* (Charlottesville: University Press of Virginia, 2001).

7. Richard E. Beringer, Herman Hattaway, Archer Jones, and William N. Still Jr., *Why*

the South Lost the Civil War (Athens: University of Georgia Press, 1986); George C. Rable, *The Confederate Republic: A Revolution against Politics* (Chapel Hill: University of North Carolina Press, 1994).

8. Paul D. Escott, *Many Excellent People: Power and Privilege in North Carolina, 1850–1900* (Chapel Hill: University of North Carolina Press, 1985); Laurence Shore, *Southern Capitalists: The Ideological Leadership of an Elite, 1832–1885* (Chapel Hill: University of North Carolina Press, 1986); Anne C. Rose, *Victorian America and the Civil War* (New York: Cambridge University Press, 1992).

9. William J. Cooper Jr., *Jefferson Davis, American* (New York: Alfred A. Knopf, 2000), p. xiv.

CHAPTER ONE

1. *Congressional Record*, 53rd Cong., 2d sess., April 16, 1894, p. 3759; *Raleigh News-Observer-Chronicle*, April 18, 1894.

2. *Congressional Record*, 53rd Cong., 2d sess., April 16, 1894, pp. 3759–60; Clipping, April 19, 1894, *The Papers of Zebulon Vance*, eds. Gordon B. McKinney and Richard M. McMurry (Frederick, Md.: University Publications of America, 1987), microfilm, reel 7.

3. *Raleigh News-Observer-Chronicle*, April 18, 1894.

4. Ibid.

5. Clement Dowd, *Life of Zebulon B. Vance* (Charlotte: Observer Printing and Publishing House, 1897), pp. 321–22.

6. *Raleigh News-Observer-Chronicle*, April 18, 1894.

7. *Asheville Citizen*, April 18, 1894.

8. Ibid.

9. Ibid.

CHAPTER TWO

1. Henry D. Shapiro, *Appalachia on Our Mind: The Southern Mountains and Mountaineers in the American Consciousness, 1870–1920* (Chapel Hill: University of North Carolina Press, 1978); Cratis D. Williams, "The Southern Mountaineer in Fact and Fiction: Part I," *Appalachian Journal* 3 (Autumn 1975): 8–61; ibid., "Part II," *Appalachian Journal* 3 (Winter 1976): 100–162; ibid., "Part III," *Appalachian Journal* 3 (Spring 1976): 186–261; ibid., "Part IV," *Appalachian Journal* 3 (Summer 1976): 334–92; J. W. Williamson, *Hillbillyland: What the Movies Did to the Mountains and What the Mountains Did to the Movies* (Chapel Hill: University of North Carolina Press, 1995). See also: Kenneth W. Noe, "Toward the Myth of Unionist Appalachia, 1865–1883," *Journal of the Appalachian Studies Association* 6 (1994): 73–80; Gordon B. McKinney, "The Political Uses of Appalachian Identity after the Civil War," *Appalachian Journal* 7 (Spring 1980): 200–209.

2. Charles C. Royce, *The Cherokee Nation of Indians* (Chicago: Aldine Publishing Company, 1975).

3. David Hackett Fischer, *Albion's Seed: Four British Folkways in America* (New York: Oxford University Press, 1989), pp. 605–39.

4. Ora Blackmun, *Western North Carolina: Its Mountains and Its People to 1880* (Boone, N.C.: Appalachian Consortium Press, 1977), pp. 152–65.

5. Gordon B. McKinney, "Preindustrial Jackson County and Economic Development," *Journal of the Appalachian Studies Association* 2 (1990): 1–10.

6. John D. Reid Jr., "Antebellum Southern Rental Contracts," *Explorations in Economic History* 13 (January 1976): 69–83; John C. Inscoe, *Mountain Masters, Slavery, and the Sectional Crisis in Western North Carolina* (Knoxville: University of Tennessee Press, 1989).

7. Frontis W. Johnston, "Zebulon Baird Vance," in *The Papers of Zebulon Baird Vance*, vol. 1, *1843–1862* (Raleigh: North Carolina Division of Archives and History, 1963), pp. xvii–xix.

8. Ibid., pp. xviii–xx; Blackmun, *Western North Carolina*, p. 220.

9. H. Tyler Blethen, "The Transmission of Scottish Culture to the Southern Back Country," *Journal of the Appalachian Studies Association* 6 (1994): 59–72.

10. Clement Dowd, *Life of Zebulon B. Vance* (Charlotte: Observer Printing and Publishing House, 1897), pp. 7–8.

11. Mira M. Vance to Margaret Davidson, September 14, 1830, *The Papers of Zebulon Vance*, eds. Gordon B. McKinney and Richard M. McMurry (Frederick, Md.: University Publications of America, 1987), microfilm, reel 2; Zebulon B. Vance, "Autobiography of the Hon. Zebulon Baird Vance" (private collection).

12. Dowd, *Life of Vance*, pp. 9–14.

13. Ibid., p. 10.

14. Fischer, *Albion's Seed*, pp. 687–90; Dowd, *Life of Vance*, pp. 10–13.

15. Dowd, *Life of Vance*, p. 13; Glenn Tucker, *Zeb Vance: Champion of Personal Freedom* (Indianapolis: Bobbs-Merrill, 1965), p. 21.

16. Johnston, "Zebulon Baird Vance," pp. xxi–xxii.

17. Vance, "Autobiography Vance," p. 2; Franklin R. Shirley, *Zebulon Vance, Tarheel Spokesman* (Charlotte: McNally and Loftin, 1963), pp. 2–3.

18. Vance, "Autobiography Vance," p. 2; Dowd, *Life of Vance*, p. 13 n, Tucker, *Zeb Vance*, p. 33.

19. Marc W. Kruman, *Parties and Politics in North Carolina, 1836–1865* (Baton Rouge: Louisiana State University Press, 1983), pp. 3–139; Thomas E. Jeffrey, *State Parties and National Politics: North Carolina, 1815–1861* (Athens: University of Georgia Press, 1989), pp. 143–85.

20. Harry L. Watson, *Jacksonian Politics and Community Conflict: The Emergence of the Second American Party System in Cumberland County, North Carolina* (Baton Rouge: Louisiana State University Press, 1981); Jeffrey, *State Parties*.

21. Shirley, *Spokesman*, p. 8.

CHAPTER THREE

1. Kemp P. Battle, "As a Student at the University," in Clement Dowd, *Life of Zebulon B. Vance* (Charlotte: Observer Printing and Publishing House, 1897), pp. 16–17.

2. Augustus Merrimon Diary, February 1, 17, 20, 27, March 12, [1851], Augustus Somerville Merrimon Papers, Southern Historical Collection, University of North Carolina Library, Chapel Hill.

3. *Asheville News*, January 9, 1851.

4. Augustus Merrimon Diary, February 15, [1851], Merrimon Papers; Zebulon B. Vance to Harriett Newell Espy, March 15, April 2, May 20, October 17, [18]51, *My Beloved Zebulon: The Correspondence of Zebulon Baird Vance and Harriett Newell Espy*, ed. Elizabeth Roberts Cannon (Chapel Hill: University of North Carolina Press, 1971), pp. 3–5, 22–24.

5. Zebulon B. Vance to Harriett Newell Espy, July 18, [18]51, *Beloved*, pp. 7–9; Vance to

Martha E. Weaver, September 24, 1851, *The Papers of Zebulon Baird Vance*, vol. 1, *1843-1862*, ed. Frontis W. Johnston (Raleigh: North Carolina Division of Archives and History, 1963), pp. 9-11; Glenn Tucker, *Zeb Vance: Champion of Personal Freedom* (Indianapolis: Bobbs-Merrill, 1965), p. 54.

6. Battle, "Student," in Dowd, *Life of Vance*, p. 17.

7. Ibid., p. 22.

8. Zebulon B. Vance to Harriett Newell Espy, September 9, 1851, *Beloved*, pp. 12-15; Vance to John M. Davidson, September 14, 1851, *Vance Papers*, 1:7-9.

9. Tucker, *Zeb Vance*, p. 39; Zebulon B. Vance to John M. Davidson, September 14, 1851, *Vance Papers*, 1:7-9.

10. Franklin R. Shirley, *Zebulon Vance, Tarheel Spokesman* (Charlotte: McNally and Loftin, 1963), p. 6.

11. Battle, "Student," in Dowd, *Life of Vance*, pp. 25-26.

12. Harriett Newell Espy, "Covenant of Religious Faith," September 3, 1848, October 18, 1857, December 19, 1858, *The Papers of Zebulon Vance*, eds. Gordon B. McKinney and Richard M. McMurry (Frederick, Md.: University Publications of America, 1987), microfilm, reel 29; Espy, "Let This Be My Daily Prayer," November 22, 1857, ibid.; Augustus Merrimon Diary, May 28, 1851, Merrimon Papers.

13. Zebulon B. Vance to Harriett Newell Espy, October 2, 1851, *Beloved*, pp. 17-21.

14. Harriett Newell Espy to Zebulon B. Vance, [December 1851], *Beloved*, p. 33.

15. Harriet Newell Espy to Zebulon B. Vance, [December 1851], Vance to Espy, January 1, 1852, *Beloved*, pp. 33, 39-40.

16. Zebulon B. Vance to Harriett Newell Espy, January 1, 18, 1852, *Beloved*, pp. 37-43.

17. Zebulon B. Vance to Harriett Newell Espy, September 9, [1851], January 1, 1852, *Beloved*, pp. 12-14; W. Conard Gass, "Kemp Plummer Battle," Memory F. Mitchell, "Richard Henry Battle," W. Conard Gass, "William Smith Battle," all in *Dictionary of North Carolina Biography*, ed. William S. Powell, 6 vols. (Chapel Hill: University of North Carolina Press, 1979-96), 1:114-18.

18. Katherine F. Martin, "Charles Phillips," W. Conard Gass, "James Phillips," Allen W. Trelease, "Samuel Field Phillips," Phillips Russell, "Cornelia Phillips Spencer," all in *Dictionary*, 5:89-90, 92-93, 411-12.

19. Zebulon B. Vance to Harriett Newell Espy, December 20, [18]51, January 1, 1852, January 18, [1853], *Beloved*, pp. 35, 38, 41; Carolyn A. Wallace, "David Lowry Swain," in *Dictionary*, 5:483-86.

20. Elgiva D. Watson, "Elisha Mitchell," in *Dictionary*, 4:281-83.

21. Battle, "Student," in Dowd, *Life of Vance*, pp. 44-45, 47.

22. Zebulon B. Vance to Harriett Newell Espy, March 30, [18]52, *Beloved*, p. 72.

23. Zebulon B. Vance to Harriett Newell Espy, August 29, 1852, *Beloved*, pp. 116-17.

CHAPTER FOUR

1. Zebulon B. Vance to Harriett Newell Espy, May 13, 1853, *My Beloved Zebulon: The Correspondence of Zebulon Baird Vance and Harriett Newell Espy*, ed. Elizabeth Roberts Cannon (Chapel Hill: University of North Carolina Press, 1971), p. 229; A. R. Newsome, "The A. S. Merrimon Journal, 1853-1854," *North Carolina Historical Review* 8 (July 1931): 316.

2. E. Lee Shepard, "Breaking into the Profession: Establishing a Law Practice in Antebel-

lum Virginia," *Journal of Southern History* 48 (August 1982): 331-48; Newsome, "Merrimon," p. 301-2.

3. Zebulon B. Vance to Harriett Newell Espy, June 23, [1852], *Beloved*, pp. 96-97.

4. R. B. Vance, "Boyhood, Education Begun," in Clement Dowd, *Life of Zebulon B. Vance* (Charlotte: Observer Printing and Publishing House, 1897), p. 15; Zebulon B. Vance to Harriett Newell Espy, October 23, December 24, 1852, April 16, [1853], *Beloved*, pp. 137, 164, 214.

5. Newsome, "Merrimon," pp. 309-19; Zebulon B. Vance to Harriett Newell Espy, May 16, [1852], *Beloved*, pp. 88-89.

6. Zebulon B. Vance to Harriett Newell Espy, December 12, 1852, February 19, March 23, April 5, 1853, *Beloved*, pp. 161, 184 n, 200, 208.

7. Zebulon B. Vance to Harriett Newell Espy, July 30, December 8, 1852, April 16, April 22, July 9, [1853], *Beloved*, pp. 110, 161, 214, 219, 254-55.

8. Zebulon B. Vance to Harriett Newell Espy, May 16, [1852], *Beloved*, pp. 88-89; Newsome, "Merrimon," pp. 309-19.

9. Dowd, *Life of Vance*, pp. 102-3; Newsome, "Merrimon," pp. 300-301; Franklin R. Shirley, *Zebulon Vance, Tarheel Spokesman* (Charlotte: McNally and Loftin, 1963), pp. 8-9.

10. Clipping, April 16, 1894, *The Papers of Zebulon Vance*, eds. Gordon B. McKinney and Richard M. McMurry (Frederick, Md.: University Publications of America, 1987), microfilm, reel 7.

11. R. B. Vance, "Marriage, Public Life Begun," in Dowd, *Life of Vance*, pp. 31-32.

12. Zebulon B. Vance to Harriett Newell Espy, [August 1852], *Beloved*, p. 111.

13. Zebulon B. Vance to Harriett Newell Espy, September 25, November 2, 6, 1852, *Beloved*, pp. 126, 143, 147; Glenn Tucker, *Zeb Vance: Champion of Personal Freedom* (Indianapolis: Bobbs-Merrill, 1965), pp. 69-70.

14. Zebulon B. Vance to Harriett Newell Espy, June 7, 15, 1853, *Beloved*, pp. 235-37; Cm M. Cocke et al. to Vance, June 23, [18]55, *Papers of Vance*, reel 2.

15. Zebulon B. Vance to Kate [E. Smith], September 6, 1854, *The Papers of Zebulon Baird Vance*, vol. 1, *1843-1862*, ed. Frontis W. Johnston (Raleigh: North Carolina Division of Archives and History, 1963), p. 22; *Asheville News*, April 27, August 10, 1854; R. B. Vance, "Public Life," in Dowd, *Life of Vance*, p. 32.

16. Zebulon B. Vance to Kate [E. Smith], September 6, 1854, *Vance Papers*, 1:22-23. See also Harriett E. Vance to Zebulon B. Vance, December 14, 1854, January 6, 1855, April 11, 1860, August 8, 1867, *Papers of Vance*, reel 1.

17. Thomas E. Jeffrey, *Thomas Lanier Clingman: Fire Eater from the Carolina Mountains* (Athens: University of Georgia Press, 1998), pp. 99-101.

18. Ibid., pp. 11-55; Marc W. Kruman, "Thomas L. Clingman and the Whig Party: A Reconsideration," *North Carolina Historical Review* 64 (January 1987): 5-7.

19. Jeffrey, *Clingman*, pp. 56-98; Kruman, "Clingman," pp. 15-16.

20. *North Carolina Standard* (Raleigh), December 6, 13, 20, 1854, January 3, 6, February 10, 1855.

21. Ibid., January 20, 1855; *Asheville News*, January 25, 1855; E. Stanly Godbold and Mattie U. Russell, *Confederate Colonel and Cherokee Chief: The Life of William Holland Thomas* (Knoxville: University of Tennessee Press, 1990), p. 75.

22. William S. Powell, *North Carolina through Four Centuries* (Chapel Hill: University of North Carolina Press, 1989), p. 290.

23. *Raleigh Register*, December 20, 1854; *North Carolina Standard* (Raleigh), December 20, 1854.

24. Allan Nevins, *Ordeal of the Union*, vol. 2, *A House Dividing, 1852-1857* (New York: Charles Scribner's Sons, 1947), pp. 327-32, 341-46.

25. *North Carolina Standard* (Raleigh), January 24, 31, 1855.

26. *Asheville Spectator*, April 21, 1855.

27. Ibid.

28. Ibid.

29. *Asheville News*, June 21, 28, July 5, 1855.

30. Ibid., July 5, August 9, 1855; James S. T. Baird to Zebulon B. Vance, [July 9, 1855], *Vance Papers*, 1:29-30.

31. *Asheville News*, February 21, April 3, June 5, 1856.

32. Ibid., May 22, June 5, 19, 26, 1856; *Asheville Spectator*, June 19, July 17, 1856.

33. *Asheville News*, July 3, 24, 31, August 7, 14, 1856.

CHAPTER FIVE

1. *Asheville News*, September 6, 1855.

2. Thomas E. Jeffrey, "'A Whole Torrent of Mean and Malevolent Abuse': Party Politics and the Clingman-Mitchell Controversy, Part I," *North Carolina Historical Review* 70 (July 1993): 256-63; ibid., "Part II," *North Carolina Historical Review* 70 (October 1993): 402.

3. Jeffrey, "Clingman-Mitchell, Part I," pp. 263-65, and "Clingman-Mitchell, Part II," pp. 401-3; Zebulon B. Vance to David L. Swain, July 6, 1857, *The Papers of Zebulon Baird Vance*, vol. 1, *1843-1862*, ed. Frontis W. Johnston (Raleigh: North Carolina Division of Archives and History, 1963), pp. 30-31.

4. Jeffrey, "Clingman-Mitchell, Part II," pp. 403-4; *Asheville News*, July 16, 1857.

5. *Asheville News*, May 7, 14, 28, June 4, 11, July 16, 30, August 13, 20, 1857.

6. Zebulon B. Vance to Charles Phillips, July 8, August 4, 1856, *The Papers of Zebulon Vance*, eds. Gordon B. McKinney and Richard M. McMurry (Frederick, Md.: University Publications of America, 1987), microfilm, reel 39; Jeffrey, "Clingman-Mitchell, Part II," pp. 405-11.

7. Jeffrey, "Clingman-Mitchell, Part II," pp. 412-16; Zebulon B. Vance to Margaret Mitchell, May 25, 1858, *Vance Papers*, 1:37-38; "Agreement to Contribute to the Monument for Dr. Elisha Mitchell," [1857], *Papers of Vance*, reel 2.

8. *Asheville News*, May 20, 27, June 10, 1858.

9. Ibid., June 17, 1858.

10. Ibid.

11. Zebulon B. Vance to David F. Caldwell, February 19, 1858, *Vance Papers*, 1:34; *Asheville News*, June 17, 24, July 1, 8, 1858.

12. W. Conard Goss, "'The Misfortune of a High Minded and Honorable Gentleman': W. W. Avery and the Southern Code of Honor," *North Carolina Historical Review* 56 (July 1979): 283-96; Zebulon B. Vance to Harriett Newell Espy, November 28, [18]51, *My Beloved Zebulon: The Correspondence of Zebulon Baird Vance and Harriett Newell Espy*, ed. Elizabeth Roberts Cannon (Chapel Hill: University of North Carolina Press, 1971), pp. 30-31.

13. R. B. Vance, "Marriage, Public Life Begun," in Clement Dowd, *Life of Zebulon B. Vance* (Charlotte: Observer Printing and Publishing House, 1897), pp. 33, 119-20; Franklin R.

Shirley, *Zebulon Vance, Tarheel Spokesman* (Charlotte: McNally and Loftin, 1963), p. 11; *Asheville News*, July 22, 1858.

14. *Asheville News*, July 29, August 12, 19, September 9, 1858.

15. Jeffrey, "Clingman-Mitchell, Part II," p. 418; *Asheville News*, August 12, 19, 1858; Richard Walser, ed., *Tar Heel Laughter* (Chapel Hill: University of North Carolina Press, 1983), pp. 95–96.

16. Frontis W. Johnston, ed., *The Papers of Zebulon Baird Vance*, vol. 1, *1843–1862* (Raleigh: North Carolina Division of Archives and History, 1963), p. 23n; Zebulon B. Vance to David F. Caldwell, February 19, 1858, Vance to Robert B. Davidson, April 2, 1858, Vance to Margaret Mitchell, May 25, 1858, Vance to John E. Brown, August 22, 1859, *Vance Papers*, 1:32, 36, 38, 55.

17. *Congressional Globe*, 35th Cong., 2d sess., December 7, 1858, p. 7; ibid., January 26, 1859, p. 612; ibid., February 3, 1859, p. 802; ibid., February 7, 1859, p. 875.

18. *Congressional Globe*, 35th Cong., 2d sess., February 7, 1859, app. pp. 85–86.

19. Ibid.

20. Ibid., app. p. 87.

21. *Congressional Globe*, 35th Cong., 2d sess., February 15, 1859, pp. 1039, 1040, 1048–49; ibid., February 16, 1859, p. 1072; ibid., February 24, 1859, p. 1324; ibid., February 25, 1859, pp. 1368, 1378.

22. Zebulon B. Vance to Jane L. Smith, February 10, 1859, *Vance Papers*, 1:40–41; Vance to Saml. Smith, January 29, 1859, Vance to Isaac Toucey, February 8, 1859, *Papers of Vance*, reel 2; Vance to Toucey, February 24, 1859, *Papers of Vance*, reel 39; Horatio King to Vance, May 13, 1859, *Papers of Vance*, reel 29.

23. Zebulon B. Vance to Jane L. Smith, February 10, 1859, *Vance Papers*, 1:40–41.

24. R. B. Vance, "Public Life," in Dowd, *Life of Vance*, pp. 33–34; Dan. 5:24–28.

25. R. B. Vance, "Public Life," pp. 35–36; *Asheville News*, July 21, 28, 1859.

26. R. B. Vance, "Public Life," pp. 36–37; Luke 13:6–9; David Coleman to Zebulon B. Vance, August 15, 1859, *Vance Papers*, 1:42–43.

27. *Asheville News*, August 11, 1859; Zebulon B. Vance to John E. Brown, August 22, 1859, *Vance Papers*, 1:55; David Coleman to Vance, August 15, 16, 17, 18, 27, 1859, Vance to Coleman, August 16, 17, 18, 19, 29, 1859, J. F. E. Hardy and John W. Woodfin to Vance, August 22, 1859, Vance to J. F. E. Hardy and Woodfin, August 22, 1859, Coleman to J. F. E. Hardy and Woodfin, August 22, 1859, Coleman to Woodfin, [August 22, 1859], John D. Hyman to Vance, [August 22, 1859], W. M. Hardy and Hyman to Vance, August 25, 1859, *Vance Papers*, 1:42–53, 57–60.

CHAPTER SIX

1. Kent Blaser, "North Carolina and John Brown's Raid," *Civil War History* 24 (September 1978): 197–212.

2. Glenn Tucker, *Zeb Vance: Champion of Personal Freedom* (Indianapolis: Bobbs-Merrill, 1965), pp. 84–85.

3. W. Caleb Brown to Zebulon B. Vance, December 24, 1859, *The Papers of Zebulon Baird Vance*, vol. 1, *1843–1863*, ed. Frontis W. Johnston (Raleigh: North Carolina Division of Archives and History, 1963), pp. 62–63; Clement Dowd, *Life of Zebulon B. Vance* (Charlotte: Observer Printing and Publishing House, 1897), p. 55.

4. *Asheville News*, January 26, 1860; *Congressional Globe*, 36th Cong., 1st sess., January 31, 1860, p. 644.

5. *Congressional Globe*, 36th Cong., 1st sess., February 15, 1860, p. 796; Harriett E. Vance to Zebulon B. Vance, March 6, 1860, Robert B. Vance to Zebulon B. Vance, April 16, 1860, *Vance Papers*, 1:65–68.

6. *Salem People's Press*, March 16, 1860.

7. William W. Freehling, *The Road to Disunion: Secessionists at Bay, 1776-1854* (New York: Oxford University Press, 1990), pp. 23–24, 419–23, 443–45; John C. Inscoe, "Mountain Masters: Slaveholding in Western North Carolina," *North Carolina Historical Review* 61 (April 1984): 143–73; John C. Inscoe, *Mountain Masters: Slavery and the Sectional Crisis in Western North Carolina* (Knoxville: University of Tennessee Press, 1989); Charles B. Dew, *Bond of Iron: Master and Slave at Buffalo Forge* (New York: W. W. Norton, 1994); Kenneth W. Noe, *Southwest Virginia's Railroad: Modernization and the Sectional Crisis* (Urbana: University of Illinois Press, 1994), pp. 67–84; *Asheville News*, January 6, 1859; Harriett E. Vance to Zebulon B. Vance, March 6, 1860, *Vance Papers*, 1:65.

8. Edward H. McGee, "White Attitudes toward the Negro in North Carolina, 1850-1876" (master's thesis, University of North Carolina, 1968), pp. 95–96; D. W. Siler to Zebulon B. Vance, November 3, 1862, *Vance Papers*, 1:303.

9. *Congressional Globe*, 36th Cong., 1st sess., May 23, 1860, p. 2294; ibid., June 6, 1860, p. 2712; ibid., June 18, 1860, p. 3133.

10. W. J. Brown to Zebulon B. Vance, May 17, 1860, *Vance Papers*, 1:68–70; *Congressional Globe*, 36th Cong., 1st sess., April 6, 1860, p. 1575; ibid., April 7, 1860, p. 1603; ibid., April 20, 1860, p. 1823; ibid., May 4, 1860, pp. 1922–23.

11. *North Carolina Standard* (Raleigh), July 11, 1860.

12. *Asheville News*, August 9, 1860; *North Carolina Standard* (Raleigh), September 26, October 10, 13, 1860.

13. Dowd, *Life of Vance*, pp. 180–81.

14. *North Carolina Standard* (Raleigh), December 1, 4, 1860; Franklin R. Shirley, *Zebulon Vance, Tarheel Spokesman* (Charlotte: McNally and Loftin, 1963), pp. 21–23.

15. *North Carolina Standard* (Raleigh), December 18, 1860; Zebulon B. Vance to William Dickson, December 11, 1860, Vance to W. W. Lenoir, December 26, 1860, *Vance Papers*, 1: 71–78.

16. *North Carolina Standard* (Raleigh), December 15, 18, 1860; D. W. Siler to Rufus [S. Siler], December 7, 1860, C. D. Smith to [D. W. Siler], December 17, 1860, T. P. Siler to David [W. Siler], December 18, 1860, G. N. B. Moore to D. W. Siler, December 21, [18]60, Jacob Siler Papers, Southern Historical Collection, University of North Carolina Library, Chapel Hill.

17. Zebulon B. Vance to William Dickson, December 11, 1860, *Vance Papers*, 1:71–72.

18. Thomas Bragg Diary, January 4, 1861, Thomas Bragg Papers, Southern Historical Collection, University of North Carolina Library, Chapel Hill; *Fayetteville Observer*, January 14, 1861; *North Carolina Standard* (Raleigh), January 31, 1861.

19. W. W. Lenoir to Zebulon B. Vance, January 7, 1861, David F. Caldwell to Vance, January 13, 1861, J. M. Hamilton to Vance, January 14, 1861, George W. Logan to Vance, January 15, 1861, James C. L. Gudger to Vance, January 27, 1861, S. O. Deaver to Vance, January 28, 1861, Joseph P. Eller to Vance, January 28, 1861, *Vance Papers*, 1:79–81, 83–87, 91–93; *North Carolina Standard* (Raleigh), January 1, 8, 15, 31, 1861.

20. Zebulon B. Vance to W. W. Lenoir, December 26, 1860, Vance to Thomas G. Walton,

January 19, 1861, *Vance Papers*, 1:74-78, 88; *Congressional Globe*, 36th Cong., 2d sess., January 12, 1861, p. 345; ibid., January 14, 1861, pp. 363-64; ibid., February 6, 1861, p. 776; ibid., February 12, 1861, p. 872; ibid., February 27, 1861, p. 1263; Washington Henson to Zebulon B. Vance, December 29, 1860, *The Papers of Zebulon Vance*, eds. Gordon B. McKinney and Richard M. McMurry (Frederick, Md.: University Publications of America, 1987), microfilm, reel 2.

21. S. O. Deaver to Zebulon B. Vance, January 28, 1861, *Vance Papers*, 1:92; Thomas Bragg Diary, February 18, 1861, Thomas Bragg Papers, Southern Historical Collection.

22. Marc W. Kruman, *Parties and Politics in North Carolina, 1836-1865* (Baton Rouge: Louisiana State University Press, 1983), pp. 204-13, 273-78; Thomas E. Jeffrey, *State Parties and National Politics: North Carolina, 1815-1861* (Athens: University of Georgia Press, 1989), pp. 308-11; Robin E. Baker, "Class Conflict and Political Upheaval: The Transformation of North Carolina during the Civil War," *North Carolina Historical Review* 69 (April 1992): 156-61.

23. Daniel W. Crofts, *Reluctant Confederates: Upper South Unionists in the Secession Crisis* (Chapel Hill: University of North Carolina Press, 1989), pp. 207-13, 248-49, 280-81; Kruman, *Parties and Politics*, p. 218.

24. Dowd, *Life of Vance*, pp. 440-41; Crofts, *Reluctant Confederates*, pp. 289-307; *North Carolina Standard* (Raleigh), April 20, 1861.

25. Dowd, *Life of Vance*, pp. 440-41; Robert B. Vance et al. to John W. Ellis, April 18, 1861, *The Papers of John Willis Ellis*, vol. 2, ed. Nobel J. Tolbert (Raleigh: State Department of Archives and History, 1964), pp. 624-25; Kruman, *Parties and Politics*, pp. 219-20.

CHAPTER SEVEN

1. R. B. Vance, "Breaking Out of the War," in Clement Dowd, *Life of Zebulon B. Vance* (Charlotte: Observer Printing and Publishing House, 1897), pp. 62-63; *North Carolina Argus* (Wadesboro), February 20, 1862.

2. R. B. Vance, "Breaking Out," in Dowd, *Life of Vance*, pp. 63-64; *North Carolina Standard* (Raleigh), May 11, 1861.

3. Zebulon B. Vance to Harriett E. Vance, May 18, [1861], *The Papers of Zebulon Baird Vance*, vol. 1, *1843-1862*, ed. Frontis W. Johnston (Raleigh: North Carolina Division of Archives and History, 1963), pp. 100-101; *North Carolina Standard* (Raleigh), June 8, 12, 1861.

4. Augustus Merrimon to Zebulon B. Vance, June 13, 1861, Harriett E. Vance to Zebulon B. Vance, June 19, [1861], *Vance Papers*, 1:105-10.

5. Augustus S. Merrimon to Zebulon B. Vance, June 13, 1861, *Vance Papers*, 1:105-8; *North Carolina Standard* (Raleigh), July 10, 1861.

6. Zebulon B. Vance to Harriett E. Vance, June 19, [1861], *Vance Papers*, 1:109-10.

7. James G. Martin to Zebulon B. Vance, August 27, 1861, Zebulon B. Vance to Harriett E. Vance, September 15, 1861, *Vance Papers*, 1:113-15.

8. *North Carolina Standard* (Raleigh), September 4, 1861; *Fayetteville Observer*, September 5, 1861.

9. Zebulon B. Vance to [Henry T.] Clark, September 18, [1861], Governor's Papers (Clark), North Carolina Division of Archives and History, Raleigh.

10. Rod Gragg, *Covered with Glory: The 26th North Carolina Infantry at the Battle of Gettysburg* (New York: HarperCollins Publishers, 2000), pp. 3-7, 12; Glenn Tucker, *Zeb Vance: Champion of Personal Freedom* (Indianapolis: Bobbs-Merrill, 1965), p. 117.

11. Archie K. Davis, *Boy Colonel of the Confederacy: The Life and Times of Henry King Burgwyn, Jr.* (Chapel Hill: University of North Carolina Press, 1985), p. 106; Dowd, *Life of Vance*, pp. 192–93.

12. Davis, *Burgwyn*, pp. 99–100.

13. John P. Arthur, *History of Watauga County* (Richmond: Everett Waddy Company, 1915), pp. 160–61; *Alamance Gleaner* (Graham), February 22, 1876.

14. Davis, *Burgwyn*, pp. 99–100.

15. Ambrose E. Burnside to Lorenzo Thomas, March 16, 1862, *War of the Rebellion: A Compilation of the Official Records of the Union and Confederate Armies and Navies*, ser. 1, 53 vols. (Washington: Government Printing Office, 1880–1901), 9:197; Burnside to E. M. Stanton, April 10, 1862, *Official Records*, ser. 1, 9:201-7.

16. Zebulon B. Vance to Allen T. Davidson, March 4, [1862], *Vance Papers*, 1:120.

17. Ibid.

18. Davis, *Burgwyn*, p. 131.

19. L. O'B. Branch to T. H. Holmes, March 15, 1862, *Official Records*, ser. 1, 9:241-47.

20. Z. B. Vance to L. O'B. Branch, March 17, 1862, *Official Records*, ser. 1, 9:254-55.

21. Ibid., 9:255; John G. Barrett, *The Civil War in North Carolina* (Chapel Hill: University of North Carolina Press, 1963), pp. 99–100.

22. Z. B. Vance to L. O'B. Branch, March 17, 1862, *Official Records*, ser. 1, 9:255.

23. Ibid., 9:255-56; Zebulon B. Vance to Harriett E. Vance, March 20, [1862], *Vance Papers*, 1:128-29.

24. L. O'B. Branch to T. H. Holmes, March 15, 1862, *Official Records*, ser. 1, 9:244-45.

25. Z. B. Vance to L. O'B. Branch, March 17, 1862, *Official Records*, ser. 1, 9:256-57; Zebulon B. Vance to Harriett E. Vance, March 20, [1862], *Vance Papers*, 1:128-29; Gragg, *Covered with Glory*, p. 20.

26. Z. B. Vance to L. O'B. Branch, March 17, 1862, *Official Records*, ser. 1, 9:256-57; Davis, *Burgwyn*, p. 126; Zebulon B. Vance to Harriett E. Vance, March 20, [1862], *Vance Papers*, 1:129; Gragg, *Covered with Glory*, pp. 20-21.

27. Zebulon B. Vance to Harriett E. Vance, March 20, [1862], *Vance Papers*, 1:127-29.

28. Z. B. Vance to L. O'B. Branch, March 17, 1862, *Official Records*, ser. 1, 9:256-57; Zebulon B. Vance to Harriett E. Vance, March 20, [1862], *Vance Papers*, 1:129; *North Carolina Standard* (Raleigh), March 19, 1862; *Fayetteville Observer*, March 20, 1862.

29. *North Carolina Standard* (Raleigh), March 22, 1862; Davis, *Burgwyn*, p. 134; *Fayetteville Observer*, March 31, 1862.

30. Zebulon B. Vance to [George W. Randolph], April 3, 1862, *Vance Papers*, 1:132-33; *North Carolina Standard* (Raleigh), April 19, 1862.

31. J. G. Martin to Zebulon B. Vance, April 23, 26, 1862, Vance to William W. Holden, April 28, [1862], Vance to [George W. Randolph], May 2, 17, 1862, Zebulon B. Vance to Harriett E. Vance, May 25, 1862, *Vance Papers*, 1:135-40; *North Carolina Argus* (Wadesboro), May 1, 1862; *North Carolina Standard* (Raleigh), May 3, 1862.

32. Davis, *Burgwyn*, pp. 140-42.

33. *State Journal* (Raleigh), May 21, June 7, 1862; *North Carolina Standard* (Raleigh), June 4, 7, 1862.

34. *Fayetteville Observer*, June 19, 1862; Davis, *Burgwyn*, pp. 159-61, 164-65.

35. Davis, *Burgwyn*, pp. 165-66; Gragg, *Covered with Glory*, p. 26.

36. James M. McPherson, *Battle Cry of Freedom: The Civil War Era* (New York: Ballantine Books, 1988), pp. 464–71.

37. Davis, *Burgwyn*, pp. 166–68, 170.

38. Davis, *Burgwyn*, pp. 171–73; Gragg, *Covered with Glory*, pp. 26–27; Tucker, *Zeb Vance*, pp. 141–42.

39. McPherson, *Battle Cry*, pp. 469–70.

40. Davis, *Burgwyn*, pp. 173–75.

41. Davis, *Burgwyn*, p. 175; *State Journal* (Raleigh), July 30, 1862; Zebulon B. Vance to W. L. Scott, July 25, [1862], *The Papers of Zebulon Vance*, eds. Gordon B. McKinney and Richard M. McMurry (Frederick, Md.: University Publications of America, 1987), microfilm, reel 39.

42. *North Carolina Standard* (Raleigh), July 9, 1862; Harvey A. Davis Diary, July 1, 1862, Catawba College Archives, Salisbury, N.C.

43. *North Carolina Standard* (Raleigh), August 2, 1862; Dowd, *Life of Vance*, p. 193.

CHAPTER EIGHT

1. George C. Rable, *The Confederate Republic: A Revolution against Politics* (Chapel Hill: University of North Carolina Press, 1994).

2. Marc W. Kruman, *Parties and Politics in North Carolina, 1836–1865* (Baton Rouge: Louisiana State University Press, 1983), pp. 222–25.

3. Zebulon B. Vance to Harriett E. Vance, May 18, [1861], *The Papers of Zebulon Baird Vance*, vol. 1, *1843–1862*, ed. Frontis W. Johnston (Raleigh: North Carolina Division of Archives and History, 1963), p. 100; *North Carolina Standard* (Raleigh), June 8, 12, 1862; J. G. de Roulhac Hamilton, *Reconstruction in North Carolina* (Gloucester, Mass.: Peter Smith, 1964), p. 36.

4. *North Carolina Standard* (Raleigh), May 4, 1862; W. W. Holden to ——, June 21, 1862, Calvin J. Cowles Papers, North Carolina Division of Archives and History, Raleigh; Paul D. Escott, *Many Excellent People: Power and Privilege in North Carolina, 1850–1900* (Chapel Hill: University of North Carolina Press, 1985), p. 36.

5. Kruman, *Parties and Politics*, pp. 225–29; *Fayetteville Observer*, August 29, 1861; Jonathan Worth to W. L. Scott, September 14, 1861, William LaFayette Scott Papers, Perkins Library, Duke University, Durham, N.C.; *North Carolina Standard* (Raleigh), September 21, 1861.

6. *Fayetteville Observer*, October 17, 1861.

7. *North Carolina Standard* (Raleigh), October 12, November 16, 1862; A. J. Taylor to ——, October 13, 1862, Wm. H. Thomas to Henry T. Clark, October 17, 1862, Governor's Papers (Clark), North Carolina Division of Archives and History, Raleigh; A. T. Davidson to John M. Davidson, November 27, 1861, John Mitchell Davidson Papers, Southern Historical Collection, University of North Carolina Library, Chapel Hill; E. Stanly Godbold and Mattie U. Russell, *Confederate Colonel and Cherokee Chief: The Life of William Holland Thomas* (Knoxville: University of Tennessee Press, 1990), pp. 97–99.

8. *North Carolina Standard* (Raleigh), October 9, 19, November 2, 27, 1861; *Fayetteville Observer*, October 17, November 28, 1862; Kruman, *Parties and Politics*, pp. 229–30; William C. Harris, *William Woods Holden: Firebrand of North Carolina Politics* (Baton Rouge: Louisiana State University Press, 1987), p. 112.

9. *North Carolina Standard* (Raleigh), December 7, 1861; Kruman, *Parties and Politics*, pp. 231–32.

10. *State Journal* (Raleigh), January 22, February 8, April 16, 1862; *Fayetteville Observer*, February 6, 17, April 14, 1862; *North Carolina Standard* (Raleigh), February 19, March 26, April 5, 9, 1862; *Salem People's Press*, March 28, April 11, 1862; *Raleigh Register*, April 5, 1862; Harris, *Holden*, pp. 113–15.

11. Kruman, *Parties and Politics*, pp. 232–33; Harris, *Holden*, pp. 115–16.

12. *North Carolina Standard* (Raleigh), May 14, 31, June 4, 1862; *Fayetteville Observer*, May 15, 19, 29, 1862; *Raleigh Register*, May 17, 1862; Zebulon B. Vance to George Little, June 15, [1862], Little-Mordecai Papers, North Carolina Division of Archives and History, Raleigh.

13. *Fayetteville Observer*, June 19, 1862; Harris, *Holden*, p. 117.

14. Ibid.

15. *State Journal* (Raleigh), June 4, 18, 1862.

16. *Raleigh Register*, June 7, 25, July 9, 1862.

17. *Fayetteville Observer*, June 12, July 17, 1862; *State Journal* (Raleigh), July 16, 1862.

18. *Raleigh Register*, June 7, 1862; *North Carolina Standard* (Raleigh), July 23, 1862; *State Journal* (Raleigh), July 26, 1862.

19. *Raleigh Register*, June 21, 1862.

20. Ibid.

21. Ibid., July 12, 1862.

22. Kenneth Rayner to Thomas Ruffin, July 12, 1862, *The Papers of Thomas Ruffin*, vol. 4, ed. J. G. de Roulhac Hamilton (Raleigh: Edwards and Broughton, 1918–20), pp. 256–57; *State Journal* (Raleigh), June 28, 1862.

23. Kenneth Rayner to Thomas Ruffin, July 12, 1862, *Papers Ruffin*, 4:253–54; *Fayetteville Observer*, June 23, July 14, 17, 1862; *State Journal* (Raleigh), July 9, 1862; *Raleigh Register*, July 16, 1862.

24. Henry T. Clark, Proclamation, August 6, 1862, Clark Letterbook, pt. 2, p. 410, Governor's Papers (Clark), North Carolina Division of Archives and History, Raleigh; *North Carolina Standard* (Raleigh), August 2, 1862; *Fayetteville Observer*, August 4, 1862; *State Journal* (Raleigh), August 6, 1862; *Raleigh Register*, August 6, 1862.

25. Harris, *Holden*, p. 120; Kruman, *Parties and Politics*, pp. 237–38; *State Journal* (Raleigh), August 30, 1862.

26. Kruman, *Parties and Politics*, pp. 238–39; Robin E. Baker, "Class Conflict and Political Upheaval: The Transformation of North Carolina during the Civil War," *North Carolina Historical Review* 69 (April 1992): 166–72; William T. Auman, "Neighbor against Neighbor: The Inner Civil War in the Central Counties of Confederate North Carolina," (Ph.D. diss., University of North Carolina, 1988), pp. 118–19, 198.

27. Clement Dowd, *Life of Zebulon B. Vance* (Charlotte: Observer Printing and Publishing House, 1897), p. 193; *North Carolina Standard* (Raleigh), August 20, 1862; *Fayetteville Observer*, August 21, 1862.

28. *North Carolina Standard* (Raleigh), August 20, 1862.

29. Ibid.; *Raleigh Register*, August 20, 1862; *State Journal* (Raleigh), August 27, 1862.

30. Zebulon B. Vance to William A. Graham, August 17, 1862, *Vance Papers*, 1:155–56; *Asheville News*, August 21, 1862; *Raleigh Register*, September 6, 1862; *State Journal* (Raleigh), September 6, 13, 1862.

CHAPTER NINE

1. Gary W. Gallagher, *The Confederate War* (Cambridge, Mass.: Harvard University Press, 1997).

2. William S. Powell, *North Carolina through Four Centuries* (Chapel Hill: University of North Carolina Press, 1989), pp. 186, 279-80.

3. Glenn Tucker, *Zeb Vance: Champion of Personal Freedom* (Indianapolis: Bobbs-Merrill, 1965), pp. 169-71; Samuel H. Walkup to Zebulon B. Vance, October 11, 1862, *The Papers of Zebulon Baird Vance*, vol. 1, *1843-1862*, ed. Frontis W. Johnston (Raleigh: North Carolina Division of Archives and History, 1963), pp. 258-61; Vance to the General Assembly, November 17, 1862, *War of the Rebellion: A Compilation of the Official Records of the Union and Confederate Armies and Navies*, ser. 4, 4 vols. (Washington: Government Printing Office, 1880-1901), 2:183.

4. John K. Connally to Zebulon B. Vance, March 27, 1863, *The Papers of Zebulon Vance*, eds. Gordon B. McKinney and Richard M. McMurry (Frederick, Md.: University Publications of America, 1987), microfilm, reel 3; Robin E. Baker, "Class Conflict and Political Upheaval: The Transformation of North Carolina during the Civil War," *North Carolina Historical Review* 69 (April 1992): 161-63; Marc W. Kruman, *Parties and Politics in North Carolina, 1836-1865* (Baton Rouge: Louisiana State University Press, 1983), pp. 229-30.

5. James M. McPherson, *Battle Cry of Freedom: The Civil War Era* (New York: Ballantine Books, 1988), pp. 515-36.

6. John G. Barrett, *The Civil War in North Carolina* (Chapel Hill: University of North Carolina Press, 1963), pp. 131-33, 171-85.

7. David L. Swain to Zebulon B. Vance, August 15, 1862, *Vance Papers*, 1:152-55.

8. Jesse G. Shepherd to Zebulon B. Vance, August 28, 1862, *Vance Papers*, 1:160-62.

9. David S. Reid to Zebulon B. Vance, September 2, 1862, *Vance Papers*, 1:167-68.

10. *Fayetteville Observer*, September 11, 1862; Thomas Bragg Diary, September 9, 1862, Thomas Bragg Papers, Southern Historical Collection, University of North Carolina Library, Chapel Hill; *State Journal* (Raleigh), September 17, 1862.

11. *Fayetteville Observer*, September 11, 1862.

12. Ibid.

13. Ibid.; William J. Yates to Zebulon B. Vance, September 16, 1862, *Vance Papers*, 1:183-84.

14. Zebulon B. Vance, Proclamation, September 18, 1862, *War of the Rebellion: A Compilation of the Official Records of the Union and Confederate Armies and Navies*, ser. 1, 53 vols. (Washington: Government Printing Office, 1880-1901), 18:753-54; Tucker, *Zeb Vance*, p. 239; *North Carolina Standard* (Raleigh), September 20, 1862.

15. Zebulon B. Vance to Weldon N. Edwards, September 18, [1862], *Official Records*, ser. 4, 2:85-86; Weldon N. Edwards to David A. Barnes, October 4, 1862, *The Papers of Thomas Ruffin*, vol. 4, ed. J. G. de Roulhac Hamilton (Raleigh: Edwards and Broughton, 1920), pp. 264-67.

16. Tucker, *Zeb Vance*, pp. 219-20.

17. *Raleigh Register*, September 27, 1862; *North Carolina Standard* (Raleigh), October 1, December 16, 1862; Zebulon B. Vance to John M. Worth, October 1, 1862, Worth to Vance, October 7, 1862, *Vance Papers*, 1:243-44, 246-47.

18. Emory M. Thomas, *The Confederate Nation, 1861-1865* (New York: Harper & Row, 1979), pp. 137-38.

bibliography block:

19. Zebulon B. Vance to Francis L. Fries and Henry W. Fries, October 10, 1862, *Vance Papers*, 1:255–57.

20. Francis L. Fries and Henry W. Fries to Zebulon B. Vance, October 13, 1862, *Vance Papers*, 1:262–64.

21. *North Carolina Standard* (Raleigh), January 16, 1863; *Fayetteville Observer*, January 19, 1863; *Raleigh Daily Progress*, February 11, 1863.

22. *Raleigh Daily Progress*, November 12, 1862.

23. Edward Warren to Zebulon B. Vance, October 11, 1862, *Vance Papers*, 1:257–58; *North Carolina Standard* (Raleigh), October 14, 1862.

24. Zebulon B. Vance to Jefferson Davis, November 8, 9, 1862, *Official Records*, ser. 1, vol. 51, pt. 2, pp. 643–44; Vance to S. G. French, December 14, 1862, Vance to James A. Seddon, April 28, 1863, *Official Records,* ser. 1, 18:801, 1027–28; *North Carolina Standard* (Raleigh), December 16, 1862; *Raleigh Daily Progress*, February 21, March 19, 1863.

25. *North Carolina Standard* (Raleigh), October 21, 1862; Zebulon B. Vance to the North Carolina General Assembly, November 17, 1862, *Official Records*, ser. 4, 2:180.

26. Zebulon B. Vance to the North Carolina General Assembly, November 17, 1862, *Official Records*, ser. 4, 2:181.

27. Ibid., 2:181–82.

28. Ibid., 2:184–85.

29. Ibid., 2:183; W. A. Smith to Zebulon B. Vance, January 3, 1863, *Papers of Vance*, reel 15.

30. Zebulon B. Vance to the North Carolina General Assembly, November 17, 1862, *Official Records*, ser. 4, 2:189.

31. Ibid.; Jefferson Davis to Zebulon B. Vance, November 26, 1862, *Official Records*, ser. 4, 2:211; *North Carolina Standard* (Raleigh), October 1, 1862; *Raleigh Daily Progress*, February 3, 6, 1863.

32. Paul C. Cameron to Zebulon B. Vance, February 19, 1863, H. B. Guthrie to Vance, February 21, 1863, T. Brown Venable to Vance, February 2, 1863, R. S. McDonald to Vance, February 25, 1863, *Papers of Vance*, reel 16; John C. Inscoe and Gordon B. McKinney, *The Heart of Confederate Appalachia: Western North Carolina in the Civil War* (Chapel Hill: University of North Carolina Press, 2000), pp. 211–14.

33. Barrett, *North Carolina*, pp. 127–28.

34. Norman D. Brown, "Edward Stanly," in *Dictionary of North Carolina Biography*, ed. William S. Powell, 6 vols. (Chapel Hill: University of North Carolina Press, 1979–96), 5:423; Edward Stanly to Zebulon B. Vance, October 21, 1862, *Vance Papers*, 1:272–73; Vance to Stanly, October 29, 1862, *War of the Rebellion: A Compilation of the Official Records of the Union and Confederate Armies and Navies*, ser. 3, 5 vols. (Washington: Government Printing Office, 1880–1901), 2:846–47.

35. Edward Stanly to Zebulon B. Vance, November 7, 1862, *Official Records*, ser. 3, 2:847–49; Vance to Stanly, November 24, 1862, *Vance Papers*, 1:391–93.

36. Kenneth Rayner to Thomas Ruffin, November 22, 1862, Charles Manly to Ruffin, November 28, [18]62, *Papers Ruffin*, 4:271, 274.

37. *State Journal* (Raleigh), November 29, 1862; *Raleigh Daily Progress*, December 22, 1862; *Fayetteville Observer*, December 8, 1862; *Salem People's Press*, December 12, 1862; *North Carolina Standard* (Raleigh), November 25, December 5, 19, 1862.

38. *State Journal* (Raleigh), December 17, 1862; *North Carolina Standard* (Raleigh), January 2, 1863; *Raleigh Daily Progress*, January 13, 1863.

39. *Raleigh Daily Progress*, January 23, 1863; *State Journal* (Raleigh), January 26, 1863; *Salem People's Press*, February 27, 1863; R. S. Donnell and R. W. Lassiter, Resolutions, January 30, 1863, *Official Records*, ser. 4, 2:378.

40. *State Journal* (Raleigh), February 15, 1863; *Fayetteville Observer*, February 19, March 9, 1863; Kenneth Rayner to Thomas Ruffin, February 16, 1863, *Papers Ruffin*, 4:291.

41. *Raleigh Daily Progress*, February 13, April 6, June 1, 1863.

42. Tucker, *Zeb Vance*, p. 223; *Raleigh Daily Progress*, June 13, 24, 1863; *North Carolina Standard* (Raleigh), January 6, 1863.

CHAPTER TEN

1. See: Frank L. Owsley, *State Rights in the Confederacy* (Chicago: University of Chicago Press, 1925); George C. Rable, *The Confederate Republic: A Revolution against Politics* (Chapel Hill: University of North Carolina Press, 1994); Gordon B. McKinney and Richard M. McMurry, *A Guide to the Microfilm Edition of the Papers of Zebulon Vance* (Frederick, Md.: University Publications of America, 1987), p. 137.

2. Zebulon B. Vance to Jefferson Davis, October 20, 1862, Burton N. Harrison to Vance, October 27, 1862, *War of the Rebellion: A Compilation of the Official Records of the Union and Confederate Armies and Navies*, ser. 1, 53 vols. (Washington: Government Printing Office, 1880–1901), 18:758, 761.

3. William J. Cooper Jr., *Jefferson Davis, American* (New York: Alfred A. Knopf, 2000); William C. Davis, *Jefferson Davis: The Man and His Hour* (New York: HarperCollins Publishers, 1991); Michael Fellman, *The Making of Robert E. Lee* (New York: Random House, 2000).

4. Jefferson Davis to Zebulon B. Vance, October 17, 1862, *Official Records*, ser. 1, 18:757–58; Vance to George W. Randolph, October 10, 1862, Vance to Davis, October 25, 1862, *The Papers of Zebulon Baird Vance*, vol. 1, *1843-1862*, ed. Frontis W. Johnston (Raleigh: North Carolina Division of Archives and History, 1963), pp. 252-53, 275-278.

5. Jefferson Davis to Zebulon B. Vance, November 1, 1862, *War of the Rebellion: A Compilation of the Official Records of the Union and Confederate Armies and Navies*, ser. 4, 4 vols. (Washington: Government Printing Office, 1880-1901), 2:154.

6. Zebulon B. Vance to Jefferson Davis, December 24, 1862, *War of the Rebellion: A Compilation of the Official Records of the Union and Confederate Armies and Navies*, ser. 2, 8 vols. (Washington: Government Printing Office, 1880-1901), 5:794; T. E. Upshaw to the editor of the *Richmond Enquirer*, November 3, 1862, *The Papers of Zebulon Vance*, eds. Gordon B. McKinney and Richard M. McMurry (Frederick, Md.: University Publications of America, 1987), microfilm, reel 15; James A. Seddon to Vance, December 27, 1862, *Papers of Vance*, reel 13.

7. Zebulon B. Vance to Jefferson Davis, March 31, 1863, Davis to Vance, July 14, 1863, *Official Records*, ser. 4, 2:464-65, 632-33; John B. Jones, *A Rebel War Clerk's Diary* (Baton Rouge: Louisiana State University Press, 1993), p. 189.

8. Zebulon B. Vance to G. W. Randolph, September 11, 1862, Randolph, Endorsement, November 7, 1862, *Official Records*, ser. 4, 2:81, 148; Vance to Randolph, October 10, 1862, *Vance Papers*, 1:252-53.

9. Jones, *Clerk's Diary*, p. 111; George W. Randolph to Zebulon B. Vance, November 10, 1862, *Official Records*, ser. 4, 2:175-76; David A. Barnes to Gustavus W. Smith, November 17, 1862, *Official Records*, ser. 1, 18:779.

10. James A. Seddon to Zebulon B. Vance, February 4, 1863, Vance to Seddon, February 12, 1863, *Official Records*, ser. 4, 2:385–86, 393–94. For another assessment of Zeb's decisions in this matter, see Glenn Tucker, *Zeb Vance: Champion of Personal Freedom* (Indianapolis: Bobbs-Merrill, 1965), pp. 202–3.

11. Zebulon B. Vance to Robert E. Lee, January 6, 1865, James A. Seddon to Vance, January 31, 1865, *Official Records*, ser. 1, vol. 46, pt. 2, pp. 1016, 1166–1167; Joseph E. Johnston to John C. Breckinridge, March 2, 1865, Lee to Johnston, March 2, 1865, Vance to Breckinridge, March 18, 1865, *Official Records*, ser. 1, vol. 47, pt. 2, pp. 1311–12, 1425; Vance to Breckinridge, March 25, 1865, Breckinridge to Vance, March 31, 1865, *Official Records*, ser. 1, vol. 47, pt. 3, pp. 693, 724.

12. D. K. McRae to Zebulon B. Vance, January 28, 1863, John White to Vance, March 6, May 20, September 4, 1863, January 2, 1864, Alexander Collie to White, October 1, 28, 1863, Collie and White, Agreement, October 27, 1863, Vance to Thomas Andrea, December 28, January 7, 1864, Vance to James A. Seddon, January 7, 1864, *Papers of Vance*, reel 13.

13. George W. Randolph to Zebulon B. Vance, November 1, 18, 1862, David A. Barnes to James A. Seddon, November 20, 1862; S. P. Arrington to George Little, November 26, 1862, *Vance Papers*, 1:290–91, 375, 380, 404; Seddon to Vance, February 17, 1863, Vance to Jefferson Davis, March 7, 1863, *Papers of Vance*, reel 13; Jno. Withers, Special Order No. 58, March 10, 1863, *Papers of Vance*, reel 3.

14. Zebulon B. Vance to C. G. Memminger, November 15, 1862, *Official Records*, ser. 4, 2:178; Vance to Memminger, November 22, 1862, Treasury Department Collection of Confederate Records, Records of the Office of the Secretary of the Treasury, RG 365.2.1, National Archives, Washington, D.C.; A. R. Lawton to James A. Seddon, September 28, 1864, *Official Records*, ser. 4, 3:690–92.

15. James A. Seddon to [Zebulon B.] Vance, January 6, 14, 1864, Vance to Seddon, January 7, 1864, *Official Records*, ser. 4, 3:4, 10–11, 28–29.

16. Zebulon B. Vance to Jefferson Davis, March 17, 1864, Davis to Vance, March 26, 1864, *Official Records*, ser. 1, vol. 51, pt. 2, pp. 837–39, 841–42; Vance to C. G. Memminger, April 11, 30, 1864, Thos. L. Baynes, Report, April 12, [18]64, Confederate Secretary of the Treasury Records.

17. Stephen R. Mallory to Zebulon B. Vance, December 28, 1864, *Official Records*, ser. 4, 3:1055–57; Vance to Mallory, January 3, 1865, *Official Records*, ser. 2, 2:786–87, Mallory to Vance, January 28, 1865, *Official Records*, ser. 1, vol. 46, pt. 2, pp. 1156–58; Vance to Mallory, February 9, 1865, *Official Records*, ser. 4, 3:1076–77.

18. See: *North Carolina Standard* (Raleigh), May 24, 1864; *Raleigh Daily Progress*, June 29, 1864; *North Carolinian* (Elizabeth City), November 1, 1876. One of Vance's Civil War secretaries, A. M. McPheeters, described the trade in detail. According to McPheeters, Vance shipped "only . . . fifteen bales of cotton on his own account during the war, and that space was allotted to Vance by Power, Low, and Company from their assigned space." *Raleigh News*, November 3, 1876.

19. Zebulon B. Vance to James A. Seddon, September 19, 1864, A. R. Lawton to Seddon, September 28, 1864, *Official Records*, ser. 4, 3:671–72, 690–92.

20. Zebulon B. Vance to James A. Seddon, March 21, 25, 1863, *Papers of Vance*, reel 16; Seddon to Vance, April 2, 1863, *Papers of Vance*, reel 17; Seddon to Vance, March 25, 1863, *Official Records*, ser. 2, 5:856–57.

21. Jennifer Van Zant, "Confederate Conscription and the North Carolina Supreme Court," *North Carolina Historical Review* 72 (January 1995): 58.

22. Zebulon B. Vance to James A. Seddon, May 22, 1863, *Papers of Vance*, reel 13; Vance to Seddon, February 29, 1864, *Official Records*, ser. 4, 3:176–77; *Raleigh Daily Progress*, August 8, 1863.

23. Zebulon B. Vance to Jefferson Davis, February 9, 1864, *Official Records*, ser. 1, vol. 51, pt. 2, p. 818; *Raleigh Daily Progress*, February 20, 1864; Vance to James A. Seddon, February 29, 1864, *Papers of Vance*, reel 13; Jones, *Clerk's Diary*, p. 344; Seddon to Vance, March 5, 1864, *Official Records*, ser. 4, 3:197–98; Van Zant, "Conscription and Supreme Court," p. 68.

24. Zebulon B. Vance to James A. Seddon, February 27, 1863, *Papers of Vance*, reel 13; G. J. Rains to Vance, March 25, 1863, Vance to Rains, March 31, 1863, Vance to Jefferson Davis, March 31, 1863, *Official Records*, ser. 4, 2:458, 464–66.

25. Zebulon B. Vance to G. J. Rains, March 31, 1863, *Official Records*, ser. 4, 2:465–66; Jones, *Clerk's Diary*, p. 511.

26. *Raleigh Daily Conservative*, January 17, 1865; Van Zant, "Conscription and Supreme Court," p. 73.

27. William McKee Evans, "Daniel Lindsey Russell," in *Dictionary of North Carolina Biography*, ed. William S. Powell, 6 vols. (Chapel Hill: University of North Carolina Press, 1979–96), 5:271–72.

28. Evans, "Russell," in *Dictionary*, 5:272–73; *Raleigh Daily Conservative*, August 12, 1864; James A. Seddon to Zebulon B. Vance, May 2, 1864, Vance to Seddon, May 19, 1864, *Official Records*, ser. 4, 3:375–76, 425–28.

29. Zebulon B. Vance to James A. Seddon, February 25, 1863, *Papers of Vance*, reel 13; Seddon to Vance, March 1, 1863, *Official Records*, ser. 1, 18:902; Vance to Seddon, December 21, 1863, *Official Records*, ser. 4, 2:1061–62; Paul D. Escott, "Poverty and Governmental Aid for the Poor in Confederate North Carolina," *North Carolina Historical Review* 61 (October 1984): 465.

30. Phillip Shaw Paludan, *Victims: A True Story of the Civil War* (Knoxville: University of Tennessee Press, 1981), pp. 84–85; *Raleigh Daily Progress*, January 19, 1863; Zebulon B. Vance to [Henry] Heth, January 21, 1863, *Official Records*, ser. 1, 18:854.

31. Paludan, *Victims*, pp. 4–5; A. S. Merrimon to Zebulon B. Vance, January 31, 1863, *The Papers of Zebulon Baird Vance*, vol. 2, *1863*, ed. Joe A. Mobley (Raleigh: North Carolina Division of Archives and History, 1995), p. 17.

32. Zebulon B. Vance to W. G. M. Davis, February 2, 27, 1863, A. S. Merrimon to Vance, February 16, 24, 1863, *Official Records*, ser. 1, 18:867, 881, 893, 897; Merrimon to Vance, January 31, 1863, Vance to Merrimon, February 9, 1863, *Vance Papers*, 2:37, 55.

33. Paludan, *Victims*, pp. 104–8; John C. Inscoe and Gordon B. McKinney, *The Heart of Confederate Appalachia: Western North Carolina in the Civil War* (Chapel Hill: University of North Carolina Press, 2000), pp. 117–20; G. W. M. Davis to Zebulon B. Vance, March 30, 1863, Zebulon Baird Vance Papers, Perkins Library, Duke University, Durham, N.C.; Vance to James A. Seddon, May 18, 1863, *Official Records*, ser. 2, 5:952; Seddon to Vance, May 23, 1863, *Vance Papers*, 2:167–68.

34. Martin Reidinger, "Robert Brank Vance," in *Dictionary*, 6:83–84.

35. Zebulon B. Vance to James A. Seddon, February 1, 1865, Vance to Bradley T. Johnson, February 1, 1865, G. W. Booth to Vance, February 3, 1865, John C. Breckinridge to Vance, Feb-

ruary 8, 1865, Johnson to Vance, February 12, 1865, *Official Records*, ser. 2, 8:167-68, 178-79, 198, 211-12; Cornelia P. Spencer, *The Last Ninety Days of the War in North Carolina* (New York: Watchman, 1866), pp. 21-23.

36. Zebulon B. Vance to James A. Seddon, January 26, 1863, Wm. T. Dortch to Vance, January 31, [18]63, *Papers of Vance*, reel 13; Seddon to T. S. Ashe et al., February 23, 1863, G. J. Rains to W. Landers et al., February 25, 1863, Vance to Seddon, September 3, 1863, *Official Records*, ser. 4, 2:409, 787-88.

37. James A. Seddon to Zebulon B. Vance, January 30, 1863, *Official Records*, ser. 4, 2:377; Vance to Seddon, February 4, 1863, *Papers of Vance*, reel 13; Jefferson Davis to Vance, March 31, 1864, *Official Records*, ser. 1, vol. 51, pt. 2, pp. 844-46.

38. Zebulon B. Vance to Jefferson Davis, February 9, 1864, Davis to [Vance], February 29, 1864, *Papers of Vance*, reel 13.

39. Zebulon B. Vance to Jefferson Davis, March 9, 1864, *Official Records*, ser. 1, vol. 51, pt. 2, pp. 829-30.

40. Zebulon B. Vance to Jefferson Davis, July 6, 1863, W. H. C. Whiting to Vance, July 1[0], 1863, *Papers of Vance*, reel 13; Jones, *Clerk's Diary*, pp. 240-41.

CHAPTER ELEVEN

1. Zebulon B. Vance to the North Carolina General Assembly, November 17, 1862, in *War of the Rebellion: A Compilation of the Official Records of the Union and Confederate Armies and Navies*, ser. 4, 4 vols. (Washington: Government Printing Office, 1880-1901), 2:180.

2. Kenneth Rayner to Thomas Ruffin, November 23, 1862, *The Papers of Thomas Ruffin*, vol. 3, ed. J. G. de Roulhac Hamilton (Raleigh: Edwards and Broughton, 1920), p. 271.

3. Kenneth Rayner to Thomas Ruffin, November 23, 1862, D. W. Courts to Ruffin, November 24, 1862, *Papers Ruffin*, 3:271-72; *State Journal* (Raleigh), November 27, 1862; *Fayetteville Observer*, December 1, 1862; *Raleigh Register*, December 6, 1862.

4. *North Carolina Standard* (Raleigh), November 21, 28, 1862; *Fayetteville Observer*, December 8, 1862; *Salem People's Press*, December 12, 1862; *Raleigh Daily Progress*, December 22, 1862; Kenneth Rayner to Thomas Ruffin, November 22, 1862, Charles Manly to Ruffin, November 28, [18]62, *Papers Ruffin*, 3:271, 274; Harris, *Holden*, p. 122.

5. Zebulon B. Vance to Jefferson Davis, November 11, 1862, *The Papers of Zebulon Baird Vance*, vol. 1, *1843-1862*, ed. Frontis W. Johnston (Raleigh: North Carolina Division of Archives and History, 1963), p. 336; Glenn Tucker, *Zeb Vance: Champion of Personal Freedom* (Indianapolis: Bobbs-Merrill, 1965), p. 283; W. A. Smith to Vance, January 3, 1863, *The Papers of Zebulon Vance*, eds. Gordon B. McKinney and Richard M. McMurry (Frederick, Md.: University Publications of America, 1987), microfilm, reel 15.

6. Wayne K. Durrill, *War of Another Kind: A Southern Community in the Great Rebellion* (New York: Oxford University Press, 1990), pp. 132-33; Joseph J. Williams to Zebulon B. Vance, November 22, 1862, *Vance Papers*, 1:386-88.

7. Herman E. Stilley to Zebulon B. Vance, January 7, 1863, *Papers of Vance*, reel 15; W. T. Dortch to Vance, Jan[uar]y 7, [18]63, *The Papers of Zebulon Baird Vance*, vol. 2, ed. Joe A. Mobley (Raleigh: North Carolina Division of Archives and History, 1995), pp. 7-8.

8. John G. Barrett, *The Civil War in North Carolina* (Chapel Hill: University of North Carolina Press, 1963), p. 176; Durrill, *Southern Community*, pp. 137-39.

9. *Raleigh Daily Progress*, December 10, 1862; Zebulon B. Vance to A. C. Myers, December 26, 1862, *Vance Papers*, 1:447-48; Paul D. Escott, "Poverty and Governmental Aid for the

Poor in Confederate North Carolina," *North Carolina Historical Review* 61 (October 1984): 465-67.

10. William T. Auman, "Neighbor against Neighbor: The Inner Civil War in the Central Counties of Confederate North Carolina," (Ph.D. diss., University of North Carolina, 1988), pp. 137-39.

11. John A. Craven to Zebulon B. Vance, October 21, 1862, *Papers of Vance*, reel 15; H. W. Ayer to Vance, November 10, 1862, *Vance Papers*, 1:331; Auman, "Neighbor against Neighbor in the Central Counties," pp. 147-50.

12. R. R. Crawford to Zebulon B. Vance, [February 28, 1863], *Papers of Vance*, reel 16.

13. W. A. Joyce to Zebulon B. Vance, February 16, [1863], *War of the Rebellion: A Compilation of the Official Records of the Union and Confederate Armies and Navies*, ser. 1, 53 vols. (Washington: Government Printing Office, 1880-1901), 18:880-81; R. F. Armfield to Vance, [February 19, 1863], *Papers of Vance*, reel 16.

14. Wm. M. Swann to W. H. C. Whiting, [February 11, 1863], *Papers of Vance*, reel 16.

15. O. Goddin to [Zebulon B. Vance], [February 27, 1863], *Papers of Vance*, reel 16.

16. William T. Auman, "Neighbor against Neighbor: The Inner Civil War in the Randolph County Area of Confederate North Carolina," *North Carolina Historical Review* 61 (January 1984): 68-72.

17. Auman, "Randolph County," pp. 72-73; Auman, "Neighbor against Neighbor in the Central Counties," pp. 164-65.

18. Charles F. Bryan Jr., "'Tories' Amidst Rebels: Confederate Occupation of East Tennessee, 1861-1863," *East Tennessee Historical Society's Publications* 60 (1988): 8-18.

19. Phillip Shaw Paludan, *Victims: A True Story of the Civil War* (Knoxville: University of Tennessee Press, 1981), pp. 66-71; Marcus Erwin to Henry T. Clark, April 29, 1862, Governor's Papers (Clark), North Carolina Division of Archives and History, Raleigh.

20. *Asheville News*, November 27, December 11, 1862; David W. Siler to Zebulon B. Vance, November 3, 1862, *Vance Papers*, 1:302; Moses Wilkerson to Henry T. Clark, July 18, 1862, Governor's Papers (Clark).

21. Mily Barker to Zebulon B. Vance, February 27, 1863, [Mrs.] H. T. McLelland to Vance, February 22, 1863, *Papers of Vance*, reel 16.

22. Paul D. Escott, *Many Excellent People: Power and Privilege in North Carolina, 1850-1900* (Chapel Hill: University of North Carolina Press, 1985), p. 66; *Raleigh Daily Progress*, March 31, April 10, 1863; *North Carolina Standard* (Raleigh), April 3, 1863.

23. Zebulon B. Vance to James A. Seddon, April 27, 1863, *Official Records*, ser. 1, 18: 934-35; Richard Bardolph, "Confederate Dilemma: North Carolina Troops and the Deserter Problem, Part I," *North Carolina Historical Review* 66 (January 1989): 83-84.

24. Paul D. Escott, *After Secession: Jefferson Davis and the Failure of Confederate Nationalism* (Baton Rouge: Louisiana State University Press, 1978), pp. 68-69.

25. Auman, "Neighbor against Neighbor in the Central Counties," pp. 73-74; R. R. Crawford to Zebulon B. Vance, May 25, 1863, *Papers of Vance*, reel 16.

26. *North Carolina Standard* (Raleigh), May 1, 1863; G. W. Dobson to Zebulon B. Vance, May 25, 1863, *Papers of Vance*, reel 17. See also: John C. Inscoe and Gordon B. McKinney, *The Heart of Confederate Appalachia: Western North Carolina in the Civil War* (Chapel Hill: University of North Carolina Press, 2000), pp. 105-38.

27. Harris, *Holden*, pp. 123-24; *North Carolina Standard* (Raleigh), March 24, 1863; *Raleigh Daily Progress*, April 3, 1863; *Salem People's Press*, May 22, 1863.

28. *North Carolina Standard* (Raleigh), May 27, June 3, 17, 1863.

29. D. H. Hill to Zebulon B. Vance, April 23, [1863], *Papers of Vance*, reel 17; J. Johnston Pettigrew to Vance, May 23, 1863, *Official Records*, ser. 1, vol. 51, pt. 2, pp. 712–13.

30. Archie K. Davis, *Boy Colonel of the Confederacy: The Life and Times of Henry King Burgwyn, Jr.* (Chapel Hill: University of North Carolina Press, 1985), pp. 292–339; Rod Gragg, *Covered with Glory: The 26th North Carolina Infantry at the Battle of Gettysburg* (New York: HarperCollins Publishers, 2000), pp. 87–200; J. J. Pettigrew to Zebulon B. Vance, July 9, 1863, *Papers of Vance*, reel 3; Martin Crawford, *Ashe County's Civil War: Community and Society in the Appalachian South* (Charlottesville: University Press of Virginia, 2001), p. 119.

CHAPTER TWELVE

1. J. J. Young to Zebulon B. Vance, July 4, 1863, *The Papers of Zebulon Vance*, eds. Gordon B. McKinney and Richard M. McMurry (Frederick, Md.: University Publications of America, 1987), microfilm, reel 18; Glenn Tucker, *Zeb Vance: Champion of Personal Freedom* (Indianapolis: Bobbs-Merrill, 1965), pp. 329–32; D. H. Hill to Zebulon B. Vance, July 10, 1863, *The Papers of Zebulon Baird Vance*, vol. 2, ed. Joe A. Mobley (Raleigh: North Carolina Division of Archives and History, 1995), pp. 208–9; Saml. McD. Tate to Zebulon B. Vance, July 8, 1863, J. J. Pettigrew to Zebulon B. Vance, July 9, 1863, *Papers of Vance*, reel 13.

2. Zebulon B. Vance to Jefferson Davis, July 9, 1863, *Vance Papers*, 2:208; William T. Auman, "Neighbor against Neighbor: The Inner Civil War in the Central Counties of Confederate North Carolina" (Ph.D. diss., University of North Carolina, 1988), p. 234.

3. Zebulon B. Vance to Jefferson Davis, July 6, 1863, *Vance Papers*, 2:206.

4. Jefferson Davis to Zebulon B. Vance, July 14, 1863, *Vance Papers*, 2:214–15.

5. Ibid., July 18, 1863, *Vance Papers*, 2:215–16.

6. *Raleigh Daily Progress*, July 11, 15, 1863.

7. *North Carolina Standard* (Raleigh), July 17, 1863.

8. Ibid., July 17, 21, 1863.

9. Ibid., July 24, 1863; Jefferson Davis to Zebulon B. Vance, July 24, 1863, *Vance Papers*, 2:221–22.

10. Zebulon B. Vance to Jefferson Davis, July 26, 1863, *War of the Rebellion: A Compilation of the Official Records of the Union and Confederate Armies and Navies*, ser. 1, 53 vols. (Washington: Government Printing Office, 1880–1901), vol. 51, pt. 2, p. 740.

11. Ibid.

12. Edward J. Hale to Zebulon B. Vance, July 26, 1863, *Vance Papers*, 2:220–21.

13. Zebulon B. Vance to Edward J. Hale, July 26, 1863, *Vance Papers*, 2:226–27.

14. *North Carolina Standard* (Raleigh), July 28, 1863.

15. Ibid.

16. Ibid.; *State Journal* (Raleigh), July 29, 1863.

17. *North Carolina Standard* (Raleigh), July 31, 1863.

18. Ibid.

19. William C. Harris, *William Woods Holden: Firebrand of North Carolina Politics* (Baton Rouge: Louisiana State University Press, 1987), p. 138; James A. Seddon to Zebulon B. Vance, July 28, 1863, *Vance Papers*, 2:227; *Fayetteville Observer*, August 3, 17, 1863; *North Carolina Standard* (Raleigh), August 4, 1863.

20. *North Carolina Standard* (Raleigh), August 11, 1863.

21. Ibid., August 18, 1863; see ibid., July 28–October 13, 1863.

22. *North Carolina Standard* (Raleigh), September 4, 8, 1863; *Fayetteville Observer*, September 10, 1863.

23. *North Carolina Standard* (Raleigh), August 14, September 1, 1863.

24. Harris, *Holden*, p. 138; *North Carolina Standard* (Raleigh), September 1, 1863.

25. See *North Carolina Standard* (Raleigh), August 18, 21, 25, 28, September 1, 4, 8, 1863.

26. Ibid., August 7, 25, September 4, 8, 1863; Auman, "Neighbor against Neighbor in the Central Counties," p. 240.

27. *State Journal* (Raleigh), August 29, 1863; Zebulon B. Vance to Edward J. Hale, July 26, 1863, *Vance Papers*, 2:227.

28. *North Carolina Standard* (Raleigh), August 4, 7, 21, 1863; *Salem People's Press*, August 27, 1863.

29. Zebulon B. Vance to James A. Seddon, July 28, 1863, *War of the Rebellion: A Compilation of the Official Records of the Union and Confederate Armies and Navies*, ser. 4, 4 vols. (Washington: Government Printing Office, 1880-1901), 2:680; Seddon to Vance, August 4, 1863, *Vance Papers*, 2:232.

30. Zebulon B. Vance to Edward J. Hale, August 11, 1863, *Vance Papers*, 2:237.

31. Ibid.

32. Ibid.; Zebulon B. Vance to William A. Graham, August 13, 1863, *Vance Papers*, 2:23-28.

33. Zebulon B. Vance to John H. Haughton, August 17, 1863, *Vance Papers*, 2:242-44.

34. Ibid., 2:245-47.

35. Zebulon B. Vance to William A. Graham, August 19, 24, 1863, *Vance Papers*, 2:241, 252; Graham to Vance, August 21, 1863, *Papers of Vance*, reel 3.

36. Zebulon B. Vance to William A. Graham, August 24, 1863, *Vance Papers*, 2:252.

37. Zebulon B. Vance to William P. Bynum, August 26, 1863, *Vance Papers*, 2:252-53.

38. *Fayetteville Observer*, August 17, 1863.

39. *North Carolina Standard* (Raleigh), October 13, 1863; *Raleigh Daily Progress*, September 1, 1863.

40. Zebulon B. Vance to Edward J. Hale, September 7, 1863, *Vance Papers*, 2:270; Harris, *Holden*, pp. 137-38.

41. Zebulon B. Vance, Proclamation, September 7, 1863, *Vance Papers*, 2:268.

42. Ibid.

43. Ibid., 2:269; Zebulon B. Vance to Edward J. Hale, September 7, 1863, *Vance Papers*, 2:270.

44. *North Carolina Standard* (Raleigh), October 13, 1863.

CHAPTER THIRTEEN

1. Zebulon B. Vance to Jefferson Davis, September 10, 1863, Henry L. Benning to S. Cooper, September 28, 1863, Vance to James A. Seddon, October 15, 1863, *War of the Rebellion: A Compilation of the Official Records of the Union and Confederate Armies and Navies*, ser. 1, 53 vols. (Washington: Government Printing Office, 1880-1901), vol. 51, pt. 2, pp. 763-64, 770-71, 777-78; Jonathan Worth to Archibald McLean, September 10, 1863, *The Correspondence of Jonathan Worth*, vol. 1, ed. J. G. de Roulhac Hamilton (Raleigh: North Carolina Historical Commission, 1909), pp. 260-261; *Raleigh Daily Progress*, September 11, 1863; *North Carolina Standard* (Raleigh), October 2, 1863; Franklin R. Shirley, *Zebulon Vance, Tarheel Spokesman* (Charlotte: McNally and Loftin, 1963), p. 35.

2. *North Carolina Standard* (Raleigh), October 2, 7, 28, 1863; William C. Harris, *William Woods Holden: Firebrand of North Carolina Politics* (Baton Rouge: Louisiana State University Press, 1987), p. 139; *Raleigh Daily Progress*, September 11, 1863; Jonathan Worth to Archibald McLean, September 10, 1863, *Correspondence Worth*, 1:260-61.

3. Zebulon B. Vance to Jefferson Davis, September 10, 1863 (two letters), Vance to Davis, September 11, 1863, *Official Records*, ser. 1, vol. 51, pt. 2, pp. 710, 763-65.

4. Zebulon B. Vance to Jefferson Davis, September 11, 1863, *Official Records*, ser. 1, vol. 51, pt. 2, p. 765.

5. Ibid., pp. 764-65.

6. Jefferson Davis to Zebulon B. Vance, September 15, 1863, Vance to Davis, September 15, 1863, *Official Records*, ser. 1, vol. 51, pt. 2, pp. 767-68.

7. *North Carolina Standard* (Raleigh), October 13, 1863; *Fayetteville Observer*, September 17, 1863.

8. *Salem People's Press*, September 17, 1863; *Raleigh Daily Progress*, September 15, 1863; *North Carolina Standard* (Raleigh), October 2, 7, 28, 1863; Zebulon B. Vance to Edward J. Hale, September 20, 1863, *The Papers of Zebulon Baird Vance*, vol. 2, ed. Joe A. Mobley (Raleigh: North Carolina Division of Archives and History, 1995), p. 282.

9. Jason H. Carson to Zebulon B. Vance, September 4, 1863, Robert B. Vance to Zebulon B. Vance, August 24, 1863, *Vance Papers*, 2:251, 261. See also: A. S. Merrimon to Zebulon B. Vance, W. Murdock to [Vance], September 18, 1863, *The Papers of Zebulon Vance*, eds. Gordon B. McKinney and Richard M. McMurry (Frederick, Md.: University Publications of America, 1987), microfilm, reel 19; John C. Inscoe and Gordon B. McKinney, *The Heart of Confederate Appalachia: Western North Carolina in the Civil War* (Chapel Hill: University of North Carolina Press, 2000), p. 182.

10. Zebulon B. Vance to Edward J. Hale, September 20, 1863, *Vance Papers*, 2:282.

11. Zebulon B. Vance to Robert F. Hoke, September 7, 1863, *Vance Papers*, 2:267.

12. William T. Auman, "Neighbor against Neighbor: The Inner Civil War in the Central Counties of Confederate North Carolina," (Ph.D. diss., University of North Carolina, 1988), pp. 252-90; Zebulon B. Vance to Edward J. Hale, October 26, 1863, *Vance Papers*, 2:309.

13. Richmond M. Pearson to Zebulon B. Vance, October 3, 1863, Vance to Pearson, October 7, 1863, *Vance Papers*, 2:291, 297.

14. Marc W. Kruman, *Parties and Politics in North Carolina, 1836-1865* (Baton Rouge: Louisiana State University Press, 1983), pp. 252-55.

15. A. T. Davidson to Zebulon B. Vance, March 28, 1863, *Papers of Vance*, reel 3; Thomas E. Jeffrey, "Allen T. Davidson," in *Encyclopedia of the Confederacy*, ed. Richard N. Current (New York: Simon & Schuster, 1993), pp. 446-47.

16. *North Carolina Standard* (Raleigh), July 28, 1863; W. Murdock to Zebulon B. Vance, August 12, 1863, F. E. Johnston to Vance, August 14, 1863, *Papers of Vance*, reel 19; Inscoe and McKinney, *Confederate Appalachia*, p. 151.

17. A. T. Davidson to Zebulon B. Vance, March 23, 1863, J. D. Hyman to Vance, April 30, 1863, *Papers of Vance*, reel 3; W. Murdock to Vance, September 18, 1863, *Papers of Vance*, reel 19; A. S. Merrimon to Vance, September 21, 1863, *Papers of Vance*, reel 3.

18. L. S. Gash to Zebulon B. Vance, September 7, 11, 1863, Wm. Dedman to Vance, September 13, 1863, *Papers of Vance*, reel 19; *North Carolina Standard* (Raleigh), October 13, November 3, 10, 17, 27, 1863.

19. For different interpretations of the election results, see: Harris, *Holden*, p. 140; Paul D. Escott, *After Secession: Jefferson Davis and the Failure of Confederate Nationalism* (Baton Rouge: Louisiana State University Press, 1978), p. 155; Kruman, *Parties and Politics*, pp. 252-56; Richard E. Yates, "Governor Vance and the Peace Movement," *North Carolina Historical Review* 17 (April 1940): 19-20; J. G. de Roulhac Hamilton, *Reconstruction in North Carolina* (Gloucester, Mass.: Peter Smith, 1964), p. 55.

20. Zebulon B. Vance to Edward J. Hale, October 26, November 9, 1863, *Vance Papers*, 2:308-9, 318; *Raleigh Daily Progress*, October 14, 1863; *North Carolina Standard* (Raleigh), November 4, 1863.

21. Zebulon B. Vance to Edward J. Hale, November 9, 1863, *Vance Papers*, 2:318-19.

22. *North Carolina Standard* (Raleigh), November 27, 1863; *Raleigh Daily Progress*, December 27, 1863; Zebulon B. Vance to James A. Seddon, December 29, 1863, *War of the Rebellion: A Compilation of the Official Records of the Union and Confederate Armies and Navies*, ser. 4, 4 vols. (Washington: Government Printing Office, 1880-1901), 2:1066.

23. *North Carolina Standard* (Raleigh), November 27, 1863; Yates, "Peace Movement," p. 10; Escott, *After Secession*, pp. 190-92.

24. Zebulon B. Vance to Edward J. Hale, December 21, 1863, *Vance Papers*, 2:346.

25. Zebulon B. Vance to James A. Seddon, December 31, 1863, *Official Records*, ser. 4, 2:1072.

26. Jas. O. Simmons to Zebulon B. Vance, April 18, 1864, *Papers of Vance*, reel 23; E. R. Norton to Vance, September 27, 1864, *Papers of Vance*, reel 24.

27. J. A. Goode and J. W. Harris to Zebulon B. Vance, April 10, 1863, *Papers of Vance*, reel 16; Wm. Enloe et al. to Vance, April 10, 1863, *Papers of Vance*, reel 17; Tod R. Caldwell et al. to Vance, February 4, 1865, *Papers of Vance*, reel 26.

28. Zebulon B. Vance to Edward J. Hale, December 10, 1863, *Vance Papers*, 2:338; *Raleigh Daily Progress*, December 15, 18, 1863; *North Carolina Standard* (Raleigh), December 18, 1863.

29. William W. Holden to Thomas Settle Jr., December 22, 1863, Thomas Settle Jr. and Thomas Settle III Papers, Southern Historical Collection, University of North Carolina Library, Chapel Hill.

30. *Raleigh Daily Progress*, December 21, 1863; Richard H. Battle, "Sketch of Governor Vance," in Clement Dowd, *Life of Zebulon B. Vance* (Charlotte: Observer Printing and Publishing House, 1897), p. 162; Zebulon B. Vance to Edward J. Hale, December 21, 1863, *Vance Papers*, 2:346.

31. "Petition of Citizens of Pasquotank County," December 19, 1863, *Official Records*, ser. 1, vol. 29, pt. 2, pp. 597-98; Edward A. Wild to George H. Johnston, December 28, 1863, *Official Records*, ser. 1, vol. 29, pt. 1, pp. 911-17.

32. Jasper Spruill to Zebulon B. Vance, January 28, [18]63, *Papers of Vance*, reel 16; Wayne K. Durrill, *War of Another Kind: A Southern Community in the Great Rebellion* (New York: Oxford University Press, 1990), pp. 166.

33. Zebulon B. Vance to Edward J. Hale, December 30, 1863, *Vance Papers*, 2:359.

34. Ibid., December 21, 30, 1863, *Vance Papers*, 2:346-47, 359.

35. Zebulon B. Vance to Jefferson Davis, December 30, 1863, *Vance Papers*, 2:357-58; Davis to Vance, January 9, 1864, *Official Records*, ser. 1, vol. 51, pt. 2, pp. 808-10.

CHAPTER FOURTEEN

1. Zebulon B. Vance to [William A. Graham], [January 1], 186[4], *The Papers of Zebulon Vance*, eds. Gordon B. McKinney and Richard M. McMurry (Frederick, Md.: University Publications of America, 1987), microfilm, reel 39.

2. Zebulon B. Vance to David L. Swain, January 2, 1864, *Papers of Vance*, reel 39.

3. Ibid.

4. *Fayetteville Observer*, January 4, 1864; John A. Gilmer to Zebulon B. Vance, January 5, 1864, *Papers of Vance*, reel 2; *Raleigh Daily Progress*, January 5, 1864.

5. *North Carolina Standard* (Raleigh), January 12, 1864.

6. Ibid.; William C. Harris, *William Woods Holden: Firebrand of North Carolina Politics* (Baton Rouge: Louisiana State University Press, 1987), p. 142; Kenneth Rayner to Thomas Ruffin, January 12, 1864, *The Papers of Thomas Ruffin*, vol. 4, ed. J. G. de Roulhac Hamilton (Raleigh: Edwards and Broughton, 1918–20), pp. 362–63.

7. *Raleigh Daily Progress*, January 15, 16, 1864; *North Carolina Standard* (Raleigh), January 15, 20, 1864.

8. John B. Robbins, "The Confederacy and the Writ of Habeas Corpus," *Georgia Historical Quarterly* 55 (Spring 1971): 91; Joe A. Mobley, "Zebulon B. Vance: A Confederate Nationalist in the North Carolina Gubernatorial Election of 1864," *North Carolina Historical Review* 77 (October 2000): 441.

9. *Raleigh Daily Progress*, January 26, 1864; William T. Auman and David D. Scarborough, "The Heroes of America in Civil War North Carolina," *North Carolina Historical Review* 58 (October 1981): 348–49; William T. Auman, "Neighbor against Neighbor: The Inner Civil War in the Central Counties of Confederate North Carolina" (Ph.D. diss., University of North Carolina, 1988), p. 226.

10. Richard E. Yates, "Governor Vance and the Peace Movement," *North Carolina Historical Review* 17 (April 1940): 92–93; Auman, "Neighbor against Neighbor in the Central Counties," p. 306; Form Letter, [January 1864], Thomas Settle Jr. and Thomas Settle III Papers, Southern Historical Collection, University of North Carolina Library, Chapel Hill.

11. Harris, *Holden*, pp. 142–43; *North Carolina Standard* (Raleigh), February 5, 1864.

12. Edward J. Hale to William A. Graham, January 23, 1864, Graham to Hale, January 29, 1864, *The Papers of William Alexander Graham*, vol. 6, *1864–1865*, ed. Max R. Williams (Raleigh: North Carolina Division of Archives and History, 1976), pp. 16–17, 19–21; J. J. Sloan to James A. Seddon, February 2, 1864, *War of the Rebellion: A Compilation of the Official Records of the Union and Confederate Armies and Navies*, ser. 1, 53 vols. (Washington: Government Printing Office, 1880–1901), vol. 51, pt. 2, p. 815.

13. Paul D. Escott, *After Secession: Jefferson Davis and the Failure of Confederate Nationalism* (Baton Rouge: Louisiana State University Press, 1978), p. 202; Harris, *Holden*, p. 143; Zebulon B. Vance to Jefferson Davis, February 9, 1864, *Official Records*, ser. 1, vol. 51, pt. 2, pp. 818–20.

14. Zebulon B. Vance to Jefferson Davis, February 9, 1864, Davis, Addendum, in Vance to Davis, February 9, 1864, *Official Records*, ser. 1, vol. 51, pt. 2, pp. 818–20.

15. Julius Linebach, "Regimental Band of the Twenty-Sixth North Carolina," *Civil War History* 4 (September 1958): 233–34; C. J. Cowles to Zebulon B. Vance, February 14, 1864, Calvin J. Cowles Papers, North Carolina Division of Archives and History, Raleigh; Harris, *Holden*, p. 145; *North Carolina Standard* (Raleigh), February 12, 1864.

16. Jennifer Van Zant, "Confederate Conscription and the North Carolina Supreme Court," *North Carolina Historical Review* 72 (January 1995): 65; Escott, *After Secession*, p. 142.

17. Eugene M. Lerner, "Inflation in the Confederacy," in *Studies in the Quantity Theory of Money*, ed. Milton Friedman (Chicago: University of Chicago Press, 1956), p. 171.

18. C. J. Cowles to W. W. Holden, February 25, 1864, Cowles Papers; *Raleigh Daily Conservative*, April 16, 1864.

19. *Raleigh Daily Conservative*, April 16, 1864.

20. Ibid.

21. Ibid.

22. Ibid.

23. Ibid.

24. Ibid.

25. Ibid.

26. *Raleigh Daily Progress*, February 26, March 2, 1864; *Fayetteville Observer*, February 29, 1864; Samuel F. Phillips to William A. Graham, February 26, 1864, *Papers of Graham*, 6:31-33; C. J. Cowles to W. W. Holden, March 10, 1864, Cowles Papers.

27. *North Carolina Standard* (Raleigh), February 23, 1864; *Raleigh Daily Progress*, March 2, 1864; Glenn Tucker, *Zeb Vance: Champion of Personal Freedom* (Indianapolis: Bobbs-Merrill, 1965), p. 361.

28. Auman, "Neighbor against Neighbor in the Central Counties," p. 318; Samuel F. Phillips to William A. Graham, February 26, 1864, *Papers of Graham*, 6:35; C. J. Cowles to W. W. Holden, March 10, 1864, Cowles Papers; Zebulon B. Vance to Graham, March 3, 1864, *Papers of Graham*, 6:36.

29. *Fayetteville Observer*, March 17, 1864; *Charlotte Bulletin*, March 29, 1864; Tucker, *Zeb Vance*, pp. 337-48; Franklin R. Shirley, *Zebulon Vance, Tarheel Spokesman* (Charlotte: McNally and Loftin, 1963), p. 45.

30. *Fayetteville Observer*, April 14, 1864.

31. *Raleigh Daily Progress*, April 21, 1864; Jesse M. Frank to Jesse Hendrick, April 2, 1864, Siler Family Papers (private collection).

32. *North Carolina Standard* (Raleigh), April 6, 1864; *Raleigh Daily Progress*, April 11, 1864; Yates, "Peace Movement," p. 98; Auman, "Neighbor against Neighbor in the Central Counties," pp. 308-9.

33. Zebulon B. Vance to William A. Graham, April 9, 1864, *Papers of Graham*, 6:57; *Raleigh Daily Progress*, April 8, 15, 1864; *North Carolina Standard* (Raleigh), April 20, 1864.

34. Auman, "Neighbor against Neighbor in the Central Counties," pp. 315-22.

35. Escott, *After Secession*, pp. 204-5; *Raleigh Daily Progress*, April 7, 8, 1864; *North Carolina Standard* (Raleigh), April 20, 1864; *Fayetteville Observer*, April 21, 1864.

36. Wayne K. Durrill, *War of Another Kind: A Southern Community in the Great Rebellion* (New York: Oxford University Press, 1990), pp. 209-10.

37. Braxton Bragg to Zebulon B. Vance, April 21, 1864, *War of the Rebellion: A Compilation of the Official Records of the Union and Confederate Armies and Navies*, ser. 2, 8 vols. (Washington: Government Printing Office, 1880-1901), 7:78-79.

1. *Fayetteville Observer*, April 25, 1864.

2. Ibid.

3. Ibid.

4. Ibid.

5. Ibid.

6. *Raleigh Daily Conservative*, April 25, 1864.

7. *Raleigh Daily Progress*, April 26, 27, May 9, 1864.

8. *Raleigh Daily Conservative*, April 29, 1864.

9. Ibid., May 17, 1864.

10. Ibid., April 27, May 10, 1864.

11. Jonathan Worth to William W. Holden, April 23, 1864, *The Papers of William Woods Holden*, vol. 1, *1841–1868*, eds. Horace Raper and Thornton W. Mitchell (Raleigh: North Carolina Division of Archives and History, 2000), pp. 135–37.

12. *North Carolina Standard* (Raleigh), May 20, 1864.

13. Ibid.

14. Ibid.

15. *Raleigh Daily Conservative*, May 21, 23, 24, 1864.

16. Ibid., May 23, 24, 1864.

17. *North Carolina Standard* (Raleigh), May 24, 1864.

18. Ibid.

19. For speaking schedules, see *Raleigh Daily Conservative*, May 31, July 2, 22, 1864. Ibid., June 11, 1864; Calvin J. Cowles to William W. Holden, July 9, 1864, Calvin J. Cowles Papers, North Carolina Division of Archives and History, Raleigh.

20. *North Carolina Standard* (Raleigh), May 27, 1864.

21. William T. Auman and David D. Scarborough, "The Heroes of America in Civil War North Carolina," *North Carolina Historical Review* 58 (October 1981): 327–63.

22. Auman and Scarborough, "Heroes of America," pp. 354, 356; John B. Jones, *A Rebel War Clerk's Diary* (Baton Rouge: Louisiana State University Press, 1993), p. 391; *Raleigh Daily Confederate*, June 18, 1864; *North Carolina Standard* (Raleigh), July 1, 1864; *Raleigh Daily Conservative*, July 2, 18, 1864.

23. William Kaufman Scarborough, ed., *The Diary of Edmund Ruffin*, vol. 3, *July 1863– June 1865* (Baton Rouge: Louisiana State University Press, 1989), p. 497.

24. James M. McPherson, *Battle Cry of Freedom: The Civil War Era* (New York: Ballantine Books, 1988), pp. 718–43.

25. Albert Castel, *Decision in the West: The Atlanta Campaign of 1864* (Lawrence: University Press of Kansas, 1992); Richard M. McMurry, *Atlanta, 1864: Last Chance for the Confederacy* (Lincoln: University of Nebraska Press, 2000).

26. McPherson, *Battle Cry*, pp. 756–58; Phillip Shaw Paludan, *The Presidency of Abraham Lincoln* (Lawrence: University Press of Kansas, 1994), pp. 280–83.

27. William W. Holden to Calvin J. Cowles, July 19, 1864, *Papers Holden*, 1:162; Kenneth Rayner to Thomas Ruffin, July 18, 27, 1864, *The Papers of Thomas Ruffin*, vol. 4, ed. J. G. de Roulhac Hamilton (Raleigh: Edwards and Broughton, 1918–20), pp. 403–4, 409; *Raleigh Daily Conservative*, July 20, 1864; *Carolina Times* (Charlotte), July 22, 1864.

28. *Raleigh Daily Progress*, July 18, August 1, 1864; Richard E. Yates, "Governor Vance and the Peace Movement," *North Carolina Historical Review* 17 (April 1940): 111.

29. *Raleigh Daily Conservative*, July 20, 1864; Calvin J. Cowles to William W. Holden, July 25, August 4, 1864, Cowles Papers; Wayne K. Durrill, *War of Another Kind: A Southern Community in the Great Rebellion* (New York: Oxford University Press, 1990), p. 215.

30. William W. Holden to [Calvin J. Cowles], July 29, 1864, *Papers Holden*, 1:162; *Raleigh Daily Progress*, August 1, 1864.

31. *Raleigh Daily Progress*, July 30, August 3, 1864; Winfield S. Hancock to —— Humphreys, July 29, 1864, *War of the Rebellion: A Compilation of the Official Records of the Union and Confederate Armies and Navies*, ser. 1, 53 vols. (Washington: Government Printing Office, 1880-1901), vol. 40, pt. 3, p. 598; William C. Harris, *William Woods Holden: Firebrand of North Carolina Politics* (Baton Rouge: Louisiana State University Press, 1987), p. 151.

32. Harris, *Holden*, p. 152; Marc W. Kruman, *Parties and Politics in North Carolina, 1836-1865* (Baton Rouge: Louisiana State University Press, 1983), p. 265; *North Carolina Standard* (Raleigh), August 12, 1864; Robert P. Dick to William W. Holden, August 20, 1864, *Papers Holden*, 1:166.

33. Robin E. Baker, "Class Conflict and Political Upheaval: The Transformation of North Carolina during the Civil War," *North Carolina Historical Review* 69 (April 1992): 175; Paul D. Escott, *Many Excellent People: Power and Privilege in North Carolina, 1850-1900* (Chapel Hill: University of North Carolina Press, 1985), pp. 70-71.

CHAPTER SIXTEEN

1. Emory M. Thomas, *The Confederate Nation, 1861-1865* (New York: Harper & Row, 1979), p. 264 n; *North Carolina Standard* (Raleigh), August 12, 1864.

2. Robert E. Lee to Zebulon B. Vance, August 29, 1864, *War of the Rebellion: A Compilation of the Official Records of the Union and Confederate Armies and Navies*, ser. 1, 53 vols. (Washington: Government Printing Office, 1880-1901), vol. 42, pt. 2, pp. 1206-7.

3. William T. Auman, "Neighbor against Neighbor: The Inner Civil War in the Randolph County Area of Confederate North Carolina," *North Carolina Historical Review* 61 (January 1984): 81-83; Auman, "Neighbor against Neighbor: The Inner Civil War in the Central Counties of Confederate North Carolina," (Ph.D. diss., University of North Carolina, 1988), pp. 380-81.

4. Zebulon B. Vance, Proclamation, August 24, 1964, *Official Records*, ser. 1, vol. 51, pt. 2, pp. 1038-39.

5. James M. McPherson, *Battle Cry of Freedom: The Civil War Era* (New York: Ballantine Books, 1988), pp. 768-78.

6. Zebulon B. Vance to David L. Swain, September 22, 1864, *The Papers of Zebulon Vance*, eds. Gordon B. McKinney and Richard M. McMurry (Frederick, Md.: University Publications of America, 1987), microfilm, reel 3.

7. Ibid.

8. Ibid.

9. Zebulon B. Vance to M. L. Bonham, September 23, 1864, Joseph E. Brown to Vance, October 1, 1864, *War of the Rebellion: A Compilation of the Official Records of the Union and Confederate Armies and Navies*, ser. 4, 4 vols. (Washington: Government Printing Office, 1880-1901), 3:684-85, 706-7.

10. *Raleigh Daily Progress*, October 14, 1864; Resolutions, October 17, 1864, *Official Records*, ser. 1, vol. 42, pt. 3, pp. 1149-50.

11. Resolutions, October 17, 1864, *Official Records*, ser. 1, vol. 42, pt. 3, pp. 1149–50.

12. *Raleigh Daily Conservative*, October 21, 26, 29, 1864; *North Carolina Standard* (Raleigh), October 25, 1864.

13. *Fayetteville Observer*, September 8, 1864; *Raleigh Daily Progress*, September 30, 1864; Auman, "Randolph County," p. 84.

14. Zebulon B. Vance to W. H. C. Whiting, September 28, 1864, *Official Records*, ser. 1, vol. 42, pt. 2, p. 1300.

15. Zebulon B. Vance to T. H. Holmes, November 2, 1864, *Official Records*, ser. 4, 3:754–55; Vance to James A. Seddon, December 5, 1864, *Official Records*, ser. 1, vol. 51, pt. 2, p. 1053.

16. *Raleigh Daily Progress*, October 7, 1864; John G. Barrett, *The Civil War in North Carolina* (Chapel Hill: University of North Carolina Press, 1963), p. 231; William Lamb, Diary, November 9, [1864], *Official Records* (Navy), ser. 1, 11:742; Zebulon B. Vance to Jefferson Davis, November 15, 1864, Robert E. Lee to James A. Seddon, November 30, 1864, *Official Records*, ser. 1, vol. 42, pt. 3, p. 1214–15.

17. *Raleigh Daily Conservative*, November 23, 1864.

18. Ibid.

19. McPherson, *Battle Cry*, pp. 779–80, 803–15.

20. *Fayetteville Observer*, December 1, 1864.

21. Ibid., December 15, 1864; *Raleigh Daily Conservative*, January 21, 1865.

22. Zebulon B. Vance to Jefferson Davis, October 15, 1864, Robert E. Lee to James A. Seddon, December 8, 1864, Davis to Samuel J. Person, December 15, 1864, Zebulon B. Vance, Proclamation, December 20, 1864, *Official Records*, ser. 1, vol. 42, pt. 3, pp. 1148–49, 1259, 1273–75, 1284–85; W. H. C. Whiting to Vance, December 18, 1864, *Official Records* (Navy), ser. 1, 11:783.

23. Chris E. Fonvielle Jr., *The Wilmington Campaign: Last Rays of Departing Hope* (Mechanicsburg, Pa.: Stackpole Books, 1997), pp. 57–172.

24. *Fayetteville Observer*, December 29, 1864.

25. Fonvielle, *Wilmington*, pp. 207–96.

26. Jonathan Worth to ——, January 8, 1865, *The Correspondence of Jonathan Worth*, vol. 1, ed. J. G. de Roulhac Hamilton (Raleigh: North Carolina Historical Commission, 1909), p. 338; Cornelia P. Spencer, *The Last Ninety Days of the War in North Carolina* (New York: Watchman, 1866), p. 29; John B. Jones, *A Rebel War Clerk's Diary* (Baton Rouge: Louisiana State University Press, 1993), pp. 477–78.

27. *Raleigh Daily Conservative*, January 21, 1865; *Raleigh Daily Progress*, January 25, 1865.

28. *Raleigh Daily Conservative*, December 30, 1864; *Raleigh Daily Progress*, January 23, 24, 31, 1865.

29. John A. Campbell, Memorandum, February 1865, John A. Campbell Papers, Illinois State Historical Library, Springfield; McPherson, *Battle Cry*, pp. 821–24.

30. Zebulon B. Vance, Proclamation, February 14, 1865, *Official Records*, ser. 1, vol. 47, pt. 2, pp. 1187–92.

31. Ibid.; David L. Swain to William A. Graham, February 18, 1865, *The Papers of William Alexander Graham*, vol. 6, *1864–1865*, ed. Max R. Williams (Raleigh: North Carolina Division of Archives and History, 1976), p. 247 (n. 54).

32. Zebulon B. Vance, Proclamation, February 14, 1865, *Official Records*, ser. 1, vol. 47, pt. 2, pp. 1187–92; *Raleigh Daily Progress*, February 16, 17, 1865.

33. McPherson, *Battle Cry*, pp. 825-30.

34. Fonvielle, *Wilmington*, pp. 331-437.

35. *Raleigh Daily Conservative*, February 22, 1865; Zebulon B. Vance to Robert E. Lee, March 2, 1865, *Official Records*, ser. 1, vol. 47, pt. 2, p. 1312.

36. *Raleigh Daily Progress*, February 12, March 2, 1865; *North Carolina Standard* (Raleigh), February 3, 1865; William A. Graham to Zebulon B. Vance, February 12, 1865, *Papers of Graham*, 6:233; *Raleigh Daily Conservative*, February 17, 1865.

37. Thomas Conolly Diary, March 6, 1865, photocopy, Virginia Historical Society, Richmond; Allen W. Trelease, *The North Carolina Railroad, 1849-1871, and the Modernization of North Carolina* (Chapel Hill: University of North Carolina Press, 1991), pp. 195-96.

38. John G. Barrett, *Sherman's March through the Carolinas* (Chapel Hill: University of North Carolina Press, 1956), pp. 117-202; Ina W. Van Noppen, "The Significance of Stoneman's Last Raid," *North Carolina Historical Review* 38 (April 1961): 149-50.

39. Robert E. Lee to Zebulon B. Vance, March 9, 1865, *Official Records*, ser. 1, vol. 47, pt. 2, pp. 1353-54; Auman, "Randolph County," p. 90.

40. *Raleigh Daily Conservative*, February 23, 1865.

41. Ibid.

42. William A. Graham to David L. Swain, March 26, 1865, *Papers of Graham*, 6:289.

43. Franklin R. Shirley, *Zebulon Vance, Tarheel Spokesman* (Charlotte: McNally and Loftin, 1963), pp. 56-57; William A. Graham to David L. Swain, April 8, 1865, *Papers of Graham*, 6:294-95.

44. Barrett, *North Carolina*, pp. 368-69; McPherson, *Battle Cry*, pp. 844-49; Van Noppen, "Stoneman's Raid," pp. 163-65; Richard E. Yates, *The Confederacy and Zeb Vance* (Tuscaloosa, Ala.: Confederate Publishing Company, 1958), pp. 116-17.

CHAPTER SEVENTEEN

1. Cornelia P. Spencer, *The Last Ninety Days of the War in North Carolina* (New York: Watchman, 1866), pp. 135-43; Zebulon B. Vance to William T. Sherman, April 11, 1865, Cornelia P. Spencer Papers, Southern Historical Collection, University of North Carolina Library, Chapel Hill; Joe A. Mobley, "Zebulon B. Vance: A Confederate Nationalist in the North Carolina Gubernatorial Election of 1864," *North Carolina Historical Review* 77 (October 2000): 449.

2. Zebulon B. Vance to W. T. Sherman, April 12, 1865, *War of the Rebellion: A Compilation of the Official Records of the Union and Confederate Armies and Navies*, ser. 1, 53 vols. (Washington: Government Printing Office, 1880-1901), vol. 47, pt. 3, p. 178; Mark L. Bradley, *This Astounding Close: The Road to Bennett Place* (Chapel Hill: University of North Carolina Press, 2000), pp. 108-9.

3. Zebulon B. Vance to [Jefferson Davis], April 11, 1865, *Official Records*, ser. 1, vol. 46, pt. 3, p. 1393; Davis to [Vance], April 11, 1865, Vance to Davis, April 12, 1865, Davis to Vance, April 12, 1865, *Official Records*, ser. 1, vol. 47, pt. 3, pp. 786-87, 792; John G. Barrett, *Sherman's March through the Carolinas* (Chapel Hill: University of North Carolina Press, 1956), pp. 216-17.

4. Zebulon B. Vance to J. E. Johnston, April 19, 1865, *The Papers of Zebulon Vance*, eds. Gordon B. McKinney and Richard M. McMurry (Frederick, Md.: University Publications of America, 1987), microfilm, reel 4; Bradley, *Astounding Close*, pp. 147, 165-67.

5. Bradley, *Astounding Close*, p. 167.

6. *North Carolina Standard* (Raleigh), April 17, 18, 1865; *Raleigh Daily Progress*, April 19, 22, 1865.

7. Zebulon B. Vance to [William A. Graham], April 21, [1865], *Papers of Vance*, reel 39; J. E. Johnston to Vance, April 24, 1865, *Papers of Vance*, reel 4; Allan Nevins, *War for the Union: The Organized War to Victory* (New York: Charles Scribner's Sons, 1971), 8:352-57.

8. Joseph E. Johnston to Zebulon B. Vance, April 19, 1865 (two letters), Johnston to Vance, April 24, 1865, *Official Records*, ser. 1, vol. 53, pp. 417-19; Johnston to Vance, April 19, 1865, Vance to Johnston, April 19 (two letters), April 20, 1965, *Official Records*, ser. 1, vol. 47, pt. 3, pp. 810-12, 815; Bradley, *Astounding Close*, pp. 180-82.

9. Bradley, *Astounding Close*, p. 204; Zebulon B. Vance to William T. Sherman, April 27, 1865, Vance, Proclamation, April 28, 1865, *Papers of Vance*, reel 4; *Raleigh Daily Progress*, May 3, 1865.

10. Spencer, *Ninety Days*, pp. 214-15; Tucker, *Zeb Vance*, pp. 467-68.

11. Glenn Tucker, *Zeb Vance: Champion of Personal Freedom* (Indianapolis: Bobbs-Merrill, 1965), p. 411; Clement Dowd, *Life of Zebulon B. Vance* (Charlotte: Observer Printing and Publishing House, 1897), pp. 95-96; *North Carolina Standard* (Raleigh), May 4, 1865.

12. *North Carolina Standard* (Raleigh), May 17, 29, 1865; Dowd, *Life of Vance*, pp. 96-97; Zebulon B. Vance to D. G. Fowle, May 16, 1865, *Papers of Vance*, reel 4; Tucker, *Zeb Vance*, p. 415.

13. Dowd, *Life of Vance*, p. 97; F. N. Boney, *John Letcher of Virginia: The Story of Virginia's Civil War Governor* (Tuscaloosa: University of Alabama Press, 1966), pp. 218-19; Newton T. Colby to Zebulon B. Vance, July 8, 19, August 22, 1865, *Papers of Vance*, reel 4.

14. Boney, *Letcher*, p. 219.

15. Harriett E. Vance to Zebulon B. Vance, May 19, June 5, 9, 1865, Robert [B. Vance] to Zebulon B. Vance, June 10, July 12, 1865, *Papers of Vance*, reel 4; Tucker, *Zeb Vance*, pp. 417-18.

16. Zebulon B. Vance to Andrew Johnson, June 3, 1865, Pardon Applications, RG M1003, reel 43, National Archives, Washington, D.C.; Jonathan Truman Dorris, "Pardoning North Carolinians," *North Carolina Historical Review* 23 (July 1946): 379-80.

17. Zebulon B. Vance to Andrew Johnson, June 3, 1865, Pardon Applications.

18. Zebulon B. Vance Parole, July 6, 1865, *Papers of Vance*, reel 4; *North Carolina Standard* (Raleigh), July 15, 24, 1865; Tucker, *Zeb Vance*, p. 429.

19. Tucker, *Zeb Vance*, pp. 432-33.

20. William A. Graham to Zebulon B. Vance, October 4, 1865, *Papers of Vance*, reel 4; Vance to Kemp P. Battle, September 25, 1865, *Papers of Vance*, reel 39.

21. Zebulon B. Vance to Kemp P. Battle, September 25, 1865, *Papers of Vance*, reel 39; Charles F. Deems to Vance, August 23, 1865, *Papers of Vance*, reel 4.

22. Harriett E. Vance to Zebulon B. Vance, October 21, 1865, Robert P. Dick to Zebulon B. Vance, October 24, 1865, Andrew Johnson to Dick, October 24, 1865, *Papers of Vance*, reel 4; William W. Holden to [Andrew Johnson], July 24, 1865, *The Papers of Andrew Johnson*, vol. 8, ed. Paul Bergeron (Knoxville: University of Tennessee Press, 1989), pp. 463-64.

23. *North Carolina Standard* (Raleigh), October 23, December 6, 1865; *Raleigh Sentinel*, November 3, December 4, 1865; *Raleigh Daily Progress*, November 20, 1865; F. E. Shober to Zebulon B. Vance, November 27, 28, 1865, D. L. Swain to Vance, November 30, December 4, 1865, North Carolina General Assembly, Resolutions, December 5, 1865, *Papers of Vance*, reel 4.

24. *Raleigh Daily Progress*, May 24, August 16, September 1, October 2, 1865.

25. Cornelia P. Spencer to Zebulon B. Vance, October 30, 1865, *Papers of Vance*, reel 4; Vance to Spencer, November 1, 1865, *Papers of Vance*, reel 39.

26. Zebulon B. Vance to Cornelia P. Spencer, November 1, 15, 1865, *Papers of Vance*, reel 39.

27. Zebulon B. Vance, "Autobiography of the Hon. Zebulon Baird Vance" (private collection), p. 14.

28. "Autobiography Vance," pp. 20-21.

29. Zebulon B. Vance to [David L. Swain], November 14, 1865, Swain to [Vance], November 20, 1865, J. M. Morris to Vance, December 15, 1865, Vance to Swain, January 12, 1866, J. G. Person to Vance, January 23, 1866, J. G. Burr to [Vance], February 22, 1866, John Letcher to Vance, May 4, 1866, *Papers of Vance*, reel 4; Dorris, "Pardoning," p. 379; *Salem People's Press*, March 17, 1866.

30. John A. Young to Zebulon B. Vance, February 23, 1866, Kemp P. Battle to [Vance], May 3, 1866, *Papers of Vance*, reel 4; Vance to W. A. Graham, May 9, [1866], *Papers of Vance*, reel 39; *Charlotte Democrat*, April 3, 1866; Franklin R. Shirley, *Zebulon Vance, Tarheel Spokesman* (Charlotte: McNally and Loftin, 1963), p. 60.

31. *North Carolina Standard* (Raleigh), January 10, 1866.

32. Zebulon B. Vance to [Cornelia P. Spencer], April 27, [1866], *Papers of Vance*, reel 39.

33. Spencer, *Ninety Days*, p. 126.

34. C[ornelia] A[nn] Spencer to [Zebulon B. Vance], May 10, 1866; Vance to David L. Swain, May 24, [1866], *Papers of Vance*, reel 4; Vance to Spencer, May 6, 1866, Vance to —— Argo et al., May 19, 1866, *Papers of Vance*, reel 39.

35. Dowd, *Life of Vance*, pp. 404-10.

CHAPTER EIGHTEEN

1. Dan T. Carter, *When the War Was Over: The Failure of Self-Reconstruction in the South, 1865-1867* (Baton Rouge: Louisiana State University Press, 1985), pp. 47-54, 74-75, 77-83, 187-88, 227-29.

2. Carter, *Self-Reconstruction*, pp. 188-90; L. S. Gash to M. A. Gash, March 4, 1866, in Otto H. Olsen and Ellen Z. McGrew, "Prelude to Reconstruction: The Correspondence of Leander Sams Gash, 1866-1867, Part I," *North Carolina Historical Review* 40 (January 1963): 84.

3. Eric Foner, *Reconstruction: America's Unfinished Revolution, 1863-1877* (New York: Harper & Row, 1988), pp. 196-261.

4. *Charlotte Democrat*, July 17, 31, 1866.

5. *North Carolina Standard* (Raleigh), June 2, 1866; J. J. Jackson to Jonathan Worth, August 9, 1866, *The Correspondence of Jonathan Worth*, vol. 2, ed. J. G. de Roulhac Hamilton (Raleigh: North Carolina Historical Commission, 1909), p. 741.

6. Clement Dowd, *Life of Zebulon B. Vance* (Charlotte: Observer Printing and Publishing House, 1897), p. 109.

7. John Foster West, *Lift Up Your Head, Tom Dooley: The True Story of the Appalachian Murder That Inspired One of America's Most Popular Ballads* (Asheboro, N.C.: Down Home Press, 1993), pp. 8-39; *North Carolina Standard* (Raleigh), October 27, 1866.

8. West, *Tom Dooley*, pp. 39-45.

9. Ibid., pp. 45-52.

10. Max R. Williams, "The Johnston Will Case: A Clash of Titans," pt. 1, *North Carolina Historical Review* 67 (April 1990): 193–221; ibid., pt. 2, *North Carolina Historical Review* 67 (July 1990): 334–59. Quotation from p. 352.

11. *Charlotte Democrat*, December 18, 25, 1866; *North Carolina Standard* (Raleigh), January 8, 1867.

12. Laurence Shore, *Southern Capitalists: The Ideological Leadership of an Elite, 1832–1855* (Chapel Hill: University of North Carolina Press, 1986), pp. 116–17.

13. Gordon B. McKinney, *Southern Mountain Republicans, 1865–1900: Politics and the Appalachian Community* (Chapel Hill: University of North Carolina Press, 1978), p. 45.

14. *North Carolina Standard* (Raleigh), September 18, 1866, April 2, 1867; Alfred Dockery to Thomas Settle Jr., September 29, 1866, Thomas Settle Jr. and Thomas Settle III Papers, Southern Historical Collection, University of North Carolina Library, Chapel Hill; J. G. de Roulhac Hamilton, *Reconstruction in North Carolina* (Gloucester, Mass.: Peter Smith, 1964), p. 181; William C. Harris, *William Woods Holden: Firebrand of North Carolina Politics* (Baton Rouge: Louisiana State University Press, 1987), p. 214.

15. L. S. Gash to M. A. Gash, February 9, 1867, in "Gash Correspondence," p. 350; Olsen and McGrew, "Gash Correspondence," p. 334.

16. Andrew Johnson to [Zebulon B. Vance], March 11, 1867, *The Papers of Zebulon Vance*, eds. Gordon B. McKinney and Richard M. McMurry (Frederick, Md.: University Publications of America, 1987), microfilm, reel 4; Vance to William H. Seward, May 2, 1867, *Papers of Vance*, reel 39; Glenn Tucker, *Zeb Vance: Champion of Personal Freedom* (Indianapolis: Bobbs-Merrill, 1965), p. 430; *Charlotte Democrat*, April 16, 1867.

17. *North Carolina Standard* (Raleigh), April 13, 16, 1867; *Charlotte Democrat*, April 16, 1867.

18. Zebulon B. Vance to David L. Swain, July 26, 1867, *Papers of Vance*, reel 4; *Charlotte Democrat*, June 4, July 16, 1867; *North Carolina Standard* (Raleigh), July 27, 1867.

19. For attacks on Union League members, see *North Carolina Standard* (Raleigh), July 18, December 14, 1867. John Pool to David M. Carter, August 19, September 31, 1867, David Miller Carter Papers, Southern Historical Collection, University of North Carolina Library, Chapel Hill; Daniel R. Goodloe to R. P. Dick, September 30, 1867, Settle Papers; *Raleigh Daily Progress*, October 5, 1867.

20. William S. Powell, *North Carolina through Four Centuries* (Chapel Hill: University of North Carolina Press, 1989), p. 392.

21. Harris, *Holden*, p. 230–231; *North Carolina Standard* (Raleigh), November 7, 1867.

22. Franklin R. Shirley, *Zebulon Vance, Tarheel Spokesman* (Charlotte: McNally and Loftin, 1963), pp. 66–67.

23. *Charlotte Democrat*, February 11, 1868.

24. Ibid., March 3, 5, 1868; Paul D. Escott, *Many Excellent People: Power and Privilege in North Carolina, 1850–1900* (Chapel Hill: University of North Carolina Press, 1985), pp. 137–39.

25. Zebulon B. Vance to William A. Graham, March 2, [1868], Jos. L. Carson et al. to Graham, March 20, 1868, *The Papers of William Alexander Graham*, vol. 7, *1866–1868*, ed. Max R. Williams (Raleigh: North Carolina Division of Archives and History, 1976), pp. 507–8, 526; *North Carolina Standard* (Raleigh), March 11, 25, 1868.

26. Powell, *North Carolina*, p. 395; Susie L. Owens, "The Union League of America: Political Activities in Tennessee, the Carolinas, and Virginia, 1865–1870" (Ph.D. diss., New

York University, 1943); Foner, *Reconstruction*, pp. 283–86; H. C. Thompson to B. S. Hedrick, April 3, 1868, Benjamin Sherwood Hedrick Papers, Duke University Library, Durham, N.C.

27. Shirley, *Spokesman*, p. 69; *Charlotte Democrat*, August 25, 1868.

28. *North Carolina Standard* (Raleigh), September 3, 1868; *Milton Chronicle*, September 17, 1868, *Papers of Vance*, reel 7; Escott, *Many Excellent People*, p. 150.

29. Carolyn A. Wallace, "David Lowry Swain," in *Dictionary of North Carolina Biography*, ed. William S. Powell, 6 vols. (Chapel Hill: University of North Carolina Press, 1979–96), 5:485.

30. Zebulon B. Vance to the editor of the *New York World*, October 13, 1868, in Dowd, *Life of Vance*, p. 101.

31. Harris, *Holden*, p. 252; Dowd, *Life of Vance*, p. 196; Escott, *Many Excellent People*, p. 148.

32. Otto H. Olsen, "North Carolina: An Incongruous Presence," in *Reconstruction and Redemption in the South: An Assessment*, ed. Otto H. Olsen (Baton Rouge: Louisiana State University Press, 1980), p. 170.

33. *North Carolina Standard* (Raleigh), April 22, June 10, August 28, 1869; *Charlotte Democrat*, April 27, June 15, 22, September 14, 1869, April 26, 1870.

34. Allen W. Trelease, *White Terror: The Ku Klux Klan Conspiracy and Southern Reconstruction* (New York: Harper & Row, 1971), pp. 189–207; Otto H. Olsen, "The Ku Klux Klan: A Study in Reconstruction Politics and Propaganda," *North Carolina Historical Review* 39 (Summer 1962): 341; Olsen, "North Carolina," p. 181; *North Carolina Standard* (Raleigh), October 22, 1869.

35. *Charlotte Democrat*, January 18, 1870; Harris, *Holden*, pp. 282–83; Carole Watterson Troxler, "'To Look More Closely at the Man': Wyatt Outlaw, a Nexus of National, Local, and Personal History," *North Carolina Historical Review* 77 (October 2000): 403–4; Trelease, *White Terror*, pp. 205–6.

36. *North Carolina Standard* (Raleigh), March 7, 1870; William Woods Holden, Proclamation, March 7, 1870, Broadsides Collection, Duke University Library, Durham, N.C.; Holden to U. S. Grant, March 10, 1870, William Woods Holden Papers, Duke University Library, Durham, N.C.; Trelease, *White Terror*, pp. 212–15.

37. Harris, *Holden*, pp. 288–93; *North Carolina Standard* (Raleigh), July 2, 1870.

38. *North Carolina Standard* (Raleigh), April 20, June 20, 1870; Harris, *Holden*, pp. 268–76.

39. *Charlotte Democrat*, May 31, June 28, 1870.

40. *North Carolina Standard* (Raleigh), July 25, 30, 1870; Harris, *Holden*, pp. 295–296; J. W. Payne to William L. Scott, July 26, 1870, William LaFayette Scott Papers, Perkins Library, Duke University, Durham, N.C.

41. *Charlotte Democrat*, July 26, 1870; *Louisville Courier-Journal*, November 26, 1868; Trelease, *White Terror*, pp. 341–47; Gordon B. McKinney, "The Klan in the Southern Mountains: The Lusk-Shotwell Controversy," *Appalachian Journal* 8 (Winter 1981): 89–104.

42. Harris, *Holden*, pp. 297–98.

CHAPTER NINETEEN

1. *Charlotte Democrat*, August 16, September 6, 1870; George W. Swepson to Matt W. Ransom, September 11, 1870, Matt W. Ransom Papers, Southern Historical Collection, University of North Carolina Library, Chapel Hill.

2. George W. Swepson to Matt W. Ransom, September 11, 1870, Ransom Papers.

3. Zebulon B. Vance to [Kemp P. Battle], October 27, 1870, *The Papers of Zebulon Vance*, eds. Gordon B. McKinney and Richard M. McMurry (Frederick, Md.: University Publications of America, 1987), microfilm, reel 39.

4. *North Carolina Standard* (Raleigh), November 25, 1870.

5. *Raleigh Sentinel*, December 20, 1872.

6. *Charlotte Democrat*, January 17, 1871.

7. William C. Harris, *William Woods Holden: Firebrand of North Carolina Politics* (Baton Rouge: Louisiana State University Press, 1987), p. 301; *North Carolina Standard* (Raleigh), December 19, 1870; Zebulon B. Vance to Cornelia P. Spencer, December 27, 1870, *Papers of Vance*, reel 39.

8. Zebulon B. Vance to the editor of the *Washington Chronicle*, December 10, 1870, in *Charlotte Democrat*, January 3, 1871.

9. *Charlotte Democrat*, January 10, 17, 1871; R. M. Pearson et al. to the Congress of the United States, [January 1871], *Papers of Vance*, reel 39.

10. Sandy Smith et al. to the Senate and House of Representatives of the United States, [January 1871], *Papers of Vance*, reel 39.

11. *Charlotte Democrat*, January 10, 17, March 14, 1871, February 20, 1872; *Raleigh News*, May 6, 1872.

12. *Charlotte Democrat*, January 10, March 14, 21, 1871; James B. Mason et al. to William W. Holden, January 10, 1871, William Woods Holden Papers, Duke University Library, Durham, N.C.

13. Harris, *Holden*, p. 305–8; *Charlotte Democrat*, March 21, 1871.

14. John Pool to A. C. Cowles, March 17, 1871, in *Charlotte Democrat*, March 28, 1871.

15. Allen W. Trelease, *White Terror: The Ku Klux Klan Conspiracy and Southern Reconstruction* (New York: Harper & Row, 1971), pp. 341–46; *Asheville Pioneer*, June 22, 1871; *Charlotte Democrat*, June 13, 20, July 18, 25, October 3, 17, 1871.

16. *Raleigh News*, April 6, 1872; Zebulon B. Vance to Randolph A. Shotwell, March 8, 1872, *Papers of Vance*, reel 39.

17. *Charlotte Democrat*, April 18, May 16, 1871; *Asheville Pioneer*, July 20, August 31, 1871; Paul D. Escott, *Many Excellent People: Power and Privilege in North Carolina, 1850–1900* (Chapel Hill: University of North Carolina Press, 1985), p. 164; Gordon B. McKinney, *Southern Mountain Republicans, 1865–1900: Politics and the Appalachian Community* (Chapel Hill: University of North Carolina Press, 1978), p. 47.

18. *Asheville Pioneer*, November 16, 1871; *Charlotte Democrat*, January 30, 1872; Zebulon B. Vance to General Assembly of North Carolina, January 20, 1872, *Papers of Vance*, reel 4.

19. *Raleigh Sentinel*, December 20, 1872.

20. *Asheville Pioneer*, February 8, April 25, 1872; *Charlotte Democrat*, May 7, 1872.

21. *Raleigh News*, March 11, 1872.

22. *Asheville Pioneer*, April 25, 1872; *Charlotte Democrat*, April 23, July 16, 1872.

23. *Raleigh News*, April 6, 1872.

24. Ibid.

25. *Raleigh Sentinel*, December 20, 1872.

26. *Raleigh News*, April 25, June 12, 15, 1872; *Raleigh Sentinel*, December 20, 1872.

27. *Raleigh News*, August 8, 16, 19, September 11, 12, 1872; William S. Powell, *North Carolina through Four Centuries* (Chapel Hill: University of North Carolina Press, 1989), p. 403.

28. *Charlotte Democrat*, July 23, August 13, 1872; *Raleigh Sentinel*, December 20, 1872.

29. *Raleigh News*, August 26, September 6, November 17, 26, 1872; *Raleigh Sentinel*, December 20, 1872; McKinney, *Mountain Republicans*, p. 48.

30. *Charlotte Democrat*, December 3, 1872; J. G. de Roulhac Hamilton, *Reconstruction in North Carolina* (Gloucester, Mass.: Peter Smith, 1964), p. 594.

31. Hamilton, *Reconstruction*, p. 594; *Raleigh Sentinel*, December 20, 1872; *Charlotte Democrat*, December 10, 1872.

32. *Raleigh Sentinel*, December 20, 1872; Clement Dowd, *Life of Zebulon B. Vance* (Charlotte: Observer Printing and Publishing House, 1897), p. 118.

33. *North Carolina Citizen* (Asheville), August 7, October 9, 23, 1873.

34. Zebulon B. Vance to J. A. Early, September 27, 1873, *Papers of Vance*, reel 4; Vance to [Kemp P. Battle], May 1, 1875, April 19, 1876, *Papers of Vance*, reel 39; Dabny H. Maury and J. William Jones to Vance, December 28, 1877, *Papers of Vance*, reel 29; Receipt, American Academy of Political and Social Science, January 1, 1893, Zebulon Baird Vance Papers, Southern Historical Collection, University of North Carolina Library, Chapel Hill; *Our Living and Dead* 3 (July 1875): 65.

35. "Address Delivered by Governor Vance before the Southern Historical Society," *Our Living and Dead* 3 (November 1875): 612-14, 619, 623-24.

36. Ibid., p. 626, 626n; Robert Graham to —— Graham, November 29, 1875, *Papers of Vance*, reel 39.

37. Selig Adler, "Zebulon B. Vance and the 'Scattered Nation,'" *Journal of Southern History* 7 (August 1941): 357-77; Zebulon B. Vance, *The Scattered Nation* (New York: Press of J. J. Little & Co., 1904), pp. 34-35.

38. Vance, *Scattered Nation*, pp. 14, 19, 34-35, 39.

39. Dowd, *Life of Vance*, p. 210.

40. *Asheville Pioneer*, June 6, 1874; O. H. Dockery to D. L. Russell, June 7, 1874, Daniel Lindsay Russell Papers, Southern Historical Collection, University of North Carolina Library, Chapel Hill; *Charlotte Democrat*, August 10, 1874, February 15, 1875; McKinney, *Mountain Republicans*, p. 49; *Asheville Citizen*, August 13, 1874.

41. Michael Perman, *The Road to Redemption: Southern Politics, 1869-1879* (Chapel Hill: University of North Carolina Press, 1984), pp. 197-98; *Charlotte Democrat*, July 12, August 2, 1875.

42. *Asheville Citizen*, August 12, 1875; Hamilton, *Reconstruction*, p. 635; Otto H. Olsen, "North Carolina: An Incongruous Presence," in *Reconstruction and Redemption in the South: An Assessment*, ed. Otto H. Olsen (Baton Rouge: Louisiana State University Press, 1980), p. 190-91; Perman, *Redemption*, p. 198.

43. *Charlotte Democrat*, December 6, 1875.

CHAPTER TWENTY

1. *Winston Union Republican*, February 24, 1876; *Charlotte Democrat*, April 3, 1876; Danl. G. Fowle to [M. W. Ransom], June 2, 1876, Plummer Batchelor to [Ransom], June 3, 1876, [Jos. B. Batchelor] to Ransom, June 3, 1876, Wm. B. Meares to [Ransom], June 4, 1876, Fab. H. Busbee to Ransom, June 5, 1876, H. G. Williams to [Ransom], June 5, 1876, Matt W. Ransom Papers, Southern Historical Collection, University of North Carolina Library, Chapel Hill.

2. *Charlotte Democrat*, May 8, 15, 22, 29, June 12, 1876; Fab. H. Busbee to M. W. Ransom, June 5, 1876, Ransom Papers.

3. Zebulon B. Vance to ——, May 22, 1876, in *Tarboro Southerner*, June 9, 1876.

4. *Warrenton Gazette*, June 2, 1876; Plummer Batchelor to [M. W. Ransom], June 3, 1876, Ransom Papers; *New North State* (Greensboro), June 9, 1876.

5. *North Carolina Gazette* (Fayetteville), June 22, 1876; Clement Dowd, *Life of Zebulon B. Vance* (Charlotte: Observer Printing and Publishing House, 1897), pp. 143-44; Sandra Porter Babb, "The Battle of Giants: The Gubernatorial Election of 1876 in North Carolina" (master's thesis, University of North Carolina, 1970), pp. 25-26.

6. *Alamance Gleaner* (Graham), June 27, 1876.

7. Dowd, *Life of Vance*, pp. 144-45; *Charlotte Democrat*, June 19, 1876; *Wilmington Weekly Star*, June 23, 1876; Wm. R. Cox to M. W. Ransom, July 7, 1876, Ransom Papers.

8. *Tarboro Southerner*, July 7, 21, 1876; Babb, "Battle of Giants," pp. 62-63; *Wilmington Weekly Star*, July 21, 1876; *Raleigh Daily News*, July 23, 1876.

9. *Oxford Torch-Light*, July 11, 1876; *Raleigh Daily News*, July 25, 1876; *New North State* (Greensboro), October 13, 1876.

10. Jeffrey J. Crow, "Thomas Settle Jr., Reconstruction, and the Memory of the Civil War," *Journal of Southern History* 62 (November 1996): 691-93.

11. Ibid., pp. 694-713.

12. Ibid., pp. 713-16.

13. Thomas Settle Jr. to Zebulon B. Vance, July 13, 1876 (two letters), Vance to Settle, July 14, 1876, Thos. B. Keogh to W. R. Cox, July 15, 17, 1876, Cox to Keogh, July 14, 19, 1876, Thomas Settle Jr. and Thomas Settle III Papers, Southern Historical Collection, University of North Carolina Library, Chapel Hill; Geo. Mathes to M. W. Ransom, July 20, 1876, Ransom Papers; Babb, "Battle of the Giants," pp. 37-38; *Charlotte Democrat*, July 17, 24, 1876; *Winston Union Republican*, July 20, 1876; *North Carolinian* (Elizabeth City), August 16, 1876.

14. *Winston Union Republican*, June 22, August 10, 17, 24, September 7, 1876; *Carolina Messenger* (Goldsboro), July 17, 20, 1876; *Tarboro Southerner*, July 21, 1876; *New York Times*, July 30, 1876; *Raleigh News*, July 28, August 2, 1876; *Salem People's Press*, August 3, 1876; *Raleigh Daily Constitution*, August 9, October 16, 1876; *North Carolinian* (Elizabeth City), August 9, 16, 30, 1876; *New North State* (Greensboro), August 25, September 15, 1876; Babb, "Battle of Giants," pp. 41-42, 59.

15. *Raleigh News*, July 28, August 2, 1876; *New York Times*, July 30, 1876; *Charlotte Democrat*, July 31, August 14, 21, 1876; *Salem People's Press*, August 3, 10, 1876; *Winston Union Republican*, July 27, August 10, 24, 1876; *Raleigh Daily Constitution*, August 9, September 5, October 16, 1876; *North Carolina Gazette* (Fayetteville), August 17, 1876; *Greensboro Patriot*, August 23, 1876; *New North State* (Greensboro), August 25, 1876; *Carolina Messenger* (Goldsboro), October 5, 1876; Babb, "Battle of Giants," p. 60.

16. "The War Record of Z. B. Vance," n.d., Edward Dromgoole Papers, Southern Historical Collection, University of North Carolina Library, Chapel Hill.

17. *North Carolinian* (Elizabeth City), August 30, September 6, November 1, 1876; *Raleigh Daily Constitution*, August 9, October 16, 1876; *Winston Union Republican*, August 24, 1876; *New North State* (Greensboro), October 27, 1876; Babb, "Battle of Giants," p. 42.

18. *Raleigh News*, July 28, 1876; *Charlotte Democrat*, July 31, 1876.

19. *Raleigh Daily Constitution*, August 9, 1876; *Alamance Gleaner* (Graham), August 22, 1876; J. S. Heilig to Rutherford B. Hayes, August 14, 1876, Rutherford B. Hayes Papers, Rutherford B. Hayes Presidential Center, Fremont, Ohio.

20. *Raleigh News*, August 12, 1876; *Salem People's Press*, August 10, 1876; Franklin R. Shirley, *Zebulon Vance, Tarheel Spokesman* (Charlotte: McNally and Loftin, 1963), p. 78.

21. *Charlotte Democrat*, August 14, 1876; Edward H. McGee, "White Attitudes toward the Negro in North Carolina, 1850-1876" (master's thesis, University of North Carolina, 1968), pp. 104-5; *Warrenton Gazette*, August 25, 1876.

22. J. S. Heilig to Rutherford B. Hayes, August 14, 1876, Hayes Papers.

23. Babb, "Battle of Giants," p. 53; *Winston Union Republican*, August 17, 1876.

24. *Winston Union Republican*, August 24, 1876.

25. Ibid.

26. *New North State* (Greensboro), August 25, 1876; *North Carolina Gazette* (Fayetteville), August 31, 1876.

27. *New North State* (Greensboro), August 25, 1876.

28. *Carolina Messenger* (Goldsboro), August 17, 1876; *New North State* (Greensboro), August 25, 1876.

29. *Raleigh Daily Constitution*, October 16, 1876.

30. Ibid.

31. *Oxford Torch-Light*, October 17, 1876.

32. Ibid.; *Carolina Messenger* (Goldsboro), October 30, 1876.

33. Dowd, *Life of Vance*, p. 161.

34. *Alamance Gleaner* (Graham), September 5, 1876; *Raleigh News*, September 16, 1876; *Raleigh Daily Constitution*, October 16, 17, 1876.

35. *Raleigh Daily Constitution*, September 5, October 17, 1876; *North Carolinian* (Elizabeth City), September 20, October 4, 1876; Babb, "Battle of Giants," pp. 50-51.

36. *Warrenton Gazette*, September 1, 1876; "White Slavery in North Carolina," [1876], *The Papers of Zebulon Vance*, eds. Gordon B. McKinney and Richard M. McMurry (Frederick, Md.: University Publications of America, 1987), microfilm, reel 4; *Elizabeth City Economist*, August 23, 1876; *Alamance Gleaner* (Graham), October 17, 1876; *Raleigh News*, October 26, 1876.

37. *North Carolina Gazette* (Fayetteville), October 12, 1876.

38. *Elizabeth City Economist*, November 1, 1876; Shirley, *Spokesman*, pp. 81-82.

39. Edward Cantwell to Rutherford B. Hayes, September 13, 1876, Hayes Papers; E. R. Hampton to Thomas Settle, September 29, 1876, Settle Papers; Calvin J. Cowles to Thos. B. Keogh, October 21, 26, 1876, Calvin J. Cowles Papers, North Carolina Division of Archives and History, Raleigh.

40. *Tarboro Southerner*, June 23, 1876; *Raleigh Daily Constitution*, August 9, September 5, 1876; *New North State* (Greensboro), October 27, 1876; *North Carolinian* (Elizabeth City), November 1, 1876; *Raleigh News*, November 3, 1876.

41. *Raleigh News*, November 7, 1876; Babb, "Battle of Giants," pp. 66-67; Calvin J. Cowles to Calvin D. Cowles, October 29, 1876, Cowles Papers; *Carolina Messenger* (Goldsboro), November 2, 1876.

42. Tho. Kenan to Zebulon B. Vance, November 8, 1876, *Papers of Vance*, reel 4; *Winston Union Republican*, November 16, 1876; *New North State* (Greensboro), November 17, 1876; O. H. Blocker to Thomas Settle, December 1, 1876, Settle Papers.

43. Babb, "Battle of Giants," pp. 84-87; Donald R. Matthews, *North Carolina Votes: General Election Returns, by County* (Chapel Hill: University of North Carolina Press, 1962), pp.

5, 51, 67, 111, 156, 172, 187, 208; William D. Cotton, "Appalachian North Carolina: A Political Study, 1860–1889" (Ph.D. diss., University of North Carolina, 1954), pp. 317–18.

44. Crow, "Thomas Settle," 722–25.

45. A. V. Dockery to Rutherford B. Hayes, November 17, 1876, Hayes Papers.

46. For the best discussions of this process see: David W. Blight, *Race and Reunion: The Civil War in American Memory* (Cambridge, Mass.: Belknap Press, 2001); Gaines M. Foster, *Ghosts of the Confederacy: Defeat, the Lost Cause, and the Emergence of the New South* (New York: Oxford University Press, 1987).

CHAPTER TWENTY-ONE

1. *Warrenton Gazette*, November 11, 1876; Clement Dowd, *Life of Zebulon B. Vance* (Charlotte: Observer Printing and Publishing House, 1897), pp. 154–55.

2. John Ingram et al. to Zebulon B. Vance, November 15, 1876, W. W. Stringfield to Vance, November 20, 24, December 23, 1876, Joseph Liner to Stringfield, November 25, 1876, M. L. Brittain to Vance, November 29, 1876, Liner et al. to Vance, [1876], *The Papers of Zebulon Vance*, eds. Gordon B. McKinney and Richard M. McMurry (Frederick, Md.: University Publications of America, 1987), microfilm, reel 27; Vernon H. Crow, *Storm in the Mountains: Thomas' Confederate Legion of Cherokee Indians and Mountaineers* (Cherokee, N.C.: Press of the Museum of the Cherokee Indian, 1982), pp. 142–43.

3. W. N. H. Smith et al. to Zebulon B. Vance, December 9, 1876, John C. Watkins et al. to Vance, December 20, 1876, J. M. Neal et al. to Vance, December 1876, B. C. Manly et al. to Vance, 1876, John N. Maples to Vance, [1876], *Papers of Vance*, reel 27.

4. Thos. D. Johnston to [Zebulon B. Vance], November 21, 1876, *Papers of Vance*, reel 29; R. T. Wilson to R. Y. McAden, December 9, 1876, Appleton Oaksmith to Vance, December 15, 1876 (two letters), James Gordon to Vance, December 26, 1876, William J. Best to Vance, December 28, 1876, *Papers of Vance*, reel 27.

5. Cornelia P. Spencer to [Zebulon B. Vance], November 21, 1876, H. H. Webb to Vance, December 13, 27, 1876, *Papers of Vance*, reel 29; Jas. C. Baird to Vance, December 26, 1876, Thomas Settle to Vance, December 30, 1876, *Papers of Vance*, reel 27; Vance to Spencer, November 27, 1876, Cornelia P. Spencer Papers, Southern Historical Collection, University of North Carolina Library, Chapel Hill.

6. *Charlotte Democrat*, December 22, 1876, January 5, 1877.

7. Franklin R. Shirley, *Zebulon Vance, Tarheel Spokesman* (Charlotte: McNally and Loftin, 1963), pp. 84–85.

8. Zebulon B. Vance to Cornelia Spencer, November 27, 1876, Cornelia P. Spencer Papers; *New York Times*, January 2, 1877.

9. Shirley, *Spokesman*, pp. 86–87.

10. *Charlotte Democrat*, January 19, 1877.

11. Ibid.

12. Ibid.

13. Ibid.

14. Zebulon B. Vance to the Senate of North Carolina, January 9, [January], January 20, 1877; Thos. J. Jarvis to Vance, January 9, [January], January 23, 1877; Sherwood Haywood to Vance, [January 1877], W. G. Curtis to Vance, January 30, February 28, 1877, *Papers of Vance*, reel 14.

15. Zebulon B. Vance to Eugene Rankin, April 27, 1876, Wm. S. Carter to Vance, May 10,

1876, *Papers of Vance*, reel 14; Vance to W. S. Carter, April 30, 1877, *Papers of Vance*, reel 39; Thos. J. Jarvis et al. to Vance, [March 1877], *Papers of Vance*, reel 14.

16. Zebulon B. Vance to the Senate of North Carolina, March 9, 1877, Drury Lacy to Vance, January 4, 1877, *Papers of Vance*, reel 4; Thos. J. Jarvis to Vance, March 9, 1877, Vance to Thos. S. Kenan, March 17, 1877, Kenan to Vance, April 2, 1877, R. H. Battle Jr. and S. A. Ashe to Vance, May 9, 1877, Vance to the Senate of North Carolina, [January 1877], Vance to the Senate of North Carolina, March 9, 1877, W. S. Pearson to Vance, April 2, 1877, *Papers of Vance*, reel 14; D. L. Dix to Vance, January 12, 1877, Wm. A. B. Norcan to Vance, Feb. 9, [18]77, R. D. Johnston to Vance, February 24, 1877, *Papers of Vance*, reel 27.

17. J. J. Powell and W. P. Bodie to Zebulon B. Vance, [June 1877], Vance to Powell and Bodie, June 4, 1877, Vance to Robt. Harris, June 23, 1877, Harris to Vance, June 27, 1877, *Papers of Vance*, reel 14; "An Act to Establish Normal Schools," March 13, 1877, *Papers of Vance*, reel 27.

18. "An Act to Establish Normal Schools," March 13, 1877, "An Act to Provide an Ayslum for the Colored Insane of the State," March 12, 1877, J. H. Myrover to J. C. Scarborough, March 24, 1877, C. W. Chesnutt to Zebulon B. Vance, March 31, [18]77, Geo. T. Wassons to Vance, March 31, 1877, W. H. Day to Vance, April 4, 1877, William H. Oliver to Vance, April 5, [18]77, J. Rumple to Vance, April 5, 1877, Julius A. Bonitz to Vance, April 15, 1877, John S. Henderson to Vance, April 5, 1877, Geo. Allen to Vance, April 7, 1877, L. C. Vass et al., Statement, [April 7, 1877], J. S. Scales to Vance, April 7, 1877, M. L. Holmes to Vance, April 8, 1877, F. A. Dortete to Thos. S. Kenan, April 9, 1877, Dortete to Scarborough, April 9, 1877, Scarborough to Vance, April 9, 1877, John E. C. Smedes to Vance, April 10, 1877, A. L. DeRosset to Vance, March 21, 24, 1877, Julius A. Bonitz to Vance, March 25, 1877, H. C. Bourne to Vance, July 13, 1877, *Papers of Vance*, reel 27.

19. Zebulon B. Vance to Theodore [Davidson], October 2, 1877, *Papers of Vance*, reel 39; Jas. B. Stewart to Vance, February 10, April 18, 1878, T. D. Carter to Vance, February 12, 14, 1878, Davidson to Vance, February 22, 1878, W. W. Rollins to Vance, [March] 15, 1878, Rollins to Thos. S. Kenan, August 28, 1878, G. N. Folk to Vance, January 13, 1879, *Papers of Vance*, reel 28; Michael Perman, *The Road to Redemption: Southern Politics, 1869–1879* (Chapel Hill: University of North Carolina Press, 1984), pp. 198–99; Benjamin U. Ratchford, "The North Carolina Public Debt, 1870–1878," *North Carolina Historical Review* 10 (January 1933): 1–20; Jonathan Daniels, *Prince of the Carpetbaggers* (Philadelphia: J. B. Lippincott Company, 1958).

20. Zebulon B. Vance, Message to General Assembly, [January 1879], *Papers of Vance*, reel 14.

21. Edward L. Ayers, *Vengeance and Justice: Crime and Punishment in the 19th Century American South* (New York: Oxford University Press, 1984); Andrew C. Hutson Jr., "The Overthrow of the Convict Lease System in Tennessee," *East Tennessee Historical Society's Publications* 8 (1936): 82–103; Rebecca Hunt Moulder, "Convicts as Capital: Thomas O'Connor and the Leases of the Tennessee Penitentiary System, 1871–1883," *East Tennessee Historical Society's Publications* 48 (1976): 40–70; Karin A. Shapiro, *A New South Rebellion: The Battle against Convict Labor in the Tennessee Coalfields, 1871–1896* (Chapel Hill: University of North Carolina Press, 1998); A. Elizabeth Taylor, "The Origin and Development of the Convict Lease System in Georgia," *Georgia Historical Quarterly* 26 (June 1942): 113–28; Robert D. Ward and William W. Rogers, *Convicts, Coal, and the Banner Mine Tragedy* (Tuscaloosa: University of Alabama Press, 1987).

22. Thomas H. Briggs, George W. Thompson, and C. G. Yates to Zebulon B. Vance, March 7, 1877, Vance to Chairman, Buncombe County Commission, April 7, 1877, J. E. Rankin to Vance, April 17, 1877, Vance to Rankin, April 21, 1877, *Papers of Vance*, reel 14.

23. J. W. Wilson to [Zebulon B.] Vance, April 30, 1877, Vance to Board of Directors, State Penitentiary, June 4, 1877, Statement, Board of Directors, State Penitentiary, [December 20, 1877], *Papers of Vance*, reel 14.

24. M. H. Justice to Zebulon B. Vance, July 4, 1877, *Papers of Vance*, reel 29; Vance to Board of Directors, State Penitentiary, July 9, 1877, *Papers of Vance*, reel 14.

25. Jas. W. Wilson to [Zebulon B.] Vance, March 4, 1878, *Papers of Vance*, reel 28; Wilson to [Vance], December 18, 1878, *Papers of Vance*, reel 14.

26. Zebulon B. Vance to Board of Directors, State Penitentiary, June 10, 1878, *Papers of Vance*, reel 14.

27. William J. Abrams Jr., "The Western North Carolina Railroad, 1855-1894," (master's thesis, Western Carolina University, 1976), p. 44; W. J. Hicks to Zebulon B. Vance, March 4, 1878, *Papers of Vance*, reel 28; Vance, Message to the General Assembly, [January 1879], *Papers of Vance*, reel 14.

28. Cary Franklin Poole, *A History of Railroading in Western North Carolina* (Johnson City, Tenn.: Overmountain Press, 1995), p. 6; Herbert Stacy McKay, "Convict Leasing in North Carolina, 1870-1934" (master's thesis, University of North Carolina, 1942), p. 39.

29. Zebulon B. Vance, *Life and Character of Hon. David L. Swain* (Durham, N.C.: W. T. Blackwell & Co., 1878), pp. 5-12, 19.

30. Zebulon B. Vance Jr. to Harriett E. Vance, November 5, December 13, 1877, Zebulon B. Vance Jr. to Zebulon B. Vance, June 21, December 16, 1877, C. R. P. Rogers to Zebulon B. Vance, June 21, 1877, Harriett E. Vance to Charles Vance, January 9, 22, 31, March 8, 16, April 20, May 14, June 22, July 7, 1877, Charles Vance to Zebulon B. Vance, May 29, 1877, *Papers of Vance*, reel 29; Rogers, "Marks and Relative Standing of Midshipman Z. B. Vance," February 2, 1878, David M. Vance to Zebulon B. Vance, April 10, June 2, July 3, 5, 8, 1878, Thomas M. Vance to Zebulon B. Vance, January 31, February 8, 1878, R. Bingham to Zebulon B. Vance, June 1878, Thomas M. Vance to Harriett E. Vance, October 19, [1878], Harriett E. Vance to Charles Vance, March 26, April 14, May 7, 27, June 1, 1878, Charles Vance to Zebulon B. Vance, May 14, 1878, *Papers of Vance*, reel 30.

31. Zebulon B. Vance to Mrs. —— Alexander, April 5, 1878, Vance to [Cornelia P.] Spencer, October 21, 1878, *Papers of Vance*, reel 39.

32. Zebulon B. Vance to Cornelia P. Spencer, October 21, November 10, 1878, *Papers of Vance*, reel 39; Dowd, *Life of Vance*, pp. 213-17.

33. Zebulon B. Vance to Cornelia P. Spencer, November 10, 1878, *Papers of Vance*, reel 39; W. S. Moore to Vance, December 16, 1878, John A. Young to Vance, December 16, 1878, *Papers of Vance*, reel 7; A. J. Witherspoon to Vance, January 2, 1879, *Papers of Vance*, reel 5.

34. W. T. Everett to Zebulon B. Vance, December 21, 1878, *Papers of Vance*, reel 7; T. J. Boykin to Vance, December 12, 1877, R. G. Armfield to Vance, December 23, 1877, *Papers of Vance*, reel 29; J. C. Codner to Vance, June 11, 1878, J. D. Cameron to Vance, June 20, 1878, J. C. Newland to Vance, June 25, 1878, *Papers of Vance*, reel 30.

35. *Charlotte Democrat*, March 16, April 27, May 11, 1877; *Winston Union Republican*, May 10, 1877; M. Jewell Sink, "James Madison Brown Leach," in *Dictionary of North Carolina Biography*, ed. William S. Powell, 6 vols. (Chapel Hill: University of North Carolina Press, 1979-96), 4:38-39.

36. William D. Cotton, "Appalachian North Carolina: A Political Study, 1860–1889" (Ph.D. diss., University of North Carolina, 1954), p. 362; *Charlotte Democrat*, July 5, 1878.

37. *Charlotte Democrat*, June 14, 1879; N. London to Zebulon B. Vance, June 10, 1878, T. J. Boykin to Vance, June 10, 1878, *Papers of Vance*, reel 5; W. J. Montgomery to Vance, June 5, 1878, J. A. Sadler to Vance, June 9, 1878, W. F. Beasley to Vance, June 10, 1878, Edward Jones to Vance, June 13, 18, 1878, H. Shepperd to Vance, June 15, 1878, *Papers of Vance*, reel 30.

38. *Appleton's Cyclopedia, 1878*, p. 631; W. P. Elliott to Zebulon B. Vance, November 14, 1878, James G. Scott to Vance, November 19, 1878, Wm. A. Allen to Vance, November 20, 1878, T. J. Boykin to Vance, November 21, 1878, R. G. Armfield to [Vance], November 28, 1878, Chas. R. Jones to [Vance], November 30, 1878, Thos. J. Jarvis to [Vance], December 17, 1878, Jas. E. Englehard, Statement, December 18, 1878, T. C. D. Robins to Jarvis, December 23, 1878, J. S. Ramsey to Vance, December 29, 1878, Thos. H. McKoy to Vance, December 31, 1878, Jno. H. Sharp to Vance, January 1, [18]79, W. J. Montgomery to Vance, January 4, 1879, *Papers of Vance*, reel 28.

39. Dowd, *Life of Vance*, pp. 208–9; Zebulon B. Vance, "Message to the General Assembly," [January 1879], *Papers of Vance*, reel 14.

40. *Charlotte Democrat*, January 10, 17, 24, 1879; *Washington Post*, January 14, 16, 17, 22, 24, 1879; *Appleton's Cyclopedia, 1879*, pp. 689–90.

CHAPTER TWENTY-TWO

1. *Charlotte Democrat*, March 28, August 15, October 24, 1879.

2. Clement Dowd, *Life of Zebulon B. Vance* (Charlotte: Observer Printing and Publishing House, 1897), pp. 227–39.

3. Ibid., p. 239.

4. *Statesville Landmark*, January 23, 1880; Zebulon B. Vance to D. F. Caldwell, March 10, 1880, *The Papers of Zebulon Vance*, eds. Gordon B. McKinney and Richard M. McMurry (Frederick, Md.: University Publications of America, 1987), microfilm, reel 39; Margaret W. Morris, "The Completion of the Western North Carolina Railroad: Politics of Concealment," *North Carolina Historical Review* 52 (July 1975): 261.

5. Morris, "Western Railroad," 256–80; W. J. Best to Zebulon B. Vance, September 23, 1881, *Papers of Vance*, reel 31; Memorandum of Agreement, September 30, [18]80, D. F. Caldwell to Vance, May 4, 1881, Vance and J. M. Worth, Statement, [18]81, Thomas J. Jarvis, Vance, and Worth, Memorandum, May 25, 1881, Best to Vance, September 28, 1881, L. L. Polk to Vance, October 27, 1881, D. J. Sprague to Jarvis, November 7, 1881, Jarvis to Vance, December 15, 1881, Edmund Jones to Vance, January 22, 1882, *Papers of Vance*, reel 5; Zebulon B. Vance to Florence S. Vance, April 26, 1881, *Papers of Vance*, reel 8.

6. Frontis W. Johnston, "The Courtship of Zeb Vance," *North Carolina Historical Review* 31 (April 1954): 222–39; Zebulon B. Vance to Florence S. Martin, January 27, February 3, 1880, *Papers of Vance*, reel 7.

7. Zebulon B. Vance to Florence S. Martin, February 11, 21, 1880, *Papers of Vance*, reel 7.

8. Ibid., February 29, March 8, 1880, *Papers of Vance*, reel 7.

9. A. Burrel to Zebulon B. Vance, March 29, 1880, Zebulon B. Vance to Florence S. Martin, March 30, 1880, Martin to Zebulon B. Vance, June 1, 1880, Zebulon B. Vance to Florence S. Vance, May 3, 9 (two letters), 1881, Florence S. Vance to Zebulon B. Vance, May 12, 1881, R. T. Merrick to [Zebulon B. Vance], June 10, 1881, Mary G. Bartlett to Florence S. Vance, July 4,

[1881], N. H. to [Florence S. Vance], November 2, [18]81, Theo. F. Davidson to Zebulon B. Vance, December 12, 1882, *Papers of Vance*, reel 8.

10. Michael Fellman, *Citizen Sherman: A Life of William Tecumseh Sherman* (New York: Random House, 1995), pp. 43–50, 120–21, 202–10, 313–14, 343–48, 362–63, 399–400; Zebulon B. Vance to Florence S. Martin, February 23, March 3, 1880, *Papers of Vance*, reel 7.

11. Zebulon B. Vance to Florence S. Martin, March 3, 7, 8, 10, 1880, *Papers of Vance*, reel 7.

12. Ibid., May 17, 1880; Martin to Vance, May 19, 1880; Vance to Martin, May 20, 1880 (two letters), *Papers of Vance*, reel 8.

13. Johnston, "Courtship," pp. 236–38.

14. *Louisville Courier-Journal*, June 17, 1880.

15. Ibid.

16. Ibid.; *Charlotte Home and Observer*, October 12, 1883.

17. Anne C. Rose, *Victorian America and the Civil War* (New York: Cambridge University Press, 1992), pp. 29, 39–40, 96, 104–5, 116, 129, 150, 153, 162, 188, 206–7, 210.

18. U.S. Senate, Select Committee, *The Removal of the Negroes from the Southern States to the Northern States*, 46th Cong., 2d sess., 1880, Rept. 693, pt. 2 (Washington: Government Printing Office, 1880), pp. 16, 109, 150, 164–65.

19. Ibid., pp. 98–99, 146.

20. Ibid., pp. 131–32.

21. Gordon B. McKinney, *Southern Mountain Republicans, 1865-1900: Politics and the Appalachian Community* (Chapel Hill: University of North Carolina Press, 1978), pp. 96–109.

22. *Statesville Landmark*, March 18, June 10, 17, 24, September 23, October 28, 1881; *Charlotte Democrat*, March 18, June 17, 1881; *Winston Union Republican*, June 2, 9, 16, 30, November 3, 1881; *Memphis Weekly Appeal*, June 1, 1881.

23. "Testimony before the Senate Special Committee to Investigate the Administration of the Collection of Internal Revenue in the Sixth District of North Carolina, Appointed April 21, 1882," *Senate Miscellaneous Documents no. 116*, 47th Congress, 1st sess., pp. 285, 469, 472, 478, 538.

24. Ibid., pp. 366, 425–31.

25. Ibid., pp. 1–538 passim; R. M. Furman to [Zebulon B. Vance], January 20, 1882, W. S. Pearson to [Vance], January 23, 1882, G. M. Mathes to Vance, February 2, 1882, J. C. Brown to Vance, July 3, 1882, *Papers of Vance*, reel 8; W. H. H. Cowles to Vance, July 3, 1882, *Papers of Vance*, reel 5.

26. "Sixth District of North Carolina," pp. 362–95.

27. Zebulon B. Vance to Florence S. Vance, November 21, 23, 25, 1882, *Papers of Vance*, reel 8.

28. *Congressional Record*, 47th Cong., 2d sess., February 19, 1883, pp. 2923–24.

29. Ibid., pp. 2926–29.

30. Ibid., January 19, 1883, p. 1346.

31. Ibid., January 17, February 5, 1883, pp. 1276, 2078.

32. Ibid., February 7, 1883, p. 2215.

33. Ibid., p. 2206; ibid., 48th Cong., 1st sess., March 26, 1884, p. 2284; *Asheville News*, August 23, 1882.

34. *Congressional Record*, 47th Cong., 2d sess., January 15, February 14, 1883, pp. 2713, 2609.

35. Ibid., February 14, 1883, p. 2611.

36. Ibid., January 30, February 14, 15, 1883, pp. 1771–72, 2598, 2714.

37. Ibid., February 15, 1883, p. 2713.

38. Ibid., March 2, 1883, p. 3584.

39. Daniel W. Crofts, "The Blair Bill and Elections Bill: The Congressional Aftermath to Reconstruction" (Ph.D. diss., Yale University, 1968), pp. 48–70.

40. *Congressional Record*, 48th Cong., 1st sess., March 24, 1884, pp. 2208, 2212.

CHAPTER TWENTY-THREE

1. Gordon B. McKinney, *Southern Mountain Republicans, 1865-1900: Politics and the Appalachian Community* (Chapel Hill: University of North Carolina Press, 1978), pp. 101–6; Edward L. Ayers, *The Promise of the New South: Life after Reconstruction* (New York: Oxford University Press, 1992), pp. 46–47; James T. Moore, *Two Paths to the New South: The Virginia Debt Controversy, 1870-1883* (Lexington: University Press of Kentucky, 1974), pp. 57–108.

2. Zebulon B. Vance to Florence S. Vance, September 12, 14, 1880, April 9, 11, 1881, A. Jackson to Zebulon B. Vance, March 31, [18]81, *The Papers of Zebulon Vance*, eds. Gordon B. McKinney and Richard M. McMurry (Frederick, Md.: University Publications of America, 1987), microfilm, reel 8.

3. McKinney, *Mountain Republicans*, p. 106; Gordon B. McKinney, ed., "Coalition Rule in Danville," *Appalachian Journal* 1 (Spring 1973): 111–14; Moore, *Two Paths*, pp. 115–17; John T. S. Melzer, "The Danville Riot: November 3, 1883" (master's thesis, University of Virginia, 1963), pp. 92–93.

4. U.S. Senate, Committee on Privileges and Elections, *Report upon Danville, Va., Riot, November 3, 1883*, 48th Cong., 1st sess., 1884, Rept. 579 (Washington: Government Printing Office, 1884); U.S. Senate, *Views of the Minority on the Danville Riot*, 48th Cong., 1st sess., Rept. 579, pt. 2 (Washington: Government Printing Office, 1884); Samuel Hales to Zebulon B. Vance, March 6, [1884], *Papers of Vance*, reel 31.

5. Senate Committee on Privileges and Elections, *Views of the Minority*, p. lxv; H. Shepherd to Zebulon B. Vance, May 17, 1884, E. B. Withers to Vance, September 8, 1885, *Papers of Vance*, reel 5; Law[rence] S. Mayre to Vance, March 28, 1884, Jas. P. Harrison to Vance, April 18, 1884, *Papers of Vance*, reel 8; John A. Parker to Vance, June 23, 1884, Geo. P. Badger to Vance, February 2, 1885, *Papers of Vance*, reel 31.

6. *Charlotte Home and Observer*, October 5, 1883, September 12, October 3, 24, 1884, January 23, 1885; *Asheville Advance*, August 13, 1884; Clipping, *Wilmington Star*, [1886], *Papers of Vance*, reel 7; Zebulon B. Vance to Florence S. Vance, September 14, 28, 1884, *Papers of Vance*, reel 8; Zebulon B. Vance to Florence S. Vance, October 27, 1884, Jas. D. Glenn to Zebulon B. Vance, January 15, 1885, *Papers of Vance*, reel 9.

7. Zebulon B. Vance to Florence S. Vance, July 8, [1884], *Papers of Vance*, reel 8; A. Barney to [Matt W. Ransom], November 16, 1884, Matt W. Ransom Papers, Southern Historical Collection, University of North Carolina Library, Chapel Hill.

8. *Congressional Record*, 48th Cong., 2d sess., January 13, 1885, p. 649.

9. Ibid., p. 650.

10. Ibid.

11. Zebulon B. Vance to S. A. Ashe, January 16, 1885, *Papers of Vance*, reel 39.

12. H. Leonidas Cable to Zebulon B. Vance, March 16, 1885, John G. Potts to Vance, March 7, 1885, *Papers of Vance*, reel 32; James W. Forbes to Vance, November 26, 1884, *Papers of Vance*, reel 31.

13. Thomas J. Jarvis to Zebulon B. Vance, January 31, February 3, March 3, 30, 1885, *Papers of Vance*, reel 5.

14. Samuel McD. Tate to M[att] W. Ransom, March 21, 1885, Charles R. Jones to Ransom, May 11, 1885, Samuel T. Parson to Ransom, March 26, 1885, Ransom Papers.

15. Tho[mas] D. Johnston to M. W. Ransom, May 16, 1885, E. J. Aston to Ransom, July 2, 1885, Garland Ferguson to [Ransom], August 31, 1885, J. M. Gudger to Ransom, September 11, 1885, A. C. Avery to [Ransom], September 22, 1885, Ransom Papers.

16. A[ndrew] Johnson to James K. Polk, April 9, 1845, *The Papers of Andrew Johnson*, vol. 1, *1822–1851*, eds. LeRoy P. Graf and Ralph W. Haskins (Knoxville: University of Tennessee Press, 1967), p. 213; Jonathan M. Atkins, "The Whig Versus the 'Spoilsman' in Tennessee," *Historian* 57 (Winter 1995): 329–40; Jeff Forret, "The United States Mint at Charlotte: Superintendents, Spoils, and the Second-Party System, 1837–1841," *North Carolina Historical Review* 77 (April 2000): 151–78; William F. Mugleston, "Andrew Jackson and the Spoils System: An Historiographical Survey," *Mid-America* 59 (April–July 1977): 117–25; Robert V. Remini, *Andrew Jackson and the Course of American Freedom, 1822–1832* (New York: Harper & Row, 1981), pp. 170, 185–86, 191–92; Ari Hoogenboom, *Outlawing the Spoils: A History of the Civil Service Reform Movement, 1865–1883* (Urbana: University of Illinois Press, 1961), pp. 1–12; Marc W. Kruman, *Parties and Politics in North Carolina, 1836–1865* (Baton Rouge: Louisiana State University Press, 1983), pp. 38–39, 42, 52–53; Allan Nevins, *The Emergence of Lincoln: Douglas, Buchanan, and Party Chaos, 1857–1859* (New York: Charles Scribner's Sons, 1950), pp. 256, 275, 278, 290–91.

17. Hoogenboom, *Spoils*, pp. 88–214.

18. Ibid., pp. 215–63.

19. C. Dowd to M. W. Ransom, July 24, 1885, Ransom Papers; *Statesville Landmark*, June 5, 1885; *Charlotte Home and Democrat*, May 29, October 9, November 6, 1885.

20. H. C. Hunt to L. C. Houk, July 12, 1886, Leonidas Campbell Houk and John Chiles Houk Papers, Lawson McGhee Library, Knoxville, Tenn.; Clement Dowd, *Life of Zebulon B. Vance* (Charlotte: Observer Printing and Publishing House, 1897), p. 221.

21. *Congressional Record*, 49th Cong., 1st sess., March 31, 1886, p. 2945.

22. Ibid., pp. 2946, 2952; *Charlotte Home and Democrat*, June 25, 1886.

23. Franklin R. Shirley, *Zebulon Vance, Tarheel Spokesman* (Charlotte: McNally and Loftin, 1963), p. 98; *Congressional Record*, 49th Cong., 1st sess., January 12, 1886, p. 605.

24. *Congressional Record*, 49th Cong., 1st sess., January 12, 1886, pp. 605–7; D. Schenck to Zebulon B. Vance, January 26, 1886, J. F. Hoke to Vance, February 5, 1886, *Papers of Vance*, reel 5; Chas. R. Jones to [Vance], January 13, 1886, *Papers of Vance*, reel 9.

25. *Charlotte Home and Democrat*, October 21, December 4, 1885.

26. Glenn Tucker, *Zeb Vance: Champion of Personal Freedom* (Indianapolis: Bobbs-Merrill, 1965), p. 473; *Charlotte Democrat*, July 15, 1887; J. M. Blair to Zebulon B. Vance, May 12, 1890, C. T. Bailey to Vance, May 26, 1890, *Papers of Vance*, reel 8; Natt Atkinson to Vance, June 19, July 17, 1890, R. McBrayer to Vance, July 19, 1890, D. M. Vance to Vance, July 21, 1890, G. W. Purifoy to Vance, July 29, 1890, W. B. Shaw to Vance, August 7, 1890, Vance to Shaw, n.d., *Papers of Vance*, reel 9.

27. *Charlotte Home-Democrat*, August 7, 1885; Zebulon B. Vance to Florence S. Vance, May 15, 29, September 30, 1885, *Papers of Vance*, reel 9.

28. Frederick M. Burnett, *This Was My Valley* (Charlotte: Heritage Printers, 1960), pp.

82-83; *Asheville Advance*, October 12, 1886; Zebulon B. Vance to Florence S. Vance, [May 15], September 17, November 5, 1886, *Papers of Vance*, reel 9.

29. Burnett, *Valley*, pp. 83-84; Zebulon B. Vance to Florence S. Vance, March 22, April 5, 17, October 14, 19, 31, November 4, 1887, *Papers of Vance*, reel 9.

30. Burnett, *Valley*, pp. 83-84, 86; Adlai Ewing Stevenson, *Something of the Men I Have Known* (Chicago: A. C. McClung & Co., 1909), pp. 289-90.

31. Zebulon B. Vance to Florence S. Vance, October 16, 23, 1887, *Papers of Vance*, reel 9; *Charlotte Democrat*, October 28, 1887.

32. *Winston Union Republican*, August 5, 12, 1886; *Statesville Landmark*, September 23, 1886; *Asheville Skyland Herald*, October 6, 1886.

33. *Asheville Advance*, June 14, 1885; Paul D. Escott, *Many Excellent People: Power and Privilege in North Carolina, 1850-1900* (Chapel Hill: University of North Carolina Press, 1985), pp. 188-91.

34. *Asheville Advance*, June 14, 1885, September 19, 21, November 4, 1886; *Statesville Landmark*, September 23, 1886; *Asheville Skyland Herald*, October 6, 1886; *Winston Union Republican*, November 18, 1886.

35. *Congressional Record*, 49th Cong., 2d sess., February 25, 1887, p. 2268.

36. Ibid., 50th Cong., 1st sess., January 13, 1887, pp. 441-44.

37. *Baltimore Sun*, March 19, 23, 26, April 4, 12, 20, 27, 1888.

38. Robert C. McMath Jr., *Populist Vanguard: A History of the Southern Farmers' Alliance* (Chapel Hill: University of North Carolina Press, 1975), pp. 38-39; Ayers, *New South*, pp. 223-25; *Charlotte Democrat*, June 8, 1888; *Asheville Sun*, July 1, 1888.

39. Josephus Daniels, *Tar Heel Editor* (Chapel Hill: University of North Carolina Press, 1939), pp. 361-62; *Winston Union Republican*, October 4, 1888; *Charlotte Democrat*, October 19, 1888; Dowd, *Life of Vance*, p. 198.

40. Lala Carr Steelman, *The North Carolina Farmers' Alliance: A Political History, 1887-1893* (Greenville, N.C.: East Carolina University Publications, 1985), pp. 37-41.

41. *Charlotte Democrat*, November 30, 1888, March 29, 1889.

42. Quotation in *Congressional Record*, 50th Cong., 1st sess., December 18, 1888, p. 304. See also: ibid., December 11, 1888, p. 152; ibid., December 13, 1888, pp. 217-18; ibid., December 20, 1888, p. 350; ibid., 2d sess., January 2, 1889, pp. 493, 508; ibid., January 4, 1889, pp. 518-19; ibid., January 8, 1889, pp. 587, 591-92; ibid., January 9, 1889, p. 615; ibid., January 14, 1889, pp. 732, 734, 736, 738; ibid., January 21, 1889, p. 1036.

43. J. J. Chilton to Florence S. Vance, January 30, 1889, *Papers of Vance*, reel 6; Lizzie M. Partner to Florence S. Vance, January 28, 1889, *Papers of Vance*, reel 10; Florence S. Vance to Matt W. Ransom, January 29, 1889, Zebulon B. Vance to W. W. Holden, February 7, 1889, *Papers of Vance*, reel 39.

CHAPTER TWENTY-FOUR

1. Zebulon B. Vance to Florence S. Vance, February 22, March 17, 28, May 5, 16, October 12, November 7, 1889, Florence S. Vance to Zebulon B. Vance, April 8, 12, 1889, H. A. Herbert to Zebulon B. Vance, July 16, 1889, *Papers of Vance*, reel 10; Zebulon B. Vance to Nan ——, October 20, 1889, *Papers of Vance*, reel 39.

2. *Charlotte Democrat*, April 5, May 10, 1889; Zebulon B. Vance, *Address at the Guilford Battle Ground* (Greensboro, N.C.: Reece & Elam, [1889]); Gaines M. Foster, *Ghosts of the*

Confederacy: Defeat, the Lost Cause, and the Emergence of the New South (New York: Oxford University Press, 1987), pp. 88–103.

3. *Winston Union Republican*, February 28, 1889; Paul D. Escott, *Many Excellent People: Power and Privilege in North Carolina, 1850–1900* (Chapel Hill: University of North Carolina Press, 1985), p. 185; John B. MacLeod, "The Development of North Carolina Election Laws, 1865–1900" (master's thesis, University of North Carolina, 1946), p. 152–54.

4. *Congressional Record*, 51st Cong., 1st sess., January 30, 1890, p. 967.

5. H. A. Herbert to Zebulon B. Vance et al., April 8, [1889], *The Papers of Zebulon Vance*, eds. Gordon B. McKinney and Richard M. McMurry (Frederick, Md.: University Publications of America), microfilm, reel 6; Zebulon B. Vance, "Reconstruction in North Carolina," in *Why the Solid South? Or, Reconstruction and Its Results*, ed. Hilary A. Herbert et al. (Baltimore: R. H. Woodward & Company, 1890), pp. 70–84.

6. Vance, "Reconstruction," pp. 78–83. Quotation is from p. 80.

7. *Congressional Record*, 51st Cong., 1st sess., February 24, 1890, p. 1645; ibid., February 26, 1890, p. 1715.

8. L. L. Polk to Zebulon B. Vance, April 29, 1890, *Papers of Vance*, reel 33; E. C. Beddingfield to Vance, May 16, 1890, *Papers of Vance*, reel 6.

9. Zebulon B. Vance to E. C. Beddingfield, May 18, 1890, in Clement Dowd, *Life of Zebulon B. Vance* (Charlotte: Observer Printing and Publishing House, 1897), pp. 282–83.

10. Ibid., p. 283.

11. *Charlotte Democrat*, May 23, 1890.

12. Zebulon B. Vance to Elias Carr, June 29, 1890, *Papers of Vance*, reel 39.

13. Zebulon B. Vance to S. A. Ashe, June 29, 1890, *Papers of Vance*, reel 39; Ashe to Vance, June 30, 1890, Elias Carr to Vance, July 1, 1890, *Papers of Vance*, reel 34; Vance to Florence S. Vance, July 8, [1890], *Papers of Vance*, reel 10.

14. *Congressional Record*, 51st Cong., 1st sess., June 12, 1890, app. pp. 382–83; ibid., July 10, 1890, p. 7104.

15. Wm. J. White to Zebulon B. Vance, July 12, 1890, *Papers of Vance*, reel 34; Zebulon B. Vance to Florence S. Vance, July 25, [1890], *Papers of Vance*, reel 9; W. C. Newland to M. W. Ransom, July 22, 1890, Matt W. Ransom Papers, Southern Historical Collection, University of North Carolina Library, Chapel Hill; *Charlotte Democrat*, July 18, 1890; Alan B. Bromberg, "'The Worst Muddle Ever Seen in N.C. Politics': The Farmers' Alliance, the Subtreasury, and Zeb Vance," *North Carolina Historical Review* 56 (January 1979): 32.

16. Bromberg, "Muddle," pp. 32–33; Lala Carr Steelman, *The North Carolina Farmers' Alliance: A Political History, 1887–1893* (Greenville, N.C.: East Carolina University Publications, 1985), pp. 81–82, 122; *Charlotte Democrat*, August 22, 1890.

17. Steelman, *Farmers' Alliance*, p. 86; Bromberg, "Muddle," p. 34; S. A. Ashe to M. W. Ransom, September 8, 1890, Ransom Papers.

18. *Congressional Record*, 51st Cong., 1st sess., July 15, 1890, pp. 6688–90; *Statesville Landmark*, October 9, 1890; Gordon B. McKinney, *Southern Mountain Republicans, 1865–1900: Politics and the Appalachian Community* (Chapel Hill: University of North Carolina Press, 1978), pp. 136–37.

19. *Congressional Record*, 51st Cong., 1st sess., August 9, 11, 12, 1890, pp. 8357, 8360, 8403, 8461. Quotation is from p. 8461.

20. Ibid., September 2, 10, 1890, pp. 9556, 9938, 9942. Quotation is from p. 9556.

21. *Charlotte Democrat*, September 19, 1892.

22. Ibid.

23. Ibid., October 3, 1890; Zebulon B. Vance to Florence S. Vance, September 7, 1890, *Papers of Vance*, reel 10.

24. *Charlotte Democrat*, October 17, 1890; MacLeod, "Election Laws," p. 161.

25. Bromberg, "Muddle," p. 36; Elias Carr to Zebulon B. Vance, November 20, 1890, *Papers of Vance*, reel 34.

26. Zebulon B. Vance to Elias Carr, December 6, 1890, *Papers of Vance*, reel 35; *Charlotte Democrat*, December 12, 1890.

27. *Congressional Record*, 51st Cong., 2d sess., December 15, 1890, pp. 470-71.

28. Bromberg, "Muddle," p. 39; Dowd, *Life of Vance*, p. 290.

29. Bromberg, "Muddle," p. 39; Dowd, *Life of Vance*, p. 290.

30. *Congressional Record*, 51st Cong., 2d sess., February 13, 1891, pp. 2614-15.

CHAPTER TWENTY-FIVE

1. Clement Dowd, *Life of Zebulon B. Vance* (Charlotte: Observer Printing and Publishing House, 1897), p. 313.

2. *Charlotte Democrat*, May 29, 1891; Zebulon B. Vance to Charles N. Vance, June 15, 1891, *The Papers of Zebulon Vance*, eds. Gordon B. McKinney and Richard M. McMurry (Frederick, Md.: University Publications of America, 1987), microfilm, reel 35; Florence S. Vance to Nannie ——, June 7, 1891, Zebulon B. Vance to Nan ——, June 17, 1891, *Papers of Vance*, reel 39.

3. Zebulon B. Vance to Charles N. Vance, June 15, October 13, 1891, *Papers of Vance*, reel 35; Florence S. Vance to Nannie ——, July 7, 1891, *Papers of Vance*, reel 39.

4. Zebulon B. Vance to —— Kenan, November 4, 1891, *Papers of Vance*, reel 39.

5. Zebulon B. Vance to Charles N. Vance, October 13, 1891, *Papers of Vance*, reel 35; Zebulon B. Vance to —— Kenan, November 4, 1891, *Papers of Vance*, reel 39.

6. Paul D. Escott, *Many Excellent People: Power and Privilege in North Carolina, 1850–1900* (Chapel Hill: University of North Carolina Press, 1985), p. 245; *Statesville Landmark*, July 9, 1891; *Winston Union Republican*, July 30, September 17, 1891.

7. Dowd, *Life of Vance*, pp. 311-12.

8. *Congressional Record*, 52d Cong., 1st sess., February 25, 26, 1892, pp. 1445-47, 1473-78; *Charlotte Democrat*, April 22, 1892.

9. *Charlotte Democrat*, May 27, July 8, 22, August, 5, 1892; A. C. Avery to [Zebulon B. Vance], August 2, 1892, *Papers of Vance*, reel 6.

10. Helen G. Edmonds, *The Negro and Fusion Politics in North Carolina, 1894-1901* (Chapel Hill: University of North Carolina Press, 1951), p. 26; *Winston Union Republican*, September 15, 1892; Dowd, *Life of Vance*, p. 301.

11. Dowd, *Life of Vance*, p. 297.

12. Ibid., pp. 256-57; Zebulon B. Vance to Florence S. Vance, October 26, 30, 1892, H. E. Bynum to Florence S. Vance, October 27, 1892, *Papers of Vance*, reel 10.

13. Dowd, *Life of Vance*, pp. 256-57; Zebulon B. Vance to Florence S. Vance, November 1, 6, 1892, *Papers of Vance*, reel 10.

14. *Winston Union Republican*, October 27, 1892; William S. Powell, *North Carolina through Four Centuries* (Chapel Hill: University of North Carolina Press, 1989), pp. 429-30.

15. Zebulon B. Vance to [M. W. Ransom], May 25, 1893, C. Dowd to Ransom, July 1, 1893, Matt W. Ransom Papers, Southern Historical Collection, University of North Carolina Library, Chapel Hill.

16. W. B. Ragonly to K. Elias, June 19, 1893, [Kope Elias] to [M. W. Ransom], July 29, 1893, Ransom Papers.

17. *Charlotte Democrat*, July 28, 1893.

18. *Congressional Record*, 53rd Cong., 1st sess., September 1, 1893, pp. 1127-29.

19. Zebulon B. Vance to Florence S. Vance, September 1, 1893, *Papers of Vance*, reel 11; *Congressional Record*, 53rd Cong., 1st sess., September 19, 1893, p. 1567; ibid., 2d sess., December 14, 1893, p. 224.

20. T. R. Ransom to [M. W. Ransom], September 19, November 3, 1893; K. Elias to Ransom, December 26, 1893, Fannie R. Williams to [Ransom], January 6, 1894, Ransom Papers; *Charlotte Democrat*, October 20, 1893.

21. *Charlotte Democrat*, December 1, 1893; Z. B. Vance to [M. W.] Ransom, January 9, 26, 1894, Ransom Papers; *Charlotte Observer*, February 22, March 4, 23, April 5, 1894; F. M. Simmons to [M. W. Ransom], April 1, 1894, Ransom Papers.

22. *Charlotte Observer*, April 5, 6, 1894; Dowd, *Life of Vance*, p. 315.

CHAPTER TWENTY-SIX

1. David W. Blight, *Race and Reunion: The Civil War in American Memory* (Cambridge, Mass.: Belknap Press, 2001), pp. 255-99.

2. Charles N. Vance to T. W. Patton, May 4, 1894, A. H. Baird to Charles N. Vance, May 15, 1894, Florence S. Vance to ——, May 26, 1894, Charles N. Vance, Zebulon B. Vance Jr., and Thomas M. Vance to Florence S. Vance, May 31, 1894, Robert B. Vance to Charles N. Vance, June 7, July 8, 1894, Thomas N. Vance to ——, June 13, 1894, Thomas M. Vance to Charles N. Vance, July 10, 1894, Julius C. Martin to Charles N. Vance, August 3, 14, 1894, *The Papers of Zebulon Vance*, eds. Gordon B. McKinney and Richard M. McMurry (Frederick, Md.: University Publications of America, 1987), microfilm, reel 37; Charles N. Vance to H. A. Gudger, June 6, 1894, Charles N. Vance to Florence S. Vance, n.d., *Papers of Vance*, reel 39.

3. *Asheville Citizen*, December 22, 1897, December 21, 1951.

4. Ibid., December 22, 1897; Clipping, n.d., North Carolina Room, Pack Memorial Public Library, Asheville.

5. *Asheville Citizen*, August 22, 23, 1900.

6. Ibid., August 22, 1900; U.S. Senate, Joint Committee on Printing, *Statue of Zebulon Baird Vance*, 64th Cong., 1st sess., 1915-16 (Washington: Government Printing Office, 1917), p. 10.

7. Senate Joint Committee on Printing, *Statue Vance*, pp. 36-49.

8. Ibid., pp. 79-82, 94-97.

9. *Asheville Times*, October 14, 15, 1928.

10. Ibid.

11. *Asheville Citizen*, May 12, 14, 1938.

12. "Historical News," *North Carolina Historical Review* 21 (January 1944): 93; ibid., 21 (April 1944): 175; ibid., 28 (October 1951): 537.

13. "Historical News," *North Carolina Historical Review* 21 (January 1944): 89-90; ibid., 21 (October 1944): 389; *Zebulon B. Vance Birthplace: Appalachian Mountain Home of the*

Dynamic *"War Governor of the South"* (Raleigh: North Carolina Division of Archives and History, [1978]).

14. Frank L. Owsley, *State Rights in the Confederacy* (Chicago: University of Chicago Press, 1963); George C. Rable, *The Confederate Republic: A Revolution against Politics* (Chapel Hill: University of North Carolina Press, 1994); Joe A. Mobley, "Zebulon B. Vance: A Confederate Nationalist in the North Carolina Gubernatorial Election of 1864," *North Carolina Historical Review* 77 (October 2000): 434–54.

INDEX ✻

Gudger, H. A., 402–3
Gudger, James M., 371–72
Guilford County, N.C., 177–78, 203, 220

Habeas corpus, writ of, 105, 142, 281
Hale, Edward J., 102, 171–72, 174, 179, 182,
    188, 190, 192, 194, 196–98, 201, 204, 206,
    213, 245, 369
Hamilton, Alexander, 359
Hampton, Wade, 249–50, 312
Hancock, Winfield S., 228
Hanes, Lewis, 174–75, 241, 274–75
Hansa (ship), 137–38
Hardy, James F. E., 63
Harpers Ferry, Va., 65
Harris, James H., 359
Harris, Robert, 332
Harris, William C., 183
Haughton, John H.: Zeb's reply to, 180–81
Hayes, Rutherford, 317, 320, 322, 340–41
Haywood County, N.C., 161, 191
Heaton, James, 322
Helper, Hardie H., 292
Helper, Hinton Rowan, 65
Henderson, N.C., 375
Henderson County, N.C., 191, 356
Hendersonville, N.C., 191
Hendersonville Times, 192
Herbert, Hilary A., 384, 386
Heroes of America, 158, 160, 224–25, 227,
    232
Heth, Henry, 145
Hill, Daniel H., 166, 168
Hillsborough, N.C., 249
Historical Society of North Carolina, 279
Hoge, Moses, 1
Hoke, Robert F., 189, 215, 243
Holden, William W., 69–70, 75–76, 98,
    100–103, 106, 111, 113, 117, 165–66, 170–
    83, 186, 188–89, 192–93, 196, 198, 200–
    206, 211–13, 216–18, 221–25, 227–31, 244,
    250, 252, 256–58, 261, 264, 266, 271–
    73, 275, 279–81, 284, 287, 317, 382, 386;
    impeachment of, 285–86, 288
Holmes, Theophilus H., 91
Holston Female College, 41

Home Guard, 189
Hood, John Bell, 226, 233, 238
Huger, Benjamin, 93–94
Hunter, R. M. T., 242
Hyman, John D., 44, 46, 70, 191, 219

Idaho, 399
Immigration restriction, 44
Inflation, 119–20
Inscoe, John C., 67
Internal Revenue Service, 316, 355–56, 371,
    373, 380, 402
Internal Revenue tax, 315
Interstate trade embargo, 121
Iredell County, N.C., 158
Ireland, 397
Irvin, John, 141
Isaac (Vance slave), 68

Jackson, Andrew, 13, 359, 372
Jackson, Thomas J. "Stonewall," 94
Jackson County, N.C., 34, 74, 195
Jacobson, Moses, 410
Jarvis, Thomas, 347, 370–71
Jefferson, Thomas, 359
Jeffrey, Thomas E., 49–50, 56
Jewish community, 410–11
Johnson, Andrew, 125, 254–57, 260, 264–
    66, 270
Johnson, Edward, 253
Johnson, R. D., 261
Johnston, James C., 269; will case, 269–70
Johnston, Joseph E., 226, 245, 247–51
Johnston, Thomas D., 371–72
Johnston, William, 101, 103–7
Johnston County, N.C., 155, 163, 178, 200,
    202–3, 213, 229
Jones, Bill, 36
Jones, Henry, 331
Jonesboro, N.C., 315
Jones County, N.C., 319

Kansas-Nebraska Bill, 43, 54
Keith, James A., 145–46
Kenan, Thomas S., 331
Kilpatrick, Hugh J., 277